TERMINATION OF WAR

AND

TREATIES OF PEACE

BY

COLEMAN PHILLIPSON

M.A., LL.D., Litt.D.

Of the Inner Temple, Barrister-at-Law

AUTHOR OF "STUDIES IN INTERNATIONAL LAW," "EFFECT OF WAR ON CONTRACTS," "INTERNATIONAL LAW AND CUSTOM OF ANCIENT GREECE AND ROME," "INTERNATIONAL LAW AND THE GREAT WAR," CO-AUTHOR OF "GREAT JURISTS OF THE WORLD," EDITOR OF WHEATON'S "INTERNATIONAL LAW," ETC.

THE LAWBOOK EXCHANGE, LTD.

Clark, New Jersey

ISBN-13: 9781584778608

Lawbook Exchange edition 2008, 2010

The quality of this reprint is equivalent to the quality of the original work.

THE LAWBOOK EXCHANGE, LTD.
33 Terminal Avenue
Clark, New Jersey 07066-1321

Please see our website for a selection of our other publications and fine facsimile reprints of classic works of legal history:
www.lawbookexchange.com

Library of Congress Cataloging-in-Publication Data

Phillipson, Coleman, 1875-1958.
Termination of war and treaties of peace / Coleman Phillipson.
p. cm.
Originally published: New York, E.P. Dutton & Company, 1916.
Includes bibliographical references and index.
ISBN-13: 978-1-58477-860-8 (cloth : alk. paper)
ISBN-10: 1-58477-860-1 (cloth : alk. paper)
1. Peace treaties. 2. War (International law) I. Title.
KZ6753.P45 2007
341.6'6--dc22

2007039212

Printed in the United States of America on acid-free paper

TERMINATION OF WAR

AND

TREATIES OF PEACE

BY

COLEMAN PHILLIPSON

M.A., LL.D., Litt.D.

Of the Inner Temple, Barrister-at-Law

AUTHOR OF "STUDIES IN INTERNATIONAL LAW," "EFFECT OF WAR ON CONTRACTS," "INTERNATIONAL LAW AND CUSTOM OF ANCIENT GREECE AND ROME," "INTERNATIONAL LAW AND THE GREAT WAR," CO-AUTHOR OF "GREAT JURISTS OF THE WORLD," EDITOR OF WHEATON'S "INTERNATIONAL LAW," ETC.

NEW YORK

E. P. DUTTON & COMPANY

681 FIFTH AVENUE

1916

DEDICATED

TO

THE RIGHT HON. LORD READING

P.C., G.C.B., K.C.V.O.

LORD CHIEF JUSTICE OF ENGLAND

(PRINTED IN GREAT BRITAIN)

PREFACE

I TRUST that the present work may fill a gap in the literature of international law and international relations. So far as I know (I have searched numerous bibliographies—British, continental, and American) there is no publication in any language that deals with this most important branch of international law and practice in a systematic and comprehensive manner.

The reader will see, even from a cursory examination, that the work is, on the one hand, a comparative and analytical study, based for the most part on original documents, and accompanied throughout by critical observations founded on what I conceive to be the fundamental principles of international law and general jurisprudence; and, on the other hand, a synthetic presentation of conclusions derived from such analysis and application of first principles.

The qualities desirable in writing that is analytical and juristic are clearness, definiteness, concision, and exclusion of irrelevance. I have from beginning to end borne these desiderata in mind, and have endeavoured to write conformably thereto. One result, at least, is that I am able to present the work within moderate compass.

The plan of the book is, briefly, as follows: First, I consider the methods of terminating wars without recourse to treaties of peace, viz. by a reciprocal intermission of hostilities or by conquest and subjugation. After discussing the various claims and difficulties that arise in the one case, and the numerous problems and controverted matters in the other, I examine the questions of premature annexation and the validity of conquest, and set forth the juridical consequences of forcible annexation from the point of view of State succession. Secondly, the normal mode of ending wars, viz. by concluding a treaty of peace, is expounded much more elaborately. The reader is conducted from the field of battle, where the first pourparlers are exchanged for provisionally staying hostile operations, to the calmer atmosphere of the council-chamber of plenipotentiaries, who take up the conflict by the less sinister methods of negotiation and diplomacy. It may be, too, that these peaceable approaches have been facilitated by the mediation or good offices of a neutral State. It is, therefore, necessary to consider here the conclusion of armistice conventions, their political character, the difference between them and suspensions of arms effected by the military authorities themselves or on their own initiative; and then the nature and extent of the interposition of third Powers. Next, I deal with the preliminaries of peace, their object and functions, their constituent elements, and their relation to the definitive treaty. The groundwork for the peace plenipotentiaries having now been prepared, I turn my attention to the constitution and procedure of the peace conference, and give illustrations furnished by notable examples from previous wars. Then I look at the treaty of peace itself, its form, underlying principles, its component elements, date of operation, its ratification, breach, and modes of ensuring its performance. The main provisions, general and special, are examined separately and fully; and, finally, the legal effects of the most important of these provisions—viz. the cession of territory—are discussed, and the principles of State succession (one of the most difficult subjects of international law and custom) are set forth, and their application is exemplified.

All these and many other questions here considered will arise when the present Great War comes to an end. I hope, therefore, that this work will be found to furnish ample material, principles, and conclusions, which will explain and illustrate the various proceedings that will be adopted to effect a settlement, and the results that will ultimately be brought about.

In conclusion, I would draw the reader's attention to the texts of the treaties of peace given in the Appendix. Their sources, English and French, are indicated in the Bibliography. For the task of transcription, collation, and arrangement I am gratefully indebted to my wife.

COLEMAN PHILLIPSON.

INNER TEMPLE,
May 15, 1916.

CONTENTS

PART I

TERMINATION OF WAR BY MERE WITHDRAWAL FROM HOSTILITIES; OR BY CONQUEST AND SUBJUGATION

CHAPTER I

CHAPTER II

CHAPTER III

CHAPTER IV

PART II

TERMINATION OF WAR BY TREATIES OF PEACE. HOW THEY COME TO BE MADE; THEIR CONTENTS; AND THEIR EFFECTS

CHAPTER I

CHAPTER II

CHAPTER III

CHAPTER VII

CHAPTER VIII

CHAPTER IX

CHAPTER X

CHAPTER XI

CHAPTER XII

CHAPTER XIII

APPENDIX

TEXTS OF PEACE TREATIES FREQUENTLY REFERRED TO IN THE COURSE OF THE WORK

JUDICIAL CASES REFERRED TO

WORKS AND DOCUMENTS REFERRED TO

[Besides those given below, several other works are cited which it was not thought necessary to include in the list.]

(A) WORKS

AMERY, L. S. (Ed.). The Times History of the War in South Africa (London, 1902).

D'ANGEBERG, COMTE. Le Congrès de Vienne et les traités de 1815 (Paris, 1864).

ANZILOTTI, D. Article in Rivista di diritto internazionale (Roma, 1912).

ARIGA, N. La guerre sino-japonaise au point de vue du droit international (Paris, 1896).

BARCLAY, SIR T. The Turco-Italian War (London, 1912).

——— ——— Article in Law Quarterly Review, vol. xxi.

BERNARD, M. Four lectures on subjects connected with diplomacy (London, 1868).

BLUNTSCHLI, J. C. Das moderne Völkerrecht (Nordlingen, 1872). French trans. by C. Lardy (Paris, 1895).

BONFILS, H. Manuel de droit international public (Paris, 1912).

BOUGEANT, G. H. Histoire des guerres et des négociations qui précédèrent le traité de Westphalie. 6 vols. (Paris, 1751).

CALVO, C. Le droit international théorique et pratique. 6 vols. (Paris, 1896).

COBBETT, P. Cases and opinions on international law. 2 vols. (London, 1909–1913).

COGORDAN, G. La nationalité au point de vue des rapports internationaux (Paris, 1890).

COSTES, M. Des cessions de territoires (Paris; Toulouse, 1914).

CRANDALL, S. B. Treaties, their making and enforcement. (Studies in history. Columbia College. Vol. xxi. New York, 1904).

DILLON, E. J. Articles in Contemporary Review (London, Sept. 1913 and Oct. 1905).

FIORE, P. Nouveau droit international public. 2nd ed. Trad. de l'italien par C. Antoine. 3 vols. (Paris, 1880).

FLASSAN, G. DE. Histoire du Congrès de Vienne. 3 vols. (Paris, 1829).

FORSYTH, W. Cases and opinions on constitutional law (London, 1869).

FUNCK-BRENTANO, T., et SOREL, A. Précis du droit des gens (Paris, 1877).

GARDEN, G. DE. Histoire générale des traités de paix. 15 vols. (Paris, 1848–1887).

HALL, W. E. International Law (Oxford, 1909).

HALLECK, H. W. International Law. Ed. Sir S. Baker. 2 vols. (London, 1908).

HEFFTER, A. W. Das europäische Völkerrecht der Gegenwart (Berlin, 1882). French ed. (Paris, 1883).

HERSHEY, A. S. International Law and Diplomacy in the Russo-Japanese War (New York, 1906).

HOLLS, F. W. The Peace Conference at The Hague (New York, 1900).

HOLTZENDORFF, F. VON [and other writers]. Handbuch des Völkerrechts. 4 vols. (Hamburg, 1885–1889).

HUBER, M. Die Staatensuccession (Leipzig, 1898).

JACOMET, R. La guerre et les traités (Paris, 1909).

KEITH, A. B. The theory of State succession (London, 1907).

FUR, L. LE. La guerre hispano-américaine de 1898 envisagée au point de vue du droit international public (Paris, 1899).

MAGOON, C. E. Reports on the law of civil government in territory subject to military occupation by the military forces of the United States (Washington, 1902).

MARTENS, F. DE. La paix et la guerre (Paris, 1901).

——— Article on the Portsmouth Peace Conference in North American Review (Boston), Nov. 1905.

MARTENS, G. F. DE. Précis du droit des gens moderne de l'Europe (Gottingue, 1801).

MAURICE, SIR F. (Ed.). History of the War in South Africa, 1899–1902. Written by direction of H.M. Government. 4 vols. (London, 1906–1910).

MAY, G. Le traité de Francfort (Paris, 1909).

MOORE, J. B. Digest of International Law. 8 vols. (Washington, 1906).

——— History and Digest of the International Arbitrations to which the United States has been a party. 6 vols. (Washington, 1898).

OPPENHEIM, L. International Law. 2 vols. (London, 1912).

PHILLIMORE, SIR R. Commentaries upon International Law. 3rd ed. 4 vols. (London, 1879–1889).

PHILLIPSON, C. International Law and Custom of ancient Greece and Rome. 2 vols. (London, 1911).

——— International Law and the Great War (London, 1915).

PISTOYE, A. DE, et DUVERDY, C. Traité des prises maritimes. 2 vols. (Paris, 1855–1859).

POLITIS, N. La guerre gréco-turque au point de vue du droit international (Paris, 1898).

POORTUGAEL, GEN. DEN BEER. Article in Revue des Deux Mondes (Paris, 1901).

PRADIER-FODÉRÉ, P. Cours de droit diplomatique. 2 vols. (Paris, 1899).

——— Traité de droit international. 8 vols. (Paris, 1885–1906).

RIVIER, A. Principes du droit des gens. 2 vols. (Paris, 1896).
SOREL, A. Histoire diplomatique de la guerre franco-allemande (Paris, 1875).
STAMBLER, B. Les Roumains et les Bulgares (Paris, 1914).
TAKAHASHI, S. International Law applied to the Russo-Japanese War (London, 1908).
VALFREY, J. Histoire du traité de Francfort et de la libération du territoire français (Paris, 1874).
VATTEL, E. DE. Droit des gens (first published at Neuchâtel, 1758).
WESTLAKE, J. International Law. 2 vols. (Cambridge, 1910).
——— Collected Papers (Cambridge, 1914).
WHEATON, H. International Law. 5th English edition, partly re-written and enlarged. By C. Phillipson (London, 1916).
The Campaign of 1866 in Germany. Compiled by the Department of Military History of the Prussian Staff. English trans. 1872; reprinted 1907 (by Colonel von Wright and Captain H. M. Hozier).

(B) TEXTS OF TREATIES, OFFICIAL PAPERS, AND OTHER DOCUMENTS

American Journal of International Law (New York).
American State Papers: Foreign Relations of the United States.
Annual Register (London).
Archives Diplomatiques (Paris).
British and Foreign State Papers (London).
CLERCQ, A. J. DE. Recueil des traités de la France. 10 vols. (Paris, 1864–1872).
COBBETT. Parliamentary History.
HANSARD. Parliamentary Debates.
HERTSLET, SIR E. Collection of Treaties (London, 1827, etc.).
——— Map of Europe by Treaty. 4 vols. (London, 1875–1891).
MARTENS, G. F. DE (continued by C. de Martens, Saalfeld, Murhard, Samwer, Hopf, Stoerk, and H. Triepel). Recueil des traités. Suppléments. Nouveau Recueil (1761–1913).
Official Opinions of the Attorneys-General of the United States (Washington).
Parliamentary Papers.
Revue Générale de Droit International Public (Paris).
U.S. Senate Documents.
VILLEFORT. Recueil des traités, conventions, lois, décrets et autres actes relatifs à la paix avec l'Allemagne. 5 vols. (Paris, 1872–1879).

PART I

TERMINATION OF WAR BY MERE WITHDRAWAL FROM HOSTILITIES; OR BY CONQUEST AND SUBJUGATION

CHAPTER I

TERMINATION OF WAR BY RECIPROCAL INTERMISSION OF HOSTILITIES

Modes of terminating hostilities—*De facto* cessation of hostilities—Resulting difficulties—Claims of the contending parties—Principle of *uti possidetis*—Principle of *status quo ante bellum*—Public proclamation necessary.

Modes of terminating hostilities.

THERE are three ways of terminating hostilities between belligerent States, namely: (1) by a mere cessation of hostilities on both sides, without any definite understanding supervening; (2) by the conquest and subjugation of one of the contending parties by the other, so that the former is reduced to impotence and submission; (3) by a mutual arrangement embodied in a treaty of peace, whether the honours of war be equal or unequal.

Under the first mode the relationships between the parties remain in a condition of uncertainty; and owing to the numerous difficulties involved, combatant States have very seldom resorted to this method of withdrawing from the war, without arriving at some definite and intelligible decision. Of the second mode, history presents a larger number of instances, especially in earlier times when, on the one hand, might predominated over or was synonymous with right, and, on the other, when inequality of civilization and less settled national life conduced to territorial expansion and absorption. The third is the more usual mode of putting an end to hostilities, and offers the largest number of examples. Let us take each of the methods in turn, and examine its application and effects, as illustrated by the leading instances of modern times. First, as to the *de facto* cessation of hostilities, and the *de facto* revival of peace relations.

For our present purpose there is no need to go back further than the eighteenth century for examples. Thus, in 1716 the war between Charles XII of Sweden and Frederick Augustus, King of Poland, came to an end in this manner. An armistice was concluded, whereby the actual fighting was suspended, but the state of war between the two countries remained. For no less than ten years did this precarious condition continue, neither side being disposed to resume military operations against the other.

De facto **cessation of hostilities.**

Finally a state of peace was declared, and therefore recognized *de jure*, by means of letters exchanged between the two monarchs.

This example, however, is not an entirely satisfactory one, owing to the various exceptional features that characterized the conflict. As a result of the victories of Charles XII at Cracow and Warsaw in 1702, Frederick Augustus abdicated, and Stanislas, a nominee of the victor, ascended the throne of Poland. In 1709, however, the Swedish sovereign was defeated at Pultawa, and Stanilas was deposed. This marked a *de facto*, but not necessarily a *de jure*, cessation of hostilities. Moreover, Frederick Augustus had taken up arms against Sweden contrary to the decision of the Polish Diet, so that some doubt has been expressed as to whether the war was a *justum bellum* at all, and hence whether it furnished a legitimate precedent.[1]

In 1720 the war between Spain and France was terminated by the mere withdrawal of their respective forces.

In 1801 the Russian war with Persia, which was begun by Catherine II, was similarly ended by Paul I.

The conflict between Spain and her revolted South American colonies offers a further instance. It was in 1810 that the War of Independence began; hostilities did not actually cease till 1825, but a state of peace was not formally established until some twenty years had elapsed, when diplomatic relations were instituted. With the victory of Bolivar at Carabolo in 1820, Venezuela acquired her independence, which was not, however, formally recognized by the mother-country till 1850. After the battle of Pichincha, 1822, Ecuador asserted her freedom; but not before 1840 was shipping of the new Republic permitted to enter Spanish ports. In 1843, that is nearly twenty years after the *de facto* cessation of hostilities, the independence of Chile was formally acknowledged by Spain.

Again, in 1866 in the war between Prussia and the German States, Prussia did not reduce to submission or conclude peace with the principality of Lichtenstein, though hostilities were terminated with some of the States by conquest and subjugation and with others by means of treaties of peace.

Finally, in 1867 the war between France and Mexico came to an end by the withdrawal of the French troops, effected at the

[1] Cf. Sir R. Phillimore, *Commentaries upon International Law*, 3rd ed., 4 vols. (London, 1879–1889), vol. iii. § 511; A. W. Heffter, *Das Europäische Völkerrecht der Gegenwart* (Berlin, 1882); French ed. (Paris, 1883), § 176.

instance of the United States Government. A considerable length of time passed by before diplomatic relations were resumed between the former belligerent countries; at first Mexico appointed only commercial agents in France. However, with the fall of Napoleon III, the ill-feeling between the two States disappeared; though it is noteworthy that in 1878 France did not invite Mexico to take part in the universal exhibition held in Paris. After a good deal of negotiation, an agreement was arrived at whereby both parties engaged to waive their respective claims; in November 1880 their international reconciliation was formally signalized by a diplomatic instrument, and in November 1886 it was confirmed and completed by a treaty of friendship, commerce, and navigation.[1]

Resulting difficulties.

The above examples of the reciprocal intermission of hostilities show that there are several serious difficulties that attend this mode of procedure. In the first place, the relationships between the Governments in question remain uncertain; secondly, their subjects, so far as commercial intercourse is concerned, are in a doubtful position; thirdly, the relationship between the two Governments and third Governments gives rise to some embarrassment. When the belligerent operations cease and the forces engaged are tacitly withdrawn, do third States remain neutrals, subject to the various obligations of neutrality, until a formal declaration of peace has been made? And what is their position, should such declaration be deferred for a considerable length of time? On this point reference may be made to an American pronouncement which, notwithstanding its expression in general terms, furnishes a satisfactory answer to the questions raised. "It is certain," observed the American Secretary of State in 1868, "that a condition of war can be raised without an authoritative declaration of war, and, on the other hand, the situation of peace may be restored by the long suspension of hostilities without a treaty of peace being made. History is full of such occurrences. What period of suspension of war is necessary to justify the presumption of the restoration of peace has never yet been settled, and must in every case be determined with reference to collateral facts and circumstances." With regard to the affairs of Spain and Chile, he maintained that if either Power claimed that the war between them still existed—seeing that active hostilities had long ceased—it would be obliged to substantiate its claims. "Peru, equally with Spain, has an absolute right to decline the good offices or mediation of the United States for peace as either

[1] Cf. D'Estournelles de Constant, "Relations extérieures" [of Mexico], in *Le Mexique au début du XXe siècle*. By several writers (Paris, n.d.), vol. ii. p. 304.

has to accept the same. The refusal of either would be incon clusive as an evidence of determination to resume or continue the war. It is the interest of the United States, and of all nations, that the return of peace, however it may be brought about, shall be accepted whenever it has become clearly established. Whenever the United States shall find itself obliged to decide the question whether the war still exists between Spain and Peru, or whether that war has come to an end, it will make that decision only after having carefully examined all the pertinent facts which shall be within its reach, and after having given due consideration to such representations as shall have been made by the several parties interested." [1]

Claims of the contending parties.

Another difficulty that arises concerns the claims of the contending parties. When they merely discontinue *de facto* their armed contention, are their claims to be regarded as being dependent on the principle of the *status quo ante bellum* or on that of the *uti possidetis* (that is, the *status quo post bellum*)? In other words, are they put back into the position in which they were before the outbreak of war, or is their position in which they find themselves on the termination of active hostilities to be considered their definitive legal position? There is a difference of opinion on this question among publicists and jurists. The majority hold the second alternative—that the position of the States in question is to be considered that which exists at the time hostilities have actually terminated. On principle this is the more reasonable view.

Principle of *uti possidetis*.

The fact that the war has ceased and that neither party is disposed to prosecute hostilities further in order to obtain a more decisive solution, may justifiably be interpreted to mean that they are willing to let matters rest where they are, and to remain satisfied with their relative positions, and with their respective positions in regard to third States. This is the *status*, then, that may be held to be the point of departure for their future relations. But a final rule to cover all possible cases cannot be laid down. The circumstances of each case have to be considered. Thus it may well be that soon after an aggrieved State has taken up arms against another State for the purpose of obtaining redress, it decides to postpone its enterprise, but expressly and openly re-asserts its claims which, it is manifest, it intends to exact afterwards by warlike means. In such a case the general principle of *uti possidetis* can scarcely be supplied as the determining criterion. War is the

[1] Mr. Seward, Secretary of State to Mr. Goñi, Spanish Minister, July 22, 1868; *Diplom. Corr.* 1868, vol. ii. pp. 32, 34; J. B. Moore, *Digest of International Law*, 8 vols. (Washington, 1906), vol. vii. pp. 336–337.

final method—the *ultima ratio*—for settling international disputes; but in the absence of a definite decision in the clash of arms, the previous dispute cannot, obviously, be considered to have been settled. But some qualification is necessary to this statement, if the war has gone on for some length of time, and the aggrieved belligerent has withdrawn from the conquest, allowed its grievances to drop, and has not manifested any intention to seek further reparation. The intention is the vital consideration; and the intention of the withdrawing State is to be gathered from its conduct and its attitude.

Status quo ante bellum.

However this may be, to adopt as a general rule the principle of the *status quo ante bellum*—as does, for example, Sir R. Phillimore[1]—would be fraught with greater difficulties, especially with regard to third States. If, after a period of hostilities, one of the belligerent States takes possession of property—say, a certain portion of territory or a vessel—belonging to the other, and then, though not fully satisfied in respect of its grievance, withdraws from the war for the time being, without implying that it will not renew active hostilities, it is clearly more reasonable for third States to consider the then position—namely, the *status quo post bellum*—as the basis for future international relationships. It is impossible to hold that third States should refuse to recognize the captured territory or vessel as the captor's legitimate possession, and expect it to be restored to the dispossessed State, before normal relationships can be resumed between those third States and each of the contending Powers. Where there are such claims as have not been settled or affected by the actual condition of affairs existing at the time the warlike enterprise was abandoned, it is, of course, open to the parties to come to a mutual agreement on them. But if within a reasonable length of time after the termination of hostilities no steps are taken to come to an agreement on or to assert by force the prior claims, it is a justifiable presumption that such claims have beeen waived, and that the principle of *uti possidetis*—and not that of the *status quo ante bellum*—is to determine the starting-point of future relationships.

In any case, it is desirable that a formal declaration of the resumption of peace should be made by the belligerents. Their subjects will then know when they are entitled to recommence commercial intercourse with each other, and third States will ascertain at what date they cease to be neutrals and become again members of a normal society of nations.

[1] *Commentaries*, vol. iii. p. 511: "In such a state of things the presumption of law would be, that both parties had agreed that the *status quo ante bellum* should be revived."

A public proclamation is, similarly, desirable when a civil war is brought to a conclusion. The observations of Mr. Bayard, the United States Secretary of State, may be here referred to on this point, as well as by way of supplementing what has been said above. In reference to the American Civil War he wrote in 1886 in a despatch to the Spanish Minister: "I have yet to learn that a war in which the belligerents, as was the case with the late Civil War, are persistent and determined, can be said to have closed until peace is conclusively established, either by treaty when the war is foreign, or when civil by proclamation of the termination of hostilities on one side and the acceptance of such proclamation on the other. The surrender of the main armies of one of the belligerents does not of itself work such termination; nor does such surrender, under the law of nations, of itself end the conqueror's right to seize and sequestrate whatever property he may find which his antagonist could use for a renewal of hostilities. The seizure of such property, and eminently so when, as in the present case, it is notoriously part of the war capital of the defeated Government, is an act not merely of policy and right, but of mercy, in proportion to the extent to which the party overthrown is composed of high-spirited men who are ready to submit only when their military resources are wholly exhausted, and not until then. This, in the summer of 1865, was the condition of things in the Southern and South-western States of this nation. The period was one in which the maintenance of military rule and the taking into the possession of the United States of all the property capable of use as military resources of those States was essential to the permanent restoration of order, peace, and a common municipal law. This was so from the nature of things, and such was the course of public action. It is in accordance with this principle that the Supreme Court of the United States has formally decided that the late Civil War terminated in the particular sections of the United States at the period designated in the proclamations of the President of the United States."[1] And by the President's proclamation of April 2, 1866, "the insurrection which heretofore existed in the States of Georgia, South Carolina, Virginia, North Carolina, Tennessee, Alabama, Louisiana, Arkansas, Mississippi, and Florida is at an end, and is henceforth to be so regarded. Up to and before that date the insurrection in those States was held to exist. After that date it was held to be at an end."[2]

Public proclamation necessary.

[1] *Brown* v. *Hiatts* (1872), 15 Wallace, 177; *Adger* v. *Alston* (1872), 15 Wallace, 555; *Batesville Institute* v. *Kauffman* (1873), 18 Wallace, 151.

[2] Mr. Bayard, Secretary of State, to Mr. Muruaga, Spanish Minister, December 3, 1886, *Foreign Relations of U.S.* (1887), pp. 1015, 1019; Moore, *Digest*, vol. vii. pp. 337–338.

CHAPTER II

TERMINATION OF WAR BY CONQUEST AND SUBJUGATION

Difference between conquest and subjugation—Difference between occupation and annexation—Case of the Elector of Hesse-Cassel—Effect of treaty of cession —Treaty of cession and title of the conqueror—Surrender of the South African Republic and Orange Free State: the Peace of Vereeniging is not a peace proper—Other examples of conquest and annexation—Title by conquest.

Difference between conquest and subjugation.

A DISTINCTION may be drawn between conquest and subjugation,[1] though the two terms are frequently used as synonymous. The conquest of a territory does not necessarily involve its subjugation; for conquest implies the condition of things brought about prior to subjugation. Therefore subjugation necessarily does involve conquest. Conquest means nothing more than effective military occupation by the enemy forces; and as such it may be merely a provisional procedure, or a means to some other end contemplated by the Government, of the occupying forces. It may well happen that these occupying forces are eventually expelled by the adversary; if so, the military occupation comes *ipso facto* to an end. But in the case of subjugation—the *debellatio* of the Romans—not only have the occupying forces acquired effective possession of the territory concerned, but the adversary has been reduced to impotence and submission, or has been practically annihilated—or, at all events, all his organized resistance has disappeared[2]—and the victorious Government has clearly manifested its intention to hold the said territory permanently under its dominion. Such intention may be manifested implicitly, as, for example, by a long-continued performance, without intermission, of the functions usually performed by a ruler; or it may be manifested explicitly by some formal act, such as the despatch of a diplomatic circular to the Powers, or publishing a declaration of the transfer of sovereignty. Here, then,

[1] Cf. L. Oppenheim, *International Law*, 2 vols. (London, 1912), vol. i. p. 236; vol. ii. p. 264.

[2] Cf. Vattel, *Droit des gens*, liv. iii. ch. xiii. §§ 197, 198.

we see three steps—conquest, subjugation, and annexation. In conquest alone the military possession was simply *de facto*, depending on an actual fact, namely, superior force; after subjugation and annexation, the territorial possession becomes *de jure*, that is, sanctioned by law.

Difference between occupation and annexation.

This difference between effective military occupation (or conquest) and annexation involves a profound difference in the rights conferred by each. Whilst the rights of occupation are limited, those consequent on annexation are unlimited. The occupant[1] is entitled for the time being to govern the territory occupied, to introduce his martial law and modify the territorial law so far as the safety and the exigencies of his army imperatively demand it. In other respects the local law must not be interfered with, especially that portion of it which governs the civil relations of the inhabitants to each other. Similarly, the occupant's court-martial may, for the same urgent reasons, supersede to some extent the tribunals of the invaded State; but the latter may not be abolished indiscriminately, and especially so when their decisions are confined to settling disputes of the inhabitants themselves and do not aim at impairing the position of the army of occupation. The general administration of the territory should also be allowed to proceed, as far as possible, on the former lines, and to be conducted by the former officials. An oath may, however, be required from the latter, that in the fulfilment of their functions they will do nothing prejudicial to the occupant. But no oath of loyalty or allegiance may be exacted from the population, inasmuch as a mere occupant is not a sovereign. The inhabitants are under no legal obligation to obey his orders; their obedience depends entirely on considerations of prudence. But in no case may they be required to furnish information about the army of their country or its means of defence.

Again, the occupant may make use of the resources of the country, but only in proportion to his actual needs, and subject to certain qualifications. Thus he may use the immovable property of the invaded State, not as a proprietor but as a usufructuary. He may appropriate the State funds and realizable securities, together with arms, munitions, stores, supplies, means of transport, etc., which are necessary for his military operations. On the contrary private property, and property belonging to corporations or municipal bodies, or to institutions devoted to education, religion, charity, science, and art, are alike inviolable, which the occupant

[1] See *Hague Convention concerning the Laws and Customs of War on Land* (1907), No. IV; Arts. 42–56.

may not destroy or appropriate. Contributions and requisitions, however, may be levied, but only for the legitimate needs of the army and not for purposes of ransom, intimidation, or self-enrichment, and even then, subject to provision for payment of the articles supplied or reimbursement in respect of the sums advanced. Should taxes and other imposts be levied they must be utilized for the benefit of the State and for defraying the expenses of the administration; and they must be calculated on the basis of the previous rules of assessment and distribution. All these regulations and restrictions show that the rights of an occupant are by no means equivalent to those of a proprietor, and that occupation is, in its strict denotation, far removed from sovereignty.

In the case of the Elector of Hesse-Cassel,[1] the question of the rights of occupation and completed subjugation came up. In 1806, during the war between France and Prussia, the French occupied Hesse-Cassel and expelled the Elector. The territory remained in the hands of Napoleon for about a year, and then the greater portion of it was embodied in the newly formed kingdom of Westphalia, of which Jerome Bonaparte was acknowledged king by the treaties of Tilsit, 1807, and Schönbrunn, 1809. Napoleon and Jerome made an arrangement disposing of the private domains of the Elector and providing for the payment of debts due to the latter or to his former province. In 1810, Count von Hahn, a debtor of the Elector, paid over a part of his debt to Napoleon and received a release for the whole. Three years later, however, the Elector was restored to his dominions, and his position ensured by international conventions. Thereupon he laid claim to all his former rights, and, declining to acknowledge the validity of the transactions entered into by the intervening Governments, he dispossessed the purchasers of his former domains, and forbade the local courts to take cognizance of these acts of his. The ousted proprietors appealed first to the Congress of Vienna and then to the Diet of the Germanic Confederation, but in vain. The views of jurists, however, condemned the Elector's proceedings, on the ground that the principle of postliminium, asserted by him, did not apply to property transferred in the meantime to a third party, nor to a case in which military occupation was followed by completed subjugation, especially when the conqueror's title was confirmed not only by the acquiescence of the inhabitants but also by treaty and the recognition of foreign Powers.

Case of the Elector of Hesse-Cassel.

As to the debts, it was held in judicial decisions that the subjects of the King of Westphalia who had paid their debts to him or to his

[1] Phillimore, *Commentaries*, vol. iii. §§ 568–574; pp. 841 *seq.*; Pitt Cobbett, *Cases and Opinions on International Law*, vol. ii. (1913), pp. 248 *seq.*

exchequer were not liable to pay them a second time; and that the full release given by Napoleon to Count von Hahn, who was not a Westphalian subject, was valid, even though only a part of his original debt had been so paid. The grounds of this judgment were that the title of Napoleon was based not merely on the temporary rights due to military occupation, but on subjugation followed by the definite assumption of sovereignty intended to be permanent; that the doctrine of *restitutio in integrum* did not apply, as the Elector's return was not a mere continuation of dominion, seeing that he had abandoned armed opposition to Napoleon, and had been considered politically extinct by the treaties of Tilsit and Schönbrunn and by foreign Powers, so that the conqueror's title thereby became complete; and that, in any case, a restored owner could not claim that property disposed of should be replaced.

In reference to Napoleon's title to Hesse-Cassel, there is some doubt as to when it became valid. He conquered the territory in 1806, and a year later dealt with it as his own. It is, perhaps, not maintainable that the title was then complete, inasmuch as opposition to Napoleon was being continued by Great Britain, which might have arrested the conquest from him by force of arms. This did not happen, however; so that after several years' firm and quiet possession, and before the restoration of the Elector, the title may well be held to have been perfected.

Another point that remains to be noted in connection with the above case concerns the appropriation of the Elector's private property. Here we have to remember that a century ago the modern distinction between the private property of the sovereign and the domains of the State was not definitely recognized. Under the present system private property of the Crown would not be confiscated; though it might, of course, be liable to forfeiture under municipal law if, after the annexation of the territory, the deposed sovereign continued active hostilities against the new Government.

Effect of treaty of cession.

Sometimes the conquest and subjugation of territory is followed by a treaty of cession. This makes good any defects of title that might otherwise attach to the military possessor; but such a treaty, though desirable, is not indispensable, as a valid title may have been acquired without it. Thus, when Heligoland fell into British possession by conquest, and before its cession by the Treaty of Kiel, 1814, Lord Stowell held that the distinction, which was attempted to be made, was merely a formal one, and that the island was rightfully the property of the British Crown. He held, further, that a conqueror was entitled to alienate domains as soon as he acquired firm possession, and that the right of the defeated belligerent to such domains was but a "shadowy right," even though no treaty of cession were concluded. "I observe," he said, "that the grant from the Crown to the Lord High Admiral applies to the King's dominions generally, and that there is nothing which points to a distinction between those parts of the King's dominions over which the Crown has *plenum dominium* or otherwise. No point is more clearly settled in the courts of common law than that a conquered country forms immediately part of the King's dominions."[1]

This pronouncement must be taken subject to the qualifications set forth above. Property in territory does not vest in a conqueror immediately after he has taken possession of it. Some time must elapse, in order to allow his claim to ripen, and to obtain or enforce definitively the acquiescence of the defeated sovereign and the recognition of third States.

Treaty of cession and title of conqueror.

When there is a treaty of cession, as a sequel to a conquest, the title of the conqueror is, technically, based on the cession, though virtually it be the outcome of the acts of subjugation. In the absence of a formal international document, the title is purely and simply based on conquest and on the unilateral authority of annexation. In case the territory subjugated constitutes the whole of some particular State, there can be no question, logically, of a supervening treaty of cession or treaty of peace. If there is no territory there is no State; so that a bilateral transaction cannot well take place. There may, however, be an act of submission or surrender; this will not be the same as a treaty or a peace in the strict sense of the term, even though it be designated one or the other through considerations of prudence, or in order to avoid the further effusion of blood and to facilitate the subsequent pacification of the annexed country. The act of surrender, if not essential to validate the title of the conquering State, is desirable for the purpose of regulating the fate of the defeated army, the displaced sovereign, his family and his property, the civil officials, the position of the inhabitants, the prisoners of war, the questions of amnesty, indemnity, etc. Thus in the Prussian war of 1866, the capitulation of Langensalza, June 29, 1866, provided, *inter alia*, that the King of Hanover, together with the Crown Prince and a suite, might reside freely outside the territory of Hanover, and that the private property of the King should remain at his disposal. This property was, however, afterwards sequestrated; and the sequestration did not cease till 1892.

[1] *The Foltina* (1814), 1 Dodson, 450–451; referring to *Campbell* v. *Hall* (1774), Cowper, 208.

A more notable and more recent example of an act of surrender is that of the late South African Republic and the Orange Free State. The act in question is known as the "Peace of Vereeniging"; but, obviously, it is not a treaty of peace, as it was not this transaction which brought the war to an end—the hostilities were in reality terminated by subjugation. The transaction has not the character of a conventional compromise, whereby mutual rights and obligations are postulated. Moreover, on May 24, 1900, and on the following September 1, Lord Roberts issued proclamations annexing the Orange Free State and the South African Republic respectively. Though these annexations were premature—as will be shown presently—they became valid in 1901 when the military occupation of the countries in question was rendered effective and the resistance of the enemy was reduced to a negligible quantity. Let us recall the circumstances leading to the surrender.[1]

Surrender of the South African Republic and the Orange Free State.

On February 28, 1901, Commandant-General Botha had an interview with Lord Kitchener at Middleburg with a view to peace negotiations. General Botha intimated that his country's independence should constitute the fundamental condition. But this was rejected. The terms of submission were afterwards formulated by the Boers more specifically, as follows: (1) That representative government should be introduced without undue delay, (2) the Dutch language should have equal rights with English, (3) the franchise of Kaffirs should be deferred, (4) Dutch Church property should remain intact, (5) Great Britain should assume all the debts of the two Republics, including notes, requisitions, and other liabilities incurred during the war, (6) no war taxation should be imposed on farmers, (7) prisoners of war should be restored as soon as possible, (8) an amnesty should be extended to all, (9) financial aid should be given to ruined farmers, (10) rifles should be retained, as a protection against the natives. After Lord Kitchener had communicated with Lord Lansdowne, the Foreign Secretary, he offered (March 7, 1901) the following terms: (1) Surrender of all rifles, guns, ammunition, etc., (2) substitution of Crown Colony government for military administration, to be followed eventually by self-government, (3) equal rights for the Dutch language in schools and courts of law, (4) immunity of Church property, public trusts, and orphan funds, (5) no liability for debts to be undertaken by Great Britain, but, as an act of grace, a sum not exceeding a million pounds to be set aside to repay inhabitants for requisitions

[1] See Sir F. Maurice, *History of the War in South Africa*, 1899–1902, 4 vols. Written by direction of His Majesty's Government. Vol. iv. (1910), pp. 523 *seq.* (vol. iv. is by Captain M. H. Grant).

made by the late Governments, (6) no war tax on farmers, (7) loans to farmers taking the oath of allegiance to repair losses suffered during the war, (8) amnesty for all regular acts of war, subject to prosecution for treason of British subjects belonging to Cape Colony and Natal on their return to these colonies, (9) restoration of prisoners of war, (10) burghers taking the oath of allegiance to be allowed fire-arms by licence, (11) no franchise to Kaffirs before the introduction of representative government, and if then given the predominance of the white race to be ensured. These terms were refused by the Boer leaders; so hostilities were resumed.

The following January the Netherlands Government tendered its good offices for the purpose of putting in communication negotiators to be nominated by the belligerent parties, and offered accommodation in Holland for a peace conference. Lord Lansdowne replied that the previous announcement as to refusing foreign intervention must be adhered to, and that the negotiations must take place in South Africa between the British Commander-in-Chief and the Boer leaders.

On April 12, 1902, Lord Kitchener met the Boer leaders at Pretoria, and received their demands once more, which were to this effect: (1) Franchise, (2) equal claims of Dutch in schools, (3) customs union, (4) postal, telegraph, and railways union, (5) arbitration in case of future differences, (6) amnesty, (7) dismantling of all forts in the Transvaal and Orange River Colony. This proposal having been cabled to London, a reply was at once returned that terms involving independent government could not be entertained. The Commander-in-Chief and Lord Milner were at the same time directed to ask the Boer representatives to propose fresh terms based on the abandonment of independence. In the meantime the military situation of the Boers was rapidly becoming worse.

A conference was held at Pretoria, April 16. The Boer leaders then declared that their mission was to make peace, not to surrender the independence of their people. They proposed first, an armistice, and secondly, that one of their delegates should be summoned from Europe in order to obtain the views of the banished statesmen. The British answer was that military reasons forbade such delay, and that the deputation in Europe could not be considered a valid executive. In the meantime instructions arrived from the Foreign Secretary in regard to terms on the basis of relinquishment of independence.

At the following day's meeting, the British conditions offered in February were, in substance, presented again. The Boer delegates once more requested an armistice, and the attendance of one of their European deputies; for the third time Lord Kitchener refused. The latter, however, suggested that the delegates, under the protection of a local armistice, should get the votes of the commandos. It was thereupon arranged that sixty representatives —thirty for each country—should be elected by ballot, and should lay the wishes of the people before a general assembly to be held at Vereeniging on May 15.

On April 18 the delegates left Pretoria. The voting on the essential question of abandoning independence or continuing hostilities proceeded till May 13. On May 15 the elected representatives of the commandos assembled at Vereeniging, and for two days deliberated on the fateful alternatives. The Transvaal deputies spoke of the complete ruin of their country, the absence of horses, the scarcity of supplies, and accordingly they proposed (all but six of them) to terminate the struggle. On the other hand, the Orange Free State delegates supporting their leader, General De Wet, were for continuing resistance, if the surrender of independence was demanded. Then a compromise was suggested by one of the Transvaal representatives, namely, (1) a British protectorate, (2) cession of a portion of territory, (3) abandonment of foreign embassies and relations, (4) conclusion of a defensive treaty with Great Britain with regard to South Africa.

Lord Kitchener and Lord Milner rejected this proposal, and insisted on the following preamble as an indispensable part of the terms of peace laid down in February: "The burgher forces in the field will forthwith lay down their arms, handing over all guns, rifles, and munitions of war in their possession or under their control, and desist from any further resistance to the authority of His Majesty King Edward VII, whom they recognize as their lawful sovereign. The manner and details of this surrender will be arranged between Lord Kitchener and Commandant-General Botha, Assistant Commandant-General De la Rey, and Chief Commandant De Wet."

General Botha once again appealed for better terms; but Lord Milner could not make any departure from the main principles, though he was prepared to make certain modifications in the details. A sub-committee was then appointed, which met on May 20 and 21 and drew up, together with the above-mentioned preamble, twelve articles embodying provisional terms. Discussion thereon followed; the Boer commanders urged that Great Britain should assume their financial liabilities incurred in the field, on the ground that a conqueror acquiring the assets of the conquered should likewise undertake their debts. Lord Milner declined to accept such a principle, as a State cannot be expected to pay the adversary the expenses due to his hostilities; but he suggested, as an additional concession, that a further grant might be recommended if the Boer leaders named a reasonable sum. After consideration, they proposed the sum of three millions. The British Government objected, not to the sum, but to its allocation—for a large portion of it might go to foreigners who had supplied munitions of war to the Republican forces—and therefore suggested certain modifications as final, demanding a definitive reply by the evening of May 31 at the latest.

On May 28 the Boer representatives left Pretoria for Vereeniging; the following day the final conditions were submitted to the assembly, and for two days the meeting swayed between peace and war, when suddenly General De Wet rose and moved a resolution for peace, which was carried by 54 votes to 6. The appointed signatories hastened to Pretoria, and at 11 o'clock in the evening of May 31 the terms of peace were signed and sealed.

The "Peace" of Vereeniging is not a treaty of peace proper.

Now it cannot be validly held that the Act, described as the "Terms of surrender of the Boer forces in the field,"[1] is a peace treaty proper. It was not an ordinary case of cession, but a case of surrender. It is true that six of the Boer signatories were designated in the instrument as "acting as the Government of the South African Republic," and the four others as "acting as the Government of the Orange Free State." But this terminology is not authoritative, as against the substantial nature of the Act. Besides, this very terminology implies a difference. For it makes use of the expression "acting as the Government . . . on behalf of their respective burghers," in contrast with the expression "on behalf of the British Government," applied to the British representatives. No treaty describes the signatories of one of the parties thereto as "acting as" some particular Government, and "on behalf of" their fellow-citizens. An examination of the Peace of Vereeniging and regular peace treaties will show the radical difference between them, not only in form, but also in purport, intention, substance.[2] Further, we have already seen that the British Government throughout discountenanced all proposals for the "renewed independence" of the States which had already been validly annexed before the peace negotiations were instituted. The annexation meant loss of independence, therefore disappearance of all judicial personality, therefore absolute incapacity to enter into a peace treaty proper.

[1] Cf. *Parliamentary Papers, South Africa*, 1902, Cd. 1096.

[2] See the texts given in the Appendix, *infra*.

We may here recall that in a case in the Transvaal Supreme Court in 1903,[1] when it was argued that the Peace of Vereeniging should be regarded as a cession treaty, Chief Justice Innes expressly declined to accept this view. He observed:

"I do not so read the articles of peace signed at Pretoria. On the contrary, it seems to me that scrupulous care was taken by those who represented the British Government to refrain from any recognition of the South African Republic or its Government, while at the same time they fully recognized the position of certain leaders of a force entitled to all the privileges of belligerents, as being persons with whom it was proper and necessary to treat in regard to the terms upon which that force should lay down its arms. This is clear to my mind from the language used in describing the capacities of the several signatories and the persons they represented, and the body of the document, while referring to the burgher forces and to the burghers in the field, makes no reference whatever to the Governments of either of the two Republics."[2]

Other examples of conquest and annexation.

Other examples of subjugation and annexation may be mentioned. Thus Poland was destroyed by the Third Partition. In 1859–1860 Sardinia subjugated the Two Sicilies, the Grand Dukedom of Tuscany, the Dukedoms of Parma and Modena,[3] and with the annexation, in 1870, of the former Papal States the modern Kingdom of Italy came into being. The Southern Confederacy fell in the American Civil War, after a four years' conflict. In 1866 Prussia subjugated, and, by a proclamation of September 20, annexed to her dominion the

[1] *Van Deventer* v. *Hancke and Mossop* (1903), Transvaal Sup. Ct. Rep. 404.

[2] *Ibid.*, 411. In an article in the *Law Quarterly Review*, vol. xxi. pp. 303, 307, Sir Thomas Barclay, discussing the relation of the South African Railway case to international law, maintained that the "terms of surrender" constituted an agreement, which should be considered a convention or treaty on the ground that the Boer negotiating parties were described as acting as Governments of their respective countries. "Nor can there be any question as to the representative character of the signatories who were appointed under a resolution adopted by an assembly of the burghers held at Vereeniging." The writer stated further that the British Government had acknowledged the existence of the Boer Governments down to May 31, 1902. It has already been shown above that this claim is untenable. We have already seen that the British Government did not make such acknowledgment; for long before that date it had annexed formally and in fact the two States, and had to the last insisted on the annexations, so that it could not have admitted at the same time that the Governments of the annexed territories were in existence. Further, the representatives were described as representing the burghers, and not as representing sovereigns or governments.

[3] Cf. the Proclamations of the King of Sardinia, March 18 and March 22, 1860; *British and Foreign State Papers*, vol. lvii. pp. 1029 *seq.*

Kingdom of Hanover, the Dukedom of Nassau, the Electorate of Hesse-Cassel, and the Free Town of Frankfort-on-the-Main.[1] The territorial accessions of Great Britain in India and of Russia in Central Asia comprise areas more extensive than those of the ancient conquests. In 1885 Great Britain conquered Upper Burma, and on January 1, 1886, the Governor-General of India issued a proclamation annexing the territory thus acquired: "By command of the Queen-Empress it is hereby notified that the territories formerly governed by King Theebaw will no longer be under his rule, but have become part of Her Majesty's dominions, and will during Her Majesty's pleasure be administered by such officers as the Viceroy and Governor-General of India may from time to time appoint."[2]

Of all the titles by which sovereigns hold and govern territories, title by conquest is now generally considered the least desirable.

Title by conquest.

Nevertheless, having regard to international practice and to the fact that modern international law contains no provision to the contrary, it must be admitted that such title is juridically valid. Protests against forcible annexation may be made by the defeated monarch or other head of the country, his claims may continue to be asserted; protests may, indeed, be made too by third States. But all such protests and claims are of no avail legally, whatever moral considerations may be urged in their support. Thus in 1860 Austria protested against the annexation to Sardinia of the States of Central Italy—but without affecting the legal and political significance of the proceeding. Sometimes, on the other hand, a neutral Power may, by means of a special convention, expressly recognize the new condition of affairs. As an instance of this may be mentioned the Treaty of Prague, August 23, 1866, between Austria and Prussia, whereby (Art. VI) the Emperor of Austria pledged himself to recognize the new arrangements that were to be made by the King of Prussia in North Germany, including the territorial alterations.[3]

[1] *State Papers*, vol. lvi. p. 1050.

[2] *Ibid.*, vol. lxxvii. pp. 980, 981.

[3] See Appendix (H).

CHAPTER III

PREMATURE ANNEXATION—VIEWS AS TO VALIDITY OF CONQUESTS

Premature annexation: By Great Britain, 1900; by Italy, 1911—Current of modern opinion against forcible annexation—Consent of country annexed—Resolutions of the International American Conference.

Premature annexation.

THERE have been cases in which a belligerent has invaded the enemy territory, or a part of it, expelled the enemy armed forces therefrom, and occupied it militarily, not merely for strategic reasons or for the purpose of ministering to the success of his campaign in general, but with a view to retaining such territory permanently and making it a part of his dominions. As we have seen, the annexation cannot necessarily be effected the moment military occupation has begun. None the less the intention of the invader may be based on his assurance of ultimate victory, and therefore on his capacity to carry out his project. We have already referred to the British operations in the South African War; from the first it became evident that Great Britain determined not only to win the war, but to annex the enemy's country. Similarly, in the Franco-German War, 1870–1871, as soon as the Germans invaded Alsace-Lorraine and got possession of these provinces, they established themselves therein and resolved never to restore them again; though conformably to the law of military occupation they did not claim to exercise absolute sovereignty in the territory until it was delivered to them by the treaty of peace—for here there was no question of annihilating the enemy and simply annexing his territory by a purely unilateral act.

On August 23, 1870, General von Werder, commanding the army before Strasburg, issued a notice to the local officials, which stated that the authority of the French Government in Alsace was superseded, and added that the various departments of French administration—e.g. the "préfectures," the "sous-préfectures," and the "mairies"—would continue, but under the obligation of carrying out the orders of the General. Another proclamation was published on August 30 by the Governor-General of Alsace, which declared that the territories occupied by the German military forces were withdrawn from French authority. Soon afterwards the reconstitution of the Government of Alsace was begun. This conduct was not fundamentally inconsistent with military occupation. Full sovereignty was claimed only from the date of the Treaty of Frankfort, May 10, 1871; for shortly before this instrument of peace was drawn up, the Germans permitted the people of the occupied territory to vote for the French National Assembly, as they were still considered to be French subjects *de jure*.

Again, during the Russian occupation of Bulgaria, 1877–1878, the Russians acted throughout on the assumption that the country would never be restored to Turkey under the former conditions. Russia had conceived it to be her imperious duty—as Professor de Martens says [1]—to take advantage of the period of occupation by establishing in Bulgaria a new and more regular condition of affairs. She took upon her the task of erecting new institutions in place of the bad Ottoman régime, so as to bring the occupied country into harmony with European civilization. Accordingly, the entire local administration was placed, during the occupation, in Russian hands. This procedure was condemned in some quarters on the ground that military occupation does not confer on an occupant such wide rights, and that he is not entitled, *qua* occupant, entirely to displace the local administration and put an end to the former government. But Russia's reply was that her occupation was not an ordinary taking possession of enemy territory—that is to say, merely provisional—which was to be handed back to the previous Government at the end of the war.[2] Possibly the special circumstances of this case, arising out of the notorious mischievous policy and administration of the Sublime Porte, are to be taken into consideration in deciding as to the legitimacy of the Russian action. However this may be, a military occupant is not entitled to exercise the powers of sovereignty in a particular region before he has definitively and validly annexed it. And annexation cannot be considered definitive and valid unless certain necessary conditions have been fulfilled, e.g. the subjugation of the enemy effected so thoroughly and completely that his possible resistance may fairly and safely be

[1] F. de Martens, *La paix et la guerre* (Paris, 1901), pp. 278, 279 : "Le but de la guerre imposait à la Russie le devoir impérieux de profiter de la période d'occupation pour établir en Bulgarie un nouvel ordre de choses, plus régulier."

[2] "Ces accusations et ces insinuations pourraient s'expliquer, si l'occupation russe avait été une prise de possession ordinaire, par suite, provisoire, d'un territoire ennemi, qui à l'issue de la guerre, pouvait être restitué à l'ancien gouvernment. Tel n'était pas le cas pour la Bulgarie, au delà du Danube." (*Ibid.*)

regarded as a negligible potentiality. Consequently, if the invader issues a proclamation purporting to annex a given territory before this essential condition is fulfilled, the proclamation is invalid.

In the South African War, President Steyn issued a proclamation as early as October 14, 1899, which, supplemented by proclamations of Wessels and other Transvaal and Orange Free State commandants, amounted practically to an annexation of British territory in Cape Colony. There was, indeed, no formal declaration to this effect, but the Boer proceedings were based on such an assumption, and "wavering disloyalists were impelled to take up arms by being told that to do so was their obligation as Transvaal or Free State burghers."[1]

Premature annexation by Great Britain.

This irregular action was counterbalanced, however, by the British premature annexation of the Orange Free State and the South African Republic, in 1900. On May 24, 1900, Lord Roberts, the Commander-in-Chief of the British forces operating against the Boer States, issued the following proclamation:—

"Whereas certain territories in South Africa, heretofore known as the Orange Free State, have been conquered by Her Majesty's forces, and it has seemed expedient to Her Majesty that the said territories should be annexed to, and should henceforth form part of, Her Majesty's dominions, and that I should provisionally, and until Her Majesty's pleasure is more fully known, be appointed administrator of the said territories, with power to take all such measures, and to make and enforce such laws, as I may deem necessary for the peace, order, and good government of the said territories:

Now, therefore, I, Frederick Sleigh, Baron Roberts of Kandahar, K.P., G.C.B., G.C.S.I., G.C.I.E., V.C., Field-Marshal, Commanding-in-Chief the British Forces in South Africa, by Her Majesty's command, and in virtue of the power and authority conferred upon me in that behalf by Her Majesty's Royal Commission, dated the 21st day of May, 1900, and in accordance with Her Majesty's instructions thereby and otherwise signified to me, do proclaim and make known that, from and after the publication hereof, the territories known as the Orange Free State are annexed to, and form part of, Her Majesty's dominions, and that provisionally, and until Her Majesty's pleasure is fully declared, the said territories will be administered by me with such powers as aforesaid.

[1] *The Times History of the War in South Africa*, ed. by L. S. Amery (London, 1902), vol. ii. p. 273.

Her Majesty is pleased to direct that the new territories shall henceforth be known as the Orange River Colony.

GOD SAVE THE QUEEN.

Given under my hand and seal, at the head-quarters of the army in South Africa, Camp south of the Vaal River, in the said territories, this 24th day of May, in the year of Our Lord 1900.

(L.S.) ROBERTS,
Field-Marshal, Commanding-in-Chief Her Majesty's Forces in South Africa." [1]

A similar proclamation, published September 1, 1900, purported to annex the South African Republic.[2]

Now at this date the Boer forces had by no means been subjugated; their organized resistance still remained, and was, indeed, very vigorous and effective. Both in the Transvaal and in the Orange Free State the British subsequently met with considerable reverses; and these reverses were inflicted by burghers who could not be considered other than the legitimate combatants of States whose independence was still in existence, and whose Governments still issued orders which were obeyed. Indeed, from September 1, 1900, to September 1, 1901, the British losses amounted to 1,857 officers and 34,531 men; so that it was manifestly impossible to claim that the armed contention was at an end. The position, then, assumed by the British authorities was juridically invalid, because it was unsupported by conditions *de facto*. As General Den Beer Poortugael, a leading European authority, writing in 1901, observed on the subject: "L'annexion est un fait juridique parfait, et peut donc être reconnu, lorsque la conquête a eu lieu dans des conditions qui répondent aux exigences du droit des gens. Mais, la guerre étant une action entre deux parties, il ne suffit pas pour établir la légalité du fait, que l'une de ces parties déclare que la contestation avec l'autre a pris fin. Il y faut le consentement libre de l'autre partie, ou du moins une supériorité de force devant laquelle, en fait, la seconde partie soit obligée de s'incliner, qu'elle ne puisse nier, à laquelle elle doive se soumettre." [3]

Such annexations unjustifiable.

British statesmen, too—e.g. Sir William Harcourt and Mr. Bryce (now Lord Bryce)—condemned the proclamations. The

[1] *Parl. Papers, S. Africa,* 1900, Cd. 426; *Brit. and For. State Papers* vol. 92, p. 548.
[2] *Ibid.*
[3] *Revue des Deux Mondes,* November, 1901, p. 42.

latter, speaking in the House of Commons of that of May 24, 1900, described it as "a monstrous proclamation, a proclamation absolutely opposed to the first principles of international law, a proclamation based upon a paper annexation made seven days before, which purported to treat the inhabitants of the two Republics[1] as rebels—rebels, forsooth, on the basis of this paper annexation."[2]

As soon as these proclamations were made, the President of the Orange Free State and the President of the South African Republic protested against them (June 11 and September 3, respectively), which they declared to be null and void, and contrary to the law of nations. They added that their nations remained free and independent, and refused to submit to British authority.

Reasons for the action.

Certain reasons have been suggested for the issue of the proclamations. In the first place, it was said that the British military authorities interpreted the departure of President Kruger for Europe as implying the disappearance of the Government of the South African Republic. But the departure, or expulsion, or death of the head of a Government does not necessarily put an end to that Government or to the juridical personality of the State. The Germans in 1870, despite their licentious conduct in many respects, advanced no such pretension. The Imperial Government had fallen, but they acknowledged its temporary substitute—the Government of National Defence—as the legitimate Government.[3] Secondly, judging from a proclamation of September 9, 1900, it appears that the object of the annexation was to prevent the "late South African Republic" from granting concessions, and so on the one hand raising money for the prosecution of hostilities, and on the other compromising the future of the country by burdening it with obligations imposed through military exigencies.

Notwithstanding the formal proclamations, it is fair to add that the British authorities did not on that account consider *in fact* that the countries had thereby been annexed; at all events, they made no attempt to apply in practice the various principles underlying annexation and change of sovereignty.

The Turco-Italian War, 1911, furnished another example of premature annexation on the part of Italy. The first Italian act

[1] This was said by inadvertence; for, as we have seen, the proclamation of May 24 referred only to the Orange Free State.

[2] Wyman's *Army Debates*, Session 1902, vol. i. p. 190.

[3] Cf. A. Mérignhac, *Les pratiques anglaises dans la guerre terrestre*, in *Revue générale de droit international public* (Paris, 1901), p. 96.

of occupation took place on October 5, 1911, when Italian vessels transported landing parties to take possession of Tripoli. Already in the middle of October public opinion in Italy declared in favour of annexation; and towards the end of the same month an announcement was made that the Italian Government had notified the Powers "of the cessation of Ottoman rule in North Africa," and that the newly acquired Italian possessions there extended from the Egyptian frontier on the east to Tunis on the west, and southward to the British and French zones of influence in Central Africa. These boundaries, however, were mentioned neither in the decree of annexation nor in the circular addressed by the Marquis di San Giuliano to the Powers. On November 5, exactly a month after the first act of occupation, the King of Italy issued a decree to the effect that Tripolitana and Cyrenaica were placed under the full and complete sovereignty of the Kingdom of Italy, that an Act of Parliament would establish the final regulations for the administration of the said regions, and that until this Act was promulgated provision would be made by royal decrees; it added that the decree would be laid before Parliament for the purpose of converting it into law. At the same time, the Italian Foreign Office sent a note to the Powers as follows:—

Premature annexation by Italy.

"The occupation of the principal towns of Tripolitana and Cyrenaica, the constant success of our armies, the strong forces which we have sent there and those which we are making ready ready to send, make any further opposition from Turkey ineffective and useless; on the other hand, in order to avoid the effusion of blood, it is urgent to dispel any dangerous uncertainty in the minds of the population of these regions. For this reason, by a royal decree dated to-day, Tripolitana and Cyrenaica have been definitely and irrevocably submitted to the full and complete sovereignty of the Kingdom of Italy.

Any other less radical solution, which would have left even the shade of a nominal sovereignty to the Sultan over these provinces, would have been a permanent cause for future conflicts between Italy and Turkey—conflicts which might fatally have broken out later, even against the will of the Governments, at a time far more dangerous for European peace.

The solution which we have adopted is the only one which definitely safeguards the interest of Italy, of Europe, and even of Turkey: a peace agreed to on this basis will eliminate any cause for wide divergence between Turkey and Italy, and we shall be able much more easily to adapt our policy to the important interest which we have in the maintenance of the territorial *status quo* in the Balkan Peninsula, of which the consolidation of the Ottoman Empire is the essential condition.

We are, therefore, very desirous, if Turkey's attitude does not make it impossible, that the conditions of peace be as much as possible in accordance with her legitimate interests and her prestige. Tripolitana and Cyrenaica have ceased to be a part of the Ottoman Empire, but we are at present prepared to examine in a liberal and conciliatory spirit the means of settling in the most suitable and honourable manner for Turkey the consequences of irrevocably accomplished facts.

Certainly we could not maintain these conciliatory intentions if Turkey persisted in uselessly prolonging the war. We, however, trust that the Great Powers' work of concord will bring her to take without delay wise decisions, and resolutions responding to her true interests and those of the whole civilized world. In any case, Italy will co-operate in obtaining such results by showing herself as ready to agree upon equitable terms of peace as she is resolute in her determination to adopt the most efficacious means of imposing it with the shortest possible delay." [1]

Two days later (November 7), General Caneva, accompanied by his staff and a guard of honour, read the royal decree before the Arab notables in Tripoli.

It appears that the annexation had not been notified to the Turkish Government. None the less, the Porte hastened to protest against the proceeding. In terms similar to those used by the Presidents of the late South African Republic and Orange Free State, it was pointed out that the decree of annexation was null and void, that it was contrary to international law, that a state of war still existed between the two belligerent Powers; moreover, the Powers were reminded that the action involved also a violation of the Treaties of Paris and Berlin, which ensured the territorial integrity of the Turkish Empire. This protest is expressed so precisely and pointedly that it is desirable to give it *verbatim*:

"The Imperial Ottoman Government learns that the Italian Government, having *motu proprio* promulgated a decree proclaiming the annexation of the Ottoman provinces of Tripoli and Bengazi, communicates the same to the Powers. The Sublime Porte protests in the most energetic manner against this proclamation, which it considers as null and valueless, both in law and in fact. Such an act is effectively null because it is contrary to the most elementary principles of international law, and equally so because Turkey and Italy are still in a state of war and because the Turkish Government intends to preserve and to defend by force of arms its

[1] Cf. Sir T. Barclay, *The Turco-Italian War* (London, 1912), pp. 38–40.

sovereign rights, which are imprescriptible and inalienable, over these two provinces. On the other hand, this proclamation and its communication to the Powers constitute a double and formal violation of the engagements solemnly contracted under treaties, especially those of Paris and Berlin, as well by Italy towards the Great Powers as by the latter towards the Ottoman Government, with reference to the territorial integrity of the Empire. Under these conditions the annexation proclaimed by the Italian Government remains juridically null, just as it is inexistent in fact." [1]

In point of fact, at the date of the alleged annexation there had been no subjugation whatever.[2] The Italian army had entered into occupation of little more than the main points on the coast of the provinces. It had taken possession of only five towns at considerable distances from each other. The interior remained in the hands of the Turks and Arabs, who from time to time made assaults on the Italian forces near the ports occupied. There was not even effective occupation, according to the provisions laid down in the Hague Regulations and Article 34 of the General Act of Berlin (February 26, 1885), which forbids fictitious annexation of territory.

Like the British premature proclamations in South Africa, the Italian decree was generally condemned. According to a statement made by Sir Edward Grey in the House of Commons, November 8, 1911—that is, three days after the decree was published—the British Government then regarded the annexation as inoperative. Even in Italy objections to it were raised on the ground of international law, whatever grounds policy might furnish. Thus, Professor Diena held [3] that juridically the acts in question possessed no international validity—his phrase is "internazionalmente irrilevanti"; and that Tripolitana and Cyrenaica really ceased in law to form part of the Ottoman Empire only as a result of the Sultan's firman annexed to the treaty of peace, which Italy promptly communicated to the other Powers.[4]

On the other hand, Professor Anzilotti of Rome maintained that there were two kinds of occupation: firstly, occupation pure and simple, secondly, occupation with the object of conquest and annexation; and he held that the latter kind would entitle the occupant to transfer to himself the sovereignty over the country

[1] *Rivista di diritto internazionale* (Roma, 1912), p. 568; Barclay, *The Turco-Italian War* (London, 1912), pp. 42–43.

[2] Cf. M. Costes, *Des cessions de territoires* (Paris, Toulouse, 1914).

[3] *Vita Internazionale* (Milano), December 5, 1912, pp. 611 *seq.*; Dec. 20, 1912, pp. 644 *seq.*

[4] See Treaty of Lausanne, October 18, 1912, Appendix (V).

occupied.[1] This agrees with the view, which we have already set forth, of the eminent Russian jurist, Professor De Martens.[2] It is, however, untenable. If adopted, it would inevitably involve the suppression of the entire doctrine of military occupation as embodied in modern international law. It would, more than ever, put a weaker State at the mercy of a more powerful. The purely temporary provisional character of occupation would vanish; and the first act of invasion might well signalize one of two arbitrary and terrible alternatives—the total destruction of all on the invaded territory who offered resistance, or the immediate appropriation of the invaded territory and the bringing of all under the yoke of the invader's sovereignty. That is, the moment the invaders arrived, with a view to taking possession of the country and permanently retaining it, they would consider the people their subjects, and would thus be in a position to regard resistance as high treason, and to compel all, non-combatants and armed forces alike, to take part in military operations against their own country. Their refusal, due to their patriotism and devotion to their country, would be looked upon by the invader as a crime punishable with death; their unswerving and self-sacrificing fidelity would be treated as the vilest offence that man is capable of; their martyrdom would be regarded as the condign punishment of a traitor. Moreover, if a distinction is to be set up between invasion followed by subjugation and invasion followed merely by provisional military occupation, when is such distinction to become apparent in actual practice? It is impossible to expect a definite announcement at the very commencement of a given war that it is to be a war of subjugation and annexation of territory. It is impossible for the invader to indicate and mark out the territory he intends to appropriate as soon as he has reached the enemy's country. Even if the war were announced as a war of conquest, would it follow that every portion of territory occupied was intended to be kept for good? If only some of the territory occupied was intended to be so kept, how would the line of demarcation be established between the region of military occupation proper and that of full annexation? How would the practices and proceedings of the occupying army and of the annexing army be discriminated? These and other questions of the same character in vain call for satisfactory answers. And even supposing for one moment that theoretically satisfactory answers to them might be furnished, the varying fortunes and vicissitudes of actual warfare would still be left out of account. It might happen that the invaders were eventually expelled from

[1] *Rivista di diritto internazionale*, 1912, p. 11, note 2.

[2] *Supra*, p. 21.

the territory they had originally occupied by way of annexation, and had in turn gained a firm footing in another province, which they suddenly resolved to annex in place of that from which they were ousted. Such changes would, of course, carry with them all the dire consequences affecting the local populations. Indeed, the introduction of the more drastic species of military occupation would undoubtedly render warfare, still more than it is now, an unconscionable game of unrestrained licence and indiscriminate slaughter.

Current of modern opinion against forcible annexation.

On the contrary, the current of modern opinion is against the validity of annexation altogether, when it is the result of subjugation and has been effected without the consent of the conquered people. In earlier days—say, to the middle of the eighteenth century—an invader claimed that as soon as territory or property of the enemy fell into his hands it became his absolutely, and he was entitled to dispose of it as he pleased. But gradually mitigations were introduced; and such limitations were imposed on the severe practice and wide pretension of belligerents as to cause the earlier theory to be abandoned. The growing conception of nationality, territorial sovereignty, and State independence, together with the advocacy of jurists and publicists, and the pronouncements of judicial tribunals all contributed to bring about this amelioration.

It is now held universally that forcibly to deprive a people of territory without good and sufficient cause is a violation of right and justice. The accepted body of international jurisprudence does not cover and provide for all possible international relationships and every species of proceeding. It is urged that other considerations —for example, honour, fairness, equity—apply, and must perforce govern the conduct of the civilized society of States. These principles are fundamental. There is no need to consult codes and conventions to find them; they are implanted in the consciousness of mankind, and can never be eradicated. The main problem in private relationships as well as in public and international affairs is how to cause such principles to be regarded always and everywhere as a more desirable guide than envy, coveteousness, and greed. But even apart from the applicability of ethical doctrines, encroachment on a nation's territory is not sanctioned by international law; for its entire edifice has been built up on the assumption of the autonomy and independence of sovereign States. Territorial expansion can only be justified if the equal rights of others are respected. No matter how great a particular nation's need of additional territory may be, it cannot justify the seizure of another nation's land. Perhaps the only cases where a right of conquest may be pleaded are where the people of a country are given to savagery, cannibalism, inhuman practices, or where in a war of self-defence it is found absolutely indispensable in the interests of general and more enduring peace to take away from an aggressive State a portion of its territory. As Fiore observes: "La conquête d'un territoire ne peut pas être par elle-même une condition suffisante pour exiger la cession du territoire conquis quand le droit du vainqueur n'existe pas. Le vainqueur pourra imposer cette cession, quand elle sera justifiée par des conditions évidentes de moralité, et par un intérêt général d'assurer la paix." [1]

Furthermore, even if annexation in such circumstances be admitted, it is held by many jurists—e.g. by Bluntschli,[2] Calvo,[3] as well as the writer last quoted—that it should at all events be supported by the assent of the political and legislative authority of the country concerned; in other words, that it should not be a case of forcible annexation carried out unilaterally, but rather that it should take the form of a cession, constituting a bilateral transaction as a treaty of peace, sanctioned by the dismembered State.

Annexation and consent of country annexed.

Similarly—to quote some decisions of the United States Courts, which may serve as a corrective of the view expressed by Lord Stowell in *The Foltina*[4]—in the case of *American Insurance Co.* v. *Canter*[5] it was declared that the holding of conquered territory amounted only to military occupation until its fate was determined at the treaty of peace.

In *U.S.* v. *Hayward*,[6] the court held that when the British conquered, and entered into military occupation of, Castine on September 1, 1814, the latter passed under the temporary allegiance and sovereignty of the conqueror; so that the sovereignty of the United States over the territory was suspended. But a territory conquered by an enemy was not to be regarded as incorporated into his dominions, unless there were an express renunciation in a treaty of peace or a long and permanent possession. (Obviously, the temporary allegiance and sovereignty here spoken of mean nothing more

[1] P. Fiore, *Nouveau droit international public*, 2nd ed.; traduit de l'italien par C. Antoine, 3 vols. (Paris, 1880); § 1696.

[2] J. C. Bluntschli, *Das moderne Völkerrecht* (Nordlingen, 1872); French tran. by C. Lardy, *Le droit international codifié* (Paris, 1895); § 286.

[3] C. Calvo, *Le droit international théorique et pratique*, 6 vols., 5e éd. (Paris, 1896); vol. v. § 3141.

[4] See *supra*, pp. 12, 13.

[5] (1828) 1 Peters, 511.

[6] (1815) 2 Gallison, 485. Cf. *U.S.* v. *Rice* (1819), 4 Wheaton, 246.

than temporary control and administration—that is, military occupation in the sense we have used throughout.)

Finally, we may refer to the resolutions unanimously accepted by the International American Conference (1889–1890), which was attended by delegates of the United States and the South American States:

Resolutions of the International American Conference.

"1. That the principle of conquest shall not, during the continuance of the treaty of arbitration, be recognized as admissible under American public law.

2. That all cessions of territory made during the continuance of the treaty of arbitration shall be void if made under threats of war or the presence of an armed force.

3. Any nation from which such cessions shall be exacted may demand that the validity of the cessions so made shall be submitted to arbitration.

4. Any renunciation of the right to arbitration made under the conditions named in the second section should be null and void." [1]

The views expressed above suggest a most desirable relaxation of international practice. It is to be hoped that the society of States will one day so amend its juridical system, and fortify it by such potent sanctions, that it will be impossible for one State to annex the territory of another without the latter's free consent. In the meantime, forcible annexation, however it be deprecated and condemned by international morality, is not forbidden by international law.

[1] *Minutes of the International American Conference* (1889–1890), pp. 798–806; Moore, *Digest*, vol. i. p. 292.

CHAPTER IV

MAIN EFFECTS OF CONQUEST AND SUBJUGATION WITH REGARD TO SUCCESSION

When an entire State is annexed—Limitations imposed on the conqueror—Date of change of sovereignty—Effect on treaties: public law and administration; nationality; State property; debts, the Cuban debt; contracts and concessions; private rights and private law.

THE main effects of conquest and subjugation will be dealt with here very briefly, as fuller treatment of the consequences of annexation in general is reserved for later chapters.[1]

Either a whole State or a part of a State may be annexed to another as a result of war. A treaty of peace being usually concluded at the termination of the war, provisions are inserted in it confirming the transfer of the territory, and, it may be, regulating various matters relative to the rights and obligations consequent on the change of sovereignty.

Where an entire State is annexed.

When one entire State is subjugated, there is, as a rule, little or no necessity to conclude such a treaty of peace with it; for—as has been pointed out already—subjugation may well be taken to mean the disappearance *ipso facto* of the subjugated State, and therefore of its international personality. Consequently, having no legal entity, it necessarily cannot be a party to legal acts. An enlightened conqueror, however, may think fit to enter into a treaty with the heads of the late Government, as representing the nation—as was the case at the end of the South African War, 1902—but in thus straining a point he cannot be said to be entering into a legal international transaction, though considerations of honour and equity, not to mention expediency, will make him fulfil his engagement. Subject, then, to any stipulations contained in the treaty of peace or in the articles of surrender, as the case may be, certain rules may be submitted concerning the succession involved in the territorial change.

Subjection being the result of force, it would seem, theoretically,

[1] See *infra*, Part II, chaps. xi, xii, and xiii.

that the conqueror may deal with the annexed territory in an arbitrary manner, assume all the benefits it brings, and repudiate all its liabilities. But in practice such a procedure cannot be adopted entirely, as there are some claims that it is impossible to overlook. War, it is true, is not carried on by a Power for the purpose of saddling itself with burdens in the hour of victory. But no civilized State can rationally assume that victory gives it rights and privileges without any responsibility and obligations whatever. The important question is, what is or should be the extent of this responsibility and these obligations. The question is not settled, and there is much difference of opinion on it. Change of sovereignty affects various matters, including the public treaties of the annexed country, its public law and administration, the position of officials and the army of the annexed country, the jurisdiction of its courts, the nationality of its inhabitants, its property, debts, concessions, and contractual obligations, the operation of its private law, the private rights of its inhabitants, and the like.

Limitations imposed on the conqueror.

The date of the change of sovereignty is that on which the annexation was proclaimed, or that on which the treaty of peace was concluded. Sometimes such transfer of sovereignty has been made to operate retrospectively; that is, certain acts of the preceding Government done after the outbreak of war, or after the conquered territory had been first effectively occupied, were repudiated by the successor. Thus, in the Franco-German War, Germany declared, long before the conclusion of peace, that she would not recognize the laws passed by France after September 4, 1870 (when the Imperial régime terminated), with regard to Alsace-Lorraine, then occupied by German troops. The German courts went further, holding that the laws enacted by France since the declaration of war were not binding on districts occupied by the Germans at the date of such enactment. Similarly, in the South African War, long before the enemy countries were even effectively occupied, the British Government announced that it would regard as invalid forfeitures of or charges on property situated in enemy territory, and made after October 10, 1899; or the transfer of property, including railways, lands, mines, and mining rights, effected after March 19, 1900.[1] Whatever the object of this action was (e.g. to prevent fraudulent alienation), it was hardly justifiable on the ground of law; as rights of sovereignty cannot legitimately be exercised before the sovereignty has been properly acquired. The High Court of the Orange

Date of change of sovereignty.

[1] *Parl. Papers, S. Africa*, Cd. 53 and Cd. 128; *Brit. and For. State Papers*, vol. 94, p. 1011.

River Colony properly held that the administrative acts of the Boer forces in the field, after the ostensible annexation of May 24, 1900, were legitimate; for, as we have already seen, at that date the country had by no means been subjugated.[1] On the other hand, from the date when the annexation is validly completed, the former Government ceases to exercise rights of sovereignty in regard to the territory concerned; so that any transactions afterwards entered into or laws passed by it purporting to affect such territory will possess no legal force.

Effect on treaties.

As to the treaties that were applicable to the annexed country or province, it cannot be said that they are subject to the principles of universal succession. There is, however, as much difference of opinion among jurists as there is divergence in practice among States. Each species of treaty must be considered on its merits. Some writers[2] hold that, theoretically, all treaties devolve on the annexing State; but as certain kinds—e.g. treaties of alliance, subsidies, commerce—necessarily presuppose the continued existence of the contracting parties, they cease to apply to a State that has become extinct, or that has lost a considerable portion of its territory, so that the absorbing State cannot succeed to them. Nor can a ceding State be any longer bound by conventions of guarantee, and those relating to river navigation, boundary regulation, etc., which affect the area ceded. Other authorities maintain that as diminution of territory does not deprive the ceding State of its international and juridical personality (which does not necessarily depend on territorial extent), it retains in any case its treaty rights and obligations, whether or not any of these have been assumed by the annexing State. Others, again, hold that though annexation means cessation of independence, yet rights and obligations with regard to third States cannot be extinguished, seeing that the people and the territory of the absorbed State continue substantially to exist; so that the conqueror or cessionary succeeds to the obligations so far as they are compatible with the new condition of affairs.[3] This subject will be considered more fully later on, when we examine the practice of States as seen in treaties of peace;[4] but for the present we may say briefly that subject to provisions laid down to the contrary, treaties do not descend to the annexing Power, except, perhaps, such as specially

[1] For these cases, see A. B. Keith, *The Theory of State Succession* (London, 1907). On the subject of succession in general, the present writer is much indebted to this monograph.

[2] M. Huber, *Die Staatensuccession* (Leipzig, 1898), pp. 151, 154.

[3] Bluntschli, *op. cit.*, § 50.

[4] See *infra*, Part II, chap. xii, *in init.*

concern the annexed territory, e.g. as to river navigation, embankment of boundary rivers, etc.; but the annexing Power's treaties pass over, though not invariably, to the annexed territory.

The annexing State acquires complete legislative administration, and judicial authority over the area annexed. There can be no question of succession; for the new sovereign may introduce his own law, constitution, and administration, and abolish the law that prevailed there before. After the conquest and annexation of Hanover by Prussia, 1866, the latter at once introduced there her own military, revenue, and criminal laws, and legislation in general. Sometimes the old law is allowed to remain, either through tacit consent or by specific confirmation. Thus, after the annexation of the Transvaal, a proclamation issued in 1902 recognized the Roman Dutch law as the common law of the country, and confirmed its statute law. On the other hand, Great Britain changed the public and administrative law in the Transvaal in 1877, in Upper Burma in 1886, and frequently in India. The new sovereign has a similar discretion with regard to taking over the old officials; when the territory is annexed after conquest it is usually found necessary to dismiss most of them, when it is acquired by voluntary cession the cessionary finds it possible to retain most of them.[1]

Public law and administration.

From the date of annexation following conquest, the courts in the annexed country lose their jurisdiction, which passes over to the courts of the absorbing State. Decisions of the former are not binding on the latter.[2] Completed proceedings are recognized by British practice, those that are still incomplete may be begun again.

The official language of the annexed territory may be altered by the annexing Government. After the South African War, Great Britain allowed the teaching of Dutch in the schools of the acquired countries, and the use of the language in the courts of law.[4]

Armed forces.

There cannot be a succession in regard to the armed forces of the subjugated territory; the act of annexation does not *ipso facto* constitute them part of the military forces of the conqueror.

As to the effect of change of sovereignty on nationality, the rule generally accepted is that all persons found in the conquered

[1] These observations are intended to be supplemented by those made in regard to the effect of cession, *infra*, pp. 305 *seq.*

[2] Cf. a case in the Transvaal: *Habib Motan* v. *The Transvaal Government* (1904), Sup. Ct. Rep. 404; *Parl. Papers*, Cd. 2239, pp. 46, 48; Keith, *op. cit.*, p. 34.

[3] Proclamation No. 14 of 1901, s. 16.

[4] See the Peace of Vereeniging, Art. V; *infra*, Appendix (T).

territory at the time of annexation come under the allegiance of the conqueror, and assume his nationality, subject to the right of option on

NATIONALITY.

their part to retain their former nationality by departure or otherwise.[1] This right of option, however, is by no means unchallenged. The same act (said the eminent American judge, Chief Justice Marshall) which transfers the country transfers the allegiance of those who remain in it.[2] In *U.S.* v. *Repentigny*, Mr. Justice Nelson, delivering the decision of the Supreme Court of the United States, observed: "The conqueror who has obtained permanent possession of the enemy's country has the right to forbid the departure of his new subjects or citizens from it, and to exercise his sovereign authority over them. Hence the stipulation in the capitulation and treaties of cession providing for the emigration of those inhabitants who desire to adhere to their ancient allegiance, usually fixing a limited period within which to leave the country, and frequently extending to them the privilege, in the meantime, of selling their property, collecting their debts, and carrying with them their effects." [3]

There is an interesting continental case on the subject. In the Austro-Prussian War, 1866, Hanover, which sided with Austria, was occupied by the Prussian troops; its army capitulated, its king was put to flight, and subsequently the country was annexed to Prussia. Before the annexation, Count Platen-Hallemund, prime minister of Hanover, left his country for Vienna. Whilst there he was summoned (1868) to appear before the Supreme Court of Berlin on a charge of high treason, alleged to have been committed by him as a "Prussian subject," though after his removal from Hanover. Under the Prussian law only a Prussian subject was triable before a Prussian court for high treason committed abroad. The essential question, therefore, was whether the Count had necessarily been invested with Prussian nationality on the annexation. He did not appear at the trial in person, but by his counsel denied the jurisdiction of the court, and cited in support of his plea the opinions of two jurists, Professor Zachariae of Göttingen and Professor Neumann of Vienna, to whom the question had been submitted. The court, however, overruled this plea, found him guilty, and sentenced him in his absence to fifteen years' penal servitude.[4]

[1] *Boyd* v. *Thayer* (1891), 143 U.S. Rep. 135, 162; *U.S.* v. *Ritchie* (1854), 17 Howard, 525, 539. Cf. *Campbell* v. *Hall* (1774), 1 Cowper, 208; 20 State Tr. 239.

[2] *American Insurance Co.* v. *Canter* (1828), 1 Peters, 511, 542.

[3] *U.S.* v. *Repentigny* (1866), 5 Wall, 211, 260.

[4] W. Forsyth, *Cases and Opinions on Constitutional Law* (London, 1869), p. 335; H. W. Halleck, *International Law*, ed. Sir S. Baker (London 1908); vol. ii. pp. 510, *seq.*; Cobbett, *Cases*, vol. ii. (1913), pp. 42, 43; F. von Holtzendorff, *Handbuch des Völkerrechts*, 4 vols. (Hamburg, 1885–1889), vol. i. § 12.

The opinion of the two jurists is in harmony with the modern prevailing view, which is more logical and more rational than the earlier uncompromising rule. It is to the effect that the mere fact of conquest and annexation does not impose a new bond of allegiance on the conquered people ; such relation can result only from a submission, either express or tacit. To remain within the dominion of the new Power and fulfil the duties of a subject amounts to tacit submission. Subject to this proviso, the subjects of the ousted sovereign must be allowed to choose between accepting the new nationality and emigrating from the country.

In another case, in 1869, this view was accepted by Prussia. After the annexation of Frankfort by the latter, certain citizens of the city departed, became naturalized in Switzerland, and afterwards returned. The Government merely expelled them from its territory, and so did not act conformably to its previous claim, whereby Prussian allegiance and liability to military service would have been imposed on them.[1]

Personal character of tie of allegiance.

The personal character of the tie of allegiance is emphasized by Westlake, who sums up the more liberal doctrine in the following terms : "It cannot be doubted that the nationals of an extinguished State who continue to reside in the territory, or who, not being within it at the moment of the change, return to it for any but a temporary purpose, become the subjects of the new Government. They do so by accepting its rule and protection, even if the succession did not of itself comprise them among its objects. But what of the nationals of an extinguished State who were not within its territory at the moment of the change, or leave it after the change without any undue delay, repudiate any tie to the conqueror, and do not return to the territory except for the removal of their goods, or for some other such temporary purpose? The decisive consideration appears to be that allegiance is a purely personal tie, and therefore cannot be claimed by the successor State, which is not identified in person with the extinguished State, merely on the ground that it was due to the latter. If the individuals in question do not get themselves naturalized elsewhere, they can have only the legal position which the State in which they reside grants to resident aliens, and such an international position as depends on residence."[2]

A similar view was adopted in a series of recent judgments delivered in South Africa—in the Supreme Court of the Trans-

[1] *Revue de droit international*, vol. ii. (1870), p. 310.

[2] J. Westlake, *International Law* (Cambridge, 1910), vol. i. p. 70. Cf. his *Collected Papers* (Cambridge, 1914), p. 486.

vaal,[1] in the High Court of the Orange River Colony,[2] and in the Court of the Cape of Good Hope.[3] Exception, however, has been taken to these decisions; and it has been suggested that they would very probably have been reversed on appeal to the Privy Council.[4] British practice in previous cases of conquest and annexation—e.g. Upper Burma in 1886, and the Transvaal and the Orange Free State in the last South African War—has, indeed, followed the stricter rule, whereby persons found in the territories on the date of annexation became British subjects. It is true that we cannot say there is yet a definitely crystallized rule of international law to the contrary; but having regard to the evidence furnished by provisions in numerous treaties of cession (which we shall consider later), it may legitimately be held that the right of option has become a principle of international custom, and that its exercise should be assumed even if it is not expressly stipulated.[5]

Naturalized persons in annexed territory.

Naturalized persons residing in the annexed territory are practically in the same position as natural-born persons; though there have been cases where the right of option was not extended to the former, when it was given to the latter. But on resident aliens the new nationality cannot, in any event, be imposed. Sometimes, too, certain reservations have been made with regard to the native inhabitants of non-European annexed or ceded territory in accordance with the public law of the successor State. Thus, under American practice, the status given to the Indians and Chinese of New Mexico and California did not amount to citizenship. After the Spanish-American War, the Filipinos of the ceded Philippine Islands were divested of Spanish nationality, but by Art. IX of the Treaty of Paris, December 10, 1898, their civil rights and political status were to be specially determined by Congress.[6] Similarly, under British practice, the Crown or Parliament decides such questions. We may recall that by the Peace of Vereeniging, May 31,

[1] *Lemkuhl* v. *Kock* (1903), Sup. Ct. Rep. 77; in which the Chief Justice observed: "The fact of annexation does not make the people living in the annexed country subjects of the annexing State, unless they, within a reasonable time, show by their conduct or their acts that they acquiesce in their position and choose to become subjects of the conquering Power."

[2] *Rabie* v. *Jansen* (1902), O.R.C. Rep. 72.

[3] *The Queen* v. *Jizwa* (1894), 4 Cape Times Rep. 383. The Chief Justice here accepted the doctrine stated above, and held that to remain in the ceded territory for two months after the cession amounted to a tacit submission, entailing the assumption of the annexing State's nationality.

[4] Cf. Keith, *op. cit.*, p. 47.

[5] Cf. A. Rivier, *Principes du droit des gens*, 2 vols. (Paris, 1896), vol. ii. pp. 438, 439.

[6] See Appendix (S), Art. IX.

1902, some discrimination was drawn, in regard to franchise, between the burghers of the annexed States and the Kaffirs.[1]

STATE PROPERTY.

Public domain.

Next we come to the question of State property.[2]

The public domain on the territory of the annexed country passes over to the successor State. This class of property includes fortifications, arsenals, depots, harbours, ports, shores, bridges, roads, navigable rivers, Government buildings, prisons, barracks, hospitals, establishments devoted to charity, education, science, art, religion, etc.

Archives.

All the State archives relating to the annexed territory and found thereon at the date of annexation descend to the conqueror.

Private property of the State.

The private domain of the State, including funds of the national exchequer, railways, stores of arms, etc., pass over to the conqueror, subject to the rights possessed in them by private persons. Thus only that portion of the State treasure may be appropriated as has not been lawfully expended. Acting on this principle, the British Government, on the annexation of the Transvaal, took over the sum left at the National Bank, after deducting the amount of cheques previously drawn against the original balance and paid by the bank. Similarly, all moneys in the possession of agents were taken over, after deducting disbursements lawfully paid by them.

The private property of the monarch or other head of the State is generally assimilated to that of private individuals, and as such is not the object of succession.

Property outside the conquered territory.

Whether the annexing State is entitled to sums of money and other property not actually in the conquered territory is not clear. There are some decisions of the English courts which have been regarded, though by analogy, as supporting such title. Thus in *U.S.* v. *McRae*,[3] Vice-Chancellor James, delivering the judgment of the court, said: "Upon the suppression of a rebellion, the restored legitimate Government is entitled, as of right, to all moneys, goods, and treasure which were public property of the Government at the time of the outbreak, such right being in no way affected by the wrongful seizure of the property by the usurping Government. But with respect to property which has been voluntarily contributed to, or acquired by, the insurrectionary Government in the exercise of its usurped authority, and has been impressed in its hands with the character of public property, the legitimate Government is not, on

[1] Art. IX; Appendix (T).

[2] Cf. Keith, *op. cit.*, pp. 49 *seq.*

[3] *U.S.* v. *McRae* (1869), L.R. 8 Equity, 69.

its restoration, entitled by title paramount, but as successor only (and to that extent recognizing the authority) of the displaced usurping Government; and in seeking to recover such property from an agent of the displaced Government can only do so to the same extent, and subject to the same rights and obligations, as if that Government had not been displaced, and was itself proceeding against the agent."[1] Similarly, in a case in which the Confederate States of America had sent to England under a contract goods held by them as public property, it was held that the United States Government could not, after the Civil War was over, repudiate the contract and recover the goods.[2] The rule underlying these decisions, however, relevant as it is to private international law, cannot be considered part of the law of nations. On principle, property situated outside the territory annexed cannot devolve on the successor State. Anything that can be saved from the clutches of the invader may justifiably be carried away elsewhere—as from an approaching conflagration—before he has occupied and annexed the country. The annexing Power takes the territory, subject to the fortunes of war. If, on the other hand, the invader should in any way obtain possession of such property afterwards, he will be liable to all existing claims in regard to it.

Taxes.

As to taxes, dues, revenues, and other imposts, they are levied by virtue of the establishment of the new sovereignty, and not through any right of succession; if the successor thinks fit, he may retain the former rules of assessment and incidence. Thus, after the annexation of the Transvaal, the taxes, etc., were collected by the British authorities in accordance with the old régime.[3]

Rents.

Rents of State domains and loans to public bodies descend to the conqueror; this is a corollary of the rule that the territory of the annexed State and its private domain pass over to him.[4]

Debts due.

Whether the conqueror may legitimately exact the payment of debts due to the annexed State from its subjects has been doubted, but considering the basic principles of succession relative to the substitution of sovereignty, the question must be decided in the affirmative. Even at the provisional stage of military occupation, international law gives the occupant the right

[1] Similar views were adopted in *King of the Two Sicilies* v. *Wilcox* (1851), 1 Sim. N.S. 301, 332–336; *Hullett & Co.* v. *King of Spain* (1828), 1 Dow and Cl. 169.

[2] *U.S.* v. *Prioleau* (1866), 2 H. & M. 559; J. B. Scott, *Cases on International Law* (Boston, 1906), p. 85. Cf. *Republic of Peru* v. *Dreyfus* (1888), 38 Ch. D. 348; *Republic of Peru* v. *Peruvian Guano Co.* (1886), 36 Ch. D. 489.

[3] Cf. Proclamation, No. 13 (1900).

[4] See, however, Huber, *Die Staatensuccession*, p.75.

to take possession not only of State cash and funds, but also of realizable securities; [1] when the conquest has been completed, the conqueror's rights are incomparably larger, if not absolute and unlimited.

The main results of the above analysis may be well summarized in the following terms: [2] "The State succeeds to the property of its predecessor, whether public or private domain, or archives or claims founded on contract, in so far as that property is locally situated in the conquered or ceded territory, and so obtainable by action in its own courts, provided of course that special rules are not arranged by the terms of cession. In the case of taxes, there is no succession, but a re-imposition by sovereign authority. If the property is situated outside its jurisdiction no legal rule of succession exists."

PUBLIC DEBTS.

When a State subdues another State or annexes, by conquest, a part of its territory, the enterprise is not, of course, undertaken with the intention of incurring onerous liabilities and converting the success of arms into a failure of public policy. But as the world is constituted, as peace is regarded by the whole world as its normal condition, and considering the position of the society of nations, the ramifications of international relationships, the confidence placed in engagements, especially with Governments, we are bound to recognize that a conqueror taking another sovereign's territory must take it not merely for the advantages its possession offers, but also with its accompanying disadvantages in the form of burdens, charges, liabilities imposed on it. A country that passes over to the dominion of another ruler does not on that account undergo a kind of territorial reincarnation destructive of *all* its former ties and associations; some of these must of necessity remain for the sake of the ordered life of the community, which implies continuity and not an entirely fresh commencement. A conqueror is in the position of an adventurer, and must take the object of his quest for better *and* for worse. This is the fundamental principle that should govern forcible annexation; but certain qualifications may in some respects be admitted, as will be seen presently. It is not a written disposition of international law; but it is on the way to becoming—if it has not already become—a customary rule. It is the rule invariably followed in voluntary cessions; and it is, at all events, contrary to all elementary notions of fairness, equity, and

[1] *Hague Convention concerning the Laws and Customs of War on Land*, No. IV (1907), Art. 53.

[2] Keith, *op. cit.*, p. 57.

human justice to assume that the presence of superior physical force, in the conquest of a given territory, purges it completely of its liabilities and places it in the hands of the conqueror as an unalloyed prize. As Mr. Adams, the American Secretary of State, said a century ago: "The conqueror who reduces a nation to his subjection receives it subject to all its engagements and duties towards others, the fulfilment of which then becomes his own duty. However frequent the instances of departure from this principle may be in point of fact, it cannot with any colour of reason be contested on the ground of right." [1] The British Government has never admitted a legal obligation to assume the liabilities appertaining to a conquered territory, as a case of conquest cannot involve a universal succession; it has, rather, held that the policy to be adopted depends on the dictates of expediency and the merits and special circumstances of each case. However this may be, Great Britain has never repudiated equity, and has not acted ungenerously, towards the conquered country in regard to its previously incurred obligations. Whether the guiding principle is legal obligation or moral obligation, it matters little, especially in international affairs, so long as what is fair and right is done.

Conformably, then, to the fundamental principle suggested above, an absorbing State must take over the public debts of the extinct State; [2] or if only a part of a State's territory is annexed, it must take over an amount proportionate to the region acquired, regard being paid to its population, area, and resources, or, as Bluntschli suggests, in proportion to the amount of taxes contributed by it; and more particularly it must take over the debt that had been incurred exclusively for the benefit of such region. In 1866 when Prussia annexed the Kingdom of Hanover, the Electorate of Hesse, the Duchy of Nassau, and the Free Town of Frankfort, she declared herself (by the law of November 22, 1866) responsible for the debts and international obligations of these States. In 1877, on the annexation of the Transvaal, Great Britain assumed responsibility for the country's debt. In 1886, when Upper Burma was annexed, the British Government undertook to repay moneys lent for and expended on public purposes.[3] In 1902 all the debts of the late South African Republic and Orange Free State were taken over, including a deficit amounting to about £1,500,000. In each

[1] Mr. Adams, Sec. of State, to Mr. Everett; Chargé d'Affaires to the Netherlands, August 10, 1818, *Amer. State Papers, For. Rel.*, vol. v. p. 603; Moore, *Digest*, vol. i. p. 334.

[2] Cf. Huber, *op. cit.*, pp. 156, 282, n. 449; H. Appleton, *Des effets des annexions de territoires sur les dettes de l'État démembré ou annexé* (Paris, 1895); Moore, *Digest*, vol. i. § 97.

[3] *Parl. Papers*, Cd. 4887.

of these cases legal liability was denied, the debts having been paid on the ground of equity and expediency. At the Congress of Berlin, 1878, when the Turkish representative proposed that Russia should assume part of the Ottoman public debt relative to her annexed territory, the Russian delegates replied that though there was a partition of debts in the case of voluntary cession, it was different where there was a conquest; so that Russia refused to assume such debt in respect of her acquisitions in Asia.[1] When, on the conclusion of the Spanish-American War, Spain was obliged to relinquish her sovereignty over Cuba, the United States Government refused to take over the so-called Cuban debt, on the ground that it was not created by Cuba herself or incurred for its benefit, but was created by Spain for her own purposes and mainly for supporting a Spanish army in the island.[2] But in regard to the Philippine Islands, the United States succeeded to the rights and obligations of the former sovereign.

War debt.

The case of the Cuban debt is closely related to that of a conquered State's war debt, which forms an exception to the general principle enunciated above. In the case of loans raised for the specific purpose of prosecuting the war, there cannot properly be any succession. As Westlake says: "Those who lend money to a State during a war, or even before its outbreak when it is notoriously imminent, may be considered to have made themselves voluntary enemies of the other State, and can no more expect consideration on the failure of the side which they have espoused than a neutral ship which has entered the enemy's service can expect to avoid condemnation if captured." [3] (The point urged here is perfectly valid, so far as the question of succession is concerned, but the statement is untenable so far as the rights and obligations of neutrals are concerned; and the analogy suggested is fallacious.) A conqueror can hardly be expected to take upon himself liabilities incurred by the conquered State for the express purpose of carrying on hostilities against him.[4] It may

[1] The 17th protocol of the Berlin Congress, session of July 10, 1878: "Le Comte Schouvaloff répond qu'il ne croyait fondé à considérer comme admis que, s'il y a répartition de dettes pour les territoires qui se détachent par voie d'arrangement, de donation, ou d'échange de la contrée dont ils faisaient partie intégrante, il n'y en a point là où il y a une conquête. Son Excellence ajoute que la Russie est conquérante en Europe et en Asie. Elle n'a rien à payer pour les territoires et ne saurait être en rien solidaire de la dette turque."—*British and Foreign State Papers*, vol. lxix. (1877–1878), p. 1055.

[2] Cf. *Senate Documents*, 62, 55th Cong., 3rd sess., part ii. pp. 48 *seq.*; Moore, *Digest*, vol. i. pp. 356–380.

[3] *International Law* (1910), vol. i. p. 78.

[4] Cf. *King of the Two Sicilies* v. *Wilcox* (1851), 1 Sim. N.S. 301; *U.S.* v. *Prioleau* (1865), 2 H. & M. 559; 35 L.J. Ch. N.S. 7.

reasonably be assumed that a person who lends money to a belligerent for the purposes of the war does so with a consciousness of the hazard involved. Would he lend the money if he was absolutely certain that the belligerent would be defeated, and the country annexed by the adversary? Nethertheless, even here it is open for a victorious Power to consider the merits of any particular claims and make grants *ex gratia*, as Great Britain did after the South African War.

CONTRACTS AND CONCESSIONS.

With regard to the rights and obligations arising out of the ordinary contracts entered into and the concessions[1] made by the annexed State or by a State in respect of such part of its territory as it is deprived of, there is a consensus of opinion that the rule of universal succession applies, though there are weighty views to the contrary. Thus, in the *West Rand Gold Mining Co.* v. *Rex* (1905),[2] Lord Alverstone, C.J., delivering the judgment of the court, held that there is no principle of international law by which, after the annexation of conquered territory, the annexing State becomes liable, in the absence of express stipulations providing otherwise, to discharge financial obligations of the conquered State incurred before the outbreak of war; that the assumption of such obligations entirely depends on the discretion of the victorious Power; and that in any event having regard to the constitutional doctrine relative to "acts of State," inquiry into such obligations is not within the competence of a municipal court. To the same effect was the judgment in *Cook* v. *Sprigg* (1899),[3] and in many earlier English decisions, as well as in a number of recent cases decided in the Transvaal. In one of the latter, *Postmaster-General* v. *Taute* (1905),[4] the Postmaster-General sued on a mortgage bond entered into by the defendant in favour of the Postmaster-General of the late Republic; the defendant endeavoured to set off against the present claim a debt due to him from the late Government in respect to stock and supplies that had been requisitioned for war purposes. In the course of his judgment, the Chief Justice observed: "When, at the conclusion of a war, one of the combatant States is absorbed by the other, the conqueror becomes, by right of conquest, the successor to all the public property, corporeal and incorporeal, of the vanquished. That result follows so soon as a conquest is complete. In the present instance the conquest has been perfected by annexation, and the principle to which I have referred is one which certainly

[1] As to concessions, see Moore, *Digest*, vol. i. § 98, pp. 385 *seq.*; G. Gidel, *Des effets de l'annexion sur les concessions* (Paris, 1904).

[2] 2 K.B. 391. [3] (1899) A.C. 572. [4] (1905) Sup. Ct. Rep. 582.

cannot be questioned in the courts of the annexing State. The debt sued upon was due to the late Government; it has become the property of the present one. . . . But the conquering State cannot be sued in its own courts in respect of contractual obligations alleged to have been incurred by its adversary, because the annexation is an act of State carried out by the supreme authority of the conquering country, and neither the act itself, nor its legal consequences, can be called in question in the courts of that country. Those courts have no power to adjudicate upon it, and they are bound to recognize it. It is, therefore, impossible for them to declare that, as a result of annexation, any contractual obligations have been transferred from the one Government to the other. No doubt it is just and right that, in many cases, such obligations should be recognized; and if a conquering State were recklessly to repudiate all the liabilities of the country which it had absorbed, such conduct might lead to international complications, and would certainly be reprobated by civilized public opinion. Hence, wholesale repudiation is never likely to occur, and conquering Governments will, in practice, largely hold themselves bound by the commitments of their predecessors. But though such an attitude may be adopted for reasons of policy, or from a sense of moral obligation, no country can be compelled to adopt it by a decree of its own courts. Even if the recognition of contractual obligations formed the subject of treaty agreement between the belligerents, the conqueror could not be sued upon his promises in his own courts. Honour and policy would induce him to observe his engagements, but municipal law would have no voice in the matter. As the conscience of mankind improves, the tendency will doubtless be to take an ever-widening view of the obligations which the conquering State ought to recognize. But liabilities incurred by a vanquished nation to its own subjects, in the prosecution of warlike operations against the conqueror, will probably be among the last to commend themselves to the latter as entitled to recognition."

There are, however, other judicial decisions in which the rule of succession is recognized.[1] And the examples of annexation under British practice, such as that of the Transvaal in 1877, Upper Burma in 1886, South African Republic and Orange Free State in 1900, show that the contractual obligations of the countries concerned were by no means disregarded by Great Britain. Moreover, in voluntary cessions and (as we shall see later[2]) in cessions under treaties of peace, provision is regularly made for the devolution of these liabilities. Considering then the frequent, if not invariable,

[1] *U.S.* v. *McRae* (1869), L.R. 8 Eq. 69; *supra*, p. 39. Cf. *U.S.* v. *Smith* (1877), 1 Hughes, R. 347; Scott, *Cases*, p. 89. [2] See Part II, chap. xiii.

practice, and the widespread opinion in its favour, we may say that the rule of succession has probably ripened into a rule of international law. The fact that municipal courts of law have no jurisdiction over claims made by the private creditor of an extinct State against the annexing State (as was emphasized in the above-mentioned cases, *Cook* v. *Sprigg*, *West Rand Gold Mining Co.* v. *R.*, and *Postmaster-General* v. *Taute*) does not necessarily prove that the principle is not a rule of international law. Were there an international court to take cognizance of matters of international law, it would very probably (as Professor Oppenheim aptly points out)[1] recognize and enforce such a principle.

Transvaal Concessions Commission.

In the case of the South African War, the British authorities announced, September 8, 1900, that all concessions granted by the Transvaal Government would be considered on their merits; but that the British Government reserved to itself the right to repudiate or modify such concessions as were beyond the power of the Transvaal Government, having regard to any agreement with Great Britain, or were granted without legal authority or contrary to law, or whose conditions had not been duly fulfilled, or which conflicted with the public interest. A commission of inquiry was appointed, and on April 19, 1901, appeared its report,[2] comprising a statement of principles, a schedule of assets relative to concessions, shares in companies, etc., and an examination of some twenty-five particular concessions, e.g. as to railways and tramways, manufacture and trade, municipal rights, etc. For our present purpose, the first part of the report—the statement of principles—is of special interest.

The report declares (1) that an annexing State is not legally bound by contracts made by the annexed State, and that no court of law has jurisdiction to enforce them if the annexing State refuses to recognize them;[3] but that the tendency of the modern usage of nations is to acknowledge such contracts. "After annexation, it has been said, the people change their allegiance, but their relations to each other and their rights of property remain undisturbed;[4] and property includes rights which lie in contract.[5] . . . Concessions of the nature of those which are the subject of inquiry present examples of mixed public and private rights; they probably continue to exist after annexation until abrogated by the annexing State;[6] and as a matter of practice in modern times, where treaties have

[1] *International Law* (1912), vol. i. p. 129.

[2] *Parl. Papers, S. Africa* (1901), Cd. 623; Cobbett, *Cases*, vol. ii. pp. 234–240.

[3] *Cook* v. *Sprigg* (1899), A.C. 572.

[4] *U.S.* v. *Percheman* (1833), 7 Peters, 51 [per Chief Justice Marshall, at p. 86].

[5] *Soulard* v. *U.S.* (1830), 4 Peters, 511.

[6] Huber, *Die Staatensuccession*, p. 149.

been made on the cession of territory they have often been maintained by agreement."[1] (2) "Though we doubt whether the duties of an annexing State towards those claiming under concessions or contracts granted or made by the annexed State have been defined with such precision in authoritative statement, or acted upon with such uniformity in civilized practice, as to warrant their being termed rules of international law, we are convinced that the best modern opinion favours the view that as a general rule the obligations of the annexed State towards private persons should be respected. Manifestly the general rule must be subject to qualifications—as that an insolvent State could not by aggression, which practically left to a solvent State no other course than to annex it, convert its worthless into valuable obligations; that an annexing State would be justified in refusing to recognize obligations incurred by the annexed State for the immediate purposes of war against itself; and that probably no State would acknowledge private rights the existence of which caused or contributed to cause the war which resulted in annexation." (3) Subject to these reservations, the principle adopted in the analogous case of the annexation of Hanover by Prussia, 1866, viz. the protection of duly acquired rights,[2] may well be followed. (4) But the rights in question must have been duly acquired, and any conditions involved duly performed. (5) Conformably to these principles, a concession may be cancelled if (*a*) the late Government could not legally grant it; or (*b*) it was contrary to a treaty with the annexing State; or (*c*) it was acquired unlawfully or by fraud; or (*d*) has failed to fulfil its essential conditions without lawful excuse. In these cases, concessions may be cancelled or modified without compensation, in the absence of special circumstances. (6) The new Government may cancel or modify a concession if its maintenance is injurious to the public interest. Here compensation is payable according to the merits of each case.

The recommendations of the commission were in general followed by the British Government, though in some instances with important relaxations. Thus the concession regarding the Netherlands South African Railway (belonging to a company incorporated in Holland) was cancelled, on the ground, first, that the company, through its local manager and officers, and with the approval of the Dutch board of directors, had aided the Boers during the war and committed unwarranted acts of aggression against the British;[3] and secondly, that such a large monopoly was against the public interest, especially when owned by a foreign

[1] Certain treaties are referred to in the report; they need not be mentioned here, as they will be considered more fully in Part II, chap. xiii.

[2] Royal Prussian Patent, October 3, 1886.

[3] Cf. *Parl. Papers, S. Africa* (1901), Cd. 623, pp. 23, 28, 30, 35.

company. But the British Government took over the whole liability with regard to the debenture-holders, and, despite the recommendation of the commission, agreed to pay a full indemnity to all shareholders—except the late Government and the company's managers and agents, who had acquired their interests before the war. (The commission had held that the shareholders were responsible for the action of the directors and officials, and so forfeited their shares.[1]) Again, the dynamite concession was cancelled, because the company in which it was vested had violated the terms of its contract, and because such a monopoly was contrary to the public interest. On the other hand, the concession as to the Pretoria–Pietersburg Railway, owned by an English company, in which the late Government held three-fifths of the shares, was recognized, as its employment during the war was within the right of that Government. The shares owned by the latter were taken over, with the corresponding liabilities.

On the whole, the conclusions contained in the report of the Transvaal Concessions Commission are in harmony with those set forth above, except that it implies a too restricted interpretation of the terms "law" and "legal," and speaks only of a tendency in modern usage, in regard to an absorbing State's assumption of the absorbed State's obligations, when there is actually a pretty firmly established usage, followed with some regularity and uniformity. It is well to attribute a wider significance to law, especially when matters outside municipal jurisprudence are concerned, in accordance with the distinction drawn by Richard Hooker: "They who are thus accustomed to speak apply the name of law unto that only rule of working which superior authority imposeth; whereas we, somewhat more enlarging the sense thereof, term every kind of rule or canon, whereby actions are framed, a law." [2]

Finally, as to private property and private law.

PRIVATE RIGHTS AND PRIVATE LAW.

It has long been an established rule that in changes of government, of dynasty, of sovereignty, or of foreign relationships of States, the private rights of individuals created by the private law should be safeguarded and preserved, until alteration be regularly effected by the properly constituted legislative authority. Even during the continuance of

[1] For a criticism of the report, and of the action of the British Government, see Sir T. Barclay, *Problems of International Practice and Diplomacy* (London, 1907), pp. 49 *seq.* We must say, however, that having regard to our entire exposition of the rights and duties of a conqueror—for title by conquest is recognized by international law—the principles of the report and the action of the British Government involved no violation of international rules or practice.

[2] *Ecclesiastical Polity*, Book I, chap. iii. 1.

hostilities, in invasion or military occupation, private property receives a very large measure of protection from international law and usage.[1] With regard to English law in case of conquest, reference may be made to *Calvin's Case* (1608),[2] where it was said: "If a King come to a Christian kingdom by conquest . . . he may at his pleasure alter and change the laws of that kingdom, but until he doth make an alteration of these laws the ancient laws of that kingdom remain." It was added that the subjugation of an infidel country, on the contrary, immediately brought about the abrogation of its laws and the introduction of those of the conqueror. But this view was soon abandoned, and specifically repudiated in noteworthy judicial decisions. In 1693 Chief Justice Holt held[3] that on the conquest of Jamaica its laws remained in force until provision was made otherwise by the conquering State. Similarly Lord Mansfield declared in 1774,[4] with regard to the island of Grenada, that the laws of a conquered country continue in force until they are altered by the conqueror.[5]

The same doctrine is asserted in American cases. Thus, in *U.S.* v. *Power's Heirs*,[6] it was laid down that in cases of conquest among civilized countries that possess established laws of property the rule is that the laws, usages, and municipal regulations prevailing at the time of the conquest remain in force until they are changed by the new sovereign.

In the United States, too, there is a series of judicial decisions recognizing the rule that neither private rights nor private property, attaching or belonging to individuals in the conquered territory, should be interfered with by the conqueror. In the leading case of *U.S.* v. *Percheman* (1833) (whose authority, as we have just seen, was accepted by the Transvaal Concessions Commission), the eminent Chief Justice Marshall observed: "It is very unusual, even in cases of conquest, for the conqueror to do more than displace the sovereign and assume dominion over the country. The modern usage of nations, which has become law, would be violated; that sense of justice and of right which is acknowledged and felt by the whole civilized world would be outraged if private property

[1] Cf., for example, among written international provisions, the *Hague Convention concerning the Laws and Customs of War on Land* (1907), No. IV, Arts. 46, 47.

[2] Coke, *Rep.* vii. 1.

[3] *Blankard* v. *Galdy* (1693), 2 Salkeld, 411; 4 Mod. Rep. 215.

[4] *Campbell* v. *Hall* (1774), 1 Cowper, 204; 20 State Tr. 239. Cf. *Picton's Case* (1806), 30 State Tr. 944 [per Lord Ellenborough].

[5] Cf. W. Forsyth, *Cases and Opinions on Constitutional Law* (London, 1869), chap. i, where several other references are given.

[6] (1850), 11 Howard, 570. Cf. *Cross* v. *Harrison* (1853), 16 Howard, 164; *Airhart* v. *Massieu* (1878), 98 U.S. Rep. 491.

should be generally confiscated. The people change their allegiance; their relation to their ancient sovereign is dissolved; but their relations to each other and their rights of property remain undisturbed."[1] This principle is *a fortiori* observed in cases of cession, even—as was declared by the same judge—if no stipulation to that effect has been inserted in the treaty.[2]

A conqueror who annexes the territory of another sovereign cannot, as a general rule, acquire greater rights with regard to this territory than the displaced sovereign possessed. In no respect can this rule be more applicable than in the sphere of private rights of property.

If any change in the private law of a conquered territory is thought to be desirable, the conqueror may, after annexation, introduce alterations by virtue of his newly acquired sovereignty—not, however, in an arbitrary manner, but in conformity with his own established legal system.[3] And even when legislative changes are made they cannot operate retrospectively, and interfere with private rights and obligations resulting from previous judgments, sentences, or decrees;[4] unless such judicial pronouncements—especially so in reference to such matters as land grants—were obtained in an unlawful or fraudulent manner.

To all legal and quasi-legal dispositions determining international action must always and everywhere be added the dictates of wise public policy and enlightened expediency, together with the ineradicable behests of equity and right. The promptings of conscience should be as sacred and inviolable as the commands of external authority. As a modern writer well says: "Over and above these customary restrictions there is also a moral obligation incumbent on the conquering State to administer the conquered territory, in so far as this may consist with its own safety, in such a manner as to mitigate the sufferings and restore the prosperity of its inhabitants, and to distribute so far as possible over the population at large the burden of losses that have fallen on individuals."[5]

Practice of States.

So far as actual practice is concerned, it has generally followed the principles set forth above, though qualifications were sometimes made in accordance with the particular circumstances of each case. Great Britain has in her conquests respected private rights and property, and private law;

[1] *U.S.* v. *Percheman* (1833), 7 Peters, 51, at pp. 86, 87. Similar expressions were used by the same judge in *Delassus* v. *U.S.* (1835), 9 Peters, 117.

[2] *U.S.* v. *Soulard* (1830), 4 Peters, 511. Cf. *Strother* v. *Lucas* (1838), 12 Peters, 410; *Johnson* v. *McIntosh* (1823), 8 Wheaton, 543.

[3] *The Chicago, etc., Ry. Co.* v. *McGlinn* (1885), 114 U.S. 542.

[4] *The African Gold Recovery Co.* v. *Hay* (1904), A. C. 438.

[5] Cobbett, *Cases*, vol. ii. p. 248.

the existing Roman-Dutch law in South Africa, Ceylon, and British Guiana, and the prevailing French law in Quebec, Mauritius, and the Seychelles offer permanent examples of the application of the principle. Further, in regard to the former South African Republic and Orange Free State, the British Government appointed a commission, including local representatives, in each district, for the purpose of aiding the inhabitants to be restored to their homes, and supplying those who, owing to war losses, were unable to provide themselves with food, shelter, stock, implements, etc. A sum of three million pounds, followed by other large grants, was devoted to such purposes; and loans were advanced repayable by small instalments.[1]

In 1866, when Prussia conquered and annexed Hanover, a Royal Prussian Patent, October 3, 1866, announced that she would protect existing rights: "We will protect every one in the possession and enjoyment of his duly acquired rights."

The United States has likewise observed this principle. When she conquered and annexed New Mexico, only the allegiance of the people was considered to have been changed; their rights of property and their relations to each other remained undisturbed.[2] The provisions relating to Cuba, Porto Rico, and the Philippine Islands will be considered later in connection with treaties of peace; as we are dealing, for the present, with cases of conquest and annexation, which exclude bilateral arrangements based on the common consent of the States concerned.

France, too, followed this practice in Algeria.[3]

We have now come to the end of that portion of our subject relative to the doctrine and practice of conquest and annexation. We have seen that the progress of civilization has brought with it many mitigations of the former severe theory and unconscionable practice, whereby a conquered country was exploited merely for the advantage of the conqueror, the rights of its population were disregarded, and military adventurers were enriched at the expense of the subjugated and ill-treated nation. There is no need to recount the many arbitrary proceedings that took place, and the gross abuses that were perpetrated. Let us hope that the great step in advance that has been made may soon be followed by a still greater step—an agreement by the States of the world, reinforced by really effective sanctions, that conquests of civilized countries shall no longer be permitted.

[1] Cf. Peace of Vereeniging, Art. X; *infra*, Appendix (T).
[2] Cf. *Leitensdorfer* v. *Webb* (1857), 20 Howard, 176.
[3] Cf. Calvo, *Droit international*, § 2482.

PART II

TERMINATION OF WAR BY TREATIES OF PEACE—HOW THEY COME TO BE MADE; THEIR CONTENTS; AND THEIR EFFECTS

CHAPTER I

ARMISTICE CONVENTION

Suspension of hostilities—Sometimes no armistice before peace negotiations: examples—Cases in which armistice concluded first—Distinction between armistice and suspension of arms—The Hague Regulations—Political character of the general armistice—What may be done—Various examples of armistices—No settled rules.

WE have now reached the main part of our work; for of all the modes of terminating war the treaty of peace is the normal mode, and offers a great variety of subjects for examination. For example, we shall have to consider the question of putting a temporary stop to hostilities pending preliminary negotiations, and whether the conclusion of an armistice is indispensable; the interposition of third Powers, either by their good offices or their mediation, or even by their forcible intervention; the preliminaries of peace, their purport, their object, and their relation to the definitive treaty of peace; the meeting of the peace commissioners or plenipotentiaries, and the negotiations and proceedings at the conference; the treaty of peace, its main constituent elements and its effects.

In the previous chapters we dealt with subjugation and annexation as a mode of terminating war, and we saw that where an entire State was thus subdued and absorbed there was no reason for concluding a treaty of peace, as the imposition of the conqueror's will on the conquered nation involved merely a unilateral arrangement. But where the fortunes or misfortunes of war are more or less equally divided between the belligerent Powers, or even where one of them has been thoroughly defeated, without having its forces annihilated and its resistance completely crushed, and the other cannot or does not wish to push its success further, then a movement for peace usually begins, and the ultimate arrangement made is then a bilateral transaction. That is, it is a compromise *ad hoc*, involving an agreement as to demands made on both sides, and settling all the matters in dispute, more particularly those that brought about the war. It

Compromise *ad hoc*.

may happen, however, that the original causes of the conflict involve various complicated questions, and that during the course of hostilities further difficulties have arisen; so that the contending parties, when they come to negotiate, find it impossible to arrive at a mutually satisfactory solution of all these matters, and, both being desirous of ending the war, limit themselves to the restoration of peace and friendship, in the hope that their former difficulties may be settled at another time. This occurred at the conclusion of the Anglo-American War, 1812–1814: negotiations had been going on for five months, and on more than one occasion were on the point of being broken off; and the Treaty of Ghent, signed on December 24, 1814, provided for the exchange of prisoners, the restoration of property taken during the war, the determination by a commission of questions relating to boundaries and the islands in Passamaquoddy Bay—and left a host of problems unsolved. Instances of this kind are very rare; for when the contending Powers are less sincerely desirous of establishing and maintaining peace, or of settling their differences by pacific means, there is a possibility that one or both of them may agree to a temporary accommodation, with a view to renewing war at a more favourable moment for the extraction of more drastic terms. A treaty of peace is, of course, no guarantee that there will never be war again between the contracting parties; but what it ought to do is to settle permanently the differences that gave rise to the particular war it terminates.

Suspension of hostilities.

As soon as both sides are prepared to make peace, the first step they should take is to suspend hostilities for a given period by means of an armistice convention. This course is not always adopted; but its adoption is assuredly some indication at least that their avowed readiness to establish peace as soon as possible is conscientious. If military operations and active hostilities are allowed to continue after the Governments or other authorities of the belligerents have entered into negotiations, or whilst their respective representatives are battling for the best possible terms within the four walls of the conference chamber, great difficulties must inevitably arise; for the negotiations will sway with the fortunes in the field, thus militating against a satisfactory issue of the proceedings, and against the stability of peace, if extreme terms are extorted from the representatives of one side as a result of a sudden military success on the part of the other. In the majority of cases such an armistice was first concluded; and this procedure was coming to be regarded as a well-nigh established rule of international law, when a conspicuous exception occurred in the case of the Russo-Japanese War. The forces of the combatants were engaged in a furious conflict at the very moment the peace conferences were being held at Portsmouth, in the United States. Professor De Martens, the eminent Russian jurist, writing on the Portsmouth Peace Conference, thus comments on this undesirable condition of things: "It is only proper that diplomatic negotiations looking towards peace should never run the risk of being interrupted by fresh acts of hostility by armies in the field. This principle is so solidly established that the exception created by the Portsmouth Conference cannot overturn it. Quite the contrary; for it is this very exception which proves the practical and indisputable advantage of this principle. Thus, to cite an example drawn from this very Portsmouth Conference, during the voyage of the Russian and Japanese plenipotentiaries to America, the Japanese land and sea forces disembarked on the island of Saghalin, a large portion was conquered, and even the name of the island was changed. Up to the moment of this occupation, the Japanese had not a square foot of Russian territory in their possession; and later, in the course of the peace negotiations, this conquest was made to play an important part; the demand was made that Russia cede this great island to Japan. If an armistice, or even a suspension of arms, had been concluded before the conference was arranged, this conquest could not have taken place. Diplomatic negotiations carried on under such circumstances are liable at any moment to give rise to surprises." [1]

Sometimes no armistice before peace negotiations.

The Treaty of Portsmouth received the signatures of the plenipotentiaries on September 5, 1905. On September 1, an armistice having been proposed, a protocol was signed at Portsmouth by the same, "pending the coming into force of the treaty of peace." Some ten days later the Japanese commander informed the Russian commander-in-chief that he had been notified of the armistice treaty concluded at Portsmouth; and on September 11, a parlementaire, despatched by Lieutenant-General Linevitch, arrived at the Japanese outposts, saying that the latter had received a copy of the full text of the armistice treaty, and had appointed the Assistant-Chief of his Staff to make the necessary arrangements. Accordingly, Field-Marshal Oyama fixed the place for the negotiations; and, on the 13th the appointed representatives met and agreed to five articles, suspending hostilities in Manchuria at noon on the 16th. Not till the 18th was the naval armistice concluded. The ratifications of the definitive treaty of peace were exchanged

[1] F. De Martens, *The Portsmouth Peace Conference*; article in the *North American Review* (New York), November 1905, pp. 641–648; at p. 644.

at Washington on the 25th. The above shows that hostilities continued not only during the course of the peace negotiations, but also for some time after the treaty of peace was signed.

Other cases.

There have been several other cases, in addition to this striking instance, in which no armistice was concluded before the commencement of peace negotiations, or even before the signing of the definitive treaty of peace. Thus—to give a noteworthy early example—in the Thirty Years' War hostilities went on whilst the congresses at Münster and Osnabrück were conducting their negotiations; and this twofold conflict continued for four years before the definitive treaty was concluded.[1]

In the war between France and Austria, 1735, there was no suspension of arms before the treaty of peace was entered into; after the signing of the latter, an armistice was agreed to which was to remain valid until the exchange of ratifications.[2]

In 1761, France, Austria, Russia, Sweden, and Poland carried on peace negotiations at Augsburg for several months with Great Britain and Prussia, without concluding an armistice. These negotiations, however, proved to be fruitless.[3]

An instance similar to that of the Russo-Japanese War occurred in the war between Great Britain and the United States, 1814. The Treaty of Ghent was signed on December 24, 1814; but hostilities went on for about seven weeks longer, almost up to the date of the exchange of ratifications.

The Treaty of Guadalupe Hidalgo (1848), between United States and Mexico, was signed before the suspension of hostilities; Art. II stipulated that arrangements should be made for the latter immediately after the signature of the treaty. Accordingly, an elaborate military convention, consisting of seventeen articles, was entered into in the city of Mexico, February 29, 1848, ratified March 5, and proclaimed the following day.

In the Anglo-Boer War there was no armistice proper; the negotiations that led to the Peace of Vereeniging, May 31, 1902, began on February 28. We have already seen[4] that the Boer representatives more than once asked for a general suspension of hostilities; this was refused on account of military exigencies, though brief local armistices and safe-conducts were allowed to them so that they might communicate with the commandos, and submit the British terms to an assembly of delegates at Vereeniging.

[1] Cf. M. Bernard, *Four Lectures on Subjects connected with Diplomacy* (London, 1868), p. 16.

[2] Cf. Vattel, *Droit des gens*, liv. iv. ch. iii. § 25.

[3] *Annual Register*, 1761, p. 3.

[4] See *supra*, p. 15.

But we have to remember that this was a case of conquest and annexation of the defeated countries, and that the "peace" was virtually nothing more than an instrument specifying the articles of surrender.

Finally, in the Turco-Italian War, 1912, peace negotiations were begun on July 12 and continued for three months, the preliminaries of peace having been signed on October 15. During all this time there was no suspension of hostilities; no armistice preceded or followed these preliminaries, which were described as a *modus procedendi*. Moreover, the war went on even after the definitive Treaty of Lausanne was signed, October 18; for Art. I stipulates that the two Governments shall adopt "the necessary measures to bring about the immediate and simultaneous cessation of hostilities." [1]

Cases in which armistice concluded before the peace negotions.

The above examples show that there is no established rule requiring the conclusion of an armistice before the peace commissioners begin their negotiations in conference, or even before the signing of the definitive treaty of peace. The cases in which there was a previous suspension of hostilities are, however, more numerous; and a few of these may be given.

In 1814 when the Allied Powers invaded France and overcame Napoleon, an armistice convention was agreed to on April 17, and the Treaty of Paris was concluded on May 30.

Again, in the following year, when Wellington and Blücher arrived before Paris after the Battle of Waterloo, they signed an armistice treaty on July 3. The definitive Treaty of Paris was concluded on November 20, 1815.[2]

In the case of the Crimean War, when the peace plenipotentiaries of the various Powers concerned met in Paris, it was proposed at their very first sitting, February 25, 1856, that an armistice should first be concluded. After some discussion as to its nature and duration, it was decided that it should cease on March 31, unless renewed before then, and that the decision should be at once communicated by telegraph to the respective commanders-in-chief, who were to make the necessary arrangements. The Conference then agreed to meet on February 27, to proceed to the negotiation of the definitive treaty. The latter was signed on March 30.[3]

In the war betwen France and Austria, 1859, after the French victory at Solferino, the Emperors Napoleon and Francis Joseph met at Villafranca and concluded an armistice on July 8, which was to last till August 15. It is of interest to recall the order of the day (dated from Valleggio) which the Emperor Napoleon issued

[1] See Appendix (V), Art. I. [2] Appendix (A). [3] Appendix (D).

to his army two days afterwards: "Soldiers,—An armistice has been concluded on the 8th inst. between the belligerent parties, to extend to the 15th of August next. This truce will permit you to rest after your glorious labours, and to recover, if necessary, new strength to continue the work which you have so gloriously inaugurated by your courage and your devotion. I am about to return to Paris, and shall leave the provisional command of my army to Marshal Vaillant; but, as soon as the hour of combat shall have struck, you will see me again in your midst to partake of your dangers." [1]

On July 11, however, the preliminaries of peace were signed at Villafranca by the Emperors personally,[2] and the definitive Treaty of Zurich was concluded on November 11.[3]

In the war between Austria and Prussia on the one side, and Denmark on the other (1864), it was agreed, at a conference in London, to suspend hostilities for a month, beginning May 12.[4] The treaty of peace was not signed until October 30.

In the course of the negotiations to put an end to the war between Austria and Prussia, 1866, a military convention, stipulating the immediate cessation of hostilities, and a four weeks' truce, beginning seven days later, was entered into by General Moltke (for Prussia) and Field-Marshal Degenfeld (for Austria), at the same time as the preliminaries of peace were signed at Nikolsburg, July 26, by Count Bismarck (for Prussia) and Baron Brenner and Count Karolyi (for Austria). The definitive Treaty of Prague was concluded on August 23.

In the Franco-German War, France proposed an armistice after the capitulation of Paris. Accordingly, in the latter part of January, 1871, Jules Favre, the Minister for Foreign Affairs in the Government of National Defence, went to see Bismarck at Versailles in order to come to an arrangement as to the fate of Paris, and to conclude a general armistice. After a week's discussion, a convention was signed at Versailles, January 28, which was at once an armistice treaty and a capitulation. Hostilities were to be suspended for twenty-one days.[5] This armistice was afterwards extended, first to February 24, then to February 26, and then to March 12. On February 15, too, an additional armistice conven-

[1] *Ann. Reg.*, 1859, pp. 250, 251.

[2] Appendix (E).

[3] Appendix (F).

[4] *Ann. Reg.*, 1864, p. 227.

[5] Cf. Villefort, *Recueil des traités, conventions, lois, décrets et autres actes relatifs à la paix avec l'Allemagne*, 5 vols. (Paris, 1872–1879), vol. i. pp. 1–7; A. J. de Clercq, *Recueil des traités de la France*, 10 vols. (Paris, 1864–1872), vol. x. pp. 410–414. (The former work consists of a remarkable and most interesting collection of all kinds of documents relating to the conclusion of peace between France and Germany in 1871.

tion was concluded at Versailles for the departments of Doubs, Jura, Côte d'Or, and Belfort, as the former convention had excepted these places from its operation. On February 26 another convention was agreed upon at Versailles, prolonging the previous one to March 12, in order to facilitate the ratification of the preliminaries of peace concluded at Versailles, February 26. The definitive Treaty of Frankfort was signed May 10.

Negotiations between Russia and Turkey, in their war of 1877–1878, were begun on January 14, 1878, and continued till January 31, when the preliminary conditions of peace were agreed upon at Adrianople, and an armistice was at the same time declared.[1] On March 3 the preliminaries of peace were formally concluded at San Stefano.[2]

In the Chino-Japanese War, 1894–1895, China having suffered severe defeats, and realizing that it was hopeless to continue the struggle, despatched a peace mission to Japan, and on March 30, 1895, an armistice treaty was signed, which was followed by the definitive Treaty of Shimonoseki, April 17.[3]

Early in May 1897 the Great Powers of Europe intervened in the Greco-Turkish War, and asked the Sultan to suspend hostilities. The Sublime Porte replied, May 13, by demanding various extravagant conditions, which it was impossible for Greece to accept. On May 17, however, after a personal appeal to Abdul Hamid by Nicholas II of Russia, a twenty-four hours' suspension of arms was ordered, during which the military authorities of the combatants concluded an armistice for the armies of Epirus, on May 19, and for those of Thessaly, May 20. A long interval elapsed before the preliminaries of peace were agreed upon at Constantinople (September 6/18), which were followed by the definitive treaty signed at the same place, November 22 / December 4, 1897.

In the Spanish-American War, 1898, the United States Government agreed to discuss peace proposals, on the understanding that military and naval operations should not be interrupted until a definite armistice was established. Negotiations opened on July 27, through the medium of the French ambassador at Washington, and continued till August 12, when a protocol of peace was signed which embodied the preliminaries as well as an armistice agreement. Four months later the definitive Treaty of Paris was concluded (December 10).[4]

Finally, in the case of the second Balkan War (in which Bulgaria took the field against Roumania, Greece, Montenegro, and Serbia) a suspension of arms for five days was agreed upon (and arranged by

[1] *Ann. Reg.*, 1878, pp. 325–326.
[2] Appendix (M).
[3] Appendix (R).
[4] Appendix (S).

military representatives) as soon as the peace delegates met in conference at Bucharest, July 13, 1913. Their deliberations not having terminated at the end of that period, the armistice was renewed for three days at the sitting of August 4. The following day an incident occurred which shows the necessity of being precise and explicit in the utmost details. The president informed the conference that he received a telegram from King Constantine, to the effect that a Bulgarian military parlementaire had appeared at the Greek outposts and pointed out that there was a possibility of recommencing hostilities, seeing that the first armistice would expire at noon and the second was to begin at one o'clock in the afternoon, and that the Bulgarian army would, therefore, renew the combat between 12 and 1; King Constantine added that in that case he would order his troops to make a general attack. The Bulgarian delegates, however, declared that the telegram in question must have been the result of a misunderstanding; and the mistake was afterwards rectified. The definitive Treaty of Bucharest was signed on August 10.[1]

Distinction between armistice and suspension of arms.

Some writers, especially on the Continent, make a distinction between an armistice (or truce) and a suspension of arms. Thus German jurists hold that the former—"Waffenstillstand"—implies a general suspension of hostilities for a considerable length of time, agreed upon by the Governments themselves or their diplomatic representatives, with a view to peace negotiations; whilst the latter—"Waffenruhe"—is made for a briefer period, even a few hours, and may be confined to a particular locality, and is established by the military leaders in the field for purely military purposes, e.g. to collect the wounded or bury the dead, to negotiate for a surrender or capitulation, etc. However useful or desirable such a distinction may be, it is not always recognized in theory or observed in practice—as the examples given above show. Nor have the Hague Regulations made any distinction of the kind.

The Hague Regulations.

The provisions of the latter, contained in six articles, which merely sum up the established custom, are as follows:[2]—

"ART. 36.—An armistice suspends military operations by mutual agreement between the belligerent parties. If its duration is not defined, the belligerent parties may resume operations at any time, provided always that the enemy is warned within the time agreed upon, in accordance with the terms of the armistice.

ART. 37.—An armistice may be general or local. The first suspends the entire military operations of the belligerent States; the

[1] Appendix (X).

[2] Convention No. IV (1907).

second only between certain portions of the belligerent armies and within a fixed zone.

ART. 38.—An armistice must be notified officially and in good time to the competent authorities and to the troops. Hostilities are suspended immediately after the notification, or at the time fixed.

ART. 39.—It rests with the contracting parties to settle, in the terms of the armistice, what communications may be held in the theatre of war with and between the populations.

ART. 40.—Any serious violation of the armistice by one of the parties gives the other party the right to denounce it, and even, in case of urgency, to recommence hostilities immediately.

ART. 41.—A violation of the terms of the armistice by individuals acting on their own initiative only entitles the injured party to demand the punishment of the offenders and, if necessary, compensation for the losses sustained."

Political character of the general armistice.

The political character of the general armistice is exemplified in several wars. Thus, in the Franco-German War, the armistice convention of Versailles, January 28, 1871, was signed by Jules Favre and Bismarck; though, as is usual, the assistance of military officers was called in for making all arrangements and for drafting the detailed provisions. In this case the capitulation of Paris was involved; and Jules Favre could get no general at first to co-operate in this fateful negotiation and sign the resulting instrument. Finally, General de Beaufort d'Hautpoul was obtained, but he was too excited, and so was replaced, at the request of Bismarck, by General de Valdan. He then discussed with the German Staff the various questions relevant to the surrender of the forts, the lines of demarcation before Paris, the delivery of armament and material, and the like; but the generals did not sign the document embodying the results of their discussion. In the Russo-Japanese War, the peace commissioners decided the main elements of the armistice treaty, and allowed their respective commanders in the field to agree upon the details. Again, at the peace conference of Bucharest, the delegates of the Balkan States resolved to conclude an armistice, adjourned for a short time to allow military representatives to make the necessary arrangements, and signed the convention themselves.

What may be done.

The most important points to settle are the precise commencement and duration of the truce, and what may or may not be done during its existence. There is no consensus of opinion as to what is permissible, in the absence of specific provisions. Some writers hold that, in such circumstances, neither party may do anything which the other, but for the armistice, could have prevented. Others condemn this rule because of its vagueness and because it might well give rise to abuses, uncertainties, and recriminations (as the French official manual of the laws of war points out),[1] and hold that either may carry out any operations other than the resumption of hostilities and the making of an advance. The latter is the better view, and is more in accordance with modern practice. But, in any event, nothing may be done, whether provided for or not, that is inconsistent with the undisturbed fulfilment of the particular object for which the armistice was established.

Hostile relations not ended.

The suspension of arms does not put an end to the hostile relations of the two sides.[2] A state of war remains *de jure*, and also *de facto*—subject in the latter case to the limitations imposed as mentioned above. Sometimes, however, the armistice becomes so definitely established, and, on account of the protracted peace negotiations, occupies such a great length of time, that third States, being certain or assuming that peace will be proclaimed before the truce is ended, begin to regard it as a practical termination of the war, especially so when commercial intercourse is to some extent re-established between the two parties. Such a case occurred in the Spanish-American War: the armistice agreement was signed on August 12, 1898, and negotiations went on till December 10, when the Treaty of Paris was concluded; but before the latter date many neutral States allowed American public vessels freely to enter their ports for the purpose of docking and taking in supplies.[3]

Examples of armistices.

Next, we shall refer to special examples of armistices, not so much as illustrations of rules and principles adopted—though they serve admirably for this purpose—but primarily because of their vital relation to our present subject, viz. the course of proceedings from the moment arms are suspended to the conclusion and ratification of peace.

The armistice concluded with a view to the discussion of peace in the Crimean War, February 25, 1856, provided that the troops on both sides should retain the respective positions occupied by them at that date, and should refrain from all acts of aggression. But the blockades then existing or those to be established were not to be affected thereby, though no act of hostility was to be committed by the naval forces.

[1] Cf. also J. M. Spaight, *War Rights on Land* (London, 1911), pp. 235, 236.

[2] For a case that arose on this point in the Spanish-American War, cf. *Opinions of United States Attorneys-General*, vol. xxii. p. 190; Moore, *Digest*, vol. vii. pp. 333–334.

[3] Moore, *Digest*, vol. vii. p. 335.

In the Austro-Prussian War, 1866, a military convention was entered into on July 26, which in the first place stipulated the immediate cessation of hostilities, and secondly laid down a number of rules to be observed when the truce came into force a week later. The agreement was as follows :—

Austro-Prussian War.

"The undersigned, the Royal Prussian General of Infantry, Baron von Moltke, and the Imperial Field-Marshal, Count Degenfeld, having been empowered by His Majesty the King of Prussia and His Majesty the Emperor of Austria, and having mutually proved their credentials, conclude a truce under the following conditions :—

The preliminary articles of peace having been signed to-day, hostilities will now cease between the Royal Prussian troops on the one side, and the Imperial Austrian and Royal Saxon troops on the other side, and a four weeks' truce will commence on the 2nd of August. While it lasts, the following conditions will be observed :

1. During the truce the Royal Prussian troops will occupy a district, bounded on the west by the line Eger, Pilsen, Tabor, Neuhaus, Zlabings, Zuaym, inclusive of the forenamed places. The Thaya will form the boundary down to the influx of this river into the March, on the east, the latter river as far as Napagedl, and from thence a straight line to Oderberg.

2. An extent of 9 miles round the fortress of Olmütz, and of 4½ miles round the fortresses of Josephstadt, Königgrätz, and Theresienstadt will be exempted from the Prussian occupation, and these fortresses can draw their supplies from these rayons. The fortress Olmütz will have a line of communication over Weisskirchen to Meseritsch, leading through the Prussian rayon, on which line Prussian troops will not be quartered.

3. To enable the Prussian troops to reach the districts settled in (1) from their present positions, the routes Meissau, Scheiteldorf, Wittingau to Tabor, and Malaczka, Skalitz to Napagedl, will be given up to them, and they will be permitted to take up quarters within 9 miles on either side of these routes.

4. The Prussian troops will make free use of all land and water communications, and railways within the district settled in (1), as long as the truce lasts, and will be in no way hindered from so doing by the fortresses named in (2).

Exempted therefrom is the tract of the Prerau-Trübau railway, which passes through the wood of Olmütz.

5. The Imperial Austrian troops will not cross the line of

demarcation fixed on the 22nd of this month, until the end of the Prussian column has passed the Thaya.

A notification will be sent to the Imperial Government as soon as this has taken place.

6. The sick and the surgeons, and the officials tending them, who remain behind in the districts evacuated by the Royal Prussian troops, will remain in possession of whatever buildings they now occupy. In addition to this, the assistance of the authorities, supplies, and means of transport, will be afforded them on the part of the Austrians. Neither during nor after the truce will any obstacle be opposed to their return to their homes, which the Prussian authorities will hasten as much as possible.

7. The Royal Prussian troops will draw their supplies from the districts in which they are quartered. No contribution of money will be raised on the part of the Prussians.

8. No property, magazines, and stores belonging to the Imperial Austrian Government, which are not in possession of the Prussian troops before the commencement of the truce, will be seized by them.

9. The Imperial Government will provide for the immediate return of the civil authorities to their posts, in order that they may render assistance in provisioning the Prussian Army.

In the time intervening between the 27th of July and the 2nd of August, the Austrian-Saxon troops will keep 2¼ miles off the line of demarcation fixed on the 22nd instant, in so far as the line runs on the left bank of the Danube, and no Prussian troops will cross the aforesaid line.

(*Signed*) COUNT DEGENFELD,
Imperial Field-Marshal.
BARON VON MOLTKE,
General of Infantry.

NIKOLSBURG, *the* 26*th of July*, 1866."[1]

The twofold character of the armistice convention of January 28, 1871, in the Franco-German War, has already been pointed out.

Franco-German War.

Of the fifteen articles[2] ten concern the capitulation of Paris, but they are indiscriminately mixed up with the others. Art. I describes it as a "general" armistice, which was to take effect on the day of conclusion for Paris, and three days

[1] *The Campaign of* 1866 *in Germany.* Compiled by the Department of Military History of the Prussian Staff. Eng. tr. 1872; reprinted 1907; pp. 382–383.

[2] Text in Villefort, *Recueil*, vol. i. pp. 1–7; De Clercq, *Recueil*, vol. x. pp. 410–414.

later for the departments; [1] but certain regions were excepted, viz. the departments of Doubs, Jura, Côte d'Or, and the neighbourhood of Belfort, where the operations of the eastern army were still going on. With regard to the naval forces, the meridian of Dunkirk was adopted as the line of demarcation; the French fleet was to remain to the west of the line, and the German warships were to withdraw to the east of it, as soon as they were notified; and captures made as well as prisoners taken after the conclusion of the armistice and before its notification were to be restored. During the period stipulated—twenty-one days—the German army was not to enter Paris (Art. IV). Arts. VIII and IX gave facilities to the French commissioners for the revictualling of Paris, subject to certain restrictions depending on the line of demarcation between the armies of the belligerents. No arms were to be taken into Paris (Art. XIII). The public funds and securities were to remain intact (Art. XII)—a provision that showed the distrust of the Germans, and their intention regarding an indemnity. The remaining articles provided for the delivery of the fortresses of Paris with their guns; the surrender of the armed garrisons except a certain number of men for internal service in Paris, who were to be delivered up if peace were not concluded at the expiration of the armistice; the payment by Paris of a "war contribution" of 200 million francs—which was more like a ransom; the employment of the National Guard and gendarmerie; the disbanding of the francs-tireurs; the movement of persons subject to permits; the immediate exchange of prisoners—not mutual restoration, which takes place after the conclusion of peace—including civil prisoners, e.g. captains of the German merchant marine and French civilians interned in Germany. The entire arrangement thus possesses a one-sided character, and is far from being an armistice proper, which is essentially a bilateral transaction, giving mutual concessions and imposing mutual restrictions. Apparently, the possession of superior physical force sanctifies irregularities.

It will be noted that the above articles are expressed in general terms; so that in order to carry them out it was necessary to enter into additional conventions, prescribing detailed regulations. This was accordingly done in a series of annexes, dated January 29, 31, February 2, 3, 5, 11, 15.[2]

[1] "Un armistice général, sur toute la ligne des opérations militaires en cours d'exécution entre les armées allemandes et les armées françaises, commencera pour Paris aujourd'hui même, pour les départements dans un délai de trois jours; la durée de l'armistice sera de vingt et un jours à dater d'aujourd'hui, de manière que, sauf le cas où il serait renouvelé, l'armistice se terminera partout le dix-neuf février, à midi."

[2] Villefort, *Recueil*, vol. i. pp. 7 *seq.*; De Clercq, *Recueil*, vol. x. pp. 415 *seq.*

The armistice treaty concluded at Adrianople, January 31, 1878, between Russia and Turkey (which also included certain articles of capitulation), stipulated that the Turks should immediately surrender the Danube fortresses of Widdin, Rustchuk, and Silistria, though they would be permitted to withdraw therefrom their material of war or sell it to the Russians; and that they should evacuate Belgradjik, Razgrad, and Bazardjik. The fortifications of the line of Buyuk-Tchekmedje should be evacuated by the Turkish forces, but were not to be occupied by the Russians; the Turks should retire behind the line of Kuyuk-Tchekmedje, and the Russians advance to the line of Chatalja, the space between the respective forces—about ten miles—being a neutral zone. The towns of Bourgas and Midia on the Black Sea were to be occupied by the Russians, who were to be allowed to revictual their army through these ports. Finally, the Turks were to raise the blockade of the Black Sea ports.

Russo-Turkish War.

After Japan took Port Arthur and Wei-hai-wei in the war against China, 1894–1895, it was clear that the latter country was in sore straits. A Japanese army was preparing to proceed to Pekin; and on March 16, 1895, Prince Komatsu was placed in command of the expedition. Some six weeks before this, however, China had despatched a mission to Japan to propose peace; but as the delegates did not possess the powers necessary for negotiating, they were not received. In March the position of China became critical, so that Li Hung-Chang was appointed plenipotentiary and sent to Japan. He arrived at Shimonoseki on March 20, and on the next day asked for an armistice. The following terms were laid down by the Japanese Government: Evacuation of Tientsin, Takou, and Shan-hai-kwan, and delivery to the Japanese of the forts, barracks, arms, and other war material found in these places; administration of the railways between Tientsin and Shan-hai-kwan by the Japanese; reimbursement of all expenses of the Japanese expeditionary army. Li Hung-Chang having at once replied that these conditions were too onerous, was allowed three days in which to consider the question; but on the 24th he again expressed his inability to accept such terms, and said he would forgo a suspension of arms, and continue his negotiations without it. On the same day an attempt on his life was made by a Japanese fanatic.[1] As a token of regret for this incident the Emperor, having consulted his principal ministers, ordered that an armistice should be granted without imposing any unacceptable conditions. Accordingly, the following

Chinese-Japanese War.

[1] Cf. N. Ariga, *La guerre sino-japonaise au point de vue du droit international* (Paris, 1896), p. 247.

convention was drawn up and agreed upon: (1) Temporary suspension of hostilities on land and sea in the provinces of Mukden, Pechheli, and Shan-Tong. (The sphere was thus limited, as Formosa was excluded.) (2) The armies not to advance beyond their positions then occupied. (3) There were to be no offensive operations, reinforcements, or increase of fighting power; new troops could be distributed and transported, but not to increase the armies then in the field. (As Professor Ariga points out, this article was ambiguous, and might well have given rise to difficulties.) (4) Transport by sea of troops, munitions of war, and all contraband of war to remain liable to capture according to the usual laws of war. (5) Notice of the armistice to be sent as soon as possible to the military authorities concerned. (6) It was to last twenty-one days, unless the peace negotiations failed before the end of this period, in which case the armistice was to end at the same time.

Greco-Turkish War.

In the Greco-Turkish War, 1897, the Powers intervened, and asked the Sultan to suspend his offensive operations. After some delay—the dilatory methods of the Porte are notorious—the Turkish Government replied it would consent to an armistice if the Greeks raised the blockade of Preveza and Volo, and accepted the following terms as preliminaries of peace: Annexation of Thessaly; payment of a war indemnity of 230 million francs; abrogation of the capitulations and the treaty of extradition. It was added that Turkey expected to negotiate directly with Greece. The latter could not entertain such a proposal, which was no doubt put forward for the purpose of gaining time.[1] Hostilities went on, and the Turks soon became masters of Thessaly. The Czar of Russia having made an appeal to the Sultan (as has already been mentioned), an armistice convention was concluded on May 19 for Epirus, and on May 20 for Thessaly. Each of these conventions was regular in postulating that the relative positions of the armies should remain as they were on those dates; but both were irregular, as they contained no provisions for the period of the armistice, the military operations, or a line of demarcation; and nothing, too, was said regarding the fleets. Greece assumed apparently that the whole duration of the peace negotiations was thereby covered. After much discussion, however, in which the Powers took part, Turkey agreed to amended conventions, June 3, covering the period of the peace negotiations—that for Thessaly adding that if no agreement were reached, twenty-four hours' notice should be given before recommencing hostilities.

[1] Cf. N. Politis, *La guerre gréco-turque au point de vue du droit international* (Paris, 1898), p. 87.

On June 4 a supplementary convention was entered into, whereby the Greek blockades were raised, the right of visiting Turkish or neutral vessels was suspended, both sides could navigate the high sea and the Gulf of Arta, Turkey was forbidden to reinforce her armies by sea or transport contraband of war, but could revictual her armies twice a week by means of the occupied ports, and finally, the violation of national or occupied territory by irregular bands was to be considered a breach of the convention. This instrument proved to be defective owing to its want of precision; difficulties arose as to the movements of the troops, and mutual recriminations followed.

Spanish-American War.

On August 12, 1898, a protocol was signed at Washington on behalf of Spain and the United States. It embodied the preliminaries of peace, and also provided for the suspension of arms. Thus Art. VI says: "Upon the conclusion and signing of this protocol hostilities between the two countries shall be suspended, and notice to that effect shall be given as soon as possible by each Government to the commanders of its military and naval forces." On the same day President McKinley issued a proclamation, and at once sent telegraphic orders to the American forces. It appears that the news reached General Miles's army in Porto Rico just in time to discontinue a battle at Aibonito and another near Cayey; it prevented also the capitulation of Manzanillo—for the Spanish commander had on the previous evening drawn up a formal instrument of surrender, which was to have been despatched on the following morning; but, on the contrary, the notice arrived too late to save Manila. The last shots of the war were exchanged between an American warship and two Spanish gunboats off Cuba on the morning of August 14.

M. Cambon, the French Ambassador at Washington, having made inquiries, on behalf of Spain, as to the re-establishment of commercial intercourse, the American Department of State replied, August 17, (1) that Spanish steamers might resume their postal service beween Spain and Cuba, Porto Rico, and the Philippines (the protocol of August 12 had stipulated that Spain should relinquish her sovereignty over Cuba, cede Porto Rico to the United States, and that the United States should occupy Manila till the fate of the Philippines was determined); (2) Spanish vessels might take supplies to Cuba and the Philippines, but supplies from the United States to Porto Rico should be taken only in American vessels; and (3) a Spanish steamer, chartered by French merchants, and then lying at Havre, might proceed to Philadelphia and take mineral oil for industrial purposes, provided it was not to be transported to

Porto Rico. This consent was given on condition that American vessels should not be excluded from Spanish ports, and, if hostilities were renewed, should be allowed thirty days in which to depart therefrom with non-contraband cargo, and that such American vessels as had sailed for a Spanish port before the renewal of hostilities should be allowed to enter, discharge their cargo, and depart unmolested during their voyage to any port not blockaded. An agreement having been reached on these points, commercial intercourse was restored.[1]

On September 1, 1905, the Russian and Japanese plenipotentiaries signed an armistice protocol four days before they concluded their negotiations regarding the definitive Treaty of Portsmouth. The said protocol was as follows:—

Russo-Japanese War.

"The undersigned plenipotentiaries of Japan and Russia, duly authorized to that effect by their Governments, have agreed upon the following terms of armistice between the belligerents, pending the coming into force of the treaty of peace:

1. A certain distance (zone of demarcation) shall be fixed between the fronts of the armies of the two Powers in Manchuria, as well as in the region of the Tomamko.

2. The naval forces of one of the belligerents shall not bombard territory belonging to or occupied by the other.

3. Maritime captures will not be suspended by the armistice.

4. During the term of the armistice reinforcements shall not be despatched to the theatre of war. Those which are *en route* shall not be despatched to the north of Mukden on the part of Japan and to the south of Harbin on the part of Russia.

5. The commanders of the armies and fleets of the two Powers shall determine on common accord the conditions of the armistice in conformity with the provisions above enumerated.

6. The two Governments shall give orders to their commanders immediately after the signature of the treaty of peace in order to put this protocol into execution.

(*Signed*) JUTARO KOMURA.
K. TAKAHIRA.
SERGE WITTE.
ROSEN.

PORTSMOUTH, *September 1st*, 1905."[2]

[1] Mr. Moore, Act. Sec. of State, to M. Cambon, French Ambassador, August 17, 1898: *For. Rel. of the U.S.* (1898), p. 802; M. Cambon to Mr. Moore, September 6, 1898: *ibid.*, p. 811; Moore, *Digest*, vol. vii. pp. 332–333.

[2] S. Takahashi, *International Law applied to the Russo-Japanese War* (London, 1908), p. 219.

In pursuance of the above protocol, military commissioners of the two belligerents met (September 13) at Sha-ho-tsu, a point midway between the opposing encampments, and about a rifle range from each, and agreed to the following five articles:—

"1. Hostilities shall be suspended throughout the whole of Manchuria.

2. The ground between the first lines of the Japanese and Russian armies, as shown in the map to be exchanged together with the protocol, shall be made a neutral zone.

3. No person having any connection with either army shall be permitted to enter the neutral zone under any pretext whatever.

4. The road leading from Shahotsz to Shwangmiaotsz shall be used in common by both armies.

5. This protocol shall become effective from noon on September 16th of the 38th year of Meiji (1905), or September 3rd according to the Russian calendar.

Each respective army shall enforce the terms of armistice according to this protocol by noon on the 16th instant at the latest."[1]

Finally came the naval armistice. On September 18, the Japanese Rear-Admiral Shimamura, together with a squadron, met off Lojinpho, Korea, the Russian Rear-Admiral Jessen, with a squadron. They were each joined by a number of naval commissioners. The Russian commissioners submitted a draft of eight articles, which proved unsatisfactory, and were rejected entirely. After several hours' discussion, however, the following agreement was arrived at:—

"The sea bordering on the coasts of the belligerents is divided as follows:—

The boundary line starts from Lejionoff promontory, runs 30 nautical miles to the south-east, connects the point 42° N. Lat. and 136° E. Long.; point 46° N. Lat. and 140° E. Long.; point 48° N. Lat. and 141° E. Long.; point 50° N. Lat. and 141° 23′ E. Long.; and point 51° 48′ N. Lat. and 141° 23′ E. Long. The narrowest portion of the Mamiya Straits between the last-mentioned point and point 53° 27′ N. Lat. and 141° 27½′ E. Long. is made a neutral zone. The boundary line again starts from the point 53° 27′ N. Lat. and 141° 27½′ E. Long. and runs to the point 56° N. Lat. and 142° E. Long. and point 56° N. Lat. and 148° E. Long., and then passing

[1] Takahashi, *op. cit.*, p. 220.

through the central point of the Shumushu Straits, coincides with the parallel of 50° 50′ N. Lat.

The narrowest part of the Mamiya Straits is made a neutral zone.

The navies of both belligerents are prohibited from passing the said boundary line.

This resolution comes into force from the day of signing and will be valid during the period of armistice.

As a guarantee of the above, each representative signs his name to this protocol.

(*Signed*) REAR-ADMIRAL SHIMAMURA.
REAR-ADMIRAL JESSEN.

September 18*th*, 1905."[1]

First Balkan War.

In the first Balkan War, 1912–1913, between Turkey on the one side and the Balkan League, consisting of Greece, Bulgaria, Serbia, and Montenegro on the other, Turkey, having suffered severe defeats, sued for an armistice on November 12. In reply (November 19), the Allies demanded the surrender of all the Turkish positions in Europe that still offered resistance, including the Chatalja lines, as well as of Adrianople, Scutari, and Yanina. These terms were rejected on the 21st, and Nazim Pasha was ordered to continue operations till "reasonable and moderate conditions" were proposed. At the same time Turkish delegates were appointed to resume negotiations for an armistice. Eventually an armistice agreement was concluded (December 3, 1912), providing at once for the suspension of hostilities on the basis of the *status quo* of the respective forces, and for the commencement of peace negotiations in London ten days later. A noteworthy feature of this convention is the fact that it was not signed by Greece, though she intended to take part in the peace conference; so that hostilities for the time being went on between her and Turkey. On the 13th the plenipotentiaries of the five belligerent parties arrived in London, and on the 16th held their first meeting. The efforts made to arrive at an understanding failed; on January 6, 1913, the Balkan delegates declared the negotiations "suspended," and at the end of the month it was formally notified that the armistice was at an end.[2] It was not till May 30 that the war was terminated by the Treaty of London.[3]

[1] Takahashi, *op. cit.*, p. 223.

[2] See *infra*, p. 91, as to the intervention of the Great Powers.

[3] See *infra*, Appendix (W).

It is clear, from the preceding pages, that there are no settled rules with regard to the conclusion of armistice conventions for the purpose of instituting or carrying on peace negotiations.

No settled rules.

A belligerent is under no legal obligation to accede to a request for an armistice. Whether such compacts, if they are made at all, are to be concluded before the preliminary and fundamental conditions of peace are agreed upon, or before the preliminaries of peace proper are signed, or before the definitive treaty is solemnized; whether the armistice is to be general, applying to the whole of the forces, military and naval, or partial, applying only to certain specified territories and maritime spheres; whether it is to operate for a fixed period or indefinitely till the date of the treaty of peace, or till the date of the exchange of ratifications; whether it is to be considered abrogated at the moment peace negotiations break down or at the expiration of a certain length of time thereafter—all these questions are subject to the mutual agreement of the contending parties. Again, whether the armistice convention is to contain provisions purely and simply for regulating the suspension of hostilities, or it is to include articles of surrender, or the vital conditions on which peace proposals will be entertained, are matters also for the determination of the combatants—or depend, rather, on the will and dictation of the victorious belligerent. Diplomacy is always more effective when supported by victorious arms; but cases are not wanting—as we shall see in a subsequent chapter—where the victor in the field was not equal to his adversary's diplomacy in the conference chamber, and eventually derived little or no advantage from his martial success.

Sometimes a third Power places its services at the disposal of belligerents contemplating peace, in order to help them to begin their negotiations and to facilitate their communications with each other. Sometimes, too, neutral States intervene on their own initiative—and occasionally using more than merely moral suasion—to help to bring about the establishment of peace, and in the common interests of the society of nations to protect the weaker party against the exorbitant demands of the stronger. Such interposition of third Powers we have next to consider.

CHAPTER II

INTERPOSITION OF THIRD POWERS

Belligerents and neutrals—Forms of intervention: good offices and mediation—When a case for interposition arises—Provision in treaties—The Hague Rules—Instances of interposition.

Belligerents and neutral States.

UNDER international law every sovereign independent State is entitled to manage its own affairs, both external and internal, in peace and in war, without the interference of other States; subject, however, in the case of external relationships, pacific or warlike, to any relevant conventions to which it is a party. If, during a war, violations of law are about to be committed or have been committed, every neutral State is not only entitled but is legally obliged to intervene in order to prevent the execution of the misdeeds contemplated or their repetition; and particularly so when international agreements are endangered or broken, to which neutral Powers as well as the belligerents are parties. Further, international morality—if not international law—calls upon every State to use every means at its disposal, without giving offence—for example, friendly suggestion, moral suasion—to prevent the outbreak of war, or, when it has begun, to help the contending parties to compose their differences. A war between two nations directly or indirectly concerns all nations, members as they are of the international community. There is not and there cannot be any principle of law, of ethics, or of religion, prohibiting peaceful States from doing their utmost to bring about a cessation of carnage and devastation. Efforts made in the interests of humanity and civilization may not always succeed; but it is incumbent on third parties to make them.[1]

A war concerns all nations.

Efforts of this kind should be made at all times when peace is imperilled; but more especially during a war when it is perceived that the belligerents are disposed to begin negotiations for peace,

[1] Cf. Phillipson, *International Law and the Great War* (London, 1915), pp. 18 *seq.*, 24 *seq.*

but for reasons of their own are unwilling to make the first advances. As Vattel observes, the obvious occasion for interposition occurs when two States, though equally tired of the war, nevertheless continue it simply from a fear of taking the first steps to effect an accommodation, as this action might be imputed to weakness; or, again, when they persist in their hostilities from a feeling of animosity, and contrary to their true interests.[1]

Forms of intervention.

This intervention of third Powers, when invoked or accepted by the disputant or belligerent States, may take the form either of good offices or of mediation. When it is not voluntarily accepted, it is imposed by a more powerful State, or by several States acting in concert, in order to prevent the extermination of one or other, or even both, of the combatants; or to prevent the victorious party from forcing on the vanquished such conditions of peace as would impair the existing balance of power and the stability of the family of nations. When friendly interposition is offered, a belligerent or both belligerents may reject the offer, and if strong enough will do so successfully. But sometimes, however, it happens that the offer of mediation is refused, whilst that of good offices is accepted.

Difference between good offices and mediation.

The difference between these two kinds of intervention may be stated thus. In good offices the least pronounced form of interposition is involved, which amounts to little more than an amicable exertion of moral influence for the purpose of inducing the two hostile sides to make certain reciprocal concessions and so pave the way to a definite and solid understanding. The Power which thus uses its good offices does not take any direct part in their negotiations or arrangements, as soon as these have been set on foot. Mediation is a more accentuated form of participation, and consequently involves greater responsibility and assumes a more solemn character. The mediator is necessarily a friend of both contending parties. He is present at their conferences, or at some of them, offers his advice in regard to proposals made by one side or the other, suggests proposals to be made, indicates solutions to difficulties and problems that existed before the commencement of the negotiations, or that arise in the course of the negotiations. He is an intermediary who exercises a restraining or moderating force; he seeks to reconcile diverging interests and ostensibly incompatible demands. But he cannot, as a mediator, lay down his judgment or impose a solution irrespectively of the parties' consent; for to do so would be to usurp the functions of a judge or arbitrator. Obviously the mediator should possess

[1] *Droit des gens*, liv. iv. ch. ii. § 17.

special qualities in respect of his personality and diplomacy in order that he may smoothly, unobtrusively, and effectively perform his delicate work.

Vattel, speaking of the nature of this species of intervention and of the qualities essential thereto, aptly observes: "Mediation, in which a common friend interposes his good offices, frequently proves efficacious in engaging the contending parties to meet each other half-way—to come to a good understanding—to enter into an agreement or compromise respecting their rights, and, if the question relates to an injury, to offer and accept a reasonable satisfaction. The office of mediator requires as great a degree of integrity as of prudence and address. He ought to observe a strict impartiality; he should soften the reproaches of the disputants, calm their resentments, and dispose their minds to a reconciliation. His duty is to favour well-founded claims, and to effect the restoration, to each party, of what belongs to him; but he ought not scrupulously to insist on rigid justice. He is a conciliator, and not a judge: his business is to procure peace; and he ought to induce him who has right on his side to relax something of his pretensions, if necessary, with a view to so great a blessing." [1]

Similarly, Sir James Mackintosh, deploring the rejection by Great Britain of the proffered mediation of Russia in the Anglo-American War of 1812, said in the House of Commons that "a mediator is a common friend, who counsels both parties with a weight proportioned to their belief in his integrity and their respect for his power. But he is not an arbitrator, to whose decisions they submit their differences, and whose award is binding on them." [2]

Mr. Holls, one of the American delegates at the Hague Peace Conference, 1899, and a zealous advocate of mediation, emphasizes its advantages. He points out the elasticity of its action, and the possibility of adapting it to the special circumstances of each particular case. As it is introduced with the consent of the parties, it does not infringe their sovereignty or their liberty and independence. Without transcending the limits of conciliatory advice, it operates by merely influencing their free will, which remains unimpaired throughout.[3]

Mediation or good offices may be offered spontaneously, when and as the emergency arises, or in pursuance of a previously

[1] *Droit des gens*, liv. ii. ch. xviii. § 328 (English trans., Philadelphia, 1872).

[2] Hansard, *Parl. Debates*, vol. xxx. p. 526; April 11, 1815.

[3] F. W. Holls, *The Peace Conference at The Hague* (New York, 1900), pp. 177–178.

concluded treaty, or at the request of the parties. But a request for the employment of good offices and the consent to act in such a capacity do not confer the right of mediation proper.[1]

When a case for interposition arises.

There were formerly discussions among jurists as to whether a third Power had the right to offer its mediation to States already at war. Some held that it ought not to do so, for fear of compromising its neutrality.[2] But modern practice, provisions in treaties, and now the Hague Regulations have made such action possible without any liability of impairing the rights and duties of neutrality. First, let us look at some examples of treaties, embodying various kinds of engagements as to the employment of good offices or mediation.

Provision in treaties.

On July 20, 1806, France and Russia concluded a treaty of peace and alliance, whereby (Art. VIII) both Powers agreed to unite their good offices in order to put an end as soon as possible to the state of war then existing between Prussia and Sweden.

The treaty of peace signed at Tilsit between France and Russia, July 7, 1807, furnishes an example of a conditional acceptance of mediation (Art. XIII), and also one of an unqualified acceptance (Art. XXIII). These two articles are as follows:—

" Art. XIII.—S. M. l'Empereur Napoléon accepte la médiation de S. M. l'Empereur de toutes les Russies, à l'effet de négocier et conclure un traité de paix définitive entre la France et l'Angleterre, dans la supposition que cette médiation sera aussi acceptée par l'Angleterre, un mois après l'échange des ratifications du présent traité.

Art. XXIII.—S. M. l'Empereur de toutes les Russies accepte la médiation de S. M. l'Empereur des Français, Roi d'Italie, à l'effet de négocier et conclure une paix avantageuse et honorable aux deux Empires. Les plénipotentiaires respectifs se rendront dans le lieu dont les parties intéressées conviendront, pour y ouvrir et suivre les négociations." [3]

The Treaty of Dresden between France and Austria, June 30, 1813, stipulated both the offer and the acceptance of mediation in the interests of European peace, and to that end provided definitely for the meeting of the plenipotentiaries concerned:

" Art. I.—S. M. l'Empereur d'Autriche offre sa médiation pour la paix générale ou continentale.

Art. II.—S. M. l'Empereur des Français accepte ladite médiation.

[1] Cf. J. L. Klüber, *Droit des gens moderne de l'Europe*, 2 vols. (Paris, 1831), Part II, tit. 2, § 1, ch. ii. § 160.

[2] F. Galiani, *Dei doveri dei principi neutrali*, c. ix.

[3] De Clercq, *Recueil*, vol. ii. pp. 207, 210, 212.

ART. III.—Les plénipotentiaires Français, Russes, et Prussiens se réuniront avant le 5 juillet dans la ville de Prague." [1]

Again, the Treaty of Paris, March 30, 1856, between Great Britain, Austria, France, Prussia, Sardinia, Turkey on the one side, and Russia on the other, stipulated (Art. VIII) that if there should arise between Turkey and any of the other signatories a difference endangering peace, these Powers, before resorting to forcible measures, should afford the other contracting parties the opportunity of preventing such an extremity by means of their mediation.[2] At a subsequent conference of the Powers that signed this treaty, the wish was expressed, in their 23rd protocol, April 14, 1856, that all States, between which any serious misunderstanding might arise, should as far as possible have recourse to the good offices of a friendly Power before appealing to arms, and that the Governments not represented at the congress should unite in the sentiment that inspired this wish.[3]

The Hague Rules.

The most important of all engagements of this kind is the Hague Convention for the pacific settlement of international disputes, established in 1899 and reaffirmed in 1907, which summarizes authoritatively a number of the rules that had from time to time been observed by States. It takes a step beyond Art. VIII of the Treaty of Paris, inasmuch as it gives third States a right to mediate even when the honour and vital interests of the contending parties are concerned.

"ART. I.—With a view to obviating as far as possible recourse to force in the relations between States, the contracting Powers agree to use their best efforts to ensure the pacific settlement of international differences.

ART. II.—In case of serious disagreement or dispute, before an appeal to arms, the contracting Powers agree to have recourse, as far as circumstances allow, to the good offices or mediation of one or more friendly Powers.

ART. III.—Independently of this recourse, the contracting Powers deem it expedient and desirable [4] that one or more Powers, strangers to the dispute, should, on their own initiative and as far as circumstances may allow, offer their good offices or mediation to the States at variance.

Powers strangers to the dispute have the right to offer good offices or mediation even during the course of hostilities.

[1] De Clercq, *Recueil*, vol. ii. p. 385. [2] See Appendix (D).

[3] Sir E. Hertslet, *Map of Europe by Treaty*, 4 vols. (London, 1875-1891), vol. ii. p. 1279.

[4] The words "and desirable" were the only addition made in 1907.

The exercise of this right can never be regarded by either of the parties in dispute as an unfriendly act.

ART. IV.—The part of the mediator consists in reconciling the opposing claims and appeasing the feelings of resentment which may have arisen between the States at variance.

ART. V.—The functions of the mediator are at an end when once it is declared, either by one of the parties to the dispute or by the mediator himself, that the means of reconciliation proposed by him are not accepted.

ART. VI.—Good offices and mediation undertaken either at the request of the parties in dispute or on the initiative of Powers strangers to the dispute have exclusively the character of advice, and never have binding force.

ART. VII.—The acceptance of mediation cannot, unless there be an agreement to the contrary, have the effect of interrupting, delaying, or hindering mobilization or other measures of preparation for war.

If mediation takes place after the commencement of hostilities, the military operations in progress are not interrupted in the absence of an agreement to the contrary.

ART. VIII.—The contracting Powers are agreed in recommending the application, when circumstances allow, of special mediation in the following form:—

In case of a serious difference endangering peace, the States at variance choose respectively a Power to which they entrust the mission of entering into direct communication with the Power chosen on the other side, with the object of preventing the rupture of pacific relations.

For the period of this mandate, the term of which, unless otherwise stipulated, cannot exceed thirty days, the States in dispute cease from all direct communication on the subject of the dispute, which is regarded as referred exclusively to the mediating Powers, which must use their best efforts to settle it.

In case of a definite rupture of pacific relations, these Powers are charged with the joint task of taking advantage of any opportunity to restore peace."

The last-mentioned article, prescribing a form of special mediation, was due to the proposal of Mr. Holls, one of the delegates of the United States; [1] but there has not yet been a case of its adoption in practice.

Having set forth the fundamental principles of good offices and mediation, we may now recall some instances of this kind of interposition, whether successful or not, whether it occurred on

[1] Cf. F. W. Holls, *op. cit.*, pp. 187–203.

the initiative of the intervening Power, or at the request of the States at variance or at war, or whether it was exercised contrary to the wishes of one or both of the parties.

Instances of interposition. In connection with the long-drawn-out negotiations leading to the Peace of Westphalia, 1648, we find Pope Urban VI extorting from the belligerents as early as 1636 their consent to send delegates to Cologne to discuss peace; then Denmark acting as mediator at Hamburg (1641) in the preparation of the preliminary articles fixing the time and place of the congress; and afterwards the nuncio, Chigi, and the Venetian envoy, Contarino, taking an active part in the proceedings at Münster (1644–1648).

At the Congress of Nimeguen (1675), England and the Pope were the mediators.

In 1697, Sweden acted as mediator in the case of the Treaty of Ryswick, between France on the one part, and England, the Empire, Spain, and Holland on the other.

During the war between Russia and Sweden, 1742, Russia accepted the good offices of France, but refused her mediation.

At the Congress of Teschen, 1779, Russia and France were mediators between Austria, Prussia, and Bavaria.

In the Anglo-American War, 1812–1814, the United States requested, at the beginning of the year 1814, the mediation of Russia, which was then in alliance with Great Britain. But Lord Castlereagh, on behalf of Great Britain, rejected the proposal, probably owing to a supposed accordance between Russia and the United States in regard to questions of naval law.[1]

In the conflict between France and Spain, France refused the mediation of Great Britain, but accepted her good offices in 1823. These having failed, Canning renewed his good offices after the French invasion of Spain.[2]

Next we come to an example of mediation offered with threats. On August 16, 1827, during the sanguinary conflict between Turkey and the Greeks, Great Britain, France, and Russia addressed a declaration to the Ottoman Porte calling for a suspension of arms, and proposing their mediation. They pointed out the previous efforts made by the Powers to secure peace, the widespread evils of the protracted war, which had become their concern too; and gave the Turkish Government a month in which to return a definite answer. This document, which is of special interest, is as follows:—

Mediation with threats.

Greco-Turkish War, 1827.

[1] Cf. *American State Papers*, *For. Rel.*, vol. iii. p. 623; Moore, *Digest*, vol. vii. p. 3.

[2] Phillimore, *Commentaries*, vol. iii. pp. 888 *seq.*

"Les soussignés sont chargés par leurs gouvernements respectifs de faire à S. Ex. le Reïs-Effendi la déclaration suivante :—

Depuis près de six ans les grandes Puissances de l'Europe ont fait des efforts pour déterminer la Sublime Porte-Ottomane à pacifier la Grèce. Ces efforts sont restés infructueux, et une guerre d'extermination s'est prolongée entre Elle et les Grecs, dont les résultats ont été, d'une part, des calamités effrayantes pour l'humanité, et de l'autre, des pertes devenues intolérables pour le commerce de toutes les nations ; dès-lors il n'a plus été possible d'admettre que le sort de la Grèce concernât exclusivement la Porte-Ottomane.

Les Puissances ont par conséquent redoublé de zèle et renouvelé les instances qu'elles avaient faites pour décider la Porte à terminer à l'aide de leur médiation, et par un arrangement convenable, une lutte que son intérêt propre lui faisant une loi de ne pas prolonger.

Les Puissances se sont d'autant plus flattées de parvenir à une si heureuse conclusion que les Grecs ont témoigné, dans cet intervalle, le désir de s'y prêter ; mais la S. Porte a refusé, jusqu'ici, d'écouter des conseils dictés par des sentiments de bienveillance et d'amitié.

Dans cet état de choses, les Cours d'Angleterre, de France et de Russie, ont cru devoir réglé, par un traité spécial [1] la ligne de conduite qu'elles sont dans la résolution de suivre pour atteindre le but vers lequel tendent les vœux et les intérêts de toutes les Puissances Chrétiennes. En exécution de l'une des clauses de ce traité, elles ont chargé les soussignés de déclarer au gouvernement de la S. Porte :

Qu'elles lui proposent formellement leur médiation entre lui et les Grecs, pour faire cesser la guerre et régler par une négociation amicale les relations qui doivent, à l'avenir, exister entre eux.

Que de plus, et afin de faciliter le succès de cette médiation, elles proposent au gouvernement de la S. Porte de suspendre, par un armistice, tout acte d'hostilité envers les Grecs à qui une proposition semblable est adressée en ce moment.

Qu'enfin elles s'attendent que, dans le délai d'un mois, le gouvernement Ottoman fera connaître sa détermination précise.

Les soussignés aiment à se flatter qu'elle sera conforme aux vœux des Cours Alliées ; mais il est de leur devoir de ne pas dissimuler au Reïs-Effendi, qu'un nouveau refus, une réponse évasive ou insuffisante, ou bien même un silence complet de la part de son gouvernement, mettra les Cours Alliées dans la necessité d'avoir recours aux mesures qu'elles jugeront les plus efficaces pour faire cesser un état de choses devenu désormais incompatible avec les véritables intérêts de la Porte, avec la sûreté du commerce en général et la parfaite tranquillité de l'Europe." [2]

[1] The treaty of July 6, 1827. [2] De Clercq, *Recueil*, vol. iii. pp. 458, 460.

In 1838 Great Britain and the United States offered, independently of each other, to mediate in the struggle between France and Mexico.

The mediation of Austria was exercised in 1855–1856 to put an end to the Crimean War. Towards the close of 1855, the Allies having greatly increased their resources, France contemplated sending an army into Poland by way of Germany. Austria therefore became anxious about her own position. She ascertained the indispensable terms demanded by Great Britain and France, and on that basis endeavoured to effect an accommodation between them and Russia. Accordingly she sent Count Esterhazy to St. Petersburg with the Allies' proposal, which, she intimated, was also her own ultimatum. Soon after the latter's departure the Austrian Foreign Minister addressed a despatch to him, December 16, in which he strongly recommended to the Czar the propositions submitted, and emphasized the evils that would follow their rejection. "We entreat the Court of Russia," he observed, "to examine calmly the propositions which we submit to it. We will not dwell upon the grave consequences which would ensue from a refusal to enter into the paths which we open a second time to effect an honourable reconciliation—a refusal which would entail upon itself the weight of an immense responsibility. We prefer leaving it to its wisdom to estimate all the chances. We think that we are in this instance the interpreter of the wishes and of the real wants of Europe. It remains for us to make an appeal to the elevated sentiments of the Emperor Alexander, whose supreme determination will decide the fate of so many thousands of beings. His Imperial Majesty will take, we entertain the confident hope, that decision which appears to us alone of a nature to respond to the real interests of his people and to the wants of humanity."[1] The Austrian proposals referred to the abolition of the Russian protectorate over the Danubian principalities, the free navigation of the Danube, the neutralization of the Black Sea, the position of Christian subjects of Turkey. On January 14, 1856, Russia replied suggesting certain modifications. The reply was transmitted to the Allies, who refused to make any relaxation; and eventually Russia submitted.[2]

Austrian mediation in Crimean War.

In 1860 Russia and the United States offered their good offices in the war between Great Britain and France on the one side, and China on the other.

Two years later, in the American Civil War, France proposed to England and Russia that the three Powers should jointly offer their

[1] E. H. Nolan, *The War against Russia* (London, n.d.), vol. ii. p. 681.

[2] The negotiations are considered more fully, *infra*, pp. 133–135.

mediation to the belligerent parties. England and Russia refused to do so on the ground that the moment was inopportune. "According to the information we possess," wrote Prince Gortchakow, the Russian foreign minister, "we are led to believe that a combined movement of France, England, and Russia, however conciliatory it might be, and with whatsoever precautions it might be surrounded, if it came with an official and collective character, would incur the risk of bringing about a result opposed to the pacificatory end which the three Courts desire."[1] Had the proposal been made, it would probably have been declined; for—among other reasons—it was thought in the Northern States that France was adverse to the Union, and was anxious to recover her former American possessions. However this may be, Mr. Seward, the secretary of state, had already refused an offer to mediate which had been submitted in June 1861 by Lord Lyons, the British minister, and M. Mercier, the French minister, at Washington. "... We appreciate this generous and friendly demonstration," he replied, "but ... we cannot solicit or accept mediation from any, even the most friendly quarter."[2]

American Civil War.

The United States, in her turn, met with a refusal when she proposed her good offices in the war, 1865–1866, between Spain on the one hand, and the Republics on the west coast of South America on the other. Mediation was, again, offered on several occasions by the United States Government in the protracted war, 1866–1872, made by Spain against the allied Republics of Chile, Peru, Bolivia, and Ecuador; and eventually it was accepted, with a successful result.[3]

When war between Austria and Prussia on the one hand, and Denmark on the other, became imminent, 1864, the 23rd protocol of the Congress of Paris, 1856 (referred to above), was invoked, but without any effect. The "pious aspiration" therein expressed had little restraining influence on combatants who were much more powerful than their adversary.

In 1866, too, before the outbreak of the Austro-Prussian War, the protocol was appealed to in vain. However, after the Austrian defeat at Königgrätz, the Emperor of Austria ceded Venetia to Napoleon III, and requested his mediation to put an end to the war in Germany and Italy. Napoleon at once communicated with King William (July 4), saying that he was compelled to lay aside his reserve owing to

Austro-Prussian War.

[1] Prince Gortchakow to M. d'Oubril, Russian Chargé d'Affaires in Paris, October 27, 1862; *U.S. Diplom. Corr.*, 1863, vol. ii. p. 769.

[2] Mr. Seward to Mr. Adams, Minister to England, June 19, 1861; *Diplom. Corr.*, 1861, pp. 90, 92; Moore, *Digest*, vol. vii. p. 9.

[3] Moore, *Digest*, vol. vii. pp. 9, 10.

the rapid Prussian victories, and that he was assured the King would regard favourably his offer of mediation to obtain an armistice and establish peace. The offer was accepted, but owing to the military position Prussia could not at once grant an armistice. For some eighteen days proposals and counter-proposals were exchanged between the belligerents—in which M. Benedetti, on behalf of France, played a great part—until a military convention was concluded on July 22, 1866, suspending hostilities for five days, followed by the Preliminaries of Nikolsburg,[1] together with a definite armistice, on July 26.[2] It is to be noted that in the negotiations France was not represented at the conference, as she did not intend to play the full part of a mediator proper.[3]

Before the outbreak of the Franco-Prussian War, 1870, the British Government reminded the States at variance of the vow expressed in the protocol of April 14, 1856, and appealed to them to call in the aid of a friendly Power for the purpose of settling their differences. France replied that she appreciated the principle of mediation, but pointed out that the said protocol expressly made a reservation in regard to a nation's honour and dignity. (Under the present rules, which have been set forth above, no such plea can be made—at all events so far as the rules are concerned.) However, in September 1870, France, after serious reverses, requested the United States to endeavour, along with other Powers, to bring about peace. The United States Government replied that, despite its uniform policy to avoid all interference in European questions, it would " for humanity's sake " undertake the task if both belligerents asked for its sole mediation; it refused to participate in a joint official mediation with European States, though it would be willing to confer with the latter on the question.[4] But in any case the Government of North Germany intimated its objection to the interposition of any third Power.

After the Russo-Turkish War was ended by the Preliminaries of San Stefano, March 3, 1878, a congress of the Great Powers assembled at Berlin with the object of settling important European affairs, which involved several modifications of such articles of these preliminaries as had been deemed excessive. At this congress Germany acted as mediator.

In the Peru-Chile War, 1879–1882, the United States made an attempt to mediate. The American Minister at Santiago suggested to the Chilian Minister of Foreign Affairs, October 6, 1880, that a conference should be held for discussing terms of peace between

[1] See Appendix (G). [2] See *supra*, p. 65.

[3] See further as to these peace negotiations, *infra*, p. 135.

[4] *British and Foreign State Papers*, vol. 61, p. 784.

Peru, Chile, and Bolivia, and stated that the American Government offered its good offices or mediation for that purpose. He further proposed that the delegates of these Republics, together with the Ministers of the United States accredited to them, should meet on board an American warship off Arica. The offer of good offices was accepted. On October 22 the first meeting took place; there were present two plenipotentiaries from each of the contending States, together with the three American Ministers, of whom the one accredited to Chile presided. The proceedings were opened by Mr. Adams, the United States Minister for Bolivia, who, after expressing his country's feeling of friendship towards the three Republics and desire for the termination of the war, said that the American representatives would not take part in the discussions, though they were prepared to help by friendly co-operation. At the second meeting the negotiations broke down.

Peru-Chile War.

In the case of the war between China and Japan, 1894–1895, Great Britain and the United States endeavoured to mediate in the latter part of 1894. In November China made an appeal for mediation to England, France, Germany, Russia, and the United States. She reminded the latter Power of the treaty of 1858, whereby the United States Government undertook to exert its good offices on behalf of China, in case any State acted unjustly or oppressively towards her, for the purpose of bringing about an amicable arrangement as to any matter in dispute. The appeal concluded thus: "Will your Government do us the great favour to intervene to stop the war and re-establish peace? Such an act would be happy for China, happy for every country."[1] The Treaty of Shimonoseki, signed April 17, 1895, was to some extent due to the amicable interposition of France, Russia, and Germany.

Chinese-Japanese War.

The six Great Powers of Europe played a very great part in bringing to an end the Greco-Turkish War, 1897. Soon after the outbreak of the war there was little doubt as to the fate of Greece. Suggestions were made in many quarters that she should appeal to the Powers for their intervention; but she determined to go on with the war. On April 19, 1897, it was announced that the Powers would not interpose unless the belligerents requested their mediation. Certain Powers also required that Greece, before appealing to them, should recall Colonel Vassos and his forces from Crete. The position, however, becoming very serious, France thought fit to intervene in the sanguinary conflict, and secured the

Greco-Turkish War, 1897.

Notable intervention of the Powers.

[1] Cf. Moore, *Digest*, vol. vii. p. 19.

co-operation of Russia. At the same time Great Britain suggested that the three States should in combination make a demand for an armistice; but France considered it desirable to maintain the European concert.[1] On April 27 the Greek Minister for Foreign Affairs asked the Governments of Great Britain, France, and Russia to obtain a suspension of hostilities for a few days; but the latter held that the only cessation of arms possible in the circumstances was an armistice with a view to the establishment of peace. After some negotiation with the six Great Powers, Greece recalled her forces from Crete, May 3, and expressed a desire for intervention; but she did not wish to ask for it openly, as much dissatisfaction might thereby be caused among sections of her people. The Powers agreed to act on condition that Greece accepted their decision in regard to subsequent arrangements, and then requested the Sublime Porte to suspend hostilities. We have already referred to the exorbitant demands made by the Sultan in reply, and to the armistice that was eventually brought about (May 17) after a personal appeal by Nicholas II of Russia.[2]

When negotiations for peace were begun, the Powers, assuming the rôle of judges rather than of mediators, soon made it known that the terms proposed by Turkey were unacceptable—viz. annexation of Thessaly, a war indemnity of 230 million francs, abrogation of the capitulations and the treaty of extradition with Greece. They felt that the settlement of the struggle was also a European matter. They had declared at the commencement of the war that the victor would not be allowed to make any territorial conquest. Therefore they refused to sanction the retrocession of Thessaly to Turkey. Further, they believed the suggested indemnity to be in excess of Turkey's actual war expenditure, and to be beyond the capacity of Greece to pay. Moreover, the treaty privileges that had been secured to Greece by the Powers must remain. On the other hand, the fundamental terms conceded as a basis for the definitive treaty of peace were: a frontier rectification for strategic purposes and as a safeguard against freebooters, together with a war indemnity covering Turkey's actual war expenditure and losses, and proportionate to the resources of Greece. After a good deal of discussion, especially on the question of indemnity, an agreement was reached; the sum was reduced to 100 million francs, as a result of a report made by a special commission appointed by the six Powers.

New difficulties now arose, owing to a difference of opinion among the Powers themselves—notably England and Germany—in regard to guaranteeing the payment of this indemnity. England

[1] Cf. Politis, *La guerre gréco-turque*, p. 80. [2] See *supra*, p. 69.

was against any provision that would delay the departure of the Turkish forces from Thessaly. Negotiations dragged on for months. At length a compromise was effected, whereby an international commission should be appointed to control the financial administration of Greece until the indemnity was paid. Next came objections from Greece; she felt that such interference with her internal affairs was an invasion of her sovereignty; and she was urged by many sections of her press to repudiate altogether the intervention of the Powers. This counsel, however, she did not take, so that the preliminaries of peace were signed at Constantinople on September 18, 1897. On the 27th the Powers addressed a formal notification to the Greek Government stating that their mediation was ended, and that plenipotentiaries should be appointed for concluding the definitive treaty of peace.

Spanish-American War.

When war between the United States and Spain became imminent, many efforts were made by third parties to assure peace—first by the Pope, then by Great Britain, France, Germany, Austria, Italy, and Russia; but their efforts proved fruitless.[1] Afterwards, Spain having been reduced to sue for peace, the good offices of France were effectively used for the purpose of instituting negotiations.[2] On July 27 an official communiqué was published at Washington, which was to this effect: "The Ambassador of France, in the name of the Spanish Government, and at the request of the Spanish Minister for Foreign Affairs, handed this afternoon to the President at the White House a message from the Spanish Government, having in view the end of hostilities and the establishment of peace." Then the President consulted with his ministers for the purpose of deciding as to the fundamental conditions of peace, and the form of negotiations to be adopted. At first it was suggested that the American and Spanish ambassadors at Paris might confer with each other on this point; but afterwards the American Government thought Washington to be a more appropriate place for such negotiations. Thereupon the Spanish Government asked M. Cambon, the French Ambassador accredited to the United States, to undertake this preliminary task. At a conference between the latter and President McKinley, held on July 31, the American demands were stated; this was followed by further conferences for the elucidation of various points raised by Spain, e.g. the question of the Cuban debt, the powers of the mixed Spanish-American Commission to be appointed for regulating the fate of the Philippines. On August 7 the Spanish Government

[1] Cf. *Revue générale de droit international public* (Paris), vol. v. p. 645.
[2] *Ibid.*, vol. vii. p. 573.

forwarded, through M. Cambon, a note to the President, accepting in principle the terms proposed. Additional consultations between the President, the Secretary of State, and the French Ambassador were necessary for determining the text of the agreement and its drafting; and on August 12 the protocol of peace was ready, which thus brought to a close the good offices of France.[1]

During the Anglo-Boer War the British Government declared that the offer of good offices by any third Power would not be accepted.

Anglo-Boer War.

The reason for this decision was that the war was waged by Great Britain with the avowed object of conquest and annexation; so that the use of good offices or mediation to effect a compromise of differences would be necessarily out of place here. When, therefore, the Netherlands Government proposed its good offices on January 25, 1902, for the purpose of putting into communication representatives of the contending parties, and offered accommodation in Holland for their conference, Lord Lansdowne replied that he could not depart from the previously announced declaration, and that the peace negotiations must take place in South Africa between the Boer leaders and the Commander-in-Chief of the British forces.

In connection with the Treaty of Portsmouth, September 5, 1905, which terminated the Russo-Japanese War, the United States

Russo-Japanese War.

played a conspicuous part. In January, after the fall of Port Arthur, a movement for peace was manifested which gathered force in March after the great Japanese victory at Mukden. None the less, Russia determinedly continued hostilities; but when her Baltic fleet was destroyed in the Straits of Korea, May 27, 1905, she became more favourably disposed to consider the re-establishment of peace. The greatest difficulty was to take the first step in this direction. Here President Roosevelt came on the scene and saved the situation. After ascertaining that his interposition in the interests of peace would not prove unacceptable to both belligerents, he took definite action in pursuance of the provisions laid down in the Hague Convention. (It should be mentioned that his action was said to have been supported by the German Emperor, who, it was reported, had made independent representations to the Czar.[2]) Accordingly, on June 8, 1905, Mr. Roosevelt sent the following message, *mutatis mutandis*, to the American ministers at St. Petersburg and Tokyo:—

"The President feels that the time has come when in the interest of all mankind he must endeavour to see if it is not

[1] See *infra*, pp. 141 *seq.*, for the negotiations that followed at the conference of the peace commissioners.

[2] See a despatch from Berlin, dated June 15, to *The Times*.

possible to bring to an end the terrible and lamentable conflict now being waged. With both Russia and Japan the United States has inherited ties of friendship and goodwill. It hopes for the prosperity and welfare of each, and it feels that the progress of the world is set back by the war between these two great nations.

The President accordingly urges the Russian and Japanese Governments, not only for their own sakes, but in the interest of the whole civilized world, to open direct negotiations for peace with one another. The President suggests that these peace negotiations be conducted directly and exclusively between the belligerents; in other words, that there may be a meeting of Russian and Japanese plenipotentiaries or delegates without any intermediary, in order to see if it is not possible for these representatives of the two Powers to agree to terms of peace. The President earnestly asks that the Russian [Japanese] Government do now agree to such meeting, and is asking the Japanese [Russian] Government likewise to agree.

While the President does not feel that any intermediary should be called in in respect to the peace negotiations themselves, he is entirely willing to do what he properly can, if the two Powers concerned feel that his services will be of aid in arranging the preliminaries as to the time and place of meeting. But if even these preliminaries can be arranged directly between the two Powers, or in any other way, the President will be glad, as his sole purpose is to bring about a meeting which the whole civilized world will pray may result in peace." [1]

Japan replied at once, and agreed unconditionally to enter into negotiations; but the reply of Count Lamsdorff, the Russian Minister for Foreign Affairs, showed a feeling of hesitation and reserve, if not downright reluctance. He pointed out that the moment was scarcely opportune for discussing peace, as the war was still undecided. The Russian army, too, was anxious to continue the campaign; its leaders acknowledged their mistakes, and were sure they could atone for their reverses; they appealed to the Czar begging him "to show his confidence in his army, and not to leave the blot of defeat on its scutcheon." [2] Despite such opposition, President Roosevelt directed the American Ambassador at St. Petersburg to lay his proposal before the Czar himself. The latter received it favourably, and replied that he was prepared to appoint plenipotentiaries to conclude peace.

The President emphasized in his message that he offered only

[1] *Foreign Relations of the United States*, 1905, p. 807; Moore, *Digest*, vol. vii. pp. 21–22.

[2] E. J. Dillon, *Contemporary Review*, October 1905, pp. 457 *seq.*

his good offices, and did not wish to participate as a mediator. But in the subsequent proceedings, at a critical moment of the peace conference, when the negotiations were on the point of breaking down, his active interposition and consultations with the respective plenipotentiaries made him practically though not formally a mediator; and so, thanks to his remarkable resourcefulness and personality, a great calamity was averted.[1]

Turco-Italian War.

During the Turco-Italian War, 1912, mediation was suggested in many quarters. King George, in his speech from the throne, February 14, 1912, referred to it; but Lord Lansdowne, ex-Foreign Secretary, said the same day in the House of Lords that nothing was more dangerous or less productive of good results than a premature mediation. Attempts to intervene were afterwards made, but they failed. An international conference was then spoken of in Russia, France, and elsewhere. However, the peace eventually arrived at was due to the direct negotiations between the two belligerent Powers.

First Balkan War—Intervention of the Powers.

In the first Balkan War, 1912–1913, between Turkey on the one hand, and Greece, Bulgaria, Serbia, and Montenegro on the other, the mediation of the six Great Powers of Europe assumed a pronounced form of intervention. After a number of Turkish reverses, the Porte appealed to the Powers to mediate; the latter abstained, however, and advised the Turkish Government to make a direct request to the Allies for an armistice. A convention to this effect was concluded, as we have already seen;[2] but the subsequent peace negotiations failed. In the meantime European complications, due partly to the tension between Austria and Serbia, appeared to be imminent. Serbia, whose arms had been so signally successful against the Ottoman troops, was bent on annexing Northern Albania, including a large portion of the Adriatic coast. This the Austro-Hungarian Government would not brook; and towards the end of November, 1912, took various steps for mobilization. Thereupon Russia felt obliged to make preparations in case she was called upon to protect Serbia. On November 28 a "nationalist" movement was set on foot in Albania, thus introducing further difficulties in the situation. At this juncture Sir Edward Grey proposed that representatives of the Powers should meet in an informal conference in one of the capitals, with a view to arriving at an understanding on various points that inevitably concerned Europe at large. The proposal was accepted; and on December 11 it was announced that the ambassadors of the Powers

[1] See *infra*, pp. 145 *seq.*, for the negotiations at the Portsmouth Conference.
[2] See *supra*, p. 78.

in London were to hold non-committal consultations for the purpose suggested. London thus became the scene of two separate conferences—that of the ambassadors, who met on December 17 under the presidency of Sir Edward Grey, and that of the peace plenipotentiaries of Turkey and the Balkan Allies, who met on December 16. At the third meeting of the ambassadors (December 20) the question of Albania was discussed, and a resolution was arrived at to this effect: "The ambassadors have recommended to their Governments, and the latter have accepted, the principle of Albanian autonomy, together with a provision guaranteeing to Serbia commercial access to the Adriatic. The six Governments have agreed in principle on these two points."

The peace delegates of the belligerent countries continued their negotiations; proposals and counter-proposals were made; and several sittings proved abortive. The Allies required Turkey to surrender all the territory west of the line Rodosto–Cape Malatra, and all the Ægean islands, including Crete, except certain islands near the mouth of the Dardanelles to be specified by the Powers; the Gallipoli Peninsula was to be left to Turkey; and the Powers might decide as to Albania. The Turkish delegates made various concessions, but refused to give up Adrianople. On January 6, 1913, the negotiations ceased. Then the Powers intervened, and in a joint Note advised the Porte to yield with regard to Adrianople, and to leave the question of the Ægean islands to be settled by them. This advice was accepted, and was about to be acted upon when the Ottoman Government was overthrown by the Young Turks (January 23). A few days afterwards the armistice convention between Turkey and the Balkan Allies was declared to be at an end. Peace was not concluded till the following May 30; and Arts. III and V of the Treaty of London, with regard to the settlement of Albania and the title to the Ægean islands and Mount Athos Peninsula, formally recognized the intervention of the Powers.[1]

The conference of ambassadors differed from a peace conference proper, in that the delegates acted as ambassadors only and not as plenipotentiaries; they discussed the questions submitted to them and referred to their respective Governments for instructions in regard to the necessary decisions. Moreover, it may be said that in certain respects this conference played the part of an arbitral tribunal as between the Triple Entente and the Triple Alliance. Sir Edward Grey, speaking of the interposition of the Powers, observed: "The action of the Powers seems to me to have been influenced, in the case of each individual Power, first by a view of what its own interest

[1] See *infra*, Appendix (W).

requires, and in the case of all the Powers by a common desire between them to preserve the peace of Europe, and I imagine that their action will continue to be regulated by those interests." In reply to a question in the House of Commons, August 1, he pointed out, further, that this intervention of the Powers was not based on law, but on considerations of ethics, political expediency, and self-interest.

Duty of Europe in the interests of peace.

We may conclude this chapter with the eloquent observations of M. Léon Bourgeois (May 1913), relative to this conference and to the duty of Europe in the interests of peace: "Que d'enseignements et que d'espérances contiennent ces délibérations si confuses, si anxieuses, de la Conférence de Londres! C'est une conférence diplomatique et, à certaines heures, il semble bien que cela devienne un tribunal d'arbitrage international. Si bien qu'un jour prochain, l'on pourra reconnaître que le résultat de la catastrophe récente a été de faire prendre aux grandes puissances une intelligence plus nette de la solidarité de leurs intérêts permanents. L'Europe prend conscience qu'elle est, elle aussi, une personne morale qui existe au-dessus et en dehors de chacun des États qui la composent ; elle se sent un organisme vivant ; elle a maintenant, si je puis dire, une âme où déjà vit la honte de la violence, où s'affirment le sentiment du droit et la certitude d'un devoir moral commun à tous." [1]

[1] *Revue de droit international* (Bruxelles), vol. xv. (1913), p. 624.

CHAPTER III

PRELIMINARIES OF PEACE

Place of negotiation—Distinguished from preliminary conditions—Object and nature of the preliminaries—Chief parts: general clauses; special clauses, e.g. cession, indemnity; miscellaneous provisions—Performance of certain clauses without waiting for the definitive treaty—Modification by the definitive treaty.

Preliminaries of peace.

AFTER an armistice convention has been agreed to, with or without the interposition of third States, or—as we have seen—even whilst open hostilities are being prosecuted, the first step usually taken to bring the war to an end is the conclusion of preliminaries of peace. (In the case of a war of conquest and annexation, involving the extinction of a State's independence, the question of preliminaries of peace cannot properly arise at all; for the terms—if any—eventually imposed by the conqueror do not constitute a treaty of peace in the true sense of the term.) Sometimes, when the questions in dispute are clear and definite and there are no complicated matters to be discussed in detail before a substantial accommodation can be arrived at by the parties, such conventions are dispensed with and negotiations are set on foot with a view to establishing at once the treaty of peace itself. A conspicuous example of such procedure occurred in the Russo-Japanese War, when discussions between the plenipotentiaries of the two Powers were conducted at Portsmouth (New Hampshire), whilst the war was in progress, and ended with the definitive treaty of peace, September 5, 1905.[1]

Place of negotiation.

It happens frequently that the preliminaries of peace are discussed and signed at one place, and that the definitive treaty is discussed and signed at another place. Thus—to give a few recent instances—in the Crimean War the preliminaries were signed at Vienna, February 1, 1856, and the definitive treaty at Paris, March 30, 1856;[2] in the war between France and Austria the preliminaries were concluded at Villafranca, July 11, 1859,[3] and the definitive treaty at Zurich,

[1] See *infra*, Appendix (U). [2] Appendix (D). [3] Appendix (E).

November 10, 1859;[1] in the war between Austria and Prussia on the one side and Denmark on the other, both the preliminaries and the definitive treaty were signed at Vienna, the first on August 1, 1864, the second on October 30, 1864; in the war between Austria and Prussia the preliminaries were signed at Nikolsburg, July 26, 1866,[2] and the definitive treaty at Prague, August 23, 1866;[3] in the Franco-German War the preliminaries were entered into at Versailles, February 26, 1871,[4] and the final treaty at Frankfort, May 10, 1871;[5] the Russo-Turkish War was ended by the Preliminaries of San Stefano, February 19 / March 3, 1878,[6] but before a definitive treaty was concluded the European Powers intervened and at the Congress of Berlin made substantial modifications of the provisions by means of the Treaty of Berlin, July 13, 1878; this was, however, followed by the definitive treaty between Russia and Turkey, signed at Constantinople, January 27 / February 8, 1879,[7] which embodied the alterations thus effected, and confirmed or settled those clauses of the Preliminaries of San Stefano that had remained intact; in the Greco-Turkish War both the preliminaries and the definitive treaty of peace were concluded at Constantinople, the former on September 18, 1897, the latter on November 22 / December 4, 1897; in the Spanish-American War the Protocol of Peace, which included an armistice as well as the preliminaries, was signed at Washington on August 12, 1898, and the definitive treaty was signed at Paris, December 10, 1898;[8] in the Turco-Italian War the preliminaries—designated in the French text "accord prêliminaire de paix"[9]—were agreed to at Lausanne, October 15, 1912, and the definitive treaty of peace was signed at the same place, October 18.[10]

Preliminaries of peace distinguished from preliminary conditions (or "preliminary articles").

The preliminaries of peace are to be distinguished from the preliminary conditions (sometimes designated "preliminary articles") which are demanded by the victorious party or the party more successful in arms as a fundamental basis for negotiation, when the other party sues for peace. Not infrequently such preliminary conditions are required to be conceded by the belligerent who, finding himself in sore straits, appeals for an armistice; the successful party thus grasps the opportunity and insists first on an acceptance of such terms as he deems to be indispensable, e.g. the

[1] Appendix (F). [2] Appendix (G). [3] Appendix (H).
[4] Appendix (J). [5] Appendix (K). [6] Appendix (M).
[7] Appendix (N). [8] Appendix (S).
[9] G. F. de Martens, *Nouveau recueil général de traités*, etc., 3me série, t. vii. p. 3 (Leipzig, 1913). Continuation by H. Triepel.
[10] Appendix (V).

cession of certain territory, the payment of indemnity, or other substantial sacrifices. Formerly the preliminary articles were merely *pacta de contrahendo*; that is, they provided that negotiations were to take place, and stated the time and place of meeting, the form of the negotiations, the ceremonial to be followed, whether a third Power was to be admitted as a mediator, that the plenipotentiaries and their suites should be inviolable, if an armistice convention had not already stipulated it, the exchange of safe-conducts, etc. Thus, in connection with the negotiations relative to the Treaty of Westphalia (1648), we find that preliminary articles of this kind were signed at Hamburg on December 25, 1641. Nowadays the necessary arrangements as to formal matters are generally made at the first meeting of the conference.

Object and nature of the preliminaries.

The modern preliminaries of peace are embodied in a special convention, concluded by plenipotentiaries with almost as much formality and solemnity as is the definitive treaty of peace, and are like the latter subject to ratification; thus the Preliminaries of Nikolsburg, July 26, 1866, were negotiated and signed by Count Karolyi and Baron von Brenner on behalf of Austria, by Count von Bismarck on behalf of Prussia; the Preliminaries of Versailles, February 26, 1871, were entered into by M. Thiers, the head of the Government of National Defence, and M. Favre, the Minister for Foreign Affairs, on behalf of France, by Bismarck and other ministers on behalf of the German Empire and the confederated States; the Preliminaries of San Stefano, February 19 / March 3, 1878, by Count Ignatiew and M. Nelidow for Russia, by Safvet Pasha and Sadoullah Bey for Turkey; and in all these cases the dignity and position of the plenipotentiaries were indicated and their full powers were exchanged. It may be added that the Preliminaries of Villafranca, July 11, 1859, between France and Austria were signed, exceptionally, by the Emperors Napoleon and Francis Joseph. The preliminaries represent an important stage in the journey towards peace, and have a provisional character inasmuch as the parties, though prepared to terminate the war and compose their differences, cannot yet agree to the precise terms and their formulation; there may be numerous and complicated matters to examine, and many pourparlers may have to be exchanged in order to elucidate them and arrive at a clear and definite understanding thereon. It follows that although the preliminaries are a preparatory structure there is none the less a vital relationship between them and the final edifice—the definitive treaty. The fundamental conditions laid down in the former may not be modified substantially in the latter, unless there be a mutual agreement to the contrary. The preliminaries, then, constituting the essential groundwork of the peace treaty, will necessarily provide solutions to the very questions that gave rise to the war, and may incorporate also special conditions — e.g. as to territorial cession or war indemnity — which will depend obviously on the temper and the ulterior aims of the party whom success of arms has placed more or less in the position of a dictator. The parties may provide specifically for whatever modifications and additions it may be found necessary to embody in the final treaty. Moreover, the preliminaries usually prescribe the place where the peace commissioners are to meet to conduct their negotiations, and the delay within which the meeting is to take place. Should these negotiations break down, the preliminaries, being provisional, will *ipso facto* become null and void, unless it has been otherwise stipulated.

Protest by third States.

One of the many advantages of first concluding such a provisional convention is that third States get an opportunity to protest if, on the one hand, they are themselves prejudicially affected thereby, or, on the other, if the terms imposed on the weaker party are outrageously severe and onerous. (We have already seen instances of the intervention of Powers in signally unequal contests, even before preliminaries were concluded or hostilities suspended.) A notable example of a protest against preliminaries of peace is that aroused by the Convention of San Stefano, March 3, 1878, terminating the Russo-Turkish War; indeed, not only were protests made, but a Congress of the great European Powers met at Berlin and subjected the terms of that convention to considerable revision, so that the result was much less favourable to Russia than the preliminaries of peace had been.

Chief parts of the preliminaries.

We may now look at the principal parts of preliminaries of peace in reference to some actual cases, and in relation to the corresponding parts of the respective definitive treaties of peace that followed them.

Different designations.

It is to be noted, in the first place, that the preliminaries of peace are not always so designated. For example, in the Spanish-American War the preliminaries signed at Washington, August 12, 1898, were described as a "protocol of peace"; in the Turco-Italian War the preliminaries signed at Lausanne, October 15, 1912, were often referred to as a *modus procedendi*, and designated in the French text an "accord préliminaire de paix." In the Franco-German War the draftsmen of the Preliminaries of Versailles, concluded on February 26, 1871, appear to have attached little importance to precise and consistent terminology: Arts. VI and VII speak of the "present preliminaries"—the correct and regular expression; whilst Arts. I, III, and VIII speak of the "present treaty."[1] Preliminaries of peace are, of course, a treaty, to which they are related as species to genus; but it is more convenient, especially in one particular transaction, to refer to an act or document uniformly by its proper name as generally recognized. In a case like the present it is all the more necessary, inasmuch as a sharp and clear distinction is made between the preliminaries and the treaty itself—that is, the final definitive treaty of peace.

Main provisions.

Preliminaries of peace are necessarily less elaborate than the definitive treaty. Their contents vary naturally according to the circumstances of each case, just as the contents of definitive treaties vary. But in general they include provisions for such matter as the following: recognition of the conditional character of the convention and its dependence on the definitive treaty to be concluded thereafter; appointment of plenipotentiaries for negotiating the definitive treaty (sometimes also the number for each side being fixed), the time and place of meeting; ratification of the preliminaries; adhesion of allies, if any, when these are not signatories in the ordinary way; the conclusion of an armistice if one has not already been established, or its extension, as the case may be; the grant of an amnesty; restoration of prisoners of war; the payment of a war indemnity; military occupation as a guarantee, and maintenance of the forces; administration of occupied territory; conditions of evacuation; rectification of frontier; cession of territory; option and rights of subjects on ceded territory; revival or annulment of previous treaties; etc.

GENERAL CLAUSES.

The clauses covering matters like the above are obviously divisible into two classes—general, i.e. those found in all or most cases; special, i.e. those pertaining to this or that case, as its own peculiar conditions require. First, one or two actual examples of the former may be mentioned.

Stipulation for negotiating a definitive treaty.

In reference to the conclusion of a definitive treaty on the basis of the preparatory convention, the Preliminaries of Nikolsburg, July 26, 1866, between Austria and Prussia, say in the preamble that the parties "have agreed upon the following fundamental points as the basis of the peace to be concluded without delay"; and in Art. VIII: "Immediately after the ratification of the present convention shall have been effected and exchanged, Their Majesties the Emperor of Austria and the King of Prussia will appoint

[1] See *infra*, Appendix (J).

plenipotentiaries, who will meet at a place to be hereafter named, to conclude the peace upon the basis of the present preliminary treaty, and to agree upon the details of the conditions."[1] The Preliminaries of Versailles, February 26, 1871, between France and Germany, say in the preamble: ". . . The following has been agreed upon to serve as a preliminary basis to the definitive peace to be concluded hereafter"; and in Art. VII: "The opening of negotiations for the definitive treaty of peace to be concluded on the basis of the present preliminaries shall take place at Brussels, immediately after the ratification of the latter by the National Assembly and by His Majesty the Emperor of Germany."[2] The Preliminaries of San Stefano, February 19 / March 3, 1878, between Russia and Turkey, say (Art. XXIX) that an agreement shall be concluded at St. Petersburg "as to the place and the time at which the stipulations of the present Act shall be invested with all the solemn forms usually observed in treaties of peace."[3] The Protocol of Peace, entered into at Washington, August 12, 1898, by the United States and Spain, provided as follows (Art. V): "The United States and Spain will each appoint not more than five commissioners to treat of peace, and the commissioners so appointed shall meet at Paris not later than October 1, 1898, and proceed to the negotiation and conclusion of a treaty of peace, which treaty shall be subject to ratification according to the respective constitutional forms of the two countries."

Ratification of preliminaries.

As to the ratification of the preliminary agreement, the Preliminaries of Nikolsburg (Art. VII) stipulate: "The ratifications of the present convention shall be exchanged at Nikolsburg in the space of two days at the latest"; Art. X of the Preliminaries of Versailles says: "The present preliminary treaty shall be immediately submitted to the ratification of His Majesty the Emperor of Germany and the French National Assembly sitting at Bordeaux"; and Art. XXIX of the Preliminaries of San Stefano prescribes thus: "The present Act shall be ratified by Their Imperial Majesties the Emperor of Russia and the Emperor of the Ottomans, and the ratifications shall be exchanged in fifteen days or sooner if possible at St. Petersburg. . . . It is, however, well understood that the high contracting parties consider themselves as formally bound by the present Act from the moment of its ratification."

When the preliminaries involve such sacrifices as the cession of territory, it is necessary, according to the constitutional law of most countries, to submit their ratification to the legislative authority and not merely to the executive head. Thus, in the

[1] Appendix (G). [2] Appendix (J). [3] Appendix (M).

case of the Preliminaries of Versailles, they were signed on February 26, submitted to the French National Assembly on March 1, and ratifications were exchanged at Versailles on March 2. The preliminaries between Greece and Turkey were signed on September 18, 1897, approved by the Sultan on the 22nd, and by the Greek Chamber on the 30th. Similarly in the case of the Protocol of Peace between the United States and Spain. It was signed on August 12, 1898; on September 5 the Cortes assembled, and after some stirring sittings the ratification of the protocol was authorized first by the Senate, then by the Chamber.

Position of allies.

As to the position of allies, we find in some instances a certain irregularity. Thus, in the Preliminaries of Versailles, the contracting parties were specified thus in the preamble: on the one side, France; on the other side, Prussia and the other States of the North German Confederation, as well as the Kingdom of Bavaria, the Kingdom of Würtemberg, and the Grand Duchy of Baden. As the enemies of France had included several independent States, the French representatives appear to have thought at the opening of peace negotiations that they would have to conclude separate treaties with these States; but Bismarck soon expressed a contrary view. Having regard to the nature and object of the conflict, its strictly localized character, the solidary bond of the allies, we must admit Bismarck's opinion to have been the correct one. The fact, however, that the two kingdoms and the duchy signified their assent to the preliminaries in a separate document of the same date is a less regular proceeding. It is true that on February 26—the date in question—they had already been embodied in the German Empire; but they were set out in the preamble as contracting parties. They ought either to have been omitted from the preamble, or, if included equally with Prussia, they ought, equally with Prussia, to have figured as signatories to the principal Act.[1] Again, in the Preliminaries of Nikolsburg, provision is made for their acceptance by Italy, the ally of Prussia (Art. VI): "His Majesty the King of Prussia undertakes to prevail upon His Majesty the King of Italy, his Ally, to give his approval to the preliminaries of peace, so soon as the Venetian Kingdom shall have been put at the disposal of His Majesty the King of Italy by a declaration of His Majesty the Emperor of the French." Stipulations of this kind are open to objection; their fulfilment is problematical and precarious, so that the whole engagement is endangered, and the sphere of possible conflict is enlarged.

Sometimes hostilities continue after negotiations for the pre-

[1] Cf. Appendix (J), *in fin.*

liminaries of peace have been commenced. In that case a clause is usually included therein for the temporary suspension of arms or for the conclusion of an armistice convention which is to have effect until the definitive treaty is established. In the Preliminaries of Nikolsburg, July 26, 1866, between Prussia and Austria, Art. IX stipulates thus: ". . . The contracting States, after having decided upon these preliminaries, will conclude an armistice for the Austrian and Saxon armies on the one part, and for the Prussian army on the other part, of which the detailed conditions, from the military point of view, are to be immediately determined. That armistice shall date from the 2nd of August, the day to which the present suspension of arms shall be prolonged. The armistice shall at the same time be concluded with Bavaria, and General the Baron von Manteuffel will be instructed to conclude with the Kingdom of Würtemberg and the Grand Duchies of Baden and Hesse-Darmstadt, as soon as these States shall propose it, an armistice beginning on the 2nd of August, and founded on the state of military possession at the time." Again, Art. VI of the Protocol of Peace, signed at Washington, August 12, 1898, said that as soon as the said protocol was concluded and signed by the representatives of the United States and Spain, hostilities between the two countries would be suspended.

Provision for concluding an armistice.

An amnesty clause is not infrequently found in preliminaries of peace, though it is more often reserved for the definitive treaty. The Preliminaries of Villafranca, entered into by France and Austria, July 11, 1859, provided that a full and complete amnesty was to be granted on both sides to persons compromised on the occasion of the preceding events in the territories of the belligerents.[1] In the Preliminaries of San Stefano (1878), between Russia and Turkey, a one-sided arrangement was made; thus Art. XVII is to this effect: "A full and complete amnesty is granted by the Sublime Porte to all Ottoman subjects compromised by recent events, and all persons imprisoned on this account or sent into exile shall be immediately set at liberty"; and Art. XXVII says: "The Sublime Porte undertakes not to punish in any manner, or allow to be punished, those Ottoman subjects who may have been compromised by their relations with the Russian army during the war. In the event of any persons wishing to withdraw with their families when the Russian troops leave, the Ottoman authorities shall not oppose their departure." (It is not clear why this repetition was found necessary. The arrangement and draftsmanship of this document are by no means free from defects.) But by the definitive Treaty of Constantinople,

Amnesty clause.

[1] Appendix (E), *in fin.*

January 27 / February 8, 1879, the amnesty provision was made mutual; thus Art. VIII: "Both parties pledge themselves not to molest or to allow to be molested in any manner those Russian or Ottoman subjects who might have become compromised in consequence of their intercourse with the armies of either Empire during the war." [1] In the preliminaries the clause appears to have been the result of dictation by the victorious party; in the definitive treaty—between which and the former the Treaty of Berlin intervened—the clause is, properly, one resulting from a bilateral transaction.

Clause as to restoration of prisoners of war.

A clause as to the restoration of prisoners of war is also occasionally inserted in the preliminaries. There is no such provision, for example, in the Preliminaries of Villafranca, or in the Preliminaries of Nikolsburg, or in the Protocol of Washington. But we find one in the Preliminaries of Versailles, of which Art. VI provides thus: "The prisoners of war who shall not have been already set at liberty by exchange shall be given up immediately after the ratification of the present preliminaries. In order to accelerate the transport of French prisoners, the French Government shall place at the disposal of the German authorities in the interior of the German territory a part of the rolling-stock of its railways in such proportion as shall be determined by special arrangements and at prices paid in France by the French Government for military transport." Similarly, in the Preliminaries of San Stefano it is stipulated (Art. XXVIII): "Immediately upon the ratification of the preliminaries of peace, the prisoners of war shall be reciprocally restored under the care of special commissioners appointed on both sides, who for this purpose shall go to Odessa and Sebastopol. The Ottoman Government will pay all the expenses of the maintenance of the prisoners that are returned to them, in eighteen equal instalments in the space of six years, in accordance with the accounts that will be drawn up by the above-mentioned commissioners. The exchange of prisoners between the Ottoman Government and the Governments of Roumania, Serbia, and Montenegro will be made on the same basis, deducting, however, in the account, the number of prisoners restored by the Ottoman Government from the number of prisoners that will have to be restored to that Government."

With regard to the renewal or annulment of treaties affected by war—constituting regularly a general clause in definitive treaties of peace—we find sometimes a stipulation in the preliminaries settling that doubtful question as between the

[1] Appendix (O).

parties.[1] Thus Art. XXIII of the Preliminaries of San Stefano says: "All the treaties, conventions, and agreements previously concluded between the two high contracting parties relative to commerce, jurisdiction, and the position of Russian subjects in Turkey, and which had been abrogated by the state of war, shall come into force again, with the exception of the clauses affected by the present Act. The two Governments will be placed again in the same relation to one another, with respect to all their engagements and commercial and other relations, as they were in before the declaration of war." And so, too, in the Preliminaries of Constantinople, September 18, 1897, between Turkey and Greece, it was agreed (Arts. III, V, and IX) [2] to conclude supplementary conventions modifying the system of capitulations so as to prevent abuses.

Renewal of treaties.

Next we come to some special clauses—that is, those clauses which lay down the special terms as the price to be paid by the party suing for peace to his adversary for consenting to put an end to the war. Among such clauses we are pretty sure to find some relating to the payment of a war indemnity, and to the cession of territory, or to the abandonment of sovereignty over territory. A successful belligerent animated by the flush of victory will naturally be ready to impose at once such conditions as can be wrung from an opponent emerging from defeat. He may feel it safe to postpone the consideration of various other questions till the plenipotentiaries meet in conference to conclude the definitive treaty of peace; but he feels that demands involving territory and money should be made at the most opportune moment—namely, when the enemy is too helpless to oppose them effectively. In the case of the Franco-German War, for example, the exaction of territory and money was consigned to the very first two articles of the preliminaries.

SPECIAL CLAUSES.

Let us take first the cession of territory or the relinquishment of certain rights therein. During the Crimean War the preliminaries agreed to at Vienna, February 1, 1856, in accordance with the resolute demands of the Allies, stipulated the abolition of the Russian protectorate over the Danubian principalities, the freedom of the Danube, and the neutralization of the Black Sea. The Preliminaries of Villafranca, July 11, 1859, required Austria to cede Lombardy to France, and to give up certain rights with regard to Venetia. The Preliminaries of

Cession of territory.

[1] See *infra*, pp. 308 *seq.*, on State Succession, with respect to the effect of war on treaties.

[2] Cf. Politis, *La guerre gréco-turque*, p. 116.

Nikolsburg, July 26, 1866, required (Art. III) Austria to transfer to Prussia the Duchies of Schleswig and Holstein. By the Preliminaries of Versailles (Art. I), France was obliged to renounce in favour of the German Empire all her rights and titles over Alsace and Lorraine, the frontier being indicated in a detailed manner.[1] The position of the inhabitants of these provinces was regulated thus (Art. V): "The interests of the inhabitants of the territories ceded by France, in everything relating to their commerce and their civil rights shall be regulated in as favourable a manner as possible when the conditions of the definitive peace are settled. A certain time will be fixed, during which they will enjoy particular advantages for the disposal of their produce. The German Government will put no obstacle in the way of free emigration by the inhabitants from the ceded territories, and shall take no steps against them affecting their persons or their property." The Preliminaries of San Stefano were almost entirely devoted to territorial questions; Turkey was deprived of extensive rights. Provision was made for the independence and new boundaries of Montenegro (Arts. I and II), Serbia (Art. III), the independence of Roumania (Art. V), the constitution of Bulgaria as an autonomous tributary principality and the determination of its boundaries (Arts. VI, VII, and IX), the free commercial navigation of the Bosphorus and the Dardanelles (Art. XXIV), etc. Questions as to property situated in ceded territory, and the option of inhabitants to emigrate were also regulated (Arts. VII and XXI).[2] The Preliminaries of Constantinople, September 18, 1897, between Turkey and Greece, prescribed a frontier rectification; and the preliminaries concluded at Lausanne, October 15, 1912, between Italy and Turkey, transferred to the former the sovereignty over Cyrenaica and Tripolitana. Similarly, four of the six articles contained in the protocol of peace, signed at Washington, August 12, 1898, by the United States and Spain, concerned territorial cessions and the renunciation of sovereignty:

"ART. I.—Spain will relinquish all claim of sovereignty over and title to Cuba.

ART. II.—Spain will cede to the United States the island of Porto Rico and other islands now under Spanish sovereignty in the West Indies, and also an island in the Ladrones, to be selected by the United States.

ART. III.—The United States will occupy and hold the city, bay, and harbour of Manila pending the conclusion of a treaty of peace, which shall determine the control, disposition, and government of the Philippines.

[1] See *infra*, Appendix (J), Art. I.

[2] Appendix (M).

ART. IV.—Spain will immediately evacuate Cuba, Porto Rico, and other islands now under Spanish sovereignty in the West Indies; and to this end each Government will, within ten days after the signing of this protocol, appoint commissioners, and the commissioners so appointed shall, within thirty days after the signing of this protocol, meet at Havana for the purpose of arranging and carrying out the details of the aforesaid evacuation of Cuba and the adjacent Spanish islands; and each Government will, within ten days after the signing of this protocol, also appoint other commissioners, who shall, within thirty days after the signing of this protocol, meet at San Juan, in Porto Rico, for the purpose of arranging and carrying out the details of the aforesaid evacuation of Porto Rico and other islands now under Spanish sovereignty in the West Indies."

Secondly, as to the payment of an indemnity, in connection with which we find also the temporary occupation of territory as a guarantee, Art. IV of the Preliminaries of Nikolsburg runs thus: "His Majesty the Emperor of Austria undertakes to pay His Majesty the King of Prussia the sum of 40,000,000 thalers to cover a part of the expenses which Prussia has been put to by the war. But from this sum may be deducted the amount of the indemnity for the costs of war which His Majesty the Emperor of Austria still has the right of exacting from the Duchies of Schleswig and Holstein,[1] by virtue of Art. XII of the Treaty of Peace of the 30th October, 1864, say 15,000,000 thalers, with 5,000,000 in addition as the equivalent for the cost of providing for the Prussian army, maintained by the Austrian countries occupied by that army until the time of the conclusion of the Peace." Art. I, stipulating the withdrawal of Prussian troops from Austrian territory, makes a special reservation regarding the maintenance of forces therein until the payment of the indemnity is definitely assured.

Payment of indemnity.

The Preliminaries of Versailles laid down (Art. II) that France should pay Germany the sum of 5,000,000,000 francs (£200,000,000); of which a fifth part was to be handed over within the year 1871, and the whole of the remainder in the space of three years, dating from the ratification of the present Act. Art. III dealt, on the one hand, with the evacuation of the French territory occupied by German troops, the time and the localities being specified, and the retirement of the French forces beyond a certain fixed line, excluding the garrison of Paris, which should not comprise more than 40,000 men; on the other hand, it prescribed that the evacua-

[1] These duchies were transferred to Prussia by Art. III of the present preliminaries; *supra*, p. 104.

tion of certain other departments was to be effected in proportion as the indemnity was paid. Moreover, by Art. IV the German army of occupation was prohibited from levying contributions or requisitions in the departments occupied; but its maintenance was to be at the expense of the French Government in a manner decided upon by an agreement with the German military administration. The final provision on this subject was contained in Art. VIII, which said that the administration of these occupied departments was to be handed over to the French authorities as soon as the definitive treaty of peace was concluded and ratified; though the said authorities were to conform to the orders issued by the German commanders in the interests of the safety, maintenance, and distribution of their troops.[1]

In the Preliminaries of San Stefano there was no occupation of territory by way of assuring the payment of indemnity. Art. XXV required the Russian forces to evacuate Turkey in Europe (with the exception of Bulgaria, which was temporarily occupied for other purposes) within three months after the conclusion of the definitive treaty of peace, and Turkey in Asia within six months; and the actual evacuation was to begin immediately after the exchange of ratifications. Turkish civil and military administration was not to be resumed in the evacuated territories until all the Russian troops had withdrawn therefrom (Art. XXVI). Unlike the Preliminaries of Versailles, the Preliminaries of San Stefano specified the various items constituting the indemnity demanded. Thus, by Art. XIX Russia imposed on Turkey the payment of 1,410,000,000 roubles, this sum being made up of the following: 900,000,000 roubles for war expenses (e.g. cost of maintaining the army, replacing war material and war contracts); 400,000,000 roubles for damage done to the south coast of Russia, to her export commerce, industries, and railways; 100,000,000 roubles for injuries inflicted on the Caucasus by the invasion; and 10,000,000 roubles for costs and damages of Russian establishments and subjects in Turkey. But owing to the financial embarrassments of Turkey a bargain was struck, at the suggestion of the Sultan, whereby the latter agreed to cede to Russia certain territories as an equivalent for the greater part of the indemnity, viz. 1,100,000,000 roubles—first, the Sandjak of Toultcha (comprising a number of specified districts) to be afterwards exchanged, if Russia thought fit, for the part of Bessarabia detached from her by the treaty of 1856; and secondly, Ardahan, Kars, Batoum, Bayazet, and the territory as far as the Saganlough, the frontiers of which being delimited in detail. Of the remaining 310,000,000 roubles the sum of

[1] See *infra*, Appendix (J).

10,000,000 roubles, intended to indemnify Russian interests and establishments in Turkey, was to be paid as soon as the claims were examined by the Russian embassy at Constantinople and presented to the Porte, and the sum of 300,000,000 roubles was to be paid in accordance with an agreement to be subsequently concluded.[1] We shall see later that considerable modifications of these terms were afterwards made,[2] and that the claims of Russian subjects and institutions in Turkey for losses due to the war remained unsatisfied for many years—an arbitration agreement having been concluded at Constantinople on August 4, 1910.[3]

Miscellaneous provisions.

In addition to such general and special clauses in preliminaries of peace as have been mentioned above, there is a number of miscellaneous provisions depending on the peculiar circumstances of each case. Thus, in the Preliminaries of Vienna, February 1, 1856, the Allies demanded that the immunities of the Christian subjects of the Porte should be established without injury to the independence or dignity of the Sultan's crown. Further, the belligerent Powers reserved the right to introduce, in the general interests of Europe, some special conditions into the definitive treaty, besides the fundamental guarantees consigned to the preliminaries.

In the Preliminaries of Villafranca, July 11, 1859, the Emperors Napoleon and Francis Joseph expressed their agreement in favour of creating an Italian Confederation, under the honorary presidency of the Pope; and they engaged to request the Holy Father to introduce in his States certain essential reforms.

By the Preliminaries of Nikolsburg, July 26, 1866 (Art. II), the Emperor of Austria recognized the dissolution of the Germanic Confederation and consented to a new organization of Germany without Austria taking any part in it. On the other hand (Art. V), the King of Prussia declared his willingness to let the Kingdom of Saxony remain as it was when the contemplated modifications should be made, but reserved the right to regulate by a separate treaty of peace with Saxony the latter's part in the expenses of the war and her subsequent position in the North German Confederation.

Stipulations of an entirely different kind are found in the Preliminaries of San Stefano, March 3, 1878. Thus, after declaring Bulgaria an autonomous tributary principality, delimiting the frontiers,

[1] See *infra*, Appendix (M).

[2] Cf. the Treaty of Constantinople, January 27 / February 8, 1879; *infra*, Appendix (N), Art. V; and the protocol of the same date, Appendix (O).

[3] Appendix (P).

and providing for the election of the Prince, and the withdrawal of the Turkish army, it was laid down (Art. VIII) that Russian troops should occupy the country until the establishment of a native militia sufficient to preserve order, security, and tranquillity. The period of occupation was not to exceed two years. Regulations were also made as to the strength of the army of occupation, the cost of its maintenance, and its means of communication with Russia. Art. X reserved to Turkey the right to transport her regular troops through Bulgaria by fixed routes, and to continue her postal and telegraphic services through the principality. Further, the Sublime Porte agreed (Art. XX) to take measures to put a satisfactory end to the lawsuits of Russian subjects pending for several years, to indemnify the latter if necessary, and to execute without delay all judgments delivered; also (Art. XXII) to accord to Russian ecclesiastics, pilgrims, or monks travelling or sojourning in European and Asiatic Turkey the same rights and privileges as were granted to the foreign ecclesiastics of any other nationality.

Performance of certain clauses without waiting for the definitive treaty.

Finally, it is to be noted that although the preliminaries of peace constitute merely a provisional convention preparatory to the definitive treaty, it may happen that some of their provisions are carried out before the conclusion of the final treaty. For example, in the Preliminaries of Versailles, February 26, 1871, there were certain stipulations that were capable of being performed at once; their postponement would have served no useful purpose, and—had it been insisted upon by Germany in her position as dictator of terms—would have inflicted on France unnecessary and unjustifiable injury. Thus Art. III said that the evacuation of French territory occupied by the German troops was to begin after the ratification of the preliminaries. This took place without delay on March 2. Accordingly, on March 4 and 6 two additional conventions were drawn up by the military authorities of both sides, regulating the mode of evacuating the forts of Paris on the left bank of the Seine, and the occupation of Versailles by the French army.[1] On March 11 another convention was signed at Ferrières prescribing in detail the conditions, expenses of maintenance, the rations and lodging of the army of occupation.[2] By the convention of March 10, signed at Reims by the head of the postal department, questions as to postal service in the occupied departments were regulated.[3] Again, in pursuance of Art. VI

[1] Villefort, *Recueil*, vol. i. p. 31; De Clercq, *Recueil*, vol. x. p. 442.

[2] *Ibid.*, p. 40; *ibid.*, p. 449.

[3] *Ibid.*, p. 35; *ibid.*, p. 445.

of the preliminaries, a convention signed at Ferrières on March 11 drew up the rules to be observed regarding the restoration of prisoners of war.[1] Further, in order to fulfil the stipulation of the second paragraph of Art. VIII of the preliminaries, another convention was entered into at Rouen, March 16, regulating the levy of taxes by the French Government in the occupied departments.[2]

Modification of preliminaries by the definitive treaty.

Sometimes, too, though the preliminaries of peace are regarded as the fundamental and invariable basis for the subsequent definitive treaty, considerable modifications of the former are introduced in the latter. When these are made by mutual consent, given voluntarily by both sides, well and good; the parties may, of course, alter in this manner the preliminaries as they think fit. But departures from the preliminaries, involving substantial alterations of their terms, are undoubtedly illegitimate if they are brought about through pressure exercised by the victorious State on the defeated State, either at the final peace conference or otherwise. We find examples of such proceedings in the Franco-German settlement—the French negotiators were as easily overpowered in the council chamber as French armies had been in the field; it very rarely happens that the victor in the field is beaten in the peace conference. (It did, indeed, happen in the case of the Russo-Japanese War; but then there had been no preliminaries to work upon.) Art. III of the Preliminaries of Versailles distinctly laid down that immediately after the ratification of the latter the German troops were to evacuate certain specified territory—viz. the departments of Somme, Oise, and the parts of Seine Inférieure, Seine-et-Oise, Seine-et-Marne, Seine, and the forts on the right bank of the river Seine—after the first payment of 500,000,000 francs. But the German negotiators, alleging the unsettled condition of French internal affairs, insisted, under Art. VII of the Treaty of Frankfort, May 10, 1871, on the continuance of military occupation in several of these localities, and this in spite of the fact that the stipulated payment had been made.[3] Again, Art. IV of the preliminaries prohibited the German troops from levying contributions in the departments occupied by them; but under Art. VIII of the definitive treaty they acquired the right to levy both contributions and taxes.[4] As a French writer says, the Treaty of Frankfort was not merely a consecration of the Preliminaries of Versailles, it was a fresh diplomatic defeat for France: "Le traité du 10 mai ne fut pas seulement la consécra-

[1] Villefort, *Recueil*, vol. i. p. 54; De Clercq, *Recueil* vol. x. p. 460.

[2] De Clercq, *Recueil*, vol. x. p. 467.

[3] See *infra*, Appendix (K), Art. VII.

[4] *Ibid.*

tion des préliminaires, il fut une nouvelle défaite diplomatique, mais une défaite à laquelle nos tergiversations des mois précédents eurent autant de part que les difficultés de notre situation intérieure."[1] Finally, with regard to the considerable modifications of the Preliminaries of San Stefano, March 3, 1878, which were introduced in the definitive Treaty of Constantinople, February 8, 1879, between Russia and Turkey, we have already pointed out that they were due to the intervention of the Great Powers of Europe at the Congress of Berlin, 1878.[2]

[1] G. May, *Le traité de Francfort* (Paris, 1909), p. 66.
[2] See *infra*, Appendices (M), (N), and (O).

CHAPTER IV

CONSTITUTION AND PROCEDURE OF THE PEACE CONFERENCE

GENERAL PRINCIPLES

Allies and peace negotiations—Place of negotiation—Title of plenipotentiary—What persons are chosen—Who is represented—Distinction between congress and conference—Ceremonial and procedure—Initial proceedings—Mode of conducting the deliberations—Secrecy—Function of mediators—The protocol and the *procès-verbal*—The use of the *alternat*.

HAVING discussed the nature and the component elements of preliminaries of peace, our next step is to examine the constitution and the procedure of the peace conference, and the mode of conducting negotiations there. In this chapter the general principles will be set forth; in the following chapter notable examples of peace negotiations will be given, for purposes of illustration and in order to supply further details according to the circumstances of each case.

First we have to note the position of belligerent allies with regard to the inauguration of peace pourparlers. Unless there be a specific agreement to the contrary, it is understood that allied States prosecuting hostilities against a common enemy will not conclude peace separately; to do so might be incompatible with the alliance, and so would constitute an illegitimate repudiation of it. And this is especially the case when the alliance is a complete one, that is for offence as well as for defence. It is usual, however, to strengthen this obligation and make it more precise by means of an engagement entered into before the war, or at its commencement, or at some period during its existence.

Allies and peace negotiations.

A striking instance occurred in the case of the Great War. On September 5, 1914—about a month after the outbreak of the war—the following agreement was concluded between Great Britain, France, and Russia:

Recent instances.

"The undersigned duly authorized thereto by the respective Governments hereby declare as follows:—

The British, French, and Russian Governments mutually engage not to conclude peace separately during the present war. The three Governments agree that when terms of peace come to be discussed no one of the Allies will demand terms of peace without the previous agreement of each of the other Allies. In faith whereof the undersigned have signed this Declaration and have affixed thereto their seals.

Done at London in triplicate the 5th day of September, 1914.

E. GREY, His Britannic Majesty's Secretary of State for Foreign Affairs.

PAUL CAMBON, Ambassador Extraordinary and Plenipotentiary of the French Republic.

BENCKENDORFF, Ambassador Extraordinary and Plenipotentiary of His Majesty the Emperor of Russia."[1]

Immediately afterwards Japan acceded to this agreement.

By the Anglo-Japanese treaty of alliance, entered into August 12, 1905, in London (which replaced the agreement of January 30, 1902) for the purpose of maintaining general peace in Eastern Asia and India, assuring the independence and integrity of China and the equality of commercial and industrial opportunities of all nations therein, and maintaining the territorial rights of the contracting parties in Eastern Asia and India, a similar obligation was created so far as these objects were concerned. Thus Art. II says that if either party should be involved in war in defence of its territorial rights or special interests on account of an unprovoked attack or aggressive action by any other Power, the other must at once come to the aid of its ally, conduct the war in common, and make peace in mutual agreement with it.[2]

Similarly, the "alliance of peace and reciprocal protection" concluded at Vienna, October 7, 1879, between Prince Henry VII of Reuss on behalf of Germany, and Count Andrassy on behalf of Austria, stipulated (Art. I) that if Russia attacked one of the two Empires the other was to come to its assistance with the whole of the military power, and peace should not be concluded save conjointly and by agreement between the two parties.[3]

A few earlier instances of this kind may be mentioned. In the seventeenth century we find treaties stipulating that neither peace

[1] *The Times*, September 6, 1914, p. 1. [2] *Parl. Papers, Japan*, 1905.

[3] G. F. de Martens, *Nouveau Recueil général de traités*, etc., 2me série (ed. F. Stoerk), vol. xv. p. 477.

nor truce was to be made by the signatories independently of each other, e.g. the Treaty of Paris, February 8, 1635, between France and the States-General; the Treaty of Rivoli, July 11, 1635, between France and the Duke of Savoy, together with the Duke of Parma, and the Duke of Mantua; the Treaty of Wismar, March 20, 1636, between France and Sweden. In the eighteenth century there are the Treaty of The Hague (the "Grand Alliance"), September 7, 1701, between England, the Emperor, and the States-General (Art. VII); the treaty of January 11, 1757, between England and Prussia (Art. VIII), in view of the Austro-French danger; the Treaty of Turin, April 8, 1797 (Art. VIII), between France (the Directoire) and Charles Emmanuel IV of Sardinia, which prohibited also the conclusion of a separate armistice. In the nineteenth century there are, amongst others, the following cases: the Treaty of Palermo, March 30, 1808, between England and Ferdinand IV, King of the Two Sicilies, whereby the latter undertook (Art. X) not to make peace separately with France; the Treaty of London, January 14, 1809, between England and Spain, the common enemy being France again; the Treaty of Kalisch, February 28, 1813, between Russia and Prussia, whereby (Art. VI) the contracting parties pledged themselves neither to make a separate peace nor to negotiate separately with the enemy; the Treaty of Toeplitz, October 3, 1813, between England and Austria (Art. IV); the Treaty of Ried, October 8, 1813, between Austria and Bavaria (Art. X); the Treaty of Langres, February 2, 1814, between Austria and Sweden (Art. VI), directed against France; the Treaty of Naples, January 11, 1814, between Austria and Naples (Art. X); the Treaty of Hanover, February 8, 1814, between Russia and Denmark (Art V); the Treaty of Chaumont, March 1, 1814, between England, Austria, Russia, and Prussia, forbidding separate negotiation with France; the Treaty of Vienna, March 25, 1815, between the same parties and stipulating the same terms; the Treaty of Vienna, January 3, 1815, between England, Austria, and France, directed against Alexander I of Russia. After the Napoleonic wars, we find similar arrangements in connection with the Crimean War. Thus the Treaty of Constantinople, March 12, 1854, between England, France, and Turkey, provided (Art. II) that each of the contracting parties should immediately notify to the others all communications received from the Emperor of Russia, and that peace should not be made by them separately. This engagement was confirmed by the Treaty of London, April 10, 1854, which laid down (Art. III) that none of the parties was to accept any overture or proposal tending to bring about a cessation of hostilities without having arrived at a

Earlier examples.

common decision to that effect. The Treaty of Vienna, December 2, 1854, made the same provision (Art. I), and was signed not only by England and France again, but also by Austria; the latter Power remained only a potential belligerent in the Crimean War, and towards the end, 1855–1856, used effectively her good offices (soon converted into mediation) to establish peace between the combatant States.[1] In 1855 Napoleon III began to negotiate with Russia independently of Great Britain; but Lord Palmerston emphatically protested against the contemplated breach of the engagement. Again, in the case of the Austro-Prussian War, 1866, Prussia was obliged to obtain the consent of Italy, by reason of a previous agreement, for the conclusion of an armistice as well as for the commencement of peace negotiations.

Place of peace negotiations.

Peace negotiations may be conducted by means of letters and despatches exchanged between the parties concerned, or through the medium of representatives specially appointed to meet at a given place. The former mode is unusual; an instance occurred in 1729, between Sweden and Poland, when by correspondence between the Courts peace was successfully established; a similar effort made in 1761 in the war between England and France failed. The latter is now the regular mode; the main point to be settled is where the chosen representatives are to meet. As we have seen, the preliminaries of peace, if there be any, usually provide for this. The convenience of both parties is the main consideration in selecting a place; but it is obvious that the choice will depend on the will of the more successful belligerent who is sued for peace.

Neutral territory.

Sometimes a place in neutral territory is specified;[2] this is preferable for various reasons, mainly because all presumption of constraint and intimidation is then minimized; but if there is a mediating Power, then not infrequently some place in the latter's country is selected. Thus, Zurich was fixed for the holding of the peace conference, 1859, between France and Austria; Brussels, 1871, between France and Germany (but the conference was afterwards removed by Germany to her own territory, at Frankfort); Berlin, 1878, between Russia and Turkey, though other important matters of European concern were also settled there by the congress of the Great Powers; Paris, 1898, between the United States and Spain; Portsmouth (in the United

[1] See *supra*, p. 83, and *infra*, p. 133.

[2] We cannot agree with M. May (*Le traité de Francfort*, p. 41), who claims that international custom requires the definitive treaty to be concluded in a neutral country. The contrary examples given here show that such practice is far from being a custom.

States), 1905, between Russia and Japan. In the latter case there was some difficulty in determining the place of meeting. On the one hand Che-Foo was suggested by Japan; on the other Paris was proposed by Russia; but neither accepted the other's proposal. The Hague was then suggested by Russia, but refused by Japan. Eventually the United States was agreed to, conformably to the choice of Japan; in the first place Washington was chosen, but afterwards Portsmouth was fixed upon as a more suitable locality for the hot season. Similarly, the plenipotentiaries of Italy and Turkey met at Lausanne in 1912; and those of Turkey, Greece, Bulgaria, Serbia, and Montenegro assembled in London in 1913.

Territory of one of the belligerents.

Sometimes, again, the territory of one of the belligerents is chosen; whether it is to be that of the victorious party or that of the defeated State depends on the demand of the victor, if there are but two belligerents; and when there are more than two belligerents the choice of place depends usually on the demand of the successful Powers as well as on circumstances of general convenience. Thus in 1814 France was obliged to send her delegates to Vienna,[1] though in the following year (November 20) the definitive treaty between her on the one side and Great Britain, Austria, Prussia, and Russia on the other was concluded at Paris; at the close of the Crimean War, 1856, Russia sent her representatives to Paris; in the Austro-Prussian War, 1866, Prague was the scene of negotiations, but as between Austria and Italy, Vienna was the place; in the Franco-German War the proceedings were begun at Brussels, but ended at Frankfort; in the Russo-Turkish War the preliminaries of peace were concluded at San Stefano (in Turkey), the terms were, as has been pointed out, modified at Berlin, and the definitive treaty between Russia and Turkey was concluded, conformably to the changes made by the Berlin Congress, at Constantinople, 1879; in the war between Spain and Chile the peace delegates met at Lima, 1883; in the war between China and Japan, at Shimonoseki (in Japan), 1895; in the second Balkan War, 1913, between Bulgaria on the one side and Roumania, Greece, Montenegro, and Serbia on the other, the peace plenipotentiaries assembled at Bucharest;

[1] A French writer observes that Vienna was chosen for two reasons: First, because of its central position, its great resources for distractions and festivities, and the charming character of its inhabitants; secondly, because the allied sovereigns were desirous of giving proof of their gratitude to the Emperor of Austria for his firm and prudent conduct in the war, and for his resignation in preferring the peace of Europe to a throne for his daughter Marie Louise. (Comte d'Angeberg, *Le Congrès de Vienne et les traités de* 1815 (Paris, 1864); p. xxxiv of the Historical Introduction by M. Capefigue.)

finally, in the war between Turkey and Greece, 1913, the treaty of peace was concluded at Athens.

The peace conference is attended by representatives of the parties, who are sent not as ambassadors but in the capacity of plenipotentiaries. The title of "plenipotentiary" (i.e. possessing full powers) dates from the eighteenth century. It was devised in order to avoid the disputes that had been frequent in assemblies of the envoys of States, with regard to questions of ceremonial and relative precedence. "Ce n'est que vers le milieu du 18e siècle," says G. F. von Martens, "que le cérémonial a rangé les ministres plénipotentiaires dans la même classe avec les envoyés" (that is, ambassadors ordinary).[1] Flassan, speaking of the constitution of the Vienna Congress, points out that the delegates were invested only with the character of plenipotentiaries. Several of them, indeed, were described as "ambassadors" in their letters of credence; but this title can be properly given only to diplomatic agents accredited to some particular sovereign; whereas the congress possessing neither territory nor supreme jurisdiction could not be assimilated to a sovereign State.[2]

Title of plenipotentiary.

As to the number of peace commissioners to be appointed by each State concerned, there is no international rule or custom; it is a question depending on the circumstances of each case, and is determined on every occasion by agreement between the Powers to be represented. Usually, however—though by no means invariably—each party deputes more than one delegate. It may be, as M. Pradier-Fodéré says,[3] that one is chosen because of his persuasive powers, diplomatic skill, high rank, etc.—"l'un aura le talent de persuader, des manières insinuantes, un grand nom, l'habitude des grandes réceptions"; another, because of his special knowledge of history and international law, so that he may effectively support the arguments set forth; a third, because of his skill in draftsmanship, and so on. But such a distinction is rarely observed by States. If we look at the treaties of peace concluded in the last hundred years, we shall find that when several delegates are chosen by each Power, one of them is generally its minister for foreign affairs,

Number of peace commissioners.

[1] G. F. von Martens, *Précis du droit des gens moderne de l'Europe* (Gottingue, 1801), p. 295.

[2] G. de Flassan, *Histoire du Congrès de Vienne*, 3 vols. (Paris, 1829), vol. i. p. 13.

[3] P. Pradier-Fodéré, *Cours de droit diplomatique*, 2 vols. (Paris, 1899), vol. ii. p. 433.

another is frequently its ambassador or diplomatic agent accredited to the sovereign in whose territory the peace conference is to be held, the rest are ministers of state or special envoys. Their rank, dignity, titles, orders, and offices are stated in the instrument, and they are now invariably described in it as plenipotentiaries; as such they possess all the immunities and prerogatives of ambassadors. A few examples will illustrate these points.

What persons are chosen.

The negotiators of the treaty of peace signed at Paris, November 20, 1815, were, on behalf of Great Britain, Lord Castlereagh, the foreign secretary, and the Duke of Wellington; and on behalf of France, the Sieur Armand Emanuel du Plessis Richelieu, the French foreign secretary.

The Treaty of Paris, March 30, 1856, between Great Britain, Austria, France, Prussia, Sardinia, Turkey on the one side, and Russia on the other, is described as having been concluded by plenipotentiaries of these States, each of which sent two—one being a minister of state (in most of the cases the foreign secretary); the other being, for Great Britain, Austria, Prussia, Sardinia, Turkey, the ambassador to the Court of France, for France the ambassador to Austria, for Russia the ambassador to the Germanic Confederation.[1]

The Treaty of Zurich, November 10, 1859, between Austria and France was negotiated by two delegates on each side, of whom one was a member of the Government, and the other specially appointed for the purpose.

In the case of the Preliminaries of Nikolsburg, July 26, 1866, there were two plenipotentiaries (including the minister for foreign affairs) for Austria, and one (viz. Bismarck, the foreign minister) for Prussia; but in the definitive Treaty of Prague, August 23, 1866, there was only one for each side—the one for Prussia being Baron Werther, the royal chamberlain. In the Treaty of Vienna, October 3, 1866, we find one, a senator, for Italy; and one, the chamberlain, for Austria.

The negotiators of the Preliminaries of Versailles, February 26, 1871, were Bismarck, together with the foreign ministers of Bavaria, Würtemberg, and Baden, on one side, and M. Thiers, Chief of the Executive of the French Republic, and M. Favre, the foreign minister, on the other; but in the definitive Treaty of Frankfort, May 10, 1871, France appointed three plenipotentiaries (including M. Favre, and the minister of finance), and Germany two (Bismarck, and the German ambassador to the Papal Court).

In 1878 Russia sent to San Stefano, for concluding preliminaries

[1] See *infra*, Appendix (D), *in init.*

of peace, two plenipotentiaries who occupied ministerial positions, and Turkey sent her foreign minister, and her ambassador to Germany; but in the following year, for the definitive Treaty of Constantinople (February 8), Russia appointed only one, her ambassador to the Sultan, and Turkey two, both ministers of state (including the foreign minister).

The Treaty of Shimonoseki, April 17, 1895, was concluded by two representatives on behalf of Japan, the minister president of state, and the minister for foreign affairs; and two on behalf of China, Li Hung-Chang, the senior grand secretary of state, and the ex-minister of the diplomatic service.

In the Treaty of Paris, December 10, 1898, between United States and Spain, we find five plenipotentiaries for the former described as "citizens of the United States," consisting of the secretary of state, the chairman of the Senate Foreign Affairs Committee, the former ambassador to France, and two senators; and five for Spain, viz. the president of the Spanish Senate, a judge of the Supreme Court, the former ambassador to France, the Spanish minister to Belgium, and a general.

The negotiators of the Treaty of Portsmouth, September 5, 1905, between Russia and Japan, were, for the former, M. Witte, the secretary of state, and Baron Rosen, ambassador to the United States; and for the latter Baron Komura, the foreign minister, and M. Takahira, ambassador to the United States.

In the case of the Treaty of Lausanne, October 18, 1912, there were three plenipotentiaries for Italy, including two members of Parliament; and two for Turkey.

The delegates appointed to conclude the Treaty of London, May 30, 1913, numbered three for Turkey on the one side; and three for each of the Allies—Greece, Bulgaria, Serbia, and Montenegro—on the other.

The Treaty of Bucharest, August 10, 1913, was concluded by a large assembly of plenipotentiaries; six for Roumania—the foreign minister (M. Maïoresco), the minister of finance, the minister of the interior (M. Jonesco), the minister of public worship and public instruction, and two others; five for Greece, including M. Venizelos, the prime minister, and M. Politis, the professor of international law in the University of Paris; two for Montenegro, viz. the prime minister and the former chargé d'affaires at Constantinople; five for Serbia, including M. Pasitch, the foreign minister, and the Serbian minister at Bucharest; and five for Bulgaria, including the minister of finance, the former vice-president of the Sobranje, and the chief of staff of the Bulgarian army.

In the case of the Treaty of Constantinople, September 29, 1913, between Turkey and Bulgaria, the former appointed three plenipotentiaries, viz. the minister of the interior, the minister of marine, and the president of the Council of State; the latter appointed three, including two former ministers.

The delegates named to negotiate the Treaty of Athens, November 14, 1913, between Turkey and Greece, were one on each side—the one for Greece being the minister for foreign affairs.

All Powers directly concerned to be represented.

The above examples show that all the Powers directly concerned should be represented at the peace conference, as indeed at any other international conference, and that their representatives should be allowed to participate freely in the negotiations. This fundamental principle, demanded by law and equity alike, has not always, in practice, been observed. On several occasions have the Great Powers arrogated to themselves the right to regulate the affairs and even decide the fate of smaller States, without admitting their representatives, or—if they were formally admitted—without consulting their wishes or regarding their contentions. Thus at the Congress of Utrecht, opened January 29, 1712, England and France predominated; the proceedings were conducted primarily by their plenipotentiaries, and the delegates of the other States, viz. the United Provinces, Savoy, Spain, Portugal, intervened only by submitting notes. At the Congress of Aix-la-Chapelle (1748), only the two Great Powers, Great Britain and France, discussed the high diplomatic questions, and merely communicated the decisions reached to their allies. In the nineteenth century, examples of unjustifiable exclusion or disregard of smaller States are furnished by the Congress of Vienna (1814–1815), the Congress of Paris (1856), the Congress of Berlin (1878). In 1869, at the Conference dealing with the affairs of Crete, Greece was not represented; in 1883, at the Conference of London relating to the Danube, Roumania was not allowed to participate.[1] Another form of the predominance of the stronger Power is seen in the conclusion of peace in the case of the Franco-German War; the Preliminaries of Versailles, February 26, 1871, were signed by France and the North German Confederation—Bavaria, Würtemberg, and Baden, as allies, acceding by means of a separate document; the Treaty of Frankfort, May 10, 1871, was similarly concluded between France and the North German Confederation, the allies of the latter afterwards signing an additional protocol. Thus the allies of Prussia did not participate in the negotiations equally with the latter, and did not appear as contracting parties on the instrument itself, which embodied provisions affecting them.

[1] Cf. Pradier-Fodéré, *op. cit.*, vol. ii. pp. 428–430.

On the other hand, representatives of a neutral State are sometimes invited to a peace conference, either because it will be indirectly concerned in the transactions, or because it is desired to fortify the treaty that is eventually to be concluded. In 1856 Great Britain, Austria, France, Sardinia, and Turkey on the one side, and Russia on the other, agreed to invite Prussia to take part in the Congress of Paris, 1856, in the interest of Europe, inasmuch as her concurrence would be useful in the work of general pacification.

Sometimes representatives of a neutral State invited.

A distinction was formerly drawn between a congress and a conference; in recent times, too, some writers have claimed that there is a difference between them. Let us see to what extent, if any, this claim holds. The word "congress" in its political sense appears to have first been used in the seventeenth century. During the Thirty Years' War delegates of the belligerent States assembled in Cologne (1636), at the instance of the Pope, with a view to making peace; this meeting was then designated a congress. Their efforts, however, failed. In 1647, too, the assembly of representatives at Münster and at Osnabrück was termed a congress; this time their deliberations ended in the Peace of Westphalia (1648). Several later examples of international congresses have already been mentioned.[1]

Distinction between congress and conference.

Vattel, whose *Droit des gens* was published in 1758, makes no distinction between congress and conference. He says that a congress is an assembly of plenipotentiaries, whose object is to discover means of conciliation, to discuss and adjust reciprocal claims.[2] The same description applies to a conference. Klüber,[3] Meisel,[4] and Comte de Garden[5] regard a congress as an assembly of public ministers or plenipotentiaries of different States, and a conference as an actual sitting of the same. Flassan, writing of the Congress of Vienna (1814–1815), remarks that most of the plenipotentiaries there assembled had a very imperfect notion of the meaning and object of a congress—"les uns voulant que le congrès fût le tribunal suprême de l'Europe, avec un pouvoir illimité; d'autres ne l'envisageaient que comme centre de négociations sans formes précises." He himself gives the following definition: "Un congrès est une réunion des plénipotentiaires de plusieurs États et

[1] A list of more than a hundred official congresses and conferences is given in *American Journal of International Law*, vol. i (1907), pp. 808 *seq.*

[2] *Droit des gens*, liv. ii. ch. xviii. § 330.

[3] *Droit des gens moderne de l'Europe* (Paris, 1831), § 225.

[4] *Cours de style diplomatique* (1824), vol. ii. pp. 468 *seq.*

[5] *Traité complet de diplomatic* (1833), vol. ii. liv. viii. § 4.

gouvernemens indépendans qui conviennent de négocier dans un même lieu, sur des intérêts communs."[1] On the other hand, writers like Heffter[2] and Sir Travers Twiss[3] make little or no discrimination; the former uses the word conference both in the sense of a sitting and in that of an assembly, the latter employs the terms congress and conference indifferently. Rivier,[4] too, speaks of congress as including conference.

Another distinction that has been suggested relates to a difference in the position of the persons taking part in the negotiations. Bluntschli[5] says that formerly the members of a congress were frequently the heads of States or their ministers for foreign affairs, whilst those of a conference were usually ambassadors or envoys specially appointed for the purpose. Accordingly, a congress was entitled to come to a final decision there and then; whilst the resolutions of a conference required, for their validity, the ratification of the respective Governments. He points out that since the Congress of Paris, 1856, the attendance of heads of States is not necessary to make an assembly a congress, provided that statesmen and not merely delegates *ad hoc* take part in it. A congress, then, possesses a more solemn character and greater political authority, so that the questions it discusses have a wider importance; whilst a conference is concerned usually with ordinary and technical matters.[6] A similar point of view is adopted by F. de Martens,[7] who adds that the work of a conference is of a preliminary or preparatory character,[8] but that of a congress is definitive; a congress may establish new principles, a conference confines itself to applying those already in existence. He observes, however, that in actual practice these distinctions are not followed.

In point of fact there was formerly no sharp line of demarcation between a congress and a conference, though certain more or less vague differences were recognized. At present the difference is still less defined. It is true that in earlier days we find certain conferences engaged only in preparatory discussions, and certain

[1] Flassan, *Histoire du Congrès de Vienne* (Paris, 1829), vol i. pp. 1, 2.

[2] *Droit international de l'Europe*, liv. iii. § 240.

[3] *The Rights and Duties of Nations in Time of War* (Oxford, 1889), chap i. § 8.

[4] *Principes du droit des gens* (1896), vol. ii. p. 8.

[5] *Droit international codifié*, § 12.

[6] Cf. T. Funck-Brentano et A. Sorel, *Précis du droit des gens* (Paris, 1877), pp. 462, 463; where it is pointed out that in the case of a congress the object is general and several States participate, whereas in the case of a conference the object is more restricted.

[7] F. de Martens, *Traité de droit international*; trad. du russe par A. Leo; 3 vols. (Paris, 1883–1887), vol. i. pp. 2 , 299.

[8] Similarly, cf. C. Calvo, *Le droit international*, vol. ii. § 1478.

congresses in transactions that were regarded as final; thus the Conferences of Moerdyk and Gertruidenberg prepared the way for the Congress of Utrecht, whilst such congresses as those of Münster (1648), Aix-la-Chapelle (1668, 1748), Rastadt (1794), Châtillon (1814), Vienna (1814–1815), Laybach (1821), Verona (1822), etc., arrived at definitive results. But—as Pradier-Fodéré points out[1]—more than one congress has held a succession of sittings without reaching positive results, and more than one conference has assumed the character of a congress. A striking recent instance is that of the Algeciras Conference, 1906, which comprised the representatives of a dozen States, and settled important territorial questions. The presence or absence of sovereigns or other heads of States and their executive ministers is now no decisive criterion. Mountague Bernard, writing in 1868, remarks that the term "conference" applies to any meeting held for the purpose of discussion, and that during the preceding thirty or forty years it came to be used, on account of its more flexible and less ostentatious character, to designate assemblies that would in earlier days have been called "congresses." He added that the latter name would "probably be reserved in future, if employed at all, for assemblages extraordinarily numerous, or of extraordinary importance."[2] It is true that certain meetings of the plenipotentiaries of States are invariably called congresses, e.g. that of Vienna (1814–1815), that of Berlin (1878). But it is also true that certain recent extraordinarily numerous or important assemblages are described as conferences, e.g. the Algeciras Conference, and—most important of all—those of The Hague, 1899 and 1907, which are referred to indifferently as congresses or conferences, and that of London, 1909, which is formally designated a Naval Conference. It is clear, then, that whatever principles of division may have existed at one time or another, it cannot be said that there is now any clearly defined dividing-line between them; indeed, the term "conference" appears to be taking more and more frequently the place of "congress," and probably will before long oust it altogether. Pradier-Fodéré, after endeavouring to fasten upon this or that distinction, is bound to admit, even before the date of the above-mentioned highly significant cases, that it is impossible to find any real difference. ". . . Il faut convenir," he concludes, "qu'en réalité la différence qu'il peut y avoir entre une *conférence* et un *congrès* et difficile à percevoir, en dehors de la question de solennité, et que les conférences et les congrès ont le

No sharp line of demarcation between them.

[1] *Traité de droit international*, etc. (Paris, 1885–1906), vol. vi. p. 227.

[2] *Four Lectures on Subjects connected with Diplomacy* (London, 1868), p. 28.

même but et le même caractère dans leurs traits essentiels, car les uns et les autres sont des réunions des représentants des États, tenues en vue de discuter des questions de droit international, de travailler à amener une entente, de prendre des décisions communes et de conclure des traités." [1]

Next, as to the ceremonial and procedure of the conference. In earlier days ceremonial and formality played a great part not only in the negotiation of treaties, but also in all other public transactions—just as in the private law of States the letter, form, elaborate routine often prevailed over the essential spirit and reality. Many attempts at peace conferences to effect an accommodation of vital matters proved abortive or were unduly protracted owing to the non-observance of certain forms, or on account of persistent disputes as to the personal dignity or relative precedence of the representatives. Striking instances of such conflicts and delays are found at Münster and Osnabrück, where the negotiations dragged on for several years before the Thirty Years' War was terminated by the Peace of Westphalia (1648); [2] and also at Ryswick. Gradually, as time became more valuable and business generally came to be conducted with greater despatch, thanks to the growth of men's interests, the increase of international relationships, and the development of means of rapid communication, the elaborate ceremonial of diplomacy was little by little whittled down, until there is nowadays scarcely anything left of it. Commenting on this transformation, Bernard observes: "Those who know little else about diplomacy have heard of its reverence for forms and its punctilious etiquette. These things belonged to a state of society different from ours. In the love of mere sumptuousness and show there is a touch of barbarism; the most profusely magnificent pageants have not been exhibited by the most polished nations: but where splendour has become an established fashion, an elaborate ceremonial seems naturally to follow." [3]

CEREMONIAL AND PROCEDURE.

The initial proceedings at the conference are now simple and businesslike. As soon as the plenipotentiaries have arrived at the town appointed and have paid the usual visits to each other, they decide the time and the exact place of the meeting. Having assembled there, they proceed to exchange and verify their full powers—that is, to make sure that they

Initial proceedings.

[1] *Traité de droit international*, vol. vi. pp. 228, 229.

[2] There were, in this case, certain other causes that contributed to bring about the delay; see the following chapter, *in init.*

[3] *Op. cit.*, p. 131.

possess the necessary authority to transact the affairs in view, and thereby to bind their respective Governments, subject, however, to ratification by the latter (which, in point of fact, regularly follows in due course). If there is a mediator, he examines the full powers. When the assembly comprises a considerable number of delegates, it is usual to appoint a special committee to verify their powers. Thus, at the Vienna Congress (1814) it was decided that a commission of three of the plenipotentiaries should undertake this task and report thereon at the next sitting. In earlier days this preliminary step occupied much time; the credentials were drawn up in an elaborate and ornate style, and the language used not infrequently gave rise to difficulties of interpretation. Nowadays delegates sent in the capacity of plenipotentiaries are usually not provided with letters of credence, which other diplomatic agents take with them; their full powers (*pleins pouvoirs*) are in themselves regarded as sufficient proof of their position and authority. If the foreign minister himself attends the conference, it is not absolutely necessary that he should possess documentary authorization; and the credentials of his colleagues are countersigned by him.

Mode of conducting the deliberations.

The next step is to settle the mode of conducting the deliberations, as well as small details of ceremonial, such as the positions to be occupied at the council-table. Formerly there were many frivolous disputes as to which representatives should be at the high end of the table, and as to the order of the seats. Thus, at the Congress of Ryswick (1697) this point alone gave rise to so much wrangling, and the conclusion of peace was thereby endangered to such an extent, that the representatives finally solved the knotty problem by an agreement to sit in a circle, without a table. At Utrecht (1713) and Aix-la-Chapelle (1748) the delegates, mindful of the factitious difficulties that had beset previous conferences, consented to waive ceremonial and to take up their positions at a round table without reference to distinction of rank. At Cambrai and Soissons, too, a round table was used; "but even a round table," remarks Bernard, "loses its accommodating quality when it is discovered that the place of honour is that opposite the door, and that every place of honour has a right hand and a left."[1] The principle of alphabetical order was then introduced, and so the remaining causes of friction were removed. Thus, at the Paris Conference (1856) the members sat at a round table specially made for the occasion, and took their places in the alphabetical order, counting from right to left, of the initial letters of the French names of the Powers

[1] *Op. cit.*, p. 137.

represented. At the Congress of Berlin (1878) the plenipotentiaries took their seats in a similar alphabetical order at a table in the shape of a horseshoe.

Appointment of president.

Their places having been settled, a president is elected when the assembly is composed of several delegates of different States. If the State in whose territory the conference is held is a party thereto, the presidential chair is customarily offered to its first plenipotentiary; but where there is a mediating Power, the honour is conferred on its principal representative. The president then takes the chair, and makes an introductory speech expressing the welcome of the sovereign of the country, and emphasizing the objects of the meeting. A suitable reply to this is made by one or more of the delegates. At the suggestion of the president, a secretary and an assistant-secretary are then appointed and introduced to the assembly. (Sometimes the verification of the full powers takes place at this stage, so that the secretary may himself undertake the function.) Finally, the president points out the necessity of keeping the proceedings secret, and adjourns the meeting for a day or two, in order that the members may be able to meet privately, make each other's acquaintance, and discuss amongst themselves those questions upon whose agreement will depend the satisfactory opening of the negotiations proper.

Secrecy of proceedings.

With regard to this customary obligation of secrecy, which is all the more binding when the plenipotentiaries expressly engage to observe it, it is to be noted that during the peace negotiations at Portsmouth (New Hampshire), between Russia and Japan, American journalists managed to learn the results arrived at. It appears that the Japanese delegates had from the first consistently opposed publicity of every kind, and had throughout remained proof to the approaches of would-be interviewers. The Russian representatives, on the other hand, were not so strongly in favour of secrecy, though they consented to observe it. It is not hard to guess which side was responsible for the leakage of information that was so promptly published by the American Press. M. de Martens, the distinguished Russian publicist and jurist, commenting on this occurrence, says: "Heretofore it has been an axiom in the diplomatic world that absolute secrecy concerning the proceedings of a conference is the *sine qua non* of its success. Consequently, at the first sitting of all international congresses, the delegates of the various Governments represented agree to reveal nothing that transpires there. This rule was also observed on the opening day of the Portsmouth Conference. In European countries the keeping of the promise is nearly always possible. In the United States the contrary has been found to be true. It is an admitted fact that most of the secret negotiations of the conference were revealed and immediately published by the American newspapers." It is rather strange, to say the least, that the American Press should be condemned for the breach of faith of those who communicated the information to it. The writer adds, however—but inconsistently with the tenor of his previous observations—that though secrecy should continue to be the rule in international diplomatic meetings, circumstances sometimes demand that it should be abandoned.[1] Whether this remark was made with a view to justifying the Russian delegates' departure from the rule, there is no need to inquire; but in any case it is obvious that to admit such a relaxation, in the absence of an agreement thereto by all the parties concerned, would open the door to arbitrary procedure and enlarge the already extensive sphere of political casuistry.

Mode of conducting the negotiations.

The negotiations may be conducted by the exchange of notes, or by oral argument, or by a conjunction of these methods. At the Congress of Münster (constituted 1644) there was no general conference. The delegates presented written statements under seal to the two mediators, Chigi, the nuncio, and Contarino, the representative of the Venetian Republic. They in their turn examined the various claims and counter-claims, communicated them to the contending parties, and afterwards suggested conciliatory measures without offering definitive decisions. These negotiations dragged on for a considerable length of time without reaching any result whatever, much to the annoyance of Cardinal Mazarin, who regarded negotiation by notes as a novel procedure productive of delay, and accordingly instructed the French representatives to proceed orally. Bernard points out that the reason that impelled Mazarin to take this step was not merely in order to enforce less dilatory methods, but also that in *viva voce* communication it was easier to effect a withdrawal if necessary; quickness to recede from offer and assent was deemed an indispensable factor at a time "when negotiation meant subtle bargain-driving, and the terms on which the parties really meant to insist were approached by degrees under cover of a series of feints and artifices."[2]

Function of mediators.

At Osnabrück there was no mediation; the proposals and counter-proposals were exchanged, by means of detailed notes, between the plenipotentiaries themselves; they were carried from one to the other by a secretary of

[1] *North American Review*, November 1905, pp. 646, 647.

[2] *Op. cit.*, p. 29.

legation, who was attended by two *cavaliers d'ambassade,*[1] and were from time to time discussed in conference.

In the case of the Congress of Nimeguen (1675–1676), the King of England and the Pope being mediators, there was no general assembly; each representative presented his claims and defended his rights and interests by means of memoranda. The French delegates objected to the exchange of written communications, so that a modified plan was adopted, whereby the written form was nevertheless retained. Here the account of Sir William Temple is the best possible testimony: "They were positive to give no answer in writing nor to receive any, alleging both reason and example for their opinion; *this* from the practice of the Münster Treaty, *that* from the danger of the invective style or language that are apt to enter into the writings of each party upon such occasions. The Allies were for some time as peremptory in their resolution of delivering their answers in writing; but both at last agreed upon the expedient we proposed of dictating to us what they intended should be said to the other party, of our setting the substance down in writing, and reading it over to them first who dictated to us, so as they might be judges whether we had rightly apprehended and expressed their meaning, and yet the thing might go on in our style and not in theirs, by which all sharpness and provocation would be avoided."[2]

Again, at the Congress of Teschen (1779), where Russian and French mediators officiated between Austria, Prussia, and Bavaria, the plenipotentiaries carried on their negotiations by means of notes. At Rastadt (1798) there were personal conferences as well as the exchange of memoranda. Such combination was adopted in many subsequent cases. Obviously there cannot be any hard-and-fast method; such method will be adopted as, in the given circumstances, conduces to create smoothness, expedition, and effectiveness. Of recent instances two may be given, in the words of Dr. E. J. Dillon, to indicate different modes of procedure. The first is that of the Conference of Bucharest relative to the second Balkan War, 1913, and the next is that of the Conference of Portsmouth relative to the Russo-Japanese War, 1905.

"The Roumanian delegates contended that in public assemblies real work is hardly ever done, progress being at most reported there. The arguments that carry weight, the considerations that beget concessions, and the suasion that moves mountains, are brought to bear in private. And they concluded that the peace delegates

[1] Bernard, *op. cit.*, p. 30.

[2] Sir William Temple, *Memoirs* . . ., first edition, 1692; in *Works* (London, 1814), vol. i. p. 323; referred to by Bernard, *op. cit.*, p. 29, n.

would do well to talk over their differences, argue their claims, and set off one renunciation against another in an informal way, meeting at the tea-table in each other's rooms. And whenever they had disposed of any set of contentious questions they were to notify the conference at a plenary sitting. Meanwhile, lest the public should draw disquieting conclusions from the cessation of the negotiations, it was resolved to hold a formal plenary sitting every day. . . .

At Portsmouth the Russians and Japanese had gone to work on the old lines: the victor making his demands orally at first, and then presenting them on paper; and the vanquished considering them for a day or two before returning a written reply.[1] The discussion usually took place when the terms asked for or the concessions offered were about to be declined in writing. The less contentious matters were taken first and threshed out at plenary sittings, just as in a law court, by means of *a priori* arguments, precedents, proposals of compromise. This difference of methods may be partially accounted for by the circumstance that at Portsmouth there were but two sides pitted one against the other, and two sets of interests to be balanced, whereas at Bucharest there were five different parties whose pretensions had to be dealt with, to say nothing of the Great Powers, which were also indirectly involved. Moreover, in Bucharest there were various outside forces at work, which might at any moment influence the course of negotiations."[2]

The written record of the proceedings at the conference is generally known as the *procès-verbal*; but since the Vienna Congress of 1814–1815 the minutes have also received the special name of protocol. The latter word is used in different ways, which it is necessary to distinguish.

The protocol and *procès-verbal*.

Under the late Roman Empire the *protocollum* (πρῶτος, first, κολλᾶν, to glue) was a volume of leaves glued together containing a record of public acts; afterwards it referred to the original drafts of such acts. The term was also applied to the first leaf or sheet glued at the beginning of a bundle of manuscripts or a papyrus roll, for the purpose of entering on it particulars regarding the authority under which the manuscript was written, as well as the writer's name, etc. Nowadays the word protocol is used with the following meanings: the minutes of the sitting of a conference—e.g. the first sitting of the Paris Conference (1856) took place on

[1] At the conference held in Paris, 1898, to restore peace between the United States and Spain, there was, too, oral discussion introduced or supplemented by a number of very elaborate memoranda; see *infra*, pp. 141 *seq.*

[2] *Contemporary Review*, September 1913, pp. 418–419.

February 25, and Protocol No. 1 gives a report of the proceedings; the rough draft or the original copy of an instrument; the preliminary document recording the fundamental principles or the particular points on which an agreement has been reached, thus serving as the basis for the final instrument—e.g. the protocol of peace between the United States and Spain that was signed at Washington, August 12, 1898;[1] an ancillary document attached to the principal act for the purpose of explaining it or amplifying its provisions, e.g. the protocols appended to the Treaty of Constantinople, September 29, 1913;[2] finally, the *protocole diplomatique* or *protocole de chancellerie* is a body of rules regulating the form and ceremonial to be followed in diplomatic intercourse.[3] Other examples of most of these usages are given in the present work.

The use of the *alternat*.

The signing of documents, including definitive treaties, formerly gave rise to disputes, on account of conflicting pretensions as to priority. Nowadays this formality has been simplified by the use of the *alternat*, which will be considered in a later chapter.[4]

[1] See *supra*, p. 104. [2] See *infra*, Appendix (Y).
[3] Cf. Pradier-Fodéré, *Cours de droit diplomatique*, vol. ii. p. 499.
[4] See *infra*, p. 172.

CHAPTER V

PEACE NEGOTIATIONS

NOTABLE EXAMPLES FROM PREVIOUS WARS

Thirty Years' War—Crimean War—Franco-German War—Italian-Abyssinian War—Spanish-American War—Russo-Japanese War—Second Balkan War (1913).

WE shall take as our first example the negotiations that led to the Peace of Westphalia (1648),[1] in order that the differences between former modes of procedure and those of modern times may be readily perceived.

Thirty Years' War.

The definite movement for peace during the Thirty Years' War began twelve years before its actual conclusion. Pope Urban VI prevailed on the belligerents to enter on negotiations, and taking upon himself the task of mediator despatched to Cologne Cardinal Ginetti as his representative, who was afterwards joined by envoys from the Courts of Vienna and Madrid (1636). The following year a discussion commenced as to the form of the safe-conducts to be granted by the Emperor; and the controversy on the subject was not setted till nearly five years later.

On December 25, 1641, the preliminary arrangements were made with regard to the time and place of the peace congress; and the agreement arrived at was signed at Hamburg under the mediation of Denmark. Ratification by the respective sovereigns was necessary; so that another year and a half passed by before this was effected, and the exchange of safe-conducts took place (April 28, 1643)—"six years having been thus spent in frivolous controversies on points of form." [2]

At length (July 1643) the plenipotentiaries of the Emperor repaired to the appointed place, Münster (in Westphalia); and eight months later (March 19, 1644) the first French envoy arrived. The nuncio, Chigi, and the Venetian delegate, Contarino, came to

[1] See Bernard, *op. cit.*, lect. i.; G. H. Bougeant, *Histoire des guerres et des négociations qui précédèrent le traité de Westphalie*, 6 vols. (Paris, 1751).

[2] *Ibid.*, p. 17.

officiate as mediators. The congress having been now constituted, the nuncio directed that public prayers should be offered in all the churches of the town, for the successful issue of the peace negotiations. These solemnities lasted three days; and even here the disputatious character and personal susceptibilities of the envoys were manifested, in regard to questions of precedence during the procession and the arrangement of the seats in church. Indeed, there was so much mutual jealousy and bickering with regard to points of dignity, title, and etiquette that the contending parties found it necessary to engage in a good deal of correspondence to settle the question whether the Emperor should allow the title of "Majesty" to the King of France. In this comedy of humours the spouses and suites of the delegates did not fail to participate to such an extent that the conciliatory capacity of the leading citizens of the town as well as its police measures were severely taxed.

The verification of their full powers gave rise to further difficulties; and it took seven months to remove them. Another delay followed, in consequence of the quibbling of the French representatives.

On June 11, 1645, the actual proceedings began, not in a general conference, but by the exchange of notes through the mediators. For the most part negotiation proceeded by means of written communications, until, at the instigation of Mazarin, more oral discussion was adopted. French had not yet become the predominating language of diplomatic intercourse; for we find that various languages were used—Latin, French, Italian, and Spanish often being spoken indiscriminately in the same conversation. The first proposals delivered by France and Sweden were, as we might well expect, "frivolous and illusory"; [1] and no reply was returned for two months. Haggling and bargaining, evasion and subterfuge, approach and withdrawal, offer and counter-offer, chicanery and dissimulation were kept up to the last. This game of cross-purposes had a tragic aspect, inasmuch as the operations of war had not been suspended: despite the efforts of the mediators neither side would consent to an armistice, each hurling recriminations at the other for refusing an accommodation. In these circumstances, the bargaining fluctuated from day to day with the reported changes of military fortune; the diplomatists on each side hesitated in the hope that their respective forces might achieve such success as would justify the demand for better terms than those offered. As Bernard observes: "The French and Swedes, wearied and impoverished, but superior in the field, could not renounce the hope of further conquests: the Emperor could not reconcile himself to

[1] See Bernard, *op. cit.*, lect. i. p. 19.

inevitable humiliation and loss; and supported by the resolute obstinacy which for good and for evil has always characterized his House, kept hoping against hope for a favourable turn of fortune."[1] The period of negotiation was thus protracted, not merely because of the employment of a "captious, peevish, and punctilious diplomacy," but mainly because neither side was sincerely desirous to establish peace, or, at all events, because neither side cared to make peace without first extorting crushing terms.

Eventually, however, the provisions of the peace treaty were arrived at; before its signing was to take place, each enemy was called upon to signify formally his assent thereto, after having received the necessary instructions from his sovereign. On the day when Isaac Volmar, one of the Emperor's representatives, was to announce his definitive acceptance of the treaty, he received a despatch in cipher from Vienna, but was unable at the time to learn its contents, as he had lost the key. "Let him go to the nuncio," exclaimed the delegate of Savoy, "and borrow the Keys of St. Peter!" "Finally"—to borrow the words of the previously quoted writer—"at nine o'clock on the 24th October, 1648, the German deputies assembled, full of joyful impatience, at the palace of the Bishop of Münster, but waited three hours in vain, and separated ruefully at noon. A last question of etiquette was undergoing solution. They were doomed, however, to no more disappointments. A fresh summons soon reconvoked them to add their signatures to the momentous instrument; and in a few minutes shouts of joy and the roar of cannon from the ramparts announced the conclusion of peace."[2]

Bernard dwells on the social features of the congress — the parade, the ceremonial visits, the numerous coaches-and-six, the dances, the ballets, the entertainments, the conviviality, the intemperance. At the same time the envoys, partisans, and others engaged in pamphleteering conflicts; appeals were made to the public opinion of Europe, and bribery was not without its devotees. Carriers were stopped, and robbed of their despatches; and many other incidents occurred which are foreign to our own less spacious and less picturesque age.[3]

Next, let us pass over a couple of centuries and look at a few modern examples of peace negotiation; they will show a remarkable change, inevitable, indeed, in a world that has in some respects moved very fast. The cases are selected, not for the purpose of displaying the whole course of the procedure in each, but in order

[1] See Bernard., *op. cit.*, lect. i. p. 20.

[2] *Ibid.*, pp. 19, 20.

[3] *Ibid.*, pp. 22–27.

to indicate certain distinctive or striking aspects of modern negotiation arising out of wars.

Crimean War. The interposition of Austria during the Crimean War, and the motives which induced her to intervene as mediator have already been referred to.[1] Whilst she was endeavouring to arrive at an accommodation between Russia and the Allied Powers, discussion was going on in various parts of Europe: it was felt in general that this negotiation would fail. This feeling was intensified on January 14, 1856, when concerning the overtures of Count Esterhazy Russia replied to the Austrian Government, stating that she was willing to accept the "points" in principle if certain modifications were made. (As has already been stated, the terms of the Allies as presented to Russia by Austria related to: the abolition of the Russian protectorate over the Danubian principalities; the freedom of the Danube; the neutralization of the Black Sea; the immunities of the Christian subjects of the Porte; further special conditions to be added later.) But the modifications suggested were extensive. Thus the first point in the Austrian proposal involved a rectification of the Russian frontier, whereby the navigation of the Danube would be liberated from Russian control; for the territory to be ceded and for Kars, the Allies offered in exchange the various places conquered by them on the coast of Crimea and of Asia Minor. Russia declined to cede the former territory, but offered Kars in exchange for the places on the Black Sea held by the Allies. As to the third point, Russia was called upon to abandon her military arsenals on the Black Sea, and not to establish new ones; but in her reply she required the word "military" to be replaced by the word "naval," and claimed the right to guard her coasts with warships. Further, the fifth condition was refused altogether. When the Austrian Government communicated this reply to the Allies, the latter rejoined that they would put an end to all negotiation unless all the terms were unconditionally accepted. Count Buol, the Austrian foreign secretary, was authorized to extend the time within which a final answer was to be given to the 18th of January. The young Czar submitted, despite the opposition of the war party of his empire; and the acceptance was formally delivered to Count Esterhazy. It was now recognized that the establishment of peace was certain. The news was received in the various countries of Europe with different feelings: in France, with joy; in the neutral countries, too, with delight; in England, there was much dissatisfaction with the terms; Sardinia was disappointed; and Turkey appeared indifferent.

[1] *Supra*, p. 83.

As soon as the terms were accepted, Russia requested that a protocol should be signed, embodying the five propositions as preliminaries of peace, and certifying the assent of the Allies thereto, that the peace conference should be opened in Paris (the place suggested by Great Britain) as soon as possible, that an armistice convention should in the first place be there concluded, that she should not be called upon to pay a war indemnity or cede any territory other than that necessarily involved in the rectification of her Danubian frontier. The desired protocol was signed at Vienna on February 1.

On February 25, 1856, the conference met for the first time in Paris, at the Ministry for Foreign Affairs. The following plenipotentiaries were present: for Great Britain, the Earl of Clarendon and Lord Cowley; for Austria, Count de Buol and Baron de Hübner; for France, Count Walewski and Baron de Bourqueney; for Russia, Count Orloff and Baron de Brunnow; for Sardinia, Count de Cavour and Marquis de Villa-Marina; for Turkey, Ali Pasha and Mehemmed Djemil Bey. At the invitation of the above Powers, Prussia also sent representatives, viz. Baron de Manteuffel and Count de Hatzfeldt.

Count de Buol, the first Austrian plenipotentiary, proposed that Count Walewski, the first French delegate, should preside over the conference. He observed: "This is not only a custom sanctioned by precedents and recently observed at Vienna; it is at the same time an act of homage to the sovereign whose hospitality the representatives of Europe are at this moment enjoying." The proposal was accepted unanimously. Count Walewski accordingly took the presidential chair, thanked the conference for the honour conferred on him, and expressed his hope that the negotiations would prove successful.

The president next proposed as secretary of the congress, M. Benedetti, the director of political affairs in the French Foreign Office. The conference agreed, and M. Benedetti was introduced to the members.

Next followed the verification of the full powers. Having been found in good and due form, they were deposited among the Acts of the conference.

Count Walewski then proposed, and the plenipotentiaries unanimously resolved, that complete secrecy should be observed with regard to all the negotiations and transactions that would take place at the conference.

Then the president, having submitted suggestions respecting the order of the proceedings, proposed in the first place that the protocol that had been signed at Vienna on February 1 should constitute the preliminaries of peace, and therefore serve as a fundamental basis for the discussion of the definitive terms. The plenipotentiaries exchanged their views on this point, and agreed.

The first session was concluded by an agreement, on the motion of Count Walewski, establishing an armistice (which has already been referred to); [1] and it was decided to hold the next meeting on February 27.

Austro-Prussian War.

The negotiations arising out of the Austro-Prussian War, 1866,[2] furnish many points of interest, which exemplify or supplement the analysis set forth in the preceding chapters.[3] The interposition of the Emperor Napoleon has already been considered.[4] To the latter's suggestion (July 4) that an armistice should first be concluded, Prussia replied (July 5) that the military position and her pledge to Italy (whereby neither Power could make peace or suspend arms without the consent of the other) made this step impossible, though she was willing to commence peace negotiations. At the same time the Prussian ambassador in Florence informed the Italian Government of the condition of affairs. In the meantime the army pushed on its operations; so that the work of diplomacy had to proceed in the midst of war.

On July 7 the Prussian ambassador in Paris was instructed to declare that an armistice would be agreed to only if a guarantee of the fundamental terms of peace were obtained, and to insist, accordingly, on the similar interests of Prussia and Germany, and on the necessity for the monarchy's leadership in North Germany based on a confederacy of the States concerned. Four days later M. Benedetti, the French ambassador, arrived at King William's headquarters, in order to negotiate a suspension of arms; but the reply made before was repeated. The King of Prussia agreed, however—owing to interruptions in the telegraphic communication—not to attack the Austrian forces for three days, if the latter would evacuate the region north of the Thaya. The Austrian counter-proposals, made on July 14, were declined, on the ground that they contained conditions which would have enabled Austria to bring up reinforcements and so change entirely the military situation.

Meanwhile the Emperor Napoleon drew up and forwarded to the two contending Powers a series of propositions which, he thought, might serve as the basis of the peace conference: "Main-

[1] See *supra*, p. 84.

[2] See *The Campaign of 1866 in Germany*. Compiled by the Department of Military History of the Prussian Staff. English trans. by Colonel Von Wright and Captain H. M. Hozier, 1872; reprinted 1907; pp. 487 *seq.*

[3] Cf. especially Part II, chaps. iii. and iv.

[4] See *supra*, p. 84.

tenance of Austria's integrity, but withdrawal of this Power from Germany, which State was to be reorganized; establishment of a North German Union under the military supremacy of Prussia; right of the South German States to form an independent union, but a bond of nationality to exist between North and South Germany, to be regulated by free and mutual agreement between the German States."[1] Prussia doubted whether these terms would satisfy her requirements regarding the consolidation of her power and the national development of Germany; but she consented to suspend arms for five days, in order that Austria's intentions might be made known. If the latter accepted the said propositions, an armistice convention would be entered into, and the peace conference inaugurated, subject to the sanction of Italy. Owing to the damage done to the telegraph wires, M. Benedetti was obliged to go to Vienna; he returned to Nikolsburg on July 19, reporting Austria's acceptance, whereupon Prussia agreed to suspend hostilities for five days.

On July 21 the Austrian plenipotentiaries arrived at Berlin in order to conclude preliminaries of peace together with an armistice convention. The conference began on the following day, and was conducted by Count Karolyi and Baron Brenner on behalf of Austria, and by Count Bismarck on behalf of Prussia. Negotiations went on till the 26th, when the Preliminaries of Nikolsburg were signed.[2] On the same date Field-Marshal Degenfeld and General Moltke entered into an armistice convention, which has already been given.[3]

Count Barral, the Italian ambassador at Berlin, had been invited to participate in these peace negotiations; but he refused to do so, on the ground that his Government had not provided him with instructions to that effect. In pursuance of a previous treaty engagement with Prussia, Italy's consent was necessary to render valid the latter's conclusion of peace; but she had agreed to recognize the ultimate result of the conferences if the cession of Venetia were assured to her. Furthermore, though peace was brought about through the energetic interposition of France, yet no French representative took part in the conference, as the Emperor Napoleon was unwilling to play the rôle of a mediator in the proper sense of the term, limiting his intervention to the exercise of good offices.

The peace negotiations in the case of the Franco-German War constitute a most important example, presenting many noteworthy

[1] *The Campaign of* 1866, etc., p. 489.

[2] See *infra*, Appendix (G).

[3] See *supra*, p. 65.

features, some of which are of an exceptional character. The proceedings leading to the Preliminaries of Versailles have already been dealt with. Art. VII of this treaty said that "the opening of negotiations for the definitive treaty of peace" should take place at Brussels.[1] The French delegates were Baron Baude, the French minister in Belgium, and M. de Goulard, a member of the National Assembly, who were to be assisted by two commissioners, one civil and the other military. The German plenipotentiaries were Herr von Balan, the German minister in Belgium, and Count von Arnim, to whom were added representatives from the Kingdoms of Bavaria and Würtemberg and the Grand Duchy of Baden. A mixed military commission, too, was appointed for the delimitation of the new frontier. The abovementioned article stipulated that the conference should begin its labours immediately after the ratification of the preliminaries. Though this had been effected by the French National Assembly on March 2, 1871, it was not till the 19th and 24th of that month that the French delegates reached Brussels, the delay being due to the faulty diplomacy of the French Government—which, it may be said on its behalf, had been overburdened by internal troubles and confused by the military disasters that had so rapidly befallen the country.

Franco-German War.

On March 28 the first meeting of the conference took place.[2] This was devoted, as is usual, to purely formal matters, such as the exchange and verification of the full powers. The very next meetings at once showed that the work of negotiation would proceed under extraordinary difficulties. The methods adopted—if they can properly be called methods at all—were markedly unbusinesslike. The German plenipotentiaries were determined to exact the last ounce that could be squeezed out of the preliminaries; indeed, they were not always very scrupulous as to whether their various exactions were juridically and equitably compatible with those preliminaries. They were opposed to all suggestions that savoured of compromise, and refused to make any concessions even in details. They disregarded the customary procedure, whereby differences of views and partial agreements are recorded in the *procès-verbaux* or the protocols; they had recourse to the latter only when they succeeded in enforcing agreement or acquiescence in regard to the definite and final drafting of an article. They seem to have adopted, too, the practice of producing a number of propositions on diverse subjects at the same time, regardless of order, system, or intelligible classification; such a course could not but increase the difficulties with which the French delegates had to contend.

[1] See *infra*, Appendix (J).

[2] Cf. May, *Le traité de Francfort*, pp. 46 *seq.*

Throughout the discussions the French negotiators were no match for their opponents. Several reasons may be given for this inequality. In the first place, the latter had the moral and physical support of their military victories; their troops were still on French territory, and might, at the word of command, renew their havoc against a vanquished and well-nigh helpless nation. Their verbal arguments had therefore the sanction of force behind them. They were in a position to dictate terms, and not in the humour to submit to suggested amendments thereto. They more than once threatened to break off negotiations. There are few men who, in the position of the French representatives, would not have been disheartened by the vision of the dire consequences which such threat entailed. Secondly, the French delegates were intrinsically inferior; they had had little diplomatic experience and were manifestly deficient in those qualities that are indispensable in the work of negotiation—dexterity, penetration, decision.[1] Thirdly, they found themselves at a great disadvantage, in that they had received no instructions from their Government, preoccupied as it was with the internal disorders of France. "Si étrange que cela soit," observes an authoritative historian of the Treaty of Frankfort, "il paraît qu'ils n'avaient pas d'instructions. En vain, dans l'intervalle qui s'écoula entre l'arrivée de M. Thiers à Paris et l'insurrection du 18 mars, notre premier plénipotentiaire chercha-t-il à se rendre compte de la pensée du chef de l'État, et le provoqua-t-il à la lui faire connaître, sinon par écrit au moins verbalement; on assure qu'il n'y réussit pas. Préoccupé dans la mesure qu'on sait par les événements intérieurs, M. Thiers le laissa partir pour son poste sans lui dire un mot sur les graves questions qu'il allait avoir à traiter. En revanche, il n'est pas inutile de faire remarquer que M. le Comte d'Arnim, le principal plénipotentiaire allemand, avait assisté, le 14 et le 15 mars, avant son départ pour Bruxelles, à deux conseils de ministres, dans lesquels toutes les stipulations importantes de la paix définitive avaient été examinées et arrêtées, ainsi que les instructions dont il convenait de le pourvoir."[2] It appears[3] that the French plenipotentiaries at Brussels had received only one precise instruction, viz. to claim a plebiscite for the population of Alsace-Lorraine.[4]

In these circumstances the negotiations at the Brussels Conference dragged on throughout April. The impatience and exacer-

[1] Cf. May, *op. cit.*, p. 44.

[2] J. Valfrey, *Histoire du traité de Francfort et de la libération du territoire français* (Paris, 1874), Part I, pp. 17, 18; who refers to W. Müller, *Politische Geschichte der Gegenwart*, vol. v. p. 147: "Graf Arnim wohnte am 14 und 15 Maerz den Sitzungen der Staatsministeriums in Berlin bei und holte dort seine Instructionen."

[3] Valfrey, *op. cit.*, p. 38.

[4] As to plebiscite, see *infra*, pp. 282 *seq.*

bation of the German Government grew from day to day. France was accused of resorting to dilatory tactics deliberately, for the purpose of securing alterations in the preliminaries. On April 24 Bismarck made an open charge to that effect in the Reichstag; and a few days later (May 4) the Conference of Brussels was broken off. Bismarck and Favre agreed to meet personally at Frankfort-on-the-Main on May 6.

The principal subjects of discussion had related to the questions of the indemnity and its mode of payment, the public debt of the territory to be ceded, and the damages for losses inflicted by French warships on German commerce—and this despite the fact that international law sanctions maritime capture and, in certain circumstances, destruction of enemy vessels without making compensation. Though all these questions had not been definitely settled at Brussels, the Conference there had at least prepared the way for an understanding, by showing clearly the reciprocal claims of the contending parties and to what extent they might be regarded as irreducible.[1]

At Frankfort the French plenipotentiaries were M. Favre, the Minister for Foreign Affairs, M. de Goulard (as before), and M. Pouyer-Quertier, the Minister of Finance, added for this occasion; the German representatives were Bismarck and Count von Arnim. In four days, May 7, 8, 9, and 10, they completed their negotiations, put together the definitive treaty, and signed it.[2]

Italian-Abyssinian War.

In the case of the war between Italy and Abyssinia, 1896, peace negotiations were begun with remarkable suddenness. On March 1 the Italian army suffered a great reverse at Adoua, where out of 17,000 men more than a half were lost. On the very next day Signor Crispi made overtures for peace, and resigned immediately afterwards. On March 8 a formal order was given to General Baldissera to enter on discussion with the enemy and procure the best terms he could for the security of the Italian colony and the dignity of Italy. On March 12 pourparlers were actually begun by Major Salsa, a delegate of General Baldissera.

An understanding was soon arrived at with regard to the question of frontiers, the abrogation of the Treaty of Uccialli, 1889, and the abandonment of Italian claims to the protectorate over Abyssinia. But Menelek insisted on the payment of a war indemnity, and refused to restore the large number of Italian prisoners of war unless this was done and until the matters in dispute were satisfactorily settled by a definitive treaty. With

[1] May, *op. cit.*, p. 48.

[2] See *infra*, Appendix (K).

this object in view he kept the negotiator, Major Salsa, as a hostage.

Shortly afterwards a decree of the King of Italy (dated June 18, 1896) ordered the cessation of the state of war in Eritrea; and then Major Nerazzini was directed to prepare the way for General Valles, the special envoy of the Italian Government.

An interesting feature of the negotiations is the appeal made by the Pope, Leo XIII, to the Abyssinian ruler on behalf of the Italian prisoners. Sometimes arrangements are made in the preliminaries (as, for example, in the case of the Franco-German War) for the mutual restoration of prisoners of war; sometimes they are reserved for the definitive treaty. Having regard to the peculiar conditions and hardships attending captivity in Abyssinia, the Pope begged Menelek to liberate the Italian prisoners without imposing any delay. In a letter dated Rome, May 11, 1896, he first referred to the King's courtesies shown on the occasion of the commencement of his pontificate and on that of his sacerdotal jubilee, and then appealed to him as a monarch and a Christian to perform an act of sovereign generosity. Victory had left in his hands numerous prisoners; but their captivity did not augment the extent of his power or prestige, rather the sorrow of thousands of innocent mothers and wives. He was implored, therefore, in the name of the Divine Trinity and the Blessed Virgin, in the name of all that was dearest to him in the world, to restore them to liberty. "Do not refuse, most powerful Negus Neghest, to show yourself magnanimous in the eyes of the nations," exclaimed the Holy Father, who concluded by praying for the welfare of the royal family. On October 1, 1896, a reply was sent by "the conquering Lion of the tribe of Judah, elect of God, King of the Kings of Ethiopia," in which he referred to the moving appeal for mercy, and observed that his first impulse was to accede to it. He deplored the many innocent victims of the cruel war, which he had not provoked. But the strange attitude of the Italian Government, which, after expressing a desire for peace, yet continued to act as in a state of war, made it impossible for him to liberate the prisoners. His duty as king and father of his people forbade him, in these circumstances, to sacrifice the sole guarantee of peace that was in his hands; so that he was obliged to defer to a more fitting time proof of his esteem and affection for the Holy Father. Moreover, he expressed a hope that the latter's voice would be raised on behalf of the justice of his cause and the independence of his people; and he concluded by assuring the Pope that the prisoners were being treated in accordance with the obligations of Christian charity.

In the meantime, however, negotiations went on, which proved successful; and on October 26 the treaty of peace, drawn up in French and in the Amharic tongue, was signed at Addis-Abeba The news was telegraphed by Menelek to King Humbert.

Spanish-American War.

The negotiations in the war between the United States and Spain have already been considered to the date August 12, 1898, when the protocol of peace was signed and the good offices of France came to an end.[1] We have now to glance at the proceedings in the conference chamber, where the definitive treaty was concluded.[2]

On August 26 President McKinley appointed the following as the American peace commissioners: William R. Day, Secretary of State; Senator Davis, the Chairman of the Senate Foreign Affairs Committee; Senator Frye; Whitelaw Reid, the former ambassador to France; and Mr. Justice White, a judge of the Supreme Court. The last-mentioned nominee declining to serve was replaced by Senator Gray. The Spanish plenipotentiaries were: Señor Montero Rios, the President of the Spanish Senate; Señor de Abarzuza, a senator and the former ambassador to France; Señor de Garnica, a judge of the Supreme Court; General Rafael Cerero; and Señor de Villa-Urrutia, minister to Belgium. The first-named in each case acted as the chairman and leader of his commission.

As previously arranged, the delegates met in Paris, at the Foreign Office, on October 1. The rule as to the secrecy of the proceedings was agreed to and—unlike the case of the Portsmouth Conference, 1905—was observed throughout. In the first place, the Spanish representatives requested the liberation of Spanish prisoners of war; and, in view of the insurrection in the Philippines, asked to be allowed to send reinforcements there as the troops already stationed in the islands were insufficient to cope with the rebellion. The United States opposed the latter demand on the ground that the despatch of such forces would be incompatible with the maintenance of the *status quo*, which was a corollary of the cessation of hostilities as laid down in the protocol of peace. The American Government, however, had sent at the end of September several thousand men to reinforce General Otis. Despite the strictures of some critics, the position taken up by the United States on this question was justifiable. It is true that the Philippines had not yet been formally ceded, but there was no doubt about their fate; and

[1] See *supra*, p. 88.

[2] Cf. the account of L. Le Fur, *La guerre hispano-américaine de* 1898 *envisagée au point de vue du droit international public* (Paris, 1899), pp. 254 *seq*. The author gives a brief analysis of the documents published in the Spanish *Red Book*; but he betrays here and there prejudice against the United States.

had considerable Spanish forces been permitted to land, complications might well have arisen endangering the armistice and the conclusion of peace.

At the second meeting, on October 3, the American commissioners declined to discuss this demand, maintaining that it was beyond the powers of the peace commission to settle it. Then they presented their claims in accordance with Arts. I and II of the protocol of peace of August 12, viz. the abandonment by Spain of all rights of sovereignty over and property in Cuba, the cession of Porto Rico and her other islands in the West Indies, together with one of the Ladrones to be chosen by the United States—Guam being now selected.

On October 7 the Spanish delegates submitted a counter-proposal offering to cede the West Indian islands, and to transfer Cuba to the United States on condition that the latter would retransfer it to the Cubans, and in any case assume all the rights and obligations relative to it. This proposal was rejected (October 11) by the American commissioners,[1] who again demanded the cession of Guam and the unconditional relinquishment of Cuba. Spain was at the time in financial difficulties, and therefore she was anxious to be liberated from the so-called Cuban debt which she had contracted in the administration—one can truly say maladministration—of the island's affairs. Accordingly her plenipotentiaries advanced an elaborate argument claiming that the cession of sovereignty necessarily implied, under international law and practice, the transfer of all prerogatives, powers, rights, together with all the reciprocal charges and obligations, and that it would be unjust for a sovereign to lose his rights over a territory and its inhabitants and still remain liable to obligations incurred in the interests of their régime and government. The American reply pointed out that it was a fallacy to regard the liabilities incurred by a sovereign in the exercise of his sovereignty as a part of the sovereignty itself. Moreover, the finances of Cuba were under the exclusive control of the Spanish Government, and the debt was not created by Cuba itself or by its people; it was neither a local debt nor contracted for the benefit of Cuba, which had no voice in its creation.[2] The Spanish rejoinder was made at considerable length;[3] and the American answer thereto at still greater length, in which it was emphasized that most of the debt was incurred for the purpose of supporting a Spanish army in Cuba, and that the bonds were guaranteed by Spain.[4] The closing

[1] Cf. *Senate Documents of the United States*, 62, 55th Cong., 3 sess., part ii. pp. 22 *seq.*; Moore, *Digest*, vol. i. pp. 351–352.

[2] *Ibid.*, pp. 48–53; *ibid.*, pp. 356–360.

[3] Moore, *Digest*, vol. i. pp. 360–367.

[4] *Ibid.*, pp. 367–377.

argument of the Spanish commissioners contradicted various statements of the American representatives.[1] The discussion on the Cuban debt continued till October 14, when the difference of views seemed likely to put an end to the conference, and bring about a resumption of hostilities. To avoid this eventuality, the ambassadors of the two States at Paris endeavoured to effect an accommodation; but their interviews were without success. Then the Spanish Government requested that the meetings of the peace conference should be suspended for a time in order that its commissioners might be enabled to present a scheme suggesting certain compensation in lieu of the claims relating to the Cuban debt.

The question of the Philippines came up at the meeting of October 31. Art. III of the preliminary protocol of August 12 simply said that the "control, disposition, and government" of these islands were to be determined at the peace conference. (It appears that the word "possession" was used in the original draft of the instrument; but at the suggestion of M. Cambon "disposition" was substituted for it, as a word less offensive to Spanish susceptibilities.) President McKinley now directed the American delegates to demand the cession of the whole archipelago. This demand cannot be said to be incompatible with the said article, which Spain in the first instance accepted, knowing full well that such might be the fate of the islands. She could then have insisted on a clearer formulation of the provision, and it is very doubtful whether she would have continued a war so disastrous to her rather than agree there and then to the cession of the Philippines. If the United States Government had this cession in view at the time, it would certainly have been more regular to specify it in the protocol. This would have saved much discussion and recrimination. As it was, the Spanish plenipotentiaries protested against the demand of the American delegates. The latter persisted, and offered compensation. The Spanish Government then asked for an adjournment of the sittings, so that it might have an opportunity to consider the question.

On November 4 the twelfth meeting of the conference took place, when the Spanish Commission submitted a counter-proposal as to the Philippines, and urged that the matter should be settled in accordance with Art. III of the protocol of peace. (As we have already seen, it is difficult, indeed impossible, to say that the said article offered any definite guidance.) The counter-proposal was, however, rejected, and the cession of the whole archipelago was demanded. The conference thus found itself in an *impasse* with regard to the interpretation and purport of Art. III. The Spanish

[1] Moore, *Digest*, vol. i. pp. 377–380.

commissioners, receiving instructions from Madrid, offered to refer the point to arbitration, as they had done also in the case of the Cuban debt. But the reply given was a categorical refusal: "The commissioners of the United States and Spain have met for the purpose of concluding a treaty which is to terminate a war. The matters involved in this transaction are matters for mutual adjustment and definitive settlement. They are matters to be determined by the parties themselves. Arbitration comes before war, to avert its evils—not after war, to escape its results."[1] Thereupon the Spanish representatives asked for another suspension of the sittings, in order that they might be able to communicate with their Government.

The United States plenipotentiaries were now (November 21—the fifteenth meeting) becoming impatient owing to these repeated dilatory methods, and fixed November 28 as the last day for notifying acceptance of their proposals, including an offer of 20 million dollars by way of compensation. The precise object of this pecuniary offer is not clear; some of the American commissioners appear to have deemed the sum a consideration for the transfer of the Philippines, thus making the transaction practically a sale; but in the view of Mr. Whitelaw Reid it amounted to a payment on account of the Philippine debt.[2] Neither in the conference nor in the definitive treaty was any reason for such payment specified. As a special concession, the United States Government undertook to permit Spanish vessels and merchandise for a period of ten years to enter Philippine ports on equal terms with American traders. The Spanish Government, however, thought the sum inadequate, and so made another effort to secure better terms, but failed; therefore it decided to yield. On November 25 it despatched a telegram to its representatives, saying that it was useless to prolong resistance, and advising them to submit to the American demands under strong protest.

Certain additional demands were made by the United States, viz. the cession of the island of Kusaye in the Carolines, the right to place a submarine cable in Spanish territory, the renewal of certain treaties, the granting of religious liberty to the inhabitants of the Caroline Islands; but these were gradually withdrawn through the persistent opposition of the Spanish plenipotentiaries.

By December 5—the nineteenth sitting—the first eight articles of the treaty of peace were definitely established; and soon afterwards the other nine articles, less important than the former, were also adopted.

[1] Moore, *Digest*, vol. i. p. 373.

[2] See *infra*, p. 280, for observations on this point made by Mr. Day, the Secretary of State, Senator Gray, and Mr. Whitelaw Reid.

When the conference was drawing to a conclusion an untoward incident occurred. President McKinley, speaking in his message (December 7) of the successful issue of the war, referred to the maladministration of Cuba, and to the suspicious character of the explosion of *The Maine* in Havana harbour (which had occurred shortly before the declaration of war). These observations naturally offended the sensibilities of Spain, which was particularly indignant at the allusion to *The Maine*, on the ground that the implied allegations had never been proved. Moreover, it was ungenerous to recall the affair at the end of a war in which Spain had been severely defeated, and at a moment just before the signing of the definitive treaty of peace. As soon as a report of the message was received in Spain, her delegates were instructed to propose a fresh inquiry as to the explosion of the vessel, or failing this, a reference to arbitration; but the United States refused.

The twenty-second and final sitting took place on December 10. After the American commissioners presented a memorandum traversing some of the Spanish assertions, the treaty of peace was signed,[1] and the labours of the conference ended.

Russo-Japanese War.

With regard to the Russo-Japanese War,[2] the first steps in the peace negotiation, due to the interposition of President Roosevelt, have already been considered.[3] We have seen, too, that there were no preliminaries of peace;[4] so that the first meetings of the conference at Portsmouth were awaited everywhere with great excitement. Japan, the victorious party, had not previously disclosed her demands.

On August 9, 1905, the first session of the conference took place, two plenipotentiaries being present on each side. (In the Paris Conference, 1898, there were five on each side; it is obvious that the number does not necessarily depend on the importance of the occasion or the serious nature of the issues involved.) As usual, the opening meeting was devoted to the exchange of civilities and to the performance of various preliminary formalities. It is noteworthy that at the inauguration of the conference there was an impression in many quarters that its labours would prove unsuccessful. The correspondent of the London *Times*, for example, stated more than once that it was doomed to failure. Though the conference was pledged to the observance of secrecy, the Press—notably that of the United States—managed to obtain in the course of the negotiations a good deal of information.

[1] See *infra*, Appendix (S).

[2] Cf. A. S. Hershey, *International Law and Diplomacy of the Russo-Japanese War* (New York, 1906), pp. 347–355.

[3] See *supra*, pp. 89 *seq*.

[4] See *supra*, p. 94.

At the second meeting, held on the following day, the plenipotentiaries exchanged their full powers, which were verified and found to be in due form. Then Baron Komura presented to the Russian delegates a document specifying twelve conditions of peace demanded by the Japanese Government: (1) Russia to recognize Japan's paramount interests in Korea; (2) Russia to evacuate Manchuria and renounce all advantages and concessions therein incompatible with Chinese sovereignty or with the principle of equal opportunity; (3) Japan to restore to Manchuria the places occupied by her save those affected by the lease of the Liao-tung Peninsula; (4) neither side to obstruct any general measures which China may take for developing the commerce and industries of Manchuria; (5) Russia to cede Sakhalin to Japan; (6) Russia to transfer to Japan her leases of the Liao-tung Peninsula, including Port Arthur and Talien (Dalny); (7) Russia to transfer to Japan the section of the Southern Manchurian Railway (together with its branches) connecting Harbin with Port Arthur, as well as all the coal-mines appertaining thereto; (8) Russia to maintain the main line of the Chinese Eastern or Trans-Manchurian Railway, provided it be used only for purposes of commerce and industry; (9) Russia to pay Japan her costs of the war (the amount was not stated, but it was estimated variously at from 100 to 200 million pounds; (10) Russia to surrender to Japan all Russian warships interned in neutral ports during the war; (11) Russia to limit her naval forces in the Far East, in order to secure what Japan described as the "permanent peace of the Far East"; (12) Russia to grant Japanese subjects certain fishing rights on the Siberian coast.

The reply of the Russian plenipotentiaries was returned without delay, at the next meeting (August 12); of the above twelve conditions four, viz. the fifth, ninth, tenth, and eleventh, were categorically rejected. Baron Komura thereupon suggested that these points should be discussed, one by one, in order to facilitate agreement. But the Russian delegates, M. Witte and Baron Rosen, refused to yield so far as these four demands were concerned; they expressed their readiness to come to an understanding on every point that might be considered a *casus belli*, but declined to make other concessions. It may be truly said that the very *raison d'être* of a peace conference is, logically, a desire on the part of the contending States to settle those differences that gave rise to the war. Logical grounds, however, are always held subservient to political; a party victorious in war is ever ready to make additional demands relative to other outstanding difficulties, and not infrequently is disposed to exact further terms that have no relation whatever to the causes of the war or to any previous differences. Neither international law nor international practice furnishes any rule or authoritative precedent on this question, which is one to be solved by the parties concerned.

With regard to condition No. 5, requiring the cession of Sakhalin, the Japanese supported their demand on various grounds: that the island formerly belonged to them, that the fortunes of the war had placed it into their hands, and that the principle of *uti possidetis*, being therefore applicable, was in their favour.[1] It is clear here, however, that the question of the former proprietorship of the island was scarcely relevant, and that the principle of *uti possidetis* can apply to militarily occupied or conquered territory only with the assent or acquiescence of the dispossessed State. A political consideration was urged by the Russian envoys: the island, which they described as the sentinel at their gate, was a defence to Siberia; to cede it would be virtually to turn the Sea of Japan and the Sea of Okhotsk into a Japanese lake.

As to No. 9, Japan had avoided the expression "indemnity" as being offensive to the dignity of a great Power, and merely asked for reimbursement of expenses due to the war. In reply, M. Witte is reported to have observed: "We will pay you what you have expended to do us good—all your outlays for maintaining prisoners, and any expense of that nature which you will define to us. But for what you have spent to do us evil—not a kopeck."

The surrender by Russia of her warships interned in neutral ports—No. 10—was claimed by her representatives to be contrary to international usage. But a victorious State cannot be said to be acting illegally if it insists on such a condition.

Finally, as to No. 11—the limitation of her naval forces in the Far East—Russia naturally objected that a concession of this kind would be humiliating to her, and derogatory to her honour and dignity. She remembered the neutralization of the Black Sea by the Treaty of Paris, 1856, and the restrictions that had been imposed on her by Art. XIII regarding the maintenance or establishment of maritime and military arsenals on its coasts; she remembered, too, how she seized the first occasion that presented itself, in 1870, and liberated herself from the limitations placed on her freedom. By way of effecting a compromise with regard to the eleventh condition, M. Witte offered to make a formal declaration that his Government had no present intention to augment her fleet in Eastern waters.

After some discussion the Japanese envoys consented to waive demands No. 10 and No. 11, but they were bent on the other two

[1] As to the application of this principle, see *infra*, p. 221.

so strongly opposed by the other side, viz. No. 5, as to the cession of Sakhalin, and No. 9, as to the payment of indemnity. It was at this juncture, when the conference seemed likely to come to an end, that President Roosevelt intervened once more. He had an interview with Baron Rosen and also, it was said, with Baron Kaneko, described as the "unofficial agent of the Mikado." What occurred has not been revealed; the result was, however, that Japan undertook to waive No. 9 in addition to Nos. 10 and 11, and to *sell* the northern half of Sakhalin to Russia. But the Russian commissioners at once objected that this proposal amounted, in a disguised form, to the payment of an indemnity, and against this they made a determined stand. President Roosevelt then adopted his former successful tactics, and appealed to the Czar;[1] the latter, however, agreed at most to a division of the island between the two Powers.

The sittings of the conference now became very irregular. On August 26 the Russian representatives brought forward a proposal, which assumed the form of an Imperial ultimatum, offering to pay Japan 100 million roubles for the costs incurred on behalf of the Russian prisoners of war, and also to cede half of Sakhalin. Baron Komura and M. Takahira rejected the offer, but suggested that another meeting should be held to give them an opportunity of submitting modified terms which might prove satisfactory. Mr. Roosevelt now appealed direct to Tokio. Whatever influences prevailed is not known; but Japan showed herself to be conciliatory, a friend of peace, and a generous opponent. On August 29, Baron Komura, in accordance with instructions received from the Mikado, who had conferred with the "Gosen-Kaigi" (that is, the council before the throne, comprising the elder statesmen and the members of the cabinet), formally withdrew the demands for indemnity of any kind, and agreed to the division of Sakhalin. The last few days of the conference passed smoothly, and the definitive treaty was signed on September 5, 1905.[2]

The concessions made by Japan, and notably her renunciation of indemnity for war expenses, which indeed exceeded 120 million pounds, called forth widespread applause; even the Russians praised her "magnanimity in diplomacy" and her "moral victory," and said it was as "worthy as her heroic victory in the war." On the other hand, in Japan the treaty was denounced; many sections of the Press declared that "the fruits of victory were again nullified by weak diplomacy, and by ill-counsels of the cabinet ministers and the elder statesmen who gave advice to the Emperor." There were riots at Tokio, which was placed under martial law. At Kobe the

[1] Cf. *supra*, p. 90. [2] See *infra*, Appendix (U).

statue of Marquis Ito, one of the elder statesmen, was pulled down and dragged through the streets.[1] However this may be, and whatever failings Japan betrayed in diplomacy, the world recognized that the war left her with a most honourable position by the side of the Great Powers. Sometimes it is more blessed to be outwitted in diplomacy by an opponent than to get the better of him.

Our last example of peace negotiations shall be taken from the second Balkan War, 1913; several points of special interest will be found here, together with many apt illustrations of our previous analysis.[2]

Second Balkan War.

In more than one case have we seen a victorious belligerent refusing to grant a suspension of arms for the purpose of instituting peace overtures, unless the preliminaries of peace were at first established or, at all events, unless the fundamental conditions were definitely guaranteed. This happened also in the present instance. The heads of the allied Governments, viz. Serbia, Greece, and Montenegro, met at Nish, July 4 / 17, and determined not to enter into an armistice convention with Bulgaria without previously, or at the same time, concluding the preliminaries of peace.

The Roumanian army was now advancing to join the three allies against the common enemy, so that the complete downfall of Bulgaria seemed certain. Thereupon King Ferdinand made an urgent appeal to the Emperor of Austria, begging him to save his country and his dynasty, and intervene to stay the march of the Roumanian army. The Emperor Francis Joseph replied that the unfortunate position of Bulgaria was due to the short-sighted policy of her ruler, who had for several months been offered in vain counsels of moderation; the best course to adopt in the existing circumstances was to approach King Carol of Roumania, suggesting a frontier rectification whereby the latter would secure the line Turtucaia–Dobritch–Baltchik, and inquiring on what terms he would put a stop to his military actions, and remain neutral.

King Carol, having received a telegraphic despatch to this effect, replied, July 5 / 18, that the Roumanian demands were well known, viz. first, the frontier Turtucaia–Baltchik; and secondly, participation in the peace negotiations, in order to impart greater stability to the Balkan equilibrium. Further telegrams were exchanged; but King Carol refused to withdraw his army to the left bank of the Danube,

[1] Cf. S. G. Hishida, *The International Position of Japan* (*Columbia College. Studies*, vol. xxiv. No. 3 (1905)); *in fin.*

[2] For the account of the negotiations the writer is indebted mainly to B. Stambler, *Les Roumains et les Bulgares* (Paris, 1914), pp. 140 *seq.*

as requested, and declared that it was advanced with the object of accelerating the conclusion of peace between all the belligerents. On July 8 / 21, the Roumanian sovereign received a conciliatory communication from King Ferdinand, who expressed his readiness to establish peace if Greece and Serbia were disposed to do the same. At the same time M. Maïoresco, the Roumanian minister for foreign affairs, was informed that Bulgaria accepted the terms above mentioned.

M. Maïoresco, in his reply, drew a distinction between military pourparlers and political discussions. With regard to the former, Roumania was prepared to send a representative to any place agreed upon by Bulgaria, Serbia, and Greece, in order to conclude an armistice convention ; but as to the latter, Bucharest was suggested as the most appropriate place for negotiating the preliminaries of peace. He communicated the Bulgarian proposals and his own suggestion to the Serbian and the Greek Governments, who accepted them in principle, but pointed out that the military pourparlers at Nish—the place chosen—might end satisfactorily, whilst the diplomatic negotiations at Bucharest might be protracted or fall through ; and he insisted that it was essential not to separate the armistice convention from the preliminaries of peace.

During the exchange of these messages the war still went on ; on one occasion the Bulgarian forces made a determined attack on the Serbian and the Greek troops, but met with a severe reverse. Moreover, Sofia was already experiencing the hardships of a siege. Accordingly, Ferdinand sent another telegram to King Carol, July 11 / 24, entreating him to approach the monarchs of Serbia, Greece, and Montenegro with a view to terminating hostilities without delay. The following day Bulgarian delegates were appointed, and were declared to be ready to proceed with full powers to the conference. Then the Roumanian army was ordered to advance no farther. At this point, too, Austria and Italy intervened, and pointed out to Greece and Serbia that the conclusion of an armistice ought no longer to be retarded. On July 13 / 26 the names of the plenipotentiaries of all the States concerned were made known.[1] Those of Roumania were, in these circumstances, to play the part of mediators and moderators between the victors and the vanquished, and at the same time safeguard the interests of their own country.

The Bucharest Congress appears to have had a stormy inception. " Most of the delegates," observes Dr. Dillon, who was in Bucharest at the time, " arrived in Roumania on July 27 ; and hardly were they conveyed to their hotels when a fierce newspaper

[1] See *infra*, Appendix (X) *in init.*

war broke out among them, endangering the success of the conference before the first sitting. Interview followed interview in quick succession, and indictments were hurled by one peace delegate at another with a degree of rancour which, considering its source, was noteworthy." [1]

On July 30 the peace conference opened at the Foreign Office, under the presidency of M. Maïoresco. After the preliminary formalities, presentations, and delivery of the full powers, the latter suggested that the presidency of the conference should be taken in turn by the first plenipotentiary of each State; but M. Pasitch, head of the Serbian delegation, thought that it was more desirable to have one permanent president, and proposed M. Maïoresco for the office. This proposal having been unanimously adopted, the Roumanian foreign secretary took the chair and addressed the assembly in the following terms: "Gentlemen! My first and most agreeable duty is to welcome you here in the name of the King, my august sovereign, and to thank you for the kind reception you gave to the proposal to come to Roumania and endeavour to settle serious questions, which will have a decisive influence on the future of the States represented at this conference. I am convinced that we are all animated by the desire to bring to a successful issue the work for which we have assembled, and to assure—either by preliminary conventions or by a definitive treaty—to the Christian peoples who are still at grips on the field of battle, a lasting peace, based on a proper equilibrium between our States. It would augur well for the accomplishment of our mission if we could, at the very first sitting, agree on a most urgent and important preliminary measure, namely, a suspension of arms. . . . I believe I am fulfilling a duty of humanity in proposing to you a suspension of arms for at least five days."

M. Venizelos, the head of the Greek delegation, replied: "In the name of the delegations of the Allied States, I thank His Excellency the President for the welcome extended to us. I beg him to ask His Majesty the King to accept the assurance of our deep gratitude for the hospitality offered to us." He then went on to support the suggestion for the suspension of hostilities, which was approved by all. After the Bulgarian envoy had said a few words, the sitting was adjourned for a short time to enable the appointed military representatives, over whom General Coanda of Roumania presided, to consider the question of an armistice. Their deliberations met with no difficulty, and a protocol was drawn up embodying terms for a five days' truce. Then the conference was resumed, and the agreement sanctioned; copies were handed to the heads of

[1] E. J. Dillon, in *Contemporary Review*, September 1913, p. 416.

the missions, who telegraphed their contents to their respective military headquarters.

This done, the personal relations between the delegates became more friendly. In the evening of the very first sitting the Bulgarian plenipotentiaries paid private visits to the Greek and Serbian envoys. Informal meetings of this kind proved to be most advantageous; with a better mutual understanding, the delegates felt more disposed to enter into free and amicable discussion of knotty questions and make reciprocal concessions, so that the task of the plenary conference was enormously facilitated. The practice, indeed, received formal recognition; for at the second meeting, July 18 / 31, on the proposal of the president, the delegates agreed to group themselves according to the nature of the interests in dispute, to discuss the relevant matters privately, report solutions arrived at to the full conference, and reserve divergent views to be threshed out in the council chamber. Thus at the very outset, and without any discussion in conference, Roumania obtained the strategic line Turtukaia–Dobritch–Baltchik, together with a territory of 10 to 15 kilometres to the west and to the south; the establishment of a neutral zone without fortifications; that the fortresses of Rustchuk and Schumla should be dismantled; and that the Roumanians of Macedonia should be granted religious freedom.

Similarly, on July 19 / August 1 the delegates of Greece and Serbia held a private meeting with those of Bulgaria. The proposal submitted to the latter was to this effect: (1) The territories claimed by Greece and Serbia under the form of a *condominium* should be bounded on the east by the Struma. On the Ægean Sea the Bulgarian frontier should be about 20 kilometres from the west of Dedeagatch. The frontier starting from this point should reach the Strumnitsa, a tributary of the Struma. Thus the territory claimed by Greece and Serbia comprised almost the whole of Macedonia. On the Ægean Sea the Bulgarians were to retain only Dedeagatch. (2) No war indemnity to be demanded from Bulgaria; only a certain compensation for damage done in places belonging to Greece and Serbia. (3) The former Serbo-Bulgarian frontier to be definitely regulated. (4) Greeks inhabiting Bulgarian Thrace to enjoy religious freedom.

The Bulgarian plenipotentiaries at once reported these demands to their Government, and asked for instructions. The following day they received the following counter-proposals, which were forthwith submitted to the Greek and Serbian delegates at a private meeting: (1) The frontier to begin from the existing Serbo-Bulgarian frontier at Badovnica, follow the left bank of the Vardar at a certain distance; the towns of Kratovo, Kotchana, Ishtip and Strumnitsa, and Ghevgheli to remain to Bulgaria. From Ghevgheli the boundary was to end at the Gulf of Orphanic, Bulgaria retaining this port as well as Kavala, Porto Lagoi, and the rest of the littoral of the Ægean Sea. (2) No indemnity or damages to be paid. (3) Serbians and Greeks inhabiting Bulgarian territory to enjoy religious liberty, on the basis of reciprocity.

On July 22 / August 4 the president announced to the conference the Bulgaro-Roumanian agreement, and proposed an extension of the armistice for three days, which was agreed to. The disposition of Kavala proved to be the thorniest point; the difficulty was increased when Austria declared that whatever decision thereon the conference might reach she claimed the right to revise it. On August 5 occurred the strange incident to which we have already referred, arising out of a misunderstanding as to the armistice.[1] The same day the president read a note from the American Government expressing a desire that the definitive treaty should provide full liberty and civil and religious rights to the inhabitants of such territory as might be ceded or annexed. The president observed that the law of every State taking part in the conference prescribed such liberty, and all the delegates agreed that it would be superfluous to insert in the treaty a stipulation on the subject.[2] The following morning there was another interposition, this time on the part of Great Britain and Russia, whose ministers saw the president and declared that their Governments reserved the right to revise, conjointly with the other Powers, the treaty of peace ultimately arrived at. The same day saw a heated discussion between the Bulgarian and Greek delegations at a private meeting; eventually a partial agreement was reached. At the official sitting in the afternoon the Serbian representatives reported their successful negotiation with the Bulgarian. Then the first plenipotentiary of Montenegro read a memorandum stating the claims of his Government; he pointed out the heroic part played by his country in the recent wars, the services it rendered to the Allies in their conflict with Turkey, and therefore claimed such territorial concessions as would allow it to develop more freely.

On August 7 M. Pasitch informed the conference that the Serbo-Bulgarian agreement as to the new frontier was complete. The president, expressing the great satisfaction of the assembly, said that an understanding between the Greek and Bulgarian representatives yet remained to be established, and appealed to them to effect a compromise by sacrificing minor details in the interests of general peace. The sitting was then suspended for an hour, to give those

[1] See *supra*, p. 62. [2] Cf. *Annual Register* (1913), p. 352.

representatives another opportunity to settle their difference. This was a critical moment for the conference. On reassembling, however, the president announced that peace could be considered certain. It appears that King Carol had asked the German Emperor to use his influence with King Constantine of Greece and induce him to compromise on the question of Kavala. Accordingly, M. Venizelos was authorized to consent to a partition of this territory; and so the most difficult problem of the conference was solved.

At the meeting the following day certain Greek proposals regarding compensation for damage to property situated in the theatre of war, and also as to questions of religion, were discussed, but without success. The conference now began to consider the drafting of the articles of the treaty; and at this point the president laid before the assembly the notes he had received on August 4 and August 6 from Austria and Russia respectively. The delegates were undoubtedly aware that the Balkan affairs they were labouring to adjust concerned not only their own countries, but Europe at large. They therefore felt some misgiving as to whether the instrument they were to draw up would be final. Several of them clearly recognized that it could only be a provisional one, and hence suggested that it should begin with a preamble stating that the treaty was subject to the approval of the Great Powers, and to any territorial modifications made by them. The Roumanian delegates, it appears, objected to this suggestion, and insisted on the conclusion of a definitive treaty that should not require additional sanction.[1]

The sittings of August 9 and 10 were devoted to the drafting of the treaty. When this task was completed, M. Venizelos paid a tribute to the president, who replied. Then—and finally—followed the signing.[2] The ratifications were exchanged on August 30.

[1] Cf. E. J. Dillon, in *Contemporary Review*, September 1913, pp. 421–422.

[2] See *infra*, Appendix (X).

CHAPTER VI

THE TREATY OF PEACE

GENERAL PRINCIPLES

Treaty-making Power—Nature of Treaties of Peace, their binding force—Form and Parts—Language—Interpretation

Competence to conclude treaties—Negotiations with a revolutionary Government —Whether the head of the State, if taken prisoner, can bind his country —Binding force: effect of duress—Treaty of peace as a "real" treaty: a compromise—Form of treaty: number of copies; preamble; former invocation; designation of the plenipotentiaries; clause as to ratification; concluding formula—Language used—Use of the *alternat*—Various parts of a treaty of peace: general, special, miscellaneous, secret, additional articles; order of clauses suggested—Interpretation: arbitration clause.

In the previous chapters we have dealt with the various steps in peace negotiations, ranging from the field of battle to the conference chamber. Now we have to examine the final product thus established, viz. the treaty of peace, and a number of questions inseparably connected with it. Among the subjects of our inquiry will be such matters as the competence to conclude peace treaties, their essential nature and binding character, their form and constituent parts, the different kinds of clauses found in them, in what language they are drawn up, their interpretation, the date of taking effect, the ratification, their breach, and the means adopted to ensure their performance.

COMPETENCE TO CONCLUDE TREATIES.

First, with regard to the competence to conclude treaties of peace.[1] It is obviously of the highest importance, in international negotiations, to make sure that each party is empowered not only to negotiate, but also to bind, his sovereign, his Government, and his country. Accordingly plenipotentiaries are provided with full powers for this purpose by the proper authority in whom they inhere; that is,

[1] Cf. S. B. Crandall, *Treaties, their Making and Enforcement* (*Studies in History. Columbia College*, vol. xxi (New York, 1904)).

the competent organ simply delegates his functions and privileges for the time being to an agent or representative. If, then, those functions and privileges have been delegated irregularly, or if their exercise has been authorized by one possessing no power to do so, the resulting transactions may be repudiated by the Government or by the people of the State in whose behalf they purport to have been carried out. Now the power to enter into treaties in general is usually placed in the hands of the head of the State, be he monarch or president. It may be unlimited, or subject to certain restrictions imposed by the constitutional law and custom of each State; so that if such restrictions are not observed the treaty concluded will not be valid and binding. The power to conclude peace and the power to declare war do not necessarily reside in the same person or persons. Regard must in every case be had to the legal system and constitution of every State concerned.

As a rule it may be said that conventions established by duly appointed plenipotentiaries acting within the scope of their apparent authority are binding on all the subjects of their respective States, without the express sanction of their legislature; but in certain cases the previous consent of the legislature or subsequent ratification—as, for example, in treaties of peace—is necessary to render them valid. Treaties requiring such additional formality are sometimes described by jurists as being of imperfect obligation. The constitutional law of a given State not infrequently lays down what classes of treaties need the approval of its legislature.

Great Britain.

In the case of Great Britain, it is in general the Crown's prerogative to make peace and war, subject to the assent of a responsible minister acting on the collective advice of the cabinet. Treaties entered into for these purposes, as well as for making alliances with foreign Powers and for ceding part of the dominions of the Crown, are generally deemed to be binding on the nation without the express authorization of Parliament.[1] But when an important cession of territory is to be effected, it is the safer course to obtain first such authorization; as happened, for instance, when Heligoland was ceded to Germany in 1890.[2] It is necessary to mention that even in the case of treaties of peace, and those to prevent war made on public grounds and for the public safety, there are authorities in support of the view that the subject cannot be bound in the absence of parlia-

[1] Cf. *The Elsebe* (1804), 5 C. Rob. 174, 181; *The Parlement Belge* (1879), 4 P.D. 129, 139, 149–151.

[2] See the Anglo-German Agreement Act, 1890; 53 & 54 Vict. c. 32.

mentary sanction; there are also authorities to the contrary[1]—so that the question cannot be considered definitively settled by British constitutional law. Though there is no prescribed list of classes of treaties needing or not needing the assent of Parliament, it is clearly established that three of them do need it, viz. those involving taxation or other charge on the people, those derogating from the private rights of the subject,[2] and those modifying the established laws of trade and navigation.[3] Thus, at the Hague Conferences of 1899, 1907, the British delegates refused to accept certain articles of conventions, and signed others under reservation, on the ground that they necessitated alterations in the domestic law.

United States.

In the United States the power to enter into treaties is vested in the president, as head of the federal executive, subject to the assent of two-thirds of the senate.

France.

France: Art. 8 of the Constitutional Law of July 16, 1875, says: "The President of the Republic negotiates and ratifies treaties. He communicates them to the Chambers as soon as the interest and safety of the State permit. Treaties of peace and of commerce, treaties involving the finances of the State, and those relating to the persons and property of French citizens in foreign countries shall become definitive only after having been approved by the two Chambers. No cession, no exchange, no annexation of territory shall take place save under sanction of a law."

Germany.

Germany: The emperor may declare war only with the approval of the Bundesrath, unless German territory is invaded; but no limitation is imposed on his power to conclude peace. Art. 11 of the Constitution of 1871 empowers him to represent the empire in international affairs, to enter into alliances and other treaties with foreign States; but in the case of treaties involving matters which, under Art. 4, fall within the scope of imperial legislation, the consent of the Bundesrath is necessary for their conclusion, and that of the Reichstag for their validity.

Austria: Under Art. 6 of the Fundamental Law of the Austrian Constitution (December 21, 1867), the emperor is entitled to

[1] See *Walker* v. *Baird* (1892), A.C. 491. The point came up in this case, but it was not decided. For authorities denying the power of the Crown to bind the subject in the circumstances mentioned above, see pp. 494, 495; for authorities affirming it, see pp. 492, 493.

[2] Cf. *The Parlement Belge* (1879), 4 P.D. 129; and see *Walker* v. *Baird* (1892), A.C. 491, at p. 497.

[3] E.g. The International Copyright Acts, 1844, 1852; the Sea Fisheries Act, 1868, §§ 47, 66. Cf. *Walker* v. *Baird* (1892), H.C. 491, at pp. 494, 495.

Austria.

conclude treaties; but the consent of the Reichsrath is needed to make binding commercial treaties, those laying a burden on the country or a portion of it, and those imposing obligations on individual subjects. Similarly the approval of the Hungarian Parliament is necessary to render valid treaties affecting the internal organization of the State, imposing taxes, requiring expenditure or the raising of recruits, or causing a change of territory.

Italy.

Italy: By Art. 5 of the Fundamental Statute enacted for Sardinia, March 4, 1848, and afterwards extended to the various parts of Italy, the king makes war and peace and communicates his act to the Chambers as soon as the interests and safety of the State permit. Treaties creating financial obligations or changing the territory of the State cannot be binding without the approval of the Chambers.

Spain.

Spain: Arts. 54 and 55 of the Constitution of 1876 empowers the sovereign to conduct diplomatic and commercial relations with foreign States, to declare war, and conclude treaties of peace. But a special Act of the Cortes is needed to authorize him to alienate, cede, or exchange any part of Spanish territory, or add to it, to ratify alliances, treaties of commerce and those affecting individual subjects. In every case the Act must precede the ratification. Public articles may not be annulled by secret provisions. We have already seen that in the peace negotiations with the United States, 1898, the authorization of the Spanish Senate and of the Chamber was necessary to permit the Government to conclude peace on the basis of the protocol, which required the cession of Spanish territory. It may be mentioned that certain publicists in Spain maintained at the time that the constitutional provision applied only to a state of peace; but that in time of war *force majeure* gave a dispensation, subject to an act of indemnity passed afterwards by the Cortes.

Belgium.

Belgium: Under Art. 68 of the Constitution of 1831 the king makes treaties of peace, alliances, and commerce, reporting to the Chambers as soon as the interests and safety of the State permit. Commercial treaties and those laying a charge on the country, or affecting individuals, cannot be binding without the assent of the Chambers. A special law is necessary for the cession, exchange, or incorporation of territory. Secret articles must not be contrary to the open ones.

Holland.

Holland: Art. 59 of the Constitution (as revised in 1887) empowers the sovereign to make and ratify all treaties, reporting to the States-General when public interest permits. The assent of the States-General is necessary to enable the sovereign to ratify treaties imposing pecuniary burdens on the country, changing the territory, or affecting the legal rights of subjects.

Denmark.

Denmark: By Art. 18 of the Constitution (1849, as revised 1866) the king may conclude treaties of peace, alliances, and commerce, but may not, without the approval of the Rigsdag, cede territory or cause the public law relations to be altered.

Greece.

Greece: Under Art. 32 of the Constitution of 1864 the king makes treaties of peace, alliance, and commerce; but the assent of the Boule is necessary to validate those imposing burdens on individual subjects, and a special law is needed for the cession or exchange of territory.

Where the authorization of the legislature is necessary to give binding force to the international transactions effected by the treaty-making authority of a State, it is generally implied, and even sometimes expressly stipulated, that they shall not become operative if the authorization is withheld. In the absence of such proviso, express or implied, the State must be held responsible for the non-performance of its obligations, even if the default is due to the failure of the legislature over which the treaty-making authority has no control.[1]

Negotiations with a revolutionary Government.

When peace negotiations are conducted with a revolutionary Government, the question as to its competence to bind the nation by a treaty may arise. In such circumstances, there can be no doubt that the existing Government *de facto* may validly bind the nation by means of conventions with other Powers, and particularly by peace treaties, if the said Government and its acts are sanctioned by a national assembly recognized explicitly or tacitly by the people at large. Moreover, as no State may interfere in the internal affairs and constitutional organization of another State, it may not, as a rule, demand from a party possessing and exercising sovereign authority what title it has to conclude international engagements; for the undisturbed possession and exercise of such authority may be regarded as definite proof of contractual competence. The case of the Franco-German War furnishes an important precedent. On September 2, 1870, Napoleon III, together with an army of 83,000 men, surrendered to the enemy at Sedan; and on September 4 the downfall of the Empire and the establishment of the French Republic were proclaimed. The Government of National Defence —a Government *de facto* from the latter date—having commenced pourparlers, early in January 1871, for the conclusion of a general

[1] Cf. Cobbett, *Cases*, vol. i (1909), p. 320.

armistice, with a view to the establishment of peace, Bismarck first demanded (in a Note of January 14) that this Government should be formally recognized by a National Assembly of representatives of the French people, in order that its engagements might not afterwards be repudiated as the acts of an incompetent body.[1] Accordingly, a stipulation was inserted in the preliminary Treaty of Versailles (Art X), February 26, 1871, that it should be immediately submitted to the ratification of the French National Assembly sitting at Bordeaux; and Art. XVIII of the definitive Treaty of Frankfort, May 10, 1871, required a similar ratification within ten days.

Whether head of the State if taken prisoner can bind his country.

The question whether the head of a State who has been taken prisoner is competent to bind his country by a treaty concluded by him during his captivity, has given rise to some controversy. The case usually referred to—and it certainly is a most interesting one—is that of the Treaty of Madrid, January 14, 1526, between Francis I, King of France, and the Emperor Charles V. The former, by his bad generalship, met with a disastrous reverse at Pavia, February 25, 1525, where 8,000 of his men were killed, and a large number, including himself, taken prisoners. Having surrendered his blood-stained sword to Charles de Lannoi, Viceroy of Naples, who handed him his own in exchange, the king begged his captors "ne pas le mener dedans Pavie, pour ne servir de spectacle ni de risée à ceux auxquels il avoit donné auparavant peur, mal, et fatigue."[2] Soon afterwards he wrote to his mother the famous letter, of which certain expressions have so frequently been misquoted: "Madame, pour vous faire savoir comme se porte le reste de mon infortune, de toutes choses ne m'est demeuré que l'honneur et la vie qui est sauve. . . ." Charles V demanded the cession of Burgundy; but the royal captive resisted for some time, and even thought of abdicating rather than comply with such terms. Eventually, however, he submitted, and signed the Treaty of Madrid; though the previous evening he drew up a protest, before the French plenipotentiaries, against the signature procured "par force et contrainte," and declared such treaty "nul et de nul effet." Francis further undertook to ratify the treaty as soon as he returned to his country, and to present it without delay for ratification by the States-General and the States of Burgundy, and for approval by the parlements. His two eldest sons were to be kept as hostages till the terms were performed, and he him-

[1] Cf. P. Esperson, *Le Gouvernement de la Défense Nationale a-t-il le droit de conclure la paix au nom de la France?* (Florence, 1870).

[2] Quoted by H. Martin, *Histoire de France* (Paris, 1878), vol. viii. pp. 66–67.

self was to return to captivity—" tenir prison "—if the ratifications were not exchanged within four months, and the treaty fully carried out.[1] He was not restored to liberty till March 18—two months later—when his two sons were surrendered. Having been called upon afterwards to ratify the treaty, he replied that it was necessary to ascertain first the views of his subjects of Burgundy, as he could not effect the cession without their consent. Lannoi and other ambassadors of the Emperor then arrived at Cognac to urge Francis to fulfil his engagement. But the deputies of Burgundy, having assembled, refused to be separated from the Crown of France, and maintained that it was not within the king's competence to alienate the French provinces. Francis then offered to pay two million crowns instead of transferring the duchy; but Charles refused, and called upon him to return to captivity—" tenir prison"—in accordance with his solemn vow. The French sovereign's reply was the publication of the "Holy League" (July 8)—the alliance of France with the Italian States, to which our Henry VIII acceded (September 4)—for the deliverance of Italy. Pope Clement VII absolved Francis from his oath.

Was the French monarch's repudiation of the treaty legally justifiable? Or, rather, is a treaty valid when entered into by a sovereign in captivity? Certain earlier authors[2] drew a distinction between a king whose kingdom is patrimonial, and another who has only the usufruct of his dominions; but Vattel[3] and others long ago showed that the notion of a partimonial kingdom was false, and that the king ruled not for his own sake, but entirely for the advantage of his country. As the last-named writer observes, every legitimate Government, whatever it be, is established solely for the good and welfare of the State; so that the conclusion of peace belongs to the nation, and is not the peculiar province of the monarch.[4] Now when a king falls into the hands of the enemy, he does not cease to be king *de jure*; if he is liberated or escapes he at once resumes his former position. But during captivity he cannot exercise the various functions incidental to his high office in its proper and legitimate sphere; wherefore his kingship *de facto* is for the time being in abeyance, and any treaties concluded by him, in these circumstances, do not bind his country. Vattel compares his position to that of a king in his minority, or of one mentally deranged; accordingly it is for the person or persons whom the laws of the State designate for the regency to assume the reins of government and conclude peace.[5]

[1] J. Dumont, *Corps universel diplomatique*, vol. iv. p. 44; Martin, *op. cit.*, p. 90.

[2] For example, C. von Wolff, *Jus gentium* (1749), § 982.

[3] *Droit des gens*, liv. i. §§ 68 *seq.*

[4] *Op. cit.*, liv. iv. ch. ii. § 13.

[5] *Ibid.*

It may be said, from one point of view, that a sovereign's captivity necessarily implies an absolute incapacity to contract *as a sovereign*; and consequently agreements entered into by him, ostensibly as a sovereign, are null and void *ab initio*, and thus are non-existent so far as his nation is concerned. But the more reasonable point of view is to regard such engagements as voidable, at the discretion of the nation. That is, the nation recognizes their existence and confirms or repudiates them as it thinks fit. In other words, the validity of a captive sovereign's treaty depends on the ratification by his country. If it is ratified it comes into force and is binding; if it is not ratified it falls to the ground and so cannot bind any one.

BINDING FORCE.

A correlative question that arises is whether a treaty of peace is, apart from the above case, invariably binding, or whether it is vitiated also by the presence of fraud and violence. There can be no doubt that the use of fraud invalidates all agreements concluded in time of peace or for the purpose of terminating war. But with regard to force and violence, it is necessary to draw a distinction. In the case of conventions established during peaceful relationships, duress may generally be deemed a ground for repudiation; but in a treaty of peace, force and compulsion cannot be so held. Nearly every treaty of peace confers advantages on one side, and imposes disadvantages on the other. That is the fundamental nature of the transaction. If peace negotiation is not an actual extension, in another plane of conflict, of the military operations of the belligerents, it is at all events a substitute therefor, and cannot possibly be considered as being immune from all threats and pressure. There is not and cannot be any legal principle forbidding a peace negotiator to threaten that he will resume hostilities if his terms are not accepted; for the other party knows full well what will happen if the negotiations fail. A certain element of pressure is therefore inevitable here, and it cannot properly be described as duress. Were it regarded by the defeated party as a factor vitiating his engagement, the only course that would remain to the victor would be to go on with the war and refuse to suspend arms until he had completely subjugated or annihilated the adversary. Hence the conclusion of treaties of peace would be rendered impossible; for a vanquished belligerent chooses deliberately to make peace and accept the hardships—if any—thereby imposed, in order to avoid a much greater evil. Vattel aptly sums up the case in the following manner: "On ne peut se dégager d'un traité de paix en alléguant qu'il a été extorqué par la crainte ou arraché

Duress.

de force. Premièrement si cette exception était admise, elle saperait par les fondements toute la sûreté des traités de paix, car il en est peu contre lesquels on ne pût s'en servir pour couvrir la mauvaise foi. . . . D'ailleurs, il serait presque toujours honteux et ridicule d'alléguer une pareille exception. Il n'arrive guère aujourd'hui que l'on attende les dernières extrémités pour faire la paix : une nation, bien que vaincue en plusieurs batailles, peut encore se défendre ; elle n'est pas sans ressource, tant qu'il lui reste des hommes et des armes. Si, par un traité désavantageux, elle trouve à propos de se procurer une paix nécessaire, si elle se rachète d'un danger imminent, d'une ruine entière, par de grands sacrifices, ce qui lui reste est encore un bien qu'elle doit à la paix ; elle s'est déterminée librement à préférer une perte certaine et présente, mais bornée, à l'attente d'un mal encore à venir, mais trop probable et terrible."[1]

Armed force during negotiations.

On the other hand, if the plenipotentiaries of one State having in vain demanded certain conditions from those of the other thereupon call into the council chamber an armed force for the purpose of terrorizing them into submission, their consent thus extorted would invalidate the resulting engagement.[2] But the violence or intimidation thus resorted to must, in order to have this effect, be serious enough to influence a reasonable man—"metus qui in homine constantissimo cadit." Phillimore thus distinguishes the case of duress that nullifies an undertaking from that of legitimate force having no such effect: "The resignation of his crown and kingdom, extorted by Napoleon from Ferdinand VII at Bayonne, whither he had decoyed that monarch and his family, was clearly—the duress and condition of the party abdicating being considered—invalid; but the resignation of Napoleon at Fontainebleau was not extorted by treachery or duress, but was the consequence of defeat in open legitimate war."[3] Since 1796 Spain had been hopelessly subservient to France; and some ten years after that date Napoleon had conceived the plan of dethroning the Spanish Bourbons and substituting a Bonaparte. On March 19, 1808, a popular rising having broken out at Aranjuez, the old king, Charles IV, resigned the crown to his son and heir, the Prince of the Asturias, who was proclaimed king as Ferdinand VII. But Murat, Napoleon's "lieutenant" in Spain, refused to recognize

When duress is a ground for repudiating an engagement.

[1] *Droit des gens*, liv. iv. ch. iv. § 37.

[2] Cf. Bluntschli, *Das moderne Völkerrecht*, § 704.

[3] *Commentaries*, vol. ii. § 49; referring to T. A. Schmalz, *Das europäische Völkerrecht* (Berlin, 1817), pp. 53, 54.

the succession; whereupon Charles drew up a secret protest declaring his abdication to have been due to duress, and therefore to be null and void. No sooner, however, had Ferdinand taken possession of the royal palace than he wrote to Napoleon confirming the alliance with France, and proposing marriage with an imperial princess. The emperor now decided to visit Madrid, and sent in advance his aide-de-camp, who, according to Spanish testimony, assured the young king of the emperor's favour and intention to give him the hand of a Bonaparte princess. Accordingly Ferdinand set out, on April 10, to meet his august guest and crossed over into French territory. On reaching Bayonne, however, April 20, he was placed under guard and told that the emperor had resolved to depose him; but that if he agreed to abdicate at once he would receive as compensation the Kingdom of Etruria. Ferdinand rejecting the proposal was suddenly confronted with his parents (who had arrived in Bayonne soon after himself), and was called upon to restore the crown to his father, under pain of being held a traitor. He offered to do so in Madrid, in the presence of the Cortes; but Napoleon refused, and soon afterwards threatened that he would be tried for high treason unless he abdicated within twelve hours. The young king therefore signed an instrument restoring the crown to his father (May 6). But in the meantime (May 5) the latter had been induced to renounce all his rights to the Spanish throne and the Indies to Napoleon, in return for certain annuities and estates in France. Ferdinand was placed under military guard in Talleyrand's manor of Valençay; and then Napoleon put his brother Joseph on the vacant throne. The Spanish people, however, rose in insurrection against him, and refused to consider as binding the renunciation extorted by treachery and duress from Charles IV and Ferdinand. No refusal was ever more justifiable.

A treaty of peace as a "real" treaty.

Subject to the above qualifications, a treaty of peace possesses binding force, and must be faithfully observed. It is not made only for the life of the sovereign who is a party to it, but is binding equally on his successors. It is what many jurists call a real, as distinguished from a personal, treaty. Formerly a stipulation was inserted in it declaring that a breach of any term would furnish ground for reparation, and not for war; and in default of satisfaction war might be declared. Nowadays no such stipulation is made; though certain precautions are taken, as we shall see presently, to ensure the due performance of the treaty as a whole or of important parts of it. Whether the non-observance of any article of the treaty is to be met by reparation sought by pacific means, or by measures short of war (e.g. retorsion, reprisals, including hostile embargo, pacific blockade, etc.), or by the *ultima ratio*, viz. war, will naturally depend on the seriousness and extent of the violation, as well as on political considerations and on the exigencies of State interest. Of course, a new cause of war is produced when the injury of the offending State relates to some matter that is outside the scope and operation of the treaty of peace.

A treaty of peace as a compromise.

It follows from the above observations that a treaty of peace is of necessity a compromise, being unlike other treaties which are equal transactions—that is, those in which the consideration given by one party, A, for the promise of the other, B, is equal, or presumed to be equal, to the consideration given by B for the promise of A. But a treaty of peace is, as it has been aptly termed, a "contract of fortune,"—for one of the parties, if not for both, it may indeed be a contract of misfortune. It is inevitably a patched-up arrangement, providing for each side a roughly approximate solution of the differences between them. Where terms are dictated throughout to the utterly vanquished belligerent at the absolute discretion of the victor, the transaction cannot, strictly speaking, be designated a treaty; it is a unilateral imposition of demands. Every treaty of peace proper must have a bilateral character; it must involve reciprocal concessions, however unequal they may be. Even in earlier ages, when the *ius victoriæ* was recognized and was in certain respects more cruel than the *ius belli*, we find such restrictions placed on the victorious combatant as to make his dealings with the defeated State a compromise. The object of the treaty of peace is not merely to put a stop to the war, but also to prevent its renewal; and this latter purpose is accomplished by means of a bargain settling each side's claims and pretensions. It is not an impartial judge who effects this accommodation; it is the disputants themselves who do so, and in general they are unequally matched, so that less than justice may be done. To give each one his due is the ideal of human relationships; but in a treaty of peace much less than in man's other devices and contrivances shall we find this object attained. "Were the rules of strict and rigid justice," says Vattel, "to be observed in it, so that each party should precisely receive everything to which he has a just title, it would be impossible ever to make a peace. First, with regard to the very subject which occasioned the war, one of the parties would be under a necessity of acknowledging himself in the wrong, and condemning his own just pretensions which he will hardly do, unless reduced to the last extremity. But if he owns the injustice of his cause, he must at the same time condemn every measure he has pursued in support of it; he must restore what he has unjustly taken, must reimburse the expenses of the war, and repair the damages. And how can a just estimate of all the damages be formed? What price can be set on all the blood that has been shed, the loss of so many lives, and the ruin of families? Nor is this all. Strict justice would further demand that the author of an unjust war should suffer a penalty proportioned to the injuries for which he owes satisfaction, and such as might ensure the future safety of him whom he attacked. How shall the nature of that penalty be determined, and the degree of it be precisely regulated? In fine, even he who had justice on his side may have transgressed the bounds of justifiable self-defence, and been guilty of improper excesses in the prosecution of a war whose object was originally lawful; here, then, are so many wrongs, for which strict justice would demand reparation. He may have made conquests and taken booty beyond the value of his claim. Who shall make an exact calculation, a just estimate of this? Therefore, since it would be dreadful to perpetuate the war, or to pursue it to the utter ruin of one of the parties, and since, however just the cause in which we are engaged, we must at length turn our thoughts towards the restoration of peace, and ought to direct all our measures to the attainment of that salutary object, no other expedient remains than that of coming to a compromise respecting all claims and grievances on both sides, and putting an end to all disputes by a convention as fair and equitable as circumstances will admit of. In such conventions no decision is pronounced on the original cause of the war, or on those controversies to which the various acts of hostility might give rise; nor is either of the parties condemned as unjust—a condemnation to which few princes would submit; but a simple agreement is formed, which determines what equivalent each party shall receive in extinction of all his pretensions." [1]

In earlier days much attention was given to form in all legal transactions, and especially in international negotiation. Nowadays substance and intention are the main consideration; so that no particular form is now indispensable to the validity of a treaty of peace or any other convention. Recent treaties contain no phraseological flourishes, no elaborate formulas and courtesies; they go straight to the point in a business-like way, and in a concise, simple style—much simpler and much more concise than that of the comparatively unimportant documents of municipal law—specify the dispositions agreed to.

FORM OF TREATY.

[1] *Droit des gens*, liv. iv. ch. ii. § 18 (Chitty's trans., Philadelphia, 1872).

An example, however, of peace treaties will show that they possess certain features in common in respect of form. First there is the preamble, the introductory portion of the instrument, which specifies the motive or the object of the negotiation, or contains some other relative explanation. Thus the Treaty of Paris, November 20, 1815, between the Allied Powers and France, states it was concluded as a result of the successful efforts made by the Allies to save France and Europe from the disaster threatened by Napoleon and the Revolution, and for the purpose of restoring order to France and amicable relationship between her and her neighbours, as well as for securing to the Allies proper indemnities for the past and solid guarantees for the future.[1] The Treaty of Paris, March 30, 1856, between the Allies and Russia, declares that all the parties are anxious to put an end to the calamities of war, to prevent the recurrence of the complications that caused it, and to secure the independence and integrity of Turkey.[2] The Treaty of Zurich, November 10, 1859, between Austria and France, makes exactly the same statement, except, of course, as to the last point.[3] The Treaty of Prague, August 23, 1866, between Austria and Prussia, says simply that the parties are animated with the desire of restoring the benefits of peace.[4] The Treaty of Frankfort, May 10, 1871, between France and Germany, contains no such declaration, but observes merely that its purpose is to convert into a definitive agreement the Preliminaries of Versailles, February 26.[5] The Preliminary Treaty of San Stefano, March 3, 1878, between Russia and Turkey, speaks of restoring and securing the blessings of peace and preventing fresh complications.[6] The Treaty of Shimonoseki, April 17, 1895, between China and Japan, uses a like expression.[7] The Treaty of Paris, December 10, 1898, between the United States and Spain, is in this respect almost as reserved as the Treaty of Frankfort; it mentions only the desire of the parties to end the state of war.[8] Similarly, the Treaty of Portsmouth, September 5, 1905, between Russia and Japan, confines itself to saying that the parties wish to restore the blessings of peace.[9] And the like brevity is observed in subsequent treaties, e.g. Lausanne, October 18, 1912, between Italy and Turkey; Bucharest, August 10, 1913, between Bulgaria and the Balkan Allies; Athens, November 14, 1913, between Turkey and Greece.[10]

Preamble.

The preamble was formerly preceded by an invocation to God,

[1] Cf. *infra*, Appendix (A). [2] Appendix (D). [3] Appendix (F).
[4] Appendix (H). [5] Appendix (K). [6] Appendix (M).
[7] Appendix (R). [8] Appendix (S). [9] Appendix (U).
[10] Appendix (V), (X), (Z).

which took such forms as the following: "In the name of God, the creator and legislator of the universe"; "In the name of the most holy and indivisible Trinity";[1] "In the name of the holy Trinity"; "In the name of Almighty God";[2] and so on. The Treaty of Constantinople, January 27 / February 8, 1879, between Russia and Turkey, appears to be the last peace treaty in which such invocation was used.

Former invocation.

After the statement (if any) of the causes and objects of the treaty comes the designation of the plenipotentiaries, together with a justification of their competence to negotiate and sign the resulting instrument. This is usually expressed in some such formula as the following: "For this purpose [viz. the purpose indicated in the preamble] His Majesty the King of . . . and His Majesty the King of . . . have named as their plenipotentiaries . . .," "with this view their said Majesties have appointed as their plenipotentiaries . . . ." This is followed by the names of the plenipotentiaries of the respective parties, their rank, title, orders, etc., being given; and by a declaration that the full powers they were provided with were found in proper form, thus, "Who having exchanged their full powers, which were found to be in good and due form, have signed the following articles," or "Who having met in conference at . . ., and after having exchanged their full powers, found in good and due form, have agreed upon the following articles," or "Who, having assembled in . . . and having exchanged their full powers, which were found to be in due and proper form, have, after discussion of the matter before them, agreed upon the following articles."

Designation of the plenipotentiaries.

Next comes a list of numbered articles,[3] of which the last is usually devoted to a stipulation requiring the exchange of ratifications within a given time and at a given place; sometimes it states, too, the language or languages in which the treaty is drawn up. Thus, Art. XIX—the last—of the Treaty of Frankfort says: "The present convention, drawn up in French and German, shall be ratified . . . and the ratifications shall be exchanged in the delay of one month, or sooner if possible." Sometimes such provision is made in the penultimate article, or in the latter part of it. After this follows a stereotyped formula implying the *consensus ad idem* of the

Clause as to ratification.

[1] E.g. Treaty of Paris, November 20, 1815, Appendix (A); Treaty of Zurich, November 10, 1859, Appendix (F); Treaty of Prague, August 23, 1866, Appendix (H); Treaty of Vienna, October 3, 1866, Appendix (I).

[2] Treaty of Constantinople, February 8, 1879, between Russia and Turkey, ppendix (N).

[3] As to these, see *infra*, pp. 174 *seq.*

plenipotentiaries with regard to the preceding articles, and stating that accordingly they sign the instrument and attach their seals to it; thus: "In faith thereof the respective plenipotentiaries have signed the present treaty and have affixed their seals thereto"; or "In witness whereof the respective plenipotentiaries have hereunto affixed their names and seals." The final paragraph before the signatures states the date, the place where the treaty was signed, and sometimes the number of original copies drawn up; thus: "Done at . . . on the . . . day of the month of . . . in the year . . ."; or "Done in duplicate (or triplicate, etc.) on . . ." (as before).

Concluding formula.

In treaties in general the practice is to draw up and sign under seal as many copies as there are parties, one copy being retained by each signatory. Where there are only two parties, whose languages are different, each copy is usually drawn up in the languages of both, the texts appearing sometimes on separate sheets, and sometimes on opposite pages or in parallel columns; in the latter case the copy kept by each party contains the text in his own language on the left-hand page or column. Sometimes, however, the copy of each nation contains the text in its own language together with a translation in a third language, generally French. When there are several parties speaking different languages, the instrument frequently appears in only one language, namely French (at least so far as Europe is concerned); though each party may, for his own convenience and purposes, attach thereto an authentic translation in his own tongue.

Number of copies drawn up.

In diplomatic negotiations and in the drawing up of treaties, each State is now entitled to use it own national language. In former times the right was not so firmly established; and practice varied considerably—first Latin and then French striving for supremacy. After the revival of letters Latin became the universal language of Europe in the spheres of learning, law, and diplomacy. Several States adopted it as their official language, e.g. the Empire, England, the Papacy, the United Provinces, Denmark, Sweden, Portugal. Some Powers, such as France and Turkey, used their own language both for domestic purposes and for international communications; others, like Russia, used their national language at home in matters of state, and French in their letters of council.[1] In the sixteenth century Spain endeavoured to make Spanish the only language in diplomatic acts transacted between her and foreign nations.

Language used.

[1] Cf. G. F. de Martens, *Précis du droit des gens moderne de l'Europe*, 2nd ed. (Gottingue, 1801); liv. vi. § 179, pp. 272–275.

Till about the middle of the seventeenth century Latin occupied an important, if not the leading, place in official audiences, conferences, etc. Thus ambassadors despatched to Henry VIII addressed him in Latin; similarly in the case of the Venetian envoy, Giustiniani, who received an audience of Francis I, King of France. The Spanish envoys who came to England in 1603 to conclude a treaty of peace with James I used sometimes Latin and sometimes French.[1]

Use of Latin.

At the Congress of Nimeguen (1676) there were conflicting claims as to the language question; Latin no longer enjoyed ascendancy, and French instead was becoming the general language of diplomacy. Sir William Temple, the envoy of England, which acted as a mediating Power, opened the proceedings in French, and was answered in Latin by the Bishop of Gurk. The Danish delegation tried to use Latin and then Danish in their negotiations with the French representatives; but the latter objected, and the use of French prevailed. The incident is thus described by Sir William Temple: "The Danish ambassador stood positively upon the common use of the Latin tongue between France and them in their powers, or else to give his in Danish if they gave theirs in French. These said that it was a novelty and an impertinence; and that, if in all intercourse that had ever been between those Crowns the language had not been French on their side and Latin on the Danes', even in any one instrument, they were content they should give their powers not only in Danish but in Hebrew if they pleased. . . . The Dane's pretence about the language, being neither countenanced nor approved by any of his allies, was at last yielded by him."[2]

French.

Limojon de St. Didier, writing from personal experience, speaks of the progress of the French language in foreign countries and observes that at Nimeguen the ambassadors of the various States not only spoke French in their private conferences, but also drew up their public memoranda in that language: "L'on s'apperceut à Nimègue du progrés que la langue françoise avoit faite dans les païs étrangers; car il n'y avoit point de maison d'Ambassadeurs où elle ne fust presque aussi commune que leur langue naturelle. Bien davantage, elle devint si necessaire, que les Ambassadeurs anglois, allemans, danois, et ceux des autres nations, tenoient toutes leurs conferences en françois. Les deux ambassadeurs de Dannemarck convinrent mesme de faire leurs dépesches communes en cette langue, parce que le Comte Antoine d'Oldembourg parloit

[1] Sir H. Ellis, *Original Letters*, second series (London, 1827), iii. 207.

[2] Sir William Temple, *Works*, vol. i. p. 310; referred to by Bernard, *op. cit.*, p. 155.

bon Allemand et n'entendoit point de danois, comme son collegue. Desorte que pendant tout le cours des negotiations de la Paix, il ne parut presque que des ecritures françoises, les etrangers aimant mieux s'expliquer en françois dans leur memoires publics, que d'écrire dans une langue moins usitée que la françoise." [1] But the text of the Treaty of Nimeguen, like that of many others—e.g. the Treaty of Ryswick (1697), the Treaty of Utrecht (1713), the Treaty of the Quadruple Alliance of London (1718)—was drawn up in Latin. This continued to be a common practice till the eighteenth century, when French came to be used instead—thanks to the widespread influence of the literature of the age of Louis XIV.[2] The German princes had for a long time adhered to their native language in the business of diplomacy; but in 1742, with the Treaty of Breslau, between Austria and Prussia, they began to follow the custom of the great majority of negotiators,[3] and the same practice appeared in the Treaties of Dresden (1745), Hubertsburg (1763), Teschen (1779). In 1817, however, the Germanic Confederation decided at Frankfort to use only German in the relationships with other Powers, and to add, on terms of reciprocity, a Latin or French translation.[4] Before this date the liberty of States to use their own language in the drawing up of treaties was so definitely recognized that in several treaties in which French was employed—e.g. Aix-la-Chapelle (1748), Paris (1763), the Final Act of the Congress of Vienna (1815)—a proviso was inserted to the effect that the adoption of this language was not to be considered a precedent for the future.

English.

Nowadays English is coming to the front in diplomatic transactions, and it is very probable that in course of time it will replace French as the universal language of diplomacy. "L'anglais est aujourd'hui," remarks Rivier, "l'idiome le plus parlé; simple, clair, facile, il remplacera peut-être un jour le français comme langue diplomatique. Koelle disait en 1838: 'Die allgemeine Verkehrssprache unserer Enkel wird die englische sein.'" [5] In 1895 English was used in the negotiations for an armistice between China and Japan. But a much more important example is the Treaty of Portsmouth, Sep-

[1] *Histoire des négotiations de Nimègue* (Paris, 1680), Pt. I, pp. 125–126.

[2] Cf. A. Rivarol, *Dissertation sur l'universalité de la langue française* (Berlin, 1784), pp. 33 *seq.*

[3] J. J. Moser, *Der Teschenische Fridenschluss* (Frankfurt am Mayn, 1779), p. 49: "Unter solchen Höfen aber, die sich allerseits der Teutschen Sprache bedienen, ware der Bresslauer Fride von 1742, zwischen Oesterreich und Preussen der erste, welcher Französisch abgefasst wurde."

[4] Cf. Pradier-Fodéré, *Cours de droit diplomatique*, vol. ii. p. 456.

[5] *Principes du droit des gens* (Paris, 1896), vol. ii. p. 20.

tember 5, 1905, between Russia and Japan, when English was employed as well as French, though the latter was given priority in questions of interpretation. Thus Art. XV stipulates: "The present treaty shall be signed in duplicate in both the English and French languages. The texts are in absolute conformity, but in case of discrepancy in interpretation, the French text shall prevail." It may be added that French has remained the official language for the conventions of the various international unions (e.g. postal, patents, etc., copyright, sugar, Latin monetary, railway traffic, customs tariff, etc.), and also for those established at the Hague Conferences, 1899, 1907.

In the conclusion of peace more than two parties may be concerned, for the combatants may have been composed of several allied Powers. In such a case it may happen that peace is established not by one general conference arriving at one common instrument, but by separate negotiations between the contending States and by separate treaties. An eventuality of this kind is not necessarily avoided by an engagement made by allies during the war not to make peace independently of each other. The essential object of the undertaking is to prevent each ally from laying down arms, coming to terms with the adversary, and leaving the other allies to continue the war at a disadvantage; in other words, that none of the allies should withdraw from the conflict unless and until the common enemy is prepared to conclude peace simultaneously with them all. It may be, however, that the compact entered into stipulates expressly that the allies should not only cease hostilities together, but also that they should conduct their peace negotiations with the enemy in one common congress; so that the resulting conditions agreed to would be consigned to one instrument settling the differences of all the parties.

Where there are several belligerents.

Each party being entitled to a copy of the treaty, the question arises whether all the copies made are in every detail of form as well as of substance precisely similar. We have already referred to the disputes that formerly took place at conferences regarding the precedence of States, and how such difficulties were solved by adopting the simple device of locating the plenipotentiaries in positions according to the French alphabetical order of the initial letters of the names of their countries. The same plan was, and is now, applied in the arrangement of the signatures on all official documents of the conference, including the definitive treaty. A further device is adopted which emphasizes still more the juridical equality of States — namely, the *alternat*; whereby the copy of the treaty taken by each con-

Use of the *alternat*.

tracting party has its own name first, both at the head of the instrument, in the preamble, and at the foot, in the list of signatures—all the other parties being arranged alphabetically. Thus, in the case of the Treaty of Berlin, 1878, the signatories being Germany (Allemagne), Austria (Autriche), France, Great Britain (Grande-Bretagne), Italy (Italie), Russia (Russie), and Turkey (Turquie), Great Britain appeared first in her own copy, followed by Germany, fourth in the copies of Germany, Austria, and France, and fifth in the copies of Italy, Russia, and Turkey; similarly, Turkey figured first in her own copy, and last in every other copy. The regular use of the *alternat* dates from 1815. Before then the State that was in a position to dictate terms, or that was sued for peace, not infrequently assumed the first place both in its own copy of the instrument and in that of the other party. In the Treaty of Ghent, 1814, for example, Great Britain took precedence over the United States in both copies. But in the exchange of ratifications the United States referred to the principle of the *alternat*, and declared that the practice then adopted was not to be considered a precedent for the future, and did not imply that she waived the said principle.

VARIOUS PARTS OF A TREATY OF PEACE.

Having dealt with the form of treaties in general, the number of copies required, the language in which they are drawn up, and the use of the *alternat*, we have now to consider the constituent elements of treaties of peace—that is, the provisions agreed upon other than those already mentioned in connection with the form of the instrument. The fundamental object of a treaty of peace is: first, to put an end to the war, secondly, to settle the differences that produced it, and thirdly, to settle whatever new differences may have arisen in the course of the hostilities. Accordingly we often find a large variety of articles in the treaty of peace. Very rarely indeed do we come across a peace treaty that confines itself simply to declaring the termination of war between the contracting parties. One of the few modern instances is the Treaty of Bucharest, March 3, 1886, between Bulgaria and Serbia, which contained a single article, as follows: "La paix est rétablie entre le royaume de Serbie et la principauté de Bulgarie, à dater du jour de la signature du présent traité." Obviously such procedure is most undesirable; the causes of the war may not have been thereby removed, conflicting pretensions may still remain, maintaining and nourishing the previous ill-feeling, and so inducing an aggrieved party to recommence hostilities at an opportune moment and with greater fury than before. Here, then, as everywhere else, an ounce of prevention is worth much more than a pound of remedy. Recognizing this, conflicting nations are, as a rule, disposed not only to solve finally and permanently their outstanding differences in order to prevent the re-assertion of all claims that gave rise to their war, but also to regulate specifically their re-established pacific relationships, making therein whatever new changes they deem fit. No wonder, then, that some treaties of peace comprise a large number of articles.

These articles may conveniently be divided into two classes—general and special. The general articles are those that relate directly to the cessation of war and resumption of peace and provide for matters that the war itself has brought into existence; consequently such clauses are found in practically all treaties of peace, and some of them are often drawn up in like terms. The following subjects, then, belong to the general articles: the cessation of hostilities and the establishment of peace, and when this is to take effect; the evacuation of territory if militarily occupied; the restoration of property captured, including certain classes of prizes in a naval war, or regulation according to the principle *uti possidetis*; the liberation of prisoners of war; the granting of an amnesty to all who were compromised during the war by certain acts (we may note here that in the case of the Franco-Prussian War the amnesty clause was irregularly omitted from the definitive Treaty of Frankfort and consigned to an additional convention); the revival or abrogation of treaties concluded before the war.

General articles.

The special articles are those that relate to the essential points at issue—that is, those for which the war was made; or they comprise the terms on the acceptance of which depends the re-establishment of peace—in other words, they constitute the price of peace. These articles, therefore, vary according to the circumstances of each war and the particular relationships of the parties. But two of them are common to most treaties, and embody the principal demands imposed by the victor on the vanquished, viz. the payment of an indemnity and the cession of territory. In the case of the former, there are frequently further articles specifying the conditions and guarantees of payment; in the case of the latter, there are almost invariably accompanying articles which, on the one hand, provide for the emigration or option of nationality of the inhabitants of the ceded territory and, on the other, regulate questions of State succession relative to property, debts, contracts, etc., connected with the ceded territory. These two special subjects—indemnity and cession—will thus give rise to a considerable number of articles, seeing that it is customary to consign all these various points to separate clauses. All these accessory clauses, then, together with

Special articles.

the two principal ones, stipulating the indemnity and the cession, must be classified as special clauses. It is to be noted that the Treaty of Frankfort, May 10, 1871, makes an unusual departure, in that it actually omits the most important stipulations as to the cession of Alsace-Lorraine and the payment of the huge indemnity. The German negotiators evidently held that the Preliminaries of Versailles, February 26, 1871, sufficed for these points, and that the definitive treaty might assume agreement thereon, and simply add supplementary provisions. But why not let the preliminaries remain final for other matters also? In point of fact, the real reason for the omission was Bismarck's determination to consider the cession and the indemnity specifically fixed before the meeting of the plenipotentiaries charged to negotiate and draw up the definitive treaty, and so to deprive the French delegates of their opportunity to reopen these questions.

Miscellaneous articles.

In addition to the above there are articles dealing with subjects peculiar to this or that treaty. On account of their variety they can scarcely be classified; but it will be seen that, having regard to the classification above suggested, some of them belong, logically, to the class of general clauses, others to that of special clauses, and others, again, relate to diverse matters, either pending before the war and not serious enough to provoke it, or such as the contracting parties, having seized the opportunity offered by the great settlement between them, desire to solve, or make clear, or establish. Examples of questions covered by these miscellaneous clauses are as follows: [1] what relation the preliminaries of peace bear to the definitive treaty; provision for further arrangements to be made to complete or fulfil the stipulations of the preliminaries or definitive treaty; mediation in case of differences; the cancelling of the armistice by the treaty of peace; demobilization; destruction of fortresses; the tombs of the fallen; railway communication; canals; rivers; straits; inland seas; rights of navigation; right of fishery; customs; treatment of shipping; treatment of produce of ceded territory; recognition by one party of the other's paramount interests in a certain locality; treatment of subjects of one party residing in the territory of the other; their lawsuits; the practice of their religion; the rights of subjects of one party expelled during the war by the other party from the latter's territory; compensation to subjects of one party for losses caused by the military operations of the other party; the establishment of new States and new political

[1] They are selected from the peace treaties of the last hundred years; and the original clauses suggesting the examples are found in the Appendix of texts given at the end of this work.

organizations; the definition of the international status of certain countries, etc.

The complete execution of articles relating to some or other of the subjects enumerated above may well involve a multitude of details which it is found impossible to provide for in the body of the treaty itself. Accordingly, these details are disposed of in a series of articles variously described as annexes, or additional, separate, supplementary articles, or additional or annexed conventions, which are attached to the treaty and are declared to possess equally binding force; so that the entire instrument is given consistency and solidarity. It may happen, too, that certain points occur to the plenipotentiaries or, after persistent opposition, are ultimately agreed upon (as in the case of the three additional articles of the Treaty of Frankfort, May 10, 1871) after their treaty has been drafted, and they find it inconvenient to alter it for the purpose of incorporating them. Such points, then, may also be embodied in the supplementary articles. One or two examples may be given of additional articles attached to the principal instrument and bearing the same date. The Treaty of Paris, May 30, 1814, between the Allies and France, contained 33 articles, and was followed by a considerable number of additional articles (and several secret ones, which will presently be referred to) concluded separately between France and each of the Allies. The subjects dealt with were of many kinds, e.g. the slave trade; expenses of prisoners of war; removal of sequestrations from funds, revenues, debts; claims of subjects for illegal confiscations; annulment of certain treaties, and of French decrees. Art. IV of the Treaty of Paris, November 20, 1815, between the Allied Powers and France, required France to pay an indemnity of 700 million francs, and said that the modes, the periods, and the guarantees for the payment were to be regulated by a special convention having the same force and effect as if it were inserted in the treaty itself. The annexed convention, consisting of sixteen articles, signed by the same plenipotentiaries, prescribed the various details necessary to the fulfilment of that stipulation.[1] Similarly Art. V of the principal instrument provided for the military occupation by the Allied troops of certain military positions along the frontiers of France, to ensure the security of neighbouring States and the performance of the terms laid down. Accordingly, an additional convention of nine articles regulated the numerous questions in regard to the maintenance of these troops, the places to be occupied, etc. Moreover, this convention is itself followed by an additional article stipulating the reciprocal surrender of deserters.[2] Art. X of the

Additional or separate articles.

[1] See *infra*, Appendix (C).

[2] Appendix (B).

Treaty of Paris, March 30, 1856, stated that the ancient rule as to the closing of the Bosphorus and the Dardanelles was revised, and that the act concluded for that purpose was annexed to the treaty. The Treaty of Prague, August 23, 1866, is followed by a list of fourteen stipulations relative to the performance of Arts. III and XII, dealing respectively with the liberation of prisoners of war and the evacuation of territory.[1] The Treaty of Frankfort, May 10, 1871, is supplemented by additional articles concerning the purchase of French railways and other rights connected therewith, and the rectification of the frontier near Belfort. To the Treaty of Constantinople, February 8, 1879, between Russia and Turkey, is appended a protocol containing a number of explanations of the articles in the principal act.[2] The Treaty of Portsmouth, September 5, 1905, is followed by a supplementary agreement for the performance of Arts. III and IX as to the evacuation of Manchuria, and the division of Sakhalin.[3] The Treaty of Constantinople, September 29, 1913, between Turkey and Bulgaria, is supplemented by elaborate protocols and annexes regulating the details arising out of articles of the treaty.[4]

On the other hand, any of these matters and others that cannot be determined at the time may be reserved for separate conventions to be concluded subsequently, either by the same negotiators or by specially appointed commissioners. Thus the full performance of the Treaty of Frankfort, May 10, 1871, actually necessitated the conclusion of more than a hundred conventions.[5]

Secret articles.

Further, certain additional articles may be kept secret. We have already seen that according to the constitutional law of certain States, e.g. Belgium and Spain, the conclusion of secret articles is forbidden if they destroy or are incompatible with the open or public articles. However, contracting parties sometimes agree secretly to set aside certain clauses of the open treaty, or modify some of them for a given time, or suspend their performance or operation, or even to supplement the public treaty by means of new provisions which it is thought inexpedient to make known at the time, because they might offend the susceptibilities of third States or arouse their distrust, or even excite opposition on the part of the signatories' own subjects. In the treaty of 1741 between England and Russia there were separate and secret articles. The treaty of peace of Campo Formio, October 17, 1797, between France and the Empire, was followed by a number of

[1] Appendix (H), *in fin.*
[2] Appendix (O).
[3] Appendix (U), *in fin.*
[4] Appendix (Y), *in fin.*
[5] These are contained in the publication of Villefort, which has already been mentioned: *Recueil des traités, conventions, lois, décrets et autres actes relatifs à la paix avec l'Allemagne* (Paris, 1872-1879).

additional secret articles, of which Art. 16 said: "The two contracting parties mutually promise in the most obligatory manner to preserve the profoundest secrecy with regard to the present articles." The treaty of peace of Paris, August 24, 1801, between France and the Elector Palatine of Bavaria, was accompanied by secret articles whereby the Elector renounced his possessions and rights in Batavian territory, on condition that this renunciation should remain secret until an understanding was arrived at between France and the King of Prussia, who had possessions there. The Treaty of Paris, May 30, 1814, was followed by "separate and secret articles" between the Allies (Great Britain, Austria, Prussia, Russia) and France, providing—among other things—for the following: disposal of the territories given up by France; regulation of the Austrian and Sardinian territories in Italy, and of the Dutch frontiers; guarantee of Switzerland; freedom of navigation of the Scheldt; renunciation by France of claims for endowments, donations, revenues of the Legion of Honour, etc. There were also secret articles between Austria and France, stipulating the continued payment of the Lorraine revenue, and the delivery by France of certain Acts taken from the archives of Vienna; between France and Portugal, restoring French Guiana, settling the mutual claims of subjects, and annulling the treaties of Badajoz and Madrid, 1801, and the Convention of Lisbon, 1804; between France and Sweden, whereby France recognized the union of Norway and Sweden. In the treaty of peace of Berlin, July 2, 1850, between Prussia and Denmark, there was a secret article providing that Prussia should take part in negotiations for regulating the order of succession in Denmark.

Whatever precedents may be cited, however, and whether or no the constitutions of States formally prohibit the conclusion of secret articles destructive of those that are patent, there can be no doubt that such a practice generally countenanced and adopted would place international relations on a basis of deceit and hypocrisy. If at present the character of international relationships is not conspicuous for its frankness and sincerity, we can well imagine what it would be like if States A and B added secret articles to their public treaty for fear of, or levelled at, C, or if D, E, and F did the same as against G and H, or a group here proceeded likewise as against a group there, and then one State of one group concluded a treaty, together with secret clauses, with a State of another group, and so on. A sinister diplomacy of this kind would enmesh the society of States in a factitious tangle of duplicity and dissimulation, and would inevitably give rise to the worst features of Machiavellianism. If civilization means anything, it means candour, honesty, and purity in men's and nations' intercourse; and international morality—if not yet international law—condemns conduct based on different principles.

Having regard to the multiplicity of subjects, the conflict of interests involved, and the circumstances of negotiation, we need not wonder that treaties of peace are not always models of logical order and exactness of expression. In very few peace treaties indeed can we detect the use of a coherent and rational system in the arrangement and drafting of the various articles. Surely the adoption of some such scheme as the following would conduce to clearness and simplicity and to what the Romans called *elegantia*: first, an article stipulating the restoration of peace and the date of its taking effect; next, the general articles necessitated by the incidents of the war, e.g. restoration of territory and evacuation of troops, the return of certain captured property, or, in either case, a provision for *uti possidetis*, liberation of prisoners of war, amnesty, a provision for the revival or definite annulment of treaties affected by the war; then, the special articles constituting the nucleus of the treaty, e.g. indemnity or reimbursement of war costs, cession of territory, regulations as to the nationality and option of inhabitants in the ceded territory, and also as to State succession in respect of the ceded territory (the order of the various points that arise is suggested in the final chapters of the present work). In the absence of cession and indemnity, the other special articles (that is, appertaining to the differences that brought the war about) might be arranged according to their importance and cognate character, which could likewise be done if cession and indemnity were stipulated; next, miscellaneous questions; after this would appear clauses (if any) for guaranteeing the performance of the treaty or certain essential portions thereof, e.g. occupation of territory; and finally the provision for ratification and the exchange of ratifications. If a plan like this were adopted, the articles would then be read in their proper context, the instrument would be much easier to understand and to interpret, and the intention of the parties would be more readily discernible. Instead of this, we have to look sometimes in supplementary articles or additional conventions for most important provisions; we are obliged to rearrange mentally several parts of treaties before we can grasp the purport of this or that article, owing to the ill-assortment of the subject-matter. Several defects of the Treaty of Frankfort have already been pointed out. An examination of the texts given at the end of this work will show, if we use as a criterion some such classification as that suggested above, how indiscriminately the articles of many treaties have been thrown together.

Suggested order of clauses.

INTERPRETATION OF TREATIES.

Treaties of peace are subject to the same rules of interpretation as apply to treaties in general. But these rules so elaborately set forth by many writers are neither final nor authoritative; they are usually coloured by the particular systems of jurisprudence adopted in their respective States; so that whilst some of the rules are intrinsically reasonable, others appear to be to this or that judge or Government of doubtful applicability or entirely unjustifiable. Amongst the former class of rules, as being generally accepted, may be mentioned the following, in the convenient summary given by a recent writer:[1] "(1) In the interpretation of international agreements it is necessary, in view of the different character of the interests involved and the different conditions under which such agreements are commonly entered into, to adopt a more liberal method of construction than that which might fairly be applied in the case of private instruments." (In other words, the spirit of a provision is not to be subordinated to the letter. A striking example showing an attempt to follow a purely literal interpretation of a clause is furnished by the Treaty of Utrecht, 1713. Art. IX laid down that the port and fortifications of Dunkirk were to be destroyed and never rebuilt. The stipulation as it stands was never carried out, but afterwards France proceeded to build another port at Mardyck, within a league of Dunkirk. England naturally protested against this irrational interpretation of the article, the object of which was perfectly obvious; and eventually France admitted the reasonableness of the protest, and stopped building the port.) "(2) All international agreements must be construed in such a way as not to derogate from the fundamental principles of international law; or even from the fundamental rights of States, except in so far as a contrary intention is explicitly manifested. (3) In general the words used must be construed in their plain and ordinary sense, save where they possess some 'customary' or 'special' meaning within the knowledge and contemplation of the parties. (4) Where the words of a stipulation or provision, taken by themselves, fail to yield a plain and reasonable sense, recourse should be had either to the immediate context, or, if necessary, to the general purport and tenor of the agreement, including a consideration of its title and statement of object and headings. (5) In the case of conflicting claims it is usual to read general clauses as being subject to qualification by special clauses, and prior clauses by later. (6) In cases where a doubt or a dual meaning cannot be dispelled by a consideration of the instrument as a whole, recourse may be had to such extrinsic

Fundamental principles.

[1] Cobbett, *Cases*, vol. i (1909), pp. 332–333, who refers to several English and American authors and judicial decisions.

evidence as may serve to throw light on the true intention of the parties; and hence regard may be had (*inter alia*) to preliminary stipulations, even though these are otherwise deemed to be merged in the substantive agreement, or to contemporaneous acts, or even to subsequent acts of the parties, as corroborative evidence of a particular construction. (7) In default of express provision, and failing any other evidence of intention, recourse may be had to the following presumptions, in so far as they may be appropriate: (*a*) The clear grant of a right or the clear imposition of an obligation will be deemed to carry all necessary incidents to its full enjoyment, or adequate discharge, as the case may be. (*b*) Subject to this, the grant of a right or imposition of an obligation will be presumed to carry no wider right and no obligation more onerous than is expressly stated, and the onus of proving anything beyond this must be deemed to rest on the party who alleges it. (*c*) If the terms used have a different legal sense in different States, then there will be a presumption in favour of that sense which attaches in the State upon which the obligation is imposed." (The last presumption is expressed in too restricted terms. It is better to say that that sense should be preferred which obtains in the State to which the provision containing the terms applies. There is an apt illustration of this principle. By the treaty of peace of Vienna, October 3, 1866, between Austria and Italy, the former agreed to cede to the latter the Lombardo-Venetian kingdom (Art. III). And Art. XIV provided that "inhabitants or natives" of the ceded provinces should be permitted to withdraw with their property into Austrian territory for the space of a year from the date of the exchange of the ratifications. Now in Austria the word "inhabitants" meant only persons domiciled according to Austrian law; but in Italy it applied to all persons living in a commune and registered as residents. Which interpretation was to prevail? At the time when the treaty was negotiated and signed, the territory to which Art. XIV referred was Austrian; accordingly it was decided to interpret the word in question in the Austrian sense.[1])

Further, where two treaties concluded by the same parties conflict, the later is, usually, to predominate; but where two treaties are concluded at different times by different parties, the earlier should predominate, on the ground that no State may make an engagement with another to the prejudice of a previous convention entered into with a third party, unless the latter assent.[2]

[1] Cf. W. E. Hall, *International Law* (Oxford, 1909), p. 329.

[2] On the interpretation of treaties, the following may be consulted: Vattel, *Droit des gens*, liv. ii. ch. xvii; Moore, *Digest*, vol. v. §§ 763, 764; Phillimore, *Commentaries*, vol. ii. pt. v. ch. viii. §§ 64–95; Pradier-Fodéré, *Traité de droit*

The above principles may be considered as being almost axiomatic, and will apply to the interpretation of peace treaties as well as to other classes of treaties. Even if a dispute as to the construction of an agreement or a particular clause of it be referred to arbitration, it is difficult to imagine the court of arbitrators adopting contrary principles, unless these are demanded by the consensus of the signatories. The real intention of the parties—that is the root of the whole question. To make it readily discernible, clearness, exactness, and simplicity of expression are indispensable ; no point relative to the matters concerned should be left indecisive ; all subtlety and ambiguity should be studiously avoided. As Gérard de Rayneval observes, with special reference to treaties of peace: "Il n'est aucun acte qui se fasse avec plus de défiance, puisqu'il y a toujours une partie mécontente; il exige donc de la clarté, de la précision, une noble simplicité ; le vainqueur doit parler le langage de la modération ; le vaincu, celui de la dignité ; s'il est humilié par les choses, il ne doit point l'être par les mots ; aucun sujet grave de discussion ne doit demeurer indécis ; aucun mot ne doit fournir matière à doute et à interprétation ; aucun mot, aucune phráse parasite ne doit être admise ; les équivoques, les amphibologies, les subtilités, les surprises doivent être soigneusement évitées." [1]

Precision and simplicity indispensable.

Vattel discusses one or two additional rules, which are deemed to be more particularly adapted to treaties of peace. Thus, in the first place, where a doubt arises as to the meaning of a given article, which imposes an obligation on one of the parties, the article should be interpreted in favour of the latter, as it must be presumed to have been dictated by the other party. He who imposes terms must suffer the consequences of faulty expression ; he should not be allowed an opportunity to use vague or ambiguous terms as snares for entrapping the weaker party—" tourner des termes vagues ou ambigus en pièges pour le plus faible contractant." [2] The difficulty here, however, is that the article in question may have been proposed in the very terms by the plenipotentiaries of the country assuming the obligation ; and that the negotiators of the other country did not consider any expression vague or ambiguous. Moreover, it may be that, when the time comes for the performance of the article, the weaker party

Additional rules.

int., vol. ii. §§ 1171–1188 ; *Amer. Journ. of Int. Law*, vol. iii (1910), pp. 46 *seq.* ; *Law Magazine and Review*, 5th series, vol. xxvi. pp. 62 *seq.*, 164 *seq.* ; *Revue générale de droit int. pub.* (Paris), vol. xvii (1910), pp. 5 *seq.*

[1] J. M. Gérard de Rayneval, *Institutions du droit de la nature et des gens* (1803), p. 285.

[2] *Droit des gens*, liv. iv. ch. iii. § 32.

manifests a subtle and captious spirit, and claims that its meaning is different from that which had before, apparently, been agreed upon. Accordingly the utility of Vattel's rule is doubtful; we can at most say in such a case that he who impugns a certain clause in a treaty is bound to prove his contention, by reference to all the material circumstances of the engagement, and especially to the evidence furnished by protocols or other reports of the negotiations and by the relevant oral discussions. Secondly, if territory is ceded under its name, and without express delimitation of its boundaries, the name should be taken in the sense used at the time by competent and intelligent men, subject, of course, to the intention of the parties—" suivant l'usage reçu alors par les personnes habiles et intelligentes." [1] This rule, too, has been criticized on the ground that the confines of the territory so ceded can best be determined—failing public Acts—by usage and immemorial tradition in accordance with the testimony of inhabitants long established there. And the intention of the contracting parties with regard to the extent of the territory is not always easy to perceive. Thus, at the conference at Aix-la-Chapelle, 1748, the English and the French plenipotentiaries had different ideas as to territorial limits dealt with in the treaty.[2] Difficulties, however, may be avoided by appointing a mixed commission of delimitation and concluding a special convention in accordance with the results thus arrived at. Thirdly, whatever clauses there are that appear to be vague must naturally be understood in relation to the war. For example, a mere stipulation to restore things to their former condition does not refer to changes that have been brought about otherwise than by the operations of the war itself. A party who desires to obtain things which the general clause does not of itself comprise should clearly and specifically express his intentions to that effect. " Stipulations of every kind may be inserted in a treaty of peace; but if they bear no relation to the war which it is the view of the contracting parties to terminate, they must be expressly specified; for the treaty is naturally understood to relate only to its own particular object." [3]

Arbitration clause.

Not infrequently provision is made in treaties for referring disputes as to interpretation to an arbitral tribunal. Thus—to give but one or two recent examples—in the case of the Treaty of Constantinople, September 16/29, 1913, between Turkey and Bulgaria, Art. XVII says that all differences and disputes that might arise in the interpretation or application of Arts. XI, XII, XIII, and XVI (referring to the right

[1] *Droit des gens*, liv. iv. ch. iii. § 33.
[2] Note by Chambrier d'Oleires to § 33 of Vattel, edit. of Hauterive, vol. ii.
[3] *Ibid.*, § 34.

of holding landed property in the ceded territory, the position of vakoufs, the property of the Sultan, and railway concessions there), as well as of Annex I of the treaty (referring to the delimitation of the frontier), should be settled by arbitration at The Hague in accordance with an agreement set out in Annex III.[1] Similarly in the Treaty of Athens, November 1/14, 1913, between Turkey and Greece, Art. X declares that the two Governments agree, under a "compromis," to be concluded, to submit to an arbitral tribunal at The Hague the dispute concerning the interpretation of the protocol of surrender of Salonica, dated October 26, 1912, viz. whether or no the arms of Ottoman soldiers of the garrison of that city should be restored.[2] Art. XII specified, too, that all controversies as to the interpretation and application of its various provisions (relating to the vakoufs in the ceded territories) were to be decided by arbitration at The Hague. These submissions are in accordance with the conclusion of the Hague Conference, 1907, that certain differences, and in particular those relating to the interpretation and application of international agreements, are susceptible of being submitted to obligatory arbitration without any restriction.

[1] See *infra*, Appendix (Y). [2] Appendix (Z).

CHAPTER VII

THE TREATY OF PEACE

GENERAL PRINCIPLES (*Continued*)

Date of Peace—Ratification—Means of ensuring Performance of the Treaty

Date of peace: necessary distinctions; cessation of hostilities; effect of signature; date of notice to armed forces; clause specifying date; sometimes future date fixed—Date of operation of other clauses: if no date is specified—Ratification: when ratification not necessary; refusal to ratify; place and time of exchange of ratifications—Breach of treaty—Means of ensuring performance: oath; hostages; pledge; guarantee by third States; military occupation; examples.

DATE OF PEACE.

Necessary distinctions.

WITH regard to the date of the treaty of peace, it is necessary to make certain important distinctions, which writers on international law, in their scanty references to the question, neglect. In the first place, the expression "the date of the treaty of peace" may mean the date that appears on the instrument, indicating when it was signed by the contracting parties. Here the date simply shows when the *consensus ad idem* was definitely arrived at, and the terms of agreement have become positive and unalterable. It does not necessarily show when such terms, or any of them, begin to operate. Secondly, the said expression may mean the day on which hostilities cease and peaceful relations are re-established, without regard to the date on which the substantive clauses of the treaty come into effect. Thirdly, it may signify the date of the operation of the treaty as a whole, and the point of departure whence begins the new status or position of the States—as provided by the terms agreed upon—in relation to each other as well as to third parties. Whether peace begins with the signing, whether a provision that hostilities should cease on signing refers to that very date or to the date of the receipt of notice by the armed forces, whether the exchange of ratifications has a retroactive effect—on these and on other relevant questions international law is silent; and previous practice does not furnish any uniform rules. Regard must, therefore, be had to the circumstances of each case, to the intention, express or implied, of the parties, and to considerations of reason and common sense.

Date of cessation of hostilities.

As to the cessation of hostilities, we have already seen, in our discussion of armistice conventions, that frequently arrangements are made for a general suspension of arms by the belligerents with a view to entering on peace negotiations, or—when the preliminary terms have been settled—with a view to the meeting of plenipotentiaries for drawing up the definitive treaty. Sometimes the preliminaries require certain guarantees that some or other of the fundamental conditions of the preliminaries of peace will be performed with complete certainty. If these guarantees are given, then the armistice previously established, or to be established forthwith, as the case may be, comes to be regarded as the final cessation of hostilities, and the opposing armies may be withdrawn from their positions, subject to the maintenance of a sufficient force in or near the one country or the other for the purpose of ensuring the fulfilment of certain fundamental conditions. We find, accordingly, that some treaties say nothing as to the date of the commencement of peace, or even of the operation of the articles in general. Such is the case, for example, with the Preliminaries of Versailles, February 26, 1871, the Treaty of Frankfort, May 10, 1871—where the suspension of arms was effected by the convention signed at Versailles, January 28—and the Treaty of Paris, December 10, 1898, between the United States and Spain—where the protocol signed at Washington, August 12, provided for the general suspension of hostilities. In these cases there is not a single word referring, even in an indefinite sense, to the commencement of peace. Other treaties, again, whilst mentioning no specific date, simply say—because an armistice has been or is to be immediately or subsequently concluded—that there shall exist peace (as in the Treaty of Lima, June 12, 1883, between Spain and Chile, Art. I: "The past shall be consigned to oblivion, and there shall exist a solid and inviolable peace . . . "), or that "there shall be in future peace and friendship" (as in the Treaty of Zurich, November 10, 1859, between France and Austria, Art. I), or "there shall be peace and friendship . . . henceforth . . ." (as in the Treaty of Prague, August 23, 1866, between Austria and Prussia, Art. I; and, in equivalent terms, in the Treaty of Portsmouth, September 5, 1905, between Russia and Japan, Art. I). What is the meaning of such expressions as "henceforth," "in future," etc.? Obviously their application is relative to the date of the documents in which they respectively appear; so that if arms have not been suspended by some other arrangement, they are deemed to be suspended there and then. But this is not the inevitable result, simple and natural as it seems to be. For in the notable Treaty of Portsmouth the expression "henceforth" occurs, and yet open hostilities between the Russian and the Japanese forces went on vigorously for some time after the signature of the treaty. It was, indeed, on September 1 that the plenipotentiaries signed an armistice protocol at Portsmouth, wherein it was stipulated that orders should be given to their respective commanders to put it into execution immediately after the signature of the treaty of peace. The latter was signed on September 5; but it was not until September 13 that the military commissioners of the belligerents met and signed a military armistice, which was to take effect on the 16th, and it was not till September 18 that the naval armistice was signed and came into operation.[1] It would appear that in this case the date of the exchange of ratifications (viz. September 25) was taken as furnishing the essential point of departure. That was clearly understood by the negotiators. But they must also have considered the date of signing the treaty of peace to be a material date, seeing that they agreed to communicate to their forces, immediately after this signing, the armistice protocol drawn up previously. That a great length of time elapsed before hostilities were brought to a stop is unfortunate, but the main point to bear in mind is that had the negotiators been able to cause the warlike operations to cease the moment they affixed their signatures to the peace treaty, they would undoubtedly have done so—unless they were fully convinced that the treaty would not be ratified if arms were suspended. In other words, they must have realized that all considerations of reason and logic and even political prudence demanded the cessation of hostilities—not necessarily the withdrawal or demobilization of the armed forces—as soon as the definitive, invariable treaty of peace was concluded and signed.

Here we must refer to a case—*The Eliza Ann*—decided a century ago by Lord Stowell, who held that the expression "dès ce moment" in the Treaty of Orebro, July 18, 1812, between Great Britain and Sweden, referred to the date of subsequent ratification and not to that of the signature; and consequently that vessels seized before the exchange of ratifications were good prize. "It is said," he observed, "that the treaty when ratified refers back to the time of its signature by the plenipotentiaries, and that it does so in this case more especially on account of the terms in which it is drawn. The words in one of the articles of the treaty—"Dès ce moment tout sujet de mésintelligence qui ait pu subsister . . . sera regardé comme

[1] See *supra*, pp. 71 *seq.*

entièrement cessant et détruit "—have been pointed out, and from these it has been contended that all hostilities were to cease the moment the treaty was signed. But I take that not to be the case; the positive and enacting part of the article is that there *shall* be a firm and inviolable peace between the two countries; the other part is *descriptive* only of the pacific intention of the parties, and of their agreement to bury in oblivion all the causes of the war. It does not stand in the same substantive way as the former part of the article, and must be considered as mere explanatory description." He concluded that, in his opinion, "the ratification is the point from which the treaty must take effect. 'Dès ce moment' must be referred to the moment at which the treaty received its valid existence by mutual ratification." [1] This reasoning is by no means conclusive. We find, moreover, that in an earlier case, *The Elsebe*,[2] the same judge said that "in matters of treaty . . . the act of ratification may be said to operate with retrospective effect, to confirm the terms of the treaty from the date of the preliminary articles." This pronouncement is hardly compatible with the observations given above. If ratification operates retroactively to confirm the treaty from the date of the preliminaries, it must also do so from the date of signature in respect of hostile acts.

Effect of signature.

If no provision has been made otherwise—either by an armistice convention or by a clause in the preliminaries or the treaty of peace—then hostilities should entirely cease with the signing of the definitive treaty; and the exchange of ratifications would therefore have, in this respect, a retroactive effect.[3] This is not an established principle of international law; but, it is submitted, it is fully worthy of becoming one on the ground of reason and expediency. The vital date, so far as the whole of the relationships of the parties are concerned, is, it is true, that of the exchange of ratifications; but the latest date for ceasing hostilities should be that of the signing of the definitive treaty, unless a different agreement has been expressly made by the parties for their own good reasons. Once the definitive treaty is concluded and signed, its provisions can no longer be altered; so that there cannot be any justifiable motive for continuing the war. When a belligerent is determined to continue warlike operations after his adversary has begun peace negotiations, his only reason can be that he is anxious to gain such military successes in the meantime as will enable him to demand better terms. But after he has come to

[1] *The Eliza Ann* (1813), 1 Dodson, 244, 248–250.

[2] (1804) 5 C. Rob. 174, 190.

[3] Cf. *Davis* v. *Police Jury of Concordia* (1850), 9 Howard, 289; *Haver* v. *Yaker* (1869), 9 Wallace, 32.

an agreement upon them, and signified his assent by adding his signature and seal, the resolve to go on with the war till the date of ratification means useless butchery, as well as indefensible waste of treasure and destruction of property. Indeed, it would be more in accordance with juridical considerations, and the dictates of humanity, to put a stop to the war—to suspend it, at least, if not to withdraw the armies from their positions—as soon as the plenipotentiaries of both sides have met in conference to negotiate the terms of peace. However, whatever reasons may be urged—and no doubt in certain circumstances strong ones might well be advanced—against the adoption of the latter practice as an invariable rule, it is difficult to see what reasons can be brought forward that are strong enough to entitle any belligerent to continue his hostilities after the definitive treaty of peace has been concluded. Does he imagine that the other side is insincere in its desire for peace, that it will not eventually ratify the treaty, and that it is utilizing the period between the conclusion of the treaty and its ratification in making further military preparations with a view to offering more effective resistance, or making a renewed onslaught in the hope of reversing the situation? The records of history show that an assumption of this kind is unwarranted. There are very few treaties indeed which were not ultimately ratified. Moreover, why assume that ratification is an unfailing protection against such ulterior designs? If a successful belligerent, after having secured satisfactory terms in the definitive treaty of peace, cannot trust the pledged word of the other contracting party, he need not demobilize his forces till the date of ratification; and he can easily insist on an early ratification, so as not to prolong unduly his state of doubt and suspicion. But if he is convinced that his only safeguard is to prosecute hostilities till the very last moment, then it is difficult to see how he can become really satisfied, unless he has completely annihilated his enemy—that is, until he has made peace negotiations impossible altogether. With regard to the effect of the signature in putting an end to hostilities, we may recall an interesting case that came before the French Prize Court. The Treaty of Lunéville, between France and Austria, was signed on February 9, 1801, and was ratified March 16, 1801. Now on March 8—after the signature, but before the ratification—the *Thétis*, an Austrian vessel, was captured by the French, and brought up for adjudication. The court ordered the restoration of the vessel and cargo, on the ground that at the time of capture France was at peace with Austria, as a result of the conclusion of the Treaty of Lunéville. To say that there could be no performance of the treaty, observed the court, because it was not yet ratified, was to advance a ridiculous proposition, which was repugnant to policy and good sense alike. The plea of ignorance could scarcely be brought forward so long after the peace was signed; but if the captor proved that he was really unaware of the conclusion of the treaty at the time of capture, his good faith would protect him personally from liability to pay damages, but it would not render the capture valid.[1]

It follows from the above observations that in case the definitive treaty or the preliminaries, as the case may be, be not ratified by the time fixed in the instrument, hostilities may then justifiably be recommenced; so that what was provisionally a definitive treaty of peace has turned out to be little more than an armistice convention.

Date of notice to armed forces.

If the date of the signing of a certain agreement is contemplated as the date on which hostilities are to cease, then it is obviously much simpler and much better in every respect to insert in it a clause to that effect. Even then disputes and difficulties are not obviated unless the understanding on the point is made perfectly explicit. Take, for example, Art. VI of the preliminaries—the "protocol of peace"—signed at Washington, August 12, 1898, by the United States and Spain: "Upon the conclusion and signing of this protocol, hostilities between the two countries shall be suspended, and notice to that effect shall be given as soon as possible by each Government to the commanders of its military and naval forces." It is evident that this article is not as clear and as free from doubt as it might easily have been made. The first part of it would seem to imply that warlike operations were to cease *ipso facto* on the signing, whilst the latter part implied undoubtedly that the real date of the cessation was that on which the respective commanders received notice. The forces engaged in conflict were at a considerable distance from Washington, where the protocol was concluded, so that, despite telegraphic convenience, some time would inevitably elapse before due notice could be received by the commanding officers of the naval and military forces operating in different spheres. Accordingly, the second part of the article must be held to prevail. But it would have been better to specify a date or a definite period, as is usually done in such agreements; for example, the armistice convention of January 28, 1871, in the Franco-German War, stipulated that military operations were to cease on the date of signature in Paris, and within three days thereafter in the departments. An undertaking to communicate the notice to the forces "as soon as possible" is eminently unsatisfactory, for the

[1] Pistoye et Duverdy, *op. cit.*, vol. i. pp. 148–149.

phrase might be interpreted to cover negligences and even deliberate delays. It is more customary and more regular to promise to communicate such notice *immediately*.

The above-mentioned Art. VI subsequently gave rise to some controversy between the American and the Spanish Governments. It appears that, notwithstanding the vague phrase in it, the United States despatched notice immediately to her forces. This was presumably on August 12. On August 14, however, before the notice arrived, Manila was compelled to capitulate to the American forces. Now Art. III of the protocol of peace said that pending the conclusion of a definitive treaty the United States was to occupy and hold Manila with its bay and harbour. Thus two different measures—one depending on the force of arms, the other on the force of an agreement—empowered the United States to hold Manila. Afterwards, when peace negotiations had begun, the Spanish Government contended that the occupation of Manila was due entirely to the agreement, and not to the capitulation—on the ground that the latter was null, as it had occurred after the signing of the protocol, which had stipulated a suspension of hostilities. In reply the American Government held—and rightly so—that as the protocol had made express provision for the giving of the notice, the suspension of arms took effect "at the date of the receipt of the notice"; [1] and it instructed its plenipotentiaries at the Paris Conference that Manila and its suburbs were held "by conquest as well as by virtue of the protocol," so that the demand of the Spanish representatives to restore immediately the *status quo* on the date of the protocol was rejected.[2]

Clause specifying date of peace.

Not infrequently—it ought to be invariably—clauses are inserted in definitive treaties specifying the date of the commencement of peace, as the regular and normal condition; and this, in spite of the fact that hostilities may have practically, though conditionally, been brought to an end by means of an armistice agreement, or military convention, or by the preliminaries. We have already seen that contracting parties regard their peace treaty as setting up a provisional condition of affairs, until the date of ratification by the competent authority, or, rather, until the date of the exchange of ratifications. Accordingly, this is the date generally fixed in treaties as that on which peace is to be considered definitely established. Thus the Treaty of Paris, March 30, 1856, says (Art. I) that "from the day of the exchange of ratifications of the present treaty there shall be peace and

[1] *Foreign Relations of the United States* (1898), pp. 813 *seq.*

[2] Cf. *Senate Documents*, vol. 148, p. 6, 56th Cong., 2nd sess.; vol. 62, pp. 13 *seq.*, 55th Cong., 3rd sess.

friendship" between Great Britain, France, Sardinia, and Turkey on the one side, and Russia on the other. The Treaty of Vienna, October 3, 1866, also stipulates (Art. I) that "there shall be, from the date of the exchange of the ratifications of the present treaty, peace and friendship" between Italy and Austria. Again, the Treaty of Shimonoseki, April 17, 1895, between China and Japan, lays down (Art. X): "All offensive military operations shall cease upon the exchange of the ratifications of this act." The Treaty of London, May 30, 1913, between Turkey on the one part, and Greece, Bulgaria, Serbia, and Montenegro on the other, says (Art. I): "Upon the exchange of ratifications of the present treaty there shall be peace and friendship" between all the States concerned. Similarly, the Treaty of Bucharest, August 10, 1913, between Bulgaria on the one side, and Roumania, Greece, Serbia, and Montenegro on the other, provides (Art. I): "From the day on which the ratifications of the present treaty are exchanged there shall be peace and amity" between the signatories.

Sometimes a future date is fixed.

Sometimes, when war is carried on in widely separated spheres, and it is deemed impossible to notify immediately the various opposing forces of the conclusion of peace, a future date is fixed in the treaty for the cessation of hostilities, if they have not already ceased under another arrangement This case differs from that of the above-mentioned Protocol of Washington, in that a definite date is specified; whereas the protocol did not fix the date, which was made to depend on the commanding officers' receipt of the notification. The fixing of a date obviously implies a guarantee that hostilities will be brought to an end on or before that date, and that each State will therefore be responsible for the hostile acts committed by its forces after that date. Suppose, however, that a certain commander, who has heard indirectly of the conclusion of peace, but who has not yet received an official notice, continues hostilities before the date agreed upon arrives. Are his acts legitimate? Remembering what the object of fixing a future date is—viz. that the belligerent forces may have an opportunity of learning that peace has been established by their Governments—it is reasonable to conclude, with the majority of jurists, that if a commander has received reliable information from whatsoever source of the conclusion of peace, he is bound to abstain from further hostilities. This, it is submitted, is only a general rule, and must be taken subject to the qualification that he is not so bound if his opposing forces, ignorant of the fact, continue their operations to his or to his country's disadvantage. Of course, his duty would be first to inform the enemy of the facts, and to continue fighting or making captures only if the information thus imparted was not acted upon. In other words, this latter contingency involves simply a case of justifiable self-defence.

Apart from this contingency, then, the determining factor is the question of knowledge. An interesting case furnished by the French Prize Courts is an excellent illustration of this principle. (One or two writers of international law, however, have wrongly cited it as illustrating the application of a contrary rule.) On October 2, 1801, preliminaries of peace were concluded between England and France, and provided that on ratification (which took place on October 11) peace and friendship were to be established on land and sea, in all parts of the world, and that conquests and captures were thereafter to be invalid. Art. XI stipulated that prizes taken after the signing of the preliminaries, within specified periods of time varying according to locality between twelve days and five months, should be restored.

Test of sufficient knowledge.

Both Governments announced these provisions, the British by a proclamation, the French by a decree, and issued orders to their commanding officers to discontinue hostilities. On March 27, 1802, the definitive treaty was signed at Amiens, Art. XVI reproducing Art. XI of the preliminaries. Now before the expiration of the five months an English vessel, *The Swineherd* (designated *Le Porcher* in the French report), was captured by a French privateer, *Bellone*, in the Indian Seas. Brought before the Conseil des Prises, the Court asked the fundamental question: Did the captor, at the time of taking the prize, possess sufficient knowledge of the establishment of peace? The Court answered in the negative, and therefore condemned the captured vessel as a good prize (April 22, 1803). What constitutes sufficiency of knowledge was thus well expounded by the Procureur-Général: "La connaissance dont il s'agit doit être certaine, assurée, indubitable; elle doit émaner directement ou immédiatement de la puissance à laquelle appartient l'armateur, et si l'on veut, de l'une on de l'autre des puissances contractantes.—Cette connaissance doit être telle, qu'elle prévienne ou dissipe tous les doutes, toutes les incertitudes, toutes les craintes, tous les dangers que pourrait courir le corsaire; elle doit, en même temps qu'elle paralyse les lettres de marque, qu'elle impose au corsaire le devoir de s'abstenir de toutes hostilités, le mettre lui-même à l'abri de la capture; elle doit enfin être transmise par des pièces authentiques et légales qui prémunissent le corsaire contre le danger, en se retirant dans un des ports de sa nation, d'être pris par quelque navire ennemi non encore informé de la conclusion de la paix. . . . Au moment de l'arrestation, la saisie est bonne, ou elle est nulle, selon que le corsaire n'a point ou qu'il a la connaissance *positive* de la paix. S'il l'a, le navire doit être relâché avec dommages-intérêts ; s'il ne l'a point, la saisie est valable, et la confiscation doit être prononcée."[1] Earlier in his argument the Procureur-Général emphasized that it is not for the captor to prove his ignorance; rather, it is for the captured vessel to show that the seizure was illegitimate. ". . . La prêsomption de la légalité de la saisie doit être admise toutes les fois que l'arrestation a été faite avant l'expiration des délais, sauf au capturé à prouver le contraire. Obliger le capteur à prouver son ignorance, ce serait l'assujettir à une preuve négative à laquelle il n'est pas tenu."[2]

Again, a few days later (April 25, 1803), the same Prize Court heard the case of *The Nymph*, another English vessel that had been captured by a French privateer, *Petite Renommée*. Here the capture was pronounced to be invalid, because it was proved that, although it had been effected before the period fixed by the preliminaries had expired, the captor had had sufficient knowledge of the establishment of peace, which had indeed been communicated to him by the British authorities. "Recevoir de notre ennemi la nouvelle de la paix," said the French advocate-general, "et, par conséquent, recevoir en même temps l'assurance qu'il n'attaquera plus nos vaisseaux, exige au moins de notre part une suspension d'hostilités offensives; profiter de la sécurité qui lui inspire la communication qu'il nous a donnée, pour faire enlever, soit à la mer, soit dans ses ports, ses navires, et sabrer les hommes, qui les montent, est un acte de perfidie et de déloyauté qui ne convient qu'à des pirates et qui flétrirait l'honneur du nom français, s'il demeurait impuni."[3]

Date of operation of other clauses.

Next we have to consider the date of operation of clauses other than those relating to the cessation of hostilities. Here, as before, the expressed intention of the parties is the determining principle. But sometimes there is no express provision; then difficulties may arise with regard to certain important clauses deemed to be urgent by the one side or the other, according to the circumstances of each particular case. For example, an article in a treaty of peace stipulates the cession of territory by one State to another. In the absence of a definite provision or reasonable indications of intention, when does the

[1] A. de Pistoye et C. Duverdy, *Traité des prises maritimes*, Paris, 1855–1859, vol. i. p. 152.

[2] *Ibid.*, p. 151. Portions of this report are also given in the more accessible works of Calvo, *Droit international*, vol. v. § 3158; and Phillimore, *Commentaries*, vol. iii. p. 780.

[3] Pistoye et Duverdy, *op. cit.*, vol. i. p. 155; Calvo, *op. cit.*, vol. v. § 3159.

ceding State's sovereignty over the territory cease and the cessionary State's begin? In some American judicial cases—e.g. *Davis* v. *Police Jury of Concordia* [1] it has been held that the exercise of sovereignty on the part of a ceding State terminates, except for purely municipal purposes, on the date of the signature; but that the national character of the acquiring State is not imposed for commercial matters until the exchange of ratifications. The Court observed [2] that a cessionary State is not entitled to the "plenum dominium et utile" over the ceded territory, until it has possession together with the full right over it; and such right can be conferred only by the ratification of the ceding State. A similar decision was given in a case—*Dooley* v. *U.S.*—that arose in connection with the settlement of the American-Spanish War. It was there decided by a majority of the Supreme Court that duties on imports from the United States to Porto Rico, collected by the American military authorities from the time of taking possession of the island until the ratification of the Treaty of Paris (signed December 10, 1898) were legally exacted under war power; but the right to exact duties so imposed came to an end when the ratifications were exchanged. In other words, the United States and Porto Rico remained foreign countries to each other until the date of the exchange of ratifications (viz. April 12, 1899), notwithstanding that on the one hand Spanish authority in the island was almost entirely replaced by the American military occupation of it, and on the other that it was ceded by the treaty of December 10.[3]

This solution of the question appears to be reasonable and practicable when the ceded territory is already under the military occupation of the cessionary State. But where the territory ceded by a treaty has not been subjected to military occupation, and remains free from all control *de facto* and *de jure* on the part of the cessionary, then, it is submitted, no element of sovereignty can vest in the latter till the exchange of ratifications. For it is only on that date that the competent authority signifies formally its full and irrevocable assent to the stipulation agreed to by its plenipotentiaries and consigned to the peace treaty.

In another American case—*Haver* v. *Yaker* [4]—a distinction is drawn between the rights of the contracting Governments and those of their subjects. In the course of his judgment, Mr. Justice Davis observed that it is a principle of international law that a

[1] *Davis* v. *Police Jury of Concordia* (1850), 9 Howard, 289. Cf. *U.S.* v. *Arredondo* (1832), 6 Peters, 749.

[2] *Per* Mr. Justice Wayne.

[3] *Dooley* v. *U.S.* (1901), 182 U.S. Rep. 223. (See the judgment of Mr. Justice Brown.)

[4] *Haver* v. *Yaker* (1869), 9 Wallace, 32.

treaty becomes binding from the date of its signature, in so far as the rights of either Government under it are concerned; and that the exchange of ratifications has, in this respect, nothing more than a retroactive effect confirming the treaty from its date. But in the case of individual rights affected by the treaty, a different rule prevails. These rights were vested before the treaty was ratified, and as regards them the treaty cannot be considered as concluded and binding until the ratifications are exchanged.[1] The learned judge, setting forth the reason for the rule, pointed out that in the United States a treaty is something more than a contract—it is the law of the land. But before it can become a law, the assent of the Senate, as the ratifying authority, is necessary. Now the Senate is not called upon to adopt it or reject it as a whole, but may modify it or amend it. In this process the individual citizen's private rights may be affected; and as he has no means of knowing the contemplated change while it is under consideration of the Senate, it would be wrong in principle to hold him bound by it, as the law of the land, until it was ratified and proclaimed. And to construe the law, so as to make the ratification of the treaty relate back to the date of the signature, thereby divesting a title already vested, would be manifestly unjust, and cannot be sanctioned by a court of law.

With regard to this judgment, we must, in conformity with our previous arguments, deny the assertion that it is a principle of international law that a treaty acquires binding force from the date of its signing, in respect of the rights of the contracting Governments. Neither jurists and publicists nor Governments have ever uniformly maintained such a principle; and it certainly cannot be inferred from actual practice. The reasoning that the exchange of ratifications alone gives the date from which the treaty becomes obligatory in respect of individual rights is forcible enough so far as it goes; but it is difficult to see why such a sharp line of demarcation should be drawn between the rights of Governments and the rights of subjects. Whatever discrimination may be made between them for the purposes of formal or abstract analysis, it cannot properly be made in the actual practice of any civilized community. The rights of Governments have really no existence save in relation to the rights of the governed. A Government has no meaning whatever without subjects to be governed. What affects the one must necessarily affect the other. A Government divesting itself of its inherent rights deprives subjects of their rights too. So that if the exchange of ratifications is necessary before the rights of subjects, whether property rights or any other kind of rights, can be affected, equally

[1] Referring to *U.S.* v. *Arredondo* (1832), 6 Peters, 749.

necessary is the exchange of ratifications before the rights of Governments can be affected.

Sometimes certain, or even all, of the clauses in a treaty of peace are executed or brought into operation, owing to conditions of exceptional urgency, before the date of the exchange of ratifications. But such a proceeding is adopted in virtue of an express provision, based on mutual consent, whereby ratification of the said clauses is presumed or implied by guarantee or waived. For example, in the case of the Convention of Madrid, July 3, 1880, relating to the exercise of protection in Morocco, the contracting parties (viz. Great Britain, France, Germany, Austria, Italy, Spain, United States, the Netherlands, Portugal, Sweden and Norway, Denmark, Belgium, and Morocco) expressly agreed (Art. XVIII) that the provisions should come into effect on the date of the signature. Similarly, in the case of the Treaty of London, July 15, 1840, between Great Britain, Austria, Prussia, Russia, and Turkey, for the pacification of the Levant, a reserved protocol was annexed, in which it was stated that, owing to the distance which separated the capitals of the contracting Courts from each other, and in view of the interests of humanity and the grave considerations of European policy relative to the existing state of affairs in Syria, the signatories agreed to carry into immediate execution the measures mentioned in Art. II of the treaty, without waiting for the exchange of ratifications[1] (which was dispensed with by the negotiators under secret instructions).

Normally, date of operation is prescribed.

Apart from exceptional circumstances, however—e.g. the continuance of military occupation, and other conditions of an urgent character—the normal course is to prescribe in the treaty itself the date of its operation in general. Sometimes it is the date of the signing, at other times it is the date of the exchange of ratifications; whichever is fixed depends on the nature of each particular case and on the purpose and motives of the parties concerned. Examples of the former are: the Treaty of Lausanne, October 18, 1912, between Italy and Turkey, Art. XI: "The present treaty shall come into force on the day of its signature"; the Treaty of Constantinople, September 29, 1913, between Turkey and Bulgaria, Art. XX: "The present treaty shall come into force immediately after its signature"; the Treaty of Athens, November 14, 1913, between Turkey and Greece, Art. XVI: "The present treaty shall become effective immediately upon its signature." Examples of the latter are: the Treaty of Ghent, December 24, 1814, between Great Britain and the United States, Art. XI: "This treaty, when the same shall have been ratified on both sides without alteration

[1] Hertslet, *Map of Europe by Treaty*, vol. ii. pp. 1021–1022.

by either of the contracting parties, and the ratifications mutually exchanged, shall be binding on both parties"; the Preliminaries of San Stefano, March 3, 1878, between Russia and Turkey, Art. XXIX: "It is well understood that the high contracting parties consider themselves as formally bound by the present Act from the moment of its ratification"; the Treaty of Portsmouth, September 5, 1905, between Russia and Japan, of which Art. XIV says that the treaty "shall in all its parts come into full force" on the date of the announcement of the ratifications by the two parties, and in case of different dates on the later one.

When no other date is specified.

Finally, if no other date has been specified, the treaty comes into effect and acquires binding force on the date of the exchange of ratifications. This rule is accepted by most publicists and jurists since Vattel. Bluntschli emphasizes that it is the exchange of ratifications that renders the treaty perfect, and entitles each party to demand its performance by the other. Heffter maintains that without due ratification the treaty has no existence; hence the date of operation begins from the exchange of ratifications. Similarly, Phillimore holds that the treaty begins to take effect only after all necessary formalities have been fulfilled and the agreement has been ratified. Bernard, referring to this principle, observes: "It [the exchange of ratifications] is an extra precaution, an artificial safeguard, against improvident or ill-considered engagements. . . . That it is salutary and convenient is an opinion—sound, I have no doubt, but which may be disputed like any other opinion; that it is a settled rule is a fact which may be proved by evidence like any other fact."[1] There can be no doubt, however, that modern usage has established the rule; and, it is submitted, it may now be considered a fundamental principle of international law. Generally a condition of subsequent ratification is inserted in the full powers of plenipotentiaries or in the treaty concluded by them; and when not so inserted, it is implied, that is, of course, if it is not expressly dispensed with by the competent authorities (e.g. by previously sanctioning the very terms arrived at)—a proviso that applies to the entire sphere of treaty-making.

RATIFICATION.

One or two other points as to ratification remain to be considered. The treaty is to be ratified by the competent authority, which is determined by the constitutional law and practice of each State, and which is not necessarily the same as the treaty-making authority. When a treaty includes articles involving territorial cessions, financial engagements, and

[1] *Four Lectures . . . on Diplomacy*, p. 178.

other charges on the people, then, as has already been pointed out, the usual rule is—logic demands that it should be an invariable rule—that the sanction of the legislature is indispensable to the validity of the treaty.

The ratification of the Treaty of Paris, signed December 10, 1898, furnishes illustrations of different practices. Under the constitution of the United States the ratifying authority consists of the President and at least two-thirds of the Senate. (Art. XVII said: "The present treaty shall be ratified by the President of the United States, by and with the advice and consent of the Senate thereof, and by Her Majesty the Queen Regent of Spain. . . .") When the treaty was submitted to the Senate, a sharp discussion arose showing divergent opinions as to American policy and therefore as to the terms of the peace—many senators repudiating the annexation of Spanish territory, and emphasizing that the original object of the war had not been to make conquests. The President was then requested to lay before the Senate the Instructions given to the American plenipotentiaries, the correspondence that passed between them and the Department of State, and the various reports delivered by them to the President and to the Secretary of State. At first he refused on the ground of public interest, but afterwards, pressure continuing, he produced a portion of the documents required. However, on February 7, 1899, the Senate decided—it appears by a majority of one vote—to ratify the treaty without amendment.

Treaty of Paris, 1898.

As soon as this ratification was made known in Spain, the Cortes was summoned. The terms of peace were disapproved; and violent attacks were made against the Spanish military and naval commanding officers. In the Senate a heated discussion took place on March 2 between the adherents of the Government and the opposition. The latter maintained that as the Cortes had already authorized the Government to conclude the treaty of peace on the basis of the preliminaries of August 12, there was no necessity for the chambers to ratify it at all. But the Government replied that such ratification was essential, on the ground that the American negotiators at the conference had increased their demands since the conclusion of the preliminaries, particularly in requiring the cession of the Philippines. (We may recall Art. III of the latter: "The United States will occupy and hold the city, bay, and harbour of Manila pending the conclusion of a treaty of peace, which shall determine the control, disposition, and government of the Philippines." This clause is lamentably vague, and is undoubtedly susceptible of more than one interpretation. But whatever assurances may or may not have been given by the United

States to the contrary, it is quite clear that to demand the cession of the islands is not incompatible with the clause as it stands. It may be that on August 12 the United States had not decided as to the cession, and preferred to express the article in general terms, implying a reservation to demand the cession if it was afterwards found desirable. Such a far-reaching reservation should not be implied, it should be expressly specified; so that when the time came for negotiating the definitive treaty it could be acted upon or set aside as circumstances dictated. In the absence of an express provision, the Spanish Government might well claim that the article could not be interpreted in the American sense, and that it would not have accepted the preliminary protocol and would have continued the war rather than agree to the cession of the islands.) However this may be, the Cortes eventually decided, after the Spanish prime minister had resigned, that formal ratification by the chambers was unnecessary. Accordingly, on March 13 the definitive treaty of peace was ratified by the Queen Regent alone.

Treaty of Frankfort, 1871.

In the case of the peace negotiations following the Franco-German War, it has already been pointed out that the Germans specified by what authority in France the resulting treaties were to be ratified—a stipulation due to the unsettled condition of political affairs in that country. Thus Art. X of the Preliminaries of Versailles, February 26, 1871, says: "The present preliminary treaty shall be immediately submitted to the ratification of His Majesty the Emperor of Germany and to the French National Assembly sitting at Bordeaux." Similarly Art. XVIII of the Treaty of Frankfort, May 10, 1871, required its ratification by the Emperor of Germany and by the French National Assembly, and the Chief of the Executive of the French Republic. On the 12th it was ratified by the Reichstag, and on the 18th by the National Assembly. It was on the 13th that M. Jules Favre, the minister for foreign affairs, brought forward a motion for ratification.[1] A commission was then appointed to consider the treaty; and its report was submitted to the Assembly on the 18th. It spoke, in moving terms, of the painful and inevitable character of the treaty, of bleeding and mutilated France, of the exorbitant indemnity, of the conqueror's exactions which no considerations could mitigate: "Cette paix est, à nos yeux, la plus douloureuse mais la plus inévitable qu'ait connue notre histoire. . . . Dans cette extrémité, il ne dépendait plus de nous de disputer à l'ènnemi les portions de territoire qu'il s'était appropriées déjà; nous pouvious nous perdre,

[1] Cf. De Clercq, *Recueil*, vol. x. pp. 481–483.

nous ne pouvious plus les sauver. C'est pourquoi nous n'avions plus songé qu'à sauver la France, blessée, saignante, et mutilée; c'est pourquoi nous n'avons pas reculé devant une indemnité de guerre assurément exorbitante, et pourtant moins ruineuse encore qu'une invasion sans limite et sans obstacle. . . . Rien n'est venu, soit du dehors, soit du dedans, qui pût atténuer les exigences du vainqueur." It proceeded to examine in what respects the definitive treaty differed from the preliminaries, and finally recommended ratification.[1]

Stipulation as to ratification.

There are other treaties containing a stipulation that they shall be ratified by the respective sovereigns; but it is not implied that the monarchs are themselves the competent authorities for the purpose. Exceptional cases apart, it is better to confine treaties to the region of international transactions, and not to let them trespass in the sphere of the constitutional law or régime of the contracting parties. Accordingly, many treaties—perhaps the majority—simply stipulate that they shall be ratified, leaving it to the signatories to fulfil this stipulation conformably to their own ways and systems.

When ratification not necessary.

In one special case subsequent ratification has not been considered necessary: that is, where sovereigns in person, possessing competence to ratify, entered into treaties. Thus the Holy Alliance concluded in Paris, September 14 / 26, 1815, between Austria, Prussia, and Russia, and signed by the sovereigns—"Francis," "Frederick William," and "Alexander"—acquired binding force from the date of the signature. Similarly, the Preliminaries of Villafranca, July 11, 1859, terminating hostilities between France and Austria, were signed by Napoléon and Francis Joseph, and came into force immediately. But the definitive Treaty of Zurich that followed (November 10) was negotiated and signed by the plenipotentiaries of these sovereigns, and therefore needed ratification. Nowadays sovereigns very rarely, if ever, conduct negotiations personally; even if they did, their acts would not be necessarily exempt, in most countries, from revision by another constituted authority.

Refusal to ratify.

Notwithstanding the condition of ratification, express or implied, the refusal to ratify a treaty that has been negotiated properly and in conformity with the full powers conferred on the plenipotentiaries would be stigmatized by the society of States as a serious breach of faith, and would furnish ground for the resumption of war by the aggrieved party, and for reparation in respect of permissible acts done in anticipation of the eventual ratification. Nowadays there is less excuse for refusing

[1] Cf. De Clercq, *Recueil*, vol. x. pp. 484–486.

than there was formerly, when plenipotentiaries were in many respects left to their own wits and resources much more frequently than they are at the present day. Indeed, owing to the numerous facilities and unparalleled rapidity of communication, plenipotentiaries are now able to be in constant touch with their Governments, and so to refer to them doubtful questions that arise in the course of the negotiations, and act throughout on their instructions; so that the "full powers" possessed by these representatives are such more in form than in reality. If, however, a case should occur in which the negotiators have exceeded their patent "full powers" and the open instructions received relatively thereto, their Government will not be bound by acts outside their authority; but if they transcend secret instructions only, it will be bound. (Of course, the obligation here insisted on is a moral one, and not, strictly speaking, legal.) Practically all jurists and publicists are agreed on this point, e.g. Grotius,[1] Pufendorf,[2] Bynkershoek,[3] Vattel,[4] to name but a few of the "fathers" of international law. The latter observes that "before a prince can honourably refuse to ratify a compact made in virtue of such plenipotentiary commission, he should be able to allege strong and substantial reasons, and, in particular, to prove that his minister deviated from his [patent] instructions."

But where the ratifying authority is not the executive Government and is quite different from the treaty-making authority—e.g. where ratification belongs to Parliament and treaty-making belongs to the Crown or its responsible ministers—then the refusal to ratify on the part of the former does not constitute a breach even of moral obligation, if the latter had not previously received due authorization to conclude the engagement thus repudiated, or had delivered instructions to the plenipotentiaries contrary to any authorization that had been given. The subsequent denunciation of treaties entered into may, then, be represented in three stages, thus: the plenipotentiaries themselves denounce their contract because it was extorted from them under duress or procured by treachery or *mala fides*; the sovereign or executive ministry that appointed them may not only allege the same grounds, but may also claim that they acted inconsistently with their "full powers"; the supreme ratifying authority, if different from the sovereign or executive, may advance the latter objections, and hold in addition that its own or Parliament's authorization was exceeded, or that, such authorization not having been first obtained, the nation cannot be deemed responsible for the ill-considered proceedings of the

[1] *De iure belli et pacis*, ii. 11. 12.
[2] *De iure naturæ et gentium*, iii. 9. 2.
[3] *Quæstiones iuris publici*, ii. 7.
[4] *Droit des gens*, ii. 12. 56.

executive Government (which, therefore, would probably have to resign).

Further, as treaties in general may be avoided on the grounds of impossibility of performance (physical, or as being prejudicial to the rights of third States), serious error, and substantial change of circumstances on which the validity of the treaty was made to depend, their ratification may *a fortiori* be refused if such causes appear before they come into force.

In point of fact, very few treaties indeed in modern times have been repudiated by the ratifying authority. M. Pradier-Fodéré[1] mentions a half-dozen examples of unratified treaties between the years 1790 and 1877 : the treaty concluded at The Hague, December 10, 1790, between England, Austria, Prussia, and the Netherlands; the treaty of peace between France and Russia, July 20, 1806; the treaty between Austria and Bavaria, July 25, 1815; the treaty of 1819 between the United States and Spain; the treaty of 1869 between Great Britain and the United States, as to the *Alabama* affair; the treaty of July 6, 1877, between France and Italy. To these may be added the treaty of 1883 between Great Britain and Portugal relating to the mouth of the Congo; the treaty of 1897 between Great Britain and the United States, as to arbitration; and that of 1900 between the same parties as to the Panama Canal (when the Senate introduced such amendments as proved to be unacceptable). But we have to bear in mind that in that period thousands of conventions were concluded. Among those mentioned above is one that concerns us here more particularly, viz. the treaty of peace between France and Russia, July 20, 1806, in which case Baron d'Oubril, the plenipotentiary of the Czar, was disavowed by his Court as having exceeded his powers.

Place of exchange of ratifications.

Next we have to consider the place and time of the exchange of ratifications. In some cases no place is mentioned, e.g. in the Treaty of Paris, November 20, 1815; the Treaty of Zurich, November 10, 1859; the Preliminaries of Versailles, February 26, 1871; the Treaty of Constantinople, September 29, 1913. (In one or two instances, indeed, there is no ratification clause at all, e.g. in the Treaty of Lausanne, October 18, 1912; the Treaty of London, May 30, 1913, between Turkey and the Balkan Allies; the Treaty of Athens, November 14, 1913.) Where provision is made for ratification without naming the place where ratifications are to be exchanged, it may be presumed that, in default of a subsequent understanding on the point, the exchange is to be effected in the

[1] *Cours de droit diplom.*, vol. ii. p. 480.

place where the treaty has been concluded. Usually, however, the place is expressly specified. Sometimes it is the town in which the treaty was signed, as in the treaties of Paris, 1856; Nikolsburg, 1866; Prague, 1866; Vienna, 1866; Frankfort, 1871; Bucharest, 1913. Sometimes it is a different town, as in the treaties of San Stefano, 1878 (St. Petersburg); Constantinople, 1879 (St. Petersburg); Lima, 1883 (Santiago); Shimonoseki, 1895 (Chefoo); Paris, 1898 (Washington); Portsmouth, 1905 (Washington).

Time of exchange of ratifications.

The determination of the time, too, within which the ratifications are exchanged depends on the mutual agreement of the contracting parties. The period varies, naturally, according to the circumstances of each case, e.g. the distance of the capitals, the nature of the dispositions of the treaty, the time taken to convoke the ratifying authority, etc. In preliminaries of peace the time fixed is, as may be expected, generally short: thus the preliminary Treaty of Nikolsburg, 1866, says two days at the latest; and Art. X of the Preliminaries of Versailles, 1871, says that the treaty is to be submitted immediately to ratification. Of the definitive treaties given at the end of this work, one—the Treaty of Shimonoseki, April 17, 1795—gives the exact date, viz. May 8 (and the exchange of ratifications was duly effected on that date); another—the Treaty of Portsmouth, September 5, 1905—stipulates that the treaty shall be ratified within fifty days, and that the exchange shall take place as early as possible thereafter (this occurred September 25). The others fix a delay, varying between eight days and a year; though in such case it is said that the exchange is to be made "sooner if possible" than the maximum term indicated. The maximum terms are as follows, running from the date of signature: Prague, 1866, eight days; Frankfort, 1871, ten days; Zurich, 1859, Vienna, 1866, San Stefano, 1878, Constantinople, 1879, Bucharest, 1913, Constantinople, 1913, fifteen days; Paris, 1856, four weeks; Paris, November 20, 1815, two months; Paris, 1898, six months; Lima, 1883, one year.

If it is found, through unavoidable causes, that the exchange of ratifications cannot be effected within the time stipulated, then the period is prolonged by mutual agreement embodied frequently in a special convention.

The act of ratification.

The act of ratification is a written statement signed and sealed by the head of the State, declaring that (with the consent and approval of Parliament, or the Senate, or otherwise, according to the requirements of each case, when the head of the State does not alone constitute the ratifying authority) he confirms and ratifies the treaty concluded in his name by his plenipotentiaries, and promises to perform it in good faith in all its particulars (or to cause it to be performed according to its tenor). One copy is attached to the instrument retained, and another to an exact copy of the latter, which is then exchanged for a copy of the original instrument accompanied by a similar act of ratification from the other contracting party. A protocol recording the exchange is then usually signed by the plenipotentiaries who make it.

BREACH OF TREATY.

Unless it is otherwise provided, a treaty of peace is regarded as an indivisible whole, and no distinction is made, formally, between essential and non-essential stipulations. Some writers have attempted to draw such a distinction, by analogy with a discrimination of the kind made in the case of other conventions; and they hold that the infringement of the fundamental conditions alone will constitute such a breach of the peace treaty as to entitle the aggrieved party to cancel it altogether. The analogy, however, being imperfect, the conclusions inferred are equally defective. A commercial treaty, for example, is a purely voluntary engagement on both sides, entered into spontaneously by a mutual give-and-take process for the equal—or apparently equal—benefit of the contracting parties. Whilst certain clauses go to the root of the bargain, many other clauses may be only secondary or supplementary, the non-observance of which by one party may be readily repaired by amicable methods, or, if necessary, counterbalanced by similar omission on the part of the other. On the other hand, a peace treaty is rarely a give-and-take bargain; its terms are usually dictated by the victorious belligerent and submitted to by the defeated State, so that, for the most part, it is "give" on the one side and "take" on the other. The conditions, in their totality, represent the minimum that will just satisfy the successful Power, which would, presumably, continue the war rather than allow an abatement. It would hence be entitled to regard a subsequent infraction of any part of the treaty as a deliberate denial of its rights, consecrated in a solemn engagement that was procured by supreme sacrifice and victory. Moreover, if it were possible at all to separate primary from secondary conditions, who is to draw the line of demarcation, if no provision has been made for receiving the independent judgment of a court of arbitration?

We must therefore conclude that in the case of a peace treaty, all the constituent articles are essential, depending on each other; so that the violation of one of them abrogates the entire treaty, if the aggrieved State chooses so to regard it. That is, a violation of the treaty does not *ipso facto* make it null and void, but only voidable at the election of the injured party. This principle, however, though it is a consequence of formal analysis, should not and indeed cannot be always applied in practice. For a treaty of peace effects a restoration of the normal relationships between States, and concerns more or less the rest of the world; to treat the whole of it as cancelled the moment an article is broken, without demanding its fulfilment and waiting for amends, is scarcely justifiable on grounds of public policy and even universal legal practice. As Rivier observes: "Toutefois, à raison du caractère propre de la paix, qui constitue un retour à l'état normal des relations entre États, notamment dans le sein de la société des nations, il faut admettre, sauf volonté contraire, que le seul fait de l'inobservation ou de l'observation incomplète et défectueuse, de la part d'un des États contractants, d'une ou de plusieurs dispositions du traité ne doit pas donner d'emblée à l'autre contractant le droit de se déclarer affranchi de ses obligations, encore moins celui de rompre la paix et de recommencer les hostilités, fût-ce même sans couleur de représailles. Il faut en pareil cas insister pour que le traité soit exécuté, et c'est seulement en cas de refus on d'omission continuée qu'il y a lieu d'appliquer les principes de la résiliation pour inexécution et de l'indivisibilité." [1] Only after demanding performance, giving the offending State sufficient opportunity to make good his omission, and seeking in vain satisfaction by measures short of war, may hostilities be instituted as the final resort. If the omission or infraction concerned relates to the period during which the condition was to be fulfilled, the commencement of hostilities is merely a continuation of the former war; but if the violation was committed after this period, then the hostilities set on foot constitute a new war. It is in every case for the aggrieved State itself to decide whether to forgo such breach or take up arms; and whatever terms of the treaty have been violated, there is not, strictly speaking, a rupture of peace between the parties until the latter course has been adopted. Thus, certain clauses of the Treaty of Zurich, 1859, were never performed; nevertheless France and Austria remained at peace.

These contingencies or consequences may, of course, be avoided by an express provision that on the breach of this or that clause the rest of the treaty shall nevertheless remain in force—leaving the parties free to reach an accommodation as to such breach by way of diplomacy or by other methods that commend themselves to both.

[1] *Principes du droit des gens*, vol. ii. pp. 459–460.

Various means have from time to time been adopted with a view to ensuring the performance of treaties in their entirety or of certain clauses. Amongst these means may be mentioned the taking of a solemn oath, the delivery of hostages, the handing over of a pledge, the guarantee of a third State, and—most important of all—the continued military occupation of territory belonging to the party who is required to fulfil certain demands within a stipulated time.

Means of ensuring performance of treaties of peace.

The oath, as a sanction of treaties, is now obsolete. Formerly, when religious faith was intense, as Bonfils remarks,[1] the observance of engagements was placed under the ægis of religion; and the conclusion of treaties was accompanied by religious solemnities, including the kissing of the cross, and the administration of the oath. The penalty of excommunication—apart from other consequences—awaited those who violated their word thus pledged. A few notable examples of treaties of peace in which the oath was used are: the Treaty of Madrid, 1526, between Francis I, King of France, and the Emperor Charles V; the Peace of Cambrai, 1529 (known as the "Ladies' Peace," between Louise of Savoy, mother of Francis I, and Margaret of Austria, aunt of Charles V, in the name of these sovereigns); the Peace of Cateau-Cambrésis, 1559, between France and Spain; the Peace of Münster, 1648, between Spain and the Dutch Provinces; the Peace of the Pyrenees, 1659, between France and Spain; the Treaty of Aix-la-Chapelle, 1668, between France and Spain; the Treaty of Ryswick, 1697, between England and France. It appears that the most recent instance of such usage is the alliance between France and Switzerland, 1777, which was solemnly confirmed by the contracting parties in the cathedral of Soleure.[2]

The oath.

As the Pope claimed the power to absolve the faithful from their engagements, the protection afforded by the oath was uncertain; thus by papal dispensation Francis I was relieved of his obligations under the Treaty of Madrid, and Henry II, King of France, of his (1556) under the Peace of Vaucelles, and so on. To avoid such an eventuality, clauses were not infrequently inserted in treaties stipulating that the contracting parties would not obtain, accept, or profit by a papal absolution from their oath.[3] Sometimes the Pope on his own initiative protested against treaties, declaring them to be null and void. Thus the famous Peace of Westphalia, which concerned almost the whole of Europe, displeasing the Pope, a bull

[1] *Manuel de droit international public* (Paris, 1912), p. 536.

[2] Cf. Pradier-Fodéré, *Cours de droit diplom.*, vol. ii. p. 489.

[3] Cf. Vattel, liv. ii. § 15.

was published in which, "from his own certain knowledge and full ecclesiastical power," he declared several articles of the treaty "null, vain, invalid, iniquitous, unjust, condemned, reprobated, frivolous, void of force and effect," and that nobody was bound to observe them, though confirmed by oath.[1]

The delivery of hostages was also very frequent in former times. The earlier jurists have long dissertations on this practice, as well as on the administration of the oath; and most of them, especially the pre-Grotian writers, expound these subjects and develop rules with all the casuistical subtlety characteristic of their age. An interesting example of the use of hostages, as a precaution against the non-observance of treaties, is that in the "perpetual peace" between Henry VIII and Francis I (1527), when two archbishops, eleven bishops, twenty-eight nobles, as well as thirteen towns, were given as security on the English side. The last recorded instance, in the case of civilized nations, is that connected with the Treaty of Aix-la-Chapelle, October 18, 1748, whereby (Art. IX) two English hostages, persons of rank and importance, were to be handed over to France as a guarantee that Cape Breton Island and the English conquests in the East and West Indies would be restored to the French sovereign, Louis XV.

Hostages.

Pledges, too, were sometimes given in order to ensure the faithful execution of engagements. These were either precious objects, e.g. the diamonds of the crown of Poland handed over to Prussia; or towns and provinces mortgaged to the party to whom certain obligations were due, e.g. Corsica made over to France by the Republic of Genoa, in the treaties of 1756, 1764, and 1768, as a security for debts.

Pledge.

Another sanction of treaties is a guarantee offered by third States. With regard to this Vattel remarks: "Convinced by unhappy experience that the faith of treaties, sacred and inviolable as it ought to be, does not always afford a sufficient assurance that they shall be punctually observed, mankind have sought for securities against perfidy—for methods whose efficacy shall not depend on the good faith of the contracting parties. A guarantee is one of these means. When those who make a treaty of peace, or any other treaty, are not perfectly easy with respect to its observance, they require the guarantee of a powerful sovereign," who undertakes to see that the conditions of the treaty shall be observed. In this form guarantee has fallen into disuse. In earlier times we find instances of vassals

Guarantee by third States.

[1] Cf. G. H. Bougeant, *Histoire des guerres et des négociations qui précédèrent le traité de Westphalie*, 6 vols. (Paris, 1751), vol. vi. p. 413.

promising to bring pressure to bear on their suzerain in order to secure fidelity to his engagements, e.g. in the Treaty of Senlis, 1493, between Maximilian of Austria and Charles VIII of France; in the Treaty of Orléans, 1514, between Henry VIII and Louis XII. In modern times the method of guarantee is applied in a different manner. In some cases leading Powers on their own initiative constitute themselves guardians of certain international arrangements. Such interposition occurs in the case of neutralized States. Thus, on November 20, 1815, a Declaration was signed at Paris by Great Britain, Austria, France, Prussia, and Russia, recognizing the neutrality of Switzerland and guaranteeing the inviolability of her territory, as marked out by the Congress of Vienna. On April 19, 1839, the treaty between Holland and Belgium (January 23, 1839), effecting their separation and creating Belgian neutrality, was placed under the guarantee of the same five Powers. On May 11, 1867, the Conference of London, comprising representatives of these Powers as well as of Italy, Belgium, Holland, and Luxemburg, concluded a treaty establishing the perpetual neutrality of the Grand Duchy, under the collective guarantee of the signatories (except Belgium, being herself neutralized).[1] An example of a guarantee, other than that of neutrality—and it is more pertinent to our purpose here—is the Convention of April 15, 1856, whereby Great Britain, France, and Austria guaranteed the execution of that part of the Treaty of Paris, March 30, 1856, relating to the integrity and independence of the Ottoman Empire. Sometimes, one Power concludes a treaty with another Power, undertaking, in return for certain concessions, to protect the rights of the latter as established by a treaty of peace or other treaty; e.g. on June 4, 1878, Great Britain entered into a defensive alliance with Turkey, engaging, in consideration of the cession of Cyprus, to join the Sultan in defending, against Russian aggression, his territories in Asia, as they would be fixed by the definitive treaty of peace.[2]

Military occupation as a means of ensuring performance.

The military occupation of part of a State's territory by the forces of the other contracting party is now the most usual and most important means of ensuring the performance of certain stipulations of the treaty of peace concluded between them. When the main purpose of the occupation is to secure the payment of a war

[1] On treaties of guarantee, see M. Milanovitch, *Des traités de garantie en droit international* (Paris, 1888); E. Descamps, *La neutralité de la Belgique* (Bruxelles, 1902).

[2] This was the Treaty of Constantinople, February 8, 1879, which adopted the territorial modifications made by the Treaty of Berlin, July 13, 1878.

indemnity, it is usual to divide the latter into a number of instalments extending over a given period, and to provide for evacuation on payment of the first instalments, if the debtor State furnished adequate financial guarantees as a security for the payment of the remainder. This kind of occupation differs substantially from that consequent on warlike invasion. The occupant in the latter case is an enemy exercising a multiplicity of rights in virtue of superior belligerent force; the occupant in what may be conveniently designated conventional or precautionary occupation, or occupation of guarantee, is not an enemy, and he possesses only such rights as are given to him either in the treaty of peace or in specially concluded conventions. As a rule the occupying troops are immune from the local jurisdiction; and they are no longer entitled to levy requisitions and contributions. But these and similar questions as to what they may or may not do, and the conditions of their maintenance, rations, etc., are in general expressly regulated. One or two examples will illustrate the arrangements made in this respect.

Treaty of Paris, 1815.

The Treaty of Paris, November 20, 1815,[1] between Great Britain, Austria, Prussia, and Russia on the one side, and France on the other, said (Art. V) that owing to the state of uneasiness and fermentation prevailing in France, and with a view to the security of neighbouring countries, the Allies thought it indispensable, as a measure of precaution and temporary guarantee, to occupy certain military positions along the French frontiers. Neither the king's sovereignty nor the state of possession as recognized by the treaty was to be prejudiced. The number of troops was limited to 150,000, who were to occupy some twenty specified fortresses. The maximum period of occupation was restricted to five years, though in certain circumstances evacuation might take place before that time expired. "It may terminate before that period if, at the end of three years, the Allied Sovereigns, after having in concert with His Majesty the King of France maturely examined their reciprocal situation and interests, and the progress which shall have been made in France in the re-establishment of order and tranquillity, shall agree to acknowledge that the motives which led them to that measure have ceased to exist." An additional convention of the same date[2] stipulated that the army was to be maintained by the French Government, and regulated the various matters as to lodging, fuel, lighting, provisions, forage, and rations. With regard to the expenses due to pay, equipment, clothing, etc., France was required to contribute a sum of 50,000,000 francs per year, payable monthly. Certain neutral zones were

[1] See *infra*, Appendix (A).

[2] Appendix (B).

specified in several departments. France was permitted to maintain garrisons, each of which being limited in size, in a number of towns situated in the occupied territory. The Commander-in-Chief of the Allied troops was to exercise military command in the occupied departments, with the exception of places in which France held garrisons and within a radius of 1,000 toises round each of them. The civil and judicial administration, the collection of taxes, customs duties, etc., and the service of the gendarmerie in the occupied territory were to continue as before. Finally, the places occupied were to be restored, on evacuation, in the state in which they were at the time of occupation, subject to "damages . . . caused by time."

In the case of 1815 it is clear that the essential object of the occupation was to ensure a tranquil settlement in France, and in the interests of Europe in general to prevent a revolutionary recrudescence. The war indemnity imposed on France amounted to 700,000,000 francs; but its payment did not necessarily entail evacuation, nor was the sum to be cleared off during the period of occupation.[1] The object of the Germans in 1871 was different.[2] The military power of France being then manifestly broken, they could not have the same fears as were entertained by the Allies in 1815. Their occupation was nothing more than a precaution taken against a debtor who might make delays in payment, or who might even become insolvent. Their army of occupation remained on French soil until the payment of the last franc. The Preliminaries of Versailles had, indeed, declared (Art. III) the German Emperor's willingness to substitute a financial guarantee for the territorial; but afterwards this declaration was brushed aside, and the French were not allowed to benefit by it—the Germans placing their trust only in hard cash, and holding fast to the property of the debtor until the enormous sum was paid in full. They kept on delaying evacuation on various alleged grounds—now it was the condition of internal affairs, now the danger of French military reorganization. They were throughout given to suspicion and distrust—"injustes soupçons et incurable défiance," wrote Saint-Vallier to Thiers, May 27, 1872.[3]

Treaty of Frankfort, 1871.

It will be of interest to look at some of the arrangements relative to the German occupation, which alone necessitated the conclusion of several special conventions. Thus by the convention

[1] See Appendix (C). Cf. A. Sorel, *Histoire diplomatique de la guerre franco-allemande* (Paris, 1875), vol. ii. pp. 355–356.

[2] Cf. May, *Le traité de Francfort*, pp. 188 *seq.*

[3] Cf. L. A. Thiers, *Occupation et libération du territoire*, vol. i. p. 352.

concluded at Berlin, October 12, 1871, Germany agreed to evacuate the six departments of the Aisne, Aube, Côte-d'Or, Haute-Saône, Doubs, and Jura, and to reduce the size of the army of occupation to 50,000 men, conformably to Art. III of the Preliminaries of February 26, in consideration of the payment by France of 650 million francs by May 1, 1872. Till the conclusion of peace there were 500,000 men and 150,000 horses, all maintained at the expense of the invaded country—1,250,000 francs per day. After the exchange of ratifications of the definitive Treaty of Frankfort (which took place May 20, 1871) and the payment of the first instalment of 500,000,000 francs, there were 150,000 men and 50,000 horses. Under the convention of November 10, 1871, a further diminution took place—120,000 men and 40,000 horses; this was followed by another reduction, leaving 80,000 men and 30,000 horses. From January 1, 1872, after the payment of 2,000,000,000 francs, till the entire evacuation there were 50,000 men and 18,000 horses. For the year 1871, the cost of the army of occupation amounted to 248,625,000 francs.[1] Numerous conventions were drawn up providing for everything relating to the quartering of officers and men, officers' mess, exercise grounds, offices for the military administration, stores, sheds, etc.

Russo-Turkish War.

On the termination of the Russo-Turkish War, a Russian army entered into occupation of Bulgaria, in accordance with Art. VIII of the Preliminaries of San Stefano, March 3, 1878, for the purpose of giving armed assistance to the commissioner, pending the complete establishment of a native militia sufficient to preserve order, security, and tranquillity. The period of occupation was limited to two years; the strength of the occupying army was not to exceed 50,000 men; and the cost of maintenance was to be defrayed by the country occupied. The troops were permitted to maintain their communications with Russia through Roumania as well as by the Black Sea ports, Varna and Bourgas, where they were empowered to organize the necessary depôts for the term of the occupation.

Chino-Japanese War.

In the case of the Chino-Japanese War, the Treaty of Shimonoseki, April 17, 1895,[2] provided, *inter alià*, that China should recognize the complete independence of Korea, cede to Japan certain specified territories, pay a war indemnity of 200,000,000 Kuping taels, and, upon the exchange of ratifications, conclude with Japan a new treaty of commerce and navigation and a convention to regulate frontier intercourse and trade. In order to ensure the faithful

[1] Villefort, *Recueil*, vol. ii. p. 590.

[2] See *infra*, Appendix (R).

performance of these stipulations, it was laid down (Art. VIII) that the Japanese forces were to occupy temporarily Wei-hai-Wei in the province of Shantung. The evacuation was to be effected on payment of the first two instalments of the indemnity (which was divided into eight instalments extending over seven years), and on the exchange of ratifications of the contemplated treaty of commerce and navigation; provided China agreed to pledge, under satisfactory arrangements, her customs revenue as security for the payment of the principal and interest of the rest of the indemnity. Should no such arrangements be made, the evacuation was not to take place until the entire sum was paid.

Greco-Turkish War.

Under the Treaty of Constantinople, December 4, 1897, terminating the Greco-Turkish war, the war indemnity imposed on Greece (Art. II) amounted to the sum of £T.4,000,000,[1] which was afterwards divided into four instalments, thus: 1 million to be paid on May 15, 1898; 1 million on May 25; 1,100,000 on June 10; and the last million on July 10. But here no payment was to be made before the commencement of the evacuation of Thessaly, and the last two instalments were to be paid only after complete evacuation. The Sublime Porte had previously proposed that the withdrawal of the Turkish troops from Greek territory should be effected in proportion to the payment of the indemnity. But the Powers (especially Great Britain, whose interposition has already been considered)[2] objected to the proposal and suggested the appointment of a commission (containing representatives of the Great Powers as well as of the two parties) to regulate the mode of evacuation, the points of concentration of the Ottoman forces, the number of Greek troops to be sent to the evacuated territories for maintaining public order, and the dates of payment of the indemnity. Great Britain opposed the suggested continuance of occupation till the full discharge of the sum agreed upon, on the ground that owing to the financial difficulties of Greece the payment might take a considerable length of time. It was therefore decided that the evacuation was to be effected a month after the Greek Chamber passed a law regulating the former debts of Greece and satisfactorily organizing the financial control of the country by an international commission. In conformity with these arrangements the withdrawal of the Ottoman troops from Thessaly took place between May 6 and June 6.[3]

[1] Art. VIII required Greece to pay an additional sum of £T.100,000 to indemnify individuals for damage caused by the Greek forces.

[2] See *supra*, pp. 86 *seq.*

[3] Cf. Politis, *La guerre gréco-turque*, p. 164.

CHAPTER VIII

THE TREATY OF PEACE

ITS MAIN CLAUSES AND EFFECTS

(i) *General Clauses: Cessation of Hostilities and Restoration of Peace—Restoration of Territory and the Principle of* Uti Possidetis—*Evacuation—Restoration of Prizes and other Movables*—Postliminium.

Cessation of hostilities and restoration of peace: treaties of peace as final and "permanent"; effect of establishment of peace; captures after conclusion of peace; adjudication after peace of captures made during the war—Resumption of diplomatic intercourse, etc.—Restoration of territory, etc.: *uti possidetis; status quo ante bellum;* condition of territories restored—Restoration of movable property—*Postliminium.*

CESSATION OF HOSTILITIES AND RESTORATION OF PEACE.

Treaties of peace, "perpetual."

USUALLY the first clause of a treaty of peace stipulates the cessation of hostilities and the restoration of peace. That is the logical introduction of a series of articles regulating the relationships of the contending parties. The same clause frequently observes that the peace thus re-established shall be "perpetual." Thus the First Peace of Paris, signed on May 30, 1814, by Great Britain, Austria, Prussia, Russia, and France, spoke of establishing "peace and friendship in perpetuity"; but in the Second Peace of Paris, November 20, 1815, the phrase is omitted. It is found also in the treaties of Paris, March 30, 1856; Zurich, 1859; Prague, 1866; Vienna, 1866; London, May 30, 1913; but not in the treaties of Constantinople, 1879; Lima, 1883; Shimonoseki, 1895; Portsmouth, 1905; Lausanne, 1912; Bucharest, 1913; Constantinople, 1913; Athens, 1913. That is, in nearly all the peace treaties of the last half-century, such expressions as "in perpetuity," "for ever," as applied to the restoration of pacific relations, do not occur.

On the other hand, most of the earlier treaties of peace concluded between Turkey and European Powers (chiefly Russia) were limited to a specified number of years; in other words, they purported to be simply prolonged truces. Thus under the Treaty of Belgrade, September 10, 1739, between the Emperor Charles VI and Turkey, peace was limited to twenty-seven years. The period fixed in the Treaty of Adrianople, June 5, 1713, between Russia and Turkey, was twenty-five years; and it was eight years in the Treaty of Unkiar-Skelessi, July 8, 1833, between the same parties. Till about the middle of the eighteenth century Turkey usually regarded her peace treaties with Christian Powers as truces, conformably to the teaching of the Koran, which considered the normal relationship between the faithful and those outside the pale as a state of war. But all nations who have considered themselves the elect adopted a similar attitude with regard to the heathens, infidels, and barbarians.

Treaties of peace as truces.

However this may be, the state of peace established by a treaty must be regarded, both from a judicial and from a political point of view, as definitive and final with regard to all those matters that were previously in dispute between the parties and now have been adjusted by their treaty. As Lord Stowell said: "A treaty of peace is an agreement to waive all discussion concerning the respective rights of the parties, and to bury in oblivion all the original causes of the war." [1]

Treaties of peace as final.

In concluding peace, the signatory Powers pledge themselves either expressly or impliedly to regard as settled not only all their differences that existed before the war and led to it, but also all such mutual claims as may have arisen during the course of the war, in connection with the conduct of hostilities. Over any of these matters they are not entitled to go to war again, however dissatisfied one party or the other may be with the solution arrived at. Very rarely is the result of a war between two States a draw; very rarely, therefore, are the terms of settlement equal; never can we find the belligerent parties equally content with the issue of their warlike enterprise. Not infrequently does a defeated State submit to the terms imposed on it with deep feelings of resentment, and with a determination to avenge the reverse at the first opportune moment; we may say that this occurs invariably when both of the States are powerful, possessing extensive resources, and one of them has been vanquished but not thoroughly crushed. Notwithstanding revengeful impulses and the cherished desire to recover what has been forfeited through a disastrous war and humiliating conditions of peace, the settlement should be regarded as "perpetual"—difficult as it may be to human nature—in

[1] *The Eliza Ann* (1813), 1 Dodson, 244, 249.

reference to the questions and differences adjusted in the treaty. It is in this sense that the seemingly extravagant expressions "for ever," "in perpetuity," etc., applied to the restoration of peace, are to be understood. As Vattel aptly observes: "The effect of the treaty of peace is to put an end to the war, and to abolish the subject of it. It leaves the contracting parties no right to commit any acts of hostility on account either of the subject itself which had given rise to the war, or of anything that was done during its continuance; wherefore they cannot lawfully take up arms again for the same subject. Accordingly, in such treaties the contracting parties reciprocally engage to preserve perpetual peace; which is not to be understood as if they promised never to make war on each other for any cause whatever. The peace in question relates to the war which it terminates, and it is in reality perpetual, inasmuch as it does not allow them to revive the same war by taking up arms again for the same subject which had originally given birth to it."[1]

Effect of establishment of peace.

After the establishment of peace—the definite commencement dating from the day fixed, or, failing this, from the signature of the treaty—all hostile operations, which before constituted legitimate acts of war, must discontinue; e.g. military or naval attacks, capture of prisoners, attack on or seizure of property, the exercise of authority on the part of an occupying commander (though subject to regulations, if any, regarding the continued occupation of certain territory by way of guarantee), the collection of taxes, the levying of contributions and requisitions, the capture of prizes, interference with neutral commerce of any kind (as the rules of contraband and blockade no longer apply). Any acts whatever of a hostile character committed by forces ignorant of the restoration of peace must be made good, and the *status quo* existing on the day of the termination of the war must as far as possible be reinstated; for example, territory occupied in such circumstances must be immediately evacuated, without waiting for the evacuation of other territory regularly occupied during the war, contributions collected must at once be repaid, persons taken prisoners must be set free again, ships captured must be released, and so on.

Compensation for subsequent acts of war.

If any such acts are committed the injured party is entitled to compensation, the responsibility resting either on those who did the acts or on their Government. Thus, in 1799 the case of *The Mentor* came before the British Prize Court. An American vessel, on a voyage from the Havannah to Philadelphia, was pursued by British vessels off the Delaware and destroyed, all parties—the British and the Americans

[1] *Droit des gens*, liv. iv. ch. ii. § 19.

alike—being in complete ignorance of the cessation of hostilities. Lord Stowell, in the course of his judgment, observed: ". . . If an act of mischief was done by the King's officers, through ignorance, in a place where no act of hostility ought to have been exercised, it does not necessarily follow that mere ignorance of *that fact* would protect the officers from civil responsibility. If by articles, a place or district was put under the King's peace, and an act of hostility was afterwards committed therein, the injured party might have a right to resort to a court of prize, to show that he had been injured by this breach of the peace, and was entitled to compensation; and if the officer acted *through ignorance*, his own Government must protect him: for it is the duty of Governments, if they put a certain district within the King's peace, to take care that due notice shall be given to those persons by whose conduct that peace is to be maintained; and if no such notice has been given, nor due diligence used to give it, and a breach of the peace is committed through the ignorance of those persons, they are to be borne harmless, at the expense of the Government whose duty it was to have given that notice." [1]

Another interesting case on this point is *The John*. The Treaty of Ghent, December 24, 1814, between Great Britain and the United States, provided that on ratification (which took place on February 17, 1815) orders were to be sent to the forces on both sides to abstain from further hostilities, and that all "vessels and effects" captured by either party after the dates fixed by the treaty, varying from 12 to 120 days according to the place of capture, should be restored (Art. II). *The John*, an American ship, was captured by a British vessel in a locality the period for which had expired, both captor and prize being ignorant of the conclusion of peace. Whilst in the possession of the captor the prize was soon afterwards lost through an act of God. The owners subsequently sought reparation on the ground that the captor was personally liable. Lord Stowell held that the alleged mismanagement of the ship whilst under the captor's control was not proved, so that the only point to consider was the question of restitution in the case of a capture effected out of due time and place. As the captor's ignorance was not one of law but of fact, and of a fact depending on State transactions which he could not know without notification, and as his possession therefore was *bona fide*, he could not be personally responsible for the loss. A liability might, however, possibly attach elsewhere, though this was a point which the Court was not then called upon to decide. [2]

[1] *The Mentor* (1799), 1 C. Rob., 179, 182–183.

[2] *The John* (1818), 2 Dodson, 336.

Later, the United States Government, acting on behalf of the owners of the vessel, claimed compensation from the British Government; and this claim was, together with others, referred in 1853 to a Joint Commission. The latter pointed out that, in accordance with the decisions in *The Mentor* and *The John*, a want of due diligence in notifying the cessation of hostilities gave an injured party a right to indemnity. In order to obviate disputes as to what constituted due diligence, the practice was adopted of fixing certain periods for the discontinuance of hostile acts according to the zone concerned. The dates specified in the treaty of 1814 must be taken as equivalent to notification, so that the obligation to abstain from hostilities was thereafter imperative. The provision of Art. II as to restoration of vessels and effects applied not only to the thing itself, when practicable, but also, if this be impracticable, to its equivalent in damages. Though the vessel was lost by an act of God, the British Government was responsible, inasmuch as she was taken to the place, where she was lost, without right—i.e. after the date fixed, whereby notice was irrebuttably presumed.[1]

Captures after conclusion of peace.

In case no date is fixed for the cessation of hostilities, all captures effected after the conclusion of peace must be restored as soon as that fact becomes known.[2] And, as we have already seen in the cases of *The Swineherd* and *The Nymph*,[3] even if a period has been fixed, commanders must abstain from all hostile acts as soon as they receive reliable information as to the peace, without waiting till the said period expires.

Another question that arises is as to the position of a prize which has been captured during the war, and recaptured after the cessation of hostilities but in ignorance of the conclusion of peace. If the prize had already been duly condemned by the captor's prize court, the ownership of it had thereby passed, and so its recapture after the establishment of peace is forbidden just as much as the capture of any other property. Furthermore, if the prize had not been yet condemned, the captor's possessory rights may not, any more than his proprietary rights, be interfered with in like circumstances, inasmuch as forcible interference is incompatible with the required discontinuance of hostile acts.[4] Accordingly, if such a prize has been recaptured, even though in ignorance of the peace, it should be restored to the captor.

Again, may a prize court, after the conclusion of peace, try

[1] J. B. Moore, *History and Digest of the International Arbitrations to which the United States has been a Party*, 6 vols. (Washington, 1898); vol. iv. p. 3793.

[2] *Bain* v. *Speedwell* (1784), 2 Dallas, 40.

[3] See *supra*, pp. 193, 194.

[4] Cf. *The Schoone Sophie* (1805), 6 C. Rob. 138.

vessels that were captured during the war—i.e. in the absence of a provision to the contrary?[1] Practice appears to sanction an affirmative answer.[2] On principle, however, a negative solution is more logical, seeing that the adjudication of a prize court partakes of the nature of a hostile act, because it is a necessary complement of the capture.

Adjudication after peace of captures made during the war.

The question was raised recently, in the war between Italy and Abyssinia, in the case of the *Doelwijk*, which was a Dutch vessel—i.e. neutral—seized by an Italian cruiser, the *Etna*, for carrying contraband. The Italian Prize Court held, December 8, 1896, that it was competent to investigate whether or no the capture was legitimate; but it refrained from pronouncing a decree of condemnation, on the ground that peace had in the meantime been declared. The capture was considered to be valid; but none the less confiscation was not decreed, for the reason that the right of capture is based only on the right of defence against the enemy, and therefore against all acts which during the war tend to augment the hostile means and resources of the enemy. The war having ceased, however, the right of defence against him who is no longer an enemy and against him who increased the latter's resources ceases at the same time. Moreover, although the capture of the prize, prior to the cessation of war, was regular, yet a decision pronounced against it after peace has been re-established would be a proceeding antagonistic to the resumption of pacific relationships, inasmuch as it would thereby impose on another's property a limitation which was no longer justified by the necessity of legitimate defence. Accordingly, a decree of confiscation in such circumstances would not be in consonance either with the dictates of justice or with the fundamental principles of international law.[3] It may be added that certain juristic critics have argued that the *Doelwijk* and her cargo were not properly subject to condemnation, not owing to the cessation of hostilities, but because the enemy destination was not incontestably proved.[4]

[1] As to stipulations in treaties, see *infra*, p. 229.

[2] Cf. Pistoye et Duverdy, *op. cit.*, vol. i. p. 145. A noteworthy case that came before the French Conseil d'État, in 1815, is that of *The Ceres*, a vessel, under Dutch flag, bound for England. She was captured before the establishment of peace, but on the date of adjudication, May 16, 1814, peace had already been concluded. The capture by the French vessel, *Sophie*, was declared to be valid, and condemnation was pronounced. This judgment was delivered on the ground that it is for the Court to consider only the rules and circumstances existing at the time of the capture, and not those existing at the time of adjudication.

[3] The judgment of the Italian Court is given, in a French translation, in *Archives Diplomatiques* (Paris), January 1897, pp. 81 *seq.*, and also in *Journal du droit international privé* (Paris), vol. xxiv. pp. 850 *seq*,

[4] Cf. article by G. Diena, in *Journ. du dr. int. privé* (Paris), vol. xiv. pp. 296 *seq.*

Other consequences of the declaration of peace are the revival of such contracts with enemy aliens as had been suspended by the outbreak of war—though this depends on the operation of municipal rather than of international law—and the resumption of diplomatic intercourse and consular arrangements. With regard to these matters, especially the latter, express provision is sometimes made in the treaty of peace. Thus Art. V of the Treaty of Lausanne, October 18, 1912, between Italy and Turkey, lays down that the Governments, as well as their respective subjects, shall be placed towards one another in the same position in which they were before the outbreak of hostilities. Further, the Treaty of Lima, June 12, 1883, between Spain and Chile, provides (Art. IV) that the parties shall appoint diplomatic representatives and also consular agents. The Treaty of Constantinople, September 29, 1913, between Turkey and Bulgaria, says (Art. III) that diplomatic relations as well as postal, telegraphic, and railway communications shall be resumed immediately after the signing of the treaty. Similarly, the Treaty of Athens, November 14, 1913, between Turkey and Greece, stipulates (Art. I) that after signature the diplomatic relations and the consulates shall be restored.

Resumption of diplomatic intercourse, etc.

More frequently, however, this result is not expressly stipulated; it follows as a matter of course, usually after the exchange of ratifications. Thus in the case of the American-Spanish War, the definitive Treaty of Paris was signed on December 10, 1898, ratifications were exchanged on April 12, 1899, and diplomatic relations were formally re-established on June 4.[1] In the course of his message, December 5, 1899, President McKinley observed: "Following the exchange of ratifications of the treaty of peace the two Governments accredited ministers to each other. . . . This was followed by the respective appointment of consuls, thereby fully resuming the relations interrupted by the war. In addition to its consular representation in the United States, the Spanish Government has appointed consuls for Cuba, who have been provisionally recognized during the military administration of the affairs of that island." [2]

Formerly it became the practice, in concluding treaties of peace, to agree upon a basis constituting a fundamental point of departure for the new relations to be established between the contracting

[1] As to other relations of the parties, see further *infra*, pp. 250 *seq.*, with regard to the revival of treaties that were affected by the war.

[2] Moore, *Digest*, vol. vii. p. 336.

parties. Such point of departure was either the state of possession existing at the outbreak of the war, represented by the formula *status quo ante bellum* (which was itself sometimes divided into *status quo de facto*—the state of possession as it actually was—and *status quo de jure*—the state of possession as it should legitimately have been just before the commencement of hostilities); or the state of possession existing at the conclusion of the war, represented by the formula *status quo post bellum*, or *uti possidetis*.

RESTORATION OF TERRITORY, ETC., AND THE PRINCIPLE OF *UTI POSSIDETIS*.

Unless otherwise stipulated, conditions remain conformably to the principle of *uti possidetis*. The establishment of peace implies the recovery or renunciation, as the case may be, of previous claims, within the limits and conditions specified by the treaty; but if the treaty is silent thereon, complete renunciation is necessarily presumed. In the case of the Russo-Japanese War, the Japanese plenipotentiaries argued at the Portsmouth Peace Conference that the rule of *uti possidetis* should apply in respect of Sakhalin, which formerly belonged to Japan. The question of former ownership was not legally relevant; but the Russian representatives declined to accede to the principle on other grounds, and eventually the possession of the island was disposed of by an express provision. If, then, there is no stipulation as to conquered or occupied territory, it is considered as remaining in the hands of the occupant, who is entitled to annex it—the presumption being that the silence of the treaty on the point indicates the other party's acquiescence and consent. Further, in the absence of a provision as to movable property, all such things as were lawfully taken by the invader in virtue of his military occupation remain his, subject to the fulfilment of any obligations attaching to his appropriation at the time: e.g. contributions, requisitions; cash, funds, realizable securities, arms, munitions, provisions, etc., all belong to the State (if they belong to private persons they must be restored and compensation paid at the conclusion of peace[1]); the fruits of land and forests belonging to the State, taken by the invader in the capacity of usufructuary.[2]

Uti possidetis.

In earlier treaties, however, the principle of *uti possidetis* was sometimes expressly stipulated. Thus—to give but a few miscellaneous instances—the Treaty of Münster, 1648, between Spain and the Low Countries, allowed each of the contracting parties (Art. III) to keep the towns and territories of which it was in

[1] Cf. *Hague Convention concerning the Laws and Customs of War on Land*, No. IV (1907), Art. 53.

[2] *Ibid.*, Art. 55.

possession at the time of making peace. The Treaty of Breda, July 31, 1667, between England, France, the States General, and Denmark, stipulated that each party should retain conquests made before and during the war till May 20, 1667 (Art. III), captured vessels should belong to the captor (Art. IV), but what was taken after that date should be restored (Art. VI). Under the Treaty of Aix-la-Chapelle, 1668, between France and Spain, Arts. III and IV gave to the King of France all conquests made by him in the north, viz. Charleroi, Tournai, Douai, Courtrai, Oudenarde, Lille, Armentières, Bergues, Furnes; but Art. V required the restoration to Spain of Franche-Comté, together with Cambrai, Aire, and St. Omer. The Treaty of The Hague, 1669, between Portugal and Holland, provided that the Dutch should remain in possession of their conquests, except Cochin and Cunanor, which they had to restore on payment of three million florins; and that Portugal should keep Brazil on payment of a millions florins. The Treaty of Gulistan, 1813, between Russia and Persia, laid down (Art. II) the existing *status quo* as the basis, each party remaining in possession of the territories then in its hands.

Expressly stipulated in earlier treaties.

The *uti possidetis* clause is nowadays unusual in peace treaties, if not obsolete. In its stead, the practice is adopted of stipulating the cession of certain territory demanded by one State or the other as a result of successful invasion or successful prosecution of the war in general, all other invaded territory being restored.[1]

Nowadays unusual.

Where the principle of *uti possidetis* is not stipulated or implied, that of *status quo ante bellum* applies. In nearly every treaty of peace do we find clauses relating to the restoration or evacuation of territory that had been invaded and militarily occupied; and occasionally dates are fixed to differentiate between conquests made in previous wars and those made in the particular war terminated by each treaty, or the actual territories to be restored are designated by name. The date of the commencement of the evacuation is generally specified, being sometimes the date of the signature of the treaty and sometimes that of the exchange of ratifications. The period, too, within which the evacuation is to be completely effected is prescribed very frequently. Further, arrangements are made for the line of demarcation between the respective forces, the date on which the local authorities may resume their administration of the territories to be restored, the maintenance of the occupying troops during that period, the use of railways and other means of transport by them,

The *status quo ante bellum*.

[1] As to cession, see *infra*, pp. 277 *seq.*

their rights and obligations as to requisitions, the treatment of the sick and wounded who cannot be removed, which troops are to be withdrawn first and the order of the rest, what lines they are to follow in returning to their country, etc. Some of these and other details are either prescribed in advance—in the treaties themselves or in supplementary articles—or are left to be settled by the respective military authorities immediately after the conclusion of the treaties of peace. The following are some interesting examples, chronologically arranged, and put in the briefest terms.[1]

Treaty of the Pyrenees, 1659, between France and Spain: the possessions of the Dukes of Savoy and Modena (allies of France against Spain in the war) are restored to the state in which they were before the war (Arts. XCI–XCIX); the Prince of Monaco regains the rights and territories held by him before the war in the Duchy of Milan, Kingdom of Naples, and other countries (Art. CIV).

Treaty of Oliva, 1660, between the Empire, Sweden, Poland, Brandenburg, and France (acting as mediator): Poland and Sweden make mutual restorations of territory (Arts. V, VII), and the Elector of Brandenburg restores to Sweden all places occupied by his troops in Pomerania (Art. XXVI).

Treaty of Copenhagen, 1660, between Sweden and Denmark (England, France, and the States General being mediating Powers): Sweden gives up to Denmark all Danish towns and territories occupied by her during the war, in their actual condition (Arts. XV, XVI).

Treaty of Lisbon, 1668, between France and Spain: (Art. II) reciprocal restitution of everything taken during the war, except Ceuta which remains in the possession of Spain.

Treaty of Westminster, 1674, between England and the States General: mutual restoration of conquests.

Treaty of Nimeguen, 1678, between England, France, the Empire, Spain, the States General, Sweden: (Arts. I–V) France restores to Holland all conquests made there; (Art. VI) France restores the principality of Orange to the Duke of Nassau.

Treaty of The Hague, June 29, 1684, between France and Holland: France to restore all the places occupied since August 20, 1683.

Treaty of Ryswick, 1697, between England and France: (Art. VII) restitution of everything taken during the war.

Treaty of Baden, 1714, between the Emperor and France: (Art. XV) the Electors of Bavaria and Cologne are restored to their possessions and rights as existing before the war.

[1] A considerable number of instances are here given, owing to the great importance of this aspect of the peace settlement.

Treaty of Dresden, 1745, between Prussia and Saxony: (Art. III) Prussia to give back to the Elector everything taken from him.

Treaty of Aix-la-Chapelle, 1748, between England, France, the Empire, Spain, Sardinia, the States General, Modena, Genoa: (Arts. IV–IX) France to give up all her conquests, and England to restore to her Cape Breton Island; (Art. XVI) England restores territory taken during the war.

Treaty of St. Petersburg, 1762, between Russia and Prussia: (Art. VI) Russia to restore to Prussia all territories and places occupied by Russian troops.

Treaty of Versailles, 1783, between Great Britain and Spain: "Art. VII. His Catholic Majesty shall restore to Great Britain the islands of Providence and the Bahamas, without exception, in the same condition they were in when they were conquered by the arms of the King of Spain. Art. VIII. All the countries and territories which may have been or which may be conquered in any part of the world whatever by the arms of his Britannic Majesty, as well as by those of his Catholic Majesty, which are not included in the present treaty, neither under the head of cessions, nor under the head of restitutions, shall be restored without difficulty, and without requiring any compensation."[1]

In the treaty of the same date, signed also at Versailles, between Great Britain and Louis XVI of France, provision is likewise made for the restitution of territory: "Art. VII. The King of Great Britain restores to France the island of St. Lucia, in the condition it was in when it was conquered by the British arms. . . . Art. VIII. The most Christian King restores to Great Britain the islands of Grenada, and the Grenadines, St. Vincent's, Dominica, St. Christopher's, Nevis, and Montserrat; and the fortresses of these islands shall be delivered up in the condition they were in when the conquest of them was made. . . . Art. XIII. The King of Great Britain restores to his most Christian Majesty all the settlements which belonged to him at the beginning of the present war, upon the coast of Orixa, and in Bengal." After providing for the delivery to France of Pondicherry, Karikal (Art. XIV), and Mahé, together with the factory at Surat (Art. XV), Art. XIX reproduces the terms of Art. VIII, mentioned above, in the treaty with Spain, substituting merely "his most Christian Majesty" for "his Catholic Majesty."[2]

Treaty of Paris, 1783, between Great Britain and the United States: (Art. V) reciprocal restitution of all places taken, as well as of all captures made from individuals.

Treaty of Paris, 1784, between Great Britain and the States

[1] *Annual Register*, 1783, pp. 335–336. [2] *Ibid.*, pp. 325–327.

General: Mutual restoration of conquests, save certain places indicated.

Treaty of The Hague, 1795, between France and Holland: (Arts. X, XII) France to restore to Holland territory and other property taken during the war.

Treaty of Bâle, 1795, between France and Spain: (Art. IV) France to deliver up all places taken in Spain, and (Art. X) all property confiscated during the war to be returned.

Treaty of Amiens, 1802, between Great Britain, France, Spain, and the Batavian Republic: (Arts. III–V) Great Britain to restore numerous and extensive territories taken from them, except Trinidad and Ceylon, which are ceded to her.

Treaty of Tilsit, July 7, 1807, between France and Russia: (Art. IV) Napoleon restores to Prussia much territory.

Treaty of Paris, 1810, between France and Sweden: (Art. IV) Napoleon restores to Sweden Swedish Pomerania, Rügen, and other dependencies, as well as (Art. VI) sequestered vessels.

Treaty of Valençay, 1813, between France and Spain: (Arts. IV, V) Napoleon recognized the integrity of Spanish territory, as it was before the war, and the Spanish provinces occupied by French troops were evacuated.

Treaty of Paris, November 20, 1815, between the Allies and France: (Art. I) France restored certain territories, leaving her frontiers as they were in 1790, subject to the modifications detailed in the same article.[1] By the additional convention of the same date, they were to be delivered up (Art. IX) within ten days from the date of the signature of the treaty, in the condition in which they were on the preceding September 20.[2]

Treaty of Adrianople, 1829, between Russia and Turkey: (Art. II) Russia to restore all conquests, the principalities of Moldavia and Wallachia, the Dobridgia from the Danube to the sea, Bulgaria, and all territories occupied by her troops in Roumelia.

Treaty of Paris, March 30, 1856, between the Allies and Russia: (Art. II) the territories conquered or occupied by their armies to be reciprocally evacuated; (Art. III) Russia to restore to Turkey Kars and other territory; (Art. IV) the Allies to restore to Russia Sebastopol, Balaklava, Kamiesch, Eupatoria, Kertch, Jenikale, and other places occupied by the Allied troops. The mode of evacuation was regulated by special arrangements.[3]

Treaty of Prague, 1866, between Austria and Italy: (Art. XII) the Prussian troops to evacuate Austrian territories within three weeks after the exchange of ratifications. The appendix to the

[1] See *infra*, Appendix (A). [2] Appendix (B). [3] Appendix (D).

treaty regulates the mode of evacuation: To accelerate the withdrawal, the time between signature and ratification to be employed by Prussia in preparatory measures. Various details are specified, e.g. dates fixed for the evacuation of certain tracts; the distance to be kept by the Austrian troops from the rear of the Prussian columns in reoccupying those tracts; the use of railways by both sides; the cost of maintaining the Prussian troops during the period of evacuation (to be borne by Prussia, though Austria to provide free quarters only, and relays which are to be paid for); the treatment of the Prussian sick and wounded who cannot be removed, and the expenses incurred.[1]

Preliminaries of Versailles, 1871, between France and Germany: (Art. III) the evacuation of French territory (except that which was to be ceded within the limits prescribed by Art. I) occupied by German troops to begin after the ratification. First, they are to quit the interior of Paris and the forts on the left bank of the Seine, then—under an agreement between the military authorities—certain specified departments, as far as the left bank of the Seine. At the same time the French troops are to fall back behind the Loire, which they are not to pass before the signature of the definitive treaty of peace. The garrison of Paris, which is not to exceed 40,000 men, is excepted from this provision.[2] The evacuation of the departments between the right bank of the Seine and the eastern frontier, which remained in German occupation by way of guaranteeing the payment of indemnity, has already been considered.[3]

Preliminaries of San Stefano, 1878, between Russia and Turkey: (Art. XXV) the Russian army to evacuate Turkey in Europe, except Bulgaria, within three months, and Turkey in Asia within six months, after the conclusion of the definitive peace; and the operations to begin immediately after the exchange of ratifications. To save time and expense part of the troops may, in the first case, proceed to the ports of the Black Sea and the Sea of Marmora, to be there shipped in vessels belonging to Russia or chartered for the purpose; and in the second case troops may take ship at Trebizond in order to return by the Caucasus or the Crimea. (Art. XXVI) Turkish administration is to be resumed only after the complete departure of all the Russian troops; the entry of the forces of Turkey and the exercise of her authority in the places to be restored cannot begin until notice of evacuation has been given to the Turkish officers by the Russian commander.[4]

Treaty of Shimonoseki, 1895, between China and Japan: (Art. VII) the evacuation of China by the Japanese armies shall

[1] See Appendix (H).
[2] Appendix (J).
[3] See *supra*, pp. 211, 212.
[4] Appendix (M).

be completely effected within three months after the exchange of ratifications, subject to the provisions (Art. VIII) relative to the temporary occupation of Wei-hai-Wei, by way of guaranteeing the payment of the indemnity.[1]

Treaty of Portsmouth, 1905, between Russia and Japan: (Art. III and Art. I of the supplementary agreement) the forces of both parties to evacuate Manchuria (except the leased territory of the Liao-tung Peninsula) simultaneously within eighteen months from the exchange of ratifications, operations commencing immediately after the latter act; the forces occupying the front positions to be withdrawn first. Provision is made for the protection of their respective railways in Manchuria. The details of evacuation to be settled by the commanders.

Treaty of Lausanne, 1912, between Italy and Turkey: (Art. II) immediately after the signature of the treaty Turkey to recall her troops and civil functionaries from Tripoli and Cyrenaica, Italy to recall hers from the islands occupied by her in the Ægean Sea; the Italian departure to take place immediately after the Turkish departure is completed.

Treaty of Bucharest, 1913, between Bulgaria and the Balkan Allies: (Art. VII) the evacuation of Bulgarian territory to begin immediately after the demobilization of the Bulgarian army (as stipulated in Art. VI), and to be completed within fifteen days. For this period the zone of demarcation for the Roumanian army is indicated. (Art. VIII) During the occupation the Allied armies to retain the right of requisition for cash payment and to have free use of the railways (without paying compensation) for transporting troops and provisions.

Condition of territories restored.

With regard to the condition in which evacuated territory is to be restored, the obvious rule is that it should be delivered up in the state in which it was at the time of concluding peace. Till that date the occupying forces enjoy the extensive rights conferred by effective military occupation; after that date those rights are considerably narrowed down—as we have seen, either in the treaty itself or in supplementary conventions signed at the same time or soon afterwards—and are just sufficient to enable the evacuating troops to make a quiet and undisturbed departure with as little delay as possible. Hence, during the period beginning with the date of signature, or the date of the exchange of ratifications if expressly stipulated, every avoidable deterioration in the occupied territory is forbidden. If destruction due to the regular operations of war is not subject to claims for

[1] See *supra*, p. 213.

indemnity, all wanton or careless damage inflicted after the cessation of hostilities certainly justifies a demand for reparation. The occupant may, of course, take away things belonging to him and all structures erected by him, unless those structures consist of property which he could lawfully use only as a usufructuary and not as a proprietor. In restoring anything the departing occupant must at the same time restore all the rights that had attached thereto at the time when it was taken, subject, however, to such changes as were produced by nature or by the legitimate acts of war.[1]

Sometimes provision as to the condition of the restored territory is expressly made in treaties. Thus—to give one or two examples of different kinds of stipulations on this point—the Treaty of the Pyrenees, 1659 (mentioned above), required that occupied towns and territories should be delivered up in their actual condition; the Treaty of Versailles, 1783, provided for the restoration of certain fortresses and islands in the condition they were in when the conquests were made; the additional convention of the Treaty of Paris, November 20, 1815, stipulated the delivery of certain territories in the condition in which they were on the preceding September 20. Whatever good effect such dispositions may produce, they cannot make good the havoc wrought by the previous hostilities or settled military occupation. In the Greco-Turkish War of 1897, for instance, the evacuation of Thessaly by the Turkish troops appears to have been carried out with regularity and good order. None the less, several regions were left in a deplorable state; towns that were flourishing and prosperous before the war were delivered up completely devastated. These devastations, observed M. Politis, will for a long time be gaping wounds for Greece—"ces dévastations seront pendant longtemps pour la Grèce des plaies béantes et un souvenir cruel des tristes événements de 1897."[2] No doubt the law of military occupation, as now established, imposes numerous restrictions on the conduct of an occupant; but if he is unscrupulous he can—though seemingly observing the letter of that law—deal death and destruction in the country in which he has temporarily settled. "Military necessity" can be made to cover many violations of the spirit of law and order—not to mention breaches of literal injunctions—and many outrages against humanity and civilization. With the "gaping wounds" and the dire heritage left by war in general we are not here concerned.

It may be added that in order to enforce observance of the laws and customs of land warfare, the Hague Convention of 1907[3] has introduced a special sanction: that when all the belligerents are

[1] Cf. Vattel, liv. iv. ch. iii. §§ 30, 31.

[2] *La guerre gréco-turque*, p. 164.

[3] No. IV. Art. 3.

parties to the convention they will be liable to pay compensation, if the case demands, for violating the regulations respecting those laws and customs; and they are held responsible for all acts committed by members of their armed forces.

Restoration of movable property.

In some cases the restitution of captured movable property is also stipulated, e.g. in the treaties of Paris, 1783, between Great Britain and the United States (things taken from individuals); The Hague, 1795, between France and Holland (property in general); Bâle, 1795, between France and Spain (all property that had been confiscated); Campo Formio, 1797, between France and the Emperor (sequestrations that had been imposed on the property of individuals reciprocally removed); Paris, 1810, between France and Sweden (sequestered vessels restored); Paris, July 20, 1814, between France and Spain—one of the treaties belonging to the first peace of Paris (Art. I of the additional articles required the mutual restoration of sequestered or confiscated property); Zurich, 1859, between France and Austria (delivery of uncondemned vessels taken from Austria); Vienna, 1864, between Denmark on the one side, and Austria and Prussia on the other (restoration of uncondemned ships and cargoes captured, Art. XIII); Frankfort, 1871, between France and Germany (German vessels and their cargoes not condemned before March 2, 1871, to be restored); and the Treaty of Athens, 1913, between Greece and Turkey, of which Art. IX says that immediately after the treaty is signed Turkey is to release all ships and boats flying the Greek flag which were seized before the declaration of war and are still held by her; and claims for damages and losses by interested persons, owing to the embargo or seizure, are to be settled by arbitration under a "compromis" to be agreed upon.

A question arising out of some of the above dispositions is—What is the legal position of prizes in general captured during the war but not yet adjudicated upon by the captor's prize court before the conclusion of peace? For it is an established principle of international law and practice that a judicial condemnation is necessary for the property in the prize to vest in the captor. Whether a prize court may, in the absence of express provision, proceed to try a vessel after peace which was captured during the war has already been considered in connection with the case of the *Doelwijk*.[1] The problem, however, is best solved by an agreement embodied in the treaty between the parties concerned. A departure from earlier practice was introduced into the Treaty of Zurich, 1859, between France and Austria. Art. III is to this effect: "To diminish the

[1] See *supra*, p. 219.

evils of war, and by an exceptional departure from the law generally observed, the captured Austrian vessels which have not yet been condemned as prizes shall be restored. The vessels and cargoes shall be restored in the state in which they were at the time of their capture, after payment of all expenses and of all charges which may have been incurred on account of the convoy and keeping of the said prizes, as well as of any legal proceedings connected with them, and the usual allowance to the captors; and lastly, no indemnity will be claimable on account of prizes sunk and destroyed any more than for the capture of merchandise belonging to the enemy, even though it may not yet have been subjected to a decision of the prize court." The proviso was added that the decisions of the prize court were to hold good in favour of those to whom the prizes were adjudged. Similarly, Art. XIII of the Treaty of Vienna, October 30, 1864, stipulated the restoration of such prizes as had not been duly condemned by a prize court at the establishment of peace. Again, Art. XIII of the Treaty of Frankfort, May 10, 1871, declared that German vessels condemned by prize courts before March 2, 1871 (the day of the ratification of the preliminaries) were to be considered as definitively condemned; but those not condemned before that date were to be restored together with their cargoes if still in existence, otherwise their value, reckoned according to the price of the sale, was to be paid to the owners. In this case a date anterior to that of the definitive treaty was fixed, in view of the fact that peace was practically established by the Preliminaries of Versailles of February 26, 1871. It may be added that out of 90 captured German vessels, 13 were restored in accordance with this stipulation.

Postliminium.

In conclusion, a word may be said as to the doctrine of *postliminium,* which finds a place in most works on international law in connection with our present subject. The *ius postliminii* of the Romans implied certain principles of their private law, as well as conceptions derived from the fetial institution appertaining to the declaration of war and conclusion of peace.[1] It referred to the right by which persons or things captured in war regained their former condition on their return to the country to which they belonged;[2] so that, by a juridical fiction a Roman prisoner of war, for example,

[1] Cf. C. Phillipson, *International Law and Custom of Ancient Greece and Rome*, 2 vols. (London, 1911), vol. ii. pp. 266 *seq.*

[2] *Dig.* xlix. 15. 19, *pr.*: "Postliminium est ius amissæ rei recipiendæ ab extraneo et in statum pristinum restituendæ inter nos ac liberos populos regesque moribus legibus constitutum."—Cf. *Cod.* viii. 50; Just. *Inst.* i. 12. 5.

might avoid the ordinary consequences of captivity. The doctrine applied to Roman citizens, slaves, immovables, and certain movables, e.g. trained horses, pack-mules, transport vessels; everything else captured by the enemy became his permanent booty—notably arms, which, it was thought, could not be lost without dishonour. The doctrine did not apply to deserters, to those who yielded to the enemy through cowardice, or were formally surrendered to the enemy, or preferred to reside with the enemy, and to certain others.

The conception out of place in modern international law.

These fundamental notions of the Roman law were afterwards imported by writers into international law; and in their hands *postliminium* came to represent the general principle that if captured persons and property, and more particularly invaded territory, were liberated from the enemy's control, they were presumed to revert *ipso facto* to their former status or condition. That is, the doctrine implied that the captor's or invader's control depended only on temporary, provisional possession, and not on permanent appropriation incidental to full sovereignty. This return to the former condition might occur in different ways[1]:—(1) Voluntary evacuation by the enemy and reoccupation by the legitimate sovereign; (2) reconquest by the latter; (3) reconquest by a third State, followed by restoration to the legitimate sovereign; (4) successful levy *en masse* (though this is closely connected with No. (2); (5) in case of property, its recapture by the former owner or its abandonment by the captor; and finally (6) restoration of the occupied or conquered territory by a treaty of peace.

However, under the modern system of international law there is no need whatever to refer any rules to this notion of *postliminium*. It is not in itself an elemental conception, but rather a complex which is analysable into more fundamental principles derived from common sense and the very nature of things. It is therefore far simpler and more salutary for a regulative science like international law to base its rules on these fundamental principles rather than on complex technicalities. If law, whether international or municipal, is to serve the true interests of States and men and to command their respect, it must be made as simple and clear as possible, and must be liberated from complicated artificialities which furnish such fertile ground for the subterfuges of the unscrupulous and the bewildering argumentations of the academically minded theorist. Many of the rules, then, laid down by most writers in regard to *postliminium* we have in the preceding chapters inferred from axiomatic principles, e.g. that the society of States ought to constitute a

[1] Cf. Oppenheim, *International Law*, vol. ii. p. 339.

harmonious and orderly system, that peace is the normal condition of civilized mankind, that a sovereign independent State should be free from external interference and be allowed to develop in accordance with its particular genius and traditions, that invasion does not necessarily confer on the invader the rights of sovereignty, and so on. We have seen, accordingly, without relying on the *ius postliminii*, the effect of the recapture of property, of the expulsion of the invader, of the occupant's evacuation, of the restitution of territory; we have seen the important differences between military occupation and completed subjugation and annexation, between the restricted rights of possession based on military necessity and the unrestricted rights of ownership based on true sovereignty, between a provisional *de facto* government and a permanent *de jure* government; and we have noted certain principles flowing as corollaries from these differences, e.g. that a State temporarily deprived of its sovereignty over its territory through the occupation of the invader, is bound on restoration to respect acts duly performed by the occupant within certain limits imposed on his conduct (say, as a usufructuary) but not such dispositive acts as transcended those limits. Having regard to these considerations, we must express our agreement with the observation of a recent French writer that the importation of this ancient doctrine of *postliminium* into modern international law, especially in matters relating to the treaty of peace and its effects, is a "tentative malencontreuse," serving but to obscure rules intrinsically simple and intelligible.[1]

[1] Cf. Bonfils, *Droit international public* (1912), p. 1086.

CHAPTER IX

THE TREATY OF PEACE

ITS MAIN CLAUSES AND EFFECTS

(i) *General Clauses (continued) : Restoration of Prisoners of War—Amnesty—Revival or Annulment of Treaties*

Restoration of prisoners of war: collective delivery; when restoration to begin; liberation to be unconditional; cost of maintenance; may prisoners be detained for debts? may prisoners be detained for disciplinary offences? offences against the common law; details regulated by special conventions—Amnesty: implied, if not expressly provided for; partial amnesty; general amnesty; restrictions on; amnesty provision really superfluous and illogical —Revival or annulment of treaties: views of writers; judicial pronouncements; practice of States, various examples; rules applicable, general conclusions submitted.

RESTORATION OF PRISONERS OF WAR.

As soon as peace is concluded the taking of prisoners of war, which is an act of hostility, is no longer permissible. The rights conferred by war cease to exist—"cessante causa cessat effectus." The condition of prisoners of war at the same time disappears, and there can be no valid reason for continuing to hold them in captivity. Reason demands that the very first step in the re-establishment of pacific relations between the former belligerent States should be the reciprocal delivery of all prisoners of war. In the removal or alleviation of the calamities brought about by the conflict, the person naturally claims precedence over property. According to the Hague Regulations, the repatriation of prisoners of war must take place with the least possible delay after peace has been concluded.[1]

Formerly prisoners were regarded as the personal property of their captors; so that, through the practice of ransom, they constituted a source of enrichment to combatants. Afterwards, owing to a clearer recognition of State personality and the organization of standing armies, followed by an improvement

[1] *Hague Convention concerning the Laws and Customs of War on Land*, 1899 and 1907, No. IV, Art. 20.

in military rules and discipline, the principle was established that prisoners of war fell into the power of the State itself, which, however, continued for a long time the system of ransom, and the modified form of exchange of man for man supplemented by a money payment to the party having the larger number of captives. Nowadays, though exchange has sometimes been resorted to as a preliminary measure, before the conclusion of the definitive treaty of peace, the regular mode of liberating prisoners is by mutually delivering all in a mass regardless of rank or excess in number on one side or the other. This is now an established principle; that is, it is necessarily implied, unless contrary or modified provisions are in express terms made by the parties voluntarily. Not infrequently do we find in early treaties articles stipulating the restoration of prisoners in a mass and without ransom: e.g. the Treaty of the Pyrenees, 1659, between France and Spain (Arts. CVI, CVII); the Treaty of Utrecht, 1713, between England and France (Art. XXIII); the Treaty of Belgrade, 1739, between the Emperor Charles VI of Austria and Turkey (Art. VI); the Treaty of Bâle, April 5, 1795, between France and Prussia (Art. IX), and the Treaty of Bâle, July 23, 1795, between France and Spain (Art. XII); the Treaty of Amiens, 1802, between England, France, Spain, and the Batavian Republic; the Treaty of Tilsit, 1807, between France and Russia (Art. XXVI); the Treaty of Paris, 1814, between the Allies and France; and so on. An interesting recent example of the survival of the early practice mentioned above is found in the case of the war between Italy and Abyssinia, 1896. According to a statement made by the Italian negotiator of the peace, Major Nerazzini,[1] the Abyssinian chiefs considered the numerous Italian prisoners as their property; so that King Menelek was obliged, in order to obtain their restitution, to pay the captors compensation —partaking of the nature of ransom—in accordance with the traditional customs of the country. But Abyssinia can scarcely be regarded as a member of the civilized society of States.[2]

Formerly prisoners the property of their captors.

Exchange.

Collective delivery.

The delivery of prisoners of war forms the subject of a general clause of the preliminaries of peace or of the definitive treaty, inasmuch as it relates to matters arising out of the war itself. As to when the delivery should begin, treaties vary more or less in their stipulations. In the absence of express provision, the delivery ought to commence,

General clause.

[1] In the Italian journal *Corriere della Sera*, January 23, 1897.

[2] As to the Italian prisoners of war in Abyssinia and the Pope's intercession in their behalf, see *supra*, pp. 139, 140.

conformably to fundamental principles, immediately after the conclusion—that is, normally, the signature—of peace, and should be carried out as expeditiously as the existing resources allow. But to avoid misunderstandings and recriminations, it is better to fix by agreement the dates and delays. Whilst practically all treaties indicate when the restoration should begin, the period within which it should be completed is less frequently prescribed. The latter point is, together with the numerous details involved, usually regulated by supplementary conventions or other special arrangements.

When restoration to begin.

Some treaties stipulate that the restoration is to begin immediately on or after their signature: e.g. the Treaty of Campo Formio, 1797, between France and Austria (Art. XXI); Treaty of Lunéville, 1801, between France, Austria, and Germany (Art. XV); Treaty of Paris, 1898, between the United States and Spain (Arts. V, VI); Treaty of Constantinople, 1913, between Turkey and Bulgaria (Art. V); Treaty of Athens, 1913, between Turkey and Greece (Art. VIII: "after the conclusion of the present treaty"). In others the date of ratification, either of the preliminaries or of the definitive treaty, is fixed; e.g. the Treaty of Aix-la-Chapelle, 1748, between England, France, and the Netherlands (Art. IV); Treaty of Amiens, 1802, (Art. II); Treaty of Pressburg, December 26, 1805, between France and Austria (Art. XIX); Treaty of Paris, 1806, between France and Russia—unratified by the latter (Art. XI); Treaty of Vienna, 1809, between France and Austria; Treaty of Paris, 1810, between France and Sweden (Art. IX); the Preliminaries of Versailles, 1871 (Art. VI); the Preliminaries of San Stefano, 1878 (Art. XXVIII); Treaty of Shimonoseki, 1895 (Art. IX); Treaty of Constantinople, 1897, between Greece and Turkey (Art. IV); Treaty of Portsmouth, 1905 (Art. XIII: "as soon as possible after the present treaty comes into force," i.e. on the exchange of ratifications as provided in another article); Treaty of Bucharest, 1913, between Bulgaria and the Balkan Allies (Art. IX: "as soon as possible after the exchange of ratifications"). Others, again, make use of such expressions as "immediately," or "as soon as possible": e.g. the Treaty of Paris, 1815 (Art X: "in the shortest time possible"); Treaty of Paris, 1856 (Art. VI: "immediately"); the Treaties of Zurich, 1859 (Art. II), Prague, 1866 (Art. III), Vienna, 1866 (Art. II) also say "immediately"; Treaty of Lausanne, 1912, between Italy and Turkey (Art. III: "with the least possible delay").

With regard to the period within which the complete delivery is to be effected, some treaties specify the length of time, adding "or sooner if possible," others remain silent, implying that the act is to be carried out with all convenient despatch, and in other cases, again, subsequent agreements settle the point. The period, when indicated, varies, naturally, according to the particular circumstances; e.g. Treaty of Aix-la-Chapelle, 1748—within six weeks; Treaty of Campo Formio, 1797—within forty days; Treaty of Lunéville, 1801—within forty days; Treaty of Amiens, 1802—within six weeks; Treaty of Pressburg, 1805—within fourteen days; Treaty of Vienna, 1809—within fourteen days; Treaty of Paris, 1810, between France and Sweden—within three months; Treaty of Constantinople, 1913—within one month.

Period of complete delivery.

The liberation of prisoners of war must be unconditional. The State that receives them is alone entitled to dispose of them, in conformity with its own laws. This principle has been observed with the utmost regularity. A notable exception occurred, however, in the case of the Franco-German War, when the German negotiators, having regard to the continued military occupation of certain French territory, insisted on making a departure from the customary practice. Thus Art. X of the Treaty of Frankfort stipulated that the French Government should send to their homes such of the prisoners as could be discharged; but those who had not completed their term of service were to be sent beyond the Loire. Furthermore, 20,000 prisoners were to be sent without delay to Lyons, and then, after organization, to be immediately despatched to Algiers for service there. Another condition was sometimes inserted in the earlier treaties between Russia and Turkey—e.g. the treaties of Kutchuk-Kainardgi, 1774, Jassy, 1792, Bucharest, 1812—to the effect that all prisoners of war were to be mutually restored, with the exception of those in Russia who had embraced the religion of the Greek Church, and those in Turkey who had adopted the Mohammedan faith.

Liberation to be unconditional.

Not infrequently there is a clause providing that the cost of the maintenance of the prisoners is to be repaid by each side, or the accounts are to be subsequently liquidated by a joint commission. We may recall here two articles of the Hague Regulations: Art. VII of the Fourth Convention of 1899 and 1907 says that the Government into whose hands prisoners of war have fallen is bound to maintain them; and Art. XVII: "Officers taken prisoners shall receive the same pay as officers of corresponding rank in the country where they are detained, the amount to be repaid by their Government"—unless a difference be made in the treaty of peace or otherwise.

Cost of maintenance.

Disputes have sometimes arisen in the course of the peace negotiations in regard to this question of expenses. Thus at the Conference of Amiens, January 1802, the French plenipotentiaries at first questioned the right of a State to demand to be reimbursed for such outlay. When an agreement on the point was reached, new difficulties arose. The number of the French prisoners maintained by England having been larger than that of the English prisoners in France, England claimed to be paid the difference in expense. On behalf of France, however, it was urged that such prisoners of Russian, Bavarian, or other nationality as had been in the pay of England should be added to the number of English prisoners, and the appointment of a commission to adjust the accounts was suggested. Lord Hawkesbury instructed the English representative, Lord Cornwallis, to demand a payment in favour of England, but Napoleon, as First Consul, opposed the claim, and agreed to the appointment of a commission, provided the prisoners of foreign nationality who had been in the English service were counted as English prisoners.[1] Eventually this plan was adopted, and laid down in Art. II of the treaty of peace signed March 27, 1802: "All the prisoners made on one side and the other, as well by land as by sea, and the hostages carried off, or delivered up during the war, and up to the present day, shall be restored without ransom in six weeks at the latest, to be reckoned from the day when the ratifications of the present treaty are exchanged, and on paying the debts which they shall have contracted during their captivity. Each of the contracting parties shall respectively discharge the advances which shall have been made by any of the contracting parties, for the support and maintenance of prisoners in the countries where they have been detained. There shall be appointed by mutual consent for this purpose a commission, especially empowered to ascertain and determine the compensation which may be due to any one of the contracting parties. The time and place shall likewise be fixed, by mutual consent, for the meeting of the commissioners, who shall be entrusted with the execution of this article, and who shall take into account, not only the expenses incurred on account of the prisoners of the respective nations, but likewise on account of the foreign troops who, before being taken, were in the pay and at the disposal of one of the contracting parties."

Similarly, by Art. III of the Treaty of Ghent, December 24, 1814, Great Britain and the United States engaged to discharge in specie the advances made by each other for the sustenance and maintenance of their respective prisoners of war. The Treaty of

[1] Cf. L. A. Thiers, *Consulat et Empire*; English trans. (1893), vol. ii. p. 216.

Constantinople, 1879, laid down (Art. VI) that special commissioners were to be appointed for the purpose of drawing up an account of the expenditure caused by the maintenance of Ottoman prisoners of war, and that from this sum should be deducted the cost of maintaining Russian prisoners in Turkey; the balance to be paid by the Sublime Porte in twenty-one equal instalments within the space of seven years. The Treaty of Portsmouth, 1905, required (Art. XIII) the contracting parties to deliver to each other, after the restoration of prisoners was complete, a statement of direct expenditure incurred for the care and maintenance of prisoners from the time of capture or surrender to the time of death or delivery; and Russia was to pay Japan the difference between the amounts shown—for it was implied that the number and cost of the Russian prisoners exceeded the number and cost of the Japanese prisoners. Art. IX of the Treaty of Bucharest, 1913, is put in almost the same terms as those of the latter treaty. The Treaty of Constantinople, 1913, made a departure from the usual methods by stipulating (Art. V) that the expenses for the keeping of prisoners and hostages were to be at the charge of the Government in whose hands they were, but that—conformably to Art. XVII of the Hague Regulations—the pay given to officers should be reimbursed by the State to which they belonged. Art. VIII of the Treaty of Athens, 1913, whilst adopting the same rule of the Hague Convention, introduced a further novelty, in that it required the claims of the parties, Greece and Turkey, to be submitted to arbitration at The Hague, under a "compromis" to be concluded.

Peace having been concluded, may prisoners be detained till the payment of debts incurred by them during their captivity?

May prisoners be detained for debt?

When treaties make specific provision, no problem arises—that is, so far as the particular parties thereto are concerned. Thus the Treaty of Utrecht, 1713 (Art. XXIII), said that prisoners of war should be liberated after paying the debts contracted during their captivity. Art. IX of the Treaty of Bâle, 1795, between France and Spain, Art. II of the Treaty of Amiens, 1802 (quoted above), and Art. III of the Treaty of Ghent, 1814, were to the same effect. Sometimes treaties made their release conditional on payment, or on giving satisfactory security for the payment of debts incurred: e.g. the Treaty of Aix-la-Chapelle, 1748; the Treaty of Paris, May 30, 1814 (Art. III of the additional articles).

When the treaty of peace is silent on the question of payment of debts, and no arrangement has been made before the departure of prisoners, there is a difference of opinion among publicists and jurists as to whether detention is justifiable. Perhaps the majority of writers incline to the affirmative; so, for example, Bluntschli,[1] Heffter,[2] and others. The contrary view is held by Pradier-Fodéré, who points out that if the practice of detention till payment be adopted the system of credit in regard to prisoners would be abused; being supported by the power to detain the debtors, it would make possible the imposition of exorbitant rates and oppressive methods of extortion. In any case, the contracting of private debts is a purely individual concern; it cannot legitimately be made an excuse for preventing the release of prisoners of war, which is a matter of public interest. Actions may be brought in the ordinary courts to recover those debts in the same manner as other debts are sought to be recovered. As the last-named writer says: "Il ne me semble pas admissible, en effet, que l'intérêt individuel de simples particuliers créanciers puisse tenir en échec la libération des prisonniers de guerre, qui est d'intérêt général. Cela me semble d'autant plus inadmissible que je n'y vois aucune nécessité qui s'impose, attendu que dans l'état actuel des législations nationales des différents peuples et du droit international conventionnel, l'accès des tribunaux est généralement ouvert à tout le monde et qu'il est de principe que les nationaux d'un État peuvent être traduits devant les tribunaux de leur pays pour des obligations par eux contractées en pays étranger, même avec un étranger."[3] The latter view is the better; it is more consonant with reason and public order. Peace concluded, prisoners of war are entitled *ipso facto* to be released; at all events, to continue their internment because of civil obligations—which would generally be of a petty character—is no less than a tyrannical or arbitrary exercise of authority. Juridical considerations and the interests of re-established peace and amity between the former belligerent States and their subjects demand that debts incurred by those who were perhaps compelled to incur them owing to inadequate maintenance should be recovered by the ordinary actions at law, or by diplomatic means. One or the other of these methods would undoubtedly suffice to procure the payment of valid debts.

May prisoners be detained for disciplinary offences?

Another question that arises is whether prisoners of war may be detained, after the date of peace, for disciplinary offences. Here, again, there is a difference of juristic opinion, as well as of practice in recent wars. Thus, in the case of the Franco-German War, the Germans placed restrictions on the release of prisoners for breaches

[1] *Droit international codifié*, § 716.

[2] *Droit international de l'Europe*, § 181.

[3] *Traité de droit international public* (Paris, 1885–1906), vol. vii. p. 269.

of discipline during their internment. They held that the definitive conclusion of peace, May 10, 1871, did not operate in favour of offenders against military law, and that their release could be effected only by pardon granted by the German Emperor. Many months passed before the latter condescended to set free a handful of obscure prisoners for acts of insubordination committed during their captivity. On February 29, 1872, sixty-two were pardoned by means of an imperial decree, and not till several months later were the rest liberated by another decree—on the condition, moreover, that most of them should complete their terms of imprisonment in their own country! On the other hand, France did not resort to methods of reciprocity in this respect; and no restriction was imposed on the repatriation of German prisoners. Japan, too, in 1905 released Russian prisoners of war who had infringed disciplinary regulations. There is no doubt that the practice adopted by France and Japan is the better; it conforms to reason and justice. Rules of military discipline as applied to foreign prisoners of war are made in the interests of general internment—to enforce order and regularity. Violations of these rules may, then, be repressed by the sanction of punishment; but when general internment comes to an end, at the conclusion of peace, the rules at the same time necessarily cease to be operative, so that the consequences of their previous application may not legitimately be allowed to remain. That is, whatever penalty has been suffered by offenders against such rules has already served its proper purpose, though the term inflicted is not yet complete. To compel an offender to complete the term after his fellow-prisoners have been released is to subject him to useless and gratuitous punishment. Whatever be the object of punishment—reformative, exemplary, or even vindictive—it can have significance only in relation to a given society. When the society of prisoners of war comes to an end the continued punishment of a few of its members is meaningless. We must agree, therefore, with Calvo, who holds that logic and justice demand the liberation along with the mass of prisoners those who had been condemned for merely disciplinary offences. "Les hostilités ayant cessé et les prisonniers devant être par conséquent réintégrés dans leur état d'avant la guerre, il nous semble juste et logique que les infractions disciplinaires soient réputées non avenues, quand même il y aurait déjà condamnation; car ces infractions sont en quelque sorte le résultat de l'état de captivité, et les conséquences doivent n'en plus subsister du moment que cesse cet état."[1]

The case is, however, different when offences against the

[1] *Droit international*, 4th ed. (1888), vol. v. p. 379.

common law have been committed. Prisoners of war are not only subject to military regulations or other special rules of discipline applicable to them *qua* prisoners of war; being within the local jurisdiction, they are also subject to the laws administered by the ordinary courts. Therefore if prisoners of war during their captivity commit crimes against the common law of the country, they are punishable like other foreigners and citizens; so that if their term has not expired at the conclusion of peace, they may justifiably be detained until it has expired.

Offences against the common law.

Further, a State may, in default of other provision, defer the repatriation of such prisoners as have been found guilty, in a fair trial, of gross violations of the law of war as clearly established by international conventions or usage.[1] They may be punished for such offences, but not for other acts which are made offences by the special military regulations of that State, inasmuch as these regulations can apply only to its own subjects. The immunity conferred by a general amnesty clause does not impliedly extend to offenders against the local common law, or against the law of nations.

Offences against the laws of war.

The various details incidental to the restoration of prisoners are frequently regulated by special conventions or other arrangements between the States concerned. One or two modern examples will suffice as suitable illustrations. The supplementary stipulations annexed to the Treaty of Prague, August 23, 1866, between Austria and Prussia, provided that from the third day after the ratification of the treaty the prisoners on both sides were to be delivered up at Austrian Oderberg railway station in echelons of about one thousand men each, at a rate not exceeding six echelons each day. Prussian prisoners interned in Bohemian fortresses and in Olmütz were to be sent to the nearest division of Prussian troops on being notified of the ratification. Commissioners from both armies were required to be stationed at Oderberg to attend to the delivery and arrange for the railway transport; in addition, a detachment of two hundred Austrian troops was to be at the same place for the reception and care of the prisoners. Prisoners not well enough to be removed were to remain in the hospitals and receive the same treatment as native troops until they could be delivered; and the expenses thus arising on both sides were to be defrayed by each in accordance with the regular rates.

Details as to restoration regulated by special conventions.

In the case of the Franco-German War, the Preliminaries of Versailles, February 26, 1871, provided that, in order to accelerate

[1] Cf. *infra*, p. 244.

the transport of French prisoners, the French Government should place at the disposal of the German authorities in the interior of the German territory a part of the rolling-stock of its railways, to be determined by special arrangements, at prices paid in France for military transport by the French Government. By the Convention of Ferrières, March 11, 1871, the French Government was to inform the German minister of war of the arrival of French transports at Bremerhafen and Hamburg, and three days afterwards 10,000 men at most were to be handed over at the first place and 14,000 at the second. France undertook to furnish the necessary rolling-stock, which was to serve also for the transportation of the German army. The prisoners entering French territory were required to go to Charleville, Lunéville, and Vesoul, where the French Government was permitted to establish a staff and make provisioning and clothing arrangements. The men liberated from military service and belonging to the neighbouring departments could be there dismissed; all others were to be sent beyond the limits of the territory occupied by the German troops. Not more than four trains a day, containing from 800 to 1,000 men each, were to be despatched by the German authorities to each of the above towns. In the same way military prisoners incarcerated in the prisons of Metz and in other fortresses were to be handed over either at Lunéville or at Charleville.[1]

Franco-German War.

The Treaty of Constantinople, terminating the Greco-Turkish War, was concluded December 4, 1897; and at the end of the month all the prisoners on both sides were restored to liberty. During this process they were treated with every consideration by the Greek and the Turkish authorities. The latter sent the Greek prisoners to Athens in charge of a military doctor and three Turkish officers; and before their departure they all received new clothes and a month's pay.[2]

Greco-Turkish War.

Under the Treaty of Portsmouth, September 5, 1905, Russia and Japan agreed (Art. XIII) to appoint a special commissioner on each side to take charge of prisoners. The prisoners of one party were to be received by the commissioner (or his representative) of the other in such convenient numbers and at such convenient ports of the delivering State as would be notified beforehand to the commissioner of the receiving State. The treaty having been ratified on September 14, the Japanese Government proposed, September 18 (through the medium of the United States), that Japanese prisoners should be

Russo-Japanese War.

[1] De Clercq, *Recueil*, vol. x. pp. 460, 461.

[2] Politis, *La guerre gréco-turque*, p. 160.

delivered at the western frontier of Russia, and Russian prisoners at the ports of Nagasaki, Kobe, and Yokohama. The Russian Government expressed its willingness, through the American State Department, to accelerate the restoration, and approved the proposed places of delivery. On October 6 the Japanese War Department drew up the following rules: A special commissioner —viz. the military attaché to the Japanese legation at Berlin— was to take charge of the proceedings. Japanese prisoners handed over by Russia were to be shipped at Hamburg and Bremen and taken to Kobe under the superintendence of the officer highest in rank among the prisoners. Non-military prisoners might remain in Europe at their own expense, with the approval of the commissioner after consultation with the minister or consul. The cost of the journey was to be advanced by the Russian authorities to a cashier appointed from among the Japanese prisoners; the sum to be refunded after their return to Japan. The Japanese military prisoners arriving at Kobe should be received by the War and the Navy Department respectively. As to the Russian prisoners in Japan, the Bureau of Information was to take charge and embark them at the ports mentioned. The sick and wounded not in a fit state to be transported were to be handed over to the Russian commissioner at the hospitals of the prison barracks or the military or naval hospitals after the general delivery. The dates and other details were to be arranged. On October 9 the Russian Government suggested Wirballen as the place for delivering Japanese prisoners; and Japan agreed.[1]

AMNESTY.

An amnesty clause is found in nearly all treaties of peace. Etymologically the word "amnesty" implies the notion of forgetting, i.e. forgetfulness of wrong done. In ancient Greece a treaty of peace or pacification putting an end to civil dissension generally included a proclamation of amnesty, ἀμνηστία. It came to be regarded as an essential incident of the declaration of international peace; and the earlier writers on the law of nations maintained that it was necessarily implied in the treaty, if it was not expressly embodied in it or otherwise proclaimed. Klüber, who published his work in 1819, described the amnesty clause as a declaration of the contracting parties to regard their enmity as entirely terminated and abolished, and a promise not to revive it as a pretext for beginning a new war. He adds that it relates only to that which brought the war about,

[1] S. Takahashi, *International Law applied to the Russo-Japanese War* (London, 1908), pp. 142 *seq.*

and does not include what was not the cause or object of it.[1] In some older treaties, e.g. the Treaty of Osnabrück, 1648, between the Empire and Sweden and the Protestant estates of the Empire, and the Treaty of Oliva, 1660 (Art. II), between Sweden, Poland, the Emperor Leopold, and the Elector of Brandenburg, the provision of amnesty stipulates not only that mutual wrongs should thereafter be consigned to oblivion, but also that the property of all persons who had been dispossessed of it during the war should be restored to them. In the peace treaties at the beginning of the nineteenth century the amnesty clause implies the notion of pardon, e.g. the Final Act of the Congress of Vienna, June 9, 1815, Arts. IX, XII, and XIII, in reference to the Poles, and Art. XXII, in reference to the Saxons.

Modern conception of amnesty.

Now amnesty signifies immunity, or exemption from prosecution or other interference, conferred on belligerents, the members of their armed forces, and their subjects in general, in respect of all wrongful acts committed by them from political motives. A clause stipulating such amnesty does not affect the right of each contracting party to punish its own subjects, military or civil, for committing violations of the law of war; moreover, if there is no stipulation to the contrary, each State may justifiably punish prisoners of war who have been found guilty of the same offences.[2] Where an amnesty provision is not inserted in the treaty, it is considered by both sides as being implied: thus it is omitted from the Treaty of Paris, November 20, 1815, between the Allies and France; the Treaty of Lima, June 12, 1883, between Spain and Chile;

An implied provision, if omitted from treaty.

the Treaty of Portsmouth, September 5, 1905, between Russia and Japan; the Treaty of London, May 30, 1913, between Turkey and the Balkan Allies; the Treaty of Bucharest, August 10, 1913, between Bulgaria and the Balkan Allies. Moreover, the amnesty condition, whether express or implied, is general in its application, unless it is specifically agreed to make it limited. Treaties stipulating a partial amnesty are not wanting, though there are comparatively

Partial amnesty.

few. For example, in the Peace of Prague, May 30, 1635, between the Elector of Saxony (ally of Sweden) and the Emperor, the latter granted only a limited amnesty to those who had risen against him, excluding the Elector Palatine. The Treaty of Nystadt, August 30, 1721, between Russia and Sweden, stipulated (Art. II) a reciprocal amnesty for all, with the exception of Russian Cossacks who had entered the service of the King of Sweden; the treaty records

[1] *Droit des gens moderne de l'Europe*, § 324. [2] Cf. *infra*, p. 246.

the latter's intercession on their behalf, and states that notwithstanding his entreaties they were not included.

Coming to more modern times, we find that under the Treaty of Frankfort, May 10, 1871 (third paragraph of Art. II), the benefit of amnesty was confined—and even then within narrow limits—to the inhabitants of the territory ceded by France to Germany: they were not to be prosecuted, annoyed, or sought for, either in their persons or their property, on account of their political or military acts previous to the war. The German plenipotentiaries suggested that if it was thought fit to make supplementary arrangements, they could be consigned to additional conventions—a suggestion which is inconsistent with the usual practice. At a meeting held on July 6, 1871, the French representatives proposed that an amnesty should be granted to all French subjects, military or civil, who had been condemned in the occupied departments or in Germany for any offence, except for one against the common law.[1] The German delegates agreed to accept the proposal if France granted immunity to all Frenchmen condemned or compromised for any act in aid of Germany. The reply made was that such an extension of amnesty was unusual, and that it involved an encroachment on French sovereignty. (The objection as to encroachment on sovereignty is, however, scarcely tenable at a peace conference, where such encroachments on sovereignty as the enforced cession of territory and the enforced payment of a war indemnity may well be made.) At a subsequent sitting the German delegates pointed out that compliance with the French demands would mean the annulment of judgments of German military courts, that the matter had better be left for later diplomatic negotiation, and to the discretion of the German Emperor in respect of his right to pardon. As a recent notable instance, we may mention the Peace of Vereeniging, May 31, 1902, embodying the terms of surrender of the Boers to Great Britain. It provided that burghers in the field outside the Transvaal and Orange River Colony, and all prisoners of war then outside South Africa who were burghers, would be brought back to their homes if they accepted the position of subjects of the British Crown (Art. II); that they would not be deprived of their personal liberty or their property (Art. III); and that no proceedings, civil or criminal, would be taken against them for acts connected with the prosecution of the war, but this immunity would not extend to certain acts contrary to the usage of war which were notified by the Commander-in-Chief to the Boer generals, and which were to be tried by a military

[1] De Clercq, *Recueil*, vol. x. p. 508; Villefort, *Recueil*, vol. i. p. 137, n. 1.

court under martial law immediately after the close of hostilities (Art. IV). It may be added that under this clause a Boer officer was tried by a military court at Heidelberg on June 19, 1902, for an abuse of the white flag, and was condemned to death.[1] In regard to the latter example it is necessary to bear in mind that the Peace of Vereeniging was not a peace treaty proper, which as a rule makes reciprocal concessions as to amnesty, but was an arrangement following the subjugation and annexation of the vanquished States. However this may be, it serves to illustrate the application of an amnesty provision made subject to certain limitations.

General amnesty.

Some examples of treaties containing general amnesty clauses may be referred to. Among those concluded before the nineteenth century are the Treaty of Oliva, 1660 (mentioned above), of which Art. II stipulated a general amnesty for all acts of hostility and for all persons; the treaties of Belgrade, 1739, between the Emperor Charles VI of Austria and Turkey (Art. VIII); Hamburg, 1762, between Prussia and Sweden (Art. II); Hubertsburg, 1763, between Austria and Prussia (Art. II).

More recent instances are as follows: The Treaty of Paris, 1856, whereby (Art. V) the sovereigns of Great Britain, France, Russia, Sardinia, and Turkey agreed to grant a full and entire amnesty to those of their subjects who were compromised by participating in any way whatever in the events of the war in favour of the enemy.

Art. XXI of the Treaty of Zurich, 1859, says that with a view to contribute by every effort to quiet the public mind, the parties (France and Austria) promised that in their respective territories no individual compromised by the events of the war, no matter what his rank or position, would be prosecuted, annoyed, or troubled, in person or property, on account of his conduct or political opinions.

The Treaty of Prague, 1866 (Art. X), and the Treaty of Vienna, 1866 (Art. XXIII), are to the same effect, the latter practically reproducing the terms of the Treaty of Zurich.

Under the Treaty of Constantinople, February 8, 1879, Russia and Turkey pledged themselves not to molest or to allow to be molested in any manner those of their subjects who had become compromised through their intercourse with the armies of either empire during the war (Art. VIII); Art. IX accorded a full and general amnesty to all Ottoman subjects who had become compromised in the provinces of European Turkey, and any persons detained on that account, or sent into exile, or removed from

[1] Cf. *Wyman's Army Debates*, Session 1902, vol. ii. p. 1051.

their country were to be immediately restored to liberty. The protocol of the same date stipulated that the provisions of Art. IX were not to hinder the local administration from taking such police measures, with regard to compromised persons, as might be necessary in the interests of public order and tranquillity.

In the Treaty of Shimonoseki, April 17, 1895, the amnesty provision is one-sided, and is mixed up with that relating to the restoration of prisoners of war (Art. IX). China promised to release at once Japanese subjects accused of military espionage or of any other military offence, and also not to punish such of her own subjects as had been compromised in their relations with the Japanese army during the war.

Italy and Turkey undertook, by Art. IV of the Treaty of Lausanne, October 18, 1912, to grant a full and complete amnesty, the one to the inhabitants of Tripoli and Cyrenaica, the other to those of the islands in the Ægean Sea under Ottoman suzerainty, who participated in the hostilities or compromised themselves by their acts or opinions, excepting offences against the common law. All persons detained or deported on such grounds were to be released immediately.

A similar disposition is found in the Treaty of Constantinople, September 29, 1913 (Art. VI), together with the proviso (which is not expressed with sufficient clearness) that the benefits of the amnesty would cease in respect of the territories ceded by Turkey to Bulgaria two weeks after the latter's reoccupation, due notice having been given to the populations.

Art. III of the Treaty of Athens, November 14, 1913, between Turkey and Greece, expresses the amnesty provision in the simplest and most general form: "The two high contracting parties accord full and complete amnesty to all persons involved in the political occurrences prior to the present treaty. Consequently no individual shall be prosecuted, disturbed, or molested in person, or property, or in the exercise of his rights, because of acts relating in any manner whatever to the war, and all judicial sentences and administrative measures based upon facts of that nature shall be *ipso facto* annulled."

In some of the above treaties the terms of the amnesty clause are so comprehensive as to cover all acts, including "war crimes."

Restrictions on amnesty.

In certain cases offences against the ordinary law of the land are expressly excluded; but express exclusion of such offences is not necessary, as it is always implied, if there be no provision to the contrary. Whether immunity is to be extended to breaches of war law depends on the agreement between the parties; in default of agreement each State may detain and punish captured delinquents belonging to the other State; or by a mutual understanding, all delinquents may be handed over to their own Government for trial and punishment. In case the amnesty clause is intended to condone all violations of the law of war, then not only should all persons who have been detained for them and not yet convicted be released, but also those who had already been tried and imprisoned should be liberated. It is held by some writers that convicted offenders serving a term of imprisonment need not be set free at the conclusion of the peace or at the time the amnesty provision comes into effect; for otherwise a belligerent might be disposed to inflict always the supreme penalty rather than a less severe one, in the interest of self-preservation. This view is incompatible with all considerations of justice, fairness, and even political and military prudence. If this view were adopted a detachment of men caught in the very act of perpetrating the foulest crime against war law would go free if their captors had no opportunity of trying them before the conclusion of peace; whilst men who had been condemned for slight delinquencies might have to remain in prison for years. Again, why assume that a belligerent would sentence to death all captured offenders for fear that their restoration would be effected at the end of the war? It is wrong, too, to assume that a belligerent State would necessarily regard their death as indispensable to its own preservation. Every belligerent State makes, and is bound to make, some discrimination in regard to the gravity of offences; it knows full well that if it abandons such discrimination and inflicts the death penalty for every alleged offence whatsoever, the enemy State would, in retaliation, adopt the same measures. Where the sense of proportion is suppressed, there anarchy and carnage will prevail.

Cannot extinguish debts.

The amnesty provision cannot, of course, extinguish debts incurred during the war, in the absence of an express stipulation thereon. Nor can it have reference to offences committed during the war by belligerent subjects on neutral territory, to those committed before the declaration of war, and to such as have no relation to the war. As Vattel observes: "On ne peut étendre l'effet de la transaction, on de l'amnistie, à des choses qui n'ont aucun rapport à la guerre terminée par le traité. Ainsi des répétitions fondées sur une dette ou sur une injure antérieure à la guerre, qui n'a eu aucune part aux raisons qui l'ont fait entreprendre, demeurent en leur entier, et ne sont point abolies par le traité; à moins qu'on ne l'ait expressément étendu à l'anéantissement de toute prétention quelconque. Il en est de même des dettes contractées pendant la guerre, mais pour des sujets qui n'y ont aucun rapport, ou des injures, faites aussi pendant sa durée, mais sans relation à l'état de guerre." [1]

Amnesty provisions superfluous and illogical.

In concluding this subject we must point out that in certain respects there is something supererogatory and illogical in the introduction of the amnesty provision. In one case we have seen it stipulated that the inhabitants of ceded territory were not to be prosecuted or disturbed, in their persons or property, for acts done before the war. In several cases States were required to accord an amnesty to those of their own subjects who had compromised themselves during the war. Two contracting parties may, of course, agree upon what dispositions they think fit, so long as they do not violate the rights of third States; they may barter away their own rights and privileges or yield them to superior force, within the entire range of their competence. But the question is, are all such proceedings compatible with public order and interest, are they really beneficial even to that party which exacts from the other the abandonment of certain rights incidental to its sovereignty? Take the case of conferring immunity on inhabitants of ceded territory for their military or political acts done before the war. If the ceded territory has already passed into the dominion of the cessionary State, the latter is not entitled to regard this transference of sovereignty as operating retrospectively, and therefore cannot prosecute individuals for violating an allegiance that was not then due to it. Further, it cannot then justifiably prosecute individuals for committing wrongful acts of war even during the war, not to mention at a time prior to the war; for the war having terminated by the conclusion of the definitive treaty of peace the military occupation of the territory in question terminates with it. An occupying army may, no doubt, introduce its martial law in the places occupied with a view to self-preservation, and may justifiably punish local inhabitants for infractions of such law or of the law of war. But the moment occupation is at an end this right ceases, for the ground on which it is exercised—viz. the interests of the occupying army—no longer exists. The occupying State being no longer such cannot take cognizance of acts committed against it when it was an occupying State; for the acts were directed against a certain authority which has entirely disappeared so far as the particular war and territory are concerned. Therefore those who had offended previously and had escaped apprehension are entitled to immunity

[1] *Droit des gens*, liv. iv. ch. ii. § 22.

at the hands of the new sovereign, without the necessity to stipulate it in a treaty.

Again, an undertaking on the part of a State to grant an amnesty to its own subjects who have compromised themselves in the war—e.g. by committing acts of treason—is a sinister and most undesirable arrangement. Some jurists have assailed this provision on the ground that it involves an encroachment on sovereignty. But such criticism is entirely irrelevant; for States are at liberty to enter into agreements derogating from their sovereignty—indeed, a good many international conventions, and nearly all peace treaties do affect the sovereignty of one party or the other. No, the objection is not really one based on theoretical jurisprudence, but rather on considerations of salutary public policy. The repression of crime is a vital interest to all countries, to mankind at large. It is contrary to all wisdom and common sense to agree to a stipulation whereby the greatest crime of all—treachery to one's country—is to remain unpunished. A general amnesty clause, exonerating all indiscriminately who have compromised themselves in the war, means a condonation of crimes aiming at the very foundation of political society, and cannot but offer an encouragement to craven spirits, to wretches who would betray their country for gold, and to perverted adventurers. After the stress and strain of war is over, and the longed-for peace is established, there may, no doubt, be a tendency to let bygones be bygones. None the less, it is to be hoped that no self-respecting State may ever again agree to such an amnesty clause as would accord impunity to its own subjects whose bygones consisted of the most heinous crimes committed against itself.

REVIVAL OR ANNULMENT OF TREATIES.

The last general clause that remains to be considered relates to the revival or annulment of treaties previously concluded by the belligerent parties. This subject is a particularly difficult one because of the diversity of juristic opinion as well as of international practice. In the majority of cases a war between two States is bound to have an effect on some or other of their future relationships, involving a change in or abrogation of treaties which formerly regulated those relationships. In order to determine what treaties—or what parts of such treaties as are of a comprehensive character and are practicably divisible—spontaneously revive at the conclusion of peace, it is necessary to ascertain first to what extent the outbreak of war annuls treaties or particular dispositions in treaties between the belligerent parties. Formerly, when the intercourse between States was less regular and less frequent, and the bonds knitting together the society of nations were less close than they are now, there was a general tendency to regard a war between two countries as putting an end to all the compacts and arrangements made with each other, and therefore to regard the establishment of peace as the point of departure for whatever subsequent relationships they might choose to set up. The commencement of hostilities meant *ipso facto* the abrogation of all treaties between them, save those perhaps that had been specifically entered into for the very event of war; so that either new treaties had to be concluded or the old treaties expressly revived. The absence of express provision did not mean revival. Nowadays both doctrine and practice are less drastic. War is by no means looked upon as being such a complete solvent. It is now well recognized that there are certain kinds of treaties which war cannot affect, that there are others which it will not affect unless there be an express stipulation to the contrary, and that there are some which are necessarily abrogated by the declaration of war. But there is not unanimity as to which treaties fall within these classes. In the circumstances the best course for us to adopt is first to refer briefly to the different views of writers, secondly to consider one or two judicial pronouncements, thirdly to examine the practice of States as evidenced in their peace treaties and diplomatic negotiations, and finally to set forth a summary statement of conclusions, based on fundamental principles, and deemed worthy of general acceptance.

Views of writers.

Some writers hold that war annuls all treaties, subject to certain exceptions; but they are not agreed as to what treaties are to be included among these exceptions. Others also maintain that the general rule is abrogation, but they insist on a greater number and variety of exceptions, e.g. treaties and stipulations entered into expressly with a view to a rupture of peace, or those establishing territorial arrangements, etc. Certain writers, e.g. Wheaton,[1] divide general compacts between nations into transitory (or dispositive or executed) conventions, and treaties properly so called, *fœdera* (or executory conventions). Examples of the first are treaties of cession, boundary, or exchange of territory, those creating international servitudes,[2] and the like, which are perpetual in their nature and their applicability, and cannot be rescinded by war; but if any should be suspended through hostilities, they revive on the conclusion of peace without any necessity to stipulate expressly such effect. Examples of the second

[1] *International Law*, 5th English edition. By C. Phillipson (London, 1916), pp. 368 *seq.*

[2] Vattel, liv. ii. ch. xii. § 192; Martens, *Précis*, liv. ii. ch. ii. § 58.

class are treaties of friendship and alliance, commerce and navigation, guarantee, extradition, etc., which expire in the event of war even if they are in their terms perpetual, save those that are made to meet the case of war, e.g. providing that private debts, shares or moneys in the public funds or in banks belonging to private individuals should never, in peace or war, be sequestered or confiscated. Both classes, however, are liable to be modified by new provisions laid down at the peace. Other writers, again, suggest that the general rule is not abrogation, but suspension, subject to varying exceptions as to which there is little unanimity. Thus Bluntschli [1] says that conventions suspended by war come into force again *pleno iure*, unless they are altered by the treaty of peace, or concern matters which the war itself has modified. Notwithstanding these variations of opinion, there are certain points of agreement; for instance, regarding the immunity of those conventions whose continuance is manifestly compatible with the prosecution of hostilities, and those concluded with the intention that they shall apply to a state of war; and, on the other hand, the revocation of all engagements whose fulfilment is obviously inconsistent with the exigencies of war.

Judicial pronouncements.

As to judicial pronouncements in the English courts, we may refer first to the case of the *Frau Ilsabe* (1801),[2] in which Sir W. Scott (afterwards Lord Stowell) observed: ". . . Though by treaties with the Dutch, made in favour of the Dutch, we have considered the Scheldt as shut up, and appropriated to the use of Holland, yet those treaties being extinguished by our present war with Holland, it is too much to say that it is at this time to be legally regarded as standing upon that footing, particularly for the purposes of a blockade, which is to act upon the interests of other States, who might be no parties to those treaties, even where they did exist."

In a leading American case (1823),[3] it was held that a war does not cancel private rights acquired or confirmed by a treaty; and that in general, treaties which establish permanent rights, or are by their terms intended to be perpetual, or are made purposely for the event of war are not annulled by the outbreak of hostilities, but are at most suspended, reviving on the conclusion of peace if no contrary agreement is then arrived at. The essential facts of the case are as follows. In 1761 a tract of land in New Hampshire was granted to the plaintiff missionary society, which was incorporated by royal charter in 1702. American independence having

[1] *Droit international codifié*, § 718.

[2] 4 C. Rob. 63.

[3] *The Society for the Propagation of the Gospel in Foreign Parts* v. *The Town of New Haven and Wheeler*, 8 Wheaton, 464.

been declared in 1776, Great Britain recognized it by the treaty of 1783, which stipulated also (Art. VI) complete immunity, in person and property, for those who had participated in the war. Another treaty made in 1794 protected (Art. IX) the title to lands in the United States held by British subjects, their heirs and assigns, exempting it from impugnment on the ground of alienage. In the same year the State of Vermont passed an act purporting to confiscate the Society's lands, of which some were assigned in 1800 to the defendant Wheeler. In 1812 war broke out between Great Britain and the United States, and was terminated by the Treaty of Ghent, 1814. Subsequently the Society brought an action of ejectment against the defendant. The case first came before the Vermont Circuit Court, but owing to a difference of opinion among its judges was removed to the Supreme Court of the United States. There it was held, contrary to the defendant's pleas, that the Revolution had not affected the capacity of British subjects or corporations to hold lands or other property in the United States; that the protection afforded by the treaties of 1783 and 1794 could not be annulled by the act of the Legislature of Vermont; that even if these treaties had been abrogated, as was alleged, by the war of 1812, and had not been expressly revived by the treaty of 1814, it did not follow that the rights of property already vested under those treaties would be thereby divested, any more than the repeal of a municipal law would affect rights of property that had already vested under its provisions.[1] But apart from this principle, on which the security of all property is based, the court declined to admit the doctrine that treaties become extinguished *ipso facto* by war between the contracting parties, unless they are expressly or impliedly revived on the return of peace. "Whatever may be the latitude of doctrine laid down by elementary writers on the law of nations, dealing in general terms in relation to this subject, we are satisfied that the doctrine contended for is not universally true. There may be treaties of such a nature, as to their object and import, as that war will put an end to them; but where treaties contemplate a permanent arrangement of territorial and other national rights, or which, in their terms, are meant to provide for the event of an intervening war, it would be against every principle of just interpretation to hold them extinguished by the event of war. . . . Treaties stipulating for permanent rights and general arrangements, and professing to aim at perpetuity and to deal with the case of war as well as of peace, do not cease on the occurrence of war, but are, at most, only suspended while it lasts; and unless they are waived by the parties or new and repugnant

[1] *Chirac* v. *Chirac* (1817), 2 Wheaton, 277.

stipulations are made, they revive in their operation at the return of peace." [1]

A similar judgment was delivered by the English Court of Chancery, in 1830, in regard to American citizens holding lands in Great Britain under the treaty of 1794. To the contention that the war of 1812 effected an abrogation of the said treaty, the Master of the Rolls replied that it was a reasonable construction that the treaty intended its operation to be permanent, and not to depend upon the continuance of a state of peace.[2]

Further, there are decisions of continental courts [3] to the effect that not all treaties are abrogated by war between the parties thereto, that some of them are only suspended during hostilities if it is found impossible to allow them to remain operative then—e.g. judgments of the Court of Turin (1810),[4] of the French Cour de Cassation (1811),[5] of the Courts of Colmar (1824), Nîmes (1839), Brussels (1841). In 1854 the Cour de Cassation decided, in a noteworthy case,[6] that only treaties of friendship and commerce were annulled by war; but in 1858 the Court of Aix held that treaties of hospitality and commerce were not extinguished by war, but only suspended on the principle—"cessante causa, tollitur effectus." And in 1885 the Court of St. Quentin [7] expressed the view that though war put an end to treaties of a political character, it only suspended conventions relating to private or judicial interests and not incompatible with the state of war.

Practice of States.

Next we come to the practice of States. This, being for our present purpose of greater importance than the views of jurists and the declarations of national courts of justice, must be considered more fully. We must not expect to find uniformity in international usage as revealed in treaties of peace and diplomatic negotiation, whose character depends on considerations of time and place, and especially on the demands of State policy and interest. In some cases States have claimed by proclamation or otherwise that the outbreak of war abolished all the treaties till then in existence between the belligerent parties. In other cases such a principle was by mutual agreement embodied in the peace treaty, and a renewal of all or certain conventions not contrary thereto was expressly stipulated. In other cases, again, the same principle was adopted, together with a provision for

[1] *The Society for the Propagation of the Gospel in Foreign Parts* v. *The Town of New Haven and Wheeler* (1823), 8 Wheaton, 464; at p. 494, *per* Washington, J.

[2] *Sutton* v. *Sutton* (1830), 1 Russell & Mylne, 663.

[3] Cf. R. Jacomet, *La guerre et les traités* (Paris, 1909), pp. 87 *seq.*, pp. 169 *seq.*

[4] *Affaire Bengero.*

[5] *Champeaux-Grammont* c. *Cardon.*

[6] *Featherstonhaugh* c. *Boffi.*

[7] *Bicci* c. *Hospices de Saint-Quentin.*

making subsequent arrangements relative to conventional relationships. In many cases, too, certain treaties (or certain dispositions of treaties) were revived expressly, or a stipulation was made for agreement thereon afterwards, without mentioning the said principle. However, the insertion of a clause merely renewing prior treaties does not necessarily mean that those treaties were extinguished by the war.

Examples of earlier treaties.

The Treaty of Paris, 1763, between England, France, and Spain, renewed and confirmed (Art. II) a great number of treaties ranging from the year 1648 to 1761: the treaties of Westphalia, 1648; Madrid, 1667, 1670; Nimeguen, 1678, 1679; Ryswick, 1697; Utrecht, 1713; Baden, 1714; the Triple Alliance concluded at The Hague, 1717; the Quadruple Alliance, London, 1718; Vienna, 1738; Aix-la-Chapelle, 1748; Madrid, 1750; treaties of 1668, 1715, 1761 (between Spain and Portugal), 1713 (between France and Portugal, guaranteed by Great Britain).[1]

Treaty of Hubertsburg, 1763, between Prussia and Austria, confirmed (Art. XII) all previous treaties, especially those of Breslau, Berlin, and Dresden, so far as their provisions were not contrary to those of the present treaty.

Treaty of Teschen, 1779, between Austria, Prussia, France, Russia, the Elector Palatine, and Saxony, confirmed (Art. XII) the treaties of Westphalia, Breslau, and Dresden.

Treaty of Versailles, 1783, between England and France, renewed (Art. II) all previous treaties from the Peace of Westphalia to the Treaty of Paris, 1763.

Treaty of Versailles, 1785, between the Emperor and the States-General provided for the renewal (Art. II) of the Treaty of Münster, 1648, so far as it was compatible with the present engagement.

Treaty of Berlin, 1792, between Austria and Prussia, renewed (Art. I) the former treaties between the parties.

Treaty of Constantinople, 1798, between Russia and Turkey, confirmed (Art. II) the Treaty of Jassy of 1791.

Treaty of Lunéville, 1801, between France and Austria, revived only certain articles of the Treaty of Campo Formio, 1797.

The Peace of Amiens, 1802, between Great Britain, France, Spain, Holland, contained no provision for the revival of treaties.

Peace of Amiens.

In the debates that took place both in the House of Lords and in the House of Commons relative to the peace, the current of opinion was to the effect that the outbreak of war abrogated prior treaties.[2] Lord Grenville com-

[1] G. F. de Martens, *Recueil des traités*, vol. i. pp. 106, 107.

[2] Cobbett, *Parliamentary History*, vol. xxxvi (1801–1803), pp. 164 *seq.*

plained that the peace did not stipulate for the renewal of all or most of the treaties that were in existence between the parties before the war.[1] Lord Thurlow, the ex-Lord Chancellor, emphasized that the commencement of war put an end to all subsisting treaties between the belligerent parties, and remarked that it did not follow as a matter of course that it was necessary to revive and renew former treaties in every treaty of peace, for it was a matter depending entirely on the will of the contracting parties.[2] The opinions of Lord Carnarvon, Lord Eldon (the Lord Chancellor), and Lord Hawkesbury were to the same effect.[3] Similarly, in the House of Commons Pitt, Windham, and others maintained that treaties were abrogated by war.

Treaty of Jonkoping, 1809, between Sweden and Denmark; Art. V confirmed the former treaties concluded between the two countries, save in so far as they were contrary to the provisions of the present treaty.

Treaty of Orebro, 1812, between Great Britain and Sweden, whereby (Art. II) the relations prior to January 1, 1791, were re-established, and all treaties and conventions before that date were renewed.

Anglo-American controversy.

The controversy following the Treaty of Ghent, 1814, between Great Britain and the United States, illustrates partly the difficulties that may arise through the omission to provide in a treaty of peace for the annulment or revival of certain classes of treaties, and partly the distinction drawn between treaties that are and treaties that are not susceptible of abrogation by a subsequent war between the parties thereto. By the treaty of 1783, between Great Britain and the United States, the former Power recognized the independence of the latter and granted its inhabitants the right to fish on certain coasts of the British dominions in North America. But after the war of 1812–1814 the British Government expressed its intention to prevent the American fishing-vessels from exercising their former rights, on the ground that they had become extinguished by the war, and had not been revived in the treaty of peace. Mr. J. Q. Adams, the American minister in London, pointed out that the treaty of 1783 was not one of those that were liable to be abrogated by war between the parties. To suppose that it was would be equivalent to saying that the United States—a sovereign and independent Power—forfeited her right of sovereignty and ndependence by the act of exercising it on a declaration of war against Great Britain (seeing that the latter recognized this right

[1] Cobbett, *Parliamentary History*, vol. xxxvi (1801–1803), pp. 587, 588.

[2] *Ibid.*, p. 596.

[3] *Ibid.*, pp. 714, 725, 761.

by treaty). But the treaty did not grant, but merely recognized, the right as being already in existence. The rights of fishery were of the same nature, and were not grants from the British Crown. They were not liable to be forfeited through a supervening war with Great Britain, and were affected neither by the declaration of her plenipotentiaries at Ghent, that she did not intend to renew them, nor by the omission to revive them in the treaty.[1]

Lord Bathurst replied that Great Britain had always held that the claimed right of fishery was derived only from Art. III of the treaty of 1783. The claim of one State to make use of another's territory, without a corresponding indulgence or other consideration, could rest only on a convention. Now the treaty of 1783, like many others, contained widely different provisions: some permanent and irrevocable, e.g. those relating to the acknowledgment of sovereignty, others temporary and revocable, e.g. grants of fishing privileges. It could not then be said that as the former were not affected by the war, therefore the latter were not affected by it. Though they appeared in the same instrument, there was no real connection between them. The independence of the United States was acknowledged, not established, by the treaty of 1783; the liberty to fish within certain limits was created by a certain article therein which was of the nature of ordinary treaties extinguishable by war. Great Britain knew of no exception to the rule that war puts an end to all treaties between the belligerent parties.[2]

Mr. Adams contended, however, that the whole scope and object of the treaty of 1783 were intended to establish a new and permanent state of relations between the two countries. And to say there were no exceptions to the rule that war abrogates all treaties was a novel assertion, unwarranted by the accepted authorities on the law of nations, unsanctioned by the usages of States, calculated to multiply the incitements to war, and to weaken the ties of peace between States. If there were no exception, what could be the purpose or meaning of the usually inserted articles in treaties of commerce providing expressly for the contingency of war, e.g. Art. X of the treaty of 1794, between the United States and Great Britain, forbidding in the event of war the sequestration or confiscation of debts due from individuals of the one nation to individuals of the other, or of their shares in the public funds and banks? Such a

[1] Mr. J. Q. Adams to Lord Bathurst, September 25, 1815: *American State Papers* (1834), vol. iv. p. 352; Wheaton, *International Law*, 5th Eng. ed. (1916), by C. Phillipson, pp. 370–372.

[2] Earl Bathurst to Mr. J. Q. Adams, October 30, 1815: *American State Papers*, vol. iv. p. 354; Wheaton (ed. Phillipson), pp. 372–374.

provision, then, must be excepted from the rule. Indeed, there were several exceptions to the rule: (1) engagements contracted on the understanding that they were to operate equally in war and peace, or exclusively during war, e.g. Art. X of the treaty of 1794; (2) those whereby the parties superadd the sanction of a formal compact to principles dictated by the eternal laws of morality and humanity, e.g. treaties or articles of treaties stipulating the abolition of the slave trade; (3) those that are of the nature of perpetual obligation, e.g. (as claimed by the American minister) the treaty of peace of 1783.[1]

Thus the American Government continued to insist that the articles of the said treaty constituted one homogeneous whole, whereas Great Britain claimed that they were different and separable, appertaining to entirely different objects; and this claim was scarcely disproved in the controversy. However, the difference was finally settled, on a basis of compromise, by the convention of 1818, which confined the right of fishery to certain geographical limits.[2]

The Treaty of Paris, November 20, 1815 (Art. XI), confirmed the Treaty of Paris, May 30, 1814, and the Final Act of the Congress of Vienna, June 9, 1815, excepting such of their provisions as were modified by the present treaty.

Treaty of Adrianople, 1829, between Russia and Turkey, confirmed in all their force all treaties and conventions concluded at different times between the two Powers, except any articles thereof modified by the present treaty.

In 1846, in the course of the international discussion that took place with regard to the "Spanish marriages" of Louis Philippe, Lord Palmerston, Guizot, and the Spanish minister, Xavier de Isturiz, admitted the validity of the provision contained in the Treaty of Utrecht, 1713, whereby the Duke of Orleans had renounced, for himself and his successors, his claims to the throne of Spain. Thus the articles of the Treaty of Utrecht regarding the relationships of France and Spain were deemed to hold good in 1846, notwithstanding the intervening wars between them in 1807 and 1823.[3]

The Treaty of Guadalupe Hidalgo, 1848, between the United States and Mexico, revived (Art. XVII) the treaty of commerce and navigation of April 5, 1831, with the exception of the additional article contained therein.

[1] Mr. J. Q. Adams to Lord Castlereagh, January 22, 1816: *American State Papers*, vol. iv. p. 356; Wheaton (ed. Phillipson), pp. 374–377.

[2] Cf. *British and Foreign State Papers*, vol. vi (1818–1819).

[3] Cf. Phillimore, *Commentaries*, vol. iii. § 537.

In 1854 arose the case of the Russo-Dutch loan. By a convention of May 19, 1815, between Great Britain, Holland, and Russia, Great Britain agreed (in consideration of being allowed to retain certain Dutch colonies and dependencies acquired during the war) to pay Holland half of a loan that had been advanced by Holland to Russia; the British payments were to cease if the Belgic provinces were severed from Holland, though they were not to be interrupted by the outbreak of war between the contracting parties. In 1831 the separation of Belgium from Holland legally released Great Britain from her engagement; but considering herself equitably bound thereby she entered into a new convention with Russia, November 10, 1831, agreeing to continue the payments. In 1854, when war broke out between Great Britain and Russia, a proposal was brought forward in Parliament that the obligation to make further payments should be renounced, on the ground that Russia had violated certain provisions of the Congress of Vienna. But this proposal was rejected for the reason that considerations of national honour forbade the repudiation of justly contracted debts due to the enemy. Accordingly the interest on the loan was paid throughout the Crimean War to the agents of the Russian Government.[1]

Russo-Dutch loan.

The Treaty of Paris, March 30, 1856, terminating the Crimean War, expressly stipulated (Art. XXXII) that until the treaties or conventions which existed before the war between the belligerent parties were renewed or replaced by new agreements, commercial intercourse should be carried on reciprocally on the basis of the regulations in force before the war; and in all other matters their subjects should be treated on the footing of the most-favoured nation. It is to be noted that this provision is not concerned with a general revival of treaties. In the conference held at Vienna in the preceding year, between the plenipotentiaries of Austria and the belligerent Powers, the French plenipotentiary (Baron de Bourqueney) maintained that the abrogation by war of all previous treaties was an incontestable principle of international law.[2] At the time the conference was discussing the question of commercial conventions; so that the contention was undoubtedly not intended to apply also to all non-commercial treaties. Again, a few days before the definitive treaty was signed (March 25, 1856), Count Walewski, on behalf of France, observed at the Paris Conference that as the state of war had extinguished the treaties that had existed between Russia and the

Treaty of Paris, 1856.

[1] *Parliamentary Debates*, 3rd series, vol. cxxxv. p. 1096; Cobbett, *Cases*, vol. ii. pp. 38–40.

[2] G. F. de Martens, *Nouveau Recueil général de traités*, vol. xv. p. 633.

Allies, it was desirable to insert in the treaty a provisional stipulation regarding the commercial relations of the parties.

Under the Treaty of Vienna, October 30, 1864 (Art. II), between Austria and Prussia on the one side, and Denmark on the other, all the treaties concluded before the war, that were not annulled or modified by the present treaty of peace, were re-established.

Treaty of Vienna, 1864.

The provisions on the subject embodied in the Treaty of Prague, August 23, 1866, between Austria and Prussia, are more explicit. Art. XIII brought again into force all the treaties and conventions previously concluded between the parties, in so far as they had not lost their effect by the dissolution of the relations of the Germanic Confederation. In particular, the General Cartel Convention, February 10, 1831, between the German Federal States, was renewed as between the present parties. The Monetary Treaty, January 24, 1857, having lost its value for Austria through the dissolution of the German Federal relations, Prussia agreed to enter into negotiations with Austria and the other signatories thereto with a view to its annulment. Finally, the contracting parties undertook to revise, by a subsequent agreement, their commercial and customs treaty, April 11, 1865; meanwhile it was to come into force, subject to its renunciation by either after six months' notice.

Treaty of Prague.

The Treaty of Frankfort, May 10, 1871 (Art. XI), said that as the treaties of commerce between France and the various States of Germany were annulled by the war, the two Governments agreed to adopt as the basis of their commercial relations the most-favoured-nation treatment, relative to import and export duties, transit dues, customs formalities, etc., but excluding certain specified favours. However, the treaties of navigation (subject to certain reservations on the part of France), and conventions as to the international service of railways and the protection of literary works, were renewed. Further, by the additional convention of December 11, 1871 (Art. XVIII), the contracting parties agreed to renew the other treaties between them, excepting that as to the canal of the Sarre, as well as postal relations, with the reservation of the declarations of adhesion to be supplied by them on the exchange of ratifications of the present convention. Finally, three treaties between France and German States were to be provisionally extended to Alsace-Lorraine, and were to serve as a basis for the relations between France and the ceded territories, viz. the convention with Baden, 1846, as to the execution of sentences; the extradition treaty, 1845, with Prussia; and the copyright convention, 1865, with Bavaria.

Treaty of Frankfort.

Art. X of the Treaty of Constantinople, February 8, 1879, between Russia and Turkey, provided as follows: "All treaties, conventions, and engagements concluded between the two high contracting parties relating to commerce, jurisdiction, and the position of Russian subjects in Turkey, which had been suppressed in consequence of the state of war, shall be put in force again, and the two Governments will again be placed, with regard to all their commercial and other engagements and undertakings, in the same position, in relation to one another, as they stood before the declaration of war, with the exception of such articles as may have been altered by the present treaty, or in virtue of the Treaty of Berlin."

Treaty of Constantinople, 1879.

In the Treaty of Lima, June 12, 1883, between Spain and Chile, the parties declared that until new treaties were concluded between them, their relations as existing before the war were revived.

Treaty of Lima.

The Treaty of Shimonoseki, April 17, 1895, between China and Japan, stated (Art. VI) that all the treaties between them having been annulled by the war, a new treaty of commerce and navigation and a convention regulating frontier intercourse and trade were to be concluded immediately after the exchange of ratifications, on the basis of similar treaties between China and the European Powers. Till then China agreed to accord Japan most-favoured-nation treatment. No mention was made of other kinds of treaties.

Treaty of Shimonoseki.

In the case of the Greco-Turkish War, 1897, Turkey claimed in the preliminary peace negotiations[1] that the capitulations relative to Greek subjects in the Ottoman dominions were extinguished by the war. But the Great Powers having intervened in the conflict opposed the claim, on the ground that the privileges and immunities enjoyed by Greek subjects had been granted to them in virtue of arrangements concluded between themselves (the Powers) and Turkey, so that the outbreak of hostilities between Greece and Turkey could have no prejudicial effect thereon.

On the commencement of hostilities between the United States and Spain the Spanish Government issued a decree, April 23, 1898, declaring, *inter alia*, that the war put an end to the treaty of 1795, the protocol of 1877, and all other agreements, compacts, and conventions till then in force between the two countries. This was as drastic and far-reaching a pronouncement as could well be. But there is no doubt that it went beyond legitimate limits. Art. XIII of the treaty of 1795 stipulated that in case of war between the two

Spanish-American War.

[1] Cf. the Turkish Memorandum of May 14, 1897.

parties, the merchants inhabiting towns should be allowed the space of a year after its outbreak for collecting and removing their goods and merchandise. A rumour having got abroad that Spain intended to expel American subjects found within her territories, the United States Government requested the British ambassador at Madrid to draw the attention of the Spanish Government to the said Art. XIII. The latter replied that no exception could be made to the decree already issued, but offered to conclude a special agreement for carrying out the article during the war. The offer was rejected, on the ground that as the stipulation in question was made expressly for the event of war it could not be annulled by it. Mr. Moore, Acting Secretary of State, aptly observed in reference to the Spanish claim: "If it were true that war abrogates such stipulations, they would be subject to the singular fate of ceasing to be in force whenever they should become applicable."[1] However, no decree of expulsion was issued.

Another question arose, after the conclusion of peace, as to the continuance of treaties relating to debts. The Treaty of Paris, December 10, 1898, contained no provision for the revival or abrogation of treaties. During the war between Spain and her colonies American vessels and cargoes were wrongfully seized and confiscated by the Spanish authorities. The United States Government on behalf of the owners demanded reparation; and Spain agreed, by the Convention of Madrid, 1834, to pay an indemnity in the form of annuities—an obligation that was made perpetual by the terms of the agreement. But after the outbreak of the war of 1898 payment was not made. In July 1899 the United States reminding Spain of the overdue interest, the latter replied that as the debt arose out of a treaty which was suspended by the war, the matter could be settled only by an agreement between the two States regarding the renewal of the previous conventions between them; but that "the Government of His Majesty, wishing to give a proof of its constant good faith," had already taken steps to ensure the payment of the interest, without prejudice to the agreement that was to be concluded. The Department of State replied that the treaty of 1834 being perpetual in its nature, there was no connection between it and treaties relating to commerce, navigation, extradition, etc.; so that the subsequent negotiation of the latter treaties could not affect the continuing obligation of the former. In November 1899, however, the Spanish Government decided to pay at once all the suspended annuities. And on July 3, 1902, the two States concluded the Treaty of Madrid, of which Art. XXIX

[1] *Foreign Relations of the United States*, 1898, p. 972; Moore, *Digest*, vol. v. p. 376.

expressly annulled all the treaties, engagements, conventions, and contracts existing between them prior to the war, except the treaty of 1834.[1] The abrogation of treaties existing before the war, by a convention concluded some three and a half years after the signing of the treaty of peace, was an exceptional departure, but was in this case due to the fact that the relative positions of the two countries had become radically transformed since the war.

Anglo-French agreement, 1904.

By the Anglo-French agreement (respecting Newfoundland and West and Central Africa), signed in London, April 8, 1904, France renounced, under Art. I, the privileges established to her advantage by Art. XIII of the Treaty of Utrecht, 1713, and confirmed or modified by subsequent provisions. The said privileges consisted of the liberty to catch fish and to land for the purpose of drying and curing them along the coasts of Newfoundland stretching from C. Bonavista to the north of the island, thence running down by the western side, and reaching as far as Point Riche. This concession was confirmed by Art. V of the Treaty of Paris, 1763, and renewed, with certain modifications, by Art. VI of the Treaty of Versailles, 1783. But it was not renewed by the Peace of Amiens, 1802, or by subsequent treaties between the parties. Despite the supervening Napoleonic wars, it was thought necessary to abrogate by an express provision a stipulation of a treaty concluded two centuries ago.

Treaty of Portsmouth, 1905.

The negotiations between Russia and Japan in connection with the Treaty of Portsmouth, 1905, furnish an excellent recent illustration of the different views entertained by States respecting the effect of war on treaties. The Japanese plenipotentiaries suggested that as the war had annulled the treaties of commerce between Japan and Russia, an article should be inserted in the treaty of peace stipulating on both sides the most-favoured-nation treatment, until other commercial arrangements were made. M. Witte, the first Russian delegate, thought that as soon as the war was terminated the previously existing treaties and conventions were *ipso facto* revived; but he added that he would like to take the opinion of M. de Martens on the question. The latter explained that it was usual to embody an article expressly stipulating that the treaties concluded prior to the war remained in force. In reply, Baron Komura pointed out that the very practice of inserting such an article seemed to prove that the mere fact of concluding peace did not necessarily revive treaties. If the insertion of one were indispensable, then it proved, on the contrary, that the outbreak of war effected the abrogation,

[1] Moore, *Digest*, vol. v. pp. 377–380. Cf. *British and Foreign State Papers*, vol. xcv. p. 816.

and not the suspension, of treaties. He thought that in the present case there were two courses open—either to revive by a special article the treaty of commerce that was in force before the war, or to enter into a new treaty; and believing the latter alternative to be more advantageous for the commercial relations between the two countries, he proposed the adoption of the most-favoured-nation clause in the meantime.[1] Thus the principle of abrogation was assumed as regards the treaty of commerce; though nothing was said as to other kinds of treaties. The Japanese proposal was accordingly followed in Art. XII of the Treaty of Portsmouth.

Treaty of Lausanne, 1912.

The Treaty of Lausanne, 1912, between Italy and Turkey, stipulated (Art. V) the immediate renewal of all the treaties, conventions, and engagements of every kind that were in force between the contracting parties prior to the war. But Italy agreed (Art. VI) to conclude with Turkey, when the latter would renew her treaties of commerce with the other Powers, a treaty of commerce on the basis of European public law, i.e. leaving her full economic independence and the right to renounce the capitulations and other such acts.

Treaty of Constantinople, 1913.

By the Treaty of Constantinople, September 29, 1913 (Art. IV), Turkey and Bulgaria renewed for the period of one year, dating from the signature, the convention of commerce and navigation of February 19, 1911, and the consular declaration of December 2, 1909, and pledged themselves to nominate as soon as possible a mixed commission for the purpose of negotiating a new treaty of commerce and a consular convention. Further (Art. XIX), such provisions of the Treaty of London, May 30, 1913, as concerned the two contracting Powers were renewed, in so far as they were not abrogated or modified by the present treaty.

Treaty of Athens, 1913.

The Treaty of Athens, November 14, 1913, between Turkey and Greece, restored in full force (Art. II) all the treaties, conventions, and acts that bound the two countries at the time of the rupture of diplomatic relations, and also confirmed (Art. XV) the Treaty of London so far as the present parties were concerned.

Divergent international practice.

On the basis of examples drawn from divergent international practice and diplomatic negotiations, it is impossible to establish a comprehensive body of universally applicable rules respecting the effect of war on treaties. The demands of the particular circumstances of each case, together with the express agreement of the parties concerned,

[1] *Protocols of the Portsmouth Conference*, p. 71.

will constitute the predominating factors, to which most rules—so far as they do not affect third States—must be subordinated. But there are undoubtedly some rules which neither circumstance nor intention can affect, because they spring from fundamental principles that cannot be disregarded without throwing the society of States into chaos.

But certain rules applicable.

From time to time attempts have been made by writers to formulate a number of rules on the subject, and for this purpose they have adopted different points of departure, e.g. some have started with the general rule that war abrogates treaties and then have proceeded to enumerate certain exceptions as forming special rules in themselves, whilst others have started with the general rule that war respects treaties, and have added supplementary rules by way of exceptions thereto.[1] Both these methods have serious disadvantages. A third scheme is therefore submitted here as being practically the most convenient.

A preliminary observation is necessary. It may happen that a treaty deals with a number of entirely different subjects, and that its articles are consequently separable. If the provisions relative to one of these subjects are abrogated by war, it does not follow that all the others are also abrogated; for a complex treaty of this kind is in reality nothing more than a number of different engagements entered into at the same time and consigned to one instrument. It would be an outrage on common sense to hold that because this or that particular clause in a treaty is alone incapable of performance owing to the existence of hostilities, therefore the whole treaty, containing several other kinds of stipulations, must necessarily be considered abrogated or suspended—for some of the clauses may have been made expressly for the event of war, and others may be of the nature of perpetual dispositions, and so on. The treaty of 1783, between Great Britain and the United States (which has already been considered),[2] is an example: some of its articles embodied a recognition of title to sovereignty and independence, and so were permanent and incapable of annulment; others merely granted concessions and were voidable in the event of war. Accordingly, what is said in the following analysis of treaties *may* apply also to separate stipulations in treaties. To

[1] An example of the latter method is the *Projet d'un règlement concernant les effets de la guerre sur les obligations internationales*, in *Annuaire de l'Institut de droit international*, vol. xxiv (1911), pp. 200–223; drawn up by N. S. Politis. The project was submitted to the criticism of members of the Institute, who failed to agree. Vol. xxiii (1910), pp. 251 *seq.*, contains a preliminary report presented to the Institute.

[2] See *supra*, pp. 256 *seq.*

determine whether it *does* apply in a given case, the particular circumstances of the case must be considered.

I. TREATIES NOT AFFECTED BY WAR BETWEEN THE PARTIES.

(*a*) *Treaties in which belligerents only are parties.*

General conclusions submitted.

(1) Those entered into expressly for the event of war.

E.g. Art. X of the treaty of 1794 between Great Britain and the United States, forbidding the sequestration or confiscation of debts and certain funds in the case of war between the two countries.

Treaties neutralizing certain parts of the belligerents' territories.

(2) Those which, though not entered into expressly in contemplation of war, are specially protected from its consequences.

E.g. The treaty between Great Britain and Russia, 1815, guaranteeing the payment of interest on the Russo-Dutch loan, even in case of war between the parties.

(3) Dispositive or transitory treaties, establishing a permanent condition of territorial rights.

E.g. Treaties of cession, delimitation of boundaries, creation of servitudes, etc.

(4) Treaties recognizing other permanent conditions, such as titles to sovereignty and independence, the rights of certain dynasties.

(As the above treaties concern the belligerent parties only, the latter are naturally at liberty to make in their peace negotiations whatever changes they may think fit. The essential point is that the outbreak and existence of the war cannot alone affect those treaties.)

(*b*) *Treaties in which other Powers besides the belligerents are parties.*

(1) Law-making treaties, especially those relating to war (subject in some cases to provisos as to ratification).

E.g. The Hague Conventions, 1899, 1907.

The Declaration of Paris, 1856.

The Declaration of St. Petersburg, 1868.

(2) Treaties effecting international settlements, etc.

E.g. Those relating to the neutralization of States, the navigation of international rivers, the territorial limits and autonomy of certain countries, the neutralization of canals, the division of territories or spheres of influence in uncivilized regions, etc.

(3) Treaties establishing international unions.

E.g. Those relating to postal and telegraphic communication, railway traffic, the protection of industrial property (patents, trade-marks, etc.), artistic and literary property, matters of private international law, etc.

(Subject to suspension as between the belligerent parties only.)

(4) Treaties of guarantee, when all the belligerents are parties thereto.

II. Treaties suspended during the War.

(1) Those provisions of international settlements—as between the belligerents—whose performance is incompatible with the war.

(2) Financial engagements, such as conventions regulating the repayment of loans, public or private; unless the repayment was stipulated to be unconditional, in which case the convention could not be suspended.

(3) Treaties establishing certain permanent relations between the parties, e.g. as to the acquisition of nationality, rights conceded to the subjects of the one when within the jurisdiction of the other, the power to hold property, to carry on trade, etc.

(Treaties under (2) and (3) are not necessarily suspended by the war, but may be suspended at the option of either of the belligerents.)

III. Treaties suspended during the War, or annulled on the Declaration of War, at the Option of either of the Belligerents.

Non-political treaties which do not establish permanent relations, and which are necessarily dependent on the existence of peace and amity, such as treaties of commerce, navigation, customs, etc.

IV. Treaties annulled ipso facto on the Outbreak of War.

(1) Political treaties, setting up alliances, providing for the furnishing of subsidies or other aid.

(2) Conventions, the interpretation or application of which is in dispute and has given rise to the war.

In conclusion, we may say that the vital determining principle is that, subject to the agreement of the parties in their peace treaty, only treaties that are inconsistent with the interests of the war are annulled or suspended, with the exception of such treaties as have contributed to establish the law of nations or the permanent settlement of the society of States.

CHAPTER X

THE TREATY OF PEACE

ITS MAIN CLAUSES AND EFFECTS (*Continued*)

(ii) *Special Clauses : Indemnity—Cession of Territory*

War indemnity : when none imposed, or equivalent demanded ; increasing practice in modern times ; examples of imposition of indemnities ; examples in which no indemnity stipulated—Cession of territory : how cession may be effected ; title to cede territory ; *de facto* and *de jure* sovereignty ; sometimes compensation offered ; delimitation commission ; act of delivery ; cession and plebiscite, instances of plebiscites ; examples of cessions.

ONE of the chief special clauses of a peace treaty is that relating to the payment of a war indemnity. Nearly all jurists, both the earlier and the modern, agree that a victorious State is justified in demanding a pecuniary indemnity as a means of making good the losses incurred during the war. But the mode of calculating the amount presents the greatest difficulty, for not all the losses incurred and damage inflicted can be made good. It may be possible to arrive at a fair numerical estimation of the extent of the material losses, e.g. territory devastated, property destroyed, cost of mobilization and maintenance of the armed forces ; it may be possible even to calculate the amount necessary wherewith to grant pensions or aid to the wounded, and to the widows and orphans of those who have fallen. But it is not possible to estimate in figures the sufferings, physical, moral, and mental, of combatants and non-combatants alike ; and also the indirect damage inflicted on the general fortune of the State, on its social, industrial, and commercial organization. It is thought, therefore, that as war is an established method of settling international conflicts, the victorious party is entitled to be reimbursed for the direct losses and expenses caused by the war—which the victor assumes to have been undertaken by him for the sake of seeking just redress ; but that the exaction of damages for indirect, incalculable losses

WAR INDEMNITY.

is not justified, inasmuch as it would entail an arbitrary calculation and might well become a means of enriching the victor and impoverishing the vanquished. As MM. Funck-Brentano and Sorel remark: "En dehors de ces réparations très-strictement déterminées, l'indemnité de guerre est toujours le résultat d'une évaluation arbitraire, et a toujours plus ou moins pour objet d'enrichir le vainqueur et d'appauvrir le vaincu."[1] In the proper sense of the term, then, indemnity is neither a ransom nor a penalty for an offence; it is a pecuniary reparation for actual and specific damages and extraordinary expenses brought about by the prosecution of hostilities.

When no indemnity imposed.

It may happen that in this or that war no indemnity is imposed. This results probably from reasons of prudence or moderation that weigh with the victorious party, or from the fact that the strength of neither belligerent preponderated sufficiently to enable him to back up a demand; or, again, because the vanquished Power was in such financial difficulties that to demand from it the payment of an indemnity would be for all practical purposes futile. In the latter case the victorious State sometimes calls for a substitute in the form of territorial cessions. Thus by the Preliminaries of San Stefano, March 3, 1878 (Art. XIX), Russia demanded from Turkey the sum of 1,410,000,000 roubles—consisting of 900,000,000 roubles for war expenses (maintenance of the army, replacing of war material, and war contracts), 400,000,000 roubles for damage done to the south coast of Russia, to her export trade, industries, and railways, 100,000,000 roubles for injuries inflicted on the Caucasus by the invasion, and 10,000,000 roubles for costs and damages of Russian establishments and subjects in Turkey. The article goes on to say: "Taking into consideration the financial embarrassments of Turkey, and in accordance with the wishes of His Majesty the Sultan, the Emperor of Russia consents to substitute for the payment of the greater part of the moneys enumerated in the above paragraph the following territorial cessions," viz. the Sandjak of Toultcha in Europe, together with certain islands (subject to exchange for the part of Bessarabia detached from Russia by the Treaty of Paris, 1856), and Ardahan, Kars, Batoum, Bayazet, etc., in Asia. These territories were considered as an equivalent for 1,100,000,000 roubles. The terms of the Preliminaries of San Stefano, however, were modified by the Berlin Congress, 1878; and the modifications were adopted by the definitive Treaty of Constantinople, February 8, 1879, between Russia and Turkey.

Equivalent demanded.

[1] *Précis du droit des gens* (Paris, 1877), pp. 323–324.

Art. IV thereof states that after deducting the value of the territories ceded to Russia, conformably to the Treaty of Berlin, the war indemnity remained assessed at the sum of 802,500,000 francs, the mode of paying which was to be settled by a subsequent agreement;[1] and under Art. V, the claims of Russian subjects and establishments in Turkey were not to exceed the sum of 26,750,000 francs.

In earlier times valuable objects, etc., substituted for indemnity.

Further, in several cases—notably in the first Italian campaign of Napoleon[2]—we find the pecuniary indemnity replaced or supplemented by valuable objects, provisions, and other things. Thus, under the armistice of Piacenza, May 8, 1796, the Duke of Parma not only had to pay the sum of 2,000,000 livres, but also was obliged to deliver 700 horses to the French army, 20 pictures chosen by the Commander-in-Chief, and a certain quantity of provisions and fodder. By the Armistice of Bologna, June 23, 1796, the Pope was required to pay the French Republic 15,000,000 livres in cash, 5,500,000 livres in goods, provisions, etc., and also to hand over 100 pictures, busts, vases, or statues, and 500 MSS., to be chosen by commissioners expressly sent to Rome. The King of the Two Sicilies engaged, by an additional secret article to the Treaty of Paris, October 10, 1796, to supply France with 8 millions' worth of provisions. The Peace of Tolentino, February 19, 1797, required the Pope to pay 15,000,000 livres in cash, diamonds, or other valuables. By the Convention of Milan, March 16, 1797, Venice had to pay the paymaster of the Italian army 3,000,000 livres in cash, and to deliver 3 millions' worth of hemp, ropes, tackle, etc., 3 ships of the line, 2 frigates, 20 pictures, and 500 MSS. Similarly, by the Armistice of Baden, July 17, 1796, the Duke of Würtemberg was obliged to pay 4,000,000 livres in cash and also to furnish provisions; and by that of Stuttgart, July 25, 1796, the Margrave of Baden had to pay 2,000,000 livres and to deliver 1,000 horses, 500 oxen, 2,500 quintals of corn, 12,000 sacks of oats, and 25,000 pairs of shoes. Provisions and other articles were demanded also in the armistice conventions of Stuttgart, July 27, 1796; Würzburg, August 7, 1796; Pfaffenhofen, September 7, 1796. And by the Treaty of Madrid, September 29, 1801, an indemnity of 15,000,000 livres

[1] See *infra*, p. 276.

[2] Calvo, *Droit international*, vol. iv. pp. 267 *seq.*; and the references there given to Martens, *Recueil des principaux traités*, 2nd ed. vol. vi, and G. de Garden, *Histoire générale des traités de paix*, 15 vols. (Paris, 1848–1887), vol. v.

was imposed on Portugal, payable partly in cash and commercial securities, partly in precious stones and Brazil-wood.

Increasing practice in modern times.

Before the French Revolutionary wars there were comparatively few examples of the imposition of war indemnity; the practice became much more frequent during these wars, and increased afterwards, until it reached its culminating point in the Franco-German War, 1871. It has been estimated that from 1795 to 1871, by a very moderate calculation, the sum of 7,235,000,000 francs was exacted by belligerent States in the form of war indemnities. Of this less than one-eighth part (viz. 875,000,000 francs) represents those imposed by France, notwithstanding the numerous victories gained by the French arms during that period; 1,135,000,000 francs by the various Powers; and the overwhelming sum of 5,525,000,000 francs imposed by Prussia in her wars only of 1866 and 1870-1871[1]—that is, about three-quarters of the entire total. Calvo, writing in 1888, and having in his mind the case of the Franco-Prussian War, asks where this unceasing progression is to stop; there is a world of difference, he says, between demanding the reimbursement of expenses and imposing disproportionate and ruinous exactions, calculated to prolong the evils of the war after the cessation of hostilities; he thinks, therefore, that the question of indemnity might well be settled, on the basis of a liquidation of accounts, by an impartial court of arbitration: "Devant de telles énormités, il y a lieu de se demander où s'arrêtera cette progression sans cesse croissante. On conçoit jusqu'à un certain point qu'un ennemi victorieux prétende se faire indemniser par son adversaire vaincu des dépenses dans lesquelles l'a entraîné la guerre, surtout quand il n'a pas été le provocateur; mais il y a loin de là à émettre des exigences hors de toute proportion avec les calculs les plus rationnels, exigences plutôt propres à ruiner le pays auquel elles s'adressent et à prolonger les maux de la guerre après la cessation effective des hostilités. N'y a-t-il pas place ici pour une intervention modératrice et conciliatrice? Pourquoi cette liquidation de comptes ne serait-elle pas soumise à un arbitrage désintéressé, équitable, impartial?"[2]

Examples of imposition of indemnities.

A few examples of the imposition of indemnities, in addition to those already given, may now be referred to.

Treaty of Münster, 1648—the sum of 5,000,000 crowns was paid to Sweden.

[1] J. Guelle, *Précis des lois de la guerre*, 2 vols. (Paris, 1884), vol. ii. pp. 359-361.

[2] *Droit international*, vol. iv (1888), p. 275.

In the Napoleonic wars: The Treaty of Bologna, January 10, 1797—the Grand Duke of Tuscany to deliver to the paymaster of the Italian army 1,000,000 livres; Treaty of The Hague, May 16, 1795—the Netherlands to pay 100,000,000 florins as indemnity and damages for war expenses; Treaty of Paris, August 10, 1797—Portugal to pay 10,000,000 francs; Treaty of Badajoz, June 6, 1801—Portugal to pay 15,000,000 livres.

Napoleonic wars.

In the German campaigns, ending with the battle of Austerlitz, the Austrian provinces occupied by the French armies had to pay 100,000,000 francs.

Treaty of Pressburg, 1805—the sum fixed was 40,000,000 francs.

In the following campaign a further sum of 200,000,000 francs was imposed on the invaded Austrian provinces; but the Treaty of Schönbrunn, 1809, reduced the sum to 85,000,000.

Convention of Paris, September 8, 1808—Prussian States were required to pay France 140,000,000 francs; but through the intervention of the Emperor of Russia, the sum was reduced at Erfurt in October.

In 1815 came the turn of France to pay an indemnity. By the Treaty of Paris, November 20 (Art. IV), France was required to pay the Allied Powers 700,000,000 francs. An additional convention of the same date[1] prescribed the modes, periods, and guarantees of payment. The sum was to be discharged, day by day, in equal portions, in the space of five years, by means of *bons au porteur* (drafts payable to bearer) on the Royal Treasury of France; and no interest thereon was demanded, except (5 per cent.) on payments delayed by the act of France.

Some instances relating to Eastern countries are worthy of mention. By the Treaty of Nankin, August 29, 1842, the Emperor of China engaged to pay Great Britain 21,000,000 dollars; of which, however, 6,000,000 represented the value of opium delivered up in 1839 at Canton for the lives of the British superintendent and certain British subjects, and 3,000,000 dollars was for debts due to British subjects from Chinese merchants. Thus the sum of 12,000,000 dollars was left as equivalent to the amount of expenses incurred in sending out the expedition. The Treaty of Tientsin, 1858, required the province of Kwantung to pay Great Britain 2,000,000 taels; and under the Treaty of Pekin, 1860, China had to pay Great Britain 8,000,000 taels. Two similar treaties were concluded with France, which had taken part with Great Britain in the expeditions of 1858 and 1860.

Instances relating to Eastern countries.

[1] See *infra*, Appendix (C).

By the Treaty of Saigon, 1862, the King of Annam (Cochin China) had to pay France and Spain 4,000,000 dollars within a period of ten years. By the Convention of Yokohama, 1864, Japan was obliged to pay the sum of 3,000,000 dollars to Great Britain, France, United States, and Holland.

The Treaty of Tetouan, 1860, between Spain and Morocco imposed on the latter an indemnity of 100,000,000 francs.

The Treaty of Callao, 1865, between Spain and Peru, imposed on the latter an indemnity of 65,000,000 francs.

Treaty of Prague.

By the Treaty of Prague, 1866 (Art. XI), the Emperor of Austria engaged to pay the King of Prussia 40,000,000 Prussian thalers "to cover part of the expenses" to which Prussia was put by the war. From that sum, however, was to be deducted 15,000,000 thalers due to Austria from Schleswig and Holstein, in accordance with Art. XII of the Treaty of Vienna, 1864, as well as an additional sum of 5,000,000 thalers as an equivalent for the cost of maintaining the Prussian army in the Austrian territories it occupied till the conclusion of the peace. One half of the balance was required to be paid upon the ratification of the present treaty, the second half three weeks later at Oppeln in cash. Further, none of the German States that had fought against Prussia in the war of 1866 escaped indemnity: thus Würtemberg was called upon to pay 8,000,000 florins, Baden 6,000,000 florins, Hesse 3,000,000 florins, Saxony 10,000,000 thalers. The whole sum obtained from German States amounted to 217,000,000 francs.

Preliminaries of Versailles.

The Preliminaries of Versailles, February 26, 1871 (Art. II), imposed on France an indemnity of 5,000,000,000 francs (£200,000,000) — the largest ever demanded in the history of the world. At the conference of February 21, Bismarck demanded 6,000,000,000 francs, and even claimed that this sum was not excessive.[1] M. Thiers charged the Duc de Broglie, French ambassador in London, to request the good offices of Great Britain in determining the amount of the indemnity. When the amount first proposed by Bismarck was mentioned to Mr. Gladstone, the latter was shocked at the exorbitant demand; and at his instance the sum was reduced (on February 24) to that stated above. One who, on account of his position at the French embassy, had often met Mr. Gladstone, thus wrote of his interposition: "Le cabinet de M. Gladstone s'est cependant fait honneur d'avoir cédé aux pressantes instances du duc de Broglie, et d'avoir, à sa demande, obtenu de l'Allemagne une reduction d'un milliard sur le chiffre

[1] May, *Le traité de Francfort*, pp. 163 *seq.*

de notre rançon. . . . La conscience économique de M. Gladstone se souleva à l'idée du déplacement de numéraire qu'on nous imposait; il a sincèrement cru, comme sans doute M. de Bismarck, que c'était chose impossible à exécuter, et depuis, il m'a souvent avoué qu'il n'avait pas réussi à comprendre comment la chose avait pu se faire."[1]

During the negotiations M. Thiers and M. Favre urged that the war should not be regarded as a financial speculation, and that only the actual costs should be demanded. Bismarck accepted this view, and conformably thereto justified the amount insisted on by specifying the main items of which it was composed, thus: 2,000,000,000 francs for the war expenditure itself; and the remaining 3,000,000,000 francs for the restoration of material, indemnities to German subjects expelled from France, to shipowners and crews of captured vessels, expenses due to the maintenance of French prisoners, indemnities due to German wounded and to the widows and orphans of the fallen.[2] This calculation was questioned by the French negotiators, but in vain.[3] In the report on the preliminaries laid before the National Assembly it was stated that Germany was desirous of enriching herself with the spoils extorted from France, and that she believed she would indirectly disarm the vanquished country by abandoning it to financial impotence.

According to Art. II of the preliminaries the sum of 1,000,000,000 francs at least was to be paid within the year 1871, and the whole of the remainder in the space of three years, dating from the ratification of the preliminaries (which took place on March 2). Art. VII of the Treaty of Frankfort made the mode of payment more explicit. Thus half a milliard (i.e. 500,000,000 francs) was to paid within thirty days after the re-establishment of the authority of the French Government in Paris, one milliard in the course of the year 1871, and half a milliard on May 1, 1872. The rest (viz. 3 milliards) was to be paid by March 2, 1874—i.e. within three years after the date of exchanging the ratifications of the Preliminaries of Versailles—together with three years' interest thereon at 5 per cent. per annum; but no interest was to be paid on sums paid in advance. The payments could be made only in the principal German commercial towns, in gold or silver, in Prussian, Dutch,

[1] C. Gavard, *Un diplomate à Londres—Lettres et Notes*, 1871–1877 (Paris, 1895), pp. 3, 4.

[2] Cf. the bill before the Reichstag, May 25, 1872, as to the employment of the indemnity; Villefort, *Recueil*, vol. ii. pp. 548–550.

[3] Cf. A. Sorel, *Histoire diplomatique de la guerre franco-allemande* (Paris, 1875), vol. ii. pp. 233–234, 237–238, 245–246; May, *op. cit.*, p. 165.

or Belgian bank-notes, in negotiable bills to order or letters of exchange, payable at sight. Thus French bank-notes were excluded. (The value of the Prussian thaler was fixed at 3 francs 75 centimes.) But the first instalment falling due, and France having to pay also 1,250,000 francs each day for the German army of occupation (which has been considered in a previous chapter),[1] Germany was asked to accept for once only payment in French bank-notes. As she had liabilities to meet in the occupied departments and in Alsace-Lorraine, she consented on condition that 125,000,000 francs were paid by June 15. On June 27, 1871, the French Government invited subscriptions to a public loan at 5 per cent.; and such was the strength of French credit that the offers amounted to two and a half times the sum asked for! Again, on July 28, 1872, France resorted to a loan, this time asking for 3 milliards (3,000,000,000 francs) at 5 per cent., and the offers actually totalled the amazing sum of 43 milliards (43,000,000,000 francs), of which more than three-fifths was offered by foreign countries, with Germany at the head! The period of the complete discharge of the indemnity was prolonged by a year; but the German authorities insisted on keeping the army of occupation on French territory during the extended delay, so determined were they to make sure of getting the last sou.

Russo-Turkish War.

The amount of indemnity demanded in the case of the Russo-Turkish War, 1878, has already been mentioned. A dispute having arisen between the parties as to the payment of that part of the indemnity representing the claims of Russian subjects and establishments in Turkey for losses suffered during the war, an agreement was signed at Constantinople, August 4, 1910—that is, more than thirty years after the war—for submitting the difference (which diplomatic negotiation had failed to settle) to a court of arbitration at The Hague.[2]

Chino-Japanese War.

Under the Treaty of Shimonoseki, 1895 (Art. IV), China engaged to pay Japan 200,000,000 Kuping taels, in eight instalments, within a period of seven years after the exchange of ratifications. Interest at 5 per cent. per annum was to begin to run on all unpaid portions of the indemnity from the date the first instalment fell due (i.e. six months after the exchange of ratifications). Instalments might be paid in advance; and if the whole debt were discharged within three years after the exchange of ratifications, all interest would be waived, and the interest for two years and a half, or for any less period if then already paid, would be included as a part of the principal amount of the indemnity.

[1] See *supra*, p. 212.

[2] See *infra*, Appendix (P).

The indemnity in the Greco-Turkish War, 1897, has already been considered.[1]

As a set-off against the above instances, we may mention the following cases in which no payment of indemnity was stipulated :—

Examples in which no indemnity was stipulated.

The Treaty of Zurich, 1859, between France and Austria.

The Treaty of Paris, 1898, between the United States and Spain. Art. VII provided thus: "The United States and Spain mutually relinquish all claims for indemnity, national and individual, of every kind, of either Government, or of its citizens and subjects, against the other Government, that may have arisen since the beginning of the late insurrection in Cuba and prior to the exchange of the ratifications of the present treaty, including all claims for indemnity for the cost of the war. The United States will adjudicate and settle the claims of its citizens against Spain relinquished in this article."

Art. IX of the Peace of Vereeniging, 1902, declared that no tax would be imposed on landed property in the Transvaal and Orange River Colony to defray the expenses of the war. Indeed, generous provision was made (Art. X) for the restoration of the people to their homes, and for financial aid in the case of their losses caused by the war.

No indemnity clause appears in the Treaty of Portsmouth, 1905, between Russia and Japan. When, during the negotiations, the Japanese plenipotentiaries demanded reimbursement for war expenses, the determined opposition of the Russian representatives was tersely summed up by their exclamation, "Not a kopeck." They were prepared to pay for the good done by Japan to Russia during the war, e.g. maintenance of prisoners, tending the sick, etc., but not for the evil done by belligerent operations.

The foregoing precedents appear to have exerted some influence on the minds of the parties to subsequent peace treaties; for no indemnity stipulation is found in the treaties of Lausanne, 1912, between Italy and Turkey; London, 1913, between Turkey and the Balkan Allies; Bucharest, 1913, between Bulgaria and the Balkan Allies; Constantinople, 1913, between Turkey and Bulgaria; and Athens, 1913, between Turkey and Greece.

CESSION OF TERRITORY.

The second of the two most important special clauses in a treaty of peace is that relating to the cession of territory. This clause is found so frequently in treaties that we are forced to the conclusion that, whatever be the ostensible purpose of war, its real object is territorial aggrandizement. Usually the territory ceded is that which has been occupied by the troops of

[1] See *supra*, p. 87.

the cessionary State; sometimes other territory is demanded by the victorious belligerent for strategic reasons, or with a view to regularizing boundaries, etc.

Voluntary or friendly cession may be effected by gift, or purchase, or exchange of territory, or by the entire merger of a small independent State in a greater and more powerful one. In former times territorial transfers not infrequently resulted from the marriage contracts and testamentary dispositions of sovereigns, and sometimes from pledge transactions. In our own day, too, the lease of territory—as, for example, in China—almost amounts for all practical purposes to its cession. The operative terms employed in the instrument of voluntary cession usually differ from those used in the case of a forced cession as the outcome of war. Thus—as an example of the former—in the treaty of March 24, 1860, between France and Sardinia, with regard to the union of Savoy and Nice to France, Art. I says that the King of Sardinia "consents" to the annexation; whilst in the case of the latter the sovereign of the dismembered State "cedes" a portion of his territory, or "renounces" his rights therein, or it is simply said that the new boundaries of the States concerned are to be as indicated. In any event, the nature of the expressions used is a minor consideration; the main point is the character of the transaction itself.

How cession may be effected.

Every sovereign and independent State is entitled to cede a portion of its territory; and its treaty of cession, or stipulation in the peace treaty relative to cession, is valid and binding on the nation, if its municipal regulations on the subject have been observed. In reference to the Preliminaries of Versailles, February 26, 1871, which provided for the cession of Alsace-Lorraine, we may recall that at a meeting of the French National Assembly, on February 17, the deputies of the departments threatened with annexation protested against the contemplated transaction, and denied the power of that body to dispose by vote of a part of French territory. They protested, too, against the suggested plebiscite. This contention was, however, overruled by the Assembly, which by voting its acceptance of the terms of the preliminaries asserted its title to renounce, in the name of the entire nation, sovereignty over a portion of the country's territory.[1] On the contrary, a State that is permanently neutralized, under the guarantee of other Powers, does not appear to be vested with the full right to surrender a part of its territory, without the sanction of those Powers.[2] But the neutralized parts of a not permanently

Title to cede territory.

[1] Cf. Villefort, *Recueil*, vol. ii. pp. 1–5.

[2] Cf. Descamps, *La neutralité de la Belgique*, pp. 508 *seq.*

neutralized State may perhaps be ceded. Thus in 1860 Sardinia ceded to France her neutralized provinces of Chablais, Faucigny, and the Genevese (districts of Savoy); though the Swiss Government, as well as the Great Powers, protested against the annexation as being contrary to the provisions of the treaties of Vienna and Paris, 1815, which neutralized those provinces in the interest of Swiss neutrality. (France and Sardinia contended, on the other hand, that the neutrality guaranteed to Savoy was in favour of Sardinia alone; and they were prepared to ensure that France, as successor to Sardinia, would perform the obligations arising out of the neutrality.) In such a case, however, the guaranteeing States may intervene on the ground of public policy and political equilibrium. As the determining factor of a State's capacity to cede territory is the possession of complete sovereignty and independence, it is clear that a protectorate or a vassal State cannot effect a transfer of any of its territory without the consent of the protecting Power or the suzerain respectively. Thus the Ionian Islands were annexed to Greece in 1863, but not without the necessary consent of Great Britain, which had exercised a protectorate over those islands.

Treaty of peace converts *de facto* sovereignty into *de jure* sovereignty.

The distinction drawn above between a voluntary cession and a compulsory cession was made only for the purpose of convenience; for it is not formally recognized by international law. Indeed, in the eyes of international law every case of the surrender and annexation of territory is deemed to be a "voluntary" cession, effected by means of a bilateral transaction; this mode of territorial acquisition being distinguished from that of subjugation and annexation, consequent on the use of such superior force as renders a treaty transaction unnecessary. A cessionary State, then, acquiring territory under a treaty of peace obtains a good title to it, not by reason of the fact that it may have militarily occupied it and ousted the former Government from it, but from the fact that the former Government "cedes" it, whether the act of ceding be carried out voluntarily or involuntarily. That is, in the case of territory already in the possession and under the control of the victorious belligerent, a cession clause is essential in the treaty of peace in order to convert the purely *de facto* sovereignty into full *de jure* sovereignty. And such territory is ceded in its old name, despite any alteration in this respect that may have been made by the occupant. Thus in 1905, though the Japanese had sought to change the name of Sakhalin, after they had taken undisputed firm possession of the island, the southern part was ceded to Japan "in perpetuity and full sovereignty" in the name by which it was known to the ceding State, Russia.

For the cession of territory effected and consecrated by a treaty of peace the ceding State is not entitled to compensation. By way of exception, however, we sometimes find that a cessionary State, though victorious in the war, offers compensation for the ceded territory. An example of this action, which is dictated by political and not by juridical considerations, is found at the conclusion of the Spanish-American War, 1898. Art. III of the Treaty of Paris states that "Spain cedes to the United States the archipelago known as the Philippine Islands, and comprehending the islands lying within" the lines specified, and concludes abruptly with the words: "The United States will pay to Spain the sum of twenty million dollars within three months after the exchange of the ratifications of the present treaty"—without indicating that this is a consideration for the cession. The sum was, however, regarded by some of the American commissioners who negotiated the treaty as a consideration for the transfer, and therefore as the ground of the American title to the islands. Senator Gray is reported to have said in New York on February 25, 1899, that the United States had to choose to take the Philippines either "by the ruthless hand of conquest or by some concessions that comported with the greatness and character of this country. . . . We believed it was better . . . to take them by voluntary cession and by purchase, so to speak." Mr. Day, the Secretary of State, said too on October 12, 1899, in approval of this statement: "It was not claimed that the United States had a right to the Philippine Islands as a matter of conquest. By the cession for a consideration we obtained an indisputable title." On the other hand, the opinion of Mr. Whitelaw Reid does not appear to have been in agreement with this view.[1] There is no need here to examine the various relevant circumstances in order to ascertain whether the Philippines were really acquired by a contract of sale and purchase. Obviously it was not a cession consequent on peaceable negotiation unaffected by the fortunes of war. For our present purpose it suffices to consider it simply as a cession obtained by the victorious party from the defeated party in their treaty of peace.

Sometimes compensation is offered.

Where the territory to be ceded is not clearly defined, a clause is usually inserted in the treaty of peace providing for the appointment of commissioners on both sides for the purpose of determining its limits or rectifying the boundaries of the States concerned.

Delimitation commission.

If the ceded territory was occupied by the cessionary State before

[1] Cf. R. H. Titherington, *History of the Spanish-American War* (New York, 1900), pp. 393–394, note; see *infra*, p. 324.

the peace negotiations, then the ratification of the treaty transfers the ownership in it to the new sovereign who, having possession already, therefore acquires full sovereignty over it. If the ceded territory was not already in the possession of the acquiring State, the act of delivery must supplement the conventional disposition before the latter can exercise full sovereignty in it as well as over it. But delivery is not indispensable to render the cession juridically valid—though some writers hold a contrary view; the fundamental criterion is the intention of the parties and the delivery of the document of title—viz. the instrument embodying the terms of peace—to the cessionary. A notable example is that of the Treaty of Zurich, November 10, 1859, between Austria and France. Under Art. IV the Emperor of Austria ceded Lombardy to the Emperor of the French, and under Art. V the latter agreed to hand over the ceded country to the King of Sardinia, without having taken actual possession of it. In the American case, *Davis* v. *Police Jury of Concordia*, the court observed: "It is true that in a treaty for the cession of territory its national character continues for all commercial purposes; but full sovereignty, for the exercise of it, does not pass to the nation to which it is transferred until actual delivery. But it is also true that the exercise of sovereignty by the ceding country ceases, except for strictly municipal purposes, especially for granting lands. And for the same reason in both cases; because after the treaty is made there is not in either the union of possession and the right to the territory which must concur to give *plenum dominium et utile*. To give that there must be the *jus in rem* and the *jus in re*, or what is called in the common law of England the *juris et seisinæ conjunctio*." [1]

Act of delivery.

From the point of view of the acquiring State the assumption of sovereignty over the ceded territory is consummated by a legislative enactment or by a decree of the head of the Government, as the case may be. Thus a month after the signature of the Treaty of Frankfort an Imperial law was passed (June 9, 1871) formally proclaiming the union of Alsace-Lorraine to the German Empire, authorizing the introduction therein of certain parts of the Imperial Constitution, and providing for the representation of the new provinces in the Reichstag.

Completion of annexation by act of the annexing State.

As soon as the exercise of sovereignty over the newly added territory begins the annexing State's rights and obligations with regard to it commence—in the first place, by reason of the fact

[1] *Davis* v. *Police Jury of Concordia* (1850), 9 Howard, 280, at p. 289 (per Mr. Justice Wayne).

that it constitutes part of the new sovereign's dominions, and secondly, because of the application of the principles of succession.[1] But so far as the ceding State is concerned, the cession is an act of a purely divestitive character. By renouncing its authority thus over a portion of its territory, it contracts no obligation of guarantee—subject, of course, to any stipulations in the treaty of peace—towards the annexing State, or foreign Powers, or towards the inhabitants of the transferred territory. It does not and cannot guarantee that the sentiments of the alienated population—sentiments due to the subtle influences of national character, customs, traditions, intellectual and moral development, political constitution—will become assimilated to those of the people of the cessionary State. It does not guarantee that third States will respect the frontiers of the annexed territory as they did before the annexation. The cession remains nothing more than a fact for the annexed population as well as for foreign Governments.[2]

Position of the ceding State.

Having regard to such considerations as are mentioned above, several writers maintain that no cession should be effected—and some even hold that no cession can be legitimately effected—unless sanctioned by a previous plebiscite on the part of the population of the territory whose transfer is contemplated. It is argued, too, that the right of the stronger ought not to be allowed to prevail, that the conditions are now different from those existing in earlier ages when such a right was universally exercised, that public opinion has changed, that the general democratic movement is to be taken into account, that popular suffrage is now almost everywhere the fount of political authority, that the sovereignty of the people is now the governing factor in the political and social life of nearly all civilized States. Why—it is asked—should the people of a given territory be handed over to another State, deprived of their old citizenship (and perhaps of their nationality, if they are not allowed to exercise the power of option), and of all their old associations, without consulting them as to whether they approve of the change?

Cession and plebiscite.

An early example of the use of the plebiscite is that of 1552, when Henry II of France, after capturing Toul, Metz, and Verdun, and before annexing them, resorted to a vote of the inhabitants. The Bishop of Verdun said to his people "que le roi de France était venu comme libérateur, qu'il voulait traiter les bourgeois comme de bons Français et que,

Early example

[1] See *infra*, pp. 290 *seq.*

[2] Cf. Funck-Brentano et Sorel, *Précis du droit des gens*, p. 334.

bien éloigné d'user de mesures de rigueur, il en appelait au vote libre du peuple." [1]

The principle was again proclaimed by the French Revolutionary Government and applied in several cases.[2] Thus during the war of France with Sardinia, 1792, General de Montesquiou after invading Savoy entered Chambéry on September 24. On October 14 the communes elected delegates for the purpose of discussing and deciding the question of annexation. A great majority voted in its favour. Accordingly, on November 27 the convention decreed the union of Savoy to the the Republic, of which it constituted the eighty-fourth department.[3]

Later instances.

Nice was taken by General Anselme, September 29, 1792, without any opposition on the part of the King of Sardinia's troops. A local assembly was constituted, which resolved, by a large majority, in favour of annexation to France.[4]

Similarly, after Mayence was entered by the French troops, October 21, 1792, and the greater part of the territory now forming Rhenish Bavaria was occupied, an assembly was summoned, and decided on incorporation; so that by a decree of the convention, March 30, 1793, the towns and communes of Mayence, Worms, etc., became part of the French Republic.[5]

Belgium, too (then designated the Austrian Netherlands) fell into the hands of Dumouriez by the victory of Jemapes, November 6, 1792. A decree of the convention, December 15, ordered the French generals to proclaim the sovereignty of the people, to abolish taxes and privileges, to suppress all established authority, and to summon an assembly of the people for the purpose of organizing provisional administration and justice. The defeat at Neerwinden restored Belgium to the Austrians, but two years later it was declared part of the French dominions.[6]

Napoleon III was an adherent of the system of plebiscite, to which he had recourse in the annexation of Nice and Savoy to France (treaty of March 24, 1860, Art. I), [7] and in the cession of Venetia and its annexation to Italy (treaty of October 3, 1866;

[1] Cf. E. Ollivier, *L'Empire libéral* (Paris, 1895), vol. i. p. 165.

[2] See J. Heimweh, *Droit de conquête et plébiscite* (Paris, 1896); Rouard de Card, *Études de droit international* (Paris, 1890), "Les annexions et les plébiscites dans l'histoire contemporaine."

[3] See Victor de St. Genis, *Histoire de la Savoie* (Chambéry, 1869), vol. iii. pp. 137 *seq.*

[4] J. B. Toselli, *Précis historique de Nice depuis sa fondation jusqu'en* 1860, 4 vols. (Nice, 1867–1869).

[5] A. Chuquet, *Mayence* (Paris, 1892).

[6] A. Chuquet, *Jemapes et la conquête de la Belgique* (Paris, 1890).

[7] G. Cogordan, *La nationalité au point de vue des rapports internationaux* (Paris, 1890), pp. 344–356; *Revue des deux mondes*, March 1, 1896.

plebiscite, October 21, 22). Other plebiscites proclaimed the union of Parma, Modena, Tuscany, and Emilia to Piedmont and Lombardy, March 11, 12, 1860; Sicily and the Kingdom of Naples to Italy, October 21, 1860; Umbria and the Marches, November 30; Rome and its territory, October 1870. Thus the principle of voluntary incorporation played a great part in the creation of a new Power—Italy.

In the treaty of peace between Austria and Prussia, signed at Prague, August 23, 1866, Art. V stipulated that Austria should transfer to Prussia the rights over Schleswig and Holstein, with the condition that the inhabitants of the northern districts of Schleswig should be transferred to Denmark if, by a free vote, they expressed a wish to that effect. But Prussia afterwards refused to carry out this provision.

The island of St. Bartholomew (Antilles) was ceded by Sweden to France, under the Treaty of Paris, August 10, 1877, subject to the express consent of its population (Art. I).

In the treaty of peace of October 20, 1883, between Chile and Peru, it was stipulated that the territories of Tacna and Arica should remain in the possession of Chile for ten years, and that on the expiration of this term a plebiscite should decide whether they were to remain definitively annexed to Chile or were to form part of Peru. Numerous difficulties arose between the two States in regard to the organization of the plebiscite; negotiations between them were more than once instituted and then broken off.[1]

Anglo-American practice against plebiscite.

The few examples given above, though they are interesting precedents, scarcely go to prove that the plebiscite is likely to become a recognized part of international usage. It is not capable of acquiring universal applicability. In some cases it may well be fitting and practicable; in others it may produce more evils than it is intended to avoid. In forcible cessions a powerful State will repudiate it if it suspects that a vote of the people may not ratify it. Or if the victorious party has ventured to allow recourse to the plebiscite and the resulting vote was against annexation, the war would be simply resumed, unless the defeated party consented to disregard the voice of the majority. We have already noted the conduct of Prussia, as a successful belligerent, in regard to the Treaty of Prague, 1866. The policy and practice of many leading States are against the plebiscite. The United States has always been opposed to the use of the procedure in the case of her acquisitions, whether forcible or resulting from peaceable negotiation. On

[1] Bonfils, *Droit international*, p. 372. Cf. *Revue de droit international* (Bruxelles), vol. xxix (1897), pp. 660 *seq.*

one occasion, however, the inhabitants of the Danish West Indies were allowed to vote on the question of annexing the islands to the United States; but Mr. Seward, the Secretary of State, protested against it.[1] As for Great Britain, Lord Salisbury once declared in the House of Lords that " the plebiscite is not among the traditions of this country."[2] It has, indeed, serious disadvantages. The vote of the majority is not always for the best. In the internal government of a State a bad choice may be revoked; but in the case of annexation the choice of the majority is irrevocable. Is it desirable that the will of a bare majority should be allowed to decide the destiny of a territory and its population? And are we certain that the votes would in every case be given freely, and uninfluenced by malpractices and sinister motives? Had this principle been applied in 1861, there would have been no American Civil War and also no United States—for there is no doubt that a majority in the Confederate States of the South would have voted against the maintenance of the Union. The case involved here was, of course, one of secession; but the principle is no more logically applicable to a case of forcible cession. The only way out of the difficulty is to allow each inhabitant to choose for himself whether he is prepared to remain in the ceded territory as a subject of the new sovereign, or to remove from it with his possessions. This is not a perfect solution, but it is a considerable relaxation. The practice of option, indeed, has become deeply rooted in the modern international system.[3]

Examples of cessions.

In concluding this chapter we may look at a few examples of cessions stipulated in treaties of peace, in order to supplement what has already been said, especially in regard to the delivery of the ceded territory to the cessionary State and the delimitation of boundaries where necessary.

Treaty of Paris, 1815.

The Treaty of Paris, 1815 (Art. I), required France to make such cessions as would restore her frontiers to the position in which they were in 1790, subject to the modifications specified. The latter were then indicated in detail, and the new boundary lines were marked out. Moreover, a delimitation commission (to be appointed within three months) was to complete the task afterwards. Under Art. II the fortresses, places, and districts falling outside those lines were to be placed at the disposal of the Allied Powers within ten days of the signature of the

[1] Cf. F. Bancroft, *Life of William H. Seward* (New York and London, 1900), vol. ii. pp. 483–485.

[2] Hansard, 3rd series, vol. cccxlv. p. 1311.

[3] As to the practice of option, see *infra*, pp. 294 *seq*.

treaty, the King of France renouncing for himself, his heirs, and successors for ever the rights of sovereignty and property he had hitherto exercised over the said fortresses and places.[1]

Treaty of Paris, 1856.

The Treaty of Paris, 1856, Art. XX, states that the Emperor of Russia "consents to the rectification of his frontier in Bessarabia," in exchange for the restoration of the towns and places occupied by the Allies, and in order to secure more fully the free navigation of the Danube. The new frontier was indicated,[2] and provision was made for the appointment of delegates of the contracting parties for arranging the necessary details. Art. XXI stipulated that the ceded territory was to be annexed to the principality of Moldavia under Turkish suzerainty.

Treaty of Vienna, 1866.

Under the Treaty of Vienna, 1866, the Emperor of Austria "agreed to the union" of the Lombardo-Venetian Kingdom to Italy (Art. III). Its frontier was determined by its actual administrative confines, and was to be traced out as soon as possible by a military commission appointed by the signatories (Art. IV). The evacuation of the ceded territory was to begin immediately after the signature of the treaty and was to be completed in the shortest possible delay conformably to the arrangements made by the commission (Art. V).

Preliminaries of Versailles, 1871.

The Preliminaries of Versailles, February 26, 1871, disposed of Alsace-Lorraine in the following terms (Art. I): "France renounces in favour of the German Empire all her rights and titles over the territories situated on the east of the frontier hereafter described." The line of demarcation was then traced out.[3] The definitive Treaty of Frankfort, May 10, 1871, introduced certain amendments in the territorial delimitation in favour of France—it spoke of "ceding" certain territories ceded by the preliminaries, which in this respect were irregularly regarded as final—subject to a frontier rectification on the part of France. The ceded territories were to belong to the German Empire "in perpetuity in all sovereignty and property." Provision was made for the nomination of an international commission, composed of an equal number of representatives of the contracting parties, for the purpose of proceeding to the spot immediately after the ratification of the treaty to execute the functions entrusted to them and to mark out the new frontier in accordance with the stipulations. The commission was also required to divide the property—both lands and funds—belonging to the districts and communes that were cut in two by the new line of demarcation; in case of difficulty or disagreement regarding the tracing and the measures of execution it was to refer to the two Governments.

[1] See *infra*, Appendix (A). [2] Appendix (D). [3] Appendix (J).

The work of the boundary commission took six years: it began in May 1871, and ended April 26, 1877; and ratifications thereof were exchanged at Metz, May 31, 1877.

Treaty of Shimonoseki, 1895.

Under the Treaty of Shimonoseki, 1895 (Art. II), China ceded to Japan "in perpetuity and full sovereignty" certain territories specified, "together with all fortifications, arsenals, and public property thereon." Art. III provided for the appointment, immediately after the exchange of ratifications, of a joint commission of delimitation, consisting of two or more representatives on each side. It was empowered to trace out and verify the alignments of the frontiers described in Art. II and shown on an accompanying map, and also to rectify such boundaries laid down in the treaty as were found to be defective at any point, "either on account of topography or in consideration of good administration." The commission was to begin its duties as soon as possible, and conclude its labours within the space of one year after appointment. In the meantime the alignments indicated in the treaty were to be maintained. Among the territories ceded was the island of Formosa. This needing no delimitation, it was laid down in Art. V that immediately upon the exchange of the ratifications of the treaty the two Governments should send two or more commissioners to the island in order to effect its final transfer, which was to be completed within two months after the exchange of ratifications.

Treaty of Constantinople, 1897.

The case of the Greco-Turkish boundary delimitation deserves notice, if only for one interesting point. The preliminaries of peace, introducing territorial alterations, were concluded on September 18, 1897; and without waiting for the conclusion of the definitive treaty (which afterwards took place at Constantinople, on December 4, 1897) a commission was appointed, and began its work in October. Owing to bad weather its labours were suspended till December. In May 1898 its work was completed, and the new frontier was agreed upon. The village of Koutchufliani, which was formerly on Greek soil, finding itself assigned to Turkey, the inhabitants burnt down their houses, and removed, with whatever property they could take, into Greek territory.

Treaty of Paris, 1898.

The territorial rearrangements following the Spanish-American War are noteworthy for the fact that not only was Spain required, by the Treaty of Paris, December 10, 1898, to cede to the United States Porto Rico and other Spanish islands in the West Indies, the island of Guam in the Ladrones (Art. II), and the Philippine Islands comprised within specified lines, but also to relinquish all claim of sovereignty over and title to Cuba (Art. I). As the latter island would, when evacuated by Spain, be occupied by the United States, the American Government pledged itself to assume and discharge, during the occupation, all the obligations imposed by international law for the purpose of protecting life and property.[1] Art. XVI emphasized that such obligations were limited to the period of occupation, and added that when this period came to an end the United States would "advise any Government established in the island to assume the same obligations." The payment of twenty million dollars to Spain, in connection with the cession of the Philippines, has already been referred to.[2] It had already been stipulated in the Protocol of Washington, August 12, 1898, that Spain should immediately evacuate Cuba, Porto Rico, and the other Spanish islands in the West Indies, and that within thirty days after signing the protocol commissioners should meet in Havana and San Juan in order to arrange and carry out the details of the evacuation. Similarly, Art. V of the definitive treaty required Spain to evacuate the Philippines and Guam conformably to the regulations laid down by those commissioners, and within a period of time to be agreed upon by the two Governments.

Treaty of Portsmouth, 1905.

By the Treaty of Portsmouth, 1905, Russia agreed (Art. V) to transfer to Japan, with the consent of China, the lease of Port Arthur, Ta-lien, and adjacent territory and territorial waters, together with all the incidental rights and privileges. Under Art. IX Russia ceded to Japan "in perpetuity and full sovereignty" the southern part of the island of Sakhalin and all the adjacent islands. The additional Art. II appended to the treaty provided for the appointment, as soon as possible after the exchange of ratifications, of a delimitation commission, which was to proceed to the spot and mark out in a permanent manner the exact boundary between the Russian and Japanese possessions in Sakhalin. So far as topographical considerations allowed, the fiftieth parallel of north latitude was to be followed as the line of demarcation. Where deflections were found necessary at any points, they were to be counterbalanced by equal deflections made at other points. The commissioners were also required to prepare a list and description of the adjacent islands included in the cession, and to prepare and sign maps showing the boundaries of the ceded territory. The results reached were subject to the approval of the contracting parties.

The Treaty of London, May 30, 1913, made an attempt (which proved to be futile) to settle the Balkan question. The Sultan

[1] By the treaty of June 12, 1901, Cuba was made over to the Cuban people.

[2] See *supra*, p. 280.

ceded to the Balkan Allies all his European territories to the west of a line drawn from Enos on the Ægean Sea to Midia on the Black Sea, with the exception of Albania. An international commission was to determine the exact line of the new frontier (Art. II). By Art. III the contracting parties agreed to remit to the Great Powers the delimitation of the Albanian frontier and all other questions concerning Albania. Further, Turkey ceded Crete to the Allies (Art. IV).

Treaty of London, 1913.

The Treaty of Bucharest, 1913, between Bulgaria and the Balkan Allies, is almost entirely devoted to the rectification of frontiers. Art. II prescribed the line for a new boundary between Bulgaria and Roumania, which was to be delimited in detail by a mixed commission of Bulgarian and Roumanian delegates in accordance therewith. The commission was charged also with the division of the lands and funds belonging to districts and communes intersected by the new frontier. Any disagreement as to the line or as to the method of marking it was to be submitted to an arbitrator appointed by a friendly Government, and his decision was to be regarded as final. Arts. III and V indicated the new frontiers between Bulgaria and Serbia, and between Bulgaria and Greece, respectively, and made similar arrangements for the appointment of mixed commissions and for referring disputes to arbitration. Bulgaria also renounced, under Art. V, all claim to Crete.

Treaty of Bucharest, 1913.

In a most elaborate article (I) of the Treaty of Constantinople, 1913, the new frontier between Turkey and Bulgaria was described. And Art. II laid down that ten days after the signature of the treaty the armies of each party were to evacute as soon as possible the territories assigned to the other party, and within the fifteen succeeding days to hand them over to the proper authorities "conformably to rules and usages." The appended protocol furnished further details regarding the delimitation, the establishment of mixed commissions, the division of their labour, the mode of procedure, the treatment of rivers, the islands in the bed of the Maritza (for which a special commission was to be appointed), the exchange of Bulgarian and Moslem populations and properties, compensation for differences (if any) arising out of such exchange. Finally provision was made (Art. XVII) for submitting disputes to arbitration at The Hague, in accordance with an agreement set out in Annex III.[1]

Treaty of Constantinople, 1913.

[1] See *infra*, Appendix (Y).

CHAPTER XI

EFFECT OF CESSION

STATE SUCCESSION: NATIONALITY

State succession: significance—Nationality: sometimes stipulated that nationality not to be affected; operation of treaty, difference between subjects and citizens; what persons should be vested with the new nationality; practice of option, who may opt, married women and minors, period of option, mode of exercising the option.

State Succession.

THE cession of territory raises many important questions relating to State succession. We have already considered the effects of a change of sovereignty in regard to a territory acquired by conquest and subjugation, i.e. without resorting to a treaty transaction.[1] Now we have to examine briefly the main results consequent on the acquisition of territory by means of cession effected by treaty. Here, as before, there is neither unanimity of juristic opinion nor uniformity of international practice. But certain principles may be set forth and conclusions inferred. In the first place, State succession must not be confounded with civil law succession. A State's personality—attributed to it by a juridical fiction—has not the same significance as an individual's personality. Both the State and the individual, as successors, step into the place of their predecessors and continue their respective rights and obligations. But the State successor assumes them as though they were its own; whilst the individual successor assumes them as though he were himself the predecessor. The former succeeds only to the *jura*; the latter succeeds to the full civil personality. The individual is capable of representing more than one person; the State is one and indivisible, its legal personality simply being extended to its new dominion.[2] The State succeeds to the rights and obligations to an extent determined by its political and legal institutions and its public policy; the act—unlike that of the individual successor—depends on its own will and is subject to its discrimination. The

[1] See *supra*, pp. 32 *seq.*

[2] Cf. M. Huber, *Die Staatensuccession* (Leipzig, 1898), §§ 23, 24.

succession of the individual under civil law is a universal succession; that of the State in the case of territorial cession is under international practice a partial—or, as it has also been designated, a "singular"—succession.[1] To make State succession a universal one the express consent of the transferee is necessary. Some jurists hold, indeed, that there is no such process as State succession, inasmuch as the annexation of a State involves *ipso facto* the loss of its international personality, and consequently the disappearance of its rights and obligations. But this reasoning is based on a purely abstract conception, and disregards incidents that invariably occur in practice. Certain rights and duties—varying, of course, in extent and nature, according to the circumstances of each case—are, in point of fact, always taken over by the cessionary State along with the territory ceded. And in this respect the guiding principles may be conveniently, though not strictly, represented by the maxims of Roman law—"Res transit cum suo onere,"[2] and "Nemo plus juris ad alium transferre potest quam ipse habet."[3]

The rights and duties of the cessionary State appertain to a large number of subjects:[4] the nationality[5] and allegiance of the ceding State's subjects and other inhabitants belonging to the ceded territory; treaties relative to this territory; its public law and administration; property; debts; concessions; private rights and private law, and so forth.

NATIONALITY.

The generally accepted rule is (subject to certain exceptions) that the annexation of territory by treaty implies collective denationalization of its people on the one hand and collective naturalization on the other—simultaneous results that arise on the date of the exchange of the ratifications, if no other date is expressly provided. (Some writers hold that in such a case the date of the signature is the crucial one, but it is open to objection.) The main question is what persons are affected as to their nationality and political status by the change of sovereignty—is it natives of the ceded territory whether domiciled therein or not, is it all domiciled inhabitants whether they are natives or not?[6] Is a distinction to be made between natural-born subjects and

[1] Cf. A. B. Keith, *The Theory of State Succession* (London, 1907), p. 5.

[2] *Dig.*, liv. 50, 17.

[3] *Ibid.*, xx. 41, 1.

[4] Following, for the most part, the classification adopted by Huber and Keith.

[5] The term "nationality" is used throughout in the legal, and not in the ethnological, sense.

[6] As to nationality in case of conquest and subjugation, see *supra*, pp. 86 *seq.* It is to be noted that what is said there applies in nearly every respect to the present case; so that it must be taken as supplementary thereto.

naturalized subjects, according to the judicial pronouncement in an American case[1] that the latter owing a purely statutory allegiance are, when released therefrom, remitted to their original status? In general, the persons directly concerned are the ceding State's subjects domiciled in the transferred territory at the time the transfer takes effect, unless other provisions are made in the treaty of peace and subsequent conventional arrangements. The matter is nowadays invariably settled by agreement; the ceding State, losing a portion of its dominions, seizes the last opportunity afforded it for the protection of its former subjects by stipulating in their behalf as favourable conditions as possible, and obtaining guarantees from the cessionary Power, in regard to their nationality, their persons, and their property. Sometimes, indeed, though rarely, the contracting parties agree that the nationality of their subjects belonging to ceded lands shall not be affected. Thus—to give a recent case, which is not, however, connected with war—in the Franco-German Convention of November 4, 1911, involving mutual cessions, i.e. exchange of colonial territory, no regulations were made for the condition of subjects of the one party in the territory ceded to the other; and shortly afterwards (February 2, 1912) the two Powers signed at Berlin an agreement which provided that the exchange of territory should not modify the nationality of their respective citizens and subjects not being natives of the land ceded: "L'annexion ne modifiera en rien la nationalité des citoyens français, européens ou autres, et des sujets français non originaires des territoires qui ont donné lieu à des échanges, alors même qu'ils continueraient à résider sur les territoires cédés par la France à l'Allemagne, et ils ne seront pas tenus d'émigrer dans un délai déterminé." The following paragraph contains a similar stipulation for German subjects.[2]

Sometimes stipulated that nationality not to be affected.

But no such provision was made for the natives resident in the territories at the time the annexation took effect: "Les indigènes originaires des territoires qui ont donné lieu à des échanges et résidant au jour de l'annexion définitive dans les territoires cédés par la France à l'Allemagne, perdront la qualité de sujets français pour entrer dans la sujétion coloniale allemande."[3] Similarly, in the case of the cessions consequent on the Spanish-American War a discrimination was made between the native inhabitants of Porto Rico and the Philippines and those Spanish subjects who were "natives of the Peninsula." By Art. IX of the Treaty of Paris, December 10,

Operation of treaty—difference between subjects and citizens.

[1] *Tobin* v. *Walkinshaw* (1856), McAllister, 186.

[2] *Archives Diplomatiques* (Paris), mai–juillet, 1912; pp. 5, 6.

[3] *Ibid.*

1898, the latter were permitted to remain or remove, without prejudice to their rights of property and all other rights applicable to foreigners; and if they remained they could continue to be Spanish subjects by making a declaration to that effect. But with regard to the natives of those islands, their "civil rights and political status" were to be specially determined by Congress. In the meantime the American Government decided that native inhabitants of Porto Rico (those of the Philippines not being included owing to the native insurrection there) residing abroad temporarily might register themselves in the legations and consulates of the United States, and then would be entitled to "official protection . . . in all matters where a citizen of the United States similarly situated would be entitled thereto"; that is, protection would be extended to them not as American citizens, but simply as native inhabitants of the island.[1] And in judicial decisions, too, it was held that the Treaty of Paris did not make the inhabitants of the ceded territories citizens of the United States,[2] but that they ceased to be "aliens" within the meaning of the immigration laws.[3] Further, by the Acts of April 12, 1900, and July 1, 1902, all inhabitants of Porto Rico and the Philippines, respectively, who were Spanish subjects on April 11, 1899 (the date of the exchange of ratifications), and who then resided there, were declared to be citizens of those islands (not of the United States) and entitled to the protection of the American Government, with the exception of those who had elected to preserve their allegiance to Spain within the year stipulated, i.e. on or before April 11, 1900.[4]

What persons should be vested with the new nationality.

International law provides no definite rule for the denationalization of the people of the ceded territory. There is a difference of opinion among jurists and there is a divergence of practice in treaties as to what classes of persons should be vested with the nationality of the cessionary State. The determining principles are chosen from among the elements of domicile and birth (or origin)—in the case of the latter, either the *jus soli*, relating to the place of birth, or the *jus sanguinis*, relating to the parentage.[5] These taken separately or in varying combinations constitute the criteria that are adopted in modern international practice. The object of the acquiring State, in regard to the population of the territory acquired, is to

[1] Mr. Hay, Secretary of State, to the diplomatic and consular officers of the United States, May 2, 1899: *U.S. Foreign Relations*, 1900, p. 894; Moore, *Digest*, vol. iii. pp. 315–316.

[2] *Goetze* v. *U.S.* (1900), 103 Fed. Rep. 72.

[3] *Gonzales* v. *Williams* (1904), 192 U.S. Rep. 1.

[4] Moore, *Digest*, vol. iii. pp. 315–316.

[5] Cf. M. Costes, *Des cessions de territoire* (Paris; Toulouse, 1914), pp. 101 *seq.*

obtain as many new citizens as possible—citizens on whose loyalty it may count. This object, it is thought, may perhaps be best achieved by conferring the new nationality on those of the inhabitants who are permanently resident in the territory, who have definitively established their home in it, and who will probably continue to associate themselves with it despite the change of sovereignty. On such grounds the principle of domicile is chosen as the governing factor—it is usually the domicile as determined by the law of the ceding State. The persons affected thereby will include not only natural-born subjects and naturalized subjects of the ceding State, but also domiciled aliens. This course is the most rational and the most expedient, and is in harmony with the whole trend of modern jurisprudence. If birth is taken as the criterion, then it may relate either to such persons as were born in the territory of parents themselves born there or established there a certain length of time, or simply to those persons born there, whatever be their domicile or residence at the time of annexation. Such classes of persons may well comprise those who have little or nothing but the chance tie of birth connecting them with the territory in question: their real interests may lie elsewhere. If the treaty imposes the cessionary State's nationality on those qualified either by birth or domicile, the ceding Power will obviously be deprived of a larger number of subjects; but if this nationality is imposed on persons satisfying the test of both birth and domicile, then the number of the subjects gained by the new sovereign will be smaller.

Now in order that a new nationality and a new bond of allegiance may not be imposed on the inhabitants against their will, the practice of option is adopted. For nationality is a juridical status, which is essentially voluntary. In the modern world every individual is allowed to divest himself of his own nationality and assume another, subject to the fulfilment of certain requirements; that is, he is entitled to choose between two nationalities. In treaties of cession, then, various classes of persons are permitted to preserve their old nationality and allegiance, provided they satisfy certain given conditions. It cannot be to the interest of the acquiring State to retain aliens as its subjects in spite of themselves. Indeed, in the case of a cession resulting from war, to do so might well be the cause of serious embarrassment and trouble. The annexing State is therefore entitled, in the interests of self-preservation, to ascertain by appropriate methods whether the people belonging to the acquired territory consent to be its subjects or prefer to maintain their former allegiance. The consent of the individual is, in this respect, regarded as all-important—a point of view that is now universal, and which came to be emphati-

Practice of option.

cally insisted on towards the end of the eighteenth century. And it is at that period that the practice of option was definitely established. An early and important example is that of the Treaty of Campo Formio, 1797, between France and the Empire; Art. IX provided as follows: " . . . Those who may wish to quit, for the future, the said countries (those ceded, acquired, or exchanged) shall be obliged to make a declaration to that effect three months after the publication of the said treaty. They shall then have the term of three years to sell their effects, movable or immovable, or to dispose of them at their pleasure." Succeeding treaties adopted the practice, subject to varying conditions according to the circumstances of each case. This exercise of option (implying a choice between two alternatives) presupposes, as a rule, only a partial dismemberment of a State—the surrender of only a portion of its territory by a treaty of cession or by stipulations in a treaty of peace. If an entire State is annexed, the question of nationality—i.e. in the legal sense—does not arise, for the nationality of the annexed State vanishes by the very act of annexation; but it is, of course, within the discretion of the absorbing Power to permit the old subjects of the absorbed State to retire to another country. In either event, whether partial dismemberment or total annexation, the actual value of the right or the privilege (as the case may be) of option depends on the ability of the inhabitants concerned to find homes elsewhere. In every instance where territory is transferred there are many people who do not exercise the option conceded to them, when it necessitates also removal. But their acquiescence does not necessarily imply their willing consent to be invested with the new nationality; it may well be the result of their helplessness and of the hopeless view they take of an emigration enterprise. However this may be, many are ready to avail themselves of the opportunity. We have, therefore, to consider three questions: What persons connected with the ceded territory are allowed to exercise the option? Within what time have the conditions stipulated to be fulfilled? What are the conditions stipulated (or what method of option is required)? As international law prescribes no positive principles, we have to answer these questions on the basis of international practice, which varies in accordance with the exigencies of time and place and with the nature of the relationships of the parties involved.

Who may opt.

As a general rule, the right of option ought to be granted to persons whose nationality would be changed by the fact of annexation. The stipulations of treaties sometimes follow this rule, sometimes they go beyond it, and sometimes, again, they fall short of it. The competing principles of residence, domicile, and origin are introduced; but nowadays that of domicile predominates. The Treaty of Paris, 1815 (Art. VII), conferred the right of option on the "inhabitants" of all the territories that were to change sovereigns, whether they were natives or foreigners, whatever their condition and nationality might be. The treaties of Paris, 1856 (Art. XXI), Constantinople, 1879 (Art. VII), Shimonoseki, 1895 (Art. V), also make use of the comprehensive expression "inhabitants." The Treaty of Portsmouth, 1905 (Art. X), speaks of the ceding State's "subjects, inhabitants of the territory ceded." Similarly, the Treaty of Paris, 1898, between the United States and Spain, applies (Art. IX) to "Spanish subjects . . . residing in the territory over which Spain by the present treaty relinquishes or cedes her sovereignty." But as the territories in question were Cuba, Porto Rico, and the Philippines, and the subjects included natives of Spain as well as natives of these islands, a discrimination was expressly drawn whereby subjects other than natives of Spain (the peninsula being taken to include the Balearic and Canary Islands[1]) were excluded from the provision. That is, Spanish subjects born elsewhere than in Spain, the Balearic Islands, and the Canary Islands became American subjects (not necessarily citizens) *pleno jure* by the very fact of annexation. The Treaty of Vienna, 1866 (Art. XIV), provides for "inhabitants or natives of the territory ceded." The Treaty of Zurich, 1859 (Art. XII), introduces the more definite expression—"subjects domiciled on the territory ceded." But it is doubtful whether the contracting parties in the case of earlier treaties intended to make a sharp distinction between the word "domiciled," which has a precise legal significance, and the words "residing" or "inhabiting." There can be scarcely any ambiguity in the use of the former word—that is, when used as a term of law; but in the case of the latter, uncertainty arises from the fact that the treaties using such words rarely specify whether the provision applies to persons residing in or inhabiting the territory at the moment the cession comes into effect, or to the regular, settled inhabitants present or not at the time, or to purely temporary inhabitants.

Certain difficulties arose in the Franco-German adjustment of this question of denationalization. The Preliminaries of Versailles, February 26, 1871, offered no solution at all; Art. V stated, in vague terms, that the commercial interests and civil rights of the "inhabitants" of the ceded territories would be regulated as favourably as possible in the definitive treaty. Probably—though it is not certain from the *prima facie* interpretation of the word "inhabitants"—the

Difficulties in the Franco-German settlement.

[1] Mr. Hay, Secretary of State, to the Spanish minister, November 27, 1899; Moore, *Digest*, vol. iii. p. 321.

principle of domicile was intended to be adopted as the governing factor. But the Treaty of Frankfort,[1] May 10, 1871 (Art. II), introduced a further qualification by the employment of the more precise words, "French subjects, natives of the ceded territory, actually domiciled on that territory"; that is, subject to option, only those would be denationalized who answered to the tests both of birth and domicile. This is one of the least rigorous forms of denationalization, since—if terms of logic may be used—the connotation being made large the denotation becomes small. In the subsequent negotiations (at the conference of November 28, 1871) there was a difference of opinion between the French and the German representatives with regard to the meaning of the word "natives"—the French term was "originaires," the German being "herstammend." The French negotiators maintained that these terms applied to persons born in Alsace-Lorraine of parents who were themselves born there; but the German negotiators held that they referred to all persons born there, and this view was adopted.[2] Thus under the definitive treaty only domiciled natives of Alsace-Lorraine were to become German subjects if they failed to exercise their option in favour of French allegiance. An encroachment was, however, made on this rule by the additional convention signed at Frankfort, December 11, 1871, whereby (Art. I) natives not domiciled in Europe would also lose their French nationality, in default of option. Finally, to these two classes of persons the circular of March 16, 1872, issued by the "superior president" of Alsace-Lorraine, added a third, viz. those who though not born in the provinces were domiciled there on March 2, 1871 (the date of the formal transfer of sovereignty, i.e. the date on which the ratifications of the Preliminaries of Versailles were exchanged), unless they emigrated within a certain time. The stringent conditions insisted on by Germany practically deprived a good many Alsatians and Lorrainers from exercising the option, and so unduly interfered with their nationality. It was undoubtedly an illegitimate proceeding to insist on making regulations contrary to both the spirit and the letter of the definitive treaty. What is the use of entering into a definitive treaty at all if the stronger party is to play fast and loose with it? We may quote, in this respect, the forcible words of a French writer to whom we have already referred: "La conquête des individus et des familles apparaissait avec un caractère de gravité tragique qu'on ne lui avait pas reconnu jusqu'alors. Que l'Allemagne préoccupée de sa defense prît du terrain à la France, on

[1] Cf. May, *Le traité de Francfort*, pp. 141 *seq.*; Cogordan, *La nationalité*, etc., pp. 358–396.

[2] Villefort, *Recueil*, vol. i. p. 185; De Clercq, *Recueil*, vol. x. p. 528.

pouvait l'admettre. C'était la pénalité habituelle des luttes entre nations, la règle du triste jeu de la guerre. Mais les victorieux ne s'étaient pas arrêtés là. Avec toutes les terres, il leur avait fallu toutes les personnes. Par une série de manœuvres captieuses, d'interprétations arbitraires, sans souci de l'accord primitivement écrit dans le traité de paix, ils avaient poursuivi partout, comme jadis on faisait des serfs, ceux que le hasard de la naissance ou de l'habitation avait faits leurs hommes. D'être né en pays alsacien-lorrain ou d'y être résident au moment de la conquête était comme une marque qui autorisait la revendication de l'Allemagne. Telle était l'œuvre d'une diplomatie insatiable et d'une administration qui usurpait le rôle de la diplomatie pour pousser plus avant la conquête. Non contente d'empiéter sur un domaine qui n'était pas le sien, cette administration réussissait par ses exigences intolérantes à rendre l'option presque impossible pour une foule d'Alsaciens-Lorrains."[1]

Treaties of Constantinople, 1913; Athens, 1913.

The Treaty of Constantinople, 1913 (Art. VII), provided for the denationalization of only the domiciled natives of the territories ceded by Turkey to Bulgaria, subject to the right of option. Under the Treaty of Athens, 1913 (Art. IV), "persons domiciled" in the Ottoman territories passing under the dominion of Greece were to become Greek subjects, in default of option. In the course of the negotiations prior to the conclusion of the treaty the Sublime Porte, desirous of minimizing the number of subjects to be lost by the cession, contended that the rule should apply only to domiciled natives, as being more in harmony with modern conceptions. On the other hand, the Greek Government emphasized that the annexation of the territory in question was in conformity with the wish of its population in general, so that the rule of denationalization should apply to the domiciled inhabitants at large.

Married women and minors.

With regard to the position of married women and minors, nearly all the treaties are silent; and not infrequently disputes have arisen owing to the failure to make provision for them. Having regard to the general principle that the nationality of a wife is that of her husband, it would be either supererogatory or impolitic to call upon each of them to exercise option separately; the wife must abide by the choice or the default of her husband. In the case of minors, a reasonable solution is to make the period of option begin to run from the date of their attaining majority. Such a rule was adopted in the protocol of October 31, 1877, annexed to the Treaty of Paris, August 10, 1877, which effected the friendly cession of the island of St. Bartholomew (Antilles) by Sweden to

[1] May, *Le traité de Francfort*, p. 161.

France. In the annexation of Alsace-Lorraine Germany did not allow either married women or minors a separate option. The treaty of peace signed at Vienna, October 30, 1864, between Austria and Prussia on the one side and Denmark on the other, provided (Art. XIX) that the domiciled subjects on the ceded territories were to be allowed six years in which to withdraw and remove their possessions, after a declaration before the competent authority. Different constructions were placed on this article by the German and Danish Governments. The former held the sons of those who had opted for Danish nationality to be Danish; the latter regarded them as Prussians if they were not born in Danish territory. The result was that there were some 10,000 persons without a recognized nationality, who were liable to be expelled by Germany at her discretion. The difficulty was settled by the treaty of January 11, 1907, between Germany and Denmark, whereby Prussian nationality was conferred on such children of those who had opted as were then without nationality, provided they made an application and were domiciled on Prussian territory. Denmark, on her part, agreed to allow those who had not thus become Prussian subjects to reside freely within her territory. Under the Treaty of Constantinople, 1913 (Art. VII), between Turkey and Bulgaria, and the Treaty of Athens, 1913 (Art. IV), between Turkey and Greece, minors were allowed to exercise the option within the specified period commencing on the date of their reaching majority. Married women were not specially provided for by these treaties, as the classes designated "domiciled natives" and "domiciled persons" were deemed to apply equally to them.

Period of option.

Next, as to the period within which the option may be exercised. It varies considerably in different treaties. Thus it is six years in the treaties of Vienna, October 14, 1809, between France and Austria (Art. X); Paris, May 30, 1814, and November 20, 1815, between the Allied Powers and France (Art. XVII and Art. VII respectively); Vienna, October 30, 1864, between Austria, Prussia, and Denmark (Art. XIX). A delay of four years is allowed in the Treaty of Constantinople, 1913 (Art. VII). Three years: the Bloemfontein Convention, 1854; the treaties of Paris, 1856 (Art. XXI); Constantinople, 1879 (Art. VII); Constantinople, 1897 (Art. VII); Athens, 1913 (Art. IV), but Protocol No. 1 appended to the treaty provided that natives of the ceded territories who were domiciled outside the Ottoman Empire were to have a period of six months within which to decide in favour of Greek nationality. In the Treaty of Shimonoseki, 1895 (Art. V), an interval of two years is stipulated. In the following treaties it is one year, subject to the exceptions stated: Zurich, 1859 (Art. XII), but two years for natives of the ceded territory who were outside the ceding State; Turin, 1860, between France and Sardinia (Art. VI); Paris, 1861, as to the union of Mentone and Roccabruna to France (Art. VII); Vienna, 1866 (Art. XIV), but two years for the subjects, natives of the ceded territory of Lombardy, who were outside the Austrian monarchy on the date of the exchange of ratifications; Frankfort, 1871 (Art. II), an additional year being allowed by Art. I of the convention of December 11, 1871, for natives of Alsace-Lorraine resident outside Europe; Paris, 1898 (Art. IX), but by a protocol signed at Washington, March 29, 1900, the period was extended for six months in the case of the Philippines (but not for Cuba and Porto Rico), at the request of the Spanish minister, who pointed out that no adequate machinery existed there for recording the declarations of Spanish subjects—though those who were shown to have had an opportunity to make the declaration during the originally specified year were excepted from the extension.[1]

Mode of exercising the option.

Finally, as to the modes of exercising the option. In the first place, a personal declaration of adhesion to the old nationality is usually required to be made before a competent authority as prescribed, as well as registration at the diplomatic or consular chancelleries. Thus Art. VII of the Treaty of Constantinople, 1913, provided that domiciled natives of the Ottoman territories ceded to Bulgaria were to become Bulgarian subjects, but that for a period of four years they might declare, where they were, in favour of Ottoman nationality "by a simple declaration to the local Bulgarian authorities and registration at the Imperial Ottoman consulates." If the declaration was made abroad it was to be delivered to the chancelleries of the Bulgarian consulates and registered by the Ottoman consulates. The option pertained to the individual and was not obligatory for the Ottoman Government. Under the Treaty of Paris, 1898, the declaration had to be made before a court of record. In some cases treaties do not mention either option or declaration, but take the fact of emigration to be sufficient; they simply state that certain classes of persons have a given length of time in which to remove from the ceded territory, and in default will be considered subjects of the cessionary State—e.g. the Treaty of Utrecht, 1713; the Treaty of Paris, 1815; the Treaty of Constantinople, 1879; the Treaty of Shimonoseki, 1895. Many treaties impose the obligation to emigrate on those who opt for their old allegiance when they make the declaration required; that is, both the *animus* and the

[1] *Foreign Relations of the United States*, 1899, pp. 715 *seq.*; Moore, *Digest*, vol. iii. pp. 321–322.

factum are insisted on. The question arises here, When may the emigrant return without being invested with the new nationality? He ought certainly to be allowed to do so after the period for option has expired, if he can prove that he has established his domicile elsewhere. But the solution depends on the particular circumstances connected with the settlement of the ceded territory and the policy of the acquiring State. In the case of Alsace-Lorraine the German authorities annulled considerably more than half of the number of options on the ground of ineffective transfer of domicile; and they regarded as void the acts of declaration and emigration of those who afterwards returned to the ceded lands, despite the fact that they had established their permanent homes elsewhere. Furthermore, by a decree of the Statthalter of Alsace-Lorraine, August 28, 1884, Alsace-Lorrainers who had duly opted for French nationality were required to naturalize themselves as Germans if they wished to return to their former country; failing which, they were liable to expulsion.

Some treaties, though stipulating emigration, allow the emigrant to retain his landed property in the ceded territory: e.g. the treaties of Zurich, 1859; Vienna, 1866; Frankfort, 1871; Constantinople, 1897; Constantinople, 1913; Athens, 1913. Other treaties, more stringent, require both emigration and the sale of immovables, though, invariably, no export duties are levied on the property and proceeds of the sale taken away: e.g. the treaties of Paris, 1815; Constantinople, 1879; Shimonoseki, 1895; Portsmouth, 1905. The most liberal regulations in regard to the system of option require merely a declaration, without imposing the obligation either to remove or to dispose of property. Such regulations are found more frequently in friendly cessions or exchanges of territory: e.g. the treaty of 1848, relative to the cession of California to the United States; the Anglo-French convention of April 8, 1904, with regard to the part of Gambia and the islands of Los ceded to France (Arts. V, VI, VII); the protocol of February 26, 1909, as to the cession to Austria of Bosnia and Herzegovina—but they are also found in some instances of cessions demanded in treaties of peace: e.g. the Treaty of Paris, 1898, relative to the Spanish possessions relinquished or ceded to the United States; the Treaty of Portsmouth, 1905, relative to the cession of the south of Sakhalin to Japan, though the following proviso was added (Art. X): "Japan shall have full liberty to withdraw the right of residence or to deport from such territory any inhabitants who labour under political or administrative disability. She engages, however, that the proprietary rights of such inhabitants shall be fully respected."

CHAPTER XII

EFFECT OF CESSION (*Continued*)

STATE SUCCESSION: TREATIES—PUBLIC LAW AND ADMINISTRATION

Treaties: between cessionary and ceded State; between ceding State and third parties; between cessionary and third parties; relating to the annexed territory; exception to rule of dissolution—Public law and administration: practice of States; effect of public law and policy of annexing State; sometimes law of ceded territory continued; revenue laws; official language of the acquired territory; religion; officials; armed forces; the courts of law, judicial proceedings pending, untried offenders.

It has already been pointed out in an early chapter[1] that with regard to the question of State succession as appertaining to treaties,[2] there are no settled rules of international law, and there is neither uniformity in international practice nor unanimity in juristic opinion. Various problems arise, inasmuch as several parties are affected by the transference or cancellation, as the case may be, of treaty rights and obligations consequent on the cession of an entire State or a portion of its territory. There are first the transferor, secondly the transferee, thirdly the territory transferred, fourthly other parties which are bound by treaties to one or more of these. Accordingly, the questions necessary to answer relate to the following classes of treaties: those of the annexed State with third States, or those involving the annexed territory as between the ceding State and third States, those of the ceding State with third States involving other matters, those of the cessionary with other States, or with the ceded State, or with the ceding State. The position of treaties in general between the cessionary and the ceding State, in the case where they were parties to a forced cession following war between them, has already been considered in our examination of the effect of war on treaties.[3] It is beyond the scope of the present work to discuss these controverted matters in detail; only a few principles can be pointed out

[1] See *supra*, p. 34.
[2] Cf. Keith, *op. cit.*, pp. 17–26.
[3] See *supra*, pp. 250 *seq.*

briefly, and two or three examples of international practice given by way of illustration.

Treaties between cessionary and ceded State.

If the territory ceded constitutes an entire State, then it is obvious that all treaties between the cessionary and the ceded State necessarily cease to exist as from the date of annexation, since the international personality of one of the contracting parties disappears. Thus the Transvaal Supreme Court held that the conventions of 1881 and 1884, whereby certain privileges were conferred on the natives of the late South African Republic, were abrogated by the subsequent annexation.[1]

Treaties of ceding State with third parties.

Where a State loses a portion of its territory, by cession or by any other form of dismemberment, it is not thereby liberated from its conventional engagements with other States; for it retains its international personality. The loss of territory may, no doubt, have an important effect on its political and economic conditions; but a change of this kind does not of necessity operate to dissolve its treaties with third Powers; any more than an individual's loss of a part of his estate releases him from his ordinary obligations. But treaties whose object was so closely connected with the lost territory that it becomes impossible to perform them expire, on the ground that the essential subject-matter of the agreement ceases to exist as between the contracting parties—e.g. treaties for river navigation, servitudes, boundary regulation, and the like. The clause "rebus sic stantibus," express or tacit, may only be interpreted to apply to such a radical change of circumstances as alters entirely the basis of the relationships between the parties.

Treaties of cessionary with third parties.

Similarly, the cessionary State, despite the addition to its dominions, remains bound by its treaties with third parties, and may not advance the territorial change as a ground for withdrawing from its treaty obligations.

Treaties relating to the annexed territory.

In the case of the annexation of a State, its juridical individuality is lost, and the treaties previously concluded by it with other Powers fall to the ground. The annexed part of a State also ceases to be subject to the treaties of the ceding State. Thus Algiers having been annexed by France in 1831, the United States held her treaties with the former to be dissolved; likewise her treaties with the Two Sicilies on their incorporation into Italy, 1860; and with Hanover and Nassau when the latter were annexed to Prussia, 1866. In 1860 Sardinia proclaimed that the treaties of the annexed State of Lombardy were abrogated; and in 1867 Holland declared

[1] *Tsewu* v. *Registrar of Deeds* (1905), Transv. Sup. Ct. Rep. 130.

that her extradition treaty with Hanover was cancelled through the latter's annexation to Prussia. In subsequent cases treaties were considered to be dissolved in like circumstances: those relating to Madagascar, when it was annexed to France, 1896; to the Spanish possessions, when relinquished or ceded by Spain, 1898; to the Transvaal and Orange River Colony, when these countries were acquired by Great Britain, 1901.

At the same time the conventions of the annexing State apply, and should be extended *pleno jure*, to the annexed State or territory.

Extension of cessionary's treaties to ceded territory.

Thus in 1815, when Piedmont acquired the Duchy of Genoa, the treaties that bound the former were considered binding also on the latter. The Treaty of Zurich, 1859, whereby Austria ceded Lombardy to France, which, by the same act, ceded it to Sardinia, declared that the conventions concluded by the latter were extended to the acquired territory. In 1860 the treaties of Sardinia replaced those of the annexed States—Parma, Modena, Romagna, Tuscany, Naples, Umbria, the Marches, and Sicily. The treaties of France superseded those of Savoy, which was acquired in 1860. In 1866 the treaties of Prussia were substituted for those of Frankfort, Hesse, Nassau, and Hanover; and in 1871 German treaties were applied to Alsace-Lorraine. By the Treaty of Paris, 1898, Spain ceded to the United States Porto Rico and the Philippines, and relinquished her sovereignty over Cuba; accordingly the treaties of the United States were extended to the former islands, whilst Cuba, not having been annexed, entered into treaties of its own. After the annexation of the Transvaal and the Orange River Colony their treaties were superseded by those of Great Britain. On the cession of the southern half of Sakhalin, by the Treaty of Portsmouth, 1905, the Russian treaties relating to the territory were superseded by those of Japan. When Korea was annexed to Japan by the treaty of August 22, 1910, the Japanese Government issued a declaration (August 29), of which Rule 1 was as follows: "Treaties hitherto concluded by Korea with foreign Powers ceasing to be operative, Japan's existing treaties will, so far as practicable, be applied to Korea." But this rule of the extension of the acquiring State's conventions to the territories acquired is by no means an invariable one. Whether it is to be applied or not in the case of this or that class of treaties depends on the public policy of the cessionary State, on the nature of the situation with regard to third Powers as established by the annexation, and on considerations of reciprocity. In other words, the implied condition "rebus sic stantibus" may be resorted to if it be clearly and reasonably applicable to a given case. Some treaties, for instance (viz. respecting alliances, subsidies, and commercial relationships), are entered into by the contracting parties with the understanding, express or tacit, that certain conditions then existing will continue without any substantial modification, e.g. the extent of their territory, the number of their population, the amount of their natural produce, etc. Such treaties, therefore, will not necessarily be extended when these conditions have been very much altered by the acquisition of new territory. On the other hand, other treaties appertain to the political, administrative, and judicial organization of the contracting States, and for the most part involve matters of comity and private international law, e.g. execution of judgments, patents, copyright, extradition, etc. These treaties may well be extended at once to the territory acquired if its government resembles, or is to be immediately assimilated to, that of the acquiring State.

Exception to dissolution of treaties.

To the general rule that the treaties relating to an annexed State or part of a State are dissolved by the fact of annexation there is an important exception. Though treaties of alliance, subsidy, guarantee, and commerce do not pass over to the cessionary, in default of stipulation to the contrary (a proviso that is, of course, applicable throughout the whole range of contractual transactions), it may be said that transitory or dispositive treaties, servitudes, and those that particularly and directly concern the ceded territory (e.g. relative to fluvial navigation, the embankment of boundary rivers, regulation of boundaries, railway communication, main roads, etc.) devolve normally, and on principle should devolve, on the cessionary. However, the recognition of even this class of treaties on the part of the acquiring State is due less to legal obligation—for there is no definite rule of international law on the subject—than to considerations of convenience and advantage.

PUBLIC LAW AND ADMINISTRATION.

It has already been pointed out, in our examination of the effects of conquest and subjugation,[1] that the annexing sovereign acquires full legislative, administrative, and judicial authority over the territory annexed. (What applies to annexation consequent on subjugation applies also to annexation resulting from a friendly cession or a forced cession in a treaty of peace, subject, of course, in the latter cases to express treaty stipulations.) The assumption of sovereignty necessarily implies the assumption of all rights and privileges comprised therein. Hence the constitution and the laws of the ceding Government do not go with the ceded lands as inseparable concomitants.[2] Such laws as possess a political character and concern the

[1] See *supra*, p. 35. [2] Cf. *Pollard* v. *Hagan* (1845), 3 Howard, 212, 225.

prerogatives of the ceding sovereign cease to have any validity in the transferred territory as soon as the cession has been effected. To quote the words of a judgment in an American case: "Those laws of the former Government which have for their object a certain governmental policy, of which character are laws for the disposition of the public domain and the granting of quasi-public franchises, rights, and privileges to private individuals or corporations, ceased to have any force or effect after the sovereignty of the former Government ceased."[1] If conditions attached to a grant of land by a prior sovereign are inconsistent with the policy of the acquiring Power, they will not be enforced by the latter after the annexation of the territory containing the land granted.[2] Similarly, the acquiring Power need not recognize any rights of sovereignty enjoyed by individuals or corporations, e.g. the possession of monopolies, rights to dispose of offices, and other privileges and exemptions conferred by the former sovereign or Government in virtue of his or its prerogative. All such rights naturally pass, with the acquisition of the full sovereignty, into the hands of the annexing sovereign or Government. No compensation therefor is legally due, though it is frequently granted; Germany, for example, did so in 1872 in the case of those who held saleable appointments in the judicial administration of Alsace-Lorraine. Moreover, the political rights, the constitutional and the public law of the annexing State extend to the new territory, without the necessity for special legislation or formal promulgation.

Practice of States.

The practice of States is in accordance with these doctrines. Thus when California was annexed by the United States the American rule at once superseded the Mexican, and the authority of Mexican officials to alienate the public domain at the same time fell to the ground.[3] In the case of the cession of Alsace-Lorraine, 1871, a German law of June 9, 1871, fixed January 1, 1873, as the date of the introduction into the ceded provinces of the Imperial administration, and in the meantime placed the legislative authority into the hands of the Emperor, subject to the assent of the Bundesrath, and, if charges were to be imposed on the Empire, of the Reichstag also. In 1877 and 1886 Great Britain altered the public and administrative law in the Transvaal and in Upper Burma respectively. When Madagascar was subjected to French sovereignty in 1896, the United States Government recognized that its ex-territorial rights in that island and the judicial powers of its consul dependent

[1] *Harcourt* v. *Gaillard* (1827), 12 Wheaton, 523, cited by the American Attorney-General, September 9 and November 21, 1899: *Opinions of the U.S. Attorneys-General*, vol. xxii. pp. 574, 577, 627, 631; Moore, *Digest*, vol. i. p. 304.

[2] Cf. *U.S.* v. *Vaca et al.* (1855), 18 Howard, 556.

[3] *Alexander* v. *Roulet* (1871), 13 Wallace, 386.

thereon terminated *pari passu* with the termination of the local authority.[1] After the cession of Porto Rico by Spain under the Treaty of Paris, 1898, the authority of the Spanish governor-general and of all other officers exercising Royal prerogatives delegated to them ceased; and the powers given them by the Royal Decree of 1878, respecting the establishment of corporations, did not pass to the United States Government.[2] Under the Peace of Vereeniging, 1902, the late South African Republic and Orange Free State surrendered to Great Britain, which subsequently introduced a new system of government.

Whether the whole or only a part of the administrative, legislative, and judicial system of the annexing State is to be applied to the annexed territory is a question to be determined only by the public law and policy of the former, and does not concern international law.

Effect of public law and policy of annexing State.

In the exercise by the annexing State of the powers of municipal government, "it may change or modify the form or constitutions of the municipal establishment, and may provide the method, terms, and conditions under which internal improvements may be carried on, or forbid them to be carried on, although inchoate or even completed contracts therefor have previously been entered into."[3]

Changes in municipal law.

Until the municipal laws of the acquired territory relative to its internal organization are changed by the acquiring State they remain in force, not, indeed, by reason of the ceding Government's authority, since it no longer exists there, nor owing to the intrinsic virtue or applicability of those laws, but simply because of the acquiescence of the new sovereign. Sometimes the annexing State confirms certain laws prevailing in the acquired territory, either for a specified length of time or for indefinite duration. Thus, in the case of the South African War, the British military authorities issued a number of proclamations (some of which, however, appeared before the annexation of the States to which they referred had been perfected)[4] whereby the postal and telegraphic services under the old laws were resumed, the customs regulations maintained, the local criminal law recognized, and the Roman-Dutch law as the common law of the Transvaal, as well as the existing statute law of the Transvaal, was confirmed.

[1] Mr. Olney, Secretary of State, to Mr. Eustis, ambassador to France, December 10, 1896: *U.S. Foreign Relations* (1897), pp. 152, 153; Moore, *Digest*, vol. i. p. 308.

[2] C. E. Magoon, *Reports on the Law of Civil Government under Military Occupation* (Washington, 1902), p. 490; Moore, *Digest*, vol. i. p. 307.

[3] *Opinions of U.S. Attorneys-General* (July 10, 1899), vol. xxii. p. 526.

[4] See *supra*, Part I, chap iii. pp. 22 *seq.*

Sometimes, too, stipulations are inserted in treaties of cession providing for the continuance of certain portions of the annexed territory's legislative system, or fixing a delay at the expiration of which the laws of the cessionary State are to be applied. In some cases the cessionary State on its own initiative grants such a delay. Thus when Nice and Savoy were united to France by the treaty of 1860 a decree of the French Government, issued June 12, 1860, fixed January 1, 1861, as the date on which French law was to be extended to the new possessions. On the annexation of Korea the Japanese Government issued a declaration, August 29, 1910, agreeing to maintain for ten years the existing regulations respecting import and export duties, tonnage dues, and navigation, independently of any conventional engagements formerly applicable to these matters.[1]

Sometimes the law of the ceded territory continued.

The annexing State is entitled to introduce into annexed territory its own or any other revenue laws; and it may lay down the conditions under which commercial intercourse is to be carried on with it by other countries.[2] If the annexation is the result of subjugation, the military authorities occupying the territory may themselves make rules and regulations with regard to foreign trade, and may impose on imports whatever duties they think fit.[3] In the case of the Philippine Islands ceded by Spain the Government set up there by the President of the United States regulated commerce with the archipelago and imposed import and export duties.[4]

Revenue laws.

Whether an annexed country ceases to be a foreign country within the meaning of the annexing State's tariff laws depends on the latter's public law and policy. On principle an annexed territory should be regarded, for such purposes, as part of the acquiring State. In a case that came before the United States Supreme Court it was decided—two judges dissenting—that on the cession of Porto Rico it became in every respect American territory, and therefore was no longer a foreign country within the sense of the United States tariff laws.[5]

[1] E. Hertslet, *Collection of Treaties*, vol. xxvi (1913), p. 93.

[2] Cf. *Cross* v. *Harrison* (1853), 16 Howard, 164.

[3] Cf. *Opinions of U.S. Attorneys-General* (1899), vol. xxii. p. 560.

[4] Magoon, *Reports*, etc., p. 210.

[5] *De Lima* v. *Bidwell* (1901), 182 U.S. Rep. 1. Cf. *Dooley* v. *U.S.* (1901), 182 U.S. Rep. 222; *Goetze* v. *U.S.* (1901), 182 U.S. Rep. 221; *Downes* v. *Bidwell* (1901), 182 U.S. Rep. 244; *The Fourteen Diamond Rings Case* (1901), 183 U.S. Rep. 176. There has been a great deal of discussion in the United States on the questions involved in the "insular cases." In every case the decision pronounced was that of a bare majority of the judges constituting the court. See Moore, *Digest*, vol. i. p. 331, for numerous references.

Official language.

The official language of the annexed country, including that used in the courts of law, may be changed by the annexing Government. The latter may, if it thinks fit and if the circumstances are appropriate, preserve the old language both for use in legal proceedings and for purposes of public education. Thus Art. V of the Peace of Vereeniging, May 31, 1902, provided that the Dutch language would be taught in public schools in the Transvaal and the Orange River Colony if the children's parents desired it, and would be allowed in courts of law when necessary for the better and more effectual administration of justice.

Religion.

Whether the language be interfered with or not, there is no doubt nowadays that it is incumbent on the acquiring sovereign to allow to the inhabitants of the annexed territory the free exercise of their religion, when it is not incompatible with good order and the fundamental dictates of morality. The obligation is not, of course, a legal one; but its sanction is rooted more deeply than that of positive enactments. In former times stipulations in treaties for the protection of religion were not infrequent; and even in our own day we find instances. Thus in the Transvaal conventions of 1881 and 1884 provisions were inserted in the interests of religious freedom. Art. X of the Treaty of Paris, 1898, declared that the inhabitants of the territories over which Spain relinquished or ceded her sovereignty (Cuba, Porto Rico, the Philippines) would be secured by the United States Government in the free exercise of their religion. Similarly, by Art. IX of the Treaty of Constantinople, 1913, the Moslem inhabitants on the territories ceded by Turkey to Bulgaria (indeed, on all Bulgarian territories) were to enjoy not only the same civil and political rights equally with subjects of Bulgarian origin, but also liberty of conscience and liberty and outward practice of religion; and their customs were to be respected. The name of the Sultan, as Caliph, was to continue to be pronounced in the public prayers of Moslems; and Moslem communities, their hierarchical organization, and their endowments were to be respected. Subject to express provision to the contrary, however, the annexing Government is, by reason of its sovereignty, entitled to modify the existing ecclesiastical establishments in conformity with its own public policy. Sometimes stipulations are inserted in treaties for the purpose of ensuring the unrestricted disposition of property belonging to those religious societies whose maintenance might not be authorized—e.g. in the cession of Lombardy by Austria, Treaty of Zurich, 1859 (Art. XVI). It may also consider as dissolved any concordats that formerly bound the annexed territory. In the case of the cession of Alsace-Lorraine, Germany held the ecclesiastical conventions between France and the Pope relative to these provinces to have been *ipso facto* cancelled; but after withdrawing the various religious communities there from the authority of their former French heads (Art. VI of the Treaty of Frankfort) she agreed (under Art. IX of the additional convention of December 11, 1871) to allow the bishops of the dioceses intersected by the new frontier to preserve their spiritual authority over the populations until the conclusion of special arrangements for regulating the diocesan circumscriptions of the ceded territories.

Officials.

The new sovereign may dismiss all the officers who had been invested by the former Government with the authority to preserve peace and order. Until they are replaced they may continue to exercise their powers, in conformity with the previous regulations, if no others have been made by the succeeding Government. The fact that the agents of the latter have not been appointed instead does not, of course, imply that those officers, though continuing to act in the old way, retain their authority by virtue of the former sovereignty.[1] Nor is the annexing State bound to take over any other classes of officials. In the case of British annexations—e.g. Upper Burma in 1886, the Transvaal and the Orange River Colony in 1901—some of the old officials were deprived of their offices, and some were retained when their retention was not inconsistent either with the fulfilment of their new duties or with the new régime. Under Art. II of the additional convention signed at Frankfort, December 11, 1871, Germany pledged herself to protect the former rights of those officials whose appointments might be confirmed by her. By the Treaty of Vienna, 1866, Austria ceded to Italy the Lombardo-Venetian Kingdom, and under Art. XV it was agreed that the civil servants born in the ceded territory should have the choice either of remaining in the service of Austria or of entering that of Italy; in case of the latter the Italian Government was to place them in positions analogous to those they occupied, or allot them pensions, the amount of which was to be fixed according to the Austrian regulations.

Armed forces.

There is no State succession with regard to the military and naval forces belonging to the annexed territory. As soon as the annexation is effected they necessarily lose their military status if they are withdrawn from the sovereignty of their former Government. Where option is permitted to be exercised, they are entitled, equally with the civilian inhabitants, to opt for the old or the new nationality. In the eyes of the annexing

[1] Cf. *U.S.* v. *Reynes* (1850), 9 Howard, 127; *Davis* v. *Police Jury of Concordia* (1850), 9 Howard, 280.

State they are civilians, and become soldiers again there only when they have opted for the new nationality and have entered the military service of their new sovereign in accordance with the local law. Nor may the ceding State retain in its service such soldiers as belong to the ceded lands, unless they, like others, have elected to preserve their old nationality and to remain in the service of the ceding sovereign. These conclusions, based on fundamental principles, may, however, be modified by express agreement between the contracting parties, subject to the consent of the soldiers concerned, if any change is to be made in their former position. By the Treaty of Zurich, 1859, whereby Austria ceded Lombardy, it was provided (Art. XIII) that the Lombard subjects in the Austrian army should be immediately discharged from military service and sent back to their homes, and that those who declared their wish to remain in the Austrian service should not on that account be disturbed either in person or property. Similar provisions were made in the Treaty of Vienna, 1866, whereby Austria ceded to Italy the Lombardo-Venetian Kingdom (Arts. XV, XVI). In the cession of Alsace-Lorraine, 1871, French soldiers were allowed to exercise option, and were not taken over as such by the German Government. Under British practice, too—e.g. in the case of the Transvaal, 1877, Upper Burma, 1886, the late Republics of South Africa, 1901—no claim is made, whether the territory be annexed by cession or subjugation, that the British Government succeeds to the rights of the ceding or ousted Government in regard to the military forces of the territory.

THE COURTS OF LAW.

As soon as a territory is annexed the courts of law therein lose their jurisdiction. If they are allowed to continue their work, it is not by reason of their inherent competence as conferred by the former Government, but simply through the consent, express or tacit, of the acquiring Government. The courts of the latter are not necessarily bound by the judgments pronounced in those of the predecessor.[1] As a rule they would be respected, if they had been duly and lawfully delivered, with the exception of those whose effects were antagonistic to the public policy of the annexing State.

Judicial proceedings pending.

In the case of judicial proceedings pending on the date of the annexation it would be inconvenient—and perhaps unjust—to disregard the legal steps that had taken place before the annexation, if they were not prejudicial to the public interests of the successor. In civil litigation acts of procedure effected before the transfer have already

[1] See the references cited *supra*, p. 35, n. 2.

created for the interested parties certain rights. They could validly interrupt the operation of rules of prescription, and they might well furnish proof of admissions that had been made.[1] Where a decision has been pronounced but not yet executed on the date of annexation, subject to the proviso just mentioned, it cannot be annulled by the annexing State, which, rather, should provide for its enforcement according to its own regulations and methods. But a difficulty arises when the party against whom the decision was given feels that justice has not been done and has good grounds for an appeal. Problems of this kind may then be settled by the ordinary rules of private international law. Not infrequently, however, they are provided for by express stipulations in the treaty of cession, or by the public declarations of the annexing Government. Thus by Art. III of the additional convention signed at Frankfort, December 11, 1871, provision was made for the definitive character of judgments, pleas as to lack of jurisdiction, the principle of *lex fori*, and appeal. The article says that in order to obviate difficulties, the contracting parties agree:

"(1) Que tout jugement prononcé par les tribunaux français entre citoyens français, et ayant acquis l'autorité de la chose jugée avant le 20 mai 1871, sera considéré comme définitif et exécutoire de plein droit dans les territoires cédés;

(2) Qu'aucune exception d'incompétence, à raison du changement des frontières respectives, ne pourra être élevée contre les jugements d'un tribunal civil ou d'une cour d'appel français, rendus avant le 20 mai 1871 et qui seraient encore possibles d'appel ou de recours en cassation;

(3) Que la solution des procès engagés sur des matières non personnelles appartiendra au tribunal de la situation de l'objet litigieux;

(4) Que le tribunal du domicile du défendeur sera seul compétent pour vider les procès de première instance engagés sur des matières personnelles;

(5) Que le même principe sera appliqué aux procès vidés en première ou en seconde instance qui n'auraient pas encore acquis force de chose jugée, mais dont les pourvois d'appel ou les recours en cassation ne seraient interjetés que postérieurement au 20 mai 1871;

(6) Qu'en ce qui concerne la procédure d'appel et les pourvois en cassation régulièrement engagés avant le 20 mai 1871, ils seront vidés par les tribunaux qui s'en trouvent saisis, à moins que, par suite de la nouvelle démarcation des frontières respectives, les parties en cause ne se trouvent toutes deux soumises, en matières personnelles, à la compétence des tribunaux de l'autre État."[2]

[1] Bonfils, *Droit international public*, p. 188.

[2] De Clercq, *Recueil*, vol. x. pp. 532–533.

Similarly, Art. XII of the Treaty of Paris, 1898, stipulated, conformably to common law, that judgments delivered before the exchange of ratifications were to be considered final if not subject to appeal under Spanish law, and were to be carried out by the competent authority. Civil suits pending in any other court on that date were to be continued there or in any other court substituted for it. Criminal cases pending before the Supreme Court of Spain against subjects of the ceded territory were to remain under its jurisdiction till final judgment, which was to be executed by the competent authority of the place in which the case arose. Again, on the annexation of Korea by Japan, 1910, whereby the capitular régime in the annexed country was suppressed, the Japanese Government in its declaration of August 29, 1910 (Rule 1), nevertheless consented that the jurisdiction in respect of cases pending in a foreign consular court in Korea on the date of the annexation should remain in such court until final decision.[1]

Untried offenders.

In the absence of express provisions to the contrary, the annexing State is entitled, in the interests of public safety and good order, to try and punish offenders who have been remitted for trial and have not yet been tried. Questions of procedure and evidence are to be determined by the law of the successor. But if the act committed, being an offence under the superseded law of the territory, is not an offence under the new law, the person arrested ought to be liberated; and if not in custody, no proceedings should be taken against him. And it would follow, as a corollary, that if an offender was tried and convicted before the annexation, but the penalty imposed not yet inflicted, he should be released by the annexing Government if his act is not punishable under its own law. If, however, the act was punishable under its own law, but a different penalty in respect of severity was applicable, then the lighter punishment ought, in general, to be inflicted.

[1] Hertslet, *Collection of Treaties*, vol. xxvi. p. 93.

CHAPTER XIII

EFFECT OF CESSION (*Continued*)

STATE SUCCESSION: STATE PROPERTY—PUBLIC DEBTS—CONCESSIONS, ETC.—PRIVATE RIGHTS

Public property of the State: questions in the Spanish-American War; what is public property; charitable foundations, etc.; State archives—Private domain of the State: unpaid taxes, etc.; private property of the sovereign—Contractual obligations of the annexed territory: public debts, general, local; cases in which none of the general debt taken over; frequently, part of the general debt taken over; local debts regularly taken over—Concessions and contracts other than public debts: British practice; examples furnished by treaties—Other obligations: deposits; pensions; claims based on war losses —Private rights and private law.

PUBLIC PROPERTY OF THE STATE.

THE public domain of the acquired country—that is, the property exclusively used for the public service—passes over in its juridical condition to the annexing State, whether the annexation is due to cession or to subjugation. Such property includes shores, ports, harbours, navigable rivers, roads, fortifications, barracks, prisons, schools, and other public buildings belonging to the State. The property of the Crown—not of the sovereign or other head of the State in his private capacity—is assimilated to that of the State. This result follows necessarily from the fact of annexation, so that no express stipulation to that effect is necessary in any treaty that may be concluded by the parties concerned. Sometimes, however, mention is made of the State property as being included in the transferred territory to which it is attached. Thus under Art. II of the Treaty of Shimonoseki, 1895, China ceded to Japan certain territories, "together with all fortifications, arsenals, and public property thereon." Similarly, under Art. V of the Treaty of Portsmouth, 1905, Russia transferred to Japan the lease of Port Arthur, Ta-lien, and adjacent territory and territorial waters, "and all rights, privileges, and concessions connected with or forming part of such lease . . . and all public works and properties in the territory affected . . ."; and under Art. IX she ceded also the southern portion of the island of Sakhalin and all adjacent islands, "and public works and properties thereon."

Questions that arose in the American-Spanish negotiations.

The negotiations between the United States and Spain in 1898 in regard to this question of public property, as arising out of Spain's relinquishment of Cuba and cession of Porto Rico and the Philippines, are of special interest and deserve fuller attention. In pursuance of the provisions of the protocol of peace (Art. IV) signed at Washington, August 12, commissioners of both sides met at Havana and San Juan to carry out the details of the evacuation of those islands. As the surrender of the latter included all "immovable property" thereon belonging to the Spanish Government, the American commissioners were instructed to take over "all public buildings and grounds, forts, fortifications, arsenals, depots, docks, wharves, piers, and other fixed property heretofore belonging to Spain"; and they were further instructed as follows: "The small arms and accoutrements, batteries of field artillery, supply and baggage wagons, ambulances, and other impedimenta of the Spanish army in Cuba and the adjacent Spanish islands you will permit to be removed, if desired, by the representatives of Spain, provided such removal shall be effected within a reasonable time. The armament of forts, fortifications, and fixed batteries, being in the nature of immovable fixtures, will not be permitted to be taken, but will, in connection with the said forts, fortifications, and batteries, be taken over by you into the possession of the United States."[1] But the Spanish commissioners claimed that their troops should "carry with them their flags, arms, munitions, equipment, clothing, saddles, stores, artillery pieces of all kinds, with the mountings, sets of arms, and other accessories, as also all material of war and sanitation, the machines and stock on hand of the establishments of military industry, besides the records and documents of the military dependencies and army corps." To this claim the United States commissioners replied "that under the law movable things became immovable property when constructed or destined for the permanent use or service of immovable property. This is not only in accord with the civil law of Spain, but also with the common law. Under this rule we have claimed, and do now claim, that all the ordnance in fortifications or fixed batteries, of whatever character, kind, or condition—no matter from whence brought or what its origin may have been—all machinery attached to buildings used as arsenals, or military or naval construction repair shops, or navy-yards, and the shears on the docks in

[1] *U.S. Foreign Relations* (1898), pp. 910, 913; Moore, *Digest*, vol. i. p. 286.

Havana are immovable property, and that Spain has no right to dismount, or remove, or in any manner dispose of the same, or any part thereof." This opinion the Spanish commissioners refused to accept. They preferred to refer the question to their Government, and added that "they desired to state that they hold the same views as to the real estate and public buildings, the property of Spain in the island of Cuba."

On November 16, 1898, however, an agreement as to the evacuation was concluded, whereby it was provided that the Spanish troops should "carry with them their flags, small arms, with the ammunition thereto belonging, accoutrements, clothing, batteries of field artillery, siege guns not mounted in fixed batteries, and ammunition thereto belonging, horses, saddles, supply and baggage wagons, and their animals, ambulances, medical stores, subsistence stores, camp equipments, and records and archives of the various organizations of the Spanish forces, and of their respective bureaus." The commission decided that the floating steel dry dock at Havana should be considered as movable property belonging to Spain; and this the United States afterwards purchased.

As to other property, the agreement recited that there was an irreconcilable difference between the commissioners with respect to "the disposition of the public property of Spain in the island of Cuba and the adjacent Spanish islands, consisting (1) of artillery in fixed batteries and fortifications, the fixtures and other property thereto belonging, as heretofore inventoried"; (2) "of the machinery and fixtures and other property and material of war heretofore in dispute in the 'Maestranza,' in the 'Pirotecnia Militar,' and in the 'Arsenal' in Havana, and of other military and naval property of a fixed character in barracks, hospitals, quarters, and other buildings, and (3) of the real estate and public buildings on said islands belonging to or under the control of Spain"; and it stipulated that "in respect to said property, the *status quo ante* shall be preserved until existing differences concerning the disposition of said property shall have been finally settled by the proper authorities."

The question relating to the third class of property, viz. the real estate and buildings belonging to Spain in the ceded territories, was disposed of in the peace negotiations of Paris. On October 3, 1898, the American Peace Commission proposed that Spain should cede to the United States Cuba, Porto Rico, and other Spanish islands in the West Indies, and the island of Guam in the Ladrones; and this proposal was accompanied by a stipulation that the cession included "all right and claim to the public domain, lots and squares, vacant lands, public buildings, fortifications, and the armaments thereof, and barracks and other structures which are not private individual property," as well as the public archives. On October 7 the Spanish representatives put forth a counter-proposal undertaking to relinquish or cede "all the buildings, wharves, barracks, fortresses, establishments, public ways of communication, all other immovable property which according to law attaches to the public domain, and which so attaching belongs to the Crown of Spain," but stipulated that all immovable property "which under the civil law belongs to the State as patrimonial property, and all rights and property of whatsoever kind, which up to the ratification of the present treaty have been peacefully enjoyed and held in ownership by provinces, municipalities, public and private establishments, ecclesiastical and civil corporations, or any other collective bodies lawfully incorporated and having legal authority to acquire and hold property in the island of Cuba, and by private individuals, whatsoever their nationality, are therefore excluded from the above relinquishment and transfer."

To this negative clause the American commission objected on the following grounds: "So far as it affects the question of legal title it is unnecessary, since such title, if not held by Spain, would not pass to the United States by Spain's transfer of sovereignty. On the other hand, so far as it affects the question of sovereignty, it is illogical, since the sovereignty, which includes the right of eminent domain, would, if excepted from the relinquishment, remain with Spain. We should thus have the singular spectacle of Spain relinquishing her sovereignty over property belonging to the Crown, but retaining it over all other property."

The clause concerning "patrimonial property" was afterwards waived by the Spanish commissioners: "The State, under the Spanish laws, exercises all rights of ownership over the property declared by law to be public property, and it is plain that in this case the cession of the sovereignty carries with it the cession of all those rights. But the State in Spain can also, in the capacity of a body politic or corporation, acquire and hold real property by the same means, and through the same processes, as private persons can do under civil municipal law. This peculiar kind of property was the one referred to in the exception suggested by the Spanish commissioners. Notwithstanding this fact . . . the Spanish commissioners do hereby waive the said exception, and agree that the patrimonial property of the State be also included in the cession and transfer of the sovereignty of Spain."

An agreement was also reached, during the peace negotiations at Paris, in reference to the heavy guns and armaments in the Philippines, but not with regard to those in Cuba and Porto Rico. The protocol says: "The president of the Spanish commission and his colleagues maintained that the cession of the archipelago did not carry and could not carry with it anything except what was of a fixed nature; they explained the character of the siege artillery and heavy ordnance which the Americans claimed for themselves, and after some discussion to the end of determining precisely what each commission understood as portable and fixed material it was agreed that stands of colors, uncaptured war vessels, small arms, guns of all calibers, with their carriages and accessories, powder, ammunition, live stock, and materials and supplies of all kinds belonging to the land and naval forces shall remain the property of Spain; that pieces of heavy ordnance, exclusive of field artillery, in the fortifications, shall remain in their emplacements for the term of six months, to be reckoned from the ratification of the treaty; and that the United States might in the meantime purchase such material from Spain if a satisfactory agreement between the two Governments on the subject should be reached."[1] This agreement was embodied in Art. V of the definitive treaty of peace concluded on December 10, 1898. The United States Government held that under this article the Spanish guns and other war material captured by the navy at Cavite during the war were to be considered the property of Spain. The proposed distinction between the property rights belonging to the Crown of Spain and those belonging to the "public of Porto Rico" was not accepted by the United States; so that both alike went to the latter by the treaty of cession.[2]

What is public property.

Subject to stipulations to the contrary, the test as to what is and what is not public property, and therefore as to what may or may not be directly appropriated by the annexing State, depends on the law of the latter. In the application of this test any appropriation interfering with private rights is the result of an act of sovereignty, and not of the operation of the principle of succession. Usually individuals thereby deprived of their private rights receive compensation.

Public establishments in the nature of charitable foundations

[1] *Senate Documents of the United States*, 62, 55th Cong., 3rd sess., part ii. pp. 22, 28, 34, 90, 228–229; Moore, *Digest*, vol. i. pp. 287–289.

[2] *Opinions of the Attorneys-General of the United States*, vol. xxii. p. 544; Moore, *Digest*, p. 290.

pass over to the annexing State along with the particular territory to which they belong, subject, as a rule, to the payment of compensation to inhabitants of unannexed territory, whose needs were provided for by them equally with those of the inhabitants of the territory annexed.

Charitable foundations, etc.

A peculiar class of property in Moslem countries is that of vakoufs, involving mosques, colleges, schools, and other pious and charitable institutions. Where these are concerned in the cession of territories, special provisions are usually made—e.g. as between Greece and Turkey, in the Protocol of London, 1830, in the convention of 1881 (whereby Greece acquired Thessaly), in the Treaty of Athens, 1913 (Art. XII); as between Turkey and Bulgaria, in the Treaty of Constantinople, 1913 (Art. XII).

Vakoufs.

The State archives relating to the territory annexed pass with it to the annexing Government. If only part of a province or other political and administrative division is transferred, its archives go to the State that retains its capital, with the exception of such records as appertain exclusively to the part transferred; but in the former case the State that keeps the originals is obliged to furnish copies to the other. Documents concerning taxation go to the party entitled to collect the taxes in question; and those recording the services of officers go to the party whose subjects the officers remain.[1] When the treaty of cession is silent these rules will normally apply. But sometimes special stipulations are inserted in treaties. Thus in the Treaty of Zurich, 1859, whereby Austria ceded Lombardy, it was provided (Art. XV) that the archives containing the titles to property and documents regarding the administration of justice, which were applicable to the ceded country, were to be handed over to its Government. Similar clauses are found in the Treaty of Vienna, 1864 (Art. XX), respecting the cession by Denmark of Schleswig, Holstein, and Lauenburg to Prussia and Austria; the Treaty of Vienna, 1866 (Art. XVIII), under which Austria ceded to Italy the Lombardo-Venetian Kingdom (included therein are the political and historical documents of the old Venetian Republic). Art. III of the Treaty of Frankfort, 1871, required the French Government to deliver to Germany the archives, documents, or registers relating to the civil, military, and judicial administration of Alsace-Lorraine. And to the same effect is Art. VIII of the Treaty of Paris, 1898, in regard to Cuba, Porto Rico, and the Philippines.

State archives.

[1] Cf. Huber, *op. cit.*, pp. 68 *seq.*

The private domain of the State, including lands, railways, funds, objects of art and science, military material, etc., also passes to the Government that annexes the territory to which such property belongs. But the rights therein of other parties are to be taken into account.[1]

PRIVATE DOMAIN OF THE STATE.

Thus the successor may take only the balance of funds remaining either in the treasury or in the hands of agents after deducting the amount of cheques previously drawn or disbursements made in due form. As to property situated outside the territory at the time of annexation, the successor is not as a rule entitled to it, in default of provisions stipulating its transference. It may be that a territory ceded by a treaty of peace had been fought for by the contracting parties prior to the conclusion of peace, and that the ceding State had managed, during the conflict, to save and carry off to a place of security certain treasures which had been on the said territory. In such a case it would be the height of unreason to maintain that the eventual transfer of the territory necessarily implies also the transfer of those treasures. This question has already been referred to in an earlier chapter, and certain cases were there cited, to which reference may be made for the purpose of supplementing the above observations.[2] In the event of a friendly cession, however, property temporarily outside the territory ceded may well be expected to pass with it. In either case the parties concerned may agree upon what terms they think fit in regard to the disposition of the private domain of the State. The Spanish-American negotiations (set forth above) dealt with certain kinds of property of this category. In the Treaty of Constantinople, 1913, whereby Turkey ceded territory to Bulgaria, it was provided (Art. XIII) that the private property of the State found there should not pass to the Bulgarian Government, but that the Ottoman authorities should be allowed to let it or sell it; and in the case of the latter, that preference should be given, under equal conditions, to Bulgarian purchasers. The Treaty of Athens, 1913, between Turkey and Greece, shows that on this question there was disagreement between the two Governments to the last. The Sublime Porte maintained that the private property of the State situated in the territories ceded to Greece should still belong to it, whereas Greece claimed that she was entitled to it. Accordingly, under Protocol No. II appended to the treaty, the contracting parties agreed to refer the question to an arbitral tribunal at The Hague under a "compromis" to be concluded.

[1] As to railway concessions, see *supra*, pp. 47–48; *infra*, pp. 326 *seq.*

[2] See *supra*, pp. 39–40.

The annexing Government is entitled, in the public interest, to enforce the payment of taxes and other national imposts which fell due before the annexation and which were not paid to the preceding Government. But such title is not the outcome of the law of succession; it depends solely on the sovereign power of the new Government. It is usual in practice, however, to fix a limit beyond which arrears will not be exacted.[1] It is likewise entitled to receive the rents of State property found within the ceded country and the debts due from the municipalities or individual inhabitants to the former Government (e.g. as arising out of loans that had been advanced), unless in the latter case the territory ceded constitutes only a portion of the country subject to that Government.[2]

Unpaid taxes, etc.

Though the property of the Crown is assimilated to that of the State, and as such devolves on the successor, the private property of the sovereign or other head of the State in his personal capacity (as distinguished from his representative capacity) does not pass over, any more than that of individual subjects. A stipulation to this effect is not necessary, but it is sometimes inserted in treaties. Thus by the Treaty of Vienna, 1866, whereby the Lombardo-Venetian Kingdom was ceded by Austria to Italy, it was provided (Art. XXII) that the princes and princesses of the House of Austria as well as the princesses who had entered into the Imperial family by marriage should be allowed, on proving their title, to recover their private property, real and personal, and enjoy it or dispose of it without being molested in any manner. In the Treaty of Athens, 1913, under which Turkey ceded territory to Greece, it was stipulated (Art. VII) that the private property of the Sultan and of the members of his dynasty should be maintained and respected, and that they should be at liberty to sell or rent it through their agents. Disputes on this point were anticipated by the contracting parties, for in the same article they undertook to submit differences that might arise to arbitration at The Hague. If, however, the ceding sovereign claims and proves his title to an inordinate amount of property, altogether disproportionate to the extent and value of the ceded territory, the annexing Government is not bound to recognize the claim, but may, by reason of its sovereign power, grant what it deems equitable.

Private property of the sovereign.

[1] As to the British practice in the case of the annexation of the Transvaal, see *supra*, p. 40.

[2] See *supra*, pp. 11–12, the case of the Elector of Hesse-Cassel, for other questions relative to debts.

It has been shown in an early chapter,[1] in our discussion of the effects of a conqueror's annexation of territory, that the conquering sovereign is bound—not legally, but for reasons of equity, common sense, and international solidarity—to assume in general the contractual obligations of his predecessor; he must take the burdens with the benefits. To do so is to promote the harmony and continuity of public life, to preserve the coherence and orderliness of foreign relationships; to do otherwise is to introduce precarious conditions and arbitrary proceedings which tend to produce chaos in the society of States. If a conqueror is so bound, then a cessionary, acquiring territory by treaty, is—in default of express provisions to the contrary—*a fortiori* bound by the contractual obligations attaching thereto. But express provisions to the contrary are found in comparatively few cases, as we shall presently see. In point of fact, most treaties contain stipulations in conformity with the general principle of succession. It does not, of course, necessarily follow that such frequent practice is evidence of a definitely established rule of international law, for the practice is the result of an agreement, and not of a preexisting injunction. However this may be, the very frequency of similar agreements bears witness to the recognition of a line of conduct, i.e. a principle of action, i.e. a rule, as befitting and demanded by certain circumstances. "Res transit cum suo onere"—this is found in practice to be a salutary rule, and it commends itself to the juridical consciousness of mankind.

CONTRACTUAL OBLIGATIONS OF THE ANNEXED TERRITORY.

One of the most important of these contractual obligations relates to public debts, which may be divided into two classes, viz. general and local. General debts are those contracted by the ceding Government for the purposes of the whole of its country, including the portion ceded. Local debts are those relating exclusively to the portion ceded. Let us consider the former class first. As the general debt was incurred partly for the benefit—as we must assume—of the transferred territory, he who succeeds to the territory ought, conformably to the fundamental principle set forth above, to assume a fair proportion of the debt. Where an entire State is ceded, its entire debt is taken over along with its existing treasure and other fiscal resources. If the debts are found to exceed the latter, it cannot be categorically said that the successor must assume them—unless he has agreed to do so by treaty. Such an obligation does, indeed, follow if we apply our principle absolutely; and some writers have asserted that an acquiring Power is bound to take upon itself all the liabilities of the acquired State

Public debts.

General debts.

[1] See *supra*, pp. 44 *seq.*

irrespectively of the value of its assets.[1] But other considerations are to be borne in mind: a State does not demand or accept territory mainly for the sake of its burdens; so that no more than a reasonable adjustment can be expected to be made. Where a part only of a State is ceded, what amount of the public debt of the ceding State should devolve on the successor? Different bases of calculation have been suggested—the number of the population, the extent of the territory, its general wealth and natural resources. Perhaps the most practicable means of calculating it is in reference to the proportion of the taxes it contributed to the ceding State.

War debts.

With regard to war debts it has already been shown that the principle of succession hardly applies.[2] A cessionary State acquiring territory in a treaty of peace which terminates a state of war between it and the ceding State cannot be under any obligation to defray the costs of the war which the latter had incurred.

No legal claim against cessionary.

If the succeeding Government refuses to take over debts and other financial obligations, a creditor of the ceded territory has no legal claim against the new sovereign.[3] If the creditor is or becomes a subject of the latter, he may receive compensation *ex gratia*; if he is a subject of a foreign Power, diplomatic negotiation may result in amicable settlement.

Local debts.

Secondly, as to the local debt. Whatever reasons may be urged in favour of the assumption of part of the general debt, much stronger reasons may be advanced in favour of the devolution of the local debt, which was incurred solely in the interests of the territory transferred and is inseparable from it.

Cases in which none of the general debt taken over.

Let us now look at a few treaties, in order to see how this question of public debts was solved in actual international practice. In 1783 the United States did not take over any of the general debt of Great Britain; in 1803 of France, in the cession of Louisiana; in 1821 of Spain, in the cession of Florida; in 1848 of Mexico, in the cession of New Mexico, California, etc. In the treaties of Great Britain with the Transvaal, 1852, with the Orange Free State, 1854, and with the Transvaal in 1881, 1884, none of the British general debt was taken over by these countries. In 1871, on the cession of Alsace-Lorraine, no apportionment of the French national debt was made. In 1898 the United States refused to take over not only any of the Spanish national debt, in respect of Cuba, Porto Rico, and the

[1] Huber, *op. cit.*, p. 158; Heffter, *Droit international de l'Europe*, § 25.
[2] See *supra*, p. 43. [3] Cf. *supra*, p. 44.

Philippines, but also (as has already been pointed out [1]) the so-called Cuban debt. It has been suggested that the United States Government, by resorting to the ingenious procedure—"procédé ingénieux," as a French writer says [2]—of compelling Spain to relinquish her rights over Cuba without indicating the transferee, did not assume sovereignty over the island; so that by merely entering into a provisional military occupation no responsibility was undertaken for obligations incurred by Spain in respect of Cuba. This is undoubtedly true; but it is none the less true that the American refusal to take over the Cuban debt was chiefly due to the fact that it was neither local nor incurred for the benefit of the island, that Cuba had had no voice in its creation, and the Spanish Government had created it for its own purposes. It may be added that in February 1909, when the American occupation ceased, the Cuban Government was asked by Spain to contribute a portion of the latter's colonial debt that had been contracted before Cuba was relinquished. The request, however, was refused on the ground that under the Treaty of Paris, 1898, Cuba was surrendered free from all such burdens. There can be no doubt, however, that Cuba was equitably bound to assume such part of the debt as had been incurred by the execution of improvements in the island—e.g. harbours, railways, and other public works.[3] Further, the American Government, remembering the origin of the Cuban debt, and having ascertained (as Mr. Whitelaw Reid stated [4]) that more than a quarter of the Philippine debt "had actually been transferred to Cuba to carry on the war against the Cuban insurgents," similarly refused to take over the debts in respect of the Philippines. The sum of twenty million dollars paid to Spain was a compensation for the cession of the archipelago, and was not offered in discharge of the debt.[5]

On the other hand, the cases in which part of the national debts of the ceding Government was taken over are much more numerous.

More frequently part of the general debt taken over.

In 1814 (Treaty of Kiel, Art. VI) Sweden took over a part of the Danish debt when Denmark ceded Norway to her: "As the whole debt of the Danish Monarchy is contracted, as well upon Norway as the other parts of the kingdom, so His Majesty the King of Sweden binds himself . . . to be responsible for a part of that debt, proportioned to the population and revenue of Norway. By public debt is to be understood that which has been contracted by the Danish Government, both at home and abroad. The latter consists of Royal and

[1] See *supra*, p. 43. [2] Bonfils, *Droit international*, p. 136.

[3] Cf. L. von Bar, in an article contributed to the German periodical, *Die Nation*, April 2, 1899.

[4] Article in the *Anglo-Saxon Review*, June 1899. [5] See *supra*, p. 280.

State obligations, bank-bills, and paper money formerly issued under Royal authority, and now circulating in both kingdoms." The latter part of the article provided for the appointment of commissioners to take an exact account of the debt in question. By the Treaty of London, April 19, 1839, effecting a separation of Belgium from Holland, provision was made (Art. XIII) for a division of the public debt. The Final Act of the Congress of Vienna, June 9, 1815, provided for the division of the debts of the former Grand Duchy of Frankfort (Art. XL), of Poland and the Duchy of Warsaw (Annex II, Arts. XXXI–XXXVII), and of Saxony (Annex IV, Art. IX). When Texas was incorporated in the American Union in 1845, the United States Government set aside a sum of 7,500,000 dollars to be divided *pro rata* among the holders of the Texas bonds.[1] The Treaty of Zurich, 1859, required the new Government of Lombardy to undertake three-fifths of the Monte-Lombardo-Veneto debt, and a portion of the Austrian national loan of 1854, fixed at 40,000,000 florins (Art. VII). The mode of payment was regulated by an additional article;[2] and the apportionment of the debts and assets was to be carried out by a mixed commission (Art. VIII). Under the Treaty of Turin, 1860 (Art. IV), France, acquiring Nice and Savoy, undertook to pay a part of the national debt of Sardinia. By the Treaty of Paris, September 15, 1864 (Art. IV), Italy declared herself ready to enter into arrangements in order to take upon herself a part of the Pontifical debt. (A convention was concluded, December 7, 1866, between France and Italy with regard to it.) Denmark having ceded Schleswig, Holstein, and Lauenburg to Austria and Prussia, Treaty of Vienna, October 30, 1864 (Arts. VIII–XI), the cessionary Governments assumed part of the Danish general debt. Under the Treaty of Vienna, October 3, 1866 (Art. VI), Italy took upon herself a part of the Monte-Lombardo-Veneto debt, together with obligations arising out of other public loans. The Treaty of Berlin, 1878, declaring Montenegro, Serbia, and Roumania independent, made provision for the apportionment among the latter of part of the Ottoman public debt. Under the Treaty of Lausanne, 1912, whereby Turkey handed over Cyrenaica and the Tripolitana to Italy, the Italian Government agreed (Art. X) to pay to the administration of the Ottoman public debt an annual sum corresponding to the average of the sums which in the three years before the war had been assigned for the use of the public debt from the revenues of the ceded provinces. The amount of the annuity was

[1] This case gave rise to a good deal of controversy: cf. Moore, *Digest*, vol. i. pp. 343–347; Moore, *International Arbitrations*, vol. iv. pp. 3591–3594.

[2] See Appendix (F).

to be determined by a mixed commission; and in case of disagreement, by arbitration. Italy reserved to herself the right to replace the said annuity (which was not to be less than 2,000,000 lire) by a single payment of a sum capitalized at 4 per cent.

Local debts regularly taken over.

Local debts incurred for the purposes of the ceded territory or charged upon it are, according to the practice evidenced by treaties, regularly taken over by the cessionary State. In addition to the examples mentioned above (some of which involved local as well as general debts), we may refer to one or two cases that lay down express stipulations regarding that class of debts. The Treaty of Paris, May 30, 1814, whereby France was required by the Allies to hand over various territories, provided (Art. XXI) that the debts mortgaged thereon or contracted for the support of their internal administration were to pass over to the respective cessionaries. The Final Act of the Congress of Vienna, 1815, laid down, with regard to Saxony, that debts hypothecated on provinces which passed or remained, entire, under one Government were to be assumed, entire, by that Government. A special rule was agreed to by the Kings of Prussia and Saxony in respect of debts concerning divided provinces or divided Saxony. When Great Britain renounced her protectorate over the Ionian Islands, by the Treaty of London, 1864, Greece assumed responsibility for all obligations that had been contracted by their Government. Under the Treaty of Prague, 1866, following (as it says) the example of the Treaty of Zurich, 1859, it was provided (Art. II) that on the union of the Lombardo-Venetian Kingdom with Italy the debts charged on the ceded territories were to be recognized by the latter. The British practice in the case of the annexation of the Transvaal, 1877, Upper Burma, 1886, the Transvaal and Orange River Free State, 1901, which has already been referred to,[1] was similar, despite the fact of subjugation.

CONCESSIONS AND CONTRACTS OTHER THAN PUBLIC DEBTS.

In an earlier chapter[2] it was pointed out that the rule of succession is, on principle, applicable to the case of concessions and contracts relating to the public service, when the annexing State's acquisition is a result of conquest and subjugation. The rule applies *a fortiori* to territory acquired by means of a cession, either amicable or forcible (i.e. exacted in a peace treaty). We have seen that there are conflicting judicial decisions on the point, and divergent international practices; that the annexing State's action depends (as it is asserted) on considerations of policy and expediency. On the whole, however, both opinion and practice

[1] See *supra*, p. 42.

[2] See *supra*, pp. 44 *seq.*

—not to mention the dictates of reason and equity—are in favour of the rule. The noteworthy Transvaal Concessions Commission Report, though it declares that an acquiring State is not legally bound by contracts made by the acquired State, admits that the modern usage of nations tends towards their recognition. To determine the binding obligations of a State by the tests applied to those of an individual subject is to take a narrow and irrational view of the nature of international relationships. But there is no need to enlarge further on this point here and discuss the various relevant cases; it is sufficient to refer to the chapter cited, which applies equally, *mutatis mutandis*, to our present purpose, viz. to show that the rule of succession governs, in general, a ceding State's contractual obligations relative to the ceded territory. Absolute invariability is not claimed for the rule; exceptions might occur in regard to certain concessions, for example, which it would be clearly impolitic to recognize in their full extent. The rule holds under normal conditions, when they have been created regularly and in good faith; where there are abnormal conditions, each case must be considered on its merits, regard being paid to the requirements of fairness and justice. Great Britain acted conformably to this rule in the annexation of the Transvaal in 1877, Upper Burma in 1886, and the Transvaal and Orange River Colony in 1901: practically all obligations were taken over, except in some cases certain incomplete contracts, and in others one or two concessions that were injurious to the public interest. And a similar practice was adopted in many treaties of peace (to say nothing of amicable conventions), some of which may be referred to as illustrative examples of different kinds of obligations involved.

British practice.

Examples furnished by various treaties.

Treaty of Campo Formio, 1797, between France and Austria (Art. XII): "All sales or conveyances, all obligations contracted either by the cities or by the Government or civil and executive authorities of the countries heretofore Venetian for the maintenance of the French and German armies up to the date of this treaty, shall be confirmed and considered as valid."

Treaty of Paris, 1814.

Treaty of Paris, May 30, 1814, between the Allied Powers and France (Art. XXX): "The sums due for all works of public utility on the Rhone and in the departments separated from France by virtue of this treaty, not yet completed, or which shall be completed after December 31, 1812, shall be charged to the future owners of the territory and be liquidated by the commission entrusted with the liquidation of the debt of the two countries."

Treaty of Zurich, 1859: Sardinia, acquiring Lombardy, succeeded to the rights and obligations arising out of contracts regularly concluded by the Austrian Government for objects of public interest concerning the ceded territory (Art. IX), and confirmed various railway concessions, together with all the agreements involved therein (Art. XI).

Treaty of Zurich, 1859.

Treaty of London, 1864, between Great Britain, France, Russia, and Greece (Art. VII): Greece, acquiring the Ionian Islands through Great Britain's renunciation of her protectorate, took over all the engagements and contracts lawfully concluded by the former Government of the islands or in their name by the protecting Power, either with companies or with individuals, and in particular the privileges that had been conceded to the Ionian Bank, to the Austrian Lloyds, and to the Malta and Mediterranean Gas Co.

Treaty of London, 1864.

The Treaty of Vienna, 1864 (Art. XVII), whereby Denmark ceded Schleswig, Holstein, and Lauenburg to Austria and Prussia, and the Treaty of Vienna, 1866 (Art. VIII), whereby Austria ceded the Lombardo-Venetian Kingdom to Italy, both transferred to the respective cessionary States the contractual rights and obligations established by the former Governments in respect of the ceded territories. Railway concessions were confirmed and special arrangements were made therefor in the latter treaty (Arts. X, XI).

Treaty of Vienna, 1864.

By an additional article to the Treaty of Frankfort, May 10, 1871, provision was made for the transfer to Germany of the Eastern Railway in Alsace-Lorraine; and by the additional convention of December 11, 1871 (Art. XIII), Germany recognized and confirmed the concessions relating to roads, canals, and mines, and all contracts concerning the letting or working of public property, and declared herself subrogated to all the rights and obligations arising therefrom. Patents granted to Frenchmen in the ceded territory were also confirmed.

Treaty of Frankfort, 1871.

After the Chile-Peru War (1879–1882) the former took possession of the guano deposits belonging to the latter, but subject to all the liens existing at the time of cession.

Treaty of Berlin, 1890, whereby Great Britain ceded Heligoland to Germany in exchange for other territory (Art. IX): Trading and mineral concessions and rights to real property, held by companies or individuals, subjects of one Power, were, if their validity was established, to be recognized in the sphere of the other Power. These concessions were to be worked in conformity with the local laws and regulations.

Treaty of Berlin, 1890.

During the peace negotiations at Paris between the American

and the Spanish commissioners the latter proposed (December 1, 1898) that all grants and contracts relating to public works and services in the islands to be ceded should be recognized by the succeeding Government, and the resulting rights and obligations taken over from Spain. The American commissioners rejected the proposal as set forth, on the ground that the nature, extent, and liabilities of the contracts in question were unknown to them, but they agreed to take over such engagements as would be found on investigation to be binding under international law.[1] The Treaty of Paris, December 10, 1898, guaranteed (Art. VIII) the preservation of the rights of property in general, and those of copyrights and patents in particular (Art. XIII). In reference to cable concessions that had been granted by Spain to certain companies, the British Government pointed out (January 18, 1899) that the successor was bound to recognize them: ". . . The obligations contracted by Spain under those concessions are of a local nature . . . and binding on the United States Government on their taking possession of the islands or assuming effective control of them, whether under a formal protectorate or otherwise. On the faith of those concessions the company has expended vast sums for the benefit of the islands, and the obligations in question clearly belong to that class of local obligations which have always been held to be transferred with the sovereignty and to pass with the territory."[2]

Treaty of Paris, 1898.

The Franco-German convention signed at Berlin, November 4, 1911, whereby the contracting Powers effected an exchange of territory in their possessions of Equatorial Africa, stipulated (Art. V) that concessions of all kinds should remain inviolable: "The present exchanges of territory are made subject to the circumstances by which these territories are affected at the moment the present agreement is concluded—that is to say, subject to the condition that the two Governments will respect the public and private concessions which may have been granted by either of them. The two Governments will deliver to each other the text of the acts by which these concessions have been granted. The German Government is substituted for the French Government in all the benefits, rights, and obligations resulting from the acts referred to above with respect to companies holding concessions, which will come under the sovereignty,

Treaty of Berlin, 1911.

[1] *Senate Documents*, 62, 55th Cong., 3rd sess., part ii. pp. 240, 241, 258, 262; Moore, *Digest*, vol. i. pp. 389–390.

[2] For various cases relating to Cuba and Porto Rico, see Moore, *Digest*, vol. pp. 390 *seq.*; for the case of the Manila Railway Co., *ibid.*, pp. 395–406, and Magoon, *op. cit.*, pp. 177 *seq.*

authority, and jurisdiction of the German Government. A special convention will regulate the application of the above provisions. The same rule will hold for France in regard to concessions which may be located in the territories which will come under her sovereignty, authority, and jurisdiction."

Treaty of Constantinople, 1913.

The Treaty of Constantinople, 1913, under which Turkey ceded territories to Bulgaria, provided (Art. XVI) that Bulgaria should assume the rights and obligations in respect of the part of the line of the Oriental Railway Co. situated in the ceded territory, and which had been conceded to it by the Ottoman Government. In case of dispute, recourse should be had to arbitration at The Hague (Art. XVII).

OTHER OBLIGATIONS.

Certain other obligations of the annexing Government may be briefly referred to, e.g. those relating to deposits in national banks (deposits in private banks belong to the sphere of purely private property and private law, to be presently considered), judicial deposits, the pay and pension of officials, and claims based on torts. As to deposits, the ceding State's obligations to depositors are undoubtedly transferred to the cessionary State—even in cases of annexation founded on conquest alone such obligations are invariably taken over by the conqueror. The cessionary State is, of course, empowered by reason of its sovereignty to put an end to the contracts involved in the deposit; but it is incumbent upon it to repay to the depositors the amount of their deposit, together with such interest as was due at the date of the cession. Special stipulations are sometimes inserted in treaties, requiring repayment on the part of the ceding State or on that of the acquiring State, as the case may be.

Deposits.

Thus the Treaty of Zurich, 1859, laid down, with regard to the cession of Lombardy (Art. X), that the Austrian Government should reimburse all sums paid by Lombard subjects, communal districts, public establishments, and religious societies, into the Austrian public banks, in the form of caution-money, deposits, or consignments, which were to be punctually repaid by the cessionary Government (viz. Sardinia).

The Treaty of Vienna, 1866 (Art. IX), made a similar stipulation in exactly similar terms with regard to the deposits, caution-money, etc., relating to the Lombardo-Venetian Kingdom ceded by Austria to Italy.

The Treaty of Frankfort, 1871 (Art. IV), required France to make over to Germany the sums deposited by the departments, communes, and public establishments of the ceded territories of

Alsace-Lorraine, the premiums of enlistment and discharge belonging to those soldiers and sailors born there who opted for German nationality, the caution-money of agents of the State, and judicial deposits.

A succeeding Government is not bound to take over the officials engaged in the ceded territory. If it takes them over, it is not bound to continue the former rate of pay. But the obligation to continue the payment of pensions already earned devolves on it. In the case of forcible annexations on the part of Great Britain (e.g. Upper Burma, 1886, the late South African Republics, 1901), the British Government disclaimed all liability in regard to pensions, but made payments, even in respect of arrears of salaries, *ex gratia*. An amicable cessionary State, too, is not bound legally (in the absence of special treaty provisions) to discharge such claims; but it is morally bound to do so, for the service of the officials had contributed, presumably, to the advantage of the acquired territory. Sometimes express stipulations are made requiring the new Government to pay the pensions, military and civil, to the persons entitled to them, and, if need be, to their widows and children—e.g. the Treaty of Paris, 1814; the Treaty of Vienna, 1866 (Art. XVII); the Additional Convention of Frankfort, December 11, 1871 (Art. II).

Pensions.

On the other hand, an acquiring State is not bound to recognize the claims of subjects for damages due to the tortious acts or omissions generally of the preceding Government, and in particular to the belligerent operations prior to the annexation of the territory. In some cases, however, compensation has been offered to those who suffered as a result of the latter. Thus in 1871 Germany, under an Imperial law of June 14, made good the losses suffered by the inhabitants of Alsace-Lorraine on account of commandeering or devastation on the part of either the German or the French troops. By Art. VII of the Treaty of Paris, 1898, both the United States and Spain renounced all claims for indemnity, national and individual; but the former undertook to adjudicate and settle the claims of its citizens against Spain. Similarly, under Art. X of the Peace of Vereeniging, 1902, Great Britain paid liberal compensation to those of her new subjects who had suffered through the operations of war.[1]

Claims based on war losses.

Finally, the change of sovereignty through territorial cession cannot affect private rights already vested in individuals or corporations, whether municipal or commercial. Private property of every kind remains sacred and inviolable. In this respect the

[1] See *supra*, p. 51.

principle of succession has no applicability whatever. Private law, as distinguished from constitutional and administrative law, remains valid, and the population of the transferred territory continues to be subject to it and bound by it, until legislative alterations are introduced by the competent law-making authority of the cessionary State. The new sovereign possesses no greater power to interfere with the private rights of his new subjects than he has with regard to his old subjects. As he cannot deprive the latter of their titles to real estate, notwithstanding any theory of feudal tenure that may obtain in his country, so he is not empowered to divest the former of their grants of land if lawfully and validly executed before the cession. An exception may, however, arise—as has been mentioned in reference to concessions—in a case involving serious injury to the public interests. Modifications may then be made by the the sovereign in virtue of his prerogative, or by the legislature, according to circumstances. Whatever stipulations are made in a treaty of cession in order to ensure the immunity of private rights, they are merely declaratory of the established principle of the law of nations and serve but to reinforce it by the additional sanction of an express engagement.

PRIVATE RIGHTS AND PRIVATE LAW.

In our previous survey of the effects of annexation as a result of conquest we referred to British and American judicial pronouncements, and to examples of international practice as evidence of the inviolability of the private rights of the inhabitants on subjugated territory. The rule applies all the more forcibly to the case of cession. To avoid repetition, then, we may refer to what has already been said in an earlier chapter.[1] We may add, however, one or two further judicial and Government pronouncements, and give some examples of treaty stipulations which were not considered in that chapter. In the recent important British case of *Cook* v. *Sprigg*[2] it was laid down that conformably to the well-understood rules of international law, a change of sovereignty by cession should not affect private property. The judgment of the United States Supreme Court in *Coffee* v. *Groover*[3] is explicit and emphatic: "It is no doubt the received doctrine that in cases of ceded or conquered territory the rights of private property in lands are respected. Grants made by the former Government, being rightful when made, are not usually disturbed. . . . It is true that the property rights of the people, in those cases, were protected by stipulations in the treaties of cession, as is usual in such treaties; but the court took

[1] See *supra*, pp. 48 *seq.*

[2] (1899) A.C. 572.

[3] (1887) 123 U.S. Rep. 1, at p. 9. Cf. *Townsend* v. *Greeley* (1866), 5 Wallace 326.

broader ground, and held, as a general principle of international law, that a mere cession of territory only operates upon the sovereignty and jurisdiction, including the right to the public domain, and not upon the private property of individuals which had been segregated from the public domain before the cession."

Resident aliens.

A resident alien possesses, in this respect, the same rights of immunity as does a subject in the ceded territory; and neither is to be prejudicially affected by the cessionary's legislation purporting to be retrospective. Thus observes an American Secretary of State: "The rights of a resident neutral, having become fixed and vested by the law of the country, cannot be denied or injuriously affected by a change in the sovereignty or public control of that country by transfer to another Government. His remedies may be affected by the change of sovereignty, but his *rights* at the time of the change must be measured and determined by the law under which he acquired them. . . . Title to land and landed improvements is, by the law of nations, a continuous right not subject to be divested by any retroactive legislation of new Governments taking the place of that by which such title was lawfully granted." [1]

Sometimes maintenance of private rights expressly stipulated—but always implied in other cases.

Frequently clauses are inserted in treaties in conformity with these fundamental principles, though it is not necessary to do so. Thus the Treaty of Paris, 1898, declared (Art. VIII) that the cession or relinquishment of the Spanish possessions could not impair the lawful rights and property of provinces, public or private bodies of every kind, and individuals of any nationality whatever; and Art. XIII assured the continued respect of copyrights and patents held by Spaniards in the ceded islands.

Under the Anglo-French convention signed in London, April 8, 1904, whereby certain territories in Gambia and the Los Islands were ceded to France, it was stipulated (Art. VII) that the existing native laws and customs should as far as possible remain undisturbed.

The Treaty of Portsmouth, 1905, guaranteed the inviolability of the proprietary rights of Russian subjects in Port Arthur, Ta-lien, and the adjacent territory (Art. V), as well as in the southern portion of Sakhalin (Art. X), which were ceded to Japan.

The Treaty of Constantinople, 1913, under which Bulgaria acquired territories from Turkey, laid down (Art. X) that rights in general vested before the cession, including those specified in judicial documents and official title-deeds, emanating from the

[1] Mr. Bayard, U.S. Secretary of State, to Mr. Roberts, March 20, 1886; Moore, *Digest*, vol. i. p. 422.

competent Ottoman authorities, were to be respected until their invalidity was legally established, and more especially (Art. XI), that the rights of landed proprietors were not to be interfered with.

Similarly, the Treaty of Athens, 1913, whereby Turkey ceded territories to Greece, stipulated (Art. VI) that property rights in immovables held by individuals on those territories by virtue of deeds issued by the Ottoman Government should be recognized by the Greek Government; and Art. XI provided, more comprehensively, that the life, property, honour, religion, and customs of the inhabitants subjected to Greek sovereignty were to be scrupulously respected.

APPENDIX

A CENTURY OF PEACE TREATIES

(A) TREATY OF PARIS

November 20, 1815

GREAT BRITAIN, AUSTRIA, PRUSSIA, RUSSIA—FRANCE

In the Name of the Most Holy and Undivided Trinity.

The Allied Powers having by their united efforts, and by the success of their arms, preserved France and Europe from the convulsions with which they were menaced by the late enterprise of Napoleon Bonaparte, and by the revolutionary system reproduced in France, to promote its success; participating at present with His Most Christian Majesty in the desire to consolidate, by maintaining inviolate the Royal authority, and by restoring the operation of the Constitutional Charter, the order of things which had been happily re-established in France, as also in the object of restoring between France and her neighbours those relations of reciprocal confidence and goodwill which the fatal effects of the Revolution and of the system of conquest had for so long a time disturbed; persuaded, at the same time, that this last object can only be obtained by an arrangement framed to secure to the Allies proper indemnities for the past and solid guarantees for the future, they have, in concert with His Majesty the King of France, taken into consideration the means of giving effect to this arrangement; and being satisfied that the indemnity due to the Allied Powers cannot be either entirely territorial or entirely pecuniary, without prejudice to France in the one or other of her essential interests, and that it would be more fit to combine both the modes, in order to avoid the inconvenience which would result, were either resorted to separately, their Imperial and Royal Majesties have adopted this basis for their present transactions; and agreeing alike as to the necessity of retaining for a fixed time in the frontier provinces of France a certain number of allied troops, they have determined to combine their different arrangements, founded upon these bases, in a definitive treaty. For this purpose, and to this effect, His Majesty the King of the United Kingdom of Great Britain and Ireland, for himself and his allies on the one part, and His Majesty the King of France and Navarre on the other part, have named their plenipotentiaries to discuss, settle and sign the said definitive treaty; namely, His Majesty the King of the United Kingdom of Great Britain and Ireland, the Right Honourable Robert Stewart, Viscount Castlereagh, Knight of the Most Noble Order of the Garter, His said Majesty's Principal Secretary of State for Foreign Affairs, etc., and the Most Illustrious and Most Noble Lord Arthur, Duke, Marquess, and Earl of Wellington, Marquess of Douro, Viscount

Wellington, of Talavera and of Wellington, and Baron Douro of Wellesley, a member of His said Majesty's Most Honourable Privy Council, a Field Marshal of his Armies, Colonel of the Royal Regiment of Horse Guards, Knight of the Most Noble Order of the Garter, etc.

And His Majesty the King of France and of Navarre, the Sieur Armand Emanuel du Plessis Richelieu, Duke of Richelieu, Peer of France, First Gentleman of the Chamber of His Most Christian Majesty, his Minister and Secretary of State for Foreign Affairs, and President of the Council of his Ministers, etc.,

Who having exchanged their full powers, found to be in good and due form, have signed the following articles:—

Frontiers of France.

ART. I.—The frontiers of France shall be the same as they were in the year 1790, save and except the modifications on the one side and on the other, which are detailed in the present article.

1st, on the northern frontiers the line of demarcation shall remain as it was fixed by the Treaty of Paris, as far as opposite to Quievrain, from whence it shall follow the ancient limits of the Belgian provinces, of the late Bishopric of Liége, and of the Duchy of Bouillon, as they existed in the year 1790, leaving the territories included within that line (*enclavés*), of Philippeville and Marienburg, with the fortresses so called, together with the whole of the Duchy of Bouillon without the frontiers of France. From Villers, near Orval, upon the confines of the department Des Ardennes, and of the Grand Duchy of Luxemburg, as far as Perle, upon the great road leading from Thionville to Treves, the line shall remain as it was laid down by the Treaty of Paris. From Perle it shall pass by Lauensdorff, Walwich, Schardorff Niederveiling, Pellweiler (all these places with their banlieues or dependencies remaining to France) to Houvre; and shall follow from thence the old limits of the district (*pays*) of Sarrebruck, leaving Sarrelouis and the course of the Sarre, together with the places situated to the right of the line above-described, and their banlieues or dependencies without the limits of France. From the limits of the district of Sarrebruck the line of demarcation shall be the same which at present separates from Germany, the departments of the Moselle and of the Lower Rhine, as far as to the Lauter, which river shall from thence serve as the frontier until it falls into the Rhine.

Delimitation Commission.

All the territory on the left bank of the Lauter, including the fortress of Landau, shall form part of Germany. The town of Weissenburg, however, through which the river runs, shall remain entirely to France, with a rayon on the left bank, not exceeding 1,000 toises, and which shall be more particularly determined by the commissioners who shall be charged with the approaching designation of the boundaries.

2ndly, leaving the mouth of the Lauter, and continuing along the departments of the Lower Rhine, the Upper Rhine, the Doubs, and the Jura to the Canton de Vaud, the frontiers shall remain as fixed by the Treaty of Paris.[1] The thalweg of the Rhine shall form the boundary between France and the States of Germany, but the property of the islands shall remain in perpetuity, as it shall be fixed by a new survey

[1] I.e. that of May 30, 1814.

of the course of that river, and continue unchanged whatever variations that course may undergo in the lapse of time. Commissioners shall be named on both sides, by the high contracting parties, within the space of three months, to proceed upon the said survey. One half of the bridge between Strasburg and Kehl shall belong to France, and the other half to the Grand Duchy of Baden.

3rdly, in order to establish a direct communication between the canton of Geneva and Switzerland, that part of the Pays de Gex, bounded on the east by the lake Leman; on the south by the territory of the canton of Geneva; on the north, by that of the canton de Vaud; on the west, by the course of the Versoix, and by a line which comprehends the communes of Collex-Bossy, and Meyrin, leaving the commune of Ferney to France, shall be ceded to the Helvetic Confederacy, in order to be united to the canton of Geneva. The line of the French custom-houses shall be placed to the west of the Jura, so that the whole of the Pays de Gex shall be without that line.

4thly, from the frontiers of the canton of Geneva, as far as the Mediterranean, the line of demarcation shall be that which in the year 1790 separated France from Savoy and from the county of Nice.

The relations which the Treaty of Paris of 1814 had re-established between France and the principality of Monaco shall cease for ever, and the same relations shall exist between that principality and His Majesty the King of Sardinia.

5thly, all the territories and districts included within the boundary of the French territory (*enclavés*), as determined by the present article shall remain united to France.

6thly, the High Contracting Parties shall name within three months after the signature of the present treaty, commissioners to regulate everything relating to the designation of the boundaries of the respective countries, and as soon as the labours of the commissioners shall have terminated, maps shall be drawn, and landmarks shall be erected, which shall point out the respective limits.

Fortresses, etc., outside the new French frontiers.

ART. II.—The fortresses, places, and districts, which, according to the preceding article are no longer to form part of the French territory, shall be placed at the disposal of the Allied Powers, at the periods fixed by Art. IX of the Military Convention annexed to the present treaty;[1] and His Majesty the King of France renounces for himself, his heirs, and successors for ever, the rights of sovereignty and property which he has hitherto exercised over the said fortresses, places, and districts.

Fortifications of Huninguen.

ART. III.—The fortifications of Huninguen having been constantly an object of uneasiness to the town of Bâle, the High Contracting Parties, in order to give to the Helvetic Confederacy a new proof of their goodwill and of their solicitude for its welfare, have agreed among themselves to demolish the fortifications of Huninguen, and the French Government engages from the same motive not to re-establish them at any time, and not to replace them by any other fortifications at a distance of less than that of three leagues from the town of Bâle.

[1] See *infra*, pp. 342 *seq.*

The neutrality of Switzerland shall be extended to the territory situated to the north of a line to be drawn from Ugine, that town being included, to the south of the lake of Annecy, by Faverge, as far as Lecheraine, and from thence by the lake of Bourget, as far as the Rhone, in like manner as it was extended to the provinces of Chablais and of Faucigny, by Art. XCII of the Final Act of the Congress of Vienna.

Indemnity.

Art. IV.—The pecuniary part of the indemnity to be furnished by France to the Allied Powers is fixed at the sum of 700,000,000 francs. The modes, the periods, and the guarantees for the payment of this sum shall be regulated by a special Convention, which shall have the same force and effect as if it were inserted, word for word, in the present treaty.[1]

Military occupation by Allies.

Art. V.—The state of uneasiness and of fermentation, which after so many violent convulsions, and particularly after the last catastrophe, France must still experience, notwithstanding the paternal intentions of her King, and the advantages secured to every class of his subjects by the Constitutional Charter, requiring, for the security of the neighbouring States, certain measures of precaution and of temporary guarantee, it has been judged indispensable to occupy, during a fixed time, by a corps of Allied troops certain military positions along the frontiers of France, under the express reserve, that such occupation shall in no way prejudice the sovereignty of His Most Christian Majesty, nor the state of possession, such as it is recognized and confirmed by the present treaty. The number of these troops shall not exceed 150,000 men. The Commander-in-Chief of this army shall be nominated by the Allied Powers. This army shall occupy the fortresses of Condé, Valenciennes, Bouchain, Cambray, Le Quesnoy, Maubeuge, Landrecies, Avesnes, Rocroy, Givet with Charlemont, Mezières, Sedan, Montmedy, Thionville, Longwy, Bitsch, and the Tête-de-Pont of Fort Louis. As the maintenance of the army destined for this service is to be provided by France, a special convention shall regulate everything which may relate to that object.

Maintenance of the army of occupation.

This convention,[2] which shall have the same force and effect as if it were inserted word for word in the present treaty, shall also regulate the relations of the army of occupation with the civil and military authorities of the country. The utmost extent of the duration of this military occupation is fixed at five years. It may terminate before that period if, at the end of three years, the Allied Sovereigns, after having, in concert with His Majesty the King of France, maturely examined their reciprocal situation and interests, and the progress which shall have been made in France in the re-establishment of order and tranquillity, shall agree to acknowledge that the motives which led them to that measure have ceased to exist. But whatever may be the result of this deliberation, all the fortresses and positions occupied by the Allied troops, shall, at the expiration of five years, be evacuated

Duration.

[1] See the Annexed Convention, *infra*, p. 347.

[2] See the Additional Convention, *infra*, p. 342.

without further delay, and given up to His Most Christian Majesty, or to his heirs and successors.

Evacuation.

ART. VI.—The foreign troops, not forming part of the army of occupation, shall evacuate the French territory within the term fixed by Art. IX. of the Military Convention annexed to the present treaty.

Right of option.

ART. VII.—In all countries which shall change Sovereigns, as well in virtue of the present treaty as of the arrangements which are to be made in consequence thereof, a period of six years from the date of the exchange of the ratifications shall be allowed to the inhabitants, natives or foreigners, of whatever condition and nation they may be, to dispose of their property, if they should think fit to do so, and to retire to whatever country they may choose.

Application of previous treaty.

ART. VIII.—All the dispositions of the Treaty of Paris of 30th May, 1814, relative to the countries ceded by the treaty, shall equally apply to the several territories and districts ceded by the present treaty.

Claims arising out of non-execution of previous treaty.

ART. IX.—The High Contracting Parties having caused representation to be made of the different claims arising out of the non-execution of Art. XIX and following of the treaty of 30th May, 1814, as well as of the additional articles of that treaty signed between Great Britain and France, desiring to render more efficacious the stipulations made thereby, and having determined, by two separate conventions, the line to be pursued on each side for that purpose, the said two conventions, as annexed to the present treaty, shall, in order to secure the complete execution of the above-mentioned articles, have the same force and effect, as if the same were inserted, word for word, herein.

Prisoners of war.

ART. X.—All prisoners taken during the hostilities, as well as all hostages that may have been carried off or given, shall be restored in the shortest time possible. The same shall be the case with respect to the prisoners taken previously to the treaty of the 30th May, 1814, and who shall not already have been restored.

Maintenance of former treaties.

ART. XI.—The Treaty of Paris of the 30th May, 1814, and the final act of the Congress of Vienna of the 9th June, 1815, are confirmed, and shall be maintained in all such of their enactments which shall not have been modified by the articles of the present treaty.

Ratifications.

ART. XII.—The present treaty, with the conventions annexed thereto, shall be ratified in one Act, and the ratifications thereof shall be exchanged in the space of two months, or sooner, if possible.

In witness whereof the respective plenipotentiaries have signed the same, and affixed thereunto the seals of their arms.

Done at Paris, this 20th day of November, in the year of our Lord, 1815.

(L.S.) CASTLEREAGH. (L.S.) RICHELIEU.
(L.S.) WELLINGTON.

(B) ADDITIONAL CONVENTION

Paris, November 20, 1815

GREAT BRITAIN, AUSTRIA, PRUSSIA, RUSSIA—FRANCE

(Occupation of a Military Line in France by an Allied Army)

ART. I.—The composition of the army of 150,000 men, which, in virtue of Art. V of the treaty of this day, is to occupy a military line along the frontiers of France, the force and nature of the contingents to be furnished by each Power, as well as the choice of the generals who are to command these troops, shall be determined by the Allied Sovereigns.

Composition of army of occupation.

ART. II.—This army shall be maintained by the French Government in the manner following:—

Maintenance.

The lodging, the fuel and lighting, the provisions and forage, are to be furnished in kind.

Rations.

It is agreed that the total amount of daily rations shall never exceed 200,000 for men and 50,000 for horses, and that they shall be issued according to the tariff annexed to the present convention.

Pay, etc.

With respect to the pay, the equipment, the clothing, and other incidental matters, the French Government will provide for such expense by the payment of a sum of 50,000,000 francs per annum, payable in specie from month to month, from the 1st of December of the year 1815, into the hands of the Allied commissioners.

But the Allied Powers, in order to concur as much as possible in everything which can satisfy His Majesty the King of France, and relieve his subjects, consent that only 30,000,000 francs on account of pay shall be paid in the first year, on condition of the difference being made up in the subsequent years of the occupation.

Fortresses.

ART. III.—France engages equally to provide for the keeping up of the fortifications, and of the buildings of the military and civil administrations, as well as for the arming and provisioning of the fortresses which, in virtue of Art. V of the treaty of this day, are to remain as a deposit in the hands of the Allied troops.

These respective services, which are to be regulated upon the principles adopted by the French administration of the War Department, shall be executed upon a demand, addressed to the French Government by the Commander-in-Chief of the Allied troops, with whom some plan shall be agreed upon for ascertaining what may be needful, and concerting the measures necessary to remove all difficulties which may arise, and for accomplishing the object of this stipulation, in a manner equally satisfactory to the interests of the respective parties.

The French Government will take such measures as it shall judge to be the most effectual for securing the accomplishment of the different services stated in this and in the preceding article, and will concert to that effect with the Commander-in-Chief of the Allied troops.

Military line to be occupied by Allied troops.

ART. IV.—In conformity with Art. V of the principal treaty, the military line to be occupied by the Allied troops shall extend along the frontiers which separate the departments of the Pas de Calais, of the North, of the Ardennes, of the Meuse, of the Moselle, of the Lower Rhine, and of the Upper Rhine, from the interior of France.

It is further agreed that neither the Allied troops nor the French troops shall occupy (except it be for particular reasons, and by common consent) the territories and districts hereafter named:

In the department of the Somme, all the country north of that river from Ham to where it falls into the sea.

In the department of the Aisne, the districts of St. Quentin, Vervins, and Laôn.

In the department of the Marne, those of Rheims, St. Ménéhould, and Vitry.

In the department of the Upper Marne, those of St. Dizier and Joinville.

In the department of the Meurthe, those of Toul, Dieuze, Sarrebourg, and Blamont.

In the department of the Vosges, those of St. Diez, Brugères, and Remiremont.

The district of Lure, in the department of the Upper Saône, and that of St. Hippolyte, in the department of the Doubs.

Notwithstanding the occupation by the Allies of the portion of territory fixed by the principal treaty, and by the present convention, His Most Christian Majesty may, in the towns situated within the territory occupied, maintain garrisons, the number of which, however, shall not exceed what is laid down in the following enumeration:—

At Calais	1,000 men
„ Gravelines	500 „
„ Bergues	500 „
„ St. Omer	1,500 „
„ Bethune	500 „
„ Montreuil	500 „
„ Hesdin	250 „
„ Ardres	150 „
„ Aire	500 „
„ Arras	1,000 „
„ Boulogne	300 „

At St. Venant	300 men
,, Lille	3,000 ,,
,, Dunkirk and its forts	1,000 ,,
,, Douay and Forte de Scarpe	1,000 ,,
,, Verdun	500 ,,
,, Metz	3,000 ,,
,, Lauterburg	200 ,,
,, Weissenburg...	150 ,,
,, Lichtenberg	150 ,,
,, Petite Pierre...	100 ,,
,, Phalsburg	600 ,,
,, Strasburg	3,000 ,,
,, Schlestadt	1,000 ,,
,, Neuf Brisach and Fort Mortier	1,000 ,,
,, Belfort	1,000 ,,

It is, however, well understood that the "matériel" belonging to the Engineer and Artillery Departments, as well as such articles of military equipment as do not properly belong to those fortresses, shall be withdrawn from them, and shall be transferred to such places as the French Government shall think fit, provided those places are situated without the line occupied by the Allied troops, and without the districts in which it is agreed not to leave any troops, either Allied or French.

If any infraction of the above stipulations should come to the knowledge of the Commander-in-Chief of the Allied armies, he shall make his representations on the subject to the French Government, which engages to do what is right thereupon.

The fortresses above mentioned being at this moment unprovided with garrisons, the French Government can place therein, as soon as it shall think fit, the number of troops fixed as above; apprising always beforehand the Commander-in-Chief of the Allied troops, in order to avoid any difficulty or delay which the French troops might experience in their march.

Military Command of Allied troops.

ART. V.—The military command in the whole extent of the departments which shall remain occupied by the Allied troops shall belong to the General-in-Chief of those troops; it is, however, distinctly understood, that it shall not extend to the fortresses which the French troops are to occupy, in virtue of Art. IV of the present convention, nor to a rayon of 1,000 toises around each of those places.

Civil Administration.

ART. VI.—The civil administration, the administration of justice, and the collection of taxes and contributions of all sorts, shall remain in the hands of the agents of His Majesty the King of France.

The same shall be the case with respect to the customs. They shall remain in their present state, and the commanders of the Allied troops shall throw no obstacle in the way of the measures to be taken by the officers employed in that service to prevent frauds; they shall even give them, in case of need, succour and assistance.

ART. VII.—To prevent all abuses which might affect the regulations of the customs, the clothing and equipments, and other necessary articles destined for the Allied troops, shall not be allowed to enter, except they be furnished with a certificate of origin, and in pursuance of a communication to be made by the commanding officers of the different corps, to the General-in-Chief of the Allied army, who will, on his part, cause information to be given thereon to the French Government, who will, in consequence thereof, issue the proper orders to their officers employed in the administration of the customs.

Prevention of customs abuses.

ART. VIII.—The service of the "gendarmerie" being acknowledged as necessary to the maintenance of order and public tranquillity shall continue, as hitherto, in the countries occupied by the Allied troops.

Gendarmerie.

ART. IX.—The Allied troops, with the exception of those that are to form the army of occupation, shall evacuate the territory of France in twenty-one days after the signature of the principal treaty.

Evacuation by Allied troops.

The territories which, according to that treaty, are to be ceded to the Allies, as well as the fortresses of Landau and Sarre-Louis, shall be delivered up by the French authorities and troops in ten days from the date of the signature of the treaty.

Delivery of ceded territories.

Those places shall be given up in the state in which they were on the 20th September last.

Commissioners shall be named on both sides, to ascertain and declare that state, and to deliver and receive respectively the artillery, the military stores, plans, models, and archives, belonging as well to the said places as to the different districts ceded by France, according to the treaty of this day.

Commissioners shall also be named, to examine and ascertain the state of those places still occupied by the French troops, and which, according to Art. V of the principal treaty, are to be held in deposit, for a certain time, by the Allies.

These places shall also be delivered up to the Allied troops in ten days from the date of the signature of the treaty.

Commissioners shall also be named by the French Government, on the one part, and by the General Commanding-in-Chief the Allied troops destined to remain in France, on the other; also by the General commanding the Allied troops which are at present in possession of the fortresses of Avesnes, Landrecies, Maubeuge, Rocroy, Givet, Montmedy, Longwy, Mezières, and Sedan, to ascertain and declare the state of those places, and of the military stores, maps, plans, models, etc., which they shall contain, at the moment which shall be considered as that of the occupation in virtue of the treaty.

Restoration after the temporary occupation.

The Allied Powers engage to restore, at the expiration of the temporary occupation, all the places named in Art. V of the principal treaty, in the state in which they shall have been found at the time of that occupation, save and except the damages which may have been caused by time, and which the French Government should not have provided against by the necessary repairs.

Done at Paris, this 20th day of November, in the year of our Lord, 1815.

(L.S.) RICHELIEU.

(L.S.) CASTLEREAGH.
(L.S.) WELLINGTON.

ADDITIONAL ARTICLE

Paris, November 20, 1815

(Deserters)

The High Contracting Parties having agreed, by Art. V of the treaty of this day, to occupy for a certain period with an Allied army military positions in France; and being desirous of anticipating all that might hazard the order and discipline which it is so important to maintain in that army, it is determined upon by the present additional article, that every deserter who, from either of the corps of the said army, should go over to the French side, shall immediately be arrested by the French authorities, and delivered up to the nearest commander of the Allied troops, in like manner as all deserters from the French troops who might come over towards the Allied army shall be immediately delivered up to the nearest French commandant.

Mutual delivery of deserters.

The tenor of this article is to apply equally to such deserters from either side, who may have forsaken their colours previously to the signature of the treaty; the same to be without delay restored and delivered up to the respective corps to which they may belong.

The present additional article shall have the same force and validity as if it were inserted, word for word, in the military convention of this day.

In faith whereof the respective plenipotentiaries have signed it, and have affixed thereunto the seal of their arms.

Done at Paris, the 20th November, in the year of our Lord, 1815.

(Seals and signatures, as before.)

(C) ANNEXED CONVENTION

Paris, November 20, 1815

GREAT BRITAIN, AUSTRIA, PRUSSIA, RUSSIA—FRANCE

(Relative to the Pecuniary Indemnity to be paid by France to the Allies)

THE payments to which France has bound herself to the Allied Powers, as an indemnity, by Art. IV of the treaty of this day, shall take place in the form and at the periods prescribed by the following articles:—

Indemnity.

ART. I.—The sum of 700,000,000 francs, being the amount of the indemnity, shall be discharged, day by day, in equal portions, in the space of five years, by means of "bons au porteur" on the Royal Treasury of France, in the manner that shall be now set forth.

Time of payment.

ART. II.—The Treasury shall give over, immediately, to the Allied Powers, fifteen engagements for 46,000,000 and two-thirds each, forming together the sum of 700,000,000; the first engagement payable on the 31st March, 1816, the second on the 31st July of the same year, and so on in every fourth month during the five successive years.

Mode of payment.

ART. III.—These engagements shall not be negotiable, but they shall be periodically exchanged against "bons au porteur," negotiable, drawn in the form used in the ordinary service of the Royal Treasury.

Engagements to be exchanged for "bons au porteur."

ART. IV.—In the month which shall precede the four, in the course of which an engagement is to be paid, that engagement shall be divided by the Treasury of France into "bons au porteur" payable in Paris, in equal portions, from the first to the last day of the four months.

Time of exchange.

Thus the engagement of 46,000,000 and two-thirds, falling due 31st March, 1816, shall be exchanged in the month of November, 1815, against "bons au porteur," payable in equal portions from the 1st December, 1815, to 31st March, 1816.

The engagement of 46,000,000 and two-thirds, which will fall due 31st July, 1816, shall be exchanged in the month of March of the same year, against "bons au porteur," payable in equal portions from the 1st April, 1816, to the 31st July of the same year, and so in every four months.

Mode of issue of "bons au porteur."

Art. V.—No single "bon au porteur" shall be delivered for the sum due each day, but the sum so due shall be divided into several "coupures," or bills, of 1,000, 2,000, 5,000, 10,000, and 20,000 francs, the which sums, added together, will amount to the sum total of the payment due for each day.

Limit to amount of "bons au porteur."

Art. VI.—The Allied Powers, convinced that it is as much their interest as that of France that too considerable a sum of "bons au porteur" should not be issued at once, agree that there never shall be in circulation "bons" for more than 50,000,000 francs at a time.

Non-payment of interest.

Art. VII.—No interest shall be paid by France for the delay of five years, which the Allied Powers allow to her for the payment of the 700,000,000 of francs.

Guarantee by France to Allied Powers.

Art. VIII.—On the 1st January, 1816, there shall be made over by France to the Allied Powers, as a guarantee for the regularity of the payments, a fund of interest inscribed in the "Grand Livre" of the public debt of France, of 7,000,000 francs, on a capital of 140,000,000. This fund of interest shall be used to make good, if there should be need of it, the deficiencies in the "acceptances" of the French Government, and to render the payments equal, at the end of every six months, to the "bons au porteur" which shall have fallen due, as shall be hereafter detailed.

Inscription of fund of interest.

Art. IX.—This fund of interest shall be inscribed in the name of such persons as the Allied Powers shall point out; but these persons cannot be the holders of the inscriptions, except in the case provided for in Art. XI ensuing.

The Allied Powers further reserve to themselves the right to transfer the inscriptions to other names, as often as they shall judge necessary.

Deposit of inscriptions.

Art. X.—The deposit of these inscriptions shall be confined to one treasurer named by the Allied Powers, and to another named by the French Government.

Appointment of mixed commissions.

Art. XI.—There shall be a mixed commission, composed of an equal number on both sides, of Allied and French commissioners, who shall examine every six months the state of the payments, and shall regulate the balance.

Payments.

The "bons" of the Treasury paid shall constitute the payments; those which shall not yet have been presented to the Treasury of France shall enter into the account of the subsequent balance; those also which shall have fallen due, been presented and not paid, shall constitute the arrear, and the sum of inscriptions to be applied, at the market price of the day, to cover the deficit.

Arrears.

As soon as that operation shall have taken place, the "bons" unpaid shall be given up to the French commissioners, and the mixed commission shall order the treasurers to pay over the sum so determined upon, and the treasurers shall be authorized and obliged to pay it over to the commissioners of the Allied Powers, who shall dispose of it as they think proper.

Art. XII.—France engages to replace immediately in the hands of the treasurers an amount of inscriptions equal to that which may have been made use of, according to the foregoing Article, in order that the fund stipulated in Art. VIII may be always kept at its full amount.

Full amount of inscriptions to be in hands of treasurers always.

Interest on "bons au porteur."

Art. XIII.—France shall pay an interest of 5 per cent. per annum, from the date of the "bons au porteur" falling due, upon all such "bons" the payment of which may have been delayed by the act of France.

Facilities for payment of indemnity.

Art. XIV.—When the first 600,000,000 francs shall have been paid, the Allies, in order to accelerate the entire liberation of France, will accept, should it be agreeable to the French Government, the fund mentioned in Art. VIII, at the market price of that day, to such an amount as will be equal to the remainder due of the 700,000,000. France will only have to furnish the difference, should any exist.

Art. XV.—Should this plan not be convenient to France, the 100,000,000 francs which would remain due may be discharged in the manner pointed out in Arts. II, III, IV, and V; and, after the complete payment of the 700,000,000, the inscriptions stipulated for in Art. VIII shall be returned to France.

Clothing and equipment of Allied armies.

Art. XVI.—The French Government engages to execute, independently of the pecuniary indemnity stipulated by the present convention, all the engagements stipulated for in the special conventions concluded with the different Powers and their co-Allies relative to the clothing and equipment of their armies; and engages for the exact deliverance and payment of the "bons" and "mandats" arising from the said conventions, in as far as they shall not have been already discharged, at the time of the signature of the principal treaty, and of the present convention.

Done at Paris, this 20th day of November, in the year of our Lord, 1815.

(L.S.) Castlereagh.
(L.S.) Wellington.
(L.S.) Richelieu.

(D) TREATY OF PARIS

March 30, 1856

GREAT BRITAIN, AUSTRIA, FRANCE, PRUSSIA, SARDINIA, TURKEY—RUSSIA

In the Name of Almighty God.

Their Majesties the Queen of the United Kingdom of Great Britain and Ireland, the Emperor of the French, the Emperor of All the Russias, the King of Sardinia, and the Emperor of the Ottomans, animated by a desire of putting an end to the calamities of war, and wishing to prevent the return of the complications which occasioned it, resolved to come to an understanding with His Majesty the Emperor of Austria as to the bases on which peace might be re-established and consolidated, by securing, through effectual and reciprocal guarantees, the independence and integrity of the Ottoman Empire.

For this purpose their said Majesties named as their plenipotentiaries, that is to say:

Her Majesty the Queen of the United Kingdom of Great Britain and Ireland, the Right Honourable George William Frederick, Earl of Clarendon, Baron Hyde of Hindon, a Peer of the United Kingdom, a member of Her Britannic Majesty's Most Honourable Privy Council, Her Majesty's Principal Secretary of State for Foreign Affairs, etc.; and the Right Honourable Henry Richard Charles, Baron Cowley, a Peer of the United Kingdom, a member of Her Majesty's Most Honourable Privy Council, Her Majesty's Ambassador Extraordinary and Minister Plenipotentiary to His Majesty the Emperor of the French, etc.;

His Majesty the Emperor of Austria, the Sieur Charles Ferdinant Count of Buol-Schauenstein, his Chamberlain and actual Privy Councillor, his Minister of the House and of Foreign Affairs, President of the Conference of Ministers, etc.; and the Sieur Joseph Alexander Baron de Hübner, his actual Privy Councillor, and his Envoy Extraordinary and Minister Plenipotentiary to the Court of France, etc.;

His Majesty the Emperor of the French, the Sieur Alexander Count Colonna Walewski, a Senator of the Empire, his Minister and Secretary of State for Foreign Affairs, etc.; and the Sieur Francis Adolphus Baron de Bourqueney, his Envoy Extraordinary and Minister Plenipotentiary to His Imperial and Royal Apostolic Majesty, etc.;

His Majesty the Emperor of All the Russias, the Sieur Alexis Count Orloff, his Aide-de-Camp General and General of Cavalry, Commander of the Head-quarters of His Majesty, a Member of the Council of the Empire and of the Committee of Ministers, etc.; and the Sieur Philip Baron de Brunnow, his Privy Councillor, his Envoy Extraordinary and Minister Plenipotentiary to the Germanic Confederation, and to the Grand Duke of Hesse, etc.;

His Majesty the King of Sardinia, the Sieur Camille Benso, Count of Cavour, President of the Council of Ministers, and his Minister Secretary of State for Finance, etc.; and the Sieur Salvator Marquis de Villa-Marina, his Envoy Extraordinary and Minister Plenipotentiary to the Court of France, etc.;

And His Majesty the Emperor of the Ottomans, Mouhammed Emin Ali Pasha, Grand Vizier of the Ottoman Empire, etc.; and Mehemmed Djemil Bey, his Ambassador Extraordinary and Plenipotentiary to His Majesty the Emperor of the French, accredited in the same character to His Majesty the King of Sardinia, etc.;

Which plenipotentiaries assembled in congress at Paris.

Prussia invited to the Congress, in the interest of Europe.

An understanding having been happily established between them, their Majesties the Queen of the United Kingdom of Great Britain and Ireland, the Emperor of Austria, the Emperor of the French, the Emperor of All the Russias, the King of Sardinia, and the Emperor of the Ottomans, considering that in the interest of Europe, His Majesty the King of Prussia, a signing party to the convention of the 13th of July, 1841, should be invited to participate in the new arrangements to be adopted, and appreciating the value that the concurrence of His said Majesty would add to a work of general pacification, invited him to send plenipotentiaries to the congress.

In consequence, His Majesty the King of Prussia named as his plenipotentiaries, that is to say:

The Sieur Otho Theodore Baron de Manteuffel, President of his Council, and his Minister for Foreign Affairs, etc.; and the Sieur Maximilian Frederick Charles Francis, Count of Hatzfeldt Wildenburg-Schoenstein, his actual Privy Councillor, his Envoy and Minister Plenipotentiary to the Court of France, etc.;

The plenipotentiaries, after having exchanged their full powers, found in good and due form, have agreed upon the following articles:—

Restoration of peace.

ART. I.—From the day of the exchange of the ratifications of the present treaty there shall be peace and friendship between Her Majesty the Queen of the United Kingdom of Great Britain and Ireland, His Majesty the Emperor of the French, His Majesty the King of Sardinia, His Imperial Majesty the Sultan, on the one part, and His Majesty the Emperor of All the Russias, on the other part; as well as between their heirs and successors, their respective dominions and subjects, in perpetuity.

Evacuation of territories.

ART. II.—Peace being happily re-established between their said Majesties, the territories conquered or occupied by their armies during the war shall be reciprocally evacuated.

Special arrangements shall regulate the mode of the evacuation, which shall be as prompt as possible.

ART. III.—His Majesty the Emperor of All the Russias engages to restore to His Majesty the Sultan the town and citadel of Kars, as well as the other parts of the Ottoman territory of which the Russian troops are in possession.

Restoration of Ottoman territory.

ART. IV.—Their Majesties the Queen of the United Kingdom of Great Britain and Ireland, the Emperor of the French, the King of Sardinia, and the Sultan, engage to restore to His Majesty the Emperor of All the Russias the towns and ports of Sebastopol, Balaklava, Kamiesch, Eupatoria, Kertch, Jenikale, Kinburn, as well as all other territories occupied by the Allied troops.

Restoration of Russian territory.

ART. V.—Their Majesties the Queen of the United Kingdom of Great Britain and Ireland, the Emperor of the French, the Emperor of All the Russias, the King of Sardinia, and the Sultan, grant a full and entire amnesty to those of their subjects who may have been compromised by any participation whatsoever in the events of the war in favour of the cause of the enemy.

Amnesty.

It is expressly understood that such amnesty shall extend to the subjects of each of the belligerent parties who may have continued, during the war, to be employed in the service of the other belligerents.

Prisoners.

ART. VI.—Prisoners of war shall be immediately given up on either side.

ART. VII.—Her Majesty the Queen of the United Kingdom of Great Britain and Ireland, His Majesty the Emperor of Austria, His Majesty the Emperor of the French, His Majesty the King of Prussia, His Majesty the Emperor of All the Russias, and His Majesty the King of Sardinia, declare the Sublime Porte admitted to participate in the advantages of the public law and system of Europe. Their Majesties engage, each on his part, to respect the independence and the territorial integrity of the Ottoman Empire; guarantee in common the strict observance of that engagement; and will, in consequence, consider any act tending to its violation as a question of general interest.

Turkey admitted into the public system of Europe.

ART. VIII.—If there should arise between the Sublime Porte and one or more of the other signing Powers, any misunderstanding which might endanger the maintenance of their relations, the Sublime Porte, and each of such Powers, before having recourse to the use of force, shall afford the other contracting parties the opportunity of preventing such an extremity by means of their mediation.

Mediation in case of difference between Turkey and any of the other parties.

ART. IX.—His Imperial Majesty the Sultan having, in his constant solicitude for the welfare of his subjects, issued a firman, which, while ameliorating their condition without distinction of religion or of race, records his generous intentions towards the Christian population of his Empire, and wishing to give a further proof of his sentiments in that respect, has resolved to communicate to the contracting parties the said firman, emanating spontaneously from his sovereign will.

Christian population of Turkey.

The contracting Powers recognize the high value of this communication.

It is clearly understood that it cannot, in any case, give to the said Powers the right to interfere, either collectively or separately, in the relations of His Majesty the Sultan with his subjects, nor in the internal administration of his Empire.

The Bosphorus and Dardanelles.

ART. X.—The Convention of 13th of July, 1841, which maintains the ancient rule of the Ottoman Empire relative to the closing of the straits of the Bosphorus and of Dardanelles, has been revised by common consent.

The Act concluded for that purpose, and in conformity with that principle, between the High Contracting Parties, is and remains annexed to the present treaty, and shall have the same force and validity as if it formed an integral part thereof.

The Black Sea neutralized.

ART. XI.—The Black Sea is neutralized; its waters and its ports, thrown open to the mercantile marine of every nation, are formally and in perpetuity interdicted to the flag of war, either of the Powers possessing its coasts, or of any other Power, with the exceptions mentioned in Arts. XIV and XIX of the present treaty.

ART. XII.—Free from any impediment, the commerce in the ports and waters of the Black Sea shall be subject only to regulations of health, customs, and police, framed in a spirit favourable to the development of commercial transactions.

In order to afford to the commercial and maritime interests of every nation the security which is desired, Russia and the Sublime Porte will admit consuls into their ports situated upon the coast of the Black Sea, in conformity with the principles of international law.

ART. XIII.—The Black Sea being neutralized according to the terms of Art. XI, the maintenance or establishment upon its coast of military-maritime arsenals becomes alike unnecessary and purposeless; in consequence, His Majesty the Emperor of All the Russias, and His Imperial Majesty the Sultan, engage not to establish or to maintain upon that coast any military-maritime arsenal.

ART. XIV.—Their Majesties the Emperor of All the Russias and the Sultan having concluded a convention for the purpose of settling the force and the number of light vessels, necessary for the service of their coasts, which they reserve to themselves to maintain in the Black Sea, that convention is annexed to the present treaty, and shall have the same force and validity as if it formed an integral part thereof. It cannot be either annulled or modified without the assent of the Powers signing the present treaty.

The Danube.

ART. XV.—The Act of the Congress of Vienna having established the principles intended to regulate the navigation of rivers which separate or traverse different States, the Contracting Powers stipulate among themselves that those principles shall in future be equally applied to the Danube and its mouths. They declare that its arrangement henceforth forms a part of the public law of Europe, and take it under their guarantee.

The navigation of the Danube cannot be subjected to any impediment or charge not expressly provided for by the stipulations contained in the following articles; in consequence, there shall not be levied any toll founded solely upon the fact of the navigation of the river, nor any duty upon the goods which may be on board of vessels. The regulations of police and of quarantine to be established for the safety of the States separated or traversed by that river shall be so framed as to facilitate, as much as possible, the passage of vessels. With the exception of such regulations, no obstacle whatever shall be opposed to free navigation.

ART. XVI.—With a view to carry out the arrangements of the preceding article, a commission, in which Great Britain, Austria, France, Prussia, Russia, Sardinia, and Turkey shall each be represented by one delegate, shall be charged to designate and to cause to be executed the works necessary below Isatcha, to clear the mouths of the Danube, as well as the neighbouring parts of the sea, from the sands and other impediments which obstruct them, in order to put that part of the river and the said parts of the sea in the best possible state for navigation.

In order to cover the expenses of such works, as well as of the establishments intended to secure and to facilitate the navigation at the mouths of the Danube, fixed duties, of a suitable rate, settled by the commission by a majority of votes, may be levied, on the express condition that, in this respect as in every other, the flags of all nations shall be treated on the footing of perfect equality.

River Commission.

ART. XVII.—A commission shall be established, and shall be composed of delegates of Austria, Bavaria, the Sublime Porte, and Würtemberg (one for each of those Powers), to whom shall be added commissioners from the three Danubian Principalities, whose nomination shall have been approved by the Porte. This commission, which shall be permanent, (1) shall prepare regulations of navigation and river police; (2) shall remove the impediments, of whatever nature they may be, which still prevent the application to the Danube of the arrangements of the Treaty of Vienna; (3) shall order and cause to be executed the necessary works throughout the whole course of the river; and (4) shall, after the dissolution of the European Commission, see to maintaining the mouths of the Danube and the neighbouring parts of the sea in a navigable state.

ART. XVIII.—It is understood that the European Commission shall have completed its task, and that the River Commission shall have finished the works described in the preceding article, under Nos. 1 and 2, within the period of two years. The signing Powers assembled in conference having been informed of that fact, shall, after having placed it on record, pronounce the dissolution of the European Commission, and from that time the permanent River Commission shall enjoy the same powers as those with which the European Commission shall have until then been invested.

ART. XIX.—In order to ensure the execution of the regulations which shall have been established by common agreement, in conformity with the principles above declared, each of the Contracting Powers shall have the right to station, at all times, two light vessels at the mouths of the Danube.

ART. XX.—In exchange for the towns, ports, and territories enumerated in Art. IV of the present treaty, and in order more fully to secure the freedom of the navigation of the Danube, His Majesty the Emperor of All the Russias consents to the rectification of his frontier in Bessarabia.

Cession of Russian territory.

Rectification of frontier.

The new frontier shall begin from the Black Sea, one kilometre to the east of the lake Bourna Sola, shall run perpendicularly to the Akerman Road, shall follow that road to the Val de Trajan, pass to the south of Bolgrad, ascend the course of the river Yalpuck to the height of Saratsika, and terminate at Katamori on the Pruth. Above that point the old frontier between the two Empires shall not undergo any modification.

Delegates of the contracting Powers shall fix, in its details, the line of the new frontier.

ART. XXI.—The territory ceded by Russia shall be annexed to the principality of Moldavia, under the suzerainty of the Sublime Porte.

Right of option.

The inhabitants of that territory shall enjoy the rights and privileges secured to the principalities; and during the space of three years, they shall be permitted to transfer their domicile elsewhere, disposing freely of their property.

ART. XXII.—The principalities of Wallachia and Moldavia shall continue to enjoy under the suzerainty of the Porte, and under the guarantee of the contracting Powers, the privileges and immunities of which they are in possession. No exclusive protection shall be exercised over them by any of the guaranteeing Powers.

Rights of Wallachia and Moldavia.

There shall be no separate right of interference in their internal affairs.

ART. XXIII.—The Sublime Porte engages to preserve to the said principalities an independent and national administration, as well as full liberty of worship, of legislation, of commerce, and of navigation.

The laws and statutes at present in force shall be revised. In order to establish a complete agreement in regard to such revision, a special commission, as to the composition of which the High Contracting Powers will come to an understanding among themselves, shall assemble, without delay, at Bucharest, together with a commissioner of the Sublime Porte.

The business of this commission shall be to investigate the present state of the principalities, and to propose bases for their future organization.

ART. XXIV.—His Majesty the Sultan promises to convoke immediately in each of the two provinces a divan *ad hoc*, composed in such a manner as to represent most closely the interests of all classes of society. These divans shall be called upon to express the wishes of the people in regard to the definitive organization of the principalities.

Organization of the principalities.

An instruction from the congress shall regulate the relations between the commission and these divans.

ART. XXV.—Taking into consideration the opinion expressed by the two divans, the commission shall transmit, without delay, to the present seat of the conferences, the result of its own labours.

The final agreement with the Suzerain Power shall be recorded in a convention to be concluded at Paris between the High Contracting Parties; and a Hatti-sheriff, in conformity with the stipulations of the convention, shall constitute definitively the organization of those provinces, placed thenceforward under the collective guarantee of all the signing Powers.

Collective guarantee of the Powers.

Art. XXVI.—It is agreed that there shall be in the principalities a national armed force, organized with the view to maintain the security of the interior, and to ensure that of the frontiers. No impediment shall be opposed to the extraordinary measures of defence which, by agreement with the Sublime Porte, they may be called upon to take in order to repel any external aggression.

Art. XXVII.—If the internal tranquillity of the principalities should be menaced or compromised, the Sublime Porte shall come to an understanding with the other contracting Powers in regard to the measures to be taken for maintaining or re-establishing legal order.

No armed intervention can take place without previous agreement between those Powers.

Art. XXVIII.—The principality of Serbia shall continue to hold of the Sublime Porte, in conformity with the Imperial Hats which fix and determine its rights and immunities, placed henceforward under the collective guarantee of the Contracting Powers.

Serbia.

In consequence, the said principality shall preserve its independent and national administration, as well as full liberty of worship, of legislation, of commerce, and of navigation.

Art. XXIX.—The right of garrison of the Sublime Porte, as stipulated by anterior regulations, is maintained. No armed intervention can take place in Serbia without previous agreement between the High Contracting Powers.

Russian and Turkish possessions in Asia.

Art. XXX.—His Majesty the Emperor of All the Russias and His Majesty the Sultan maintain in its integrity the state of their possessions in Asia, such as it legally existed before the rupture.

Frontier commission.

In order to prevent all local dispute the line of frontier shall be verified, and, if necessary, rectified, without any prejudice as regards territory being sustained by either party.

For this purpose a mixed commission, composed of two Russian commissioners, two Ottoman commissioners, one English commissioner, and one French commissioner, shall be sent to the spot immediately after the re-establishment of diplomatic relations between the Court of Russia and the Sublime Porte. Its labours shall be completed within the period of eight months after the exchange of the ratifications of the present treaty.

Art. XXXI.—The territories occupied during the war by the troops of their Majesties the Queen of the United Kingdom of Great Britain and Ireland, the Emperor of Austria, the Emperor of the French, and the King of Sardinia, according to the terms of the conventions signed at Constantinople on the 12th of March, 1854, between Great Britain, France, and the Sublime Porte; on

Evacuation of troops.

the 14th of June of the same year, between Austria and the Sublime Porte; and on the 15th of March, 1855, between Sardinia and the Sublime Porte; shall be evacuated as soon as possible after the exchange of the ratifications of the present treaty. The periods and the means of execution shall form the object of an arrangement between the Sublime Porte and the Powers whose troops have occupied its territory.

Commercial relations until new treaties concluded.

ART. XXXII.—Until the treaties or conventions which existed before the war between the belligerent Powers have been either renewed or replaced by new Acts, commerce of importation or of exportation shall take place reciprocally on the footing of the regulations in force before the war; and in all other matters their subjects shall be respectively treated upon the footing of the most favoured nation.

Aland Islands.

ART. XXXIII.—The convention concluded this day between Their Majesties the Queen of the United Kingdom of Great Britain and Ireland, the Emperor of the French, on the one part, and His Majesty the Emperor of All the Russias, on the other part, respecting the Aland Islands, is and remains annexed to the present treaty, and shall have the same force and validity as if it formed a part thereof.

Ratification.

ART. XXXIV.—The present treaty shall be ratified, and the ratifications shall be exchanged at Paris in the space of four weeks, or sooner if possible.

In witness whereof the respective plenipotentiaries have signed the same, and have affixed thereto the seal of their arms.

Done at Paris, the 30th day of the month of March, in the year 1856.

(Here follow signatures and seals.)

ADDITIONAL AND TRANSITORY ARTICLE

Paris, March 30, 1856

Warships employed in the evacuation.

The stipulations of the convention respecting the straits, signed this day, shall not be applicable to the vessels of war employed by the belligerent Powers for the evacuation, by sea, of the territories occupied by their armies; but the said stipulations shall resume their entire effect as soon as the evacuation shall be terminated.

Done at Paris, the 30th day of the month of March, in the year 1856.

(Here follow signatures and seals.)

(E) PRELIMINARIES OF VILLAFRANCA[1]

July 11, 1859

FRANCE—AUSTRIA

BETWEEN His Majesty the Emperor of Austria and His Majesty the Emperor of the French, it has been agreed as follows:—

The two Sovereigns favour the creation of an Italian Confederation. This confederation shall be under the honorary presidency of the Holy Father.

Cession of Lombardy. The Emperor of Austria cedes to the Emperor of the French his rights over Lombardy, with the exception of the fortresses of Mantua and Peschiera, so that the frontier of the Austrian possessions shall start from the extremity of the rayon of the fortress of Peschiera, and extend in a straight line along the Mincio as far as Legrazia, thence to Szarzarola, and Lugano on the Po, whence the existing frontiers continue to form the boundaries of Austria.

The Emperor of the French shall present the ceded territory to the King of Sardinia.

Venetia. Venetia shall form part of the Italian Confederation, remaining, however, subject to the Crown of the Emperor of Austria.

The Grand Duke of Tuscany and the Duke of Modena return to their States, granting a general amnesty.

The two Emperors shall request the Holy Father to introduce in his States some indispensable reforms.

Amnesty. Full and complete amnesty is granted on both sides to persons compromised on the occasion of the recent events in the territories of the belligerents.

Done at Villafranca, 11th July, 1859.

NAPOLÉON. FRANCIS JOSEPH.

[1] See the definitive treaty of peace, signed at Zurich, November 10, 1859; *infra* (F).

(F) TREATY OF ZURICH

November 10, 1859

AUSTRIA—FRANCE

In the Name of the Most Holy and Indivisible Trinity.

His Majesty the Emperor of Austria, and His Majesty the Emperor of the French, desirous of putting an end to the calamities of war, and of preventing the recurrence of the complications which gave rise to it, by assisting to place on solid and durable bases the internal and external independence of Italy, have resolved to convert into a definitive treaty of peace, the preliminaries signed by their hand at Villafranca.

With this view their Imperial Majesties have named as their plenipotentiaries, that is to say:

His Majesty the Emperor of Austria, the Sieur Alois Count Karolyi of Nagy Karoly, his Chamberlain and Minister Plenipotentiary, etc., etc.; and the Sieur Otho Baron de Meysenbug, his Minister Plenipotentiary and Aulic Councillor, etc.;

And His Majesty the Emperor of the French, the Sieur François Adolphe Baron de Bourqueney, Senator of the Empire, etc.; and the Sieur Gaston Robert Morin Marquis de Banneville, Officer of the Imperial Order of the Legion of Honour, etc., etc.

Who, having met in conference at Zurich, and after having exchanged their full powers, found in good and due form, have agreed upon the following Articles:—

Restoration of peace.

ART. I.—There shall be in future peace and friendship between His Majesty the Emperor of Austria and His Majesty the Emperor of the French, as also between their heirs and successors, their respective States and subjects, for ever.

Prisoners of war.

ART. II.—The prisoners of war shall be immediately given up on either side.

Restoration of prizes not yet condemned.

ART. III.—To diminish the evils of war, and by an exceptional departure from the law generally observed, the captured Austrian vessels which have not yet been condemned as prizes shall be restored.

The vessels and cargoes shall be restored in the state in which they were at the time of their capture, after payment of all expenses, and of all charges which may have been incurred on account of the convoy and keeping of the said prizes, as well as of any legal proceedings connected with them, and the usual allowance to the captors; and lastly no indemnity will be claimable on account of prizes sunk or destroyed, any more than for the capture of merchandise belonging to the enemy, even though it may not yet have been subjected to a decision of the prize court.

It is well understood, on the other hand, that the decisions pronounced by the prize court hold good in favour of those to whom the prizes have been adjudged.

Cession of Lombardy.

ART. IV.—His Majesty the Emperor of Austria renounces, for himself and all his descendants and successors, in favour of His Majesty the Emperor of the French, his rights and titles to Lombardy, with the exception of the fortresses of Peschiera and Mantua, and of the territories determined by the new limitation, which remain in the possession of His Imperial and Royal Apostolic Majesty.

Frontier.

The line of frontier, starting from the southern limit of the Tyrol, on the Lac de Garda, will pass along the middle of the lake, as far as the height of Bardolino and Manerba, from whence it will rejoin in a straight line the point where the circle of defence of the fortress of Peschiera intersects the Lac de Garda.

This circle will be determined by a circumference of which the radius, reckoned from the centre of the fortress, is fixed at 3,500 mètres, plus the distance from the said centre to the glacis of the most advanced fort. From the point where the circumference thus designated intersects the Mincio, the frontier will follow the thalweg of the river as far as Le Grazie, will extend from Le Grazie in a straight line to Scorzarolo, will follow the thalweg of the Po to Luzzara, from which point there is no change in the present limits as they existed before the war.

A military commission, appointed by the Governments interested, will be charged with the duty of tracing the line on the ground with the least possible delay.

France to cede Lombardy to Sardinia.

ART. V.—His Majesty the Emperor of the French declares his intention of handing over to His Majesty the King of Sardinia the territories ceded by the preceding Article.

Evacuation of occupied territories.

ART. VI.—The territories still occupied in virtue of the armistice of the 8th July last, shall be reciprocally evacuated by the belligerent Powers, the troops of which will retire immediately beyond the frontier line stipulated in Art. IV.

ART. VII.—The new Government of Lombardy will undertake three-fifths of the debt of the Monte Lombardo-Veneto.

Public debt and loan.

It will equally be charged with a portion of the national loan of 1854, fixed between the High Contracting Powers at 40,000,000 florins ("Conventions-münz").

The manner of the payment of these 40,000,000 florins will be determined by an additional article.

ART. VIII.—An international commission shall be immediately appointed to wind up the affairs of the Monte Lombardo-Veneto; the creditor and debtor balance to be drawn on the principle of three-fifths to the new Government, and two-fifths to Austria.

Of the assets of the sinking fund of the Monte and its deposits, consisting of public securities, the new Government will receive three-fifths and Austria two-fifths; and as to that part of the assets which consist of lands or mortgages, the commission will effect the partition with reference to the situation of the real property in question, so as to allot the property, as far as possible, to that one of the two Governments upon whose territory it may be situated.

Affairs to be adjusted by international commission.

As to the different categories of debts inscribed in the Monte Lombardo-Veneto, and to the capital placed at interest in the deposit bank of the sinking fund, the new Government undertakes three-fifths and Austria two-fifths, either for the payment of interest, or the reimbursement of the capital, in conformity with the regulations hitherto in force. The credits of Austrian subjects will, by preference, form part of the quota of Austria, who will transmit to the new Government of Lombardy specified lists of these papers, in three months' time from the exchange of ratifications, or sooner, if possible.

Succession to contracts.

ART. IX.—The new Government of Lombardy succeeds to the rights and obligations resulting from contracts regularly stipulated by the Austrian Administration for objects of public interest, especially concerning the ceded territory.

Deposits of subjects.

ART. X.—The Austrian Government is charged with the reimbursement of all sums paid by Lombard subjects, communal districts, public establishments, and religious societies, into the Austrian public banks, in the shape of caution-money, deposits, or consignments, which will be punctually reimbursed by the new Government.

Railway concessions.

ART. XI.—The new Government of Lombardy recognizes and confirms the concessions granted to the railroads by the Austrian Government on the ceded territory, to the full extent of all their arrangements and duration, and particularly the concessions resulting from the contracts passed under date of 14th March, 1856, 8th April, 1857, and 23rd September, 1858.

From the time of the exchange of the ratifications of this treaty, the new Government is bound by all the agreements and obligations resulting to the Austrian Government from the above-mentioned concessions, in regard to the lines of railway situated in the ceded territory; consequently the right of devolution which belonged to the Austrian Government in respect to these railroads is transferred to the new Government of Lombardy.

The payments which are still to be made on the sum due to the State by the concessionaries in view of the contract of 14th March, 1856, as an equivalent for the expenses of construction of the said railroads, will be paid in full into the Austrian Exchequer.

The credits of the building contractors and tradesmen, as well as the compensation-money for appropriation of land, which appertain to the time when the railways in question were administered on account of the State, and which have not yet been paid, will be paid by the Austrian Government, and, in so far as they may be due from them in virtue of the act of concession, by the grantees of the Austrian Government. A special Convention will make arrangements, as soon as possible, for the international service of the railways, between the respective countries.

ART. XII.—Lombard subjects domiciled on the territory ceded by the present treaty will have, for the space of a year, from the date of the day on which the ratifications are exchanged, and conditionally on a previous declaration before the competent authorities, full and entire power to export their movables, free of duty, and to retire with their families into the States of His Imperial and Royal Apostolic Majesty, in which case their quality of Austrian subjects will be retained by them. They will be at liberty to keep their immovable property situated in the Lombard territory.

Right of option.

The same power is granted reciprocally to the natives of the ceded territory of Lombardy living in the States of His Majesty the Emperor of Austria.

The Lombards who profit by these arrangements cannot be, on account of their choice, disturbed on either side, in their person or in their properties situated in the respective States.

The delay of one year is extended to two years, for the subjects, natives of the ceded territory of Lombardy, who at the time of the exchange of the ratifications of this treaty are not within the territory of the Austrian Monarchy. Their declaration may be received by the nearest Austrian Mission, or by the superior authority of any Province of the Monarchy.

ART. XIII.—The Lombard subjects in the Austrian army, excepting those who are natives of the part of the Lombard territory reserved to His Majesty the Emperor of Austria by this treaty, will be immediately discharged from military service, and sent back to their homes.

Lombard subjects in the Austrian army.

It is understood that those amongst them who declare their wish to remain in the service of His Imperial and Royal Apostolic Majesty will not be disturbed on this account, either in person or in property.

The same guarantees are assured to the civil employés, natives of Lombardy, who manifest the intention of keeping the offices they occupy in the Austrian service.

Civil employés.

ART. XIV.—The pensions, both civil and military, regularly paid, and which were paid out of the public funds of Lombardy, remain due to those entitled to them, and, if need be, to their widows and children, and will be paid in future by the new Government of Lombardy.

Pensions.

This stipulation is extended to the pensioners, both civil and military, as well as to their widows and children, without distinction of origin, who keep their domicile in the ceded territory, and whose salaries, paid up to 1814 by the former Kingdom of Italy, then became payable by the Austrian treasury.

ART. XV.—The archives containing the titles to property, and documents regarding the administration of justice, applying either to the part of Lombardy of which the possession is reserved to His Majesty the Emperor of Austria by this treaty, or by

Archives.

the Venetian Provinces, will be handed over to the Commissioners of His Imperial and Royal Apostolic Majesty as soon as possible.

Reciprocally, any titles of property, and documents connected with the administration of justice applying to the ceded territory, which may be in the archives of the Emperor of Austria, will be handed over to the Commissioners of the new Government of Lombardy.

The High Contracting Parties engage to consult each other, at the request of the superior administrative authorities, respecting all the documents and informations relative to the affairs which concern both Lombardy and Venetia.

Religious societies.

ART. XVI.—The religious societies established in Lombardy will be at liberty to dispose of their movable and immovable property, in case the new legislation, under which they pass, does not authorize the keeping up of their establishments.

ART. XVII.—His Majesty the Emperor of the French reserves to himself the power of transferring to His Majesty the King of Sardinia, in the form usual to international transactions, the rights and obligations esulting from Arts. VII, VIII, IX, X, XI, XII, XIII, XIV, XV, XVI of this treaty.

Confederation of Italian States.

ART. XVIII.—His Majesty the Emperor of Austria and His Majesty the Emperor of the French engage to make every effort to encourage the creation of a confederation among the Italian States, to be placed under the honorary presidency of the Holy Father, and the object of which will be to uphold the independence and inviolability of the confederated States, to assure the development of their moral and material interests, and to guarantee the internal and external safety of Italy by the existence of a Federal army.

Venetia, which remains subject to the Crown of His Imperial and Royal Apostolic Majesty, will form one of the States of this confederation, and will participate in the obligations, as in the rights, resulting from the Federal pact, the clauses of which will be determined by an Assembly composed of the representatives of all the Italian States.

Rights of Tuscany, Modena, and Parma.

ART. XIX.—As the territorial delimitations of the independent States of Italy, who took no part in the late war, can be changed only with the sanction of the Powers that presided at their formation and recognized their existence, the rights of the Grand Duke of Tuscany, of the Duke of Modena, and of the Duke of Parma, are expressly reserved for the consideration of the High Contracting Parties.

Reforms.

ART. XX.—Desirous of seeing the tranquillity of the States of the Church and the power of the Holy Father assured; convinced that such object could not be more efficaciously attained than by the adoption of a system suited to the wants of the populations and conformable to the generous intentions already manifested by the Sovereign Pontiff, His Majesty the Emperor of the French and His Majesty the Emperor of Austria will unite their efforts to obtain from His Holiness that the necessity of introducing into the administration of his States the reforms admitted as indispensable shall be taken into serious consideration by his Government.

Art. XXI.—With a view to contribute by every effort to quiet the public mind, the High Contracting Parties declare and promise that in their respective territories, and in the lands restored or ceded, no individual compromised by the recent events in the Peninsula, no matter what his rank or position in society, shall be prosecuted, annoyed, or troubled, in person or property, on account of his conduct or political opinions.

Amnesty.

Art. XXII.—The present treaty shall be ratified, and the ratifications exchanged within a fortnight, or earlier if possible. In faith of which the respective plenipotentiaries have signed it, and have affixed their seals thereunto.

Ratification.

Done at Zurich, on the 10th day of the month of November, of the year of Grace, 1859.

(L.S.) Karolyi.
(L.S.) Meysenbug.
(L.S.) Bourqueney.
(L.S.) Banneville.

Additional Article

The Government of His Majesty the Emperor of the French engages itself towards the Government of His Imperial and Royal Apostolic Majesty to pay to it, on account of the new Government of Lombardy, which will guarantee its repayment, 40,000,000 florins ("Conventions-münz"), stipulated by Art. VII of the present treaty, in the manner and at the periods hereinafter determined:—

Provisions as to the national loan.

Payments and dates.

8,000,000 florins shall be paid cash, by a bill payable at Paris, without interest, on the expiration of the third month, dating from the day on which the present treaty was signed, and which will be handed to the plenipotentiaries of His Imperial and Royal Apostolic Majesty when the exchange of ratifications takes place.

The payment of the remaining 32,000,000 florins shall take place at Vienna, cash, in ten successive instalments, to be made every two months, by bills on Paris, at the rate of 3,200,000 florins each.

The first of these payments will be made two months after the payment of the bill of 8,000,000 florins above stipulated. For that date, as for the other following, the interest will be reckoned at 5 per cent., dating from the first day of the month which will follow the exchange of the ratifications of the present treaty.

The present additional article shall have the same force and value as if inserted verbatim in the treaty of this day.

It shall be ratified in one single act, and the ratifications exchanged at the same time.

In faith of which the respective plenipotentiaries have signed the present additional article, and affixed their seals thereunto.

Done at Zurich, on the 10th day of the month of November, of the year of Grace, 1859.

(*Here follow signatures and seals.*)

(G) PRELIMINARIES OF NIKOLSBURG

July 26, 1866

AUSTRIA—PRUSSIA

THEIR Majesties the Emperor of Austria and the King of Prussia, animated with the desire of restoring the benefits of peace to their countries, have for that purpose, and in order to settle the preliminaries of peace, appointed plenipotentiaries, that is to say:

His Majesty the Emperor of Austria, the Count Aloisius Karolyi, and the Baron Adolphus von Brenner-Felsach;

And His Majesty the King of Prussia, Otho, Count von Bismarck-Schönhausen, his President of the Council and Minister for Foreign Affairs;

Who, after exchanging their full powers, which were found in good and due form, have agreed upon the following fundamental points as the basis of the peace to be concluded without delay.

Withdrawal of troops—conditions.

ART. I.—With the exception of the Lombardo-Venetian Kingdom, the territory of the Austrian Monarchy remains intact. His Majesty the King of Prussia engages to withdraw his troops from the Austrian territories occupied by them as soon as the Peace shall be concluded, under reservation of the arrangements to be made upon the definite conclusion of the Peace for guaranteeing the payment of the war indemnity.

New organization of Germany.

ART. II.—His Majesty the Emperor of Austria recognizes the dissolution of the Germanic Confederation as it has existed hitherto, and consents to a new organization of Germany without the participation of the Empire of Austria. His Majesty likewise promises to recognize the closer union which will be founded by His Majesty the King of Prussia, to the north of the line of the Main, and he declares that he consents to the German States south of that line entering into a Union, the national relations of which with the North German Confederation are to be the subject of an ulterior agreement between the two parties.

Cession of Schleswig-Holstein.

ART. III.—His Majesty the Emperor of Austria transfers to His Majesty the King of Prussia all the rights which the Treaty of Vienna of 30th October, 1864, recognized as belonging to him over the Duchies of Schleswig and Holstein, with this reservation, that the people of the northern districts of Schleswig shall be again united to Denmark, if they express a desire to be so by a vote freely given.

Art. IV.—His Majesty the Emperor of Austria undertakes to pay His Majesty the King of Prussia the sum of 40,000,000 thalers to cover a part of the expenses which Prussia has been put to by the war. But from this sum may be deducted the amount of the indemnity for the costs of war which His Majesty the Emperor of Austria still has the right of exacting from the Duchies of Schleswig and Holstein, by virtue of Art. XII of the treaty of peace of 30th October, 1864, before cited, say 15,000,000 thalers, with 5,000,000 in addition, as the equivalent for the cost of providing for the Prussian army, maintained by the Austrian countries occupied by that army until the time of the conclusion of the Peace.

Indemnity.

Art. V.—In conformity with the wish expressed by His Majesty the Emperor of Austria, His Majesty the King of Prussia declares his willingness to let the territorial State of the Kingdom of Saxony continue in its present extent, when the modifications are made which are to take place in Germany; reserving to himself, however, to regulate in detail, by a special peace with His Majesty the King of Saxony, the questions as to Saxony's part in the expenses of the war, as well as the future position of the Kingdom of Saxony in the North German Confederation.

Saxony.

On the other hand, His Majesty the Emperor of Austria promises to recognize the new organization which the King of Prussia will establish in the north of Germany, including the territorial modifications consequent thereon.

Art. VI.—His Majesty the King of Prussia undertakes to prevail upon His Majesty the King of Italy, his Ally, to give his approval to the preliminaries of peace, so soon as the Venetian Kingdom shall have been put at the disposal of His Majesty the King of Italy by a declaration of His Majesty the Emperor of the French.

Italy and the Preliminaries of Peace.

Art. VII.—The ratifications of the present convention shall be exchanged at Nikolsburg in the space of two days at the latest.

Ratification.

Art. VIII.—Immediately after the ratification of the present convention shall have been effected and exchanged, their Majesties the Emperor of Austria and the King of Prussia will appoint plenipotentiaries, who will meet at a place to be hereafter named, to conclude the Peace upon the basis of the present preliminary treaty, and to agree upon the details of the conditions.

Provision for concluding a definitive treaty.

Art. IX.—For that purpose the Contracting States, after having decided upon these preliminaries, will conclude an armistice for the Austrian and Saxon armies on the one part, and for the Prussian army on the other part, of which the detailed conditions, from the military point of view, are to be immediately determined. That armistice shall date from the 2nd of August, the day to which the present suspension of arms shall be prolonged.

Agreement to conclude an armistice.

The armistice shall, at the same time, be concluded with Bavaria and General the Baron von Manteuffel will be instructed to conclude with the Kingdom of Würtemberg and the Grand Duchies of Baden and Hesse-Darmstadt, as soon as those States shall propose it, an armistice, beginning on the 2nd of August, and founded on the state of military possession at the time.

In faith whereof the respective plenipotentiaries have signed the present convention, and to it have affixed the seals of their arms.

Done at Nikolsburg, 26th July, 1866.

(L.S.) Bismarck.

(L.S.) Karolyi.
(L.S.) Brenner.

(H) TREATY OF PRAGUE

August 23, 1866

AUSTRIA—PRUSSIA

In the Name of the Most Holy and Indivisible Trinity.

His Majesty the Emperor of Austria and His Majesty the King of Prussia, animated with the desire of restoring to their countries the benefits of peace, have determined to convert the preliminaries signed at Nikolsburg, on the 26th July, 1866, into a definitive treaty of peace, and for that purpose Their Majesties have appointed as their plenipotentiaries, that is to say:

His Majesty the Emperor of Austria, the Baron Adolphus Maria von Brenner-Felsach, his actual Privy Councillor and Chamberlain, Envoy Extraordinary and Minister Plenipotentiary, etc.; and

His Majesty the King of Prussia, the Baron Charles von Werther, his Chamberlain, actual Privy Councillor and Plenipotentiary, etc.;

Who met together in conference at Prague, and after exchanging their full powers, which were found in good and proper form, agreed upon the following articles:—

Restoration of peace.

ART. I.—There shall be peace and friendship between His Majesty the Emperor of Austria and His Majesty the King of Prussia, and between their heirs and successors, as well as between their respective States and subjects, henceforth and for ever.

Union of Lombardy and Venetia with Italy.

ART. II.—For the purpose of carrying out Art. VI of the preliminaries of peace concluded at Nikolsburg on the 26th July, 1866, and as His Majesty the Emperor of the French officially declared through his accredited ambassador to His Majesty the King of Prussia, on the 29th July, 1866, "qu'en ce qui concerne le Gouvernement de l'Empereur, la Vénétie est acquise à l'Italie pour lui être remise à la Paix,"—His Majesty the Emperor of Austria also accedes on his part to that declaration and gives his consent to the union of the Lombardo-Venetian Kingdom with the Kingdom of Italy, without any other burdensome condition than the liquidation of those debts which, being charged on the territories ceded, are to be recognized in accordance with the precedent of the Treaty of Zurich.

Ceded territories and debts.

Prisoners of war.

ART. III.—The prisoners of war shall be set at liberty immediately on both sides.

ART. IV.—His Majesty the Emperor of Austria acknowledges the dissolution of the Germanic Confederation as hitherto constituted, and

Dissolution of the Germanic Confederation, and new organization of Germany.

gives his consent to a new organization of Germany without the participation of the Imperial Austrian State. His Majesty likewise promises to recognize the more restricted Federal relations which His Majesty the King of Prussia will establish to the north of the line of the Main; and he declares his concurrence in the formation of an association of the German States situated to the south of that line, whose national connection with the North German Confederation is reserved for further arrangement between the parties, and which will have an independent international existence.

Cession of Schleswig-Holstein.

ART. V.—His Majesty the Emperor of Austria transfers to His Majesty the King of Prussia all the rights which he acquired by the Vienna Treaty of Peace of 30th October, 1864, over the Duchies of Holstein and Schleswig, with the condition that the population of the northern districts of Schleswig shall be ceded to Denmark if, by a free vote, they express a wish to be united to Denmark.

Saxony.

ART. VI.—At the desire of His Majesty the Emperor of Austria, His Majesty the King of Prussia declares his willingness to let the present territorial condition of the Kingdom of Saxony remain to the same extent as before, in the alterations which are about to be made in Germany; but he reserves to himself the right of arranging the contribution of Saxony to the expenses of the war, and the future position of the Kingdom of Saxony in the North German Confederation, by a special treaty to be concluded with His Majesty the King of Saxony.

On the other hand, His Majesty the Emperor of Austria promises to recognize the new arrangements that will be made by His Majesty the King of Prussia in North Germany, including the territorial alterations.

Questions of property to be settled by a commission.

ART. VII.—For the purpose of making arrangements respecting the late Federal property, a commission will meet at Frankfort-on-the-Main within six weeks at the latest from the ratification of this treaty, to which commission all claims and demands on the German Confederation are to be sent in, and they will be liquidated within six months. Austria and Prussia will send representatives to that commission, and all the other late Federal Governments are at liberty to do the same.

Movable property.

ART. VIII.—Austria has the right of removing or otherwise disposing of the Imperial property in the Federal fortresses, and the part of the movable Federal property belonging to Austria, according to specification; the same is the case with all the movable effects of the Confederation.

Pensioners.

ART. IX.—The pensions to which the regular officials, servants, and pensioners of the Confederation are entitled or which have already been granted, will be secured to them *pro rata* of the register.

The Royal Prussian Government, however, undertakes the pensions and allowances hitherto paid out of the Federal matriculation fund to the officers of the former Schleswig-Holstein army and their survivors.

Art. X.—The persons interested in the pensions granted by the Imperial Royal Austrian Lieutenancy in Holstein will still be allowed to draw them.

State bonds. The sum of 449,500 thalers of Danish currency in 4 per cent. Danish State bonds, which is still in the custody of the Imperial Royal Austrian Government, and which belongs to the Holstein treasury, will be restored to it immediately after the ratification of the present treaty.

Amnesty. No one belonging to the Duchies of Holstein or Schleswig, and no subject of their Majesties the Emperor of Austria and the King of Prussia will be prosecuted, molested, or obstructed in his person or property on account of his political conduct during the late events and the war.

Indemnity: mode of payment. Art. XI.—His Majesty the Emperor of Austria undertakes to pay to His Majesty the King of Prussia the sum of 40,000,000 Prussian thalers, to cover part of the expenses which Prussia has been put to by the war. From that sum is, however, to be deducted the amount of the war expenses which His Majesty the Emperor of Austria has still to demand from the Duchies of Schleswig and Holstein, according to Art. XII of the aforesaid Treaty of Vienna of the 30th October, 1864, to the extent of 15,000,000 Prussian thalers, as well as a further sum of 5,000,000, as an equivalent for the free maintenance which the Prussian army is to have in those parts of the Austrian territories which it occupies until the conclusion of peace; so that there only remain 20,000,000 to be paid in ready money.

One half of that sum is to be settled when the ratification of the present treaty takes place, the second half three weeks later at Oppeln in cash.

Evacuation of troops. Art. XII.—The evacuation of the Austrian territories held by the Royal Prussian troops shall be completed within three weeks after the exchange of the ratifications of the treaty of peace. From the day of the exchange of the ratifications the Prussian General Governments will confine their functions to the purely military sphere of operations.

The special stipulations according to which the evacuation is to take place are settled in a separate protocol which forms an appendix to the present treaty.

Revival of treaties. Art. XIII.—All the treaties or conventions concluded between the High Contracting Parties before the war are hereby again brought into force, in so far as they by their nature must not lose their effect by the dissolution of the relations of the Germanic Confederation. The General Cartel Convention between the German Federal States, of the 10th February, 1831, together with the supplementary stipulations belonging thereto, will especially retain its validity between Austria and Prussia. The Imperial Royal Austrian Government declares, however, that the Monetary Treaty concluded the 24th January, 1857, loses its most essential value for Austria by the dissolution of the German Federal relations, and the Royal Prussian

Government declares its willingness to enter into negotiations with Austria and the other participators in that treaty for the abrogation thereof.

In like manner, the High Contracting Parties reserve to themselves to enter into a negotiation as soon as possible for the revision of the commercial and customs treaty of the 11th April, 1865, for the further facilitation of their reciprocal traffic. Meanwhile the said treaty shall again come into force, on the condition that each of the High Contracting Parties reserves the right of putting an end to its operation after six months' notice.

Ratification. ART. XIV.—The ratifications of the present treaty shall be exchanged at Prague within the space of eight days, or sooner if possible.

In witness whereof the respective plenipotentiaries have signed the present treaty, and have affixed to it the seals of their arms.

Done at Prague, on the 23rd day of the month of August, in the year of Grace, 1866.

(L.S.) BRENNER. (L.S.) WERTHER.

APPENDIX.

For the execution of Arts. III and XII of the treaty of peace concluded this day, the High Contracting Parties have agreed upon the following stipulations :—

Provisions for delivery of prisoners of war. 1. On the third day after the ratification of the treaty all the Royal Prussian prisoners of war, and from the same day the Imperial Royal Austrian prisoners of war, will be delivered up at Austrian Oderberg (railway station) in echelons of about 1,000 men each, which are to follow on the successive days (not more than six echelons within twenty-four hours).

2. The Royal Prussian prisoners of war who are in the Bohemian fortresses or in Olmütz are to be delivered, so soon as the account of the ratification of this treaty reaches those fortresses, to the nearest division of the Royal Prussian troops.

3. Commissioners from both armies will be stationed at Austrian Oderberg to attend to the delivery, so far as it takes place at Oderberg, and to arrange jointly for the railway transport to the south.

On the Imperial Royal Austrian side a detachment of troops of 200 men will be stationed at Austrian Oderberg for the reception and care of the prisoners.

4. Prisoners of war who are too unwell to be removed are to remain in the hospitals on both sides, with the regular treatment and maintenance of the native troops, until they can be delivered up at Oderberg.

5. The expenses arising from the attendance upon the sick prisoners of war left behind will be liquidated and defrayed on both sides, from the third day after the ratification, at the regular rates for hospital attendance in both armies.

6. For the accomplishment of the evacuation of the Imperial Royal Austrian territories, which is to be effected within three weeks after

the ratification of this treaty, the tract south of the line of Napagedl, Brünn, Iglau, Tabor (exclusive of those places), will be evacuated on the Royal Prussian side on the seventh day, and all the country lying south of the Pilsen-Prague-Littau railway line, and beyond a straight line from Littau to the mouth of the Oppa in the Oder, on the fifteenth day after the ratification.

Evacuation of troops.

For all possible acceleration of this evacuation the time between the signing and the ratification of this treaty will be employed on the Royal Prussian side in preparatory measures.

7. The Imperial Royal Austrian troops during the time of evacuation will, in re-occupying the country, keep themselves at a distance of three miles from the rear of the Royal Prussian columns. The times of retreating on each line of march are therefore left to the arrangement of the commanders on both sides.

8. On the Imperial Austrian side the use of the railway line leading by Pilsen to the Kingdom of Bavaria will be allowed for the Royal Prussian military transports for the purpose of evacuating Bohemia.

9. During the time of evacuation the Royal Prussian army will retain the unrestricted control over the railway lines within the range which it occupies, for sending back troops and war materials, under application of the convention dated Brünn, the 1st August, 1866, and definitively concluded on the 17th August. It is settled, as a rule, that even during the evacuation there shall be a train in each direction for public traffic every day on all the railways; only unforeseen interruptions of the military transports can justify any departure from this rule for the particular day.

10. From the day following the ratification the Royal Prussian Government undertakes all the expenses of maintenance for the Royal Prussian troops, which however are to have free quarters without maintenance in the territories which they occupy. The local authorities are bound to provide the relays required by the Royal Prussian troops, for which the troops are to pay immediately in ready money according to the Imperial Royal Austrian tariffs for relays now in force. That tariff is in the possession of the national or local authorities.

11. The sick of the Royal Prussian army who cannot be removed are to remain in the military hospitals or local infirmaries, under the superintendence and treatment, so far as necessary, of the Royal Prussian military physicians. The Imperial Royal Austrian Government promises to make arrangements for the most careful treatment of those left behind, and for complying as far as possible with the necessary requisitions of the physicians for the treatment of the sick.

12. Before the evacuation the Royal Prussian commanders will send in to the Imperial Royal Lieutenancies of Bohemia, Moravia, and Silesia, through the Royal Prussian General Governments at Prague and Brünn, a list of the sick who are to be left behind, with a statement of the place where they lie.

13. For the delivery of the hospitals at Brünn, Prague, Pardubitz, and Königinhoff, commissioners of the respective armies will meet

at the places named on the day of the evacuation of those towns, to complete the delivery and draw up a protocol.

14. The expenses of attending on the sick will be paid by the Royal Prussian Government immediately after liquidation, according to the established regulations for the Imperial Royal Austrian troops.

Prague, 23rd August, 1866.

WERTHER.
BRENNER.

(I) TREATY OF VIENNA

October 3, 1866

AUSTRIA—ITALY

In the Name of the Most Holy and Indivisible Trinity.

His Majesty the King of Italy and His Majesty the Emperor of Austria having resolved to establish between their respective States a sincere and lasting peace, His Majesty the Emperor of Austria having ceded to His Majesty the Emperor of the French the Lombardo-Venetian Kingdom, His Majesty the Emperor of the French on his part having declared himself ready to recognize the union of the said Lombardo-Venetian Kingdom to the States of His Majesty the King of Italy, with the reservation of the consent of the populations being duly consulted; His Majesty the King of Italy and His Majesty the Emperor of Austria have appointed as their plenipotentiaries, namely:

His Majesty the King of Italy, the Sieur Louis Frederic Count Menabrea, Senator of the Kingdom, Lieutenant-General, etc.;

His Majesty the Emperor of Austria, the Sieur Felix Count Wimpffen, his actual Chamberlain, Envoy and Minister Plenipotentiary, on an Extraordinary Mission, etc.;

Who, after having exchanged their respective full powers, found to be in good and due form, have agreed upon the following articles:—

Restoration of peace.

ART. I.—There shall be, from the date of the exchange of the ratifications of the present treaty, peace and friendship between His Majesty the King of Italy and His Majesty the Emperor of Austria, their heirs and successors, their States and their respective subjects in perpetuity.

Prisoners of war.

ART. II.—The Italian and Austrian prisoners of war shall immediately be delivered up on both sides.

Cession of Lombardo-Venetian Kingdom.

ART. III.—His Majesty the Emperor of Austria agrees to the union of the Lombardo-Venetian Kingdom to the Kingdom of Italy.

Frontier of ceded territory.

ART. IV.—The frontier of the ceded territory is determined by the actual administrative confines of the Lombardo-Venetian Kingdom.

A military commission appointed by the two Contracting Powers shall be entrusted with the execution of the tracing on the spot with the shortest possible delay.

ART. V.—The evacuation of the ceded territory determined by the preceding article shall begin immediately after the signature of peace, and shall be terminated with the shortest possible delay, in conformity with the arrangements agreed upon between the special commissioners appointed to that effect.

Evacuation of ceded territory.

ART. VI.—The Italian Government will take upon itself:

1stly. The portion of the Monte Lombardo-Veneto debt which devolved upon Austria in virtue of the Convention concluded at Milan in 1860 for the execution of Art. VII of the Treaty of Zurich.

Succession —debts and loans.

2ndly. The debts added to the Monte Lombardo-Veneto since the 4th June, 1859, up to the day of the conclusion of the present treaty;

3rdly. A sum of 35,000,000 florins, Austrian currency, in cash, for the portion of the loan of 1854 allotted to Venetia, and for the price of the non-transportable war material. The manner of paying that sum of 35,000,000 florins, Austrian currency, in cash, shall, in conformity with the precedent of the Treaty of Zurich, be determined in an additional article.

ART. VII.—A commission, composed of Italian, Austrian, and French delegates, shall proceed to the liquidation of the different classes mentioned in the first two paragraphs of the preceding article, taking into account the sinking fund already paid, and the property, assets of every kind, constituting the sinking fund.

Liquidation by mixed commission.

That commission shall proceed with the definitive regulation of the accounts between the Contracting Parties, and shall fix the time and method to be employed for the liquidation of the Monte Lombardo-Veneto debt.

ART. VIII.—The Government of His Majesty the King of Italy succeeds to the rights and obligations resulting from contracts regularly stipulated by the Austrian Administration for objects of public interest, especially concerning the ceded territory.

Contractual rights and obligations.

ART. IX.—The Austrian Government is charged with the reimbursement of all sums paid by subjects of the ceded territory, communal districts, public establishments, and religious societies into the Austrian public banks in the shape of caution-money, deposits, or consignments. In the same manner, Austrian subjects, communes, public establishments, and religious societies, who have paid money into the banks of the ceded territories in the shape of caution-money, deposits, or consignments, will be punctually reimbursed by the Italian Government.

Deposits.

ART. X.—The Government of His Majesty the King of Italy recognizes and confirms the concessions granted to the railroads by the Austrian Government in the ceded territory to the full extent of all their arrangement and duration, and particularly the concessions resulting from the contracts passed under date of 14th March, 1856, 8th April, 1857, and 23rd September, 1858. The Italian Government also recognizes and confirms the stipulations of the convention of 20th November, 1861, between the Administration

Railway concessions.

of the South Lombardo-Venetian and Central Italian Railway Company, as well as the convention of 27th February, 1866, between the Imperial Minister of Finance and Commerce and the South Austrian Society.

From the time of the exchange of the ratifications of this treaty the Italian Government is bound by all the rights and obligations resulting to the Austrian Government by the above-mentioned convention, in regard to the lines of railway situated on the ceded territory; consequently the right of devolution which belonged to the Austrian Government in regard to these lines of railway is transferred to the Italian Government.

The payments which are still to be made of the sum due to the State by the concessionaries in virtue of the contract of 14th March, 1856, as an equivalent for the expense of construction of the said railroads, shall be paid in full into the Austrian Exchequer.

The credits of the building contractors and tradesmen, as well as the indemnities for the appropriation of land, which appertain to the time when the railways in question were administered on account of the State, and which have not yet been paid, will be paid by the Austrian Government, and, in so far as they may be due from them in virtue of the Act of Concession by the grantees of the Austrian Government.

Rights as to railways in ceded territory.

Art. XI.—It is understood that the recovery of the debts, resulting from Paragraphs 12, 13, 14, 15, and 16 of the contract of the 14th March, 1856, will give Austria no right of control or superintendence over the construction and working of railways in the ceded territory. The Italian Government engages on its part to communicate all the information which may be asked for on the subject by the Austrian Government.

Art. XII.—In order to extend to the Venetian railways the stipulations of Art. XV of the convention of the 27th February, 1866, the High Contracting Parties engage to enter as soon as possible, in concert with the South Austrian Railway Company, into a convention for the administrative and economical separation of the Venetian and Austrian railways.

In virtue of the convention of 27th February, 1866, the guarantee that the State has to pay to the South Austrian Railway Company shall be calculated on the basis of the net produce of the whole of the Venetian and Austrian lines forming the networks of the South Austrian railways actually conceded to the company. It is understood that the Italian Government will take upon itself a proportionate part of that guarantee corresponding to the lines in the ceded territory, and that the basis of the net produce of the Austrian and Venetian lines conceded to the said Company shall still form the basis for the evaluation of that guarantee.

Engagement to increase railway communications.

Art. XIII.—The Italian and Austrian Governments, desirous of extending the relations between the two States, engage to facilitate railway communications and to favour the establishment of new lines to unite the Italian and Austrian networks. The Government of His Imperial Royal Apostolic Majesty promises besides to hasten as much as possible the conclusion of the Brenner line destined to unite the valley of the Adige with that of the Inn.

Art. XIV.—Inhabitants or natives of the territory ceded by the present treaty will have, for the space of a year, from the date on which the ratifications are exchanged, and conditionally on a previous declaration before the competent authorities, full and entire power to export their movables, free of duty, and to retire with their families into the States of His Imperial Royal Apostolic Majesty, in which case their quality of Austrian subjects will be retained by them. They will be at liberty to keep their immovable property situated on the ceded territory.

Right of option.

The same power is granted reciprocally to nations of the ceded territory of Lombardy living in the States of His Majesty the Emperor of Austria.

The Lombards who profit by these arrangements cannot be, on account of their choice, disturbed on either side, in their person or in their properties situated in the respective States.

The delay of one year is extended to two years for the subjects, natives of the ceded territory of Lombardy, who at the time of the exchange of the ratifications of this treaty are not within the territory of the Austrian Monarchy. Their declaration may be received by the nearest Austrian Mission, or by the superior authority of any province of the Monarchy.

Art. XV.—The Lombardo-Venetian subjects in the Austrian army will be immediately discharged from military service and sent back to their homes.

Lombardo-Venetian subjects in Austrian army.

It is understood that those amongst them who declare their wish to remain in the service of His Imperial and Royal Apostolic Majesty shall be free to do so, and will not be disturbed on this account, either in person or in property.

The same guarantees are assured to the civil employés, natives of the Lombardo-Venetian Kingdom, who manifest their intention of keeping the offices they occupy in the Austrian service.

Civil employés.

Civil servants born in the Lombardo-Venetian Kingdom shall have the choice either of remaining in the Austrian service or entering the Italian Administration, in which case the Government of His Majesty the King of Italy engages either to place them in positions analogous to those which they occupied, or allot them pensions, the amount of which shall be fixed according to the laws and regulations in force in Austria. It is understood that the said civil servants shall act under the disciplinary laws and regulations of the Italian Administration.

Art. XVI.—Officers of Italian origin, who are actually in the Austrian service, shall have the choice, either of remaining in the service of His Imperial and Royal Apostolic Majesty or of entering the army of His Majesty the King of Italy, with the rank they hold in the Austrian army, provided they make the request within six months after the ratification of the present treaty.

Italian officers in Austrian army.

Art. XVII.—The pensions, both civil and military, regularly paid, and which were paid out of the public funds of the Lombardo-Venetian Kingdom, remain due to those entitled to them, and, if need be, to their widows and children, and will be paid in future by the Government of His Italian Majesty.

Pensions.

This stipulation is extended to the pensioners, both civil and military, as well as to their widows and children, without distinction of origin, who keep their domiciles in the ceded territory, and whose salaries, paid up to 1814 by the then Government of the Lombardo-Venetian provinces, then became payable by the Austrian Treasury.

Archives.

ART. XVIII.—The archives of the ceded territories containing the titles to property, and documents regarding the administration of justice, as well as the political and historical documents of the old Republic of Venice, will be handed over to the Commissioners who shall be appointed thereto, to whose care shall be delivered the objects of art and science specially belonging to the ceded territory.

Reciprocally, the titles to property, and documents connected with the administration and civil justice applying to the Austrian territories, which may be in the archives of the ceded territory, will be handed over to the Commissioners of His Imperial and Royal Apostolic Majesty.

The Governments of Italy and Austria engage to consult each other, at the request of the superior administrative authorities, respecting all the documents and information relative to the affairs which concern both the ceded territory and the adjoining country.

They also engage to allow authentic copies to be taken of historical and political documents which may interest the territories remaining respectively in the possession of the other Contracting Power, and which, in the interest of science, cannot be taken from the archives to which they belong.

Customs facilities.

ART. XIX.—The High Contracting Powers engage reciprocally to grant the greatest possible customs facilities to the bordering inhabitants of the two countries for the improvement of their property and the exercise of their trade.

Renewal of treaties.

ART. XX.—The treaties and conventions which have been confirmed by Art. XVII of the treaty of peace signed at Zurich on the 10th November, 1859, shall be temporarily renewed for one year, and shall extend to all the territories of the Kingdom of Italy. In the case where those treaties and conventions shall not be denounced three months before the expiration of a year dating from the exchange of the ratifications, they shall remain in force, and so on, from year to year.

Commercial relations.

ART. XXI.—The two High Contracting Powers reserve to themselves to enter, as soon as possible, into negotiations on the widest bases reciprocally to facilitate business between the two countries.

Until then, and for the term fixed in the preceding article, the Treaty of Commerce and Navigation of the 18th October, 1851, shall remain in force and shall apply to the whole territory of the Kingdom of Italy.

Property of Austrian Royal House.

ART. XXII.—The princes and princesses of the House of Austria, as well as the princesses who have entered into the Imperial family by marriage, shall, on proving their titles, recover their private property in full and entire possession, as well personal as real, which they shall be allowed to enjoy and to dispose of without being molested in any manner in the enjoyment of their rights.

Nevertheless, all the rights of the State and of individuals are reserved to be prosecuted by legal means.

Amnesty.

ART. XXIII.—With a view to contribute by every effort to quiet the public mind, the King of Italy and His Majesty the Emperor of Austria declare and promise that in their respective territories there shall be a full and entire amnesty for all individuals compromised on account of political events in the peninsula up to the present time; consequently no individual, no matter what may be his rank or position in society, shall be prosecuted, annoyed, or troubled, in person or property, or in the exercise of his rights, on account of his conduct or political opinions.

Ratification.

ART. XXIV.—The present treaty shall be ratified, and the ratifications exchanged at Vienna within a fortnight, or earlier if possible.

In faith of which, the respective plenipotentiaries have signed it and have affixed their seals thereunto.

Done at Vienna, on the 3rd day of the month of October, of the year of Grace, 1866.

(L.S.) MENABREA.
(L.S.) WIMPFFEN.

(J) PRELIMINARIES OF VERSAILLES

February 26, 1871

FRANCE—GERMANY

BETWEEN the Chancellor of the Germanic Empire, Count Otto de Bismarck-Schönhausen, furnished with full powers from His Majesty the Emperor of Germany, King of Prussia; the Minister of State and of Foreign Affairs of His Majesty the King of Bavaria, Count Otto de Bray-Steinburg; the Minister for Foreign Affairs of His Majesty the King of Würtemberg, Baron Auguste de Wächter; the Minister of State, President of the Council of Ministers of His Royal Highness the Grand Duke of Baden, Monsieur Jules Jolly, representing the Germanic Empire, on the one part; and on the other part, the Chief of the Executive Power of the French Republic, Monsieur Thiers, and the Minister for Foreign Affairs, Monsieur Jules Favre, representing France; the full powers of the two Contracting Parties having been found in good and due form, the following has been agreed upon, to serve as a preliminary basis to the definitive peace to be concluded hereafter.

ART. I.—France renounces in favour of the German Empire all her rights and titles over the territories situated on the east of the frontier hereafter described.

Cession of Alsace-Lorraine.

Delimitation of the frontier.

The line of demarcation begins at the north-west frontier of the Canton of Cattenom, towards the Grand Duchy of Luxemburg, follows on the south the western frontiers of the cantons of Cattenom and Thionville, passes by the canton of Briey, along the western frontiers of the communes of Montjois-la-Montagne and Roncourt, as well as the eastern frontiers of the communes of Marie-aux-Chênes, St. Ail, Habonville, reaches the frontier of the canton de Gooze, which it crosses along the communal frontiers of Vionville, Bouxières, and Onville, follows the south-west frontier, south of the district of Metz, the western frontier of the district of Chateau-Salins, as far as the commune of Pettoncourt, taking in the western and southern frontiers thereof to follow the crest of the mountains between Seille and Moncel, as far as the frontier of the district of Sarreburg, to the south of Garde. The demarcation afterwards coincides with the frontier of that district as far as the commune of Tanconville, reaching the frontier to the north thereof, from whence it follows the crest of the mountains between the sources of the White Sarre and Vezouze, as far as the frontier of that canton of Schirmeck, skirts the western frontier of that canton, includes the communes of

Saales, Bourg-Bruche, Colroy-la-Roche, Plaine, Ranrupt, Saulxures, and St. Blaise-la-Roche of the canton of Saales, and coincides with the western frontier of the departments of the lower Rhine and the upper Rhine, as far as the cantons of Belfort, the southern frontier of which it leaves not far from Vourvenons, to cross the canton of Delle at the southern limits of the communes of Bourogne and Froide Fontaine, and to reach the Swiss frontier skirting the eastern frontiers of the communes of Jonchery and Delle.

The German Empire shall possess these territories in perpetuity in all sovereignty and property. An international commission, composed of an equal number of representatives of the two High Contracting Parties, shall be appointed immediately after the exchange of the ratifications of the present treaty, to trace on the spot the new frontier, in conformity with the preceding stipulations.

This commission shall preside over the division of the lands and funds, which have hitherto belonged to districts or communes divided by the new frontiers; in case of disagreement in the tracing and the measures of execution, the members of the commission shall refer to their respective Governments.

The frontier, such as it has just been described, is marked in green on two identical copies of the map of the territory forming the Government of Alsace, published at Berlin in September 1870 by the geographical and statistical division of the Staff, and a copy of which shall be annexed to both copies of the present treaty.

Nevertheless, the alteration of the above tracing has been agreed to by the two Contracting Parties. In the former department of the Moselle, the villages of Marie-aux-Chênes near St. Privat-la-Montagne, and Vionville to the west of Rezonville, shall be ceded to Germany. In exchange thereof, France shall retain the town and fortifications of Belfort, with a radius which shall be hereafter determined upon.

ART. II.—France shall pay to His Majesty the Emperor of Germany the sum of 5,000,000,000 francs (5 milliards).

Indemnity.

The payment of at least 1,000,000,000 (1 milliard) francs shall be effected within the year 1871, and the whole of the remainder of the debt in the space of three years, dating from the ratification of the present Act.

ART. III.—The evacuation of the French territory occupied by German troops shall begin after the ratification of the present treaty by the National Assembly sitting at Bordeaux. Immediately after that ratification the German troops shall quit the interior of Paris, as well as forts on the left bank of the Seine, and within the shortest possible delay agreed upon between the military authorities of the two countries, they shall entirely evacuate the departments of Calvados, Orne, Sarthe, Eure-et-Loire, Loiret, Loire-et-Cher, Indre-et-Loire, Yonne, and also the departments of the Seine-Inférieure, Eure, Seine-et-Oise, Seine-et-Marne, Aube, and Côte-d'Or, as far as the left bank of the Seine. The French troops shall fall back at the same time behind the Loire, which they shall not be allowed to pass before the signature of the definitive treaty of peace. The

Evacuation of French territory.

garrison of Paris is excepted from this disposition, the number of which shall not exceed 40,000 men, and the garrisons indispensably necessary for the safety of the strongholds.

Occupation of territory as guarantee of payment of indemnity.

The evacuation of the departments between the right bank of the Seine and the eastern frontier by German troops shall take place gradually after the ratification of the definitive treaty of peace and the payment of the first 500,000,000 (½ milliard) of the contribution stipulated by Art. II, beginning with the departments nearest to Paris, and shall continue gradually, according to the proportion of the payments made on account of the contribution; after the first payment of 500,000,000 (½ milliard) that evacuation shall take place in the following departments: Somme, Oise, and the parts of the departments of the Seine-Inférieure, Seine-et-Oise, Seine-et-Marne, situated on the right bank of the Seine, as well as the part of the department of the Seine, and the forts situated on the right bank.

After the payment of 2,000,000,000 (2 milliards) the German occupation shall only include the departments of the Marne, Ardennes, Haute Marne, Meuse, Vosges, Meurthe, as well as the fortress of Belfort, with its territory, which shall serve as a pledge for the remaining 3,000,000,000 (3 milliards), and in which the number of the German troops shall not exceed 50,000 men. His Majesty the Emperor will be willing to substitute for the territorial guarantee, consisting in the partial occupation of the French territory, a financial guarantee, should it be offered by the French Government under conditions considered sufficient by His Majesty the Emperor and King for the interests of Germany. The 3,000,000,000 (3 milliards), the payment of which shall have been deferred, shall bear interest at the rate of 5 per cent., beginning from the ratification of the present convention.

Maintenance of the army of evacuation.

ART. IV.—The German troops shall abstain from levying contributions either in money or in kind in the occupied departments. On the other hand the maintenance of the German troops remaining in France shall be at the expense of the French Government in the manner decided upon by an agreement with the German military administration.

Interests of inhabitants of ceded territories.

ART. V.—The interests of the inhabitants of the territories ceded by France, in everything relating to their commerce and their civil rights shall be regulated in as favourable a manner as possible when the conditions of the definitive peace are settled. A certain time will be fixed, during which they will enjoy particular advantages for the disposal of their produce. The German Government will put no obstacle in the way of free emigration by the inhabitants from the ceded territories, and shall take no steps against them affecting their persons or their property.

Prisoners of war.

ART. VI.—The prisoners of war who shall not have been already set at liberty by exchange shall be given up immediately after the ratification of the present preliminaries. In order to accelerate the transport of French prisoners, the French Government shall place at the disposal of the German authorities in the interior of the German territory a part of the rolling-stock of its railways in such proportion as shall be determined by special arrangements, and at prices paid in France by the French Government for military transport.

ART. VII.—The opening of negotiations for the definitive treaty of peace to be concluded on the basis of the present preliminaries shall take place at Brussels, immediately after the ratification of the latter by the National Assembly and by His Majesty the Emperor of Germany.

Definitive treaty—place and time of negotiation.

ART. VIII.—After the conclusion and ratification of the definitive treaty of peace, the administration of the departments which are still to remain occupied by the German troops shall be made over to the French authorities. But the latter shall be bound to conform to the orders which the commanders of the German troops may think necessary to give in the interests of the safety, maintenance, and distribution of the troops.

Administration of occupied territory.

After the ratification of the present treaty, the taxes in the occupied departments shall be levied on account of the French Government, and by its own officers.

ART. IX.—It is well understood that these stipulations do not give to the German military authority any right over the parts of territory which it does not actually occupy.

ART. X.—The present preliminary treaty shall be immediately submitted to the ratification of His Majesty the Emperor of Germany and to the French National Assembly sitting at Bordeaux

Ratification.

In testimony whereof the undersigned have signed the present preliminary treaty, and sealed it with the seal of their arms.

Done at Versailles, 26th February, 1871.

(L.S.) BISMARCK.

(L.S.) A. THIERS.

(L.S.) JULES FAVRE.

The Kingdoms of Bavaria and Würtemberg, and the Grand Duchy of Baden, having taken part in the actual war as allies of Prussia, and now forming part of the Germanic Empire, the undersigned adhere to the present convention in the name of their respective Sovereigns.

Adhesion of Bavaria, Würtemberg, and Baden.

Versailles, 26th February, 1871.

CTE. DE BRAY-STEINBURG.

BN. DE WÄCHTER.

MITTNACHT.

JOLLY.

(K) TREATY OF FRANKFORT

May 10, 1871

FRANCE—GERMANY

M. JULES FAVRE, Minister for Foreign Affairs of the French Republic, M. Augustin Thomas Eugène de Pouyer-Quertier, Minister of Finance of the French Republic, and M. Marc Thomas Eugène Goulard, Member of the National Assembly, stipulating in the name of the French Republic, of the one part;

On the other, Prince Otho de Bismarck-Schœnhausen, Chancellor of the German Empire, Count Harry d'Arnim, Envoy Extraordinary and Minister Plenipotentiary of His Majesty the Emperor of Germany at the Papal Court, stipulating in the name of His Majesty the Emperor of Germany; having agreed to convert into a definitive treaty the preliminaries of peace of the 26th February of the present year modified as it is about to be by the following dispositions, have agreed:

Ceded territory and the new frontier.

ART. I.—The distance between the town of Belfort and the line of frontier such as it had been proposed during the negotiations of Versailles, and such as it is marked on the map annexed to the ratifications of the preliminaries of the 26th February, is considered as describing the radius which, by virtue of the clause relating thereto in Art. I of the preliminaries, is to remain to France with the town and fortifications of Belfort.

The German Government is disposed to extend that radius so as to include the cantons of Belfort, Delle, and Giromagny, as well as the western part of the canton of Fontaine, to the west of a line to be traced from the spot where the canal from the Rhone to the Rhine leaves the canton of Delle to the south of Montreux-Chateau, to the northern limits of the canton between Bourg and Félon where that line would join the eastern limit of the canton of Giromagny.

The German Government will, nevertheless, not cede the above territories unless the French Republic agrees, on its part, to a rectification of frontier along the western limits of the cantons of Cattenom and Thionville which will give to Germany the territory to the east of a line starting from the frontier of Luxemburg between Hussigny and Redingen, leaving to France the villages of Thil and Villerupt, extending between Erronville and Aumetz, between Beuvillers and Boulange, between Trieux and Lomeringen, and joining the ancient line of frontier between Avril and Moyeuvre.

The international commission mentioned in Art. I of the preliminaries shall proceed to the spot immediately after the ratification of the present treaty to execute the works entrusted to them and to trace the new frontier, in accordance with the preceding dispositions.

Option.

ART. II.—French subjects, natives of the ceded territories, actually domiciled on that territory, shall up to the 1st October, 1872, and on their making a previous declaration to that effect to the competent authority, be allowed to change their domicile into France and to remain there, that right in nowise infringing on the laws on military service, in which case the title of French citizen shall be maintained.

They shall be at liberty to preserve their immovables situated in the territory united to Germany.

Amnesty.

No inhabitant of the ceded territory shall be prosecuted, annoyed, or sought for, either in his person or his property, on account of his political or military acts previous to the war.

Archives, registers, etc.

ART. III.—The French Government shall deliver over to the German Government the archives, documents, and registers relating to the civil, military, and judicial administration of the ceded territories. Should any of the documents be found missing, they shall be restored by the French Government on the demand of the German Government.

Deposits.

ART. IV.—The French Government shall make over to the Government of the Empire of Germany within the term of six months, dating from the exchange of the ratifications of this treaty: (1) The amount of the sum deposited by the departments, communes, and public establishments of the ceded territories. (2) The amount of the premium of enlistment or discharge belonging to soldiers and sailors, natives of the ceded territory, who shall have chosen the German nationality. (3) The amount of security of responsible agents of the State. (4) The amount of sums deposited for judicial consignments on account of measures taken by the administrative or judicial authorities in the ceded territories.

Rights of navigation.

ART. V.—The two nations shall enjoy equal privileges as regards the navigation on the Moselle, the Canal of the Marne to the Rhine, the Canal of the Rhone to the Rhine, the Canal of the Sarre and the navigable waters communicating with those channels of navigation. The right of floatage shall be maintained.

Ecclesiastical authority.

ART. VI.—The high contracting parties being of opinion that the diocesan circumscriptions of the territories ceded to the German Empire must agree with the new frontier determined upon by Art. I above, will consider, without delay, after the ratification of the present treaty, upon the measures to be taken in common upon the subject.

The communities belonging either to the Reformed Church or to the Augsburg Confession, established on the territories ceded by France, shall cease to be under French ecclesiastical authority.

The communities of the Church of the Augsburg Confession established in the French territories shall cease to be under the Superior Consistories and of the Directors residing at Strasburg.

The Jewish communities of the territories situated to the east of the new frontier shall cease to depend on the Central Jewish Consistory residing at Paris.

Art. VII.—The payment of 500,000,000 (½ milliard) shall be made within thirty days after the re-establishment of the authority of the French Government in the City of Paris. 1,000,000,000 (1 milliard) shall be paid in the course of the year, and 500,000,000 (½ milliard) on the 1st May, 1872. The last 3,000,000,000 (3 milliards) shall remain payable on the 2nd March, 1874, as stipulated in the preliminary treaty. From the 2nd March of the present year the interest on those 3,000,000,000 francs (3 milliards) shall be paid each year on the 3rd March, at the rate of 5 per cent. per annum.

Indemnity—mode of payment.

All sums paid in advance on the last 3,000,000,000 shall cease to bear interest from the day on which the payment is made.

The payment can only be made in the principal German commercial towns, and shall be made in metal, gold or silver, in Prussian bank-notes, in Netherlands bank-notes, in notes of the National Bank of Belgium, in first-class negotiable bills to order or letters of exchange, payable at sight.

The German Government having fixed in France the value of a Prussian thaler at 3 francs 75 centimes, the French Government accepts the conversion of the moneys of both countries at the rate above stated.

The French Government will inform the German Government, three months in advance, of all payments which it intends to make into the treasury of the German Empire.

After the payment of the first 500,000,000 (½ milliard) and the ratification of the definitive treaty of peace, the departments of the Somme, Seine-Inférieure, and Eure shall be evacuated in so far as they shall be found to be still occupied by German troops. The evacuation of the departments of the Oise, Seine-et-Oise, Seine-et-Marne, and Seine, as well as the forts of Paris, shall take place so soon as the German Government shall consider the re-establishment of order, both in France and Germany, sufficient to ensure the execution of the engagements contracted by France.

Evacuation on payment.

Under all circumstances, the evacuation shall take place after the payment of the third 500,000,000 (½ milliard).

The German troops, for their own security, shall have at their disposal the neutral zone between the German line of demarcation and the Paris enclosure on the right bank of the Seine.

The stipulations of the treaty of 26th February, relative to the occupation of French territories after the payment of the 2,000,000,000 (2 milliards), shall remain in force. None of the deductions which the French Government might have a right to make shall be made on the payment of the first 500,000,000 (½ milliard).

Art. VIII.—German troops shall continue to abstain from levying contributions either in kind or money in the occupied territories; that obligation on their part being correlative to the obligations contracted for their maintenance by the French Government, in case the French

Government, notwithstanding the reiterated demands of the German Government, was behindhand in the execution of the said obligations, the German troops will have the right to procure what is necessary to their wants by levying taxes and contributions in the occupied departments, and even outside of them, should their resources not be sufficient.

Maintenance of army of occupation.

With reference to the maintenance of the German troops, the system actually in force shall be continued until the evacuation of the Paris forts.

In virtue of the Convention of Ferrières, of 11th March, 1871, the reductions pointed out by that convention shall be put into force after the evacuation of the forts.

As soon as the effective of the German army shall be reduced below the number of 500,000 men, account shall be taken of the reductions made below that number to establish a proportionate diminution in the price of the maintenance of the troops paid by the French Government.

ART. IX.—The exceptional treatment at present granted to the produce of the industry of the ceded territories for imports into France shall be continued for six months, from the 1st March, under the conditions made with the commissioners of Alsace.

Produce of ceded territories.

ART. X.—The German Government shall continue to deliver up prisoners of war, making arrangement with the French Government. The French Government shall send to their homes such of the prisoners as can be discharged. As for those who shall not have completed their term of service, they shall be sent beyond the Loire. It is understood that the army of Paris and Versailles, after the re-establishment of the authority of the French Government at Paris, and until the evacuation of the forts by German troops, shall not exceed 80,000 men. Until that evacuation, the French Government shall not concentrate troops on the right bank of the Loire, but it shall provide garrisons in the towns within that circuit, according to the necessities for the maintenance of public order and peace.

Prisoners of war.

As the evacuation shall proceed, the commanders of regiments shall agree together as to a neutral circuit between the armies of the two nations.

20,000 prisoners shall be sent without delay to Lyons on condition that they are immediately sent to Algiers, after their organization, to be employed in that colony.

ART. XI.—The treaties of commerce with the different States of Germany having been annulled by the war, the French Government and the German Government will adopt as the basis of their commercial relations the system of reciprocal treatment on the footing of the most-favoured nation.

Renewal of certain treaties.

Are included therein import and export duties, transit dues, customs formalities, the admission and treatment of both nations as well as their agents.

Shall nevertheless be excepted from the above rule the favours which one of the Contracting Parties has granted or may grant, by treaties of commerce, to other States than the following: Great Britain, Belgium, Netherlands, Switzerland, Austria, Russia.

The treaties of navigation, as well as the convention relative to the international service of railways in its relation with the cantons, and the convention for the reciprocal guarantee of literary works, shall be renewed.

The French Government nevertheless reserves to itself the right of levying tonnage and shipping duties (*droits de pavillon*) on German vessels and their cargoes, under the reservation that those duties shall not be higher than those imposed on vessels and cargoes of the above-mentioned nations.

ART. XII.—All expelled Germans shall preserve the full and entire enjoyment of all property which they may have acquired in France.

Rights of expelled Germans.

Such Germans who had obtained the authority required by French laws to establish their domicile in France shall be reinstated in all their rights, and may consequently again establish their domicile in French territory.

The delays stipulated by French laws to obtain naturalization shall be considered as not having been interrupted by the state of war for persons who shall take advantage of the above-mentioned facility of returning to France within six months after the exchange of the ratifications of this treaty, and the time which has elapsed between their expulsion and their return to the French territory shall be taken into account, as if they had never ceased to reside in France.

The above conditions shall be applicable in perfect reciprocity to the French subjects residing, or wishing to reside, in Germany.

ART. XIII.—German vessels condemned by prize courts before the 2nd March, 1871, shall be considered as definitively condemned.

Restoration of prizes.

Those not condemned at the above-mentioned date shall be restored with the cargo in so far as it still exists. If the restoration of the vessel and cargo is no more possible, their value, fixed according to the price of the sale, shall be restored to their owners.

Canalization of the Moselle.

ART. XIV.—Each of the two Parties shall continue on his territory the works undertaken for the canalization of the Moselle. The common interests of the separate parts of two Departments of the Meurthe and the Moselle shall be liquidated.

Rights of subjects.

ART. XV.—The High Contracting Parties mutually engage to extend to their respective subjects the measures which they may consider necessary to adopt in favour of those of their subjects who, in consequence of the events of the war, may have been prevented from arriving in time for the safety or the preservation of their rights.

Tombs of the fallen.

ART. XVI.—The two Governments, French and German, reciprocally engage to respect and preserve the tombs of soldiers buried in their respective territories.

Provision for further arrangements.

ART. XVII.—The regulation of additional stipulations upon which an understanding is to be come to, in consequence of this treaty and the preliminary treaty, will be the object of further negotiations, which shall take place at Frankfort.

ART. XVIII.—The ratifications of the present treaty by the National Assembly and by the Chief of the Executive of the French Republic, on the one part, and on the other by the Emperor of Germany, shall be exchanged at Frankfort, in the delay of ten days, or sooner if possible.[1]

Ratifications.

In faith whereof the respective plenipotentiaries have signed it and affixed thereto the seal of their arms.

Done at Frankfort, 10th May, 1871.

(Here follow the signatures and seals.)

[1] Ratifications were exchanged at Frankfort on May 20.

(L) ADDITIONAL CONVENTION

Frankfort, December 11, 1871

FRANCE—GERMANY

THE President of the French Republic, on the one part, and His Majesty the Emperor of Germany, on the other part, having determined, in conformity with Art. XVII of the treaty of peace concluded at Frankfort on the 10th May, 1871, to negotiate an additional convention to that treaty, have to that effect appointed as their plenipotentiaries, namely:—

The President of the French Republic, M. Marc Thomas Eugène de Goulard, Member of the National Assembly, and M. Alexandre Johann Henry de Clercq, Minister Plenipotentiary of the First Class; and

His Majesty the Emperor of Germany, M. Weber, Councillor of State of His Majesty the King of Bavaria, and Count Uxkull, Intimate Councillor of Legation of His Majesty the King of Würtemberg;

Who, after having communicated to each other their full powers, found in good and due form, have agreed upon the following articles:—

Ecclesiastical authority.

ART. IX.—Until the conclusion of the arrangements alluded to in the first paragraph of Art. VI of the treaty of peace of 10th May, 1871, it is agreed that the bishops established in the dioceses crossed by the new frontier shall preserve, in their entirety, the spiritual authority actually vested in them, and shall remain free to provide for the religious necessities of the populations committed to their charge.

Canals.

ART. XIV.—The canal of the Sarre, the canal of the Salt Works of Dieuse, and the junction of Colmar, which forms the communication between that town and the Rhine, being entirely included within the territories ceded to Germany, the latter takes upon herself the payment of the expenses of those three canals remaining due.

The annuities still due on the sum advanced to the French State by the town of Colmar, and by the manufacturers of the east, shall, dating from 1871, be payable by the German Government.

The canal of the Rhone to the Rhine being crossed by the new frontier, it has been agreed that the twelve annuities remaining to be paid to the old subscribers on the purchase of their shares shall be divided between the High Contracting Parties in the proportion of the extent reverting to each of the two countries.

The commission mentioned in Art. XI shall be entrusted with the accounts of the above-mentioned canals, as well as the liquidation of the accounts relative to the canalization of the Moselle, and of the common interests of the separate parts of the departments of the Meurthe and the Moselle.

The French Government undertakes to furnish the commission with all contracts, documents, etc., necessary for the fulfilment of their labours.

The High Contracting Parties shall appoint commissioners, who shall be entrusted with the regulation, in so far as regards the canal from the Rhone to the Rhine and the canal from the Marne to the Rhine, of the supply of the dividing mill-courses.

ART. XVIII.—Besides the international arrangements mentioned in the treaty of peace of 10th May, 1871, the High Contracting Parties have agreed to renew the different treaties between France and the German States existing previous to the war, with the reservation of the declarations of adhesion, to be supplied by the respective Governments at the time of the exchange of the ratifications of the present convention.

Renewal of treaties.

The special convention between France and Prussia, relative to the canal of the Sarre, being excepted.

Neither are the stipulations of the present article applicable to postal relations, which are reserved for a subsequent arrangement between the two Governments.

It is also agreed that the dispositions of the convention between Baden and France, of the 16th April, 1846, relative to the execution of sentences, of the treaty of extradition, concluded between France and Prussia on the 21st July, 1845, and of the copyright convention between Bavaria and France, of the 24th March, 1865, shall be provisionally extended to Alsace-Lorraine, and that in matters to which they relate these three arrangements shall serve as a rule for the relations between France and the ceded territories.

ART. XIX.—The present convention, drawn up in French and German, shall be ratified, on the one part by the President of the French Republic after the approval of the National Assembly, and on the other part by His Majesty the Emperor of Germany, and the ratifications thereof shall be exchanged in the delay of one month, or sooner, if possible.

Ratification.

In faith whereof the respective plenipotentiaries have signed it, and have affixed thereto the seal of their arms.

Done at Frankfort, 11th December, 1871.

(L.S.) E. DE GOULARD. (L.S.) WEBER.
(L.S.) DE CLERCQ. (L.S.) UXKULL.

(M) PRELIMINARIES OF SAN STEFANO[1]

February 19 / March 3, 1878

RUSSIA—TURKEY

HIS Majesty the Emperor of Russia and His Majesty the Emperor of the Ottomans, inspired with the wish of restoring and securing the blessings of peace to their countries and people, as well as of preventing any fresh complication which might imperil the same, have named as their plenipotentiaries, with a view to draw up, conclude, and sign the preliminaries of peace:

His Majesty the Emperor of Russia on the one side, the Count Nicolas Ignatiew, Aide-de-Camp General of His Imperial Majesty, Lieutenant-General, Member of the Council of the Empire, etc.; and the Sieur Alexander Nelidow, Chamberlain of the Imperial Court, Councillor of State, etc.;

And His Majesty the Emperor of the Ottomans on the other hand, Safvet Pasha, Minister for Foreign Affairs, etc.; and Sadoullah Bey, His Majesty's Ambassador at the Imperial Court of Germany, etc.;

Who, after having exchanged their full powers, which were found to be in good and proper form, have agreed to the following articles:—

ART. I.—In order to put an end to the perpetual conflicts between Turkey and Montenegro, the frontier which separates the two countries will be rectified conformably to the map hereto annexed, subject to the reserve hereinafter mentioned, in the following manner:—

New frontier between Turkey and Montenegro.

From the mountain of Dobrostitza the frontier will follow the line indicated by the Conference of Constantinople as far as Korito by Bilek. Thence the new frontier will run to Gatzko (Metochia-Gatzko will belong to Montenegro), and towards the confluence of the Piva and the Tara, ascending towards the north by the Drina as far as its confluence with the Lim. The eastern frontier of the principality will follow this last river as far as Prijepoljé, and will proceed by Roshaj to Sukha-Planina (leaving Bihor and Roshaj to Montenegro). Taking in Bugovo, Plava, and Gusinje, the frontier line will follow the chain of mountains by Shlieb, Paklen, and along the northern frontier of Albania by the crests of the mountains Koprivnik, Babavik, Borvik, to the

[1] The provisions of this treaty were revised by the Congress of Berlin, 1878, as was recognized by the Treaty of Constantinople between Russia and Turkey, January 27 / February 8, 1879; *infra*, p. 403.

highest peak of Prokléti. From that point the frontier will proceed by the summit of Biskaschik, and will run in a straight line to the lake of Tjiceni-hoti. Dividing Tjiceni-hoti and Tjiceni-kastrati, it will cross the lake of Scutari to the Boyana, the thalweg of which it will follow as far as the sea. Nichsich, Gatzko, Spouje, Podgoritza, Zabliak, and Antivari will remain to Montenegro.

European boundary commission.

A European commission, in which the Sublime Porte and the Government of Montenegro shall be represented, will be charged with fixing the definitive limits of the principality, making on the spot such modifications in the general tracing as it may think necessary and equitable, from the point of view of the respective interests and tranquillity of the two countries, to which it will accord in this respect the equivalents deemed necessary.

The navigation of the Boyana, having always given rise to disputes between the Sublime Porte and Montenegro, will be the subject of a special regulation, which will be prepared by the same European commission.

Independence of Montenegro.

ART. II.—The Sublime Porte recognizes definitively the independence of the principality of Montenegro.

An understanding between the Imperial Government of Russia, the Ottoman Government, and the principality of Montenegro will determine subsequently the character and form of the relations between the Sublime Porte and the principality as regards particularly the establishment of Montenegrin agents at Constantinople, and in certain localities of the Ottoman Empire, where the necessity for such agents shall be recognized, the extradition of fugitive criminals on the one territory or the other, and the subjection of Montenegrin travelling or sojourning in the Ottoman Empire to the Ottoman laws and authorities, according to the principles of international law and the established usages concerning the Montenegrins.

Resulting questions to be settled by convention.

A convention will be concluded between the Sublime Porte and Montenegro to regulate the questions connected with the relations between the inhabitants of the confines of the two countries and with the military works in the same confines. The points upon which an understanding cannot be established will be settled by the arbitration of Russia and Austria-Hungary.

Henceforward, if there is any discussion or conflict, except as regards new territorial demands, Turkey and Montenegro will leave the settlement of their differences to Russia and Austria-Hungary, who will arbitrate in common.

Withdrawal of troops.

The troops of Montenegro will be bound to evacuate the territory not comprised within the limits indicated above within ten days from the signature of the preliminaries of peace.

ART. III.—Serbia is recognized as independent. Its frontier, marked on the annexed map, will follow the thalweg of the Drina, leaving Little Zwornik and Zakar to the principality, and following the old limit as far as the sources of the stream Dezevo, near Stoilac. Thence the new line will follow the course of that stream as far as the river Raska, and then the course of the latter as far as Novi-Bazar.

Independence and boundaries of Serbia.

From Novi-Bazar, ascending the stream which passes near the villages of Mekinje and Irgoviste, as far as its source, the frontier line will run by Bosur Planina, in the valley of the Ibar, and will then descend the stream which falls into this river, near the village of Ribanic.

The line will then follow the course of the rivers Ibar, Sitnitza, and Lab, and of the brook Batintze to its source (upon the Grapachnitza Planina). Thence the frontier will follow the heights which separate the waters of the Kriva and the Veternitza, and will meet the latter river by the shortest route at the mouth of the stream Miovatzka, which it will ascend, crossing the Miovatzka Planina and redescending towards the Morava, near the village of Kalimanci.

From this point the frontier will descend to the Morava as far as the river Vlossina, near the village of Staïkovtzi. Reascending the latter river, as well as the Linberazda, and the brook Koukavitze, the line will pass by the Sukha Planina, will run along the stream Vrylo as far as the Nisawa, and will descend the said river as far as the village of Kronpatz, whence the line will rejoin by the shortest route the old Serbian frontier to the south-east of Karaoul Baré, and will not leave it until it reaches the Danube.

Ada-Kale will be evacuated and razed.

A Turco-Serbian commission, assisted by a Russian commissioner, will, within three months, arrange upon the spot the definite frontier line, and will definitely settle the questions relating to the islands of the Drina. A Bulgarian delegate will be admitted to participate in the work of the commission when it shall be engaged on the frontier between Serbia and Bulgaria.

Real estate in ceded territories.

ART. IV.—The Mussulmans holding lands in the territories annexed to Serbia, and who wish to reside out of the principality, can preserve their real property by having them farmed out or administered by others. A Turco-Serbian commission, assisted by a Russian commissioner, will be charged to decide absolutely, in the course of two years, all questions relating to the verification of real estate in which Mussulman interests are concerned.

This commission will also be called upon to settle within three years the methods of alienation of State property and of religious endowments (vakoufs), as well as the questions relative to the interests of private persons which may be involved. Until a direct treaty is concluded between Turkey and Serbia determining the character of the relations between the Sublime Porte and the principality, Serbian subjects travelling or sojourning in the Ottoman Empire shall be treated according to the general principles of international law.

The Serbian troops shall be bound to evacuate the territory not comprised within the above-mentioned limits within fifteen days from the signature of the preliminaries of peace.

Art. V.—The Sublime Porte recognizes the independence of Roumania, which will establish its right to an indemnity, to be discussed between the two countries.

Independence of Roumania.

Until the conclusion of a direct treaty between Turkey and Roumania, Roumanian subjects will enjoy in Turkey all the rights guaranteed to the subjects of other European Powers.

Art. VI.—Bulgaria is constituted an autonomous tributary principality, with a Christian Government and a national militia.

Bulgaria a tributary principality. Its frontiers.

The definitive frontiers of the Bulgarian Principality will be traced by a special Russo-Turkish commission before the evacuation of Roumelia by the Imperial Russian army.

This commission will, in working out the modifications to be made on the spot in the general tracing, take into account the principle of the nationality of the majority of the inhabitants of the border districts, conformably to the bases of peace, and also the topographical necessities and practical interests of the intercommunication of the local population.

The extent of the Bulgarian Principality is laid down in general terms on the accompanying map, which will serve as a basis for the definitive fixing of the limits. Leaving the new frontier of the Serbian Principality, the line will follow the western limit of the Caza of Wrania, as far as the chain of the Kara-dagh. Turning towards the west, the line will follow the western limits of the Cazas of Koumanovo, Kotchani, Kalkandelen, to Mount Korab; thence by the river Welestchitza as far as its junction with the black Drina. Turning towards the south by the Drina and afterwards by the western limit of the Caza of Ochride towards Mount Linas, the frontier will follow the western limits of the Cazas of Gortcha and Starovo as far as Mount Grammos. Then by the Lake of Kastoria, the frontier line will rejoin the river Moglénitza, and after having followed its course, and passed to the south of Yanitza (Wardar Yenidje), will go by the mouth of the Wardar and by the Galliko towards the villages of Parga and of Saraï-keui; thence through the middle of Lake Bechik-Guel to the mouth of the rivers Strouma and Karassou, and by the sea-coast as far as Buru-Guel; thence striking north-west towards Mount Tchaltépé by the chain of Rhodope as far as Mount Krouschowo by the Black Balkans (Kara-Balkan), by the mountains Eschek-koulatchi, Tchepelion, Karokolas and Tschiklar, as far as the river Arda.

Thence the line will be traced in the direction of the town of Tchermin, and leaving the town of Adrianople to the south, by the villages of Sutgutlion, Kara-Hamza, Arnaout-keui, Akardji, and Enidje as far as the river Tékéderessi. Following the rivers Tékéderessi and Tchorlouderessi as far as Loulé-Bourgaz, and thence, by the river Soudjak-déré as far as the village of Serguen, the frontier line will go by the heights straight towards Hakim-tabiassi, where it will strike the Black Sea. It will leave the sea-coast near Mangalia, following the southern boundaries of the Sandjak of Toultcha, and will come out in the Danube above Rassova.

Art. VII.—The Prince of Bulgaria shall be freely elected by the population and confirmed by the Sublime Porte, with the assent of the Powers. No member of the reigning dynasties of the great European Powers shall be capable of being elected Prince of Bulgaria.

Election of Prince of Bulgaria.

In the event of the dignity of Prince of Bulgaria being vacant, the election of the new prince shall be made subject to the same conditions and forms.

Before the election of the prince an assembly of Bulgarian notables, to be convoked at Philippopolis (Plowdiw) or Tyrnowo, shall draw up, under the superintendence of an Imperial Russian commissioner, and in the presence of an Ottoman commissioner, the organization of the future administration, in conformity with the precedent established in 1830 after the Peace of Adrianople, in the Danubian Principalities.

In the localities where Bulgarians are mixed with Turks, Greeks, Wallachians (Koutzo-Vlachs), or others, proper account is to be taken of the rights and interests of these populations in the elections and in the preparation of the Organic Laws.

The introduction of the new system into Bulgaria, and the superintendence of its working, will be entrusted for two years to an Imperial Russian commissioner. At the expiration of the first year after the introduction of the new system, and if an understanding on this subject has been established between Russia, the Sublime Porte, and the Cabinets of Europe, they can, if it is deemed necessary, associate special delegates with the Imperial Russian commissioner.

Withdrawal of Turkish army from Bulgaria.

ART. VIII.—The Ottoman army will no longer remain in Bulgaria, and all the ancient fortresses will be razed at the expense of the local government. The Sublime Porte will have the right to dispose, as it sees fit, of the war material and of the other property belonging to the Ottoman Government which may have been left in the Danubian fortresses already evacuated in accordance with the terms of the Armistice of the 19th / 31st January, as well as of that in the strongholds of Schoumla and Varna.

Temporary occupation by Russian army.

Until the complete formation of a native militia sufficient to preserve order, security, and tranquillity, and the strength of which will be fixed later on by an understanding between the Ottoman Government and the Imperial Russian Cabinet, Russian troops will occupy the country, and will give armed assistance to the commissioner in case of need. This occupation will also be limited to a term approximating to two years.

The strength of the Russian army of occupation, to be composed of six divisions of infantry and two of cavalry, which will remain in Bulgaria after the evacuation of Turkey by the Imperial army, shall not exceed 50,000 men. It will be maintained at the expense of the country occupied. The Russian troops of occupation in Bulgaria will maintain their communications with Russia, not only through Roumania, but also by the ports of the Black Sea, Varna and Bourgas, where they may organize, for the term of the occupation, the necessary depots.

ART. IX.—The amount of the annual tribute which Bulgaria is to pay the Suzerain Court, by transmitting it to a bank to be hereafter named by the Sublime Porte, will be determined by an agreement between Russia, the Ottoman Government, and the other Cabinets, at the end of the first year during which the new organization shall be in operation. This tribute will be calculated on the average revenue of all the territory which is to form part of the principality.

Tribute of Bulgaria to Turkey.

Bulgaria will take upon itself the obligations of the Imperial Ottoman Government towards the Rustchuck and Varna Railway Company, after an agreement has been come to between the Sublime Porte, the Government of the principality, and the directors of this company. The regulations as to the other railways which cross the principality are also reserved for an agreement between the Sublime Porte, the Government established in Bulgaria, and the directors of the companies concerned.

Transport of Turkish troops.

ART. X.—The Sublime Porte shall have the right to make use of Bulgaria for the transport by fixed routes of its troops, munitions, and provisions to the provinces beyond the principality, and *vice versa*. In order to avoid difficulties and misunderstandings in the application of this right, while guaranteeing the military necessities of the Sublime Porte, a special regulation will lay down the conditions of it within three months after the ratification of the present Act by an understanding between the Sublime Porte and the Bulgarian Government.

It is fully understood that this right is limited to the regular Ottoman troops, and that the irregulars, the Bashi-Bazouks, and the Circassians will be absolutely excluded from it.

Turkish postal service.

The Sublime Porte also reserves to itself the right of sending its postal service through the principality, and of maintaining telegraphic communication. These two points shall also be determined in the manner and within the period of time indicated above.

Turkish property in Bulgaria.

ART. XI.—The Mussulman proprietors or others who fix their personal residence outside the principality may retain their estates by having them farmed or administered by others. Turco-Bulgarian commissions shall sit in the principal centres of population, under the superintendence of Russian Commissioners, to decide absolutely in the course of two years all questions relative to the verification of real property in which either Mussulmans or others may be interested.

Similar commissions will be charged with the duty of regulating within two years all questions relative to the mode of alienation, working, or use for the benefit of the Sublime Porte of the property of the State, and of the religious endowments (vakoufs).

At the expiration of the two years mentioned above, all properties which shall not have been claimed shall be sold by public auction, and the proceeds thereof shall be devoted to the support of the widows and orphans, Mussulman as well as Christian, victims of the recent events.

The Danube.

ART. XII.—All the Danubian fortresses shall be razed. There shall be no strongholds in future on the banks of this river, nor any men-of-war in the waters of the principalities of Roumania, Serbia, and Bulgaria, except the usual *stationnaires* and the small vessels intended for river-police and custom-house purposes.

The rights, obligations, and prerogatives of the international commission of the Lower Danube are maintained intact.

Passage of Soulina.

Art. XIII.—The Sublime Porte undertakes to render the passage of Soulina again navigable and to indemnify the private individuals who have suffered loss by the war and the interruption of the navigation of the Danube, applying for this double charge a sum of 500,000 francs from the amount due to the Sublime Porte from the Danubian commission.

Bosnia and Herzegovina.

Art. XIV.—The European proposals communicated to the Ottoman plenipotentiaries at the first sitting of the Constantinople Conference shall be immediately introduced into Bosnia and Herzegovina, with any modifications which may be agreed upon in common between the Sublime Porte, the Government of Russia, and that of Austria-Hungary.

The payment of arrears of taxes shall not be required, and the current revenues of those provinces until the 1st March, 1880, shall be exclusively applied to indemnify the families of refugees and inhabitants, victims of recent events, without distinction of race or creed, as well as to the local needs of the country. The sum to be received annually after this period by the Central Government shall be subsequently fixed by a special understanding between Turkey, Russia, and Austria-Hungary.

Crete.

Art. XV.—The Sublime Porte engages to apply scrupulously in the Island of Crete the Organic Law of 1868, taking into account the previously expressed wishes of the native population.

Turkey in Europe.

An analogous law adapted to local requirements shall likewise be introduced into Epirus, Thessaly, and the other parts of Turkey in Europe, for which a special constitution is not provided by the present act.

Special commissions, in which the native population will be largely represented, shall in each province be entrusted with the task of elaborating the details of the new organization, and the result of their labours shall be submitted to the Sublime Porte, who will consult the Imperial Government of Russia before carrying it into effect.

Armenia.

Art. XVI.—As the evacuation by the Russian troops of the territory which they occupy in Armenia, and which is to be restored to Turkey, might give rise to conflicts and complications detrimental to the maintenance of good relations between the two countries, the Sublime Porte engages to carry into effect, without further delay, the improvements and reforms demanded by local requirements in the provinces inhabited by Armenians and to guarantee their security from Kurds and Circassians.

Amnesty.

Art. XVII.—A full and complete amnesty is granted by the Sublime Porte to all Ottoman subjects compromised by recent events, and all persons imprisoned on this account or sent into exile shall be immediately set at liberty.

Turco-Persian boundary.

Art. XVIII.—The Sublime Porte will take into serious consideration the opinion expressed by the commissioners of the mediating Powers as regards the possession of the town of Khotour, and engages to have the works of the definitive delimitation of the Turco-Persian boundary carried into effect.

ART. XIX.—The war indemnity and the losses imposed on Russia which His Majesty the Emperor of Russia claims, and which the Sublime Porte has bound itself to reimburse to him, consist of—

Indemnity.

(*a*) 900,000,000 roubles for war expenses (maintenance of the army, replacing of war material, and war contracts);

(*b*) 400,000,000 roubles on account of damage done to the south coast of Russia, to her export commerce, to her industries, and to her railways;

(*c*) 100,000,000 roubles for injuries inflicted on the Caucasus by the invasion; and

(*d*) 10,000,000 roubles for costs and damages of Russian establishments and subjects in Turkey.

Total, 1,410,000,000 roubles.

Taking into consideration the financial embarrassments of Turkey, and in accordance with the wishes of His Majesty the Sultan, the Emperor of Russia consents to substitute for the payment of the greater part of the moneys enumerated in the above paragraph the following territorial cessions:—

Cessions substituted for indemnity.

(*a*) The Sandjak of Toultcha, that is to say, the districts (Cazas) of Kilia, Soulina, Mahmoudié, Isaktcha, Toultcha, Matchine, Babadagh, Hirsowo, Kustendje, and Medjidie, as well as the Delta Islands and the Isle of Serpents.

Not wishing, however, to annex this territory and the Delta Islands, Russia reserves the right of exchanging them for the part of Bessarabia detached from her by the Treaty of 1856, and which is bounded on the south by the thalweg of the Kilia branch and the mouth of the Stary-Stamboul.

The question of the apportionment of waters and fisheries shall be determined by a Russo-Roumanian commission within a year after the ratification of the treaty of peace.

(*b*) Ardahan, Kars, Batoum, Bayazet, and the territory as far as the Saganlough.

In its general outline, the frontier line, leaving the Black Sea coast, will follow the crest of the mountains which separate the affluents of the river Hopa from those of the river Tcharokh, and the chain of mountains to the south of the town of Artwin up to the river Tcharokh, near the villages of Alat and Bechaget; then the frontier will pass by the peaks of Mounts Dervenikghek, Hortchesor, and Bedjiguin-Dagh, by the crest which separates the affluents of the rivers Tortoum-tchaï and the Tcharokh by the heights near Zaily-Vihine, coming down at the village Vihine-Kilissa to the river Tortoum-tchaï; thence it will follow the Sivridagh Chain to the pass (*col*) of the same name, passing south of the village of Noriman; then it will turn to the south-east and go to Zivine, whence the frontier, passing west of the road which leads from Zivine to the villages of Ardozt and Horassan, will turn south by the Saganlough Chain to the village of Gilitchman; then by the crest of the Charian-Dagh it will arrive, ten versts south of Hamour, at the Mourad-tchai defile; then the line will follow the crest of the Alla-Dagh, and the summits of the Hori and Tandourek, and,

Delimitation of frontiers.

passing south of the Bayazet valley, will proceed to rejoin the old Turco-Persian frontier to the south of the lake of Kazligueul.

The definitive limits of the territory annexed to Russia, and indicated on the map hereto appended, will be fixed by a commission composed of Russian and Ottoman delegates.

This commission in its labours will take into account the topography of localities, as well as consideration of good administration and other conditions calculated to assure the tranquillity of the country.

(*c*) The territories mentioned in paragraphs (*a*) and (*b*) are ceded to Russia as an equivalent for the sum of one milliard and one hundred million (1,100,000,000) roubles. As for the rest of the indemnity, apart from the 10,000,000 roubles intended to indemnify Russian interests and establishments in Turkey—namely, 300,000,000 roubles—the mode of payment and guarantee of that sum shall be settled by an understanding between the Imperial Government of Russia and that of His Majesty the Sultan.

(*d*) The 10,000,000 roubles claimed as an indemnity for the Russian subjects and establishments in Turkey shall be paid as soon as the claims of those interested are examined by the Russian Embassy at Constantinople and handed to the Sublime Porte.

Lawsuits of Russian subjects.

ART. XX.—The Sublime Porte will take effective steps to put an amicable end to the lawsuits of Russian subjects pending for several years, to indemnify the latter if need be, and to carry into effect without delay all judgments passed.

Ceded territory and option of inhabitants.

ART. XXI.—The inhabitants of the districts ceded to Russia who wish to take up their residence out of these territories will be free to retire on selling all their real property. For this purpose an interval of three years is granted to them, counting from the date of the ratification of the present act.

On the expiration of that time those of the inhabitants who shall not have sold their real property and left the country shall remain as Russian subjects.

State property in ceded territory.

Real property belonging to the State, or to religious establishments situated out of the locality aforesaid, shall be sold within the same interval of three years as shall be arranged by a special Russo-Turkish commission. The same commission shall be entrusted with determining how the Ottoman Government is to remove its war material, munitions, supplies, and other State property actually in the forts, towns, and localities ceded to Russia, and not at present occupied by Russian troops.

Russian ecclesiastics in Turkey.

ART. XXII.—Russian ecclesiastics, pilgrims, and monks travelling or sojourning in Turkey, in Europe, or in Asia shall enjoy the same rights, advantages, and privileges as the foreign ecclesiastics of any other nationality.

The right of official protection by the Imperial Embassy and Russian Consulates in Turkey is recognized, both as regards the persons above-mentioned, and their possessions, religious houses, charitable institutions, etc., in the Holy Places and elsewhere.

The monks of Mount Athos, of Russian origin, shall be maintained in all their possessions and former privileges, and shall continue to enjoy in the three convents belonging to them and in the adjoining buildings the same rights and privileges as are assured to the other religious establishments and convents of Mount Athos.

Revival of treaties.

ART. XXIII.—All the treaties, conventions, and agreements previously concluded between the two High Contracting Parties relative to commerce, jurisdiction, and the position of Russian subjects in Turkey, and which had been abrogated by the state of war, shall come into force again, with the exception of the clauses affected by the present Act. The two Governments will be placed again in the same relation to one another, with respect to all their engagements and commercial and other relations, as they were in before the declaration of war.

The Bosphorus and Dardanelles.

ART. XXIV.—The Bosphorus and the Dardanelles shall remain open in time of war as in time of peace to the merchant vessels of neutral States arriving from or bound to Russian ports. The Sublime Porte consequently engages never henceforth to establish at the ports of the Black Sea and the Sea of Azow a fictitious blockade ("blocus fictif"), at variance with the spirit of the declaration signed at Paris on the 4th/16th April, 1856.

Evacuation of Russian troops.

ART. XXV.—The complete evacuation of Turkey in Europe, with the exception of Bulgaria, by the Russian army will take place within three months after the conclusion of the definitive peace between His Majesty the Emperor of Russia and His Majesty the Sultan.

In order to save time and to avoid the cost of the prolonged maintenance of the Russian troops in Turkey and Roumania, part of the Imperial army may proceed to the ports of the Black Sea and the Sea of Marmora, to be there shipped in vessels belonging to the Russian Government or chartered for the occasion.

The evacuation of Turkey in Asia will be effected within the space of six months, dating from the conclusion of the definitive peace, and the Russian troops will be entitled to take ship at Trebizond, in order to return by the Caucasus or the Crimea.

The operations of the evacuation will begin immediately after the exchange of ratifications.

Administration of occupied localities.

ART. XXVI.—As long as the Imperial Russian troops remain in the localities which, in conformity with the present Act, will be restored to the Sublime Porte, the administration and order of affairs will continue in the same state as has existed since the occupation. The Sublime Porte will not participate therein during all that time, nor until the entire departure of all the troops.

The Ottoman forces shall not enter the places to be restored to the Sublime Porte, and the Sublime Porte cannot begin to exercise its authority there until notice of each fortress and province having been evacuated by the Russian troops shall have been given by the commander of these troops to the officer appointed for this purpose by the Sublime Porte.

Amnesty.

ART. XXVII.—The Sublime Porte undertakes not to punish in any manner, or allow to be punished, those Ottoman subjects who may have been compromised by their relations with the Russian army during the war. In the event of any persons wishing to withdraw with their families when the Russian troops leave, the Ottoman authorities shall not oppose their departure.

Prisoners of war.

ART. XXVIII.—Immediately upon the ratification of the preliminaries of peace the prisoners of war shall be reciprocally restored under the care of special commissioners appointed on both sides, who for this purpose shall go to Odessa and Sebastopol. The Ottoman Government will pay all the expenses of the maintenance of the prisoners that are returned to them, in eighteen equal instalments in the space of six years, in accordance with the accounts that will be drawn up by the above-mentioned commissioners.

The exchange of prisoners between the Ottoman Government and the Governments of Roumania, Serbia, and Montenegro will be made on the same basis, deducting, however, in the account, the number of prisoners restored by the Ottoman Government from the number of prisoners that will have to be restored to that Government.

Ratification.

Provision for conversion into definitive treaty of peace.

ART. XXIX.—The present Act shall be ratified by their Imperial Majesties the Emperor of Russia and the Emperor of the Ottomans, and the ratifications shall be exchanged in fifteen days, or sooner if possible, at St. Petersburg, where likewise an agreement shall be come to as to the place and the time at which the stipulations of the present Act shall be invested with all the solemn forms usually observed in treaties of peace.[1] It is, however, well understood that the High Contracting Parties consider themselves as formally bound by the present Act from the moment of its ratification.

In witness whereof the respective plenipotentiaries have appended their signatures and seals to the present Act.

Done at San Stefano, the 19th February / 3rd March, one thousand eight hundred and seventy-eight.

(Here follow signatures and seals.)

[1] See *infra*, p. 403, the Treaty of Constantinople, concluded January 27 / February 8, 1879.

(N) TREATY OF CONSTANTINOPLE

Jan. 27 / Feb. 8, 1879

RUSSIA—TURKEY

In the Name of Almighty God.

His Majesty the Emperor of All the Russias, and His Majesty the Emperor of the Ottomans, wishing to perpetuate the restoration of peace between the two Empires, and to settle permanently by a treaty such articles of the Preliminary Treaty of San Stefano as are to form the subjects of a direct understanding between the two States, have appointed for their plenipotentiaries:

His Majesty the Emperor of All the Russias, on the one part, Prince Alexis Lobanow-Rostovsky, his Ambassador Extraordinary and Plenipotentiary to His Imperial Majesty the Sultan, Secretary of State, etc.;

And His Majesty the Emperor of the Ottomans, on the other part, Al. Carathéodory Pacha, his Minister for Foreign Affairs, etc., and Ali Pacha, his Minister presiding over the Council of State, etc.;

Who, after having communicated to each other their full powers, found in good and due form, have agreed upon the following articles:—

Restoration of peace.

ART. I.—Peace and friendship shall henceforth exist between the two Empires.

The Treaty of Berlin overriding Preliminaries of San Stefano.

ART. II.—The two Powers agree in declaring that the stipulations of the treaty concluded at Berlin by the seven Powers have been substituted for such articles of the Preliminaries of Peace of San Stefano as have been abrogated or modified by the Congress.[1]

ART. III.—The stipulations of the Treaty of San Stefano which have not been abrogated or modified by the Treaty of Berlin are permanently settled by the following articles of the present treaty.

ART. IV.—After deducting the value of the territories ceded by Turkey to Russia in conformity with the Treaty of Berlin, the war indemnity remains assessed at 820,500,000 francs.

Indemnity.

The mode of payment of that sum, and also the securities by which it is to be guaranteed (save the declarations contained in the 11th Protocol of the Congress of Berlin with regard to the question of territories, and to the rights of creditors), will be settled by an understanding between the Governments of His Majesty the Emperor of All the Russias and His Majesty the Emperor of the Ottomans.

[1] See Protocol, *infra*, p. 406.

Art. V.—The claims of Russian subjects and establishments in Turkey to compensation for losses sustained during the war shall be settled as soon as they shall have been inquired into by the Russian Embassy at Constantinople and transmitted to the Sublime Porte.

Losses of subjects during the war.

The total amount of those claims shall not, under any circumstances, exceed the sum of 26,750,000 francs.

The term of one year after the ratifications shall have been exchanged is assigned as the date from which claims can be presented to the Sublime Porte, and that of two years as the date after which claims shall no longer be admitted.[1]

Art. VI.—Special commissioners shall be appointed by the Imperial Government of Russia and the Sublime Porte in order to draw up an account of the expenditure caused by the maintenance of Ottoman prisoners of war. This account shall be made up to the date of the signing of the Treaty of Berlin. From it shall be deducted the expenses incurred by the Ottoman Government for the maintenance of Russian prisoners, and the balance, once settled, shall be paid by the Sublime Porte in twenty-one equal instalments within the space of seven years.

Cost of prisoners of war.

Art. VII.—The inhabitants of the localities ceded to Russia who should wish to establish their residence beyond those territories will be free to retire upon selling their real property. A delay of three years from the date of the ratification of the present treaty will be granted to them for that purpose.

Ceded territories and option.

After that delay those inhabitants who should not have left the country and sold their immovable estates shall remain Russian subjects.

Art. VIII.—Both parties pledge themselves not to molest or to allow to be molested in any manner those Russian or Ottoman subjects who might have become compromised in consequence of their intercourse with the armies of either Empire during the war. In case any persons should wish to retire with their families after the withdrawal of the Russian troops, the Ottoman authorities will not oppose their departure.

Amnesty.

Art. IX.—A full and general amnesty is secured to all Ottoman subjects who shall have become compromised during the late events in the provinces of European Turkey, and all persons either detained on that account, or sent into exile or removed from their country, shall immediately be restored to the enjoyment of their liberty.[2]

Art. X.—All treaties, conventions, and engagements concluded between the two High Contracting Parties relating to commerce, jurisdiction, and the position of Russian subjects in Turkey, which had been suppressed in consequence of the state of war, shall be put in force again, and the two Governments will again be placed, with regard to all their commercial and other engagements and under-

Revival of treaties.

[1] See Protocol, *infra*, p. 406; and Arbitration Agreement, *infra*, p. 408.

[2] See Protocol, *infra*, p. 407.

takings, in the same position, in relation to one another, as they stood before the declaration of war, with the exception of such articles as may have been altered by the present treaty, or in virtue of the Treaty of Berlin.

Claims of Russian subjects in Turkey.

ART. XI.—The Sublime Porte will take effective steps in order to terminate amicably all litigation of Russian subjects which has been pending for several years, to compensate the latter, should there be cause for it, and to cause the judgments given to be executed without delay.

Ratification.

ART. XII.—The present treaty shall be ratified, and the ratifications shall be exchanged at St. Petersburg within two weeks, or sooner if possible.

In testimony whereof the plenipotentiaries of Russia and Turkey have affixed to it their signatures and their seals.

Done at Constantinople, $\frac{\text{27th January}}{\text{8th February}}$, 1879.

(L.S.) LOBANOW.
(L.S.) AL. CARATHÉODORY.
(L.S.) ALI.

(O) PROTOCOL BETWEEN RUSSIA AND TURKEY RESPECTING THE TREATY OF PEACE OF JAN. 27 / FEB. 8, 1879

Signed at Constantinople, Jan. 27 / Feb. 8, 1879

THEIR Excellencies the Plenipotentiaries of Turkey and Russia, having met at the Ministry for Foreign Affairs, on the 27th January / 8th February, 1879, in order to proceed to the signature of the treaty negotiated by them, examine, article by article, the text of that Act, as well as the draft treaty previously communicated to the Sublime Porte by the Russian plenipotentiary.

The Treaty of Berlin and the Preliminaries of San Stefano.

With regard to Art. II, the Ottoman plenipotentiaries record the fact that it remains understood that that article has only a declaratory character in the sense that the statements contained therein cannot bear any interpretation which may be in disagreement with the nature of the engagements entered into in the Treaty of Berlin. His Excellency Prince Lobanow, in accepting this declaration of the Ottoman plenipotentiaries, records the fact that the Imperial Russian Government on its part has only in view the strict and faithful execution of the Treaty of Berlin in letter as well as in spirit.

Art. V gives rise to the following explanation by the Russian plenipotentiary:

Losses of Russian subjects during the war.

His Excellency Prince Lobanow declares that the sum which is therein specified constitutes a maximum to which the total amount of claims will probably never reach; he adds that a commission *ad hoc* will be established at the Russian Embassy for the careful examination of the claims which shall be laid before it, and that, according to the instructions of his Government, an Ottoman delegate shall be allowed to take part in the examination of those claims. As to the term of one year fixed by this article as the date from which the claims may be presented to the Sublime Porte, it is understood that an exception will be made in favour of the claim of the Russian Hospital, amounting to the sum of £11,200.

With reference to the last part of paragraph (*c*) (Art. IV) of the original draft, it is understood, without prejudice, that the Principalities of Roumania, Serbia, and Montenegro, being now independent, those stipulations of the Treaty of San Stefano can find no place in the new treaty unless the interested parties come to a direct understanding respecting them.

Paragraph (*d*) of the said draft being suppressed, the Russian plenipotentiary refers to the declaration made on that subject by Count Schouvaloff, in the sitting of the 2nd of July, of the Congress of Berlin (Protocol II), according to which no obligation could fall upon Russia through the interruption of the navigation of the Danube caused by the breaking out of war.

Paragraph (*f*) of the Russian draft is also eliminated; but to prevent any misunderstanding, His Excellency Prince Lobanow declares that this elimination can in no way be invoked against the administrative system existing in Eastern Roumelia, and that the *status quo* will be provisionally maintained there until the introduction of the new organization elaborated by the European Commission.

Eastern Roumelia.

On their side the Ottoman plenipotentiaries declare that they have demanded the suppression of that paragraph, precisely because they do not mean in any way to deal with Eastern Roumelia, the position of which is determined by the treaty concluded between the seven Powers at Berlin, and because they are neither qualified, nor is it their mission, to discuss the matter at the present time.

Paragraph (*g*) of the same draft is also suppressed, and it is agreed that the Russian Ambassador shall address a note to the Sublime Porte declaring that the Imperial Government engages to give orders, immediately after the ratification of the treaty of this day, for the evacuation of the territories occupied by the Russian troops outside the limits of Bulgaria and Eastern Roumelia. Moreover, the Russian Ambassador gives notice that he will call the attention of the Sublime Porte to the necessity of taking certain temporary measures for the maintenance of public order and tranquillity in the territories evacuated. The Ottoman plenipotentiaries, on their part, affirm that their Government has always given it attention, in so far as it is concerned, to a change of administration in the territories evacuated by the Russian armies.

Evacuation.

With reference to Art. IX, it is understood that the amnesty therein mentioned shall not hinder the local administration from taking such police measures, with regard to compromised persons, as may be rendered necessary by the exigencies of public order and tranquillity.

Amnesty.

The signature of the treaty is then proceeded with; His Excellency the Russian Ambassador hands in the note respecting the evacuation, and the plenipotentiaries append their signatures to the present protocol.

Constantinople, $\frac{\text{27th January}}{\text{8th February}}$, 1879.

AL. CARATHÉODORY. LOBANOW.
ALI.

(P) ARBITRATION AGREEMENT

Constantinople, July 22 / August 4, 1910

RUSSIA—TURKEY

THE Imperial Russian Government and the Imperial Ottoman Government, co-signatories of the Hague Convention of October 18, 1907, for the peaceful settlement of international disputes :

Considering the provisions of Art. V of the treaty signed at Constantinople between Russia and Turkey, January 27 / February 8, 1879, as follows :

The claims of Russian subjects and institutions in Turkey for indemnity on account of damages suffered during the war will be paid as soon as they are examined by the Russian Embassy at Constantinople and transmitted to the Sublime Porte.

Claims of private persons for losses due to war.

The total of these claims shall in no case exceed 26,750,000 francs.

Claims may be presented to the Sublime Porte beginning one year from the date on which ratifications are exchanged, and no claims will be admitted which are presented after the expiration of two years from that date ;

Considering the additional explanation contained in the protocol bearing the same date :

"As to the expiration of one year, fixed by this article as the date from which claims may be presented to the Sublime Porte, it is understood that one exception will be made in favour of the Russian Hospital's claim, amounting to 11,200 pounds sterling ; "

Considering that a disagreement has arisen between the Imperial Russian Government and the Imperial Ottoman Government as to the questions of law arising from the dates on which the Imperial Ottoman Government made the following payments on the amounts of the indemnities regularly presented in pursuance of the said Art. V, to wit :

	Turkish pounds.	Piastres.	Paras.
In 1884	50,000	0	0
,, 1889	50,000	0	0
,, 1893	75,000	0	0
,, 1894	50,000	0	0
,, 1902	42,438	67	22

Considering that the Imperial Russian Government holds that the Imperial Ottoman Government is responsible to the Russian claimants for damages because of the delay in settling its debt;

Considering that the Imperial Ottoman Government contests, both in fact and in law, the grounds of the Imperial Russian Government's contention;

Considering that it has not been possible to settle the dispute through diplomatic channels;

And having resolved, in conformity with the stipulations of the said Hague Convention, to end this controversy by submitting the question to arbitration;

Have authorized to this effect their representatives designated below, to wit:

For Russia:

His Excellency Monsieur Tcharikow, Ambassador of His Majesty the Emperor of Russia at Constantinople;

For Turkey:

His Excellency Rifaat Pasha, Minister of Foreign Affairs, to conclude the following "compromis":

ART. I.—The Powers in controversy decide that the arbitral tribunal to which the question will be submitted as a last resort shall be composed of five members, who shall be appointed in the following manner:

Constitution of the arbitral tribunal.

Each party must name, as soon as possible, and within two months from the date of this "compromis," two arbitrators, and the four arbitrators thus appointed shall choose an umpire. In case the four arbitrators shall not, within two months of their appointment, have chosen an umpire either unanimously or by a majority, the choice of an umpire devolves upon a third party agreed upon by the parties. If, after the lapse of two more months, an agreement is not reached upon this question, each party designates a different Power and the umpire is chosen by the Powers thus designated.

If, after the lapse of two more months, these two Powers have not been able to agree, each of them presents two candidates selected from the list of members of the Permanent Court, exclusive of the members of the said court selected by the two Powers or by the parties and being nationals neither of the former nor of the latter. These candidates, moreover, cannot belong to the nationality of the arbitrators appointed by the parties in the present arbitration. The umpire is chosen by lot from the two candidates thus presented.

The drawing of lots will be done by the International Bureau of the Permanent Court at The Hague.

ART. II.—The Powers in controversy will be represented before the arbitral tribunal by agents, counsel, or advocates, in conformity with the provisions of Art. 62 of the Hague Convention of 1907 for the peaceful settlement of international disputes.

Agents and counsel.

These agents, counsel, or advocates will be appointed by the parties in ample time to prevent any delay in the arbitration.

Art. III.—The questions in dispute and upon which the parties ask the arbitral tribunal to render a definitive decision are as follows:

Questions in dispute.

1. Whether or not the Imperial Ottoman Government must pay the Russian claimants damages by reason of the dates on which the said Government made payment of the indemnities determined in pursuance of Art. V of the treaty of January 27 / February 8, 1879, as well as of the protocol of the same date?

2. In case the first question is decided in the affirmative, what would be the amount of these damages?

Place and date of meeting.

Art. IV.—The arbitral tribunal, as soon as it is constituted, will meet at The Hague at a date which will be determined by the arbitrators and within one month from the appointment of the umpire. After settling—in conformity with the letter and the spirit of the Hague Convention of 1907—all questions of procedure which may arise and which may not be provided for in the present "compromis," the said tribunal will determine the date of its next meeting.

However, it is agreed that the tribunal cannot open the arguments on the questions in dispute either before the expiration of two months or after the expiration of three months from the filing of the counter-case or the counter-reply provided for by Art. VI and eventually of the demands stipulated in Art. VIII.

Procedure.

Art. V.—The arbitral procedure will include two distinct phases: the written statement of the case, and the arguments which will consist in the oral development of the pleas of the parties before the tribunal.

French is the only language which the tribunal will use and which may be used before it.

Statement of claims.

Art. VI.—Within eight months at most after the date of the present "compromis" the Imperial Russian Government must deliver to each of the members of the arbitral tribunal one complete copy, written or printed, of its case containing every argument in support of its claim and with reference to the two questions mentioned in Art. III; and to the Imperial Ottoman Government ten copies.

Within eight months at most after this delivery the Imperial Ottoman Government must deliver to each of the members of the tribunal, as well as to the Imperial Russian Government, the same number of complete copies as specified above, written or printed, of its counter-case with all supporting arguments, but confining itself to Question 1 of Art. III.

Reply.

Within one month after this delivery the Imperial Russian Government will inform the president of the arbitral tribunal whether it intends to present a reply. In that case it will have an extension of three months at most from the date of such notification in which to communicate the said reply under the same conditions as the case. The Imperial Ottoman Government will then have an extension of four months from the date of this communication to present its counter-reply under the same conditions as the counter-case.

The extensions fixed by the present article may be lengthened if agreed to by both parties, or if the tribunal deems it necessary in order to reach a just decision.

But the tribunal will not take into consideration cases, counter-cases, or other communications which are presented to it by the parties after the expiration of the last extension which it has granted.

Production of documents.

ART. VII.—If in the cases or other papers exchanged either of the parties has referred or alluded to a document or paper of which it alone is in possession and of which it has not furnished a copy, it must furnish the other party with a copy, if the other party so requests, within thirty days.

ART. VIII.—In case the arbitral tribunal decides Question 1 of Art. III in the affirmative, it must, before taking up Question 2 of the same article, grant the parties further extensions, which may not be less than three months each, for the presentation and exchange of their demands and arguments in support.

Date of decision.

ART. IX.—The decisions of the tribunal on the first, and contingently on the second question at issue, shall be rendered, in so far as possible, within one month from the closing by the president of the arguments relating to each of these questions.

Judgment final.

ART. X.—The judgment of the arbitral tribunal shall be final and must be executed strictly and without any delay.

Expenses.

ART. XI.—Each party bears its own expenses and half of the expenses of the tribunal.

Other questions governed by the Hague Convention.

ART. XII.—Whatever questions arise in this arbitration which are not provided for by the present "compromis" shall be governed by the stipulations of the Hague Convention for the peaceful settlement of international disputes, except, however, those articles the acceptance of which has been reserved by the Imperial Ottoman Government.

Done at Constantinople, July 22 / August 4, 1910.

N. TCHARYKOW. RIFAAT.

(Q) TREATY OF LIMA

June 12, 1883

SPAIN—CHILE

THE Republic of Chile on the one part, and His Majesty the King of Spain on the other, being most desirous of re-establishing friendly relations between the two countries and of consigning to oblivion the events which interrupted them, have determined to conclude a treaty of peace and friendship which shall always unite Chilean citizens and Spanish subjects; and for that purpose have named and constituted as their plenipotentiaries, that is to say: His Excellency the President of the Republic of Chile, Don Jovino Novoa; His Majesty the King of Spain, Don Enrique Vallés, Commander of the Royal Order of Isabel the Catholic, Knight of the Royal and distinguished Order of Charles III, Commander of the Order of Albert of Saxony, wearing the Cross of the second class of the Royal Crown of Prussia, and that of the third class of Medjidié of Turkey, Knight of the Holy Sepulchre, etc., Chargé d'Affaires of Spain in Peru;

Who, after having communicated to each other their full powers, and found them to be in good and due form, have agreed on the following articles:—

Restoration of peace. ART. I.—The past shall be consigned to oblivion, and there shall exist a solid and inviolable peace between the Republic of Chile and His Majesty the King of Spain.

ART. II.—In virtue of what is established in the preceding article, the articles of the armistice signed between the High Contracting Parties on the 11th April, 1871, are cancelled, and the fact shall be reported to the President of the United States.

Revival of treaties. ART. III.—Until new treaties be concluded the High Contracting Parties declare that the state of things which preceded the interruption of their relations is revived.

ART. IV.—The Governments of Chile and Spain shall appoint diplomatic representatives as well as consular agents.

Ratification. ART. V.—The present treaty shall be ratified, and the ratifications shall be exchanged at Santiago in Chile as soon as possible within the term of one year, to be reckoned from this date.[1]

In witness whereof the respective plenipotentiaries have signed it in quadruple, and affixed their private seals thereto.

Done at Lima, on the 12th June, 1883.

(L.S.) JOVINO NOVOA.
(L.S.) ENRIQUE VALLÉS.

[1] Ratifications were exchanged at Santiago, May 21, 1884.

(R) TREATY OF SHIMONOSEKI

April 17, 1895

CHINA—JAPAN

HIS Majesty the Emperor of Japan and His Majesty the Emperor of China, desiring to restore the blessings of peace to their countries and subjects, and to remove all cause for future complications, have named as their plenipotentiaries for the purpose of concluding a treaty of peace, that is to say:

His Majesty the Emperor of Japan, Count Ito Hirobumi, Junii, Grand Cross of the Imperial Order of Paullownia, Minister President of State, and Viscount Mutsu Munemitsu, Junii, First Class of the Imperial Order of the Sacred Treasure, Minister of State for Foreign Affairs;

And His Majesty the Emperor of China, Li Hung-Chang, Senior Tutor to the Heir Apparent, Senior Grand Secretary of State, Minister Superintendent of Trade for the Northern Ports of China, Viceroy of the Province of Chihli, and Earl of the First Rank, and Li Ching-fong, ex-Minister of the Diplomatic Service, of the Second Official Rank;

Who, after having exchanged their full powers, which were found to be in good and proper form, have agreed to the following articles:—

Independence of Korea.

ART. I.—China recognizes definitely the full and complete independence and autonomy of Korea, and, in consequence, the payment of tribute and the performance of ceremonies and formalities by Korea to China in derogation of such independence and autonomy shall wholly cease for the future.

Cession of territories.

ART. II.—China cedes to Japan in perpetuity and full sovereignty the following territories, together with all fortifications, arsenals, and public property thereon:—

(*a*) The southern portion of the province of Fêng-tien, within the following boundaries:—

The line of demarcation begins at the mouth of the river Yalu, and ascends that stream to the mouth of the river An-ping; from thence the line runs to Fêng Huang; from thence to Haicheng; from thence to Ying Kow, forming a line which describes the southern portion of the territory. The places above named are included in the ceded territory. When the line reaches the river Liao, at Ying Kow, it follows the course of that stream to its mouth, where it terminates. The mid-channel of the river Liao shall be taken as the line of demarcation. This cession also includes all islands appertaining or belonging to the province of Fêng-tien situated in the eastern portion of the Bay of Liao Tung, and in the northern part of the Yellow Sea.

(*b*) The island of Formosa, together with all islands appertaining or belonging to the said island of Formosa.

(*c*) The Pescadores Group, that is to say, all islands lying between the 119th and 120th degrees of longitude east of Greenwich, and the 23rd and 24th degrees of north latitude.

ART. III.—The alignments of the frontiers described in the preceding article, and shown on the annexed map, shall be subject to verification and demarcation on the spot by a Joint Commission of Delimitation, consisting of two or more Japanese and two or more Chinese delegates, to be appointed immediately after the exchange of ratifications of this Act. In case the boundaries laid down in this Act are found to be defective at any point, either on account of topography or in consideration of good administration, it shall also be the duty of the Delimitation Commission to rectify the same.

Joint Delimitation Commission.

The Delimitation Commission will enter upon its duties as soon as possible, and will bring its labours to a conclusion within the period of one year after appointment.

The alignments laid down in this Act shall, however, be maintained until the rectifications of the Delimitation Commission, if any are made, shall have received the approval of the Governments of Japan and China.

ART. IV.—China agrees to pay to Japan as a war indemnity the sum of 200,000,000 Kuping taels. The said sum to be paid in eight instalments. The first instalment of 50,000,000 taels to be paid within six months, and the second instalment of 50,000,000 taels to be paid within twelve months after the exchange of the ratifications of this Act. The remaining sum to be paid in six equal annual instalments as follows: the first of such equal annual instalments to be paid within two years, the second within three years, the third within four years, the fourth within five years, the fifth within six years, and the sixth within seven years after the exchange of the ratifications of this Act. Interest at the rate of 5 per cent. per annum shall begin to run on all unpaid portions of the said indemnity from the date the first instalment falls due.

Indemnity—Mode of payment.

China shall, however, have the right to pay by anticipation at any time any or all of said instalments. In case the whole amount of the said indemnity is paid within three years after the exchange of the ratifications of the present Act, all interest shall be waived, and the interest for two years and a half, or for any less period if then already paid, shall be included as a part of the principal amount of the indemnity.

ART. V.—The inhabitants of the territories ceded to Japan who wish to take up their residence outside the ceded districts shall be at liberty to sell their real property and retire. For this purpose a period of two years from the date of the exchange of the ratifications of the present Act shall be granted. At the expiration of that period those of the inhabitants who shall not have left such territories shall, at the option of Japan, be deemed to be Japanese subjects.

Option.

Each of the two Governments shall, immediately upon the exchange of the ratifications of the present Act, send one or more commissioners to Formosa to effect a final transfer of that province, and within the space of two months after the exchange of the ratifications of this Act such transfer shall be completed.

Transfer of ceded territory.

ART. VI.—All treaties between Japan and China having come to an end in consequence of war, China engages, immediately upon the exchange of the ratifications of this Act, to appoint plenipotentiaries to conclude with the Japanese plenipotentiaries a treaty of commerce and navigation and a convention to regulate frontier intercourse and trade. The treaties, conventions, and regulations now subsisting between China and European Powers shall serve as a basis for the said treaty and convention between Japan and China. From the date of the exchange of the ratifications of this Act until the said treaty and convention are brought into actual operation the Japanese Government, its officials, commerce, navigation, frontier intercourse and trade, industries, ships, and subjects shall in every respect be accorded by China most-favoured-nation treatment.

Treaties.

China makes, in addition, the following concessions, to take effect six months after the date of the present Act:—

I. The following cities, towns, and ports, in addition to those already opened, shall be opened to the trade, residence, industries, and manufactures of Japanese subjects under the same conditions and with the same privileges and facilities as exist at the present open cities, towns, and ports of China:—

Commercial relationships.

1. Shashih, in the province of Hupeh.
2. Chungking, in the province of Szechuan.
3. Suchow, in the province of Kiang Su.
4. Hangchow, in the province of Chêkiang.

The Japanese Government shall have the right to station consuls at any or all of the above-named places.

II. Steam navigation for vessels under the Japanese flag for the conveyance of passengers and cargo shall be extended to the following places:—

1. On the upper Yang-tsze river, from Ichang to Chungking.
2. On the Woosung river and the canal, from Shanghae to Suchow and Hangchow.

The rules and regulations which now govern the navigation of the inland waters of China by foreign vessels shall, so far as applicable, be enforced in respect of the above-named routes, until new rules and regulations are conjointly agreed to.

III. Japanese subjects purchasing goods or produce in the interior of China, or transporting imported merchandise into the interior of China, shall have the right temporarily to rent or hire warehouses for the storage of the articles so purchased or transported, without the payment of any taxes or exactions whatever.

IV. Japanese subjects shall be free to engage in all kinds of manufacturing industries in all the open cities, towns, and ports of China, and shall be at liberty to import into China all kinds of machinery, paying only the stipulated import duties thereon.

All articles manufactured by Japanese subjects in China shall, in respect of inland transit and internal taxes, duties, charges, and exactions of all kinds, and also in respect of warehousing and storage facilities in the interior of China, stand upon the same footing and enjoy the same privileges and exemptions as merchandise imported by Japanese subjects into China.

In the event additional rules and regulations are necessary in connection with these concessions, they shall be embodied in the treaty of commerce and navigation provided for by this article.

Evacuation.

ART. VII.—Subject to the provisions of the next succeeding article, the evacuation of China by the armies of Japan shall be completely effected within three months after the exchange of the ratifications of the present Act.

Temporary occupation of territory.

ART. VIII.—As a guarantee of the faithful performance of the stipulations of this Act, China consents to the temporary occupation by the military forces of Japan of Wei-hai-wei, in the province of Shantung.

Evacuation and payment of indemnity.

Upon the payment of the first two instalments of the war indemnity herein stipulated for, and the exchange of the ratifications of the treaty of commerce and navigation, the said place shall be evacuated by the Japanese forces: provided the Chinese Government consents to pledge, under suitable and sufficient arrangements, the customs revenue of China as security for the payment of the principal and interest of the remaining instalments of said indemnity. In the event no such arrangements are concluded, such evacuation shall only take place upon the payment of the final instalment of said indemnity.

It is, however, expressly understood that no such evacuation shall take place until after the exchange of the ratifications of the treaty of commerce and navigation.

Prisoners of war.

Amnesty.

ART. IX.—Immediately upon the exchange of the ratifications of this Act, all prisoners of war then held shall be restored, and China undertakes not to ill-treat or punish prisoners of war so restored to her by Japan. China also engages to release at once all Japanese subjects accused of being military spies or charged with any other military offences. China further engages not to punish in any manner, nor to allow to be punished, those Chinese subjects who have in any manner been compromised in their relations with the Japanese army during the war.

When hostilities to cease.

ART. X.—All offensive military operations shall cease upon the exchange of the ratifications of this Act.

Ratification.

ART. XI.—The present Act shall be ratified by their Majesties the Emperor of Japan and the Emperor of China, and the ratifications shall be exchanged at Chefoo on the 8th day of the 5th month of the 28th year of Meiji, corresponding to 14th day of the 4th month of the 21st year of Kuang Hsü.[1]

[1] Ratifications were exchanged at Chefoo, May 8, 1895.

In witness whereof the respective plenipotentiaries have signed the same, and have affixed thereto the seals of their arms.

Done at Shimonoseki, in duplicate, this 17th day of the 4th month of the 28th year of Meiji, corresponding to 23rd day of 3rd month of the 21st year of Kuang Hsü.

(Here follow signatures and seals.)

Separate Articles

Art. I.—The Japanese military forces which are, under Art. VIII of the treaty of peace signed this day, to temporarily occupy Wei-hai-wei shall not exceed one brigade, and from the date of the exchange of the ratifications of the said treaty of peace China shall pay annually one-fourth of the amount of the expenses of such temporary occupation, that is to say, at the rate of 500,000 Kuping taels per annum.

Art. II.—The territory temporarily occupied at Wei-hai-wei shall comprise the island of Liu Kung and a belt of land 5 Japanese *ri* wide along the entire coast-line of the Bay of Wei-hai-wei.

No Chinese troops shall be permitted to approach or occupy any places within a zone 5 Japanese *ri* wide beyond the boundaries of the occupied territory.

Art. III.—The civil administration of the occupied territory shall remain in the hands of the Chinese authorities. But such authorities shall at all times be obliged to conform to the orders which the commander of the Japanese army of occupation may deem it necessary to give in the interest of the health, maintenance, safety, distribution, and discipline of the troops.

All military offences committed within the occupied territory shall be subject to the jurisdiction of the Japanese military authorities.

The foregoing separate articles shall have the same force, value, and effect as if they had been word for word inserted in the treaty of peace signed this day.

In witness whereof the respective plenipotentiaries have signed the same, and have affixed thereto the seals of their arms.

Done at Shimonoseki, in duplicate, this 17th day of the 4th month of the 28th year of Meiji, corresponding to the 23rd day of the 3rd month of the 21st year of Kuang Hsü.

(Here follow signatures and seals.)

(S) TREATY OF PARIS

December 10, 1898

UNITED STATES—SPAIN

THE United States of America and Her Majesty the Queen Regent of Spain, in the name of her august son, Don Alfonso XIII, desiring to end the state of war now existing between the two countries, have for that purpose appointed as plenipotentiaries:

The President of the United States,

William R. Day, Cushman K. Davis, William P. Frye, George Gray, and Whitelaw Reid, citizens of the United States;

And Her Majesty the Queen Regent of Spain,

Don Eugenio Montero Rios, President of the Senate, Don Buenaventura De Abarzuza, Senator of the Kingdom and ex-Minister of the Crown, Don José De Garnica, Deputy to the Cortes and Associate Justice of the Supreme Court, Don Wenceslas Ramirez De Villa Urrutia, Envoy Extraordinary and Minister Plenipotentiary at Brussels, and Don Rafael Cerero, General of Division;

Who, having assembled in Paris, and having exchanged their full powers, which were found to be in due and proper form, have, after discussion of the matters before them, agreed upon the following articles:—

Spanish sovereignty over Cuba relinquished.

ART. I.—Spain relinquishes all claim of sovereignty over and title to Cuba.

Occupation by United States, and obligations.

And as the island is, upon its evacuation by Spain, to be occupied by the United States, the United States will, so long as such occupation shall last, assume and discharge the obligations that may under international law result from the fact of its occupation, for the protection of life and property.

Cession of Porto Rico, etc.

ART. II.—Spain cedes to the United States the island of Porto Rico and other islands now under Spanish sovereignty in the West Indies, and the island of Guam in the Marianas or Ladrones.

Cession of the Philippines.

ART. III.—Spain cedes to the United States the archipelago known as the Philippine Islands, and comprehending the islands lying within the following lines:—

A line running from west to east along or near the twentieth parallel of north latitude, and through the middle of the navigable channel of Bachi, from the one hundred and eighteenth

(118th) to the one hundred and twenty-seventh (127th) degree meridian of longitude east of Greenwich to the parallel of four degrees and forty-five minutes (4 : 45) north latitude, thence along the parallel of four degrees and forty-five minutes (4 : 45) north latitude to its intersection with the meridian of longitude one hundred and nineteen degrees and thirty-five minutes (119 : 35) east of Greenwich to the parallel of latitude seven degrees and forty minutes (7 : 40) north to its intersection with the one hundred and sixteenth (116th) degree meridian of longitude east of Greenwich, thence by a direct line to the intersection of the tenth (10th) degree parallel of north latitude with the one hundred and eighteenth (118th) degree meridian of longitude east of Greenwich, and thence along the one hundred and eighteenth (118th) degree meridian of longitude east of Greenwich to the point of beginning.

The United States will pay to Spain the sum of twenty million dollars ($20,000,000) within three months after the exchange of the ratifications of the present treaty.

Spanish trade with the Philippines.

ART. IV.—The United States will, for the term of ten years from the date of the exchange of the ratifications of the present treaty, admit Spanish ships and merchandise to the ports of the Philippine Islands on the same terms as ships and merchandise of the United States.

Prisoners of war.

ART. V.—The United States will, upon the signature of the present treaty, send back to Spain, at its own cost, the Spanish soldiers taken as prisoners of war on the capture of Manila by the American forces. The arms of the soldiers in question shall be restored to them.

Evacuation of the Philippines and Guam by Spain.

Spain will, upon the exchange of the ratifications of the present treaty, proceed to evacuate the Philippines, as well as the island of Guam, on terms similar to those agreed upon by the commissioners appointed to arrange for the evacuation of Porto Rico and other islands in the West Indies, under the protocol of August 12, 1898, which is to continue in force till its provisions are completely executed.

The time within which the evacuation of the Philippine Islands and Guam shall be completed shall be fixed by the two Governments.

What may be taken by Spain.

Stands of colors, uncaptured war vessels, small arms, guns of all calibers, with their cartridges and accessories, powder, ammunition, live stock, and materials and supplies of all kinds, belonging to the land and naval forces of Spain in the Philippines and Guam, remain the property of Spain. Pieces of heavy ordnance, exclusive of field artillery, in the fortifications and coast defences shall remain in their emplacements for the term of six months, to be reckoned from the exchange of ratifications of the treaty; and the United States may, in the meantime, purchase such material from Spain, if a satisfactory agreement between the two Governments on the subject shall be reached.

ART. VI.—Spain will, upon the signature of the present treaty, release all prisoners of war, and all persons detained or imprisoned for political offences, in connection with the insurrections in Cuba and the Philippines and the war with the United States.

Prisoners of war and political offenders. Reciprocally, the United States will release all persons made prisoners of war by the American forces, and will undertake to obtain the release of all Spanish prisoners in the hands of the insurgents in Cuba and the Philippines.

The Government of the United States will at its own cost return to Spain, and the Government of Spain will at its own cost return to the United States, Cuba, Porto Rico, and the Philippines, according to the situation of their respective homes, prisoners released or caused to be released by them, respectively, under this article.

No indemnity. ART. VII.—The United States and Spain mutually relinquish all claims for indemnity, national and individual, of every kind, of either Government, or of its citizens and subjects, against the other Government, that may have arisen since the beginning of the late insurrection in Cuba and prior to the exchange of ratifications of the present treaty, including all claims for indemnity for the cost of the war. The United States will adjudicate and settle the claims of its citizens against Spain relinquished in this article.

Public domain in ceded territory. ART. VIII.—In conformity with the provisions of Arts. I, II, and III of this treaty, Spain relinquishes in Cuba, and cedes in Porto Rico and other islands in the West Indies, in the island of Guam, and in the Philippine Archipelago, all the buildings, wharves, barracks, forts, structures, public highways, and other immovable property which in conformity with law belong to the public domain, and as such belong to the Crown of Spain.

Rights of property. And it is hereby declared that the relinquishment or cession, as the case may be, to which the preceding paragraph refers, cannot in any respect impair the property or rights, which by law belong to the peaceful possession of property of all kinds, of provinces, municipalities, public or private establishments, ecclesiastical or civil bodies, or any other associations having legal capacities to acquire and possess property in the aforesaid territories renounced or ceded, or of private individuals, of whatsoever nationality such individuals may be.

Archives and records. In the aforesaid relinquishment or cession, as the case may be, are also included such rights as the Crown of Spain and its authorities possess in respect of the official archives and records, executive as well as judicial, in the islands above referred to, which relate to said islands or the rights and property of their inhabitants. Such archives and records shall be carefully preserved, and private persons shall without distinction have the right to require, in accordance with the law, authenticated copies of the contracts, wills, and other instruments forming part of notarial protocols or files, or which may be contained in the executive or judicial archives, be the latter in Spain or in the islands aforesaid.

ART. IX.—Spanish subjects, natives of the Peninsula, residing in the territory over which Spain by the present treaty relinquishes or cedes her sovereignty, may remain in such territory or may remove therefrom, retaining in either event all their rights of property, including the right to sell or dispose of such property or of its proceeds; and they shall also have the right to carry on their industry, commerce, and professions, being subject in respect thereof to such laws as are applicable to other foreigners. In case they remain in the territory they may preserve their allegiance to the Crown of Spain by making, before a court of record, within a year from the date of the exchange of ratifications of this treaty, a declaration of their decision to preserve such allegiance; in default of which declaration they shall be held to have renounced it and to have adopted the nationality of the territory in which they may reside.

Option by natives of Spain.

The civil rights and political status of the native inhabitants of the territories hereby ceded to the United States shall be determined by the Congress.

No option by natives of ceded territories.

ART. X.—The inhabitants of the territories over which Spain relinquishes or cedes her sovereignty shall be secured in the free exercise of their religion.

Exercise of religion.

ART. XI.—The Spaniards residing in the territories over which Spain by this treaty cedes or relinquishes her sovereignty shall be subject in matters civil as well as criminal to the jurisdiction of the courts of the country wherein they reside, pursuant to the ordinary laws governing the same; and they shall have the right to appear before such courts, and to pursue the same course as citizens of the country to which the courts belong.

Jurisdiction in ceded territories.

ART. XII.—Judicial proceedings pending at the time of the exchange of ratifications of this treaty in the territories over which Spain relinquishes or cedes her sovereignty shall be determined according to the following rules:—

Judicial proceedings pending.

1. Judgments rendered either in civil suits between private individuals or in criminal matters, before the date mentioned, and with respect to which there is no recourse or right of review under the Spanish law, shall be deemed to be final, and shall be executed in due form by competent authority in the territory within which such judgments should be carried out.

2. Civil suits between private individuals which may on the date mentioned be undetermined shall be prosecuted to judgment before the court in which they may then be pending, or in the court that may be substituted therefor.

3. Criminal actions pending on the date mentioned before the Supreme Court of Spain against citizens of the territory which by this treaty ceases to be Spanish shall continue under its jurisdiction until final judgment; but, such judgment having been rendered, the execution thereof shall be committed to the competent authority of the place in which the case arose.

ART. XIII.—The rights of property secured by copyrights and patents acquired by Spaniards in the island of Cuba, and in Porto Rico, the Philippines, and other ceded territories, at the time of the exchange of the ratifications of this treaty, shall continue to be respected. Spanish scientific, literary, and artistic works not subversive of public order in the territories in question shall continue

Copyrights and patents.

to be admitted free of duty into such territories for the period of ten years, to be reckoned from the date of the exchange of the ratifications of this treaty.

Spain may establish consuls in ceded territories.

ART. XIV.—Spain shall have the power to establish consular officers in the ports and places of the territories the sovereignty over which has either been relinquished or ceded by the present treaty.

Mutual treatment of merchantmen.

ART. XV.—The Government of each country will, for the term of ten years, accord to the merchant vessels of the other country the same treatment in respect to all port charges, including entrance and clearance dues, light dues, and tonnage duties, as it accords to its own merchant vessels, not engaged in the coastwise trade.

This article may at any time be terminated on six months' notice given by either Government to the other.

Nature of obligations assumed by United States in Cuba.

ART. XVI.—It is understood that any obligations assumed in this treaty by the United States with respect to Cuba are limited to the time of its occupancy thereof; but it will upon the termination of such occupancy advise any Government established in the island to assume the same obligations.

Ratification.

ART. XVII.—The present treaty shall be ratified by the President of the United States, by and with the advice and consent of the Senate thereof, and by Her Majesty the Queen Regent of Spain; and the ratifications shall be exchanged at Washington within six months from the date hereof, or earlier if possible.[1]

In faith whereof we, the respective plenipotentiaries, have signed this treaty and have hereunto affixed our seals.

Done in duplicate at Paris, the tenth day of December, in the year of our Lord one thousand eight hundred and ninety-eight.

(*Here follow the signatures and seals.*)

[1] Ratifications were exchanged at Washington on April 12, 1899, i.e. four months after the signing.

(T) PEACE OF VEREENIGING

Signed at Pretoria, May 31, 1902

SURRENDER OF THE BOERS TO GREAT BRITAIN

GENERAL LORD KITCHENER OF KHARTOUM, Commander-in-Chief, and His Excellency Lord Milner, High Commissioner, on behalf of the British Government, and Messrs. S. W. Burger, F. W. Reitz, Louis Botha, J. H. De la Rey, L. J. Meyer, and J. C. Krogh, acting as the Government of the South African Republic, and Messrs. C. R. De Wet, W. J. C. Brebner, J. B. M. Hertzog, and C. H. Olivier, acting as the Government of the Orange Free State, on behalf of their respective burghers, desirous to terminate the present hostilities, agree on the following articles:—

Surrender.

I.—The burgher forces in the field will forthwith lay down their arms, handing over all guns, rifles, and munitions of war in their possession or under their control, and desist from any further resistance to the authority of His Majesty King Edward VII, whom they recognize as their lawful Sovereign.

The manner and details of this surrender will be arranged between Lord Kitchener and Commandant-General Botha, Assistant-Commandant-General De la Rey, and Chief-Commandant De Wet.

Prisoners of war, etc.

II.—Burghers in the field outside the limits of the Transvaal and Orange River Colony, and all prisoners of war at present outside South Africa who are burghers, will, on duly declaring their acceptance of the position of subjects of His Majesty King Edward VII, be gradually brought back to their homes as soon as transport can be provided and their means of subsistence ensured.

III.—The burghers so surrendering or so returning will not be deprived of their personal liberty or their property.

Amnesty.

IV.—No proceedings, civil or criminal, will be taken against any of the burghers so surrendering or so returning for any acts in connection with the prosecution of the war. The benefit of this clause will not extend to certain acts contrary to the usage of war which have been notified by the Commander-in-Chief to the Boer generals, and which shall be tried by court-martial immediately after the close of hostilities.

Dutch language.

V.—The Dutch language will be taught in public schools in the Transvaal and the Orange River Colony where the parents of the children desire it, and will be allowed in courts of law when necessary for the better and more effectual administration of justice.

VI.—The possession of rifles will be allowed in the Transvaal and Orange River Colony to persons requiring them for their protection, on taking out a licence according to law.

Possession of rifles.

Withdrawal of military government.

VII.—Military administration in the Transvaal and Orange River Colony will at the earliest possible date be succeeded by civil government, and, as soon as circumstances permit, representative institutions, leading up to self-government, will be introduced.

Franchise to natives.

VIII.—The question of granting the franchise to natives will not be decided until after the introduction of self-government.

No indemnity.

IX.—No special tax will be imposed on landed property in the Transvaal and Orange River Colony to defray the expenses of the war.

Restoration of people to their homes, and aid in case of war losses.

X.—As soon as conditions permit, a commission on which the local inhabitants will be represented will be appointed in each district of the Transvaal and Orange River Colony, under the presidency of a magistrate or other official, for the purpose of assisting the restoration of the people to their homes and supplying those who, owing to war losses, are unable to provide themselves with food, shelter, and the necessary amount of seed, stock, implements, etc., indispensable to the resumption of their normal occupations.

His Majesty's Government will place at the disposal of these commissioners a sum of three million pounds sterling for the above purposes, and will allow all notes, issued under Law No. 1 of 1900, of the Government of the South African Republic, and all receipts given by officers in the field of the late Republics or under their orders, to be presented to a judicial commission which will be appointed by the Government, and if such notes and receipts are found by this commission to have been duly issued in return for valuable consideration, they will be received by the first-named commissions as evidences of war losses suffered by the persons to whom they were originally given. In addition to the above-named free grant of three million pounds, His Majesty's Government will be prepared to make advances as loans for the same purpose, free of interest for two years, and afterwards repayable over a period of years with three per cent. interest. No foreigner or rebel will be entitled to the benefit of this clause.

Signed at Pretoria this thirty-first day of May, in the year of our Lord one thousand nine hundred and two.

(*Here follow signatures and seals.*)

(U) THE TREATY OF PORTSMOUTH

September 5, 1905

RUSSIA—JAPAN

HIS Majesty the Emperor of Japan on the one part, and His Majesty the Emperor of All the Russias on the other part, animated by the desire to restore the blessings of peace to their countries and peoples, have resolved to conclude a treaty of peace, and have, for this purpose, named their plenipotentiaries, that is to say:

His Majesty the Emperor of Japan: His Excellency Baron Komura Jutaro, Jusammi, Grand Cordon of the Imperial Order of the Rising Sun, his Minister for Foreign Affairs, and His Excellency M. Takahira Kogoro, Jusammi, Grand Cordon of the Imperial Order of the Sacred Treasure, his Envoy Extraordinary and Minister Plenipotentiary to the United States of America;

And His Majesty the Emperor of All the Russias: His Excellency M. Serge Witte, his Secretary of State and President of the Committee of Ministers of the Empire of Russia, and His Excellency Baron Roman Rosen, Master of the Imperial Court of Russia and his Ambassador Extraordinary and Plenipotentiary to the United States of America;

Who, after having exchanged their full powers, which were found to be in good and due form, have concluded the following articles:—

Restoration of peace.

ART. I.—There shall henceforth be peace and amity between their Majesties the Emperor of Japan and the Emperor of All the Russias and between their respective States and subjects.

Japanese interests in Korea paramount.

ART. II.—The Imperial Russian Government, acknowledging that Japan possesses in Korea paramount political, military, and economical interests, engage neither to obstruct nor interfere with the measures of guidance, protection, and control which the Imperial Government of Japan may find it necessary to take in Korea.

It is understood that Russian subjects in Korea shall be treated exactly in the same manner as the subjects or citizens of other foreign Powers—that is to say, they shall be placed on the same footing as the subjects or citizens of the most-favoured nation.

It is also agreed that, in order to avoid all causes of misunderstanding, the two High Contracting Parties will abstain, on the Russo-Korean frontier, from taking any military measures which may menace the security of Russian or Korean territory.

ART. III.—Japan and Russia mutually engage:—

1. To evacuate completely and simultaneously Manchuria, except the territory affected by the lease of the Liao-tung Peninsula, in conformity with the provisions of additional Art. I annexed to this treaty, and

Evacuation of Manchuria.

2. To restore entirely and completely to the exclusive administration of China all portions of Manchuria now in the occupation or under the control of the Japanese or Russian troops with the exception of the territory above mentioned.

The Imperial Government of Russia declare that they have not in Manchuria any territorial advantages or preferential or exclusive concessions in impairment of Chinese sovereignty or inconsistent with the principle of equal opportunity.

ART. IV.—Japan and Russia reciprocally engage not to obstruct any general measures common to all countries which China may take for the development of the commerce and industry of Manchuria.

Chinese authority in Manchuria.

ART. V.—The Imperial Russian Government transfer and assign to the Imperial Government of Japan, with the consent of the Government of China, the lease of Port Arthur, Ta-lien, and adjacent territory and territorial waters and all rights, privileges, and concessions connected with or forming part of such lease, and they also transfer and assign to the Imperial Government of Japan all public works and properties in the territory affected by the above-mentioned lease.

Lease of Port Arthur, etc., transferred to Japan.

The two High Contracting Parties mutually engage to obtain the consent of the Chinese Government mentioned in the foregoing stipulation. The Imperial Government of Japan on their part undertake that the proprietary rights of Russian subjects in the territory above referred to shall be perfectly respected.

Rights of Russian subjects in territory transferred.

ART. VI.—The Imperial Russian Government engage to transfer and assign to the Imperial Government of Japan, without compensation and with the consent of the Chinese Government, the railway between Chang-chun (Kwang-cheng-tsze) and Port Arthur and all its branches, together with all rights, privileges, and properties appertaining thereto in that region, as well as all coal-mines in the said region, belonging to or worked for the benefit of the railway.

Transfer of railway in Chinese territory.

The two High Contracting Parties mutually engage to obtain the consent of the Government of China mentioned in the foregoing stipulation.

ART. VII.—Japan and Russia engage to exploit their respective railways in Manchuria exclusively for commercial and industrial purposes, and in nowise for strategic purposes.

Manchurian railways only for commercial purposes.

It is understood that this restriction does not apply to the railway in the territory affected by the lease of the Liao-tung Peninsula.

Convention to be concluded thereon.

ART. VIII.—The Imperial Governments of Japan and Russia, with a view to promote and facilitate intercourse and traffic, will, as soon as possible, conclude a separate convention for the regulation of their connecting railway services in Manchuria.

Cession of south of Sakhalin.

ART. IX.—The Imperial Russian Government cede to the Imperial Government of Japan in perpetuity and full sovereignty the southern portion of the island of Sakhalin and all islands adjacent thereto and public works and properties thereon.

The fiftieth degree of north latitude is adopted as the northern boundary of the ceded territory. The exact alignment of such territory shall be determined in accordance with the provisions of additional Art. II annexed to this treaty.

No military works to be constructed on Sakhalin.

Japan and Russia mutually agree not to construct in their respective possessions on the island of Sakhalin or the adjacent islands any fortifications or other similar military works. They also respectively engage not to take any military measures which may impede the free navigation of the straits of La Perouse and Tartary.

Right of option.

ART. X.—It is reserved to the Russian subjects, inhabitants of the territory ceded to Japan, to sell their real property and retire to their country; but if they prefer to remain in the ceded territory, they will be maintained and protected in the full exercise of their industries and rights of property on condition of submitting to Japanese laws and jurisdiction. Japan shall have full liberty to withdraw the right of residence or to deport from such territory any inhabitants who labour under political or administrative disability. She engages, however, that the proprietary rights of such inhabitants shall be fully respected.

Rights of fishery.

ART. XI.—Russia engages to arrange with Japan for granting to Japanese subjects rights of fishery along the coasts of the Russian possessions in the Japan, Okhotsk, and Behring Seas.

It is agreed that the foregoing engagement shall not affect rights already belonging to Russian or foreign subjects in those regions.

New commercial treaty to be concluded.

ART. XII.—The treaty of commerce and navigation between Japan and Russia having been annulled by the war, the Imperial Governments of Japan and Russia engage to adopt as the basis of their commercial relations, pending the conclusion of a new treaty of commerce and navigation on the basis of the treaty which was in force before the present war, the system of reciprocal treatment on the footing of the most-favoured nation, in which are included import and export duties, customs formalities, transit and tonnage dues, and the admission and treatment of the agents, subjects, and vessels of one country in the territories of the other.

Prisoners of war.

ART. XIII.—As soon as possible after the present treaty comes into force all prisoners of war shall be reciprocally restored. The Imperial Governments of Japan and Russia shall each appoint a special commissioner to take charge of prisoners.

All prisoners in the hands of one Government shall be delivered to and received by the commissioner of the other Government or by his duly authorized representative in such convenient numbers and at such convenient ports of the delivering State as such delivering State shall notify in advance to the commissioner of the receiving State.

The Governments of Japan and Russia shall present to each other, as soon as possible after the delivery of prisoners has been completed, a statement of the direct expenditures incurred by them for the care and maintenance of prisoners from the date of capture or surrender up to the time of death or delivery. Russia engages to repay to Japan, as soon as possible after the exchange of the statements as above provided, the difference between the actual amount so expended by Japan and the actual amount similarly disbursed by Russia.

ART. XIV.—The present treaty shall be ratified by their Majesties the Emperor of Japan and the Emperor of All the Russias. Such ratification shall with as little delay as possible, and in any case not later than fifty days from the date of the signature of the treaty, be announced to the Imperial Governments of Japan and Russia respectively through the French Minister in Tokio and the Ambassador of the United States in St. Petersburg, and from the date of the latter of such announcements this treaty shall in all its parts come into full force.

Ratification.

The formal exchange of ratifications shall take place in Washington as soon as possible.[1]

ART. XV.—The present treaty shall be signed in duplicate in both the English and French languages. The texts are in absolute conformity, but in case of discrepancy in interpretation, the French text shall prevail.

Language and interpretation.

In witness whereof the respective plenipotentiaries have signed and affixed their seals to the present treaty of peace.

Done at Portsmouth (New Hampshire) this fifth day of the ninth month of the thirty-eighth year of Meiji, corresponding to the twenty-third day of August (fifth September), one thousand nine hundred and five.

(*Signed*) SERGE WITTE [L.S.]
(*Signed*) ROSEN [L.S.]
(*Signed*) JUTARO KOMURA [L.S.]
(*Signed*) K. TAKAHIRA [L.S.]

SUPPLEMENTARY AGREEMENT

In conformity with the provisions of Arts. III and IX of the treaty of peace between Japan and Russia of this date, the undersigned plenipotentiaries have concluded the following additional articles:—

I.—*To Article III*

The Imperial Governments of Japan and Russia mutually engage to commence the withdrawal of their military forces from the territory of

[1] The ratifications were exchanged at Washington on September 25.

Manchuria simultaneously and immediately after the treaty of peace comes into operation, and within a period of eighteen months from that date the armies of the two countries shall be completely withdrawn from Manchuria, except from the leased territory of the Liao-tung Peninsula.

Evacuation of Manchuria.

The forces of the two countries occupying the front positions shall be first withdrawn.

The High Contracting Parties reserve to themselves the right to maintain guards to protect their respective railway lines in Manchuria. The number of such guards shall not exceed fifteen per kilometre, and within that maximum number the commanders of the Japanese and Russian armies shall, by common accord, fix the number of such guards to be employed, as small as possible, having in view the actual requirements.

The commanders of the Japanese and Russian forces in Manchuria shall agree upon the details of the evacuation in conformity with the above principles, and shall take by common accord the measures necessary to carry out the evacuation as soon as possible, and in any case not later than the period of eighteen months.

II.—*To Article IX*

Delimitation commission.

As soon as possible after the present treaty comes into force a commission of delimitation, composed of an equal number of members to be appointed respectively by the two High Contracting Parties, shall on the spot mark in a permanent manner the exact boundary between the Japanese and Russian possessions on the island of Sakhalin. The commission shall be bound, so far as topographical considerations permit, to follow the fiftieth parallel of north latitude as the boundary line, and in case any deflections from that line at any points are found to be necessary, compensation will be made by correlative deflections at other points. It shall also be the duty of the said commission to prepare a list and description of the adjacent islands included in the cession; and, finally, the commission shall prepare and sign maps showing the boundaries of the ceded territory. The work of the commission shall be subject to the approval of the High Contracting Parties.

The foregoing additional articles are to be considered as ratified with the ratification of the treaty of peace to which they are annexed.

(*Signed and sealed as before.*)

(V) TREATY OF LAUSANNE

October 18, 1912

ITALY—TURKEY

HIS Majesty the King of Italy and His Majesty the Emperor of the Ottomans, equally animated by the desire to bring to an end the state of war existing between the two countries, have appointed as their plenipotentiaries:

His Majesty the King of Italy:

MM. Pietro Bertolini, Grand Cross of the Order of the Crown of Italy, Grand Officer of the Order of Saints Maurice and Lazarus, Member of Parliament;

Guido Fusinato, Grand Cross of the Order of the Crown of Italy, Grand Officer of the Order of Saints Maurice and Lazarus, Member of Parliament, Counsellor of State;

Giuseppe Volpi, Commander of the Order of Saints Maurice and Lazarus and of the Crown of Italy.

His Majesty the Emperor of the Ottomans:

His Excellency Mehemmed Naby Bey, Grand Cordon of the Imperial Order of Osmanié, Envoy Extraordinary and Minister Plenipotentiary of His Majesty the Emperor of the Ottomans;

His Excellency Roumbeyoglou Fahreddin Bey, Grand Officer of the Order of Medjidié, Commander of the Order of Osmanie, Envoy Extraordinary and Minister Plenipotentiary;

Who, after having exchanged their respective full powers, which were found in good and due form, have agreed upon the following articles:—

Cessation of hostilities.

ART. I.—Immediately after the signing of the present treaty the two Governments pledge themselves to take the necessary measures to bring about the immediate and simultaneous cessation of hostilities. Special commissioners shall be sent to the places to assure the execution of the said measures.

Evacuation of troops.

ART. II.—Immediately after the signing of the present treaty the two Governments pledge themselves to issue orders for the recall of their respective officers and troops, as well as their civil functionaries, that is to say, the Ottoman Government will recall these officers, troops, and civil functionaries from the Tripolitana and Cyrenaica, and the Italian Government from the islands occupied by Italy in the Ægean Sea.

The actual departure of the Italian officers, troops, and civil functionaries from the said islands shall take place immediately after the Ottoman officers, troops, and civil functionaries shall have departed from the Tripolitana and Cyrenaica.

ART. III.—The prisoners of war and the hostages shall be exchanged with the least possible delay.

Prisoners of war.

Amnesty.

ART. IV.—The two Governments pledge themselves to grant full and complete amnesty, the Royal Government to the inhabitants of the Tripolitana and Cyrenaica, and the Imperial Government to the inhabitants of the islands in the Ægean Sea subject to Ottoman suzerainty who took part in the hostilities or those who have compromised themselves as a result thereof, excepting offences against the common law. In consequence, no person, to whatever class or condition he may belong, shall be prosecuted or molested in his person or property, or in the exercise of his rights, by reason of his political or military acts or of opinions expressed during the hostilities. All persons detained or deported on such grounds shall be immediately set at liberty.

Revival of treaties.

ART. V.—All the treaties, conventions, and engagements of every sort, kind, and nature concluded and in force between the two High Contracting Parties prior to the declaration of war shall immediately be put into force again, and the two Governments, as also their respective subjects, shall be placed towards one another in the same position in which they were before the outbreak of hostilities.

Agreement to conclude a new treaty of commerce.

ART. VI.—Italy pledges herself to conclude with Turkey at the same time as the latter shall renew her treaties of commerce with the other Powers a treaty of commerce on the basis of European public law, that is to say, she consents to leave to Turkey all the latter's economic independence and the right, in commercial and customs matters, to act like all other European Powers, and without being bound by the capitulations and other acts entered into up to this day. It is well understood that the said treaty of commerce shall not come into force until the treaties of commerce concluded by the Sublime Porte with the other Powers on the same basis shall have been put into force.

In addition, Italy consents to an increase from 11 per cent. to 15 per cent. of the *ad valorem* customs duties in Turkey, as well as to the creation of new monopolies or the levying of additional taxes of consumption upon the five following articles: petrol, cigarette paper, matches, alcohol, playing cards, provided that the same treatment is applied simultaneously and without distinction to the importations from other countries.

In so far as the importation of articles forming the object of a monopoly is concerned the administration of these monopolies is obliged to secure articles of Italian origin according to the percentage established on the basis of the annual importation of these same articles, provided that the prices offered for the delivery of the articles of monopoly conform to the state of the market at the time of the purchase, taking into consideration the quality of the goods and the average prices which have been current during the three years preceding that of the declaration of war.

It is, moreover, agreed that if Turkey, instead of establishing new monopolies upon the above-mentioned five articles, should decide to levy extra taxes of consumption on them, these extra taxes shall be imposed in the same measure upon similar products of Turkey and of all other nations.

Abolition of post offices in Turkey.

Art. VII.—The Italian Government pledges itself to suppress the Italian post offices employed in the Ottoman Empire at the same time as the other States having post offices in Turkey shall suppress theirs.

Abolition of the capitulations.

Art. VIII.—As the Sublime Porte proposes to open, in a conference or otherwise, with the Great Powers interested, negotiations for the purpose of doing away with the capitular system in Turkey and to replace it by the system of international law, Italy, recognizing the good grounds of these intentions of the Sublime Porte, declares her willingness henceforth to render to the Porte to that end her full and sincere support.

Former employés in public service.

Art. IX.—The Ottoman Government, wishing to show its satisfaction for the good and loyal service which it received from the Italian subjects employed in the administrations and whom it was compelled to dismiss at the time of the hostilities, declares itself ready to reinstate them in the positions which they had left.

Compensation shall be paid to them for the months during which they were not employed, and this interruption of service shall be without prejudice to those of the employés entitled to a retiring pension.

Further, the Ottoman Government pledges itself to use its good offices with the institutions with which it is connected (public debt, railway companies, banks, etc.) in order to secure similar treatment for the Italian subjects who were in their service and are in an analogous position.

The Ottoman public debt.

Art. X.—The Italian Government pledges itself to pay annually to the treasury of the Ottoman public debt to the account of the Imperial Government a sum corresponding to the average of the sums which in each of the three years preceding the declaration of war have been assigned for the use of the public debt from the revenues of the two provinces.

The amount of the said annuity shall be determined by agreement by two commissioners appointed, one by the Royal Government, the other by the Imperial Government. In case of disagreement, the decision shall be submitted to an arbitral commission composed of the said commissioners and an umpire appointed by mutual agreement between the two parties. If agreement cannot be reached in this way, each party shall nominate a different Power, and the selection of the umpire shall be made jointly by the Powers thus nominated.

The Royal Government, as well as the Administration of the Ottoman public debt, through the medium of the Imperial Government, shall have the right to request that the aforementioned annuity be replaced by a single payment of a corresponding sum, capitalized at the rate of 4 per cent.

In reference to the preceding paragraph, the Royal Government now acknowledges that the annuity cannot be less than two million Italian lire and that it is ready to pay to the Administration of the Ottoman public debt the corresponding capitalized sum as soon as the demand for it is presented.

Date of operation.

ART. XI.—The present treaty shall come into force on the day of its signature.

In faith of which the plenipotentiaries have signed the present treaty and affixed their seals thereto.

Lausanne, October 18, 1912.

(*Here follow signatures and seals.*)

(W) TREATY OF LONDON

May 17/30, 1913

TURKEY—GREECE, BULGARIA, SERBIA, MONTENEGRO

ART. I.—Upon the exchange of ratifications of the present treaty there shall be peace and friendship between His Majesty the Emperor of the Ottomans, on the one part, and their Majesties, the Allied Sovereigns, on the other part, as well as between their heirs and successors, their respective States and subjects in perpetuity.

Restoration of peace.

ART. II.—His Majesty the Emperor of the Ottomans cedes to their Majesties the Allied Sovereigns all the territories of his Empire on the continent of Europe to the west of a line drawn from Enos on the Ægean Sea to Midia on the Black Sea, with the exception of Albania.

Cession of territory.

The exact line of the frontier from Enos to Midia shall be determined by an international commission.

ART. III.—His Majesty the Emperor of the Ottomans and their Majesties the Allied Sovereigns declare that they remit to His Majesty the Emperor of Germany; His Majesty the Emperor of Austria, King of Hungary; the President of the French Republic; His Majesty the King of Great Britain and Ireland, Emperor of India; His Majesty the King of Italy; and His Majesty the Emperor of All the Russias the matter of arranging the delimitation of the frontiers of Albania and all other questions concerning Albania.

The Powers and settlement of Albania.

ART. IV.—His Majesty the Emperor of the Ottomans declares that he cedes to their Majesties the Allied Sovereigns the island of Crete and that he renounces in their favour all rights of sovereignty and all other rights which he possessed in that island.

Cession of Crete.

ART. V.—His Majesty the Emperor of the Ottomans and their Majesties the Allied Sovereigns declare that they entrust to His Majesty the Emperor of Germany; His Majesty the Emperor of Austria, King of Hungary; the President of the French Republic; His Majesty the King of Great Britain and Ireland, Emperor of India; His Majesty the King of Italy; His Majesty the Emperor of All the Russias the task of determining the title to all the Ottoman islands in the Ægean Sea (except the Island of Crete) and to the peninsula of Mount Athos.

The Powers and the Ægean Isles, etc.

Art. VI.—His Majesty the Emperor of the Ottomans and their Majesties the Allied Sovereigns declare that they refer the matter of settling questions of a financial nature resulting from the war which is ended and from the above-mentioned cessions of territory to the International Commission convened at Paris, to which they have deputed their representatives.

Special conventions.

Art. VII.—Questions concerning prisoners of war, questions of jurisdiction, of nationality, and of commerce shall be settled by special conventions.

(X) TREATY OF BUCHAREST

July 28 / August 10, 1913

BULGARIA—ROUMANIA, GREECE, MONTENEGRO, SERBIA

THEIR Majesties the King of Roumania, the King of the Hellenes, the King of Montenegro, and the King of Serbia, on the one part, and His Majesty the King of the Bulgarians, on the other part, animated by the desire to put an end to the state of war at present existing between their respective countries and wishing, for the sake of order, to establish peace between their long-suffering peoples, have resolved to conclude a definitive treaty of peace. Their said Majesties have, therefore, appointed as their plenipotentiaries, namely:

His Majesty the King of Roumania: His Excellency Titus Maïoresco, President of his Council of Ministers, Minister of Foreign Affairs; His Excellency Alexander Marghiloman, his Minister of Finance; His Excellency Take Jonesco, his Minister of the Interior; His Excellency Constantin G. Dissesco, his Minister of Public Worship and Public Instruction; Major-General C. Coanda, Aide-de-camp, Inspector-General of Artillery; Colonel C. Christesco, Assistant Chief of the General Staff of his Army;

His Majesty the King of the Hellenes: His Excellency Eleftérios Venizelos, President of his Council of Ministers, Minister of War; His Excellency Demetre Panas, Minister Plenipotentiary; M. Nicolas Politis, Professor of International Law in the University of Paris; Captain Ath. Exadactylos; Captain C. Pali;

His Majesty the King of Montenegro: His Excellency General Serdar Yanko Voukotitch, President of his Council of Ministers, Minister of War; M. Jean Matanovitch, formerly Chargé d'Affaires of Montenegro at Constantinople;

His Majesty the King of Serbia: His Excellency Nicolas P. Pasitch, President of his Council of Ministers, Minister of Foreign Affairs; His Excellency Milhaïlo G. Ristitch, his Envoy Extraordinary and Minister Plenipotentiary at Bucharest; His Excellency Dr. Miroslaw Spalaïkovitch, Envoy Extraordinary and Minister Plenipotentiary; Colonel K. Smilianitch; Lieutenant-Colonel D. Kalafatovitch;

His Majesty the King of the Bulgarians: His Excellency Dimitri Tontcheff, his Minister of Finance; Major-General Ivan Fitcheff, Chief of Staff of his Army; M. Sawa Ivantchoff, Doctor of Laws, formerly Vice-President of the Sobranje; M. Simeon Radeff; Lieutenant-Colonel Constantin Stancioff of the General Staff;

Who, in accordance with the proposal of the Royal Government of Roumania, have assembled in conference at Bucharest, with full powers, which were found to be in good and due form, and who having happily reached an accord, have agreed upon the following stipulations :—

Date of peace.

ART. I.—From the day on which the ratifications of the present treaty are exchanged there shall be peace and amity between His Majesty the King of Roumania, His Majesty the King of the Bulgarians, His Majesty the King of the Hellenes, His Majesty the King of Montenegro, and His Majesty the King of Serbia, as well as between their heirs and successors, their respective States and subjects.

New frontier between Bulgaria and Roumania—Delimitation by a mixed commission.

ART. II.—The former frontier between the Kingdom of Bulgaria and the Kingdom of Roumania, from the Danube to the Black Sea, is, in conformity with the *procès-verbal* drawn up by the respective military delegates and annexed to Protocol No. 5 of July 22 (August 4), 1913, of the Conference of Bucharest, rectified in the following manner :—

The new frontier shall begin at the Danube above Turtukaia and terminate at the Black Sea to the south of Ekrene.

Between these two extreme points the frontier line shall follow the line indicated on the 1/100,000 and 1/200,000 maps of the Roumanian General Staff, and according to the description annexed to the present article.

It is formally understood that within a maximum delay of two years Bulgaria shall dismantle the existing fortifications and shall not construct others at Rustchuk, at Shumla, in the intervening country, and in a zone of twenty kilometres around Baltchik.

A mixed commission, composed of an equal number of representatives of each of the two High Contracting Parties, shall be charged, within fifteen days from the signing of the present treaty, with delimiting the new frontier in conformity with the preceding stipulations. This commission shall supervise the division of the lands and funds which up to the present time may have belonged in common to districts, communes, or communities separated by the new frontier. In case of disagreement as to the line or as to the method of marking it, the two High Contracting Parties agree to request a friendly Government to appoint an arbitrator, whose decision upon the points at issue shall be considered final.

New frontier between Bulgaria and Serbia.

ART. III.—The frontier between the Kingdom of Bulgaria and the Kingdom of Serbia shall follow, conformably to the *procès-verbal* drawn up by the respective military delegates, which is annexed to Protocol No. 9 of July 25 (August 7), 1913, of the Conference of Bucharest, the following line :—

The frontier line shall begin at the old frontier, from the summit of Patarica, follow the old Túrco-Bulgarian frontier and the dividing line of the waters between the Vardar and the Struma, with the exception of the upper valley of the Strumitza, which shall remain Serbian territory; the line shall terminate at the Belasica Mountain, where it will bend back to the Greco-Bulgarian frontier. A detailed description of this frontier and the 1/200,000 map of the Austrian General Staff, on which it is indicated, are annexed to the present article.

A mixed commission, composed of an equal number of representatives of each of the two High Contracting Powers, shall be charged, within fifteen days from the signing of the present treaty, with delimiting the new frontier, in conformity with the preceding stipulations.

This commission shall supervise the division of the lands and funds, which up to the present time may have belonged in common to the districts, communes, or communities separated by the new frontier. In case of disagreement as to the line or as to the method of marking it, the two High Contracting Parties agree to request a friendly Government to appoint an arbitrator, whose decision upon the points at issue shall be considered final.

ART. IV.—Questions relating to the old Serbo-Bulgarian frontier shall be settled according to the understanding reached by the two High Contracting Parties, as stated in the protocol annexed to the present article.

New frontier between Greece and Bulgaria.

ART. V.—The frontier between the Kingdom of Greece and the Kingdom of Bulgaria shall follow, conformably to the *procès-verbal* drawn up by the respective military delegates and annexed to Protocol No. 9 of July 25 (August 7), 1913, of the Conference of Bucharest, the following line:—

The frontier line shall start from the new Serbo-Bulgarian frontier on the summit of Belasica Planina and terminate at the mouth of the Mesta on the Ægean Sea.

Between these two extreme points the frontier line shall follow the line indicated on the 1/200,000 map of the Austrian General Staff, in accordance with the description annexed to the present article.

A mixed commission, composed of an equal number of representatives of each of the two High Contracting Parties, shall be charged, within fifteen days from the signing of the present treaty, with delimiting the frontier in conformity with the preceding stipulations

This commission shall supervise the division of the lands and funds, which up to the present time may have belonged in common to the districts, communes, or communities separated by the new frontier. In case of disagreement as to the line or as to the method of marking it, the two High Contracting Parties engage to request a friendly Government to appoint an arbitrator, whose decision upon the points at issue shall be considered final.

It is formally understood that Bulgaria renounces from henceforth all claim to the island of Crete.

Demobilization.

ART. VI.—The headquarters of the respective armies shall be immediately informed of the signing of the present treaty. The Bulgarian Government engages to begin to reduce its army to a peace footing on the day after such notification. It shall order its troops to their garrisons, whence, with the least possible delay, the various reserves shall be returned to their homes.

If the garrison of any troops is situated in the zone occupied by the army of one of the High Contracting Parties, such troops shall be ordered to some other point in the old Bulgarian territory and may not return to their regular garrisons until after the evacuation of the above-mentioned occupied zone.

Art. VII.—The evacuation of Bulgarian territory, both old and new, shall begin immediately after the demobilization of the Bulgarian army and shall be completed within a period of not more than fifteen days.

Evacuation.

During this period the zone of demarcation for the Roumanian army of operations shall be determined by a line running as follows: Sistov–Lovcea–Turski-Isvor-Glozene-Zlatitza–Mirkovo-Araba-Konak–Orchania–Mezdra–Vratza–Berkovitza–Lom–Danube.

Art. VIII.—During the occupation of the Bulgarian territories the various armies shall retain the right of requisition in consideration of cash payment.

Occupation and right of requisition.

Such armies shall have free use of the railways for the transportation of troops and of provisions of all kinds, without compensation to the local authority.

The sick and wounded shall be under the protection of the said armies.

Art. IX.—As soon as possible after the exchange of ratifications of the present treaty all prisoners of war shall be mutually restored.

Restoration of prisoners.

The Governments of the High Contracting Parties shall each appoint special commissioners to receive the prisoners.

All prisoners in the hands of any of the Governments shall be delivered to the commissioner of the Government to which they belong, or to his duly authorized representative, at the place which shall be determined upon by the interested parties.

The Governments of the High Contracting Parties shall present to each other, respectively, as soon as possible after all the prisoners have been returned, a statement of the direct expenses incurred through the care and maintenance of the prisoners from the date of their capture or surrender to the date of their death or return. The sums due by Bulgaria to each one of the other High Contracting Parties shall be set off against the sums due by each of the other High Contracting Parties to Bulgaria, and the difference shall be paid to the creditor Government in each case as soon as possible after the exchange of the above-mentioned statements of expense.

Art. X.—The present treaty shall be ratified, and the ratifications thereof shall be exchanged at Bucharest within fifteen days, or sooner if it be possible.[1]

Exchange of ratifications.

In witness whereof the respective plenipotentiaries have hereunto affixed their names and seals.

Done at Bucharest the twenty-eighth day of the month of July (tenth day of the month of August) in the year one thousand nine hundred and thirteen.

(Here follow signatures and seals.)

[1] The ratifications were exchanged August 30, 1913.

(Y) TREATY OF CONSTANTINOPLE

September 16 / 29, 1913

TURKEY—BULGARIA

HIS Majesty the Emperor of the Ottomans and His Majesty the King of the Bulgars, animated by the desire to regulate in a friendly manner and upon a desirable basis the state of affairs caused by the events which have occurred since the conclusion of the Treaty of London, and to re-establish the relations of friendship and neighbourliness so necessary for the well-being of their peoples, have determined to conclude the present treaty, and have chosen respectively for this purpose, as their plenipotentiaries:—

His Majesty the Emperor of the Ottomans:

His Excellency Talaat Bey, Minister of the Interior; His Excellency General Mahmoud Pasha, Minister of Marine; His Excellency Halil Bey, President of the Council of State.

His Majesty the King of the Bulgars:

His Excellency General Savoff, former Minister; His Excellency M. Natchévitch, former Minister; His Excellency M. Tocheff, Minister Plenipotentiary; who, after exchanging their full powers, found to be in good and due form, have agreed as follows:

The new frontier.

ART. I.—The frontier between the two countries commences at the mouth of the river Rezvaja, south of the monastery of San Ivan, situated on the Black Sea; it follows the course of this river as far as the confluence of the rivers Pirogu and Déliva, to the west of Kamila-Köj. Between the mouth and the point of confluence above mentioned the river Rezvaja, starting from its mouth, follows first a south-westerly direction and, leaving Placa to Turkey, forms a bend and goes towards the north-west and then towards the south-west; the villages of Madzura and Pirgoplo remain in Ottoman territory. The river Rezvaja, after having followed a southerly direction beginning at Pirgoplo and for a distance of approximately five and a half kilometres, turns towards the west and the north and then goes along, slightly curved towards the north, in a generally western direction. In this portion, the villages of Likudi and Kladara remain in Bulgarian territory, and the villages of Ciknigari, Mavrodio, and Lafva return to Turkey; then the frontier, always following the Rezvaja river, leaves Torfu-Ciflik to Bulgaria, goes towards the south-east, and, leaving the village of Kamila-Köj in Ottoman territory, arrives at a point about 400 metres to the west of this village, at the point of confluence of the rivers Pirogu and Déliva.

Starting from the junction point of the rivers Pirogu and Déliva, the frontier line follows the course of the Déliva, and extending along this river in a general north-westerly direction, leaves the villages of Paspala, Kandildzik and Déli to Turkey and ends east of Souk-Sou; the latter village remains to Turkey, while Sévéligu goes to Bulgaria. After having passed between Souk-Sou and Sévéligu, the frontier line continues in a north-westerly direction, following the ridge which passes over hills 687, 619, and 563; beyond hill 563 it leaves the village of Caglaïk (Cajirlik) in Ottoman territory, and passing around this last village three kilometres to its east and north, it reaches the Goléma stream. The frontier follows the course of the Goléma for a distance of about two kilometres and reaches the junction point of this stream and the other branch of the same river, which comes from the south from Karabanlar (Karabaàlar); from this confluence the frontier line passes along the ridge to the north of the stream coming from Türk-Alatli and arrives at the old Turco-Bulgarian frontier.

The junction point of the new line and the old frontier is four kilometres east of Türk-Alatli, at the point where the ancient Turco-Bulgarian frontier forms an angle towards the north in the direction of Aykiri-Yol.

Starting at this point it exactly follows the former Turko-Bulgarian frontier as far as Balaban-Basi, west of the Toundja and north of the village of Derviska-Mog.

The new frontier line leaves the old frontier in the vicinity of Balaban-Basi and drops in a straight line towards Dermen-Déré. The point at which the new frontier leaves the former frontier is two kilometres away from the church of the village of Derviska-Mog; the frontier, leaving Derviska-Mog in Ottoman territory, follows the course of the Dermen-Déré as far as the village of Bulgar-Lefké and leaves this village in Bulgarian territory. Starting from the eastern and southern outskirts of Bulgar-Lefke the frontier line leaves the course of the Dermen-Déré and proceeds towards the west, leaves the villages Turks-Lefké and Dimitro-Kemy in Ottoman territory, and, following the watershed between Buk-Déré and Démirhan-Déré (hill 241) reaches the most northern point formed by the bend of the Marica, towards the north, east of Mustafa-Pacha. This part of the bend is three and a half kilometres away from the eastern end of the Mustafa-Pacha bridge. The frontier follows the western side of the bend of the Marica as far as the mill, and from there arrives in a straight line at Cermen-Déré, north of the railway bridge (Cermen-Déré is the stream which flows into the Maritza three kilometres east of the village Cermen), and then, passing around Cermen on the north, goes to Tazi-Tépézi. The frontier leaves Cermen to Turkey and, following the course of Cermen-Déré, crosses the railway line north-west of Cermen; it still follows the same stream and rises to Tazi-Tépési (hill 613). (The point where Cermen-Déré crosses the railway line, north-west of Cermen, is five kilometres away from the centre of the village Cermen and three thousand two hundred metres from the western end of the Mustafa-Pacha bridge.)

The frontier leaves the highest point of Tazi-Tépézi in Ottoman territory, and starting from this point follows the line of the separation of the waters of the Arda and of the Maritza, passing near the villages Yayladjik and Gjuldjuk (Goldzik), which remain in Ottoman territory.

Starting from Goldzik the frontier passes over hill 449 and then to hill 367, and, from this hill, goes southward in almost a straight line towards the Arda. This straight line passes one kilometre west of Kektachli, which remains in Ottoman territory.

The frontier line, after reaching the Arda from hill 367, follows the right bank of the Arda and comes to the mill which is one kilometre south of the village of Tchingirli; from this mill it follows the line of the watershed east of Gadjohor-Déré; it passes one kilometre east of the village Gadjohor and, leaving the village of Drébisna to Bulgaria and passing about one kilometre east of this village, descends to Atéren-Déré a kilometre south of this village; thence it goes in a south-westerly direction, by the shortest route, to the source of the stream which flows between the villages Akalan and Kajliklikeny and follows the thalweg of this waterway down to the river Kizil-Déli.

Starting from this stream the frontier, leaving Gotch-Bounar in Bulgaria, follows the course of the Kizil-Déli-Déré, and thence, following the thalweg of the stream which branches off towards the south at a point situated four kilometres south of Llandarion and three kilometres east of Soganlikli-Bala, goes to the source of this stream; it then goes by the shortest route to the source of the Mandara-Déré; it follows the thalweg of the Mandara-Déré, starting from its source, to join the Marica to the west of Mandara. In this portion the village of Krantsu remains in Bulgarian territory and the villages Bas-Kisa, Kirdjanbunar, and Mandara come to Turkey. Starting at this point the frontier follows the thalweg of the Maritza as far as the point where the river divides into two branches, three and a half kilometres south of the village of Kaldirkos; thence it follows the thalweg of the right branch, which passes not far from Férédjik, until it reaches the Aegean Sea. In this portion the marshes of Ak-Sou, as well as the lakes Quéneli-Gheul and Kazikli-Gheul, remain to Turkey, and the lakes Touzla-Gheul and Drana-Gheul go to Bulgaria.

Evacuation and delivery of ceded territories.

Demobilization.

ART. II.—Ten days after the signature of the present treaty by the above-mentioned plenipotentiaries, the armies of the two Contracting Parties at present occupying territories which are to pass into the possession of the other party shall make haste to evacuate them, and, within the fifteen succeeding days, to hand them over, conformably to rules and usages, to the authorities of the other party.

It is furthermore understood that the two States shall demobilize their armies within three weeks from the date of the present treaty.

Resumption of peaceful relations.

ART. III.—Diplomatic relations, as well as postal, telegraphic, and railway communications between the High Contracting Parties shall be resumed immediately after the signature of the present treaty.

The arrangement in regard to muftis, forming Annex No. II of the present treaty, shall be applicable in all the territories of Bulgaria.

Revival of certain conventions.

ART. IV.—With a view to encourage economic relations between the two countries, the High Contracting Parties bind themselves to put into force again, immediately after the signature of the present treaty for a period of one year from that date, the convention of commerce and navigation concluded the 6 / 19 February, 1911, and to grant to their industrial, agricultural, and other products all the customs facilities compatible with their existing engagements towards third Powers.

The Consular Declaration of the 18th November / 2nd December, 1909, shall likewise be put into force again for the same period.

However, each of the High Contracting Parties shall be able to create consulates-general, consulates, and vice-consulates "de carrière" in all localities within their territories where agents of third Powers are admitted.

Agreement to conclude new conventions.

The High Contracting Parties further bind themselves to proceed, within the shortest time possible, to the nomination of a mixed commission to negotiate a treaty of commerce and a consular convention.

Prisoners of war and hostages.

ART. V.—Prisoners of war and hostages shall be exchanged within one month from the signature of the present treaty or sooner if possible. This exchange shall take place by means of special commissioners appointed by both parties.

The expenses for the keeping of the said prisoners of war and hostages shall be at the charge of the Government in whose hands they are.

However, the pay of officers furnished by that Government shall be reimbursed by the State to which they belong.

Amnesty.

ART. VI.—A full and absolute amnesty is granted by the High Contracting Parties to all persons who have taken part in hostilities and who have compromised themselves in political events previous to the present treaty. The inhabitants of ceded territories shall enjoy the same amnesty for political events which have occurred there.

The benefits of this amnesty shall cease at the expiration of the two weeks' delay fixed by the authorities legally constituted at the time of the reoccupation of the territories which are to pass into the hands of Bulgaria and duly brought to the knowledge of the populations.

Ceded territories and nationality—time allowed for option.

ART. VII.—Natives of the territories ceded by the Ottoman Empire to the Royal Government of Bulgaria and who are domiciled there shall become Bulgarian subjects.

Those natives who have become Bulgarian subjects shall have the right for the period of four years to declare, where they are, in favour of Ottoman nationality by a simple declaration to the local Bulgarian authorities and registration at the Imperial Ottoman Consulates. This declaration, when made abroad, shall be delivered to the chancelleries of the Bulgarian consulates and registered by the Ottoman consulates. The option shall pertain to the individual and is not obligatory for the Imperial Ottoman Government.

Those who are now minors shall exercise the option within the four years following their majority.

Moslems in the ceded territories who have become Bulgarian subjects shall not be subjected to military service within this period, nor shall they pay any military tax.

After having exercised their right of option, these Moslems shall leave the ceded territories, and, until the expiration of the period of four years provided for above, shall have the right to transport their personal property without payment of export duties. They may, at the same time, keep their urban and rural property of all categories, and have it administered by third parties.

Moslem Bulgarian subjects—civil and political rights.

ART. VIII.—Moslem Bulgarian subjects of all the territories of Bulgaria shall enioy the same civil and political rights as subjects of Bulgarian origin.

They shall enjoy liberty of conscience, and liberty and outward practice of religion. The customs of Moslems shall be respected.

The name of His Imperial Majesty the Sultan, as Caliph, shall continue to be pronounced in the public prayers of Moslems.

Moslem communities already constituted or which shall be constituted in the future, their hierarchical organization, and their endowments shall be recognized and respected; their spiritual heads shall exercise authority over them without hindrance.

Bulgarian communities in Turkey.

ART. IX.—Bulgarian communities in Turkey shall enjoy the same rights as the other Christian communities of the Ottoman Empire now enjoy.

Bulgarians who are Ottoman subjects shall keep their personal property and shall not be disturbed at all in the exercise and enjoyment of their personal and property rights. Those who left their homes at the time of the recent events may return within two years at the latest.

Acquired rights in ceded territory.

ART. X.—Rights acquired previous to the annexation of the territories, as well as judicial documents and official title-deeds, emanating from the competent Ottoman authorities, shall be respected and held inviolable until there is legal proof to the contrary.

Right of holding landed property in ceded territory.

ART. XI.—The right of holding landed property in the ceded territories by virtue of the Ottoman law on urban and rural properties shall be recognized without any restriction.

The proprietors of real or personal property in the said territories shall continue to enjoy their property rights, even if they fix their personal residence temporarily or permanently outside of Bulgaria. They shall be able to let their property or administer it through third parties.

Vakoufs.

ART. XII.—The Mustesna, Mulhaka, Idjarétein, Moukata, and Idjaréi-Vahidé vakoufs, as well as the tithes which are vakouf, in the ceded territories, as they are at present recognized by the Ottoman laws, shall be respected.

They shall be managed by the proper persons.

Their systems may be modified only by just and previous indemnification.

The rights of religious and charitable establishments in the Ottoman Empire over vakouf revenues in the ceded territories, as Idjaréi-Vahidé, or Moukata, or various rights, or as the counter-value of vakouf or other tithes, and over vakoufs whether built up or not, shall be respected.

Private property of the Sultan and of the State.

ART. XIII.—The private properties of His Imperial Majesty, the Sultan, as well as those of members of the Imperial Dynasty, shall be maintained and respected. His Majesty and members of the Imperial Dynasty shall be able to sell them or let them through attorneys.

The same shall apply to private property belonging to the State. In the case of sale of property, preference shall be given, under equal conditions, to Bulgarian subjects.

Tombs of the fallen.

ART. XIV.—The High Contracting Parties bind themselves to give orders to their provincial authorities to have cemeteries and particularly the graves of soldiers fallen on the field of honour respected.

The authorities shall not prevent relatives and friends from removing the bones of victims buried in foreign soil.

Residence of subjects.

ART. XV.—The subjects of each of the Contracting States shall be able to sojourn and circulate freely as in the past in the territory of the other Contracting State.

Railway concessions in ceded territory.

ART. XVI.—The Royal Government of Bulgaria assumes the rights, duties ("charges"), and obligations of the Imperial Ottoman Government in respect to the Oriental Railways Company, for the part of the line conceded to it and situated in ceded territory.

The Royal Government of Bulgaria binds itself to restore without delay the rolling stock and the other objects belonging to the said company and seized by it.

Arbitration in disputes as to interpretation.

ART. XVII.—All differences and disputes which may arise in the interpretation or application of Articles XI, XII, XIII, and XVI, as well as Annex I, of the present treaty, shall be settled by arbitration at The Hague, in conformity with the agreement forming Annex III of the present treaty.

Annexed protocols as parts of the treaty.

ART. XVIII.—The protocol relating to the frontier (Annex I); the arrangement in regard to muftis (Annex II); the arbitration agreement (Annex III); the protocol concerning the railway and the Maritza (Annex IV) and the declaration referring to Article X (Annex V) are annexed to the present treaty, of which they form an integral part.

Revival of Treaty of London.

ART. XIX.—The provisions of the Treaty of London which concern the Imperial Ottoman Government and the Kingdom of Bulgaria are maintained in so far as they are not abrogated or modified by the preceding stipulations.

Date of operation.

ART. XX.—The present treaty shall come into force immediately after its signature.

Ratifications shall be exchanged within fifteen days from this date.

Date of ratification.

In faith whereof, the respective plenipotentiaries have signed it and affixed their seals thereto.

Done in duplicate at Constantinople, the 16/29 September, 1913.

(*Here follow signatures and seals.*)

Protocol No. I

A. The High Contracting Parties have agreed to add to the description of the frontier contained in Art. I of the treaty the following remarks:—

Delimitation of the frontier.

1. The frontier is established according to the map of the Austrian General Staff on the scale of 1:200,000, and its course is traced on an annexed sketch copied from that map.

The references to the lower part and to the tributary of the Maritza are recorded according to the topographical map on the scale of 1:50,000, and are entered upon a detailed and complete map of that region indicating the definite boundary from Mandra to the mouth.

2. Mixed commissions composed of Ottoman and Bulgarian officers shall draw the map of the new frontier line for a distance of two kilometres on both sides of that line on the scale of 1:25,000. The definitive boundary shall be marked on this map.

Mixed commissions.

These commissions shall be divided into three sections and shall begin their work simultaneously in the following regions: the coast of the Black Sea, the territory situated between the Maritza and the Arda, and that comprised between the Arda and Mandra.

After this operation the boundary line shall be established on the spot, and pyramids shall be erected under the care of the said mixed commissions. The protocols of the definitive frontier shall be drawn up by the commissions.

3. In tracing the boundary line the commissions shall draw up plans of the private and public properties left on the two sides of the line. The two high Governments shall examine the measures to be taken to avoid differences which might eventually arise from the exploitation of such properties.

It is well understood that until an agreement has been reached on this subject the owners shall continue to enjoy their properties freely as in the past.

4. The protocols previously drawn up by the two parties concerning such portions of the old Turco-Bulgarian frontier as are now maintained without change shall remain in force.

If the boundary-stones or koulés in those parts are destroyed or damaged they shall be rebuilt or repaired.

5. As for the rivers and streams other than the Toundja, the Maritza, and the Arda, the boundary line shall follow the channel (thalweg) of the watercourses. As for the three rivers mentioned, the boundary line is indicated in the protocol.

B. The delimitation in regard to the islands in the bed of the Maritza shall be entrusted to a special commission.

It is likewise agreed that the two Governments bind themselves to come to an arrangement when the time arrives for making the Maritza navigable.

C. The two Governments agree to facilitate the optional and mutual exchange of Bulgarian and Moslem populations and of their properties within a zone not exceeding fifteen kilometres along the entire common frontier.

Exchange of populations and properties along the common frontier.

The exchange shall take place by entire villages.

The exchange of rural and urban properties shall take place under the auspices of the two Governments and with the participation of the elders of the villages to be exchanged.

Mixed commissions appointed by the two Governments shall proceed to the exchange, and if there is occasion for it, to indemnification for the differences arising from the exchange of properties between these villages and individuals.

Done in duplicate at Constantinople, the 16/29 September, 1913.

(*Here follow signatures and seals as before.*)

Annex No. III

Art. I.—In case any difference or dispute should arise as provided for in Art. XVII of the treaty concluded this day between the Imperial Ottoman Government on the one hand and the Royal Government of Bulgaria on the other, this difference or this dispute shall be referred to arbitration at The Hague in conformity with the provisions below.

Provisions prescribed for submitting disputes to arbitration.

Art. II.—The plaintiff Government shall notify the defendant Government the question or questions which it intends to submit to arbitration as soon as they arise and shall give concise but precise information in regard to them.

Art. III.—The arbitral tribunal to which the question or questions will be submitted shall be composed of five members who shall be appointed in the following manner:—

Each party as soon as possible and within a delay which shall not exceed two months from the date of the notification specified in the preceding article shall name two arbitrators.

The umpire shall be chosen from among the sovereigns of Sweden, Norway, and Holland. If there is no agreement in the choice of one of these three sovereigns, it shall be decided by lot. If the defending party does not name its arbitrators within the aforementioned delay of two months, it shall be able to do so up to the day of the first meeting of the arbitral tribunal. After this delay, the plaintiff party shall indicate the sovereign who is to select the umpire. After the choice of the said umpire, the tribunal shall be validly composed of the umpire and the two arbitrators chosen by the plaintiff.

Art. IV.—The Powers in litigation shall be represented before the arbitral tribunal by agents, counsel, or advocates, in conformity with the provisions of Art. 62 of the Hague Convention for the Pacific Settlement of International Disputes.

These agents, counsel, or advocates shall be nominated in time by the parties, in order that the arbitration proceedings may not suffer any delay.

However, if the defendant party does not appear, proceedings shall go on by default as far as it is concerned.

ART. V.—The arbitral tribunal, once constituted, shall meet at The Hague at a date which shall be fixed by the arbitrators and within one month after the nomination of the umpire. After the arrangement, in conformity with the text and spirit of the convention of The Hague of 1907, of all questions of procedure which might arise and which have not been foreseen by the present mutual agreement, the said tribunal shall adjourn its next meeting to a date which it shall fix.

However, it is agreed that the tribunal shall not be able to open the discussions on the questions at issue earlier than two months nor later than three months after the delivery of counter-memorandum or the counter-reply provided for by Art. VII.

ART. VI.—The arbitral procedure shall comprise two distinct phases: the written information and the discussions, which shall consist of an oral presentation of the grounds of the parties before the tribunal.

The only language which the tribunal shall use and which shall be authorized to be used before it shall be the French language.

ART. VII.—Within a period of ten months at the latest from the notification provided for in Art. II the plaintiff party shall deliver to each of the members of the arbitral tribunal five complete copies and to the defendant party thirty copies, written or printed, of its memorandum, containing all documents in support of its demand which refer to the question or questions at issue.

Within ten months at the latest after this delivery, the defendant party shall deliver to each of the members of the tribunal, as well as to the plaintiff party, as many complete manuscript or printed copies as indicated above of its counter-memorandum with all documents in its support.

Within one month after this delivery, the plaintiff party shall notify the president of the arbitral tribunal whether it intends to present a reply. In case it so intends, it shall have four months at the most counting from this notification to communicate the said reply under the same conditions as the memorandum. The defendant party shall then have five months counting from this communication to present its counter-reply under the same conditions as the counter-memorandum.

The delays fixed by the present article may be prolonged by common accord by the parties or by the tribunal in case it shall deem it necessary for arriving at a just decision.

But the tribunal shall not take into consideration memoranda, counter-memoranda, and other communications presented to it by the parties after the expiration of the last delay fixed by it.

ART. VIII.—If in the memoranda or other documents exchanged one or other of the parties has referred to or made allusion to a document or paper in its exclusive possession and of which it shall not have attached a copy, it shall be obliged, if the other party demands it, to furnish it with a copy within thirty days at the latest.

ART. IX.—The decisions of the arbitral tribunal on the question or questions at issue shall be pronounced within a maximum delay of one month after the closure, by the president, of the discussions relative to that question or those questions.

ART. X.—The judgment of the arbitral tribunal shall be final and will have to be executed strictly without any delay.

ART. XI.—Each party shall bear its own expenses and an equal share of the expenses of the tribunal.

ART. XII.—In everything which is not provided for by the present arrangement, the stipulations of the Hague Convention of 1907 for the Pacific Settlement of International Disputes shall be applied to the arbitrations resulting from the present arrangement, with the exception, however, of the articles which have been reserved by the Contracting Parties.

Done in duplicate at Constantinople, the 16 / 29 September, 1913.

(Here follow signatures and seals.)

(Z) TREATY OF ATHENS

November 1/14, 1913

TURKEY—GREECE

HIS Majesty the Emperor of the Ottomans, and His Majesty the King of the Hellenes, animated by the common desire to strengthen the bonds of peace and friendship happily re-established between them, and to facilitate the resumption of normal relations between the two countries, have decided to conclude a treaty for this purpose, and have named as their plenipotentiaries, to wit:—

His Majesty the King of the Ottomans: His Excellency Ghalib Kémal bey;

His Majesty the King of the Hellenes: His Excellency M. D. Panas, Minister of Foreign Affairs;

Who, after having communicated to each other their full powers, which were found to be in good and proper form, have agreed upon the following:—

Establishment of peaceful relationships.

ART. I.—As soon as the present Act shall have been signed, the diplomatic relations between Turkey and Greece shall be resumed, and the respective consulates may be restored and perform their duties in the two countries.

The Imperial Ottoman Government may establish consulates in those portions of the ceded territories where there are already agents of foreign Powers, as well as in all places where the Royal Government of Greece sees no objection to their admission.

Revival of treaties.

ART. II.—The treaties, conventions, and acts concluded or in force between the two countries at the time of the breaking off of diplomatic relations, shall be fully put into force again upon the signature of the present convention, and the two Governments, as well as their respective subjects, shall be placed in the same position towards one another in which they were before the hostilities.

Protocol No. 3, annexed to the present convention, shall be applicable in all the territories of Greece.

Amnesty.

ART. III.—The two High Contracting Parties accord full and complete amnesty to all persons involved in the political occurrences prior to the present treaty.

Consequently, no individual shall be prosecuted, disturbed, or molested in person or property or in the exercise of his rights, because of acts relating in any manner whatever to the war, and all judicial sentences and administrative measures based upon facts of that nature shall be *ipso facto* annulled.

ART. IV.—Persons domiciled in those territories of the Ottoman Empire which pass under the dominion of Greece shall become Greek subjects.

Nationality and option.

They shall have the right to choose the Ottoman nationality, by making a declaration to the appropriate Greek authorities within a period of three years from this date, the declaration to be followed by registration at the Imperial Ottoman consulates. This declaration shall be sent abroad to the offices of Greek consulates and registered by Ottoman consulates. However, the exercise of this option is subject to the requirement that the persons in question shall transfer their domicile to some place outside of Greece.

Those who, during this period, shall have emigrated to the Ottoman Empire or to foreign countries, or shall have established their domicile in such places, shall remain Ottomans. They shall enjoy immunity from export duties on their movable property.

The exercise of the option shall be personal.

During the period of three years, the Mussulmans shall not be required to render military service, and shall pay no military tax.

So far as the minor children are concerned, the period during which the option may be exercised by them shall begin to run from the date when they reach their majority.

ART. V.—Rights acquired up to the time of the occupation of the ceded territories, as well as judicial decisions and official deeds given by competent Ottoman authorities, shall be respected and inviolate until legally disproved.

Rights and judicial decisions.

This article does not in any way prejudice the decisions which may be rendered by the Financial Commission on Balkan Affairs, sitting at Paris.

ART. VI.—Inhabitants of the ceded territories who, conforming to the provisions of Art. IV of the present convention, and retaining Ottoman nationality, may have emigrated to the Ottoman Empire or to foreign countries, or may have established their domicile in these places, shall continue to hold their real property situated in the ceded territories, either renting it or administering it through third parties.

Real property in ceded territory.

Property rights in urban and rural real property held by individuals by virtue of deeds issued by the Ottoman State, or by virtue of the Ottoman law in the localities ceded to Greece, and before the occupation, shall be recognized by the Royal Greek Government.

The same shall be true of property rights in the said immovables standing in the name of corporations or held by them by virtue of Ottoman laws prior to the aforesaid occupation.

No one shall be deprived of his property, either in whole or in part, directly or indirectly, except for a duly stated public purpose, and after the payment of a proper indemnity.

ART. VII.—The private property of His Imperial Majesty the Sultan, as well as that of the members of the Imperial Dynasty, shall be maintained and respected. His Imperial Majesty and the members of the Imperial Dynasty shall be able to sell or rent it through their agents

All differences or disputes which may arise in the interpretation or application of the present article shall be settled by an arbitration at The Hague, by virtue of a "compromis" to be concluded.

ART. VIII.—Prisoners of war, as well as all other persons arrested through military measures or for reasons of public order, shall be exchanged within the period of one month after the conclusion of the present treaty, or sooner if possible.

Restoration of prisoners.

Expenses incurred.

This exchange shall take place under the direction of special commissioners named by each party.

The mutual claims of the High Contracting Parties relative to prisoners of war shall be submitted to an arbitration at The Hague under a "compromis" to be concluded.

However, the salary of the officers paid by the Royal Government of Greece shall be reimbursed by the State to which they belong.

ART. IX.—Immediately after the signature of the present convention, the Imperial Ottoman Government shall release all the ships and boats flying the Greek flag which were seized before the declaration of war and are held by that Government.

Restoration of vessels seized before the declaration of war.

Claims for damages and losses by interested persons, because of the embargo or seizure of the Greek vessels and their cargoes, shall, in accordance with a "compromis" to be entered into by common agreement, be submitted to an arbitral tribunal composed of four arbitrators named by each party, and three other arbitrators to be chosen from the subjects of maritime nations by the two parties, or, in case of disagreement, by the Swiss Federal Council.

ART. X.—The two Governments agree, under a "compromis" to be concluded, to submit to an arbitral tribunal at The Hague the settlement of the dispute which has arisen concerning the interpretation of the protocol of surrender of Salonica, dated October 26, 1912 (old style), and the protocol annexed thereto, regarding the arms of Ottoman soldiers of the garrison of that city, which the Imperial Ottoman Government claims should be restored.

Questions of interpretation before an arbitral tribunal.

ART. XI.—The life, property, honour, religion, and customs of those inhabitants of the territories ceded to Greece who shall remain under the Greek administration shall be scrupulously respected.

Rights of inhabitants of ceded territories.

They shall enjoy in full the same civil and political rights as native Greek subjects. The free and public practice of their religion shall be assured to Mussulmans.

The name of His Imperial Majesty the Sultan, as caliph, shall continue to be pronounced in the public prayers of the Mussulmans.

Neither the autonomy nor hierarchical organization of the existing Mussulman communities, nor of those which may be formed, nor the control of the funds and real property which belongs to them shall be interfered with.

No interference shall be made in the relations of the individual Mussulmans or Mussulman communities with their spiritual chiefs, who shall be subject to the Cheik-ul-Islamat at Constantinople, who shall invest the chief mufti.

The muftis, each within his own community, shall be elected by Mussulman electors.

The chief mufti shall be named by His Majesty the King of the Greeks from three candidates elected and presented by an electoral assembly composed of all the muftis of Greece.

The Government of Greece shall notify the election of the chief mufti, through the Royal legation of Greece at Constantinople, to the Cheik-ul-Islamat, who shall forward to him a "menchour" and the "murassélé" authorizing him to exercise his functions and grant to the other muftis of Greece the right to exercise jurisdiction and to confer "fetvas."

The muftis, in addition to their authority over purely religious affairs and their supervision of the administration of vakouf property, shall exercise jurisdiction between Mussulmans in matters of marriage, divorce, alimony (nifaca), guardianship, trusteeship, emancipation of minors, wills of Ottomans, and succession to the office of Mutevelli (tevlict).

The judgments rendered by the muftis shall be executed by the proper Greek authorities.

As to matters of inheritance, the interested Mussulman parties may, after agreeing thereto, resort to the mufti as an arbitrator. All methods of appeal practised before the courts of the country shall be applicable to the arbitral decision thus rendered unless there is a clause expressly providing to the contrary.

Vakoufs in the ceded territories to be respected.

ART. XII.—The vakoufs Idjarié-Vahidé, Idjarétein, Moukataa, whether they be Mazbouta, Mulhaka, or Mutesna, in the ceded territories, as they were established by the Ottoman laws at the time of the military occupation, shall be respected.

They shall be governed by the Mussulman communities in the ceded territories, which shall respect the rights of Mutévellis and Gallédars.

All the vakouf real property, urban and rural, Mazbouta or Moulhaka, situated in the territories ceded to Greece and of which the revenues belong to religious and charitable institutions located in Turkey shall also be managed by the aforesaid Mussulman communities until they are sold by the ministry of the Evkaf.

It is well understood that the rights of Gallédars over the vakoufs aforesaid shall be respected by the said ministry.

The control of the vakoufs shall not be modified without previous and just compensation.

If as the result of the abolition of the vakouf tithes certain Tekkés, mosques, Médressés, schools, hospitals, and other religious institutions of a charitable character situated in the territories ceded to Greece have not sufficient revenues in the future to maintain themselves, the Royal Government of Greece shall grant to them the necessary subsidies for this purpose.

All controversies as to the interpretation or application of the provisions of the present article shall be decided by arbitration at The Hague.

Art. XIII.—The High Contracting Parties agree to issue orders to their provincial authorities to respect the cemeteries and particularly the tombs of soldiers who fell upon the field of honour.

Tombs of the fallen.

The authorities shall not prevent relatives and friends from removing the bones of victims buried in foreign ground.

Art. XIV.—The Royal Government of Greece having been subrogated to the rights, duties, and obligations of the Imperial Ottoman Government as regards the Salonica–Monastir railway companies, the Oriental railways, and the railway from the Salonica–Dedeagatch junction, over such portions of these roads as fall within the territories ceded to Greece, all questions relating thereto shall be referred to the Financial Commission on Balkan Affairs sitting at Paris.

Rights as to railways in ceded territory.

Art. XV.—The two High Contracting Parties agree to uphold, so far as they are concerned, the provisions of the Treaty of London, May 3, 1913, including the provisions of Art. V of the said treaty.

Renewal of treaty.

Date of operation of treaty.

Art. XVI.—The present treaty shall become effective immediately upon its signature.

Ratifications shall be exchanged within two weeks from this day.

In faith whereof the respective plenipotentiaries have signed it and affixed their seals thereto.

Done in duplicate at Athens, the 1/14 November, 1913.

(Here follow signatures and seals.)

Protocol No. I.

Natives of the ceded territories who are domiciled outside the Ottoman Empire shall have a period of six months within which to decide in favour of Greek nationality.

Period allowed for option.

The declaration and its effects shall be the same as those provided in Art. IV.

Protocol No. II.

Since the Imperial Ottoman Government claims that the private property of the State situated in the ceded territories should still belong to it, and the Royal Government of Greece does not accept this view and claims that these properties should belong to it, the two Contracting Parties have agreed to submit this question to an arbitral tribunal at The Hague under a "compromis" to be concluded. (The number and extent of the possessions in question are given in the list annexed to this protocol.)

Private property of the State in ceded territory.

INDEX OF SUBJECT-MATTER

[N.B.—*For references to judicial cases, see* INDEX OF CASES *at the beginning of the book; and for references to treaties, preliminaries of peace, conferences, and congresses, see* INDEX OF TREATIES *at the end of the book.*]

INDEX OF TREATIES, PRELIMINARIES OF PEACE, CONFERENCES, AND CONGRESSES

www.ingramcontent.com/pod-product-compliance
Lightning Source LLC
LaVergne TN
LVHW062244200926
848484LV00006B/1608
* 9 7 8 1 5 8 4 7 7 8 6 0 8 *